God's Scribe

JEFF RIDER

God's Scribe

The Historiographical Art of Galbert of Bruges

The Catholic University of America Press
Washington, D.C.

The paper used in this publication meets the minimum requirements of American National Standards for Information Science—Permanence of Paper for Printed Library materials, ANSI Z39.48-1984.

∞

LIBRARY OF CONGRESS CATALOGING-IN-PUBLICATION DATA
Rider, Jeff, 1954–
God's scribe : the historiographical art of Galbert of Bruges / Jeff Rider.
p. cm.
Includes bibliographical references and index.
ISBN 0-8132-1018-6 (alk. paper)
ISBN-13: 978-0-8132-1018-6 (alk. paper)
1. Galbert, de Bruges, d. 1134. De multro, traditione, et occisione gloriosi Karoli comitis Flandriarum. 2. Flanders—Historiography. 3. Charles Count of Flanders, d. 1127—Assassination. 4. Flanders — Kings and rulers—Death—Sources. I Title.
DH801.F46 R53 2001
949.3'101—dc21 00-057045

Contents

Acknowledgments

In the course of writing this book I was, both unfortunately and fortunately, given two entirely unwelcome opportunities to learn the value of friendship and loyalty in ways that I had never expected. I hope, for their sakes, that I am never given the chance to fully repay those who came to my aide, but I do want to take this opportunity to thank them. First and foremost, I want to thank my wife, JoAnn, and my children, John and Mary, for their trust, adaptability, patience, and good humor. They are the teachers of most of what I learn these days. I especially want to thank John for the constant reminder that life actually revolves around soccer rather than scholarship and for the spectacular demonstration of the importance of backing up one's files on a diskette, and Mary for an unexampled display of courage.

I also want to thank two of my colleagues, Catherine Poisson and Clark Maines, for the substantial personal and professional sacrifices they made in order to help me and my family. Their charity, since it was true charity, went far beyond what I had any right to ask or to expect. I likewise want to thank another colleague, Catherine Ostrow, for her long-time, evidently inexhaustible thoughtfulness and *serviabilité.*

I have of course acquired a large number of professional debts in the course of writing this book. The cheerful help of MaryLou Nelles, Lisa Fleury, Rosalind Eastaway, and Gail Winter enabled me to concentrate on writing in a way I could not otherwise have done. A good many of the members of the Medieval History Department of the University of Ghent have contributed to the book in one way or another; I would like to thank Professor Raoul Van Caenegem, for his encouragement and willingness to read an earlier version of the text; Professor Ludo Milis for his interest, advice, invitation to speak in Ghent, and efforts to put me in contact with historians of medieval Flanders; him again and his wife, Greta Milis-Proost, for their hospitality and conversation; and Professor Marc Boone, Professor Thérèse de Hemptinne, and Véronique Lambert for their interest and willingness to respond to queries and provide me with materials. I am indebted to a Ghent alumnus, Professor Walter Simons of Dartmouth College, for supplying me with articles and helping me with translations from Dutch, and to Professor Benoît Tock of the University of Strasbourg, who has likewise been an invaluable source of information. Large portions of this book took shape in conversation with Dr. Alan Murray of the University of Leeds, who was also kind enough to read an earlier version of it, as was Professor James Murray of the University of Cinncinnati when, rather to his surprise I imagine, I asked if he would do so.

I would like to thank Dr. David McGonagle, director of the The Catholic University of America Press, for his patience and unflagging support of this project, and Professor Leah Shopkow of the University of Indiana and the Press's two anonymous readers for their kind words—and even more for their critical ones.

I am indebted to Kathy Stefanowicz, Kate Wolfe, and the staff of Wesleyan's Interlibrary Loan Office for their help and, as always, to my colleagues in Medieval Studies at Wesleyan who continue to make the university a good place to work.

A sabbatical leave from Wesleyan and a fellowship from the National Endowment for the Humanities enabled me to finish this book far more quickly than I would otherwise have been able to do so and I am grateful to both institutions for their support.

The illumination on the cover and frontispiece is from an early eleventh-century Gospel from The Abbey of Saint Bertin in Saint-Omer, France. It is found in The Pierpont Morgan Library, New York, MSM.333f.84v. Reprinted with permission from the library. The reproduction of this illumination was made possible by a grant from the Thomas and Catharine McMahon Fund.

I would, finally, like to acknowledge once more my profound debt to the late Father Nicolas Huyghebaert, who first set me to work on Galbert's chronicle in a seminar at the Université Catholique de Louvain.

INTRODUCTION

An Open Book

Formally bizarre (it is the only journalistic history we have from Europe in the twelfth century) and almost equally offensive to all its potential audiences, Galbert of Bruges's *De multro, traditione, et occisione gloriosi Karoli comitis Flandriarum*—a contemporary, eyewitness account of the assassination of Charles the Good, count of Flanders, murdered while he was at prayer in his castral church in Bruges on March 2, 1127, and of the ensuing conflict that eventually ended with Thierry of Alsace's accession to the countship the following year—slept through the Middle Ages locked, probably, in some chest in Bruges. No medieval copies of it survive; indeed, there is no reason to believe that more than one copy of it ever existed during the period.

The *De multro* appears to have been "discovered" some time in the fifteenth century, when it was translated into French. The earliest evidence of its existence is a brief résumé, drawn from this translation, of its account of the servile and adulterous origins and ultimate fate of Charles's assassins, which Roland or Antoine de Baenst, members of one of the most important families of Flanders, with implantations both in Ghent and Bruges, copied with a certain gusto into a family register at the end of that century.[1] The chronicle was praised in the following century by the Flemish historian Jacob de Meyer, who compared it favorably to Walter of Thérouanne's contemporary *Vita Karoli comitis* in the section of his *Commentarii sive Annales rerum Flandricarum* (1561) devoted to the reign of Charles the Good, writing that "a certain monk named Walter wrote about the life and death of this Charles for John, the bishop of Thérouanne; but Galbert of Bruges did so better and in more detail."[2] In 1629, H. Jan Gooris mentioned the works of both Walter and Galbert among his sources and cited Galbert by name in his *Het Leven ende Martelie van den Heylighen Graef van Vlaenderen Carolus Bonus*,[3] and, two years later, the French royal historian and geographer André Duchesne published a series of excerpts from the *De multro* in his *Histoire généalogique des maisons de Guines, d'Ardres, de Gand et de Coucy.*[4] The complete text was first printed in 1668 in the *Acta sanctorum* by the Bollandists Godefroid Henschen and Daniel Van Papenbroeck, who praised Galbert for the "supreme diligence" with which he observed and recorded the events of 1127–1128,[5] and in the introduction to his 1776 reedition of this text, the Danish historian Jacob Langebek recommended the *De multro* to his readers for the "accuracy and . . . the richness of its information. . . . Besides the history of Charles's assassination and the events following it up to the restoration of peace in Flanders under Thierry, [Galbert] recounts clearly and pleasantly various interesting things, otherwise unknown, concerning the rites of homage in this period, its forms of punishment and arms, its instruments of war, the ways of besieging and assaulting a town, clothing, and other things. Indeed, Galbert can and should be numbered, not among the hagiographical authors, but among the good, skillful, and accurate historical writers of the twelfth century."[6] Excerpts from Henschen and Van Papenbroeck's edition were also reprinted in the *Recueil des historiens des Gaules et de la France* a decade later.[7]

Already well established as a respected source for the history of medieval France and Flanders at the end of the eighteenth century, the *De multro* enjoyed an even more remarkable success in the nineteenth. François Guizot published a French translation of it in 1825,[8] Joseph-Octave Delepierre and Jean Perneel published another in 1830,[9] and both were successful enough to be reprinted, the second one several times. In the introduction to his 1856 reedition of Henschen and Van Papenbroeck's text for the *Monumenta Germaniae Historica,* R. Köpke praised Galbert for an "accuracy . . . almost unmatched" and observed that he "composed a book, even though he was much troubled by hope, fear, and sadness, that grips and troubles the reader no less."[10] Thirty years later, Galbert earned an entry in the *Biographie nationale* of Belgium in which Alphonse Wauters observed that his "work is above all interesting for the lively and original information it provides about the role played by the burghers in Flanders at that time. Far superior to his contemporary, Walter, whose Latin was better, he is as precise but more concise, more lively, more endearing. The 'Passion of Count Charles of Flanders,' *Passio Karoli comitis Flandriae,* surely constitutes the best historical account of the time. . . . Galbert's vivacious narrative, his exact knowledge of the setting, and his judicious observations make it a precious journal."[11] At the end of the century, the *De multro* was edited anew by Henri Pirenne, while Migne reprinted Henschen and Van Papenbroeck's text yet again in the *Patrologia latina.*[12]

The chronicle's success in translation continued unabated in the twentieth century, thanks especially to James Bruce Ross's English translation, first published in 1959 and continuously in print since that time,[13] but its reception among scholars took a curious turn in the wake of the exaggerated portrait, indeed the caricature, of Galbert and his chronicle that Pirenne drew in the introduction to his edition. According to Pirenne, Galbert was a simple, naive man who had never thought much about the kinds of issues raised by Charles's assassination and the succession to the county, and thus had no profound prejudices, loyalties, or ideas that would have led him to select or repress—even unconsciously—certains facts, or to shape them—even unconsciously—as he set them down. "The more-or-less unconscious political versatility that manifests itself naively in the history of the murder of Charles the Good," Pirenne observed, "is one of [the *De multro's*] most striking characteristics." Galbert thus becomes a sort of transparent everyman—"He echoes the rumors that fly through the crowd. He shares the people's feelings"—whose record is uncomplicated by intellectual concerns: "given the nature of Galbert's work, it is almost pointless to remark that one should not expect to find in it any trace of erudition."[14] Pirenne recognized Galbert's "literary talent" and "the charm" of his work, and he praised both the liveliness and the "scrupulous exactitude" of its descriptions, but only after noting that "no one will be surprised to find many stylistic infelicities in an unfinished work. Obscure and incorrect expressions abound in Galbert. . . . Galbert's sentences are certainly less correct than Walter[of Thérouanne]'s, less in keeping with the tastes of the period, but, on the other hand, how much livelier they are!"[15] For Pirenne, Galbert's talent came from nature rather than from school and the charm of his work lay precisely in its spontaneity and artlessness.

Pirenne, followed by most subsequent scholars, also assumed that the journalistically organized *De multro* was a true journal: "Galbert's narrative," he wrote,

> . . . was composed on the basis of notes taken each day as events unfolded. As he tells us, Galbert jotted down succinctly on wax tablets . . . everything he

learned. Then, when he found the time, he wrote a few pages based on the unorganized notes that he had, in haste, scribbled in wax. It is these pages, composed in this way at irregular intervals, that we possess. In its current state, the text is something between a set of immediate notes and a finished account. It is in fact easy to see that several chapters, in the form we have them, were composed a bit later than the days whose events they report. . . . Nonetheless, with a few exceptions, the account was always written within a few days of the events it relates.[16]

This is a broadly accurate account of what Galbert tells us about his method of work during the first stage of the *De multro*'s composition, but Pirenne consistently exaggerates its immediacy and transparency and overlooks various kinds of evidence suggesting that Galbert later revised his initial account substantially. He, and not Galbert, tells us that the latter recorded "everything he learned" in the first, note-taking stage of his work (Galbert in fact tells us he did not do so), and he, not Galbert, characterizes the latter's notes as "unorganized," jotted down "in haste," "scribbled in wax," and then written up only "a few pages" at a time, and "always . . . within a few days" of being taken. "The author," Pirenne assures us a few pages later, "wrote while under the immediate influence of the events"; the text was "written under the strong and immediate influence of the events it records" and "was not revised by its author. This means that it is utterly artless, written in absolute good faith. Its narrator speaks with an open heart. Nowhere does he try to denature the events. He notes them exactly as they are reported to him [*il est d'une naïveté complète, d'une absolue bonne foi. Le narrateur y parle à coeur ouvert. Nulle part il ne s'efforce de dénaturer les évènements. Tels que ceux-ci lui sont rapportés, il les accueille*]."[17]

The *De multro,* in Pirenne's view, is an ideal source because it was not written by a historian and is not a work of history. It is an immediate record uncontaminated by its author's subjectivity, limited only by his materiality (he can only report what he has seen, heard, or read). Through it, Pirenne seems to have believed, modern historians can view the events it relates as though through the open window of a bourgeois household in Bruges, and they can use it as a kind of quarry from which to carve the building blocks of their own interpretations of these events with little thought for Galbert's intellectual background, interests, and intentions.

Pirenne's ideas about the *De multro* and its author were given new life in 1959 by James Bruce Ross's immensely valuable and successful translation of the text. In the "Introduction" to this translation, she praised Galbert's remarkable objectivity, "realism[,] and accuracy,"[18] and recognized his talent as a writer, but emphasized even more than Pirenne that his was a native genius that only suffered when he tried to cultivate it.[19] She accepted Pirenne's conclusions concerning the way in which the *De multro* was composed,[20] and underlined Galbert's simplicity, naiveté, and inability to impose any subjective order on the events he relates. Not only is Ross's Galbert characterized by "transparent honesty, loyalty, and Christian piety,"[21] he is a small-spirited man overwhelmed by the events he witnesses and the unconscious impulses that drive his life: "a devoted and perhaps compulsive functionary, deprived by circumstances of his normal work, might well have begun without conscious motive to record what was happening, and through such a substitute activity consoled himself by giving some kind of order to the appalling disorder which suddenly engulfed his quiet and routine life."[22]

This image of the *De multro* as a true journal and of Galbert as a simple, honest man of the crowd, who was nonetheless an accurate, natively gifted diarist, was accepted with little dissent or modification for eighty years. In 1974, for example, Beryl Smalley could still write that Galbert's journal is "a precious freak of historiography" that was begun because "Galbert . . . had time on his hands. . . . His normal business as a notary ceased. He resolved to keep a day-to-day record of the dreadful happenings around him. The task kept him going, and he felt a sort of compulsion, 'a little spark of charity,' as he calls it"; his "observation was unclouded by learning. Suetonius contributed nothing to the notary's shrewd, vivid character sketches. Galbert rose to his opportunity and innovated."[23] And due to the success of Ross's translation, this image is still probably the basis of the general perception of Galbert and his text.

The foundations of a new appreciation of Galbert were laid in a series of studies by Paul Bonenfant, Jan Dhondt, and especially Heinrich Sproemberg, all but one of which appeared between 1950 and 1971. In articles published in 1939 and 1951, respectively, Sproemberg and Bonenfant suggested that Galbert was not in fact an impartial and objective observer but an apologist for the citizens of Bruges.[24] A more important step was taken in 1957 when, in a pair of articles published that year, Jan Dhondt drew a richer, more complex image of Galbert, whom he portrayed as "an average intellectual," "naturally inclined to logical reasoning," who possessed "an extraordinarily concrete and positive way of thinking, one might almost call it pedagogical," and wished, above all "to understand and make others understand." "Galbert's narrative shows clearly the first stammerings of rational thought struggling with traditions," and demonstrates "a certain individualism and . . . a rationalism that were still barely perceptible in the religious sphere." Most importantly, Dhondt suggested that Galbert did have an overall design, an overarching intention, in composing the *De multro:* "[I]t is rather remarkable that Galbert tries to arrange all the events in a single plan, a divine plan of course, and one which reduces itself to the ineluctable divine punishment of those who committed the crime."[25] Dhondt's concept of Galbert was still heavily influenced by Pirenne's—Galbert is at heart only a simple man of the burgher crowd—but he credited Galbert with certain intellectual ambitions and powers and a degree of individualism (although it requires a crisis to bring them to the fore). He did not go very far in developing his idea of Galbert as a logical, critical, independent thinker, but his observations prepared and encouraged later scholars to pay more attention to Galbert himself and to consider the ways in which his particular *mentalité* determined the composition of the *De multro.*

A more radical reaction to Pirenne's views, one that emphasizes Galbert's partiality, is to be found in a series of four further essays Sproemberg composed between 1954 and 1964.[26] In the earliest of these essays, he explicitly rejected Pirenne's portrait of Galbert as a sort of naive court reporter and deplored the effects this portrait had had on the interpretation of the information provided by Galbert in the *De multro.*[27] Sproemberg portrayed Galbert as a dialectician, an experienced and knowledgeable jurist, and an original political thinker, who put his skills and knowledge to use in the service of the burghers of Bruges for whom he became an apologist, spokesman, and political theorist—indeed, "the first democratic theorist of the medieval bourgeoisie."[28] He argued that Galbert shaped the facts he reported—without falsifying them—to fit his political ideas and goals,[29] and attributed to Galbert the conception and articulation of a political theory of the selection of rulers by the "clergy and people [who, for Galbert, included the bourgeoisie]" based on the procedures for the election of bishops.[30] Sproemberg thus concluded that Galbert was a more subtle and original thinker than had previously been recognized,[31] and that his work represents a distinct point of view: "We thus perceive that Galbert was very skilled in legal matters and was well informed about the issues of constitutional law, but also that he didn't hesitate to use his legal and dialectical skills for the benefit of his fellow citizens, and thus provided a very one-sided view of the state of affairs. This clearly disproves the assertion that he was artless."[32] Galbert was, in sum, an interested apologist for the burghers of Bruges and a subtle thinker and writer, a sort of Thomas Paine for Bruges's bourgeoisie.

Constructed on the foundations laid by Bonenefant, Dhondt, and Sproemberg, a new image of Galbert has emerged from a series of studies published since the late 1970s,[33] and has achieved its fullest expression to date in a series of writings published by R. C. Van Caenegem starting in 1978.[34] Van Caenegem draws attention to Galbert's intellectual attainments,[35] praises his talent as a writer,[36] and emphasizes his independence and critical judgment: "not content to observe and report, Galbert also gives us his opinion about events, and this opinion, that of a cultivated and well situated man, is exceptionally valuable for a study of the Flemish mentality in the twelfth century. . . . Galbert sought to understand what he had observed; he applied his critical abilities not only to dishonest actions, as is only natural, but also to traditional institutions and to the detriment of the most important people."[37] He was even, Van Caenegem points out, capable of irony![38]

Scholars have thus provided a more articulate version of what one might term the pre-Pirennean view of Galbert over the last twenty years, and he has gone from being an artless, and perhaps slightly neurotic, man of the crowd and an objective, naturally gifted, note taker to a well-trained and subtle writer and the first legal and political theorist of the medieval bourgeoisie. The *De multro* itself has not been similarly rehabilitated, however, because Pirenne's ideas about the way it was composed have gone largely unchallenged. As we have seen, Pirenne's belief in the *De multro*'s artlessness and absolute good faith was not founded, or at least not founded only, on an evaluation of Galbert's character. It was based principally on ideas about the way in which the chronicle was composed and, above all, on the belief that it was not revised. The fundamental importance of this lack of revision is made clearer in two remarks by Dhondt, who writes that Galbert "did not rewrite his story afterward to make it more coherent—and false,"[39] and that "to a large degree, the extraordinary interest of the *De multro* resides in the fact that it is a narrative that was written day by day and was not subsequently reworked into a coherent whole. Galbert records the events as he learned them each day and not as they would appear, finally, to the mind of a man who knew everything that had happened."[40] Van Caenegem writes similarly that Galbert "added very little to his text subsequently and did not, happily, revise it, so that we are able day by day to follow the train of events and Galbert's reactions, just as he noted them, without foreseeing in any way the very surprising denouement of July 1128."[41] Revision is here viewed as an effort to create a coherent narrative representation of a series of events once one knows how that series ends.[42] This knowledge becomes a principle of selection and emphasis that leads historians to denature and falsify the "true" nature of the events and it must be taken into account by later historians who wish to use the accounts of earlier historians for their own work. The *De multro* is thus extraordinarily valuable, from this point of view, because it was not rewritten; because Galbert never went back and tried to create a coherent narrative representation of the events he records once he knew how they ended; because he never had to struggle with the demands of narrative history for a coherent story with a beginning, middle, and end (Van Caenegem's use of the word *denouement* is both sensitive and telling), demands that, from this point of view, inevitably lead historians to denature and falsify the unadulterated events. If the *De multro* is unrevised, that is, it offers modern historians the next best thing to raw phenomena: blocks hewn from the quarry of event in the roughest form with no precise use in mind. Scholars have generally agreed that Galbert added passages to his chronicle after May 1127, but have generally denied, or have not even entertained the idea, that he revised any portion of the work, at least in a substantial way, and the journal has not received the attention it deserves as a piece of historical writing because it has not been perceived *to be* a piece of historical writing. Their new sensitivity to Galbert's talent and personal qualities has done little to affect scholars' perception of the nature of the text because its failure to achieve the status of historical writing has been attributed to its form and the circumstances of its production and thus has been seen as largely independent of its author's personal qualities.[43]

This book thus seeks to complete the historiographical rehabilitation of Galbert and his chronicle by showing, first, that it is indeed a piece of historical writing and not a "freak of historiography," however precious.[44] The *De multro* is not, I will argue, a true journal but a journalistically organized history. This was an original form that may well be, as John Ward has recently called it, *"sui generis"* even within the "enormous . . . bewildering range of topic, form and genre" of medieval historiography,[45] but it was not, or at least not finally, an accident. It reflected an almost universally held concept of history whose consequences for the form of historical writing Galbert alone of twelfth-century historians realized in practice.

The second purpose of this book is to show that most of this journalistically organized history was revised, and a large part of it thoroughly revised: that Galbert did indeed try to create a coherent narrative representation of the events he had recorded once he knew how they ended, did indeed try to provide a coherent story with a beginning, middle, and end. Galbert's great achievement, in fact, was the composition of a bundle of gripping narratives that he managed to recount simultaneously within the original journalistic form he had created. This strong narrative element is one of the two aspects of the *De multro* that have made it such a success in translation from fifteenth-century patrician halls of Ghent to twentieth-century undergraduate classrooms. Galbert was a remarkable dramatist and raconteur who brought to brilliant fruition many of the best tendencies of twelfth-century historiography.

The other aspect of the *De multro* that has made it such a success is the opportunity it offers us to watch an intelligent and gifted human working successfully to compass the events around him with the conceptual and narrative tools of the day. This is why the *De multro* continues to please audiences who have lost all but the most tenuous connection, or never had any connection, with the events and people it describes. The pleasure comes from the triumph of the human ability to create order from evenemential chaos, from the ability to make sense, from, in a word, art.

This book thus seeks to recover to some degree the ability, whose loss was lamented by Nancy Partner a little over twenty years ago, to read one of the most complex and original of medieval histories "naturally and directly" as a work of historical literature,[46] to draw from it, as one would from any other important work of literature, its lessons about imagining worlds and making stories, and to better understand the unique historiographical instrument that a comital functionary forged in Bruges in 1127–1128. The first chapter provides a brief outline of the Flemish crisis of 1127–1128 and summarizes the little we know or can guess about Galbert. The remaining chapters trace the elaboration of the *De multro* from a set of wax notes to a nearly completed chronicle. In them, I consider Galbert's sources, the way he took and organized his notes, the distinct stages in which the chronicle was written, its literary qualities, the conceptual tools Galbert used to understand the events he related in it, and the evolution of his understanding of those events. My principal contention is that the *De multro* deserves attention for its art and that that art needs to be pointed out. This book cries out, in sum, that the *De multro* is not naked, but is as fully clothed as the most obviously artful medieval history. Such a velation might not be especially noteworthy, once the moment of recognition has passed, were the clothing not so striking and so cunningly well made. Galbert's chronicle has long been held to offer us an image of naked truth; I wish to study and draw attention to the veiled artistry with which that image was composed.

CHAPTER I

Ego Galbertus

In Lent and Easter he {Henry I of England} was at Woodstock, when a messenger said to him: "Charles, count of Flanders, who was very dear to you, has been murdered by his nobles in the church at Bruges, by abominable treachery. The French king has given Flanders to William, your nephew and enemy, who, now greatly strengthened, has punished with various torments all those who betrayed Charles." So the king, worried by these events, held a council in London at Rogationtide. And Archbishop William similarly, in the same town, at Westminster.

—Henry of Huntingdon, *The History of the English People*[1]

MURDER IN THE CHURCH

Charles, count of Flanders, rose a bit later than usual that first Wednesday of March 1127, although still well before dawn. "Troubled by a kind of anxious wakefulness," he had had a hard time falling asleep and had tossed and turned all night, "now lying on one side, now sitting up again on the bed." The darkness and the cold, humid air did not help matters. It was only the second night he had spent in his house in the *burg,* the fortified center, of Bruges since his return from a visit to his cousin, Louis VI of France, and he had "many things on his mind."[2] A carefully cultivated feud between two of the leading men from the region of Bruges—Thancmar of Straeten, whose stronghold lay to the west of town on the road to Ypres, and Thancmar's neighbor, Borsiard—had once again broken out during Charles's absence, and when he had returned to Flanders, he had been met in Ypres by a crowd of people from the region who had complained of the damage and losses they had suffered at the hands of the freebooters Borsiard had loosed on the countryside.

Borsiard had clearly been the aggressor this time, but he was not an easy man to punish. His grandfather, Erembald, had become the castellan of Bruges, the count's principal residence, around 1067 (through, rumor said, adultery and murder) and the post had been held by one of his descendants ever since. One of Borsiard's uncles, Haket, was castellan in 1127. Another uncle, Bertulf, had been the provost of Saint Donatian, the church attached to the count's house in the castle, since 1091. Bertulf was also, by virtue of his office, the receiver of the count's revenues from throughout the county and the chancellor of Flanders, in charge of the clerical personnel attached to the count's court and administration. The family's wealth and power in the county were second only to Charles's own.[3]

The situation was further complicated by the questions that had recently been raised concerning this family's legal status. Hearing them accused of servile status in his presence one day, Charles had ordered an investigation into the matter and, finding that there was good reason to believe that the members of the family were, in fact, his serfs, had summoned them to Cassel to prove their freedom on a given day in the preceding year. When the day had come, according to one report, they had shown up with three thousand armed supporters, and Charles, fearing bloodshed, had postponed the hearing. He had thus incurred the hatred of the family and all its friends and dependents—since they risked losing their wealth, offices, and power if they were found to be of servile status—but had not been able to enforce his rights: all he had gained was a large group of formidable enemies.

Faced with the need to punish a leading member of this powerful and ill-disposed family, Charles had summoned his court to meet in Ypres on Sunday, February 27, and had asked those present to advise him how to do so. Some had immediately advised him to burn down Borsiard's house while others—more politic—had suggested that he go himself and see what had been done, and then fit the punishment to the crime. He had therefore traveled to the region Monday morning—despite being told that Borsiard had recently been overheard asking: "If someone were to kill the count, who would avenge him?" (*Vita Karoli,* [20], 547, 22)—and, moved to tears by what he had seen, had burned and razed Borsiard's house. He had then gone on to spend the night in his own house in the burg of Bruges, from where he could look out and see, within the same castle walls, the houses of the provost and of the castellan, Borsiard's uncles.

He had spent Tuesday hearing suits and tending to the accumulated affairs of the county, and had again been warned, during the day, that Borsiard and his family were plotting some treachery. After dinner, Guy of Steenvoorde, who had married one of Borsiard's cousins, and a number of other prominent men had come to his house to ask him to pardon Borsiard and his allies and take them back into his favor. "'Did I requite Borsiard's outrageous deeds fittingly,'" Charles had replied, "'by burning one of his little houses, himself as yet unpunished? Does justice not demand rather that he restore to the poor everything he carried off and pay for the suffering caused by such great crimes in his own flesh? If he wishes to find the mercy he seeks, he should restore justly everything he has unjustly stolen and acknowledge the status of his lineage. For by what reckoning can he obtain forgiveness and keep what he has stolen from the poor?'" (*Vita Karoli,* [22], 548, 5/9). He had nonetheless concluded that "he would act justly and mercifully toward them [Borsiard and his supporters] if they would henceforth give up their fighting; and he assured them, moreover, that he would certainly compensate Borsiard with a house that was even better. He swore, however, that as long as he was count, Borsiard should never again have any property in that place where the house had been burned up, because as long as he lived there near Thancmar he would never do anything but fight and feud with his enemies, and pillage and slaughter the people" (*De multro,* [10], 32/39; trans., 107). The mediators had let the matter drop with surprising ease, but had stayed to drink the count's wine, "asking to be served again still more abundantly, as drinkers usually do" (*De multro,* [10], 43/44; trans., 107).

After Charles had retired that night, yet other rumors and warnings had reached him that Borsiard and his relatives were planning some kind of attack.

The count's insomnia and desire to stay in bed a little longer than usual that morning are thus easy to understand. When he did finally rise, he washed and, as was his habit, distributed food and clothing to several paupers in his house before crossing the stone archway connecting it to the gallery of Saint Donatian. Once in the gallery, he proceeded to the altar dedicated to the Virgin Mary, where he prayed and listened to mass every morning when he was in Bruges, while most of the handful of men escorting him wandered off in search of a quiet corner somewhere.

Charles began his prayers as usual. Eventually, he prostrated himself before the altar and, with his psalter open before him, began to recite the seven penitential psalms. From time to time he took a silver penny from the small pile his chaplains had placed on the psalter and gave it to a pauper whom they had led to his side. As he was reciting the fourth psalm, he reached out his right hand to give a penny to a poor woman whose turn had finally come. As he did so, he felt a light tap on the left side of his head and the woman cried out: "'Lord count, look out!'" (*Liber,* [28], 285, 37; trans., 43). He turned his head to the left and looked up, but he may never have seen Borsiard or the sword that crushed his forehead and "knocked his brains out on to the floor" (*Vita Karoli,* [25], 549, 17/18).

Borsiard had not slept well that night either. When the mediators who had gone to the count on his behalf had returned to the provost's house where he, his uncle Bertulf, and several relatives and supporters were waiting for them, the wine they had drunk gave an aggressive edge to their report. They announced "that they had not been able to secure any mercy either for the [provost's] nephews or their supporters" (*De multro,* [11], 7/8; trans., 108) and that "they would never obtain mercy from the count unless they all confessed themselves his serfs" (*Vita Karoli,* [23], 548, 18/19). Enraged by this inflammatory rendition of the count's response and fearful that he was planning to move against them in the near future,[4] Bertulf; his brother, Wulfric; their nephews, Borsiard, Robert, and Isaac (one of the count's chamberlains); and a few other men had retired to an inner room where they had sworn to kill the count as soon as they could. They had then split up, each returning to his own dwelling. When everyone in his house was asleep, Isaac had gone back out, collected Borsiard at his house, and they had gone together to the house of another knight, Walter, taking with them those members of Borsiard's household who had been chosen to murder the count. Once there, they had put out the fire and had plotted, waited, and perhaps dozed fitfully in the dark, planning to murder the count when he went to the church. Isaac, however, had left shortly before dawn. When the servants Borsiard had sent into the courtyard of the castle to watch had returned and reported that the count had gone into the gallery, "that raging Borsiard and his knights and servants, all with drawn swords beneath their cloaks, followed the count into the same gallery, dividing into two groups so that not one of those whom they wished to kill could escape from the [circular] gallery by either way, and behold! they saw the count prostrate before the altar, on a low stool, where he was chanting psalms to God and at the same time devoutly offering prayers and giving out pennies to the poor" (*De multro,* [12], 14–21; trans., 112).

After a week of indecision and confusion, the barons of Flanders collected at Bruges and drove the assassins and their accomplices into the castle, where they besieged them. Aided by friends, relatives, or large bribes, some of the besieged escaped; many of those who did, including Borsiard and Bertulf, were eventually captured and executed. Those who remained inside the castle were forced to retreat, first, to the church of Saint Donatian and then to the church's tower. They finally surrendered on April 19; on May 5, they were executed by being thrown from the tower of the count's house.

Charles died without an obvious or designated successor, and King Louis VI of France immediately seized the opportunity to exercise his rights as overlord of the county of Flanders in the choice of the new count. He summoned the barons of Flanders to meet him at Arras and, after hearing appeals from various claimants, chose William Clito (1101–1128), the nephew of Henry I of England and son of Robert Curthose, the dispossessed duke of Normandy. The choice was confirmed, in return for numerous and significant concessions, by the barons and towns of Flanders, and William was duly invested with the county and officially received as count throughout it.

Henry I's enmity toward the new count had a chilling effect on the important commercial relations between the cities of Flanders and England in the months that followed William's election and the king seems to have bribed everyone he thought could possibly make life difficult for his nephew.[5] The loss of commercial revenues, the flood of English money, and a series of unpopular actions taken by William led to rising discontent with the new count in urban centers like Lille, Bruges, Saint-Omer, and Ghent, and by March 1128 William was no longer in full control of the county. The citizens of Saint-Omer had welcomed Charles's nephew, Arnold of Denmark, and elected him count, while Thierry of Alsace, Charles's cousin and the son of Thierry II, duke of Upper Lorraine, had been received in Ghent and elected count there by its citizens. Baldwin IV, count of Hainaut, had also renewed his claim to the county. Arnold and Baldwin made no headway, but Thierry gained the support of Bruges and other cities. William finally won a decisive victory over him at the battle of Axpoel on June 21, and effectively reestablished himself as count. The defeated Thierry was pursued and besieged in Aalst on July 12 by William and Godfrey, duke of Louvain, but William was mortally wounded in the course of this siege and died on July 27 or 28. Deprived of its leader, the opposition to Thierry evaporated and he was quickly recognized as count of Flanders, a position he held for forty years until his death in 1168.[6]

GALBERT OF BRUGES

Thanks to the foresight of one of the senior canons of Saint Donatian, "the accounts and records of the revenues of the count" (*De multro,* [35], 9/10; trans., 163) were carried out of the church and the besieged castle on March 17, along with the church's relics and more valuable movable possessions, and thus saved from damage during the assault on the church and the pillaging that followed its capture. With Charles dead and Bertulf on the run, however, the comital administration could not have functioned in any regular way until after William Clito's arrival in Bruges on April 5 and the installation of a new provost on April 16. Impressed by the shocking and unprecedented events going on around him and in some way sensing their importance for the future, one of the functionaries of this administration, Galbert, decided to put his forced leisure to good use by recording them. He was an unusual and unlikely historian by the standards of the early twelfth century, and the chronicle he eventually wrote, but never quite finished, likewise stands out from other historical writing of that time.

The administration of the county of Flanders at the beginning of the twelfth century was one of the wonders of the bureaucratic world. The historical core of the county had been divided into castellanies in the course of the eleventh century, each administered from a comital castle governed by a castellan appointed by the count. Some of these fortified centers were of recent origin and may have been established as part of a deliberate comital policy intended to facilitate communications and increase commerce in the heart of Flanders and unify the county politically.[7] They usually contained a lodging for the count, a church (usually a collegiate church, sometimes recently founded, with a chapter of canons, like Saint Donatian; according to Dhondt, these churches were "in reality offices, centers of comital administration, . . . [whose] canons served first and foremost as notaries, as comital functionairies"),[8] and storehouses for revenues in kind. Each castellany was further divided into smaller administrative districts overseen by local officials serving under the castellan. The castellans and their officers were vested with the count's police and judicial powers and exercised them in his name within their jurisdictions.

The count's domain was divided into adminstrative units corresponding, for the most part, to these castellanies, and the domanial revenues corresponding to each castellany were collected at its principal castle (and at a few other centers in the larger castellanies). Most of the revenues were collected, stored, and consumed or disbursed at the castle, while any monetary surplus from cash revenues or from the sale of revenues in kind eventually made its way to the count's treasury, where it was received and administered by a chamberlain.[9]

The count needed an efficient fiscal administration to keep track of his revenues and payments throughout his domain and to oversee their collection and disbursement.[10] Perhaps the single most important step in the creation of this administration was taken in 1089 when the future Count Robert II, who was governing the county while his father, Count Robert I the Frisian, traveled to the Holy Land, appointed the provost of Saint Donatian to be "our chancellor [*cancellarium*] and that of all our successors, as well as the receiver and collector of all the revenues of the principality of Flanders [*susceptorem etiam et exactorem de omnibus redditibus principatus Flandrie*], and by my authority I entrust to his direction my notaries and chaplains and all the clergy serving in the count's court [*meorum notariorum et capellanorum et omnium clericorum in curie comitis servientum*]."[11] Robert thus gave the provost three tasks: he was to be the count's chancellor, the collector of his revenues, and the director of the clerical personnel serving in the *curia,* which in this context probably meant both the clerics in attendance on the count and all the others who worked in the administration of his domain.

Since most charters of the time were prepared by the grantee rather than by the grantor, the chancellor seems initially to have been little more than the keeper of the count's seal, responsible for verifying and sealing the charters presented to him by the beneficiaries of the count's largesse. At first, that is, it was a largely "technical" job. Indeed, the first provosts/chancellors of Saint Donatian appear to have delegated that part of their responsibilities to lesser members of their administration since no provost appears with the title of chancellor in any document until 1128, whereas several lower ranking men do.[12]

Despite the wording of the charter of 1089, the provost of Saint Donatian does not seem to have played an active role in the physical collection of the count's revenues either.[13] His principal tasks seem rather to have been to oversee the preparation and reconciliation of the accounts of the count's revenues and expenditures[14] and to direct the clerical personnel of the curia and the administration. The provost of Saint Donatian, in sum, was in charge of the count's bookkeeping and clerks, and thus ultimately in charge of the collection of the count's revenues insofar as he had the last word on what was due and whether or not it had been paid. It is not surprising, therefore, that "the accounts and records of the revenues of the count" were borne out of Saint Donatian and stored safely along with its other most prized possessions.

The chronological, quantitative, and descriptive precision of the author of the *De multro;* his method of work; and his familiarity with documents and legal proceedings all suggest that he worked in the count's administration in the burg of Bruges. Further and more precise evidence of his association with this administration comes from a charter of Thierry of Alsace dating to 1130.[15] The donation recorded in the charter was made in Bruges and its witnesses were: "Roger, provost of Bruges; Fromold, notary; Gervaise, castellan; Walter Crommelin; Froolf of Knesselare; Heio of Vulpan; Baldwin his brother, chief *preco;*[16] Hancmar of Straeten; Galbert, *clericus;* Ralph, schoolmaster and canon of Bruges." This is a heterogeneous group and the charter perhaps offers us a snapshot of a working session in the count's house. The word *clericus* is potentially ambiguous, since it means both "cleric" and "clerk," the lowest of the three ranks of clerical personnel serving in the count's administration,[17] but in the context of this charter—and given that distinct administrative positions (provost[/chancellor], notary, schoolmaster)[18] that explain their presence in the count's company are attributed to the group's other three clerical members (Roger, Fromold, and Ralph, respectively)—"clericus" probably refers here to Galbert's rank in the administration.[19]

The fact that the aristocracy is the most individuated group in the *De multro,* the group, that is, with the greatest number of differentiated individuals—singled out either by name or by description—provides further evidence that its author spent a great deal of his time in secular administrative circles. The aristocrats with whom he was most familiar were local ones like the Erembalds and the lords of Straeten; the count and court officials like the butler Didier and the chamberlains Arnold, Gervaise, and Isaac; and the great lords like Baldwin and Ivan of Aalst and Daniel of Dendermonde who were undoubtedly frequent visitors to Bruges.[20] Certain members of this group, like Borsiard and Gervaise, made a strong impression on Galbert, and he has left us lively portraits of them.[21]

It is not easy to discern Galbert's precise situation in the count's administration, however, in part because there seem to have been three more-or-less distinct organs or levels of that administration in Bruges at this time: the standing curia, or group of aulic officials and clerics in more-or-less permanent attendance on the count (and who moved throughout the county with him);[22] the "local" fiscal administration of the castellany of Bruges (the largest and most important of the castellanies of Flanders, and thus home to the largest "local" administrative center of the count's domain);[23] and the "national" fiscal administration of the count's domain in all of Flanders overseen by the provost of Saint Donatian. The witness list of the charter cited above shows Galbert in the count's presence, but, as Sproemberg noted, one never senses that Galbert was in any personal danger after Charles's murder, even though the assassins, "immediately after killing the count, . . . went out to attack those of their enemies from the court [*curia*] of the count who happened to be present" ([16], 7/9; trans., 121). Galbert seems to have "occupied no politically important position," and was not a member of the count's inner circle.[24] He never associates himself with the curia and writes about it as a group that he knew well, but to which he did not belong. He does not, that is, seem to have attended the count personally, although he does seem to have had a substantial amount of contact with him and both the secular and clerical members of his curia.

We can only speculate about the "national" administration of the count's domain in the first third of the twelfth century. In the latter part of the century, the receivers of the larger circumscriptions seem to have met periodically to reconcile their accounts,[25] and all the count's receivers, or at least representatives from each circumscription, came together once a year for a general audit under the supervision of the provost of Saint Donatian. These "national" meetings were, in effect, specialized meetings of the curia.[26] There does not, therefore, seem to have been a distinct, standing "national" administration of the domain in the first third of the twelfth century, and the only official with exclusively "national" responsibilities at the time seems to have been the provost of Saint Donatian.[27]

It is most likely, therefore, that Galbert worked in the "local" fiscal administration of the castellany of Bruges. Our earliest coherent picture of this administration comes from the *Gros Brief,* or annual account of the comital domain, for 1187, which lists six receivers of the count's revenues in the castellany of Bruges, each responsible for specific kinds of revenues or revenues from specific places. Galbert himself mentions two men, the notaries Basil and Fromold Junior, who probably served in this administration from c. 1127 to c. 1140.[28] On May 31, 1128, according to Galbert, Basil was ordered to come from Bruges to Oudenburg by Count William "because the overseers of the sheep runs and keepers of his farms and revenues had come into his presence, ready to render account of what they owed him" ([112], 16/17; trans., 294), and one may perhaps see in him a predecessor of Weitin, the receiver of the *spicaria* (principally cereal revenues) of the castellany of Bruges in 1187, since the only receipts from Oudenburg in the *Gros Brief* of that year are recorded in his account.[29] Lyon and Verhulst have pointed out that the administration of Charles's treasury seems to have been shared by Fromold Junior and the chamberlain Arnold, and they have suggested that Fromold's job was to record its receipts and expenditures.[30] He was thus perhaps a forerunner of the notary William of Mesen who was in charge of the *brevia camere* (cameral accounts) for the *Gros Brief* of 1187.[31]

Galbert calls both Basil and Fromold Junior "notaries," the highest of the three clerical ranks in the count's administration, and as many as four of the six receivers of Bruges mentioned in the *Gros Brief* of 1187 may also have been notaries. Galbert is likewise called a notary in a heading unique to one of the three early manuscript versions of the *De multro*[32] and in a variant reading of this same manuscript,[33] and, based on this heading and variant, modern scholarship has generally promoted him to this rank in the count's clerical corps. The receivers of the count's revenues in the twelfth century were not all notaries, however,[34] and nothing else suggests that Galbert ever rose above the rank of clericus. The manuscript's testimony, moreover, is dubious. As Declercq suggests, its copyist (or the copyist of its exemplar) may well have introduced this variant reading into the text because of the appelation given Galbert in the heading,[35] and since the work is unfinished and even its title, which, unlike the heading, *is* common to all the existing manuscript versions, was probably not given to it by Galbert,[36] it is fair to assume that this heading was likewise not part of the original text.

Henschen and Van Papenbroeck do refer to Galbert as a notary, however (although they call him a "public notary" of Bruges), and it is therefore possible, as Declercq suggests, that the heading of *A* was also in their early manuscript and goes back to the common ancestor of all the existing versions. Henschen and Van Papenbroeck also had a (lost) copy of *A*, however, and could have found the appelation there.[37] Even if the heading was in the lost early manuscript they used to prepare their edition, moreover, it is not necessarily due to Galbert or any of his immediate contemporaries. As the table of comital functionaries mentioned in the witness lists of the charters of Thierry of Alsace (1128–1168) shows, the title "clericus" was used only four times in these charters after 1133, while that of "notary" becomes increasingly common, especially after 1139.[38] Since the receivers of the count's domanial revenues in the later twelfth century were usually notaries, who seem to have replaced clerici as the workhorses of the comital administration during this time, a heading added to a copy of the text made at that time or later might well have "translated" Galbert's rank to conform with contemporary practice, especially if the position he held c. 1127 was held by a notary when this copy was made.[39] On the whole, then, what we know about Galbert suggests that he was probably never more than a clericus who worked principally in the fiscal administration of the count's domain in the castellany of Bruges.

Many of the receivers of the count's revenues in the twelfth century were laymen,[40] but Galbert was almost certainly a cleric. He had been decently educated—he cites Ovid[41] and Virgil,[42] paraphrases Horace,[43] makes at least three other classical allusions,[44] and had acquired the basic notions of grammar,[45] rhetoric,[46] dialectic,[47] and "psychology"[48]—although there is nothing in the *De multro* to suggest that his studies extended beyond the trivium.[49] This would, however, have been a sufficient course of study—indeed, it would have been the usual and recommended course of study—for someone preparing for a post in a secular or ecclesiastical administration at this time.[50]

Galbert mentions that students from Bruges were studying in Laon in 1127,[51] and it has been speculated, on the basis of this remark, that Galbert himself may have spent some time studying there.[52] Galbert's comment that Laon is "far away from us in France" was obviously intended to emphasize the idea that news of Charles's death traveled quickly to distant parts, but it also suggests that Laon simply lay "out there" somewhere for Galbert. It does not suggest any familiarity with the town or its school, nor would Galbert have had to travel very far to receive his basic education in the trivium. Saint Donatian itself had a school,[53] and the works of the few classical authors he cites or to whom he alludes seem to have been widely available in Flanders at the time.[54] He may thus have been educated entirely in Bruges and would certainly not have had to travel any further than Tournai,[55] Thérouanne, or Arras to complete the education he received.

Although he seems to have been well educated, Galbert was by no means a scholar and his school years were probably a somewhat distant memory when he began to write the *De multro.* He had obviously continued to write Latin over the intervening years, probably in connection with his work, and had perhaps continued to do some reading in his odd hours, but allusions to classical or patristic authors do not fall trippingly from his tongue.[56] His knowledge of the Bible is likewise neither profound nor exact[57] and is more like the familiarity one gains with it from listening to religious offices[58] than the deeper incorporation of it that comes with study or active participation in those offices. Galbert's adult education, in sum, had probably come mostly from his practical experience in the count's administration, from conversation, and from attendance at religious offices.

Galbert's historical education seems to have been more or less nil—which is perhaps what allowed him to be so original. He may have read Sallust as part of his formal education—and perhaps learned from him to write "elegant, reasoned" fictional speeches, descriptions of battles, monographic rather than universal or racial history or biography, and an "analysis of motive, informed by cynical pessimism: [to] suspect the worst"[59]—while his "theory" of history, like everyone else's at the time, seems inspired distantly by Augustine's *City of God* and, more clearly although still vaguely, by Orosius's *Seven Books of History against the Pagans.*[60] The *De multro* is, moreover, concerned almost exclusively with contemporary events, and on the couple of occasions when Galbert does relate earlier events, his source seems to have been popular, and thus unwritten, memory.[61] He shows no sign of having drawn on any existing annalistic material or, with the possible exception of Walter of Thérouanne's *Vita Karoli*[62] and Hariulf's *Vita Arnulfi,* of having read—at least recently—the work of other historians or hagiographers. He thus seems to have begun work with no practice other than half-forgotten school exercises and no more elaborate theoretical framework than could be supplied by half-remembered school readings and the broad commonplaces that underpinned the historical thought of any educated person of the time. He was not uneducated, naive, or simple—he seems rather to have been intelligent, had a basic education, a strong will, a high degree of empathy and imagination, a talent and taste for writing, and a flair for the dramatic—he had simply never planned to write history and had never thought about it too much.

This evidence of education, and the fact that Galbert writes in Latin, or indeed at all, are sufficient to tell us that he was a cleric, but his clerical state is also suggested by the fact that the clergy of Bruges form the second most frequently individuated group in the *De multro,* and the situation of the twenty clergy he mentions by name provide additional hints about his own. Eleven of these twenty belonged to the chapter, or *conventus,* as it was called in the charters of the time,[63] of Saint Donatian; Galbert identifies seven of them as also being attached in one way or another to the count's administration,[64] while the four to whom he gives no role in the administration are portrayed in a critical light.[65] Galbert associates four of the remaining nine clerics, none of whom seem to have belonged to the conventus of Saint Donatian, with the administration,[66] bringing the total number of named clerics associated with it to eleven. The last five clergy are priests of Bruges, of whom Galbert is generally, and sometimes viciously, critical.[67] The clerical side of his world, like its secular side, thus seems to have revolved around the count's administration, and it is not surprising that the most vividly and powerfully sketched clerics of the *De multro,* the provost Bertulf and the notary Fromold Junior, were both important members of it.

A number of scholars have identified Galbert as a "man of the people," and suggested that he was either a naive representative or a conscious apologist for the burghers of Bruges.[68] It is true that when he uses the first person plural, it always refers to the residents of Bruges, and he reports their opinions and deliberations in a way that suggests that he knew them well. It is possible that he, like the notary Fromold Junior, lived a secular life among them in the *suburbium,*[69] and, as we will see, there is good reason to believe that they formed the bulk of the audience he had in mind when he began to revise his journal some time after May 1127.

Galbert's clerical state and his work in the count's administration must have set him apart from most of the citizens of Bruges, however, and none of them is portrayed with the detail and interest he devotes to certain members of the aristocracy and clergy. In fact, we learn the names of only three of them.[70] During the spring of 1128, morever, Galbert grew increasingly critical of his fellow citizens and so distant from them that it is hard to think of him as a simple man of the people. He nonetheless seems to have felt closer to the citizens than to any of the other "solidarities" whose interweaving created the social tapestry of Bruges,[71] and their actions and attitudes receive a degree and kind of representation in the *De multro* that is unique in the twelfth century.

Charter evidence for the period 1089–1135 suggests the existence of as many as two other clerical Galberts in Bruges at this time, both members of the conventus of Saint Donatian. One of them was a deacon who appears in charters of 1100 and 1101, and perhaps in another charter of 1100, charters of 1116 and 1129, and a tax list of 1127/28–c. 1175.[72] It is unlikely that this Galbert is the author of the *De multro* since, on the one hand, he does not seem to have played any role in the count's administration, and, on the other, nothing in the *De multro* suggests that its author was a canon, let alone a deacon, of Saint Donatian. As we have seen, our author's opinion of the nonadministrative clergy he mentions by name is not high, and he always writes of the canons of Saint Donatian in the third person and in a way that suggests that he was not a member of that brotherhood and had no special attachment to it.[73] It is possible that this deacon Galbert was related to our author, however, and the witness lists of the charters of the counts of Flanders for 1071–1168 suggest that several senior members of the conventus found places for younger namesakes in the conventus or the administration.[74]

The second of these two other clerical Galberts whose existence is indicated by the charter evidence is called a "canon" of Saint Donatian in a charter of 1100, a "clericus" (which probably means "clergyman" here) in a charter of 1113, and is perhaps mentioned in another charter of 1100, charters of 1116 and 1129, and a tax list of 1127/28–c. 1175.[75] He is never assigned a specific rank within the conventus and he may never have risen above the rank of subdeacon.[76]

If one considers their common clerical state, and the coincidence of their names, dates, and locations, it is reasonable to identify this canon with our author/clerk.[77] This identification is satisfying both intellectually and emotionally, there are no formal, external grounds on which to exclude it (Galbert the clerk and Galbert the canon never, for example, appear together in the witness list to a charter), and it is supported by our author's familiarity with, and great, indeed elegiac, respect for, the canons of Saint Donatian in the early years of Bertulf's provostship,[78] and his affectionate pride in the church of Saint Donatian itself.[79] The notary Basilius, moreover, seems to have been a member of the conventus, as was at least one of the count's six receivers in Bruges in 1187.[80]

This identification is not required by the objective evidence available to us, however, and is not supported by the substantial subjective evidence of the *De multro.* The conventus of Saint Donatian and the administration of the count's domain were distinct and different institutions, and even though the provost of Saint Donatian was in charge of the clerics serving in the administration in Bruges, only about half of them seem to have been members of the conventus during the period 1089–1135.[81] The notary Basilius and at least one of the six receivers of Bruges in 1187 seem to have been members of it, as I mentioned above, but the notary Fromold Junior and at least two of the six receivers of 1187 do not seem to have been. Our author could have learned about the early days of Bertulf's provostship from an older relative, perhaps the deacon Galbert, or from any older member of the conventus—perhaps what he relates was simply what he had heard said around town—and any resident of Bruges might have taken a civic pride in one of the town's most prominent monuments, especially if he worked in or near it.

There is no evidence that more than two of these Galberts were active simultaneously, but the existence of even three men with the same name in the conventus or comital administration between 1089 and 1130 would not be unprecedented: two Baldwins seem to have been active between 1116 and 1136 (both simultaneously between 1116 and 1129); two Bertulfs were active simultaneously between 1096 and 1101; two Fromolds were active simultaneously between 1127 and 1129, and probably for some time before that; three Letberts were active in those two institutions between 1087 and 1145 (two of them simultaneously c. 1089); three Odgers were active between 1107 and 1147/49 (all three simultaneously between 1127 and 1138); four Reinarus were active between 1080 and 1122 (three of them simultaneously c. 1111); and three Roberts were active simultaneously c. 1129.[82] Some of these men seem to have been members of the conventus with no role in the count's administration, some of them seem to have served in the administration without being members of the conventus, and some of them seem to have been the one and done the other. Admittedly, some of these duplicates and triplicates may be mirages produced by the vagaries of the charters or their preservation, but it is unlikely that they all are.

The most compelling reason for not identifying these two Galberts, however, remains the *De multro* itself. From one end to the other, one never for a moment senses that its author associated himself with the canons of Saint Donatian.

It nonetheless remains possible that Galbert the clerk was a—marginal or alienated—member of the conventus of Saint Donatian. If he was, he belonged to a group of twenty-one men who can be identified as having been both active in the administration and members of the conventus during this period. This group can be subdivided into a group of twelve to fourteen men who appear with specific ranks in both institutions (provost, dean, priest, subdeacon, or schoolmaster in the conventus, and provost, chancellor, notary, chaplain, clerk, or schoolmaster in the administration) and another group of seven to nine men, to which this composite Galbert could be added, all of whom are given specific ranks in the administration (and some of whom had distinguished careers there), but none of whom are given a more precise rank in the conventus than that of "canon," "brother," or "member" of the conventus.[83]

These seven to nine men thus form a group of clerics who seem to have been essentially employees of the count's administration (and may have lived rather secular lives) but had a sufficient attachment, perhaps for purposes of compensation, to the conventus of Saint Donatian to be called "canons," "brothers," or "members" of that conventus in certain charters.[84] The members of such a group might, however, have been distinguished, both in their own minds and in the minds of those around them, from the core of regular canons of that church.[85] If we can admit the existence of such a group, it could explain why Galbert might be called a member of the conventus in charters without seeming to have considered himself to be one.[86]

Given our author's clerical background, administrative experience, familiarity with, but subjective distance from, both the conventus and the curia, and his identification with the citizens of Bruges, it seems most likely that he was a clericus who worked principally in the fiscal administration of the castellany of Bruges, perhaps in a position comparable to that of one of the six receivers of the count's revenues in Bruges listed in the *Gros Brief* of 1187.[87] Such work would have made him a member of the "national" administration of the domain when the various receivers met periodically for a general audit and thus a marginal member of the curia, for which he may also have performed various other, more punctual tasks.[88] It is possible that he was also a marginal member of the conventus of Saint Donatian.

The details of Galbert's education, work, and career thus remain frustratingly vague and largely speculative. The common and most remarkable characteristic that emerges from what we know or can guess about him is his central marginality, so to speak. He was probably a member of the count's curia, insofar as it included all the clerics involved in the administration of his domain, but a peripheral member of it. He was possibly a member of the conventus of Saint Donatian, but if he was, he was, again, a peripheral member of it.[89] He was a resident of Bruges, but was distinguished from most of his fellow residents by his clerical status and his work for the count. He seems to have had entrée everywhere—in the court, the conventus, and the town—but to have stood everywhere to the side or in the background, and it was perhaps a sense of his own marginality and, as his historical consciousness matured, the widening chasm between him and his fellow residents of Bruges that made his eye so keen and his voice occasionally so sharp.

Galbert's lack of an ideological home, his inability to identify fully with any one group, combined with his central position in Bruges, his access to the court, the conventus, and the gossip and councils of the citizens, and his experience in comital government,[90] make the *De multro* a unique and invaluable source. Galbert may have been, as Beryl Smalley has called him, our first civil-service historian,[91] but the civil service was not yet as organized and intellectually colonizing in his day as it would become later in the Middle Ages, and Galbert's view was not limited, physically or morally, to what he could see from his office. He used documents to which his position gave him access and was interested in political and legal matters, but he also spent time in the courtyard of the burg and the market, and was as interested in the future and destiny of Bruges and Flanders as that of his job or administration. Professor Van Caenegem is perhaps closer to the mark when he calls Galbert "our first reporter" as well as "our first bureaucrat."[92]

CHAPTER 2

"In the Midst of Such a Great Tumult"

In what I am going to relate I shall, by the help of God, write nothing but what I myself have seen and heard and know to be true, or have on good authority from the testimony or writings of reliable men.

—John of Salisbury, *Memoirs of the Papal Court*[1]

In this question it is not without value to call to mind what we see happen in the construction of buildings, where first the foundation is laid, then the structure is raised upon it, and finally, when the work is all finished, the house is decorated by the laying on of color.

So too, in fact, must it be in your instruction. First you learn history and diligently commit to memory the truth of the deeds that have been performed, reviewing from beginning to end what has been done, when it has been done, where it has been done, and by whom it has been done. For these are the four things which are especially to be sought for in history—the person, the business done, the time, and the place.

—Hugh of St. Victor, *Didascalicon*[2]

The siege of the Erembalds and their supporters in the castle of Bruges began on March 9, 1127. On March 17, the canons of Saint Donatian were permitted to climb over the castle walls in order to remove relics and fiscal records from the church. After describing this removal, Galbert adds:

And it should be noted that in the midst of such a great tumult and the burning of so many houses—set on fire by lighted arrows shot onto the roofs of the town from within the castle, and also by brigands from the outside in the hope of looting—and in the midst of so much danger by night and conflict by day, even though I, Galbert, had no suitable place for writing, I noted down on tablets a summary of events until finally, in a longed-for moment of peace during the night or day, I could set in order the present description according to the sequence of events [*locum scribendi ego Galbertus non haberem, summam re-*

rum in tabulis notavi donec aliquando, noctis vel diei expectata pace, ordinarem secundum rerum eventum descriptionem praesentem]. And in this way, though in great straits, I transcribed [*transcripsi*] for the faithful what you see and read. I did not note down individual deeds because they were so numerous and so intermingled but noted carefully only what occurred during the siege by common edict, or was done in the fighting, and its cause [*Neque quid singuli agerent prae confusione et infinitate notavi sed hoc solum intenta mente notavi quod in obsidione communi edicto et facto ad pugnam et ejus causam congestum est*], and I forced myself to do this, almost unwillingly, in order to commit it to writing [*scripturae commendarem*]. ([35], 33/45; trans., 164; trans. mod.)

This passage echoes another in the Prologue where Galbert likewise refers to the practical difficulties he faced at the beginning of his enterprise.[3] Both passages are reminiscent of common prologic protestations of a reluctance, an inability, or an unworthiness to write, but the impediments here are physical rather than moral, and the passages suggest that it truly was difficult for a reporter to do his work in war-torn Bruges. That Galbert persevered despite these obstacles suggests he had some reason and a strong desire to do so.

Scholars have proposed various motives for his decision to record the events of spring 1127. Pirenne did not think he had any precise motive.[4] Ross suggested that he had as many as four.[5] She suggested, first, that he was motivated by a simultaneously intellectual and emotional desire to bring order to chaos through writing.[6] She also suggests that he was incited to write by the tragic ends of Charles and Bertulf, two men to whom he was, in different ways, close.[7] The third and fourth motives she proposes might be termed a growing awareness of Bruges and Flanders as political entities and a concern for their fate, and an artistic or intellectual awakening to the pleasures of writing history.

Influenced by Sproemberg, Coué proposes a radically different motivation. According to her, the burghers of Bruges found themselves in "a precarious situation" after Charles's murder. They had lost their protector and the guarantor of the peace; their commerce was upset; their immediate lords, the Erembalds, were the principal assassins; and they were worried about the security of their dwellings and possessions. Faced with this crisis, familiar with writing and contracts, and predisposed to the settlement of conflict by judicial means, Coué argues, they commissioned Galbert to keep a record of the siege, taking special care to note the agreements they entered into with various aristocrats and the men from other towns, to which they could refer and use to justify their actions in any subsequent legal proceedings. Galbert's whole work, Coué concludes, "might better be named 'Collective Agreements of the Burghers with Other Parties' than the *Passio Karoli.* If Galbert was so resolute about writing down what the burghers of Bruges decided and agreed to with other parties, it was not out of a simple interest in history. He must have been commissioned to do so by the burghers of Bruges who had an interest in having a documentary record of their agreements and decisions with other parties." In its beginning the *De multro* was situation-bound and pragmatic, a text for its time, not for the future.[8]

One can, however, only speculate about Galbert's motives at this stage of the composition of the *De multro* since they seem to have changed and become more ambitious and precise at some point after May 22, 1127, and his reworking of the text on the basis of those new motives has effaced or hidden his earlier ones. He may have written for himself, perhaps initially as a means of creating some private order in the public disorder around him, or as a way of trying to understand the events he had witnessed, or with an eye to influencing public opinion about them, or simply out of a sense of their importance and significance. His decision to write, to take notes, in the face of a crisis is nonetheless significant and suggests a desire to remember, perhaps to tell, perhaps to explain, perhaps to shape understanding. It is the protogesture of a historian-to-be.[9]

The above-cited passage does tell us, fortunately, something concrete about Galbert's method of work. In it, he distinguishes between two kinds, or two stages, of activity: taking notes and writing. This distinction is clearest when he writes that "even though I, Galbert, had no suitable place for writing [*scribendi*], I noted down on tablets [*in tabulis notavi*] a summary of events," but it is also apparent when he writes "I did not note down [*notavi*] individual deeds because they were so numerous and so intermingled but noted [*notavi*] carefully only what occurred during the siege by common edict, or was done in the fighting, and its cause, and I forced myself to do this, almost unwillingly, in order to commit it to writing [*scripturae commendarem*]." Galbert forced himself to take notes on wax tablets, that is, so that he could, later, record the information in writing on, presumably, parchment.

This composition of a work in two or three stages was commonplace among medieval historians, and medieval writers in general,[10] and their drafting medium was usually, although not always, wax tablets.[11] These tablets, writes M. T. Clanchy, "were ordinarily made of wood, overlaid with coloured wax, and often folded into a diptych which could be worn on a belt. When something needed noting down, the diptych was opened, thus exposing the waxed surfaces, which were written on with a stylus."[12] Elisabeth Lalou describes these tablets in a similar way: "what is called a 'tablet' or 'table' in the Middle Ages—*tabulae* or *pugillares*—is essentially a wax tablet. A small wooden board (boxwood, cedar, beech, ebony, cypress, but also plane-tree, oak, ash, or conifer), slightly hollowed out, is covered with a skin of wax mixed with various colors: the wax may thus be black, green, or red. One wrote on these tablets with styluses or 'grafts' made of wood, of horn, or of bone, many examples of which have been preserved throughout Europe." Lalou further distinguishes three kinds of tablets: "the large wooden codex, what I call the 'notebook' (a small codex of wood and wax), and finally 'placards.'"[13] The surviving large codices can measure as much as 36 cm by 16 cm and have up to sixteen "leaves," but there are no examples of this kind of codex before the thirteenth century. Galbert is more likely to have used what Lalou terms a small codex. The most interesting surviving example (for us) of this kind of codex dates from the eleventh century and comes from the Abbey of Saint Martin in Angers. It measures 24 mm by 85 mm, originally had nine "leaves," and contains a draft of a portion of a verse chronicle.[14]

Such tablets were the lifelong companion of medieval writers—they had been taught to write on them as children,[15] and had later taken their lecture notes on them[16]—and it was convenient, relatively inexpensive, and natural for the adult writer to use them for most common writing tasks and the drafting of more enduring works. According to Clanchy, "[T]he most important equipment of the twelfth-century writer who composed for himself or wrote from dictation, as distinct from the copyist, was not the parchment book depicted in conventional portraits of scribes, but the writing tablets on which he noted down his drafts."[17] The relative frequency of taking notes on wax and writing on parchment can perhaps be judged by the fact that an eleventh-century sign-language manual from Cluny includes signs for tablets and a stylus in the section devoted to signs pertaining "to apparel" *(ad vestitum),* but does not include any signs for writing on parchment. This suggests that taking notes on wax was a normal part of daily life for which one needed a sign and that tablets and a stylus were a regular part of a monk's apparel, whereas writing on parchment was much rarer.[18]

In general, according to Lalou, the surviving tablets contain essentially three kinds of texts: "drafts (lists, notes, and administrative drafts, 'literary' drafts, or school exercises), memoranda or labels, likewise accounts. . . . Many contain lists or notes on a wide variety of different subjects. Lists of people who attended a ceremony; lists—perhaps one can call them inventories—of books or papers; lists of shoes purchased for a monastery, etc. Since most of the surviving medieval tablets were produced by what one might call royal, civil, or ecclesiastical administrations, the majority of drafts are of an administrative nature."[19] The survival of parchment accounts of the chickens and eggs received from the count's manors in the castellany of Saint-Omer c. 1120 and of the expenditures by the receiver of the *fodermolt* of Bergues-Saint-Winnoc for part of 1140–1141 shows that these accounts were ultimately put down on parchment, but it is difficult to believe, for practical reasons, that they were immediately recorded on it. It seems more likely that they were first recorded on wax tablets and then transferred to parchment, as were the tax lists of the town of Provins at the beginning of the fourteenth century.[20] This is also suggested by the fact that the verb *notare*—which Galbert uses to describe the first stage of writing—carried the specific connotation of "to note in wax": the designation given to the highest rank in the count's administration, *notarius,* thus designated first and foremost someone who wrote in wax.[21] If Galbert did indeed work in this administration, therefore, it is likely that he worked with such tablets on a daily basis and so it would be natural for him to take his notes in this way when he began to record the events of spring 1127.

The smaller notebooks, such as Galbert was likely to have used, were highly portable. They were often made to be attached to a belt, and Baudry of Bourgueil mentions a "satchel" *(saccum)* in which he kept his eight-leaved codex.[22] One can thus easily imagine Galbert carrying one around with him and noting down information as he learned it, interviewing people, summarizing speeches and the oral delivery of documents as he heard them. It is probably too much to imagine that he never went out without his notebook during the whole period from March 1127 to July 1128: in some cases he probably had to remember what he had seen or heard for at least a short period of time before he could summarize it in his notebook, but the notebook's availability, portability, and easy manipulation probably enabled him to note most things down immediately or at least soon after he learned them.

This brings us to the question of Galbert's sources of information as he walked about the streets of Bruges, tablets at the ready, that turbulent spring. He was, as we have seen, a resident of Bruges, probably worked in the burg, and probably knew a great many of the principal actors in the events of 1127–1128. He was thus well situated to observe everything that occurred within Bruges, or at least to learn of it, and undoubtedly witnessed many of the things he records.[23] It is nonetheless obvious that he cannot himself have seen or heard everything he reports as having happened in Bruges[24]—even though he imagines the scenes he describes so vividly that it is difficult to distinguish what he has witnessed from what he has learned from someone else—and we can in fact find traces of a number of different sources in the *De multro.*

I have divided these sources into three categories—oral sources, written sources, and messages—and list them in Appendices II–IV.[25] The oral sources that make up the first category range from named sources (Charles, Woltra Cruual), to specific but unnamed sources (Charles's chaplains, squires of the abbess of Origny), to hearsay, and even implicit reports of events in other towns.[26] Within this category, Galbert seems to distinguish between rumor or hearsay and eyewitness testimony. He signals the first kind of source with terms like "it is said" *(aiunt)* or "we heard" *(audivimus),* whereas he always individuates an eyewitness, even if it is only by naming the person's function (a squire, merchants, students). This list also shows us that rumor was Galbert's most important source for events outside of Bruges.[27] A report that reached Galbert in this way had been rolled around by many tongues and, worn down to a hard core by different interests and ambient narrative traditions, had an objective value as an expression of common opinion. It may not have been an accurate report of what had happened, but it was an accurate report of people's understanding of the significance and import of what had happened.[28]

Galbert refers to most of the written sources he cites as "letters" *(litterae).* He twice refers to "sealed letters" *(litterae signatae)* and calls one of the letters from Louis VI a "mandate" *(mandatum).* He refers to three "charters" *(chartae).* It is also likely that he had access to a copy of a written summary of the results of the inquest into the assassination ordered by William Clito in September 1127. I have included in this category two messages that Galbert does not call letters but does describe as having included a formal greeting ("to send greetings" [*mandare salutem*]); these may have been oral messages, but the context and the use of this term in other cases where the message is clearly written suggest that they, too, were written. I have likewise included in this category a rather curious message from the knights of Oostkerke to William Clito.[29] It is not clear whether this was a written message or an oral message accompanied by a piece of parchment on which the names of its senders had been written, but since it had a written component I included it in this category.[30]

The fact that Galbert refers to a document does not necessarily mean that he had read it. It is hard to imagine, for example, that he ever had an opportunity to inspect the "daily letters" *(quotidianae litterae)* ([49], 10/12; trans., 191) exchanged by William of Ypres and the Erembalds during the first week after the assassination, and since, as his text makes clear, written messages were frequently read aloud, or at least summarized, in public by their couriers, it is possible that he only heard a public reading, translation, or paraphrase of some of the documents he cites.[31]

Galbert's report of the first message sent by William of Ypres to the Erembalds is illustrative of the oral or performative aspect of such messages: "On March 6, Sunday, Godescalc Taihals, a messenger [*internuntius*] from Ypres, brought these words [*venit in haec verba*] to the provost at Bruges: 'My lord, and your intimate friend, William of Ypres, openly sends you and yours greetings and friendship and will help you at once in every way possible.' After they had all applauded him and taken him into the hall, he revealed [*denudavit*] to the provost and

William of Wervik and Borsiard, and a few others whom they had admitted, other matters which it would have been shameful to report publicly" ([25], 1/9; trans., 143–44). There is nothing here to suggest that Godescalc Taihals carried a letter and yet Galbert's subsequent allusions to this event make it clear that William's message was in writing, perhaps even in a sealed letter.[32]

The elision between a written message and its oral performance, or at least the oral message accompanying it, is even more evident in the case of the letter Thierry of Alsace addressed to the barons and inhabitants of Flanders:

Another messenger [*nuntius*] appeared, this one from a kinsman of Count Charles, bringing greetings [*demandans . . . salutem*] to the barons of the siege and an expression of natural affection for all the inhabitants of the land: "You all know for a certainty that the realm of Flanders pertains to my lot and power by right of kinship after the death of my lord the count. Therefore, I want you to take thought and proceed carefully concerning the election of my person, and I warn and urge you not to estrange me from the realm. If, out of respect for right and kinship, you send back a favorable reply to me, I shall hasten to become your count, and I shall be just, peaceful, tractable, and concerned for the common good and welfare." But the barons and everyone else who had heard the letter [*audierant litteras*] sent from Alsace by the count's cousin, asserting that it was not genuine, did not take the trouble to reply. ([47], 24/36; trans., 188; trans. mod.)

The messenger read (or translated or summarized) this letter aloud—the barons "heard" it—and the consequent confusion between him and Thierry is striking. Grammatically, it is the messenger who greets the barons of the siege and assures the people of Flanders of his natural affection for them; it is he who claims the realm of Flanders for himself. In the oral performance of his message, that is, the messenger incarnates Thierry who, through him, stands and speaks before the barons of Flanders.[33]

What these and the other examples of the public reading of a written message tell us is that Galbert did not necessarily read any of the written sources he cites.[34] Ganshof argued that Galbert probably did read the three written messages from the king of France that he records,[35] and it is likely that he had occasion to read a number of others, but even then, as Ganshof showed was the case with respect to the king's messages, he may have altered their contents either involuntarily, through a faulty memory or incomplete notes, or voluntarily, for the sake of narrative coherence. One can thus never assume that Galbert ever provides a verbatim reproduction of a written source he mentions.

I have placed messages in a separate category for three reasons. First, Galbert distinguishes between the kinds of oral reports I have included in the category of oral sources and a more formal transmission of information (usually signaled by the verb *mandare* [to send]) carried by designated messengers (called *nuntii* or *internuntii*), and I thought I should respect this distinction. Second, these designated messengers bearing precise messages seem to belong to a category in between oral reports and written messages insofar as they, like texts, could presumably be consulted several times in order to verify their information after its initial delivery, although their information was more liable to evolution than that contained in a written text.[36] Third, as we have seen, written messages were necessarily transmitted by couriers who sometimes, at least, read (or summarized or translated) them aloud when they delivered them. Some of the sources I have included in the category of messages, therefore, may in fact have had a written component or basis.[37]

Galbert thus seems to have drawn his information from a wide range of oral and written sources and this brings us to the question of how much he could have recorded in his wax notebook and in what form. This is, of course, impossible to answer. It depends, on the one hand, on just how summary his notes were and, on the other hand, on the size of his notebook. Since he was presumably a professional clerk used to recording information on tablets, one may suppose that he was able to compact a maximum of information into a minimum of space, and one could, it seems, record quite a bit of information on such tablets.[38] The notebooks could, moreover, contain a fair number of leaves, and, if he was a professional clerk, Galbert may have had more than one. It seems unlikely that he recorded all the information reported in chapters 15–67 and 72–85 (his running account of the events of March 2 to May 22, 1127) on wax tablets before he transferred it to parchment, but neither should we underestimate the amount of information he could record on wax before transcribing it. The passage in which he describes this transfer—"even though I, Galbert, had no suitable place for writing, I noted down on tablets a summary of events until finally, in a longed-for moment of peace during the night or day, I could set in order the present description according to the sequence of events. And in this way, though in great straits, I transcribed for the faithful what you see and read"—is ambiguous insofar as the phrase "in a longed-for moment of peace during the night or day" can be read as referring either to a single moment of peace (after March 19? after April 19?) when he was finally able to transcribe everything he had recorded on wax or to a series of intermediary moments when he transcribed smaller installments.[39] It does not in any case seem unreasonable to think that Galbert might have recorded a week's worth of information on wax tablets before he transferred it to parchment.

This raises the related question of when Galbert began taking notes. One cannot of course be certain, but his descriptions of the difficult circumstances in which he began to do so in the above-cited passages suggest that it was not until after the beginning of the siege of the castle of Bruges on March 9, a week after the assassination. If this is the case, the information found in chapters 15–27 could not have been recorded immediately, but, at the earliest, as much as a week after Galbert saw, heard, or learned it.

Another intriguing question, to which it is even more difficult to give an answer, is: Did Galbert keep his tablets or did he erase them and reuse them? Hadoard, as was already mentioned, wrote that he "'filled his tablets with accumulated impressions, and sought to keep them together without "emptying" them somewhere else; he intended to preserve them where they could be seen, while they grew into the likeness of a book *(libri)*.'"[40] And at the beginning of the fourteenth century, as we have likewise seen, the tax lists of the town of Provins were initially recorded on wax tablets, then transferred to parchment. The tablets were erased and rewaxed every year, suggesting that the records were preserved on wax for a year.[41] The use of the tablets for similar record-keeping functions by various administrations suggests that the information recorded on them was intended to be preserved for at least a certain time, and the survival of medieval tablets with legible text from as early as the seventh century shows that they could, in the right conditions, last quite long indeed.[42] It seems probable, given the state of affairs in Bruges and the private nature of his chronicle, that

Galbert did not dispose of a large number of tablets and had to erase and reuse his after he had transferred the information they contained onto parchment, but we cannot dismiss the possibility that his notes were available to him for a considerable period of time.

There are three other observations we need to make about this first step or first stage in Galbert's recording of information. First, if, as one supposes was the case, Galbert recorded information on his tablets as he learned it, that information could not have had any precise order, not even a chronological one. He witnessed many of the events that took place in Bruges, and he probably learned about most of those he did not witness on the day they happened, although it is clear that he could not have learned of some things that took place in Bruges (like the details of the conspiracy) until well after they had occurred, and he may not have had access to some of the written sources (been able, that is, to read them as well as hearing them summarized or read aloud) until some time after they had been received in Bruges. Information from outside Bruges necessarily took longer to arrive and arrived haphazardly. The information he recorded on his tablets, then, probably had an overarching chronological order, but insofar as he did not himself witness everything he records, it could not have had an exact one. And in some cases, he must of learned of events well after they had occurred and thus had to record them well out of chronological order.

Second, the information Galbert recorded was summarized, probably abbreviated, and usually translated. He himself tells us that he recorded only "a summary of events" *(summam rerum)* on his tablets and such a summary is always and necessarily subjective.[43] Given his use of the verb *notare,* the compact form of the tablets, and the universal recourse to abbreviations in medieval writing, moreover, his notes were probably highly abbreviated.[44] Since writing was, as far as we can tell, carried out almost exclusively in Latin at the time, it is also reasonable to think that he took his notes in Latin and had to translate most of what he heard said and reported from Flemish (or French), thus introducing another subjective element into this initial act of recording.

Third and finally, Galbert likewise tells us that he did not record everything he saw or heard. In the above-cited passage from chapter 14, he writes: "I did not note down individual deeds because they were so numerous and so intermingled but noted carefully only what occurred during the siege by common edict, or was done in the fighting, and its cause." Galbert seems to violate the principle he announces here in the very next chapter (although this chapter may be a later addition), but it was nonetheless his intention to be selective. He never intended to write down everything he saw, heard, or learned, and thus, to some degree at least, he must not have done so.

In this first stage or first step in recording information, then, Galbert probably noted down a summary of a selected portion of what he saw, heard, or learned, in highly abbreviated Latin, in a small codex of wax tablets. This information probably had a general chronological order, but this order was probably only rarely exact, even with respect to the events of a single day, and in some cases information must have been recorded well out of chronological order. Even during this first stage, then, Galbert's subjectivity affected what he recorded through a deliberate selectivity and processes of summarization and translation. The information he recorded, moreover, had no strong inherent organization, not even a chronological one.

The transferral of this information onto parchment—the second stage in the process of recording information—necessarily transformed it in other ways. One of the first questions Galbert had to face was that of its organization. He could have transcribed his notes onto parchment as they stood, and thus produced a true journal, but he chose instead to organize his information with a chronological rigor that a true journal could never possess. We find evidence of this intention in the above-cited passage from chapter 35, in which Galbert writes that he continued to take notes on tablets until, in a moment of peace, "I could set in order the present description according to the sequence of events" *(ordinarem secundum rerum eventum descriptionem praesentem),* a statement that also confirms that his wax notes did not already have this kind of organization since they had to be set in order, that is, reorganized, according to this chronological principle. This principle of organization resurfaces briefly in chapter 57, where Galbert interrupts his description of Bertulf's execution to remark: "And although I may seem to have a convenient place here to recount his genealogy, nevertheless, it seems to me I should let the work I have undertaken suffice and omit such an account, for I have set out to relate the outcome of the siege [*eventum obsidionis*] and not the adulterous origin of the family of the provost and his kin" ([57], 50/55; trans., 210). He thus reaffirms that his purpose is to relate the *eventum,* the chronological development, of the siege (and, as this chapter shows, of the events that grew out of it).

This decision to organize his parchment notes journalistically was eventually the most significant one Galbert made as a historian, but, initially at least, he may not have given it much thought. Few twelfth-century historians inhabited a historical crisis the way Galbert did and, faced with the immense daily volume of chronologically precise information, and the means of gathering and recording it, available to him at the time, he probably simply reacted by recording and organizing it in the way he was used to recording and organizing information in his work for the comital administration: journalistically.[45]

It also seems likely that he continued to respect the principle of selection that he used while taking notes—"I did not note down individual deeds because they were so numerous and so intermingled but noted carefully only what occurred during the siege by common edict, or was done in the fighting, and its cause"—when he transferred them to parchment, and used it both to weed out material in his notes that he had recorded in the excitement of the moment but that did not correspond to his announced intention and to keep himself from adding new extraneous material as he rewrote his notes. The continued use of this principle for this latter purpose is evident in the above-cited aside concerning the provost's genealogy. He is tempted to add this genealogy to his chronicle (and did add it in a subsequent passage when he revised it), but, reminding himself and his readers of his purpose and the discipline that it imposes, he manages to put Satan behind him.

Two other factors that are likely to have transformed Galbert's basic information when he transferred it to parchment are his amplification of the abbreviated summary of events in his notes and the common human tendency to "perfect" narrative descriptions when rewriting them by bringing them into closer conformity with common narrative models. These two processes are of course intermingled in practice. As Galbert strove to transform his abbreviated summary into a fluent prose description, he had to remember and imagine the scenes he had seen, the words he had heard, the documents he had read. In doing so, he necessarily transformed these scenes, words, and documents into *his* scenes, *his* words, *his* documents: his notes were a set of verbal indications of the impressions these things made on him when he first experienced them, and he may have noted down some of the terms and expressions he actually heard, but when it came time to fill in the blanks, to make the connections, to round out the description, the words and images necessarily came from his reservoirs of experience and Latin and were combined according to his imaginative abilities and moral and aesthetic criteria. Since memory is a narrative faculty, moreover, it is necessarily influenced by the ambient narrative traditions and the models they offer (one might even suggest that memory is formed by these traditions), and we will see in later chapters how certain common narrative models structure some of Galbert's descriptions. In the process of reconstituting, rehydrating, what he had seen, heard, and learned, Galbert necessarily injected much of himself into the mix, and reimagined it in terms of what he would have expected or liked to see, hear, and learn.

The notes that Galbert transcribed onto parchment, then, were not an immediate record of first impressions. They did not form a true journal. They were not a record of everything he saw, heard, or learned. They were, rather, the product of both what one might term a "conscious subjectivity," which articulated and strove to respect principles of selectivity and strict chronological organization in recording events, and an "unconscious subjectivity" that came unavoidably into play in the summarization, translation, and abbreviation of information on his tablets and the reconstitution of this information on parchment.

Up to now, moreover, we have been considering only the first transfer of information from tablets to parchment. What happened when Galbert transferred new information from his tablets to parchment a few days, a week, or maybe even several weeks later? Insofar as this new information concerned events occurring on days subsequent to those for which he already had an entry on parchment, the process would have been the same. This new transfer, that is, changed the existing parchment record only by extending it.

But Galbert inevitably learned things about events that had occurred on a given day well after that day had passed. What did he do when he had new information concerning events occurring on days for which he already had an entry on parchment? Perhaps, foreseeing that he might want to make additions to his entries, he left some blank space at the end of each one where he could append new information. If he did not, or if this space filled up, he probably added the new information in the margins or between the lines of the existing parchment entry. The various passages beginning with *"notandum"* (it should be noted), *"et notandum"* (and it should be noted), *"non praetereundem est"* (it should not be forgotten), or *"et memorandum"* (and it should be remembered)[46] may all be examples of such appendices or of marginal or interlinear additions that were inserted into the body of the *De multro* when it was recopied at some point.

The part of the existing *De multro* that can best help us form some idea of its material status during spring 1127 is probably chapters 102–16. This section, devoted to events of spring 1128, consists primarily of relatively short manuscript chapters, each devoted to a single day, to which a number of additions, signaled by *notandum* and the like, have been made. The most interesting from this point of view are chapters 102 and 110.

It is possible that the initial entry for chapter 102, written on a tablet during the day on March 30, 1128, was limited to lines 1–6 describing what had happened in the morning and what the citizens expected to happen later in the day.[47]

The observation concerning the calendar that occupies the next two lines (6–7)[48] was perhaps simply an idea that struck Galbert still later in the day and he jotted it down.

The next section, which runs from line 8 to line 23, describes the return of Ivan and Daniel "at evening," the news they brought with them, the evening meal, the election of Thierry as count by the people of Bruges, and the promulgation of various decrees by the new count.[49] Since everything that is described in this passage took place after vespers, and since it begins with the seemingly unnecessary notation "on the same day" *(eodem die),*[50] it may well have been written the next day.

This is followed by another observation, introduced by *et notandum,* on the irony—or significance—of the fact that exactly one year before the barons had returned from Arras to announce the election of William Clito as count (lines 23–31).[51] This observation may have been inspired by the immediately preceding description of Thierry's election, but the fact that it is preceded by *et notandum* and probably required that Galbert look back over what he had written in order to see what had happened exactly one year before, it seems more likely to be a later addition, inspired perhaps by a rereading of the passage and the earlier remark it contains concerning the evolution of the calendar from year to year.

The final lines of the chapter relate the collapse that same day in Ypres of a gallery in which William Clito and his barons were sitting (lines 31–37).[52] This passage, too, is introduced by *et notandum* and since communication between Bruges and Ypres was probably perturbed at this point by the fact that Bruges was in open rebellion against William Clito, it is likely that Galbert did not learn this bit of information right away, but added it to the entry for this day somewhat later.

This chapter thus appears to have been written not in a single moment, but in as many as five different moments, and thus gives us an idea of the way in which the initial entries of the *De multro* could grow by accretion over time.

Chapter 110 is even more fragmented, with perhaps as many as seven additions to an initial entry, dated Saturday, May 5, which may have been no more than an observation about the anniversary of the execution by precipitation of a number of the traitors (lines 1–3).[53]

What seems to be a first addition (lines 3–7)[54] begins with the phrase *et notandum* and relates the death of Lambert, son of Ledewif, and a number of other supporters of Thierry of Alsace in a battle at Oostburg "in the same week" *(in hac eadem septimana).* The battle to which he seems to refer took place on Monday, April 30, and is described in chapter 108. Galbert refers to it again here, evidently, because, as Mohr suggests, he saw a parallel between these men, "by whose counsel and treachery Thierry of Flanders was forcibly put in the place of William the Norman," and the assassins, the anniversary of whose execution he records in the first lines.[55]

A second addition (lines 7–13)[56] begins with a similar but potentially confusing temporal indication: "During this same week [*in hac eadem hebdomada*], the king of France was engaged in summoning archbishops, bishops, and all synodal persons among the clergy, and abbots, and the most responsible persons from both the clergy and people, counts and barons and other leading men to come to him at Arras on Sunday, 'Misericordia Domini,' May 6" (trans. mod.). The sense here seems to be that during the preceding week, the week of Sunday, April

29, through Saturday, May 5—during the same week that Lambert and his men were killed—the king summoned various people to meet with him at Arras on Sunday, May 6. The passage does not, that is, pertain to the meeting on May 6, but to the king's activity during the week leading up to the meeting, and was perhaps placed here because this was the day on which Galbert learned of the king's actions, or because it was the end of the week during which these actions occurred, or because the previous passage about Lambert covered the same week.

The temporal situation of a third added passage (lines 14–20)[57] is even more vague. It begins "At this time [*quo tempore*], Thierry was wandering about at Lille and William at Ypres" (trans. mod.), and goes on to describe the state of unrest and insecurity in Flanders as both sides waited to hear the results of the deliberations of the meeting of May 6. The passage thus seems to be inspired by the preceding one and to relate to the week preceding the meeting in Arras.

A fourth addition (lines 20–28)[58] begins with *et notandum* and relates the return "at this time" *(hoc tempore)* of many of those exiled for being accessories to Charles's murder, probably, as Ross notes,[59] as a result of the conditional amnesty announced a month earlier (on Friday, March 30) by Thierry at Bruges, which declared that they could return if they were willing to face any accusations made against them ([102], 15/20; trans., 279). "But," Galbert writes, "up to this time [*adhuc*] no one has been challenged or has responded." The period covered by this passage would thus seem to be more than the week of April 29–May 5 and both the *et notandum* with which it begins and the *adhuc* with which it ends suggest that it was added to this chapter after May 5.

A fifth addition (lines 29–37)[60] begins with *et memorandum* and tells how Thierry was made sick by a sorceress (who was subsequently burned alive) "when [he] . . . first went to Lille." Since Galbert reports in an earlier chapter ([107], 11/12; trans., 286) that Thierry first went to Lille on April 23, almost two weeks before the date on which this chapter begins, it is difficult to see why he added this passage to this chapter rather than to the earlier one. Perhaps, again, he only heard the story at this point (although one would think that news of such a spectacular event would have traveled more quickly); or perhaps his memory was jogged during a subsequent rereading of this chapter by its earlier reference to Thierry's presence in Lille.

The sixth addition (lines 37–43)[61] begins with yet another indefinite temporal reference—"from that time up to May 9" *(ab illo ergo tempore usque in septimum idus Maii)*—and relates depradations carried out by supporters of William Clito in the region south of Bruges, and the efforts of the citizens of Bruges to protect themselves from attack.

The last addition is very brief and notes simply that "At this time [*qua tempestate*] the village of Oostkamp was completely sacked by the knights of Count William" ([110], 43/44; trans., 292).

The various passages combined in this chapter are linked to one another in different ways. The first two additions are linked chronologically to what seems to be the precisely dated initial entry. The first refers to an event that had occurred five days earlier and has, on this the anniversary of the traitors' execution, acquired a new significance in Galbert's eyes. The second relates a continuous event that occurred during this same week.

The third addition is linked to the second in two ways. There is a weak chronological link since it relates the whereabouts of Thierry and William and the mood of Flanders "at this time." This addition provides almost no precise information, however, and serves rather to increase the reader's sense of the importance and drama of the May 6 meeting and to evoke an emotional response through its description of the two counts "wandering about" and of the deplorable state of Flanders as it awaits the outcome of the meeting. Its primary link to the preceding passage, in sum, is thematic and rhetorical.

The fourth addition is a development and precision of the third. It explains one of the reasons for the state of affairs in Flanders—the criminals have all come back—and provides an example of it: none of them have had to answer for their crimes.

The fifth addition seems largely unrelated to the previous ones and is rather out of place. Perhaps, as I suggested above, it was inspired by the mention of Thierry and Lille in the third addition.

The sixth and seventh additions, relating the raiding carried out by William's men south of Bruges, are intriguing and inspire speculation about the composition of the entire chapter. They are clearly intended to be linked chronologically to some "time" ("from that time up to May 9"; "at this time"), but to what "time"? The last "time" mentioned, in the fifth addition, is April 23 (when Thierry went to Lille). It seems unlikely, however, that it took almost two weeks to sack Oostkamp. In the preceding chapter, moreover, Galbert reports that the castellan of Bruges, Gervaise, attacked the stronghold of the marauders referred to in the sixth addition only a week before, on May 2, and it likewise seems unlikely that they were able to carry out continuous raids while he was in the area. The next "times" as one works one's way back through the chapter are May 6 (the day of the court gathering in Arras), the week of April 29 through May 5, and May 5. Since the marauders referred to in the sixth addition repulsed Gervaise on May 2, the "time" referred to in the sixth and seventh additions might well be May 3–6. Having repulsed Gervaise on May 2, that is, the marauders raided the region south of Bruges "from that time [May 3 or 4 or 5 or 6] up to May 9"; Oostkamp was sacked during "this [same] time."

How, then, did these two passages get so far separated from the "time" to which they refer? The sixth addition, at least, could not have been written before May 9, and it is possible that Galbert simply tacked these two additions on to this chapter, which seems to have become a sort of catch-all between the two shorter, precisely dated chapters that precede and follow it (chapter [109] devoted to May 2, and chapter [111], 1/4 devoted to May 14), with a vague reference to "that time" (that is, between May 2 or 5 and May 13). One can also imagine another explanation, however, which, while speculative, better illustrates the way in which I believe the first parchment version of the *De multro* evolved.

It is possible that what currently appear to be the sixth and seventh additions to the chapter were in fact the first and second additions, that the initial parchment entry went directly from the observation of the anniversary of the traitors' execution on May 5 to the passage about the pillaging south of Bruges "from that time up to May 9." The first two intervening passages (lines 3–13), introduced by an *et notandum,* would thus have been added in the margin of this chapter when Galbert made a subsequent transfer of information from wax to parchment. The next intervening passage (lines 14–20), the description of the general state of Flanders at that time, might also have been added in the margin, not from new wax notes, but spontaneously, as a rhetorical development and extension of the existing marginal note, during a subsequent rereading of the chapter. The fourth addition (lines 20–28), beginning with another *et notandum* and ending with an *adhuc,* would likewise be a later, spontaneous addition inspired by a rereading of this chapter. The fifth addition (lines 29–37), beginning with *et memorandum,* would be yet another spontaneous addition to the chapter's marginalia, likewise inspired by a rereading of the chapter and the mention in the existing marginalia of Thierry and Lille.

This last addition seems so out of place here, however, that one wants a different explanation. Could it have been written on a separate piece of parchment placed between the leaf containing chapter 107, where this addition belongs chronologically, and the leaf containing chapter 110?[62] Perhaps a later copyist found this piece of parchment between the two leaves, assumed that the addition it contained went with the material contained on the following leaf rather than with that on the preceding one, and inserted it in its current place when he recopied the entire *De multro.* This same copyist would be responsible for inserting the chapter's marginalia—maladroitly—in their current place, splitting what now appear as the final additions to the chapter from the date at the beginning of the chapter to which they refer.[63]

This explanation of the evolution of chapter 110 is speculative and is no more than one possible explanation of it. It does, however, have the value of helping us imagine the way in which Galbert may have worked in the spring of 1127: an initial transfer of information to parchment; marginal additions to the initial entry when subsequent transfers were made; subsequent spontaneous additions, inspired by rereadings of the text, in the margins or on separate pieces of parchment; followed ultimately by a final recopying that incorporated the marginalia into the text.

If, on the one hand, one assumes for the sake of illustration that Galbert transferred information from his tablets to parchment once a week between March 9 and May 22, 1127, and thus had roughly ten opportunities to add new information to chapters 15–35, roughly nine opportunities to add information to chapters 36–48, and so on, and, on the other hand, one imagines what chapter 110 might have looked like in its original condition—a relatively short initial entry surrounded by marginalia and interlinear additions, with perhaps an additional piece of parchment slipped in between the leaf on which it is found and the preceding one—it becomes clear that Galbert must have been faced with a tremendous mess after he made his last transfer from wax to parchment sometime after May 22: a series of (unbound?) parchment leaves[64] covered with marginalia, interlinear additions, and appendices, to which were attached additions written on scraps of parchment.

The surviving autograph manuscript of Richard of Devizes's *Cronicon* (c. 1192–1194) gives us a good idea of what Galbert's text may have looked like at this point. It

'is . . . a book made by an amateur on rather low-grade parchment, but this must not be exaggerated, because at least he used full sheets and not mere scraps. . . . The pages are ruled so as to (a) allow an inside margin about 9/10 in. wide, which in the annal (up to f.24*v*) is used for dates; (b) allow for a block of text, about 3⅔ in. wide; and (c) (except between ff.25 and 35) allow a generous outside margin of 1½ in. to 2 in. in width for additions. . . . The pages were clearly laid out so that the writer could insert additional passages alongside relevant passages of his main text, but it does not seem that he had any system of symbols or marks for denoting the exact place for insertion of these marginalia: such things occur only sporadically. There are a good many erasures . . . , alterations, and corrections. . . .' [This manuscript] bears all the marks of an author's draft. It starts out as a conventional chronicle, with wide margins at the outside and bottom of the page and a line left blank after each entry. Then the author starts adding bits of information in the empty spaces. There is nothing in the context to distinguish text from marginalia; the story wanders from one to the other, apparently as the items occurred to the writer. Some bits in the margin are obviously intended to fit into the text and are so marked; others carry on an entirely different story. . . . By f.40*v* things have gotten so far out of hand that the margin is entirely filled, and the space left blank for the text is used for an addition to the margin. On 42*r* the space left for the text has dwindled to about an eighth of the page; on 43*r* the writer makes the marginalia into the whole page but carefully preserves the blank line between paragraphs. Thus we have come round full circle, except that the whole width of the page is used. The writing varies from entry to entry, now careful and stately, now hurried and dashing. The ink varies throughout the manuscript. Spaces are left blank for names or better turns of speech, which are sometimes added later in a different ink. Corrections and interlineations abound.[65]

What did Galbert do with such a heap of material? This is the question we will take up in the next chapter.[66]

CHAPTER 3

The Comfort of History

Therefore he who resists the authorities resists what God has appointed, and those who resist will incur judgement.

—Romans 13.2

How hidden are your judgements, O God, and with what wondrous order do you hide what you are going to do and reveal what you have hidden.

—*The Life of the Emperor Henry IV*[1]

The judgement of God . . . is never unjust, even if it is sometimes hard to understand.

—Gerald of Wales, *The Journey through Wales*[2]

As we have seen in the preceding chapter, Galbert's intention during the spring of 1127 was to write a *descriptionem obsidionis secundum rerum eventum,* a chronologically organized description of selected events related to the siege of the traitors in Bruges and their eventual punishment. He seems, initially at least, to have thought that this sequence of events ended when "on May 22, the holy Sunday of Pentecost, the [new] count [William Clito] and the castellan Gervaise and Walter of Vladslo and the knights of Flanders who were present swore that they would preserve the peace to the best of their ability throughout the whole land of Flanders" ([85], 31/34; trans., 258). He did not make another entry until September 10, 1127, after a hiatus of almost four months.

When he looked over what must have been a crowded and difficult-to-read parchment record in late spring or early summer 1127, Galbert may at first have had no greater ambition than to make a fair copy of it, incorporating the various marginalia, interlinear additions, and appendices in their proper places. He may in fact have begun to make this fair copy, but at some point between May and, probably, early September, he seems to have decided to expand and reorient his chronicle, changing it from a description of the siege and the punishment of the traitors to a *passio Karoli,* a description of Charles's life and death and the punishment of his assassins. There is a brief statement of this new intention at the beginning of the substantial introduction (the Prologue and chapters 1–14) he added to his chronicle when he reworked it, where he writes that his purpose is "to describe the death of such a great prince" ([Prol.], 14; trans., 79), but its fullest expression is found at the end of the new introduction:

And so we, the inhabitants of the land of Flanders, who mourn the death of such a great count and prince, ever mindful of his life, beg, admonish, and beseech you, after hearing the true and reliable account of his life and death [*vera et certa descriptione et vitae et mortis ipsius*] (that is, whoever shall have heard it), to pray earnestly for the eternal glory of the life of his soul and his everlasting blessedness with the saints. In this account of his passion [*hac passionis subscriptione*],[3] the reader will find the subject divided by days and the events of those days, up to the vengeance, related at the end of this little work, which God alone wrought against those barons of the land whom he has exterminated from this world by the punishment of death, those by whose aid and counsel the treachery was begun and carried through to the end [*usque ad vindictam subnotatam in fine opusculi, quam solus Deus exercuit in principes terrae quos ab hoc seculo mortis districtione exterminavit, quorum consilio et auxilio traditio incepta est et ad finem usque producta*]. ([14], 14/25; trans., 117–18)

The last sentence of this passage also tells us that the *Passio,* as I will call the intended product of this revision, ended with God's execution of "those barons of the land . . . by whose aid and counsel the treachery was begun and carried through to the end." This seems to refer to chapters 89 and 91, the first of which begins with a reference to "the severe and horrible judgement of God" *(Dei districto et horribili examine)* ([89], 1; trans., 262) and relates the "accidental" death of Walter of Vladslo, whom Galbert had come to consider an accessory to the murder, and the second of which relates the "accidental" death of a second baron, Baldwin of Aalst, whom Galbert likewise considered an accessory, on October 24, 1127. Chapter 91 also ends with a valedictory-sounding passage beginning with a sentence whose terms are reminiscent of those Galbert uses in chapter 14.[4] Chapter 92 relates the death of yet a third suspect baron on December 17, 1127, but this chapter has the air of having been added after chapter 14 had been written, as further evidence that God's implacable vengeance was not yet complete.

If one accepts Clanchy's suggestion—based on Orderic Vitalis's comment that he was forced to summarize on wax tablets a saint's life of which he wished to have a copy "since the bearer was in haste to depart, and the winter cold prevented me from writing"—that writing on parchment may have been a largely seasonal activity confined to the warmer months of the year,[5] it seems that Galbert may have stopped work on the *Passio,* which at that point probably involved more work with parchment than wax, around December 17, adding a final, as yet unintegrated, entry to his parchment record on that day or shortly afterward. Given, on the one hand, his precision and the general orderliness of his mind, and, on the other hand, the occasional inconsistency and "tacked-on" feeling of certain passages in the chapters corresponding to the *Passio,* I suspect that he intended to return to his chronicle in the spring and give it a final revision when warmer weather made it easier to work with parchment.[6] His statement, in the same entry in which he refers to the "end" of his chronicle, that "not even yet [*sed adhuc nondum*] has the unhappy consequence of this utterance [the assassins' question: If we kill the count, who will avenge him?] reached an end, for as time goes on they do not cease to avenge [*de die in diem non desinant vindicare*] the death of the count upon all the suspect and the guilty and those who have fled in all directions and gone into exile" ([14], 11/14; trans., 117) also suggests that he anticipated new events—especially further divine chastisements of conspirators and accessories—that he would want to add to the *Passio.* He seems to have felt, though, that the chronicle was almost finished, that its general outlines had at least been sketched. As we have it, that is, the *Passio*—corresponding to the modern Prologue and chapters 1–92—is probably not quite complete, but we can perceive its general form and can imagine its finished state.

The revisions that transformed Galbert's parchment notes into the *Passio* thus seem to have been made between late May and mid-December 1127, but it is difficult to discern the rhythm with which they were accomplished. The little we know about the fiscal administration of the count's domain in the early twelfth century suggests that late

May and early June may have been the busiest time of the year for its receivers. William Clito summoned the notary Basil to Oudenburg on May 31, 1128, to record the report of "the overseers of the sheep runs and keepers of his farms and revenues [who] had come into his presence, ready to render account of what they owed him" ([112], 16/18; trans., 294), while the annual reconciliation of the count's revenues and expenses recorded in the *Gros Brief* of 1187 took place in Ypres between June 1 and 9.[7] On the basis of his analysis of the surviving register of the *fodermolt* of Bergues-Saint-Winnoc for 1140–1141, Strubbe speculated that this annual audit took place in November in 1140, but it is possible that the November audit he posited was only one of the periodic "local" audits for which we have evidence later in the century.[8] The fiscal administration's routine was probably upset by the events of spring 1127 and the annual audit may have occurred later, and may have been more difficult, that year than usual. If so, Galbert's work may have prevented him from returning to his parchment notes, completed on May 22, until, shall we say, July. One might thus speculate that Galbert's revision and recopying of his parchment notes began during the summer of 1127, and that this revision received a new impulse and took on a new direction and new dimensions some time around September 10[9] and continued until c. December 17, at which time the nearly finished work consisted of the Prologue and chapters 1–92.

Galbert's decision to transform his *descriptio* into a *passio* seems to have been motivated by a desire to answer the troubling doubts that the assassination raised about Charles's abilities as a ruler, the providential nature of history, and the divine ordainment of political authority.[10] These doubts grew out of the basic concept of secular authority that was current in learned circles in the eleventh and early twelfth centuries, a concept that Galbert shared, and of which he seems to have had some theoretical awareness. This concept, which one might term "ministerial theocracy," was founded on biblical passages like Romans 13.1 ("Let every person be subject to the governing authorities. For there is no authority except from God, and those that exist have been instituted by God") and 1 Peter 2.13 ("Be subject for the Lord's sake to every human institution, whether it be to the emperor as supreme or to the governors as sent by him to punish those who do wrong and to praise those who do right"), and buttressed by patristic authorities like Augustine and Gregory the Great. It held that all earthly power *(potestas)* either comes from God or is at least tolerated by him. "There is no power," Augustine had written, "unless it is decreed or permitted by God";[11] and he had observed elsewhere that "it is beyond anything incredible that [God] should have willed the kingdoms of men, their dominations and their servitudes, to be outside the range of laws of his providence."[12]

The prince could not, however, use his power capriciously, for God had given it to him only so that he might carry out effectively the *ministerium* or *officium,* the duty or charge, with which He had entrusted him. "The king's particular ministry," the Paris council of 829 had declared, "is to govern and rule God's people with equity and justice, and to strive to establish peace and concord among them" *(regale ministerium specialiter est populum Dei gubernare et regere cum equitate et justitia, et, ut pacem et concordiam habeant, studere),*[13] and it was echoed four centuries later by Hugh of Fleury who, in the *Tractatus de regia potestate et sacerdotali dignitate* (1102–1117) that he dedicated to Henry I of England, wrote that the king has a "ministry" which "is to keep [*corrigere*] the people subject to him from error and on the path of equity and justice. . . . He is therefore rightly called king [*rex*], who knows how to rule [*regere*] himself adequately and control those subject to him well," and "he should always help the people subject to him rather than harm them."[14] He later expanded on the prince's dual obligation—to rule both himself and his subjects—citing Hugh of Flavigny and declaring that "'the office of the' legitimate 'king is to govern the people with justice and equity and to defend the holy Church with all his strength.' He should be 'the guardian of orphans, the protector of widows, and the recourse of paupers.' . . . He should thus love omnipotent God, who set him at the head of many thousand men, with all his heart and the people entrusted to him by God like himself. . . . He should excell in four principal virtues: sobriety, justice, prudence, and temperance."[15] The political theory of the period thus taught that the ruler was bound above all to respect the law,[16] establish justice, and work for the common good of his subjects, the *utilitas communis* or *publica.*[17]

A candidate's idoneity, his concrete physical and psychological ability to successfully discharge the princely ministerium, was thus an essential consideration in the election of a new prince,[18] but unsuitable men did, of course, become rulers and, once installed, a prince might ultimately prove incapable of carrying out his ministerium, in which case he was "useless" *(inutilis),*[19] or he might abuse his God-given power, using it to pursue his own interests without regard for justice or laws, thus oppressing "God's people." In this latter case, he was a tyrant. Such men were, nonetheless, set over the people by God for a reason—"rulers," wrote Hugh, "are usually conferred according to the merits of their subjects, and thus the merits of subjects and their rulers are often connected with one another in such a way that the rulers' failings make the subjects' life worse and the subjects' merits change the rulers' life. . . . Thus a good king is given to men by a propitious God, and a bad one by an angry God, as He Himself told the Israelites through the prophets, saying: 'I will give you a king in my wrath' [Hos. 13.5] and elsewhere, 'God permits a hypocrite to reign on account of the people's sins' [Job 34.30, Vulgate]"[20]—and had to be obeyed. "All those in a position of power," wrote Hugh, "should be honored by those over whom they rule, if not for their own merits, then for the sake of the commission and rank they have accepted from God. . . . we should honor even gentiles in positions of power and patiently endure the evils that are heaped upon us, lest we seem to do an injury to God, who chose them and raised them up above men by rank, even though they may be unworthy of the rank they enjoy."[21]

According to Hugh, the only restraints on the ruler's power, be he good or evil, are his "fear of God and dread of Hell" and, ultimately, the fact that "it is in God's power to drag the proud from their exalted seat and raise the humble to the height of honor."[22] For indeed, "when kings and princes and tyrants refuse to be subject to God and to keep his precepts, they usually lose their ability to dominate and their power." And just as Adam, when he broke God's command, lost control not only of his own body—whose members immediately rebelled and were shot through with burning desires that overwhelmed his will—but of "the fishes of the sea, the birds of the air, and the beasts of the field, . . . so in the same way the people subject to a king opposed to God often rise against him and lay many snares for him of various kinds and wear him out with many adversities. . . . Men of this kind usually end their lives in an ignominious death or expire in filthy poverty. . . . Those who pervert true justice out of love, hatred, passion, mercy, negligence, thoughtlessness, or for the sake of gain are usually harrassed with horrible infirmities at the end of their lives, or suffer want or a lingering disease."[23]

The assassination of a lord by his subjects was an especially showy way of dragging him from his exalted seat and could not, according to theocratic thought, occur without divine sanction. It thus inevitably raised questions about his competence and quality as a ruler and, as Robert Jacob suggests in his study of the accounts of the murders of seven lords (including Galbert's account of Charles's assassination) that took place in Flanders, the Artois, or the Cambrésis between 1041 and 1140, it could always be portrayed in one of two ways: "Either the victim was known for his virtuous life and his sanctification was completed by his ultimate sufferings; or, on the contrary, the murdered lord had distinguished himself by his excesses, his cruelty, his lack of regard for the Church's commandments: the murder was then a punishment, the carrying out of a sanction that could only be providential. The same event may be read in two ways, with opposite meanings." The murder was thus followed by a struggle to determine "the meaning that was to be given to the death: the martyrdom of a saint or the punishment of the damned." This was a broad social struggle pitting the assassins, and their relatives, allies, and dependents, against the relatives, allies, and dependents of the victim, and it was carried out through various means including the ceremonies surrounding the burial of the victim and the efforts to punish his assassins.[24]

Galbert clearly wished to do what he—a writing man rather than a priest or a fighting man—could to turn this conflict of interpretations in favor of Count Charles, and he was thus faced with two tasks. First, he had to show that Charles had been neither a tyrant nor useless, and, second, he had to explain why God had permitted this good prince to be assassinated.[25]

He accomplished the first of these tasks in the panegyric portrait of Charles that is concentrated in the introductory material (the Prologue and first fourteen chapters) that was one of the three major additions that he made to the chronicle sometime during the summer and fall of 1127. Charles was, Galbert points out in the first sentence of the chronicle, of royal blood.[26] He was also, according to Galbert, a good knight, "renowned for his knightly valor" ([Prol.], 9; trans., 79), who "fought with distinction against his enemies" ([1], 5; trans., 82), and "engaged in tourneys" when enemies were lacking ([4], 44; trans. 92).

Charles was as noble in spirit as in birth and arms. At one point Galbert declares that, in comparison to him, all other princes were "disorderly in habits" ([6], 4/5; trans., 94), and he later writes that he possessed "noble habits [and a] . . . natural integrity of life" ([12], 28/29; trans., 112). Elsewhwere in the introduction he notes that Charles was "gentle, compassionate" ([6], 27/28; trans., 96), and "courteous and honorable among his barons, cruel and wary toward his enemies" ([Prol.], 11/12; trans., 79).

Galbert repeats several times that Charles was "pious,"[27] "devout,"[28] and "Catholic."[29] He also informs us that Charles "took the road of holy pilgrimage to Jerusalem, and after crossing the depths of the sea and suffering many perils and wounds for the love of Christ, he at last fulfilled his vow and with great joy reached Jerusalem. . . . And so, after reverently adoring the sepulcher of the Lord, he returned home" ([12], 30/35; trans., 113).

The ordered nobility of Charles's character carried over into his qualities as a ruler. Galbert declares him to have been more "experienced" and "discerning" ([6], 4; trans., 94; trans. mod.) than other rulers, mentions his "prudence" ([1], 11; trans., 83), calls him a "a prudent ruler of men" ([4], 35/36; trans., 91), and is careful to point out that he conferred "with the nobles and peers of his land" ([4], 21/22; trans., 91), with "his vassals" ([5], 10; trans., 93), with "the elders of the realm" ([7], 37; trans., 100), or with "his counselors" ([10], 9; trans., 105) before taking any action that might affect the well-being of the county.

In addition to this littany of commendable personal qualities, which prove that Charles knew "how to rule himself adequately" and excelled in the virtues of "sobriety, justice, prudence, and temperance," Galbert shows that Charles acquitted himself of his princely ministerium—to establish justice, maintain peace, defend the Church, work for the common good, and, in Hugh of Flavigny's words, be "the guardian of orphans, the protector of widows, and the recourse of paupers"—in an exemplary fashion. At the beginning of his reign, according to Galbert, his first concern was "to strengthen the peace, to reaffirm the laws and rights of the realm" ([1], 12; trans., 83),[30] and by the fourth year of his reign, "thanks to his efforts, everything was flourishing, everything was happy and joyful in the security of peace and justice" ([1], 13/15; trans., 83). Later, as Flanders was recovering from a serious famine, his first concern was again "to reestablish proper order in his realm" ([7], 6/7; trans., 96).

Galbert likewise shows Charles as a defender of the Church who, in addition to his personal piety, "fought strenuously [in the Holy Land] against the enemies of the Christian faith" ([12], 34; trans., 113), and was the "protector [*advocatus*] of the churches of God."[31]

Charles was also "generous toward the poor" ([Prol.], 11; trans., 79) and "the supporter of the poor" ([Prol.], 48/49; trans., 81), and Galbert describes at length the substantial measures he took to aid the poor during the famine of 1124–1125.[32] This sympathy for the sufferings of the poor, according to Galbert, was a result of Charles's experiences on crusade: "in the hardship and want of this pilgrimage, the pious servant of the Lord learned, as he often related when he was count, in what extreme poverty the poor labor, and with what misery the whole world is affected. And so he made it his habit to stoop to the needy, and to be strong in adversity, not puffed up in prosperity" ([12], 35/41; trans., 113). More generally, Galbert frequently calls him the "lord and father" of Flanders,[33] and describes him as "useful for the rich and poor of the realm" *(divitibus et pauperibus in regno utilem)* ([19], 33/34; trans., 131; trans. mod.).

The intimate, physical association between Charles and peace in Flanders is demonstrated negatively by Galbert's account of the consequences of his absence and death. When the count left Flanders for France in December 1126 or January 1127,[34] the Erembalds took advantage of his absence to attack their enemy, Thancmar of Straeten, and, for good measure, they also plundered the *rustici,* the defenseless country people, in the surrounding region. When the count returned to Flanders on February 27, Galbert tells us, about two hundred of these rustici went to him and "bowing down at his feet begged him for his customary paternal help. They entreated him to order their goods to be returned to them, that is, their flocks and herds, clothes and silver, and all the other furniture of their houses which the nephews of the provost had seized together with those who had fought with them continuously in that attack and siege" ([10], 2/8; trans., 105).[35]

These depradations practiced in the count's absence foreshadow what can be expected after his death, and it is clear that the merchants at the fair in Ypres, who immediately packed up their goods and fled when they heard the news of his murder, feared similar losses ([16], 53/63; trans., 123–24). Their fear was entirely justified, for Galbert, after describing the pillaging that follows the murder in the area around Bruges, goes on to note that "not only did these men pillage our vicinity but many others, who had known about the treachery in advance, ran at once to the crossroads of the merchants who were on their way to hold the fair at Ypres, and plundered them and their bundles" ([20], 21/25; trans. 133).

Bruges itself teetered on the verge of chaos throughout much of March and April 1127. Galbert evokes the general state of the city at this time when he writes that he began taking notes "in the midst of such a great tumult and the burning of so many houses . . . and in the midst of so much danger by night and conflict by day" ([35], 34/37; trans., 164) when "our place . . . was so disturbed by fear and anxiety that the clergy and people without exception were threatened continually with loss of life and property" ([Prol.], 20/23; trans., 80). The oaths and conditions that the citizens of Bruges impose on the various barons and the men of Ghent before admitting them to the town to besiege the assassins also testify to their sense of insecurity,[36] which was increased by the constant tension between them and the men of Ghent over the count's body, a tension that twice boiled up to the point of an armed clash. The reigning atmosphere is evident in the burghers' own actions once they had overrun the burg and forced the traitors to retreat into the church: "the citizens did not pursue them further but turned back to plunder and loot, running through the count's house, and the provost's house, and the dormitory and cloister of the brothers. All who had taken part in the siege did the same, hoping to lay hands on the treasure of the count and the equipment of the houses located within the walls." They stripped these buildings of everything that could be carried off—including the lead gutters of the count's house!—and "did so much looting that they kept on going and coming for that purpose from the time they entered the castle until far into the night" ([41], 64/83; trans., 176–77). This riot mentality reaches its peak in chapter 45 when the citizens of Bruges attempt to lynch the nephews of Thancmar of Straeten ([45], 1/53; trans., 182–84).

It is also significant that Galbert stopped taking notes on May 22 when "the [new] count [William Clito] and the castellan Gervaise and Walter of Vladslo and the knights of Flanders who were present swore that they would preserve the peace to the best of their ability throughout the whole land of Flanders" ([85], 31/34; trans., 258). Galbert thus associates peace with the presence of the count in an intimate way and exalts Charles as a peacemaker through his descriptions of the chaos that results from his absence and death.[37]

The justice and peace Charles's subjects enjoyed in his presence was likewise a product, Galbert suggests, of his ability to establish Flanders as a strong, independent principality. Galbert refers insistently to Flanders as a "land" *(terra),* a "fatherland" *(patria),* and a "realm" or "kingdom" *(regnum)* in the introduction,[38] and the very first sentence of the chronicle tells us that Charles "exceeded in fame and power the emperor of the Romans, Henry [V], . . . [and] surpassed in fame and strength the king of the English," Henry I ([Prol.], 4/7; trans., 79). The puissance of Flanders under Charles's rule was in fact such that he "had no enemies around his land, either in the marches or on the frontiers and borders, either because his neighbors feared him or because, united to him in the bond of peace and love, they preferred to exchange offerings and gifts with him" ([4], 37/40; trans., 91–92).

The remarkable images of both common and individual mourning at Charles's death that Galbert provides also testify to both his charisma and his fulfillment of his ministerium. Galbert describes, for example, the mood—and seems even to express the thoughts—of the count's closest friends and supporters after they have been captured in the church and shut in a room in the provost's house.[39] He draws an even more vivid image of individual grief in his description of Fromold Junior's reaction when he is finally able to mourn at the tomb of the count whose closest friend, according to Galbert, he was.[40] Indeed, writes Galbert, "the people of all lands mourned him greatly, shocked by the infamy of his betrayal" ([12], 43/45; trans., 113).[41]

As a result of the happy combination of these various qualities, Charles "held such a place among the devout sons of the Church that in his merits he excelled the leaders and many philosophers of the Christian faith" ([6], 5/7; trans., 94). The offers to Charles of the crowns of the Holy Roman Empire and the kingdom of Jerusalem which Galbert relates in chapters 4 and 5 thus seem a logical and ultimate confirmation of his "good reputation and the glory of his name among the rulers of the earth" ([1], 5/6; trans., 82; trans. mod.).

This portrait of Charles as a good prince, able, as Hugh of Fleury said he should be, to govern both himself and his subjects, is conventional, distinguished from other examples of the genre only by its extent, its dispersion over a number of chapters, and its detail.[42] It is its very conventionality, however, that, coupled with its length, dispersion, and detail—its "embeddedness" in the chronicle—enable it to achieve its task of simultaneously reassuring readers and convincing them that Charles had not been a tyrant or useless.

The second, more difficult ideological task of the *Passio* was to show that the assassination of "such a good prince, devout and strong, Catholic, the supporter of the poor, the protector, after God, of the churches of God, the defender of the fatherland, and one in whom the residue of earthly authority assumed the form of ruling well and the substance of serving God" ([Prol.], 47/51; trans., 81) represented not a withdrawal of divine power from a tyrannical or ineffective count, but a divine reward to a good one: that he died because he had been such a good count rather than because he had been such a bad one. Galbert achieves this goal in two ways. He shows, first, that the fault or failing that motivated the murder was not in Charles (as would have been the case if he had been a bad prince), but in the devil and the Erembalds, and, second, that God used this seemingly evil deed to achieve several good ends. Here again, the bulk of this ideological work is concentrated in the introductory material and the two other major additions (chapters 68–71, 86–92) that he made to the chronicle sometime during the summer and fall of 1127.

The last sentence of the Prologue suggests that the prime mover of the assassination was the devil, who, "seeing the progress of the Church and the Christian faith [under Charles's reign], . . . undermined the stability of the land, that is, of the Church of God, and threw it into confusion by guile and treachery and the shedding of innocent blood" ([Prol.], 51/55; trans., 81; trans. mod.).[43] And Galbert underlines the devil's ultimate responsibility for the assassination by portraying the assassins as his agents,[44] "full of the demon" *(pleni demonio),*[45] and the enemies of God, His Church, and His people.[46] Galbert thus simultaneously locates the blame for the murder with the devil and exalts Charles by suggesting that his murder was motivated by his success in establishing God's kingdom in Flanders.

The devil did not himself strike the blow that killed Charles, however, and Galbert was also faced with the problem of explaining why the count was killed by his own subjects, who had their own reasons for acting, even if the devil made use of them for his own purposes.[47] This was perhaps a more delicate endeavor for Galbert than it now appears to us.

The way Galbert tells it, this mutually fatal struggle between Charles and the Erembalds arose when the "the pious count, wishing to reestablish proper order in his realm, sought to find out who belonged to him, who were servile and who were free men in the realm" ([7], 6/8; trans., 96). This investigation threatened the members of the Erembald family, which "was striving by every device of craft and guile to find a way by which it could slip out of servitude and cease belonging to the count; for they belonged to him, being of servile status" ([7], 16/19; trans., 98). The spark that ignited the conflict was a knight's refusal, in the presence of the count, to fight a judicial duel with another knight, who had married one of Bertulf's nieces, because, the challenged knight claimed, his challenger had been reduced to the same servile status as his wife after a year of marriage ([7], 22/36; trans., 99–100). The implication, of course, was that the niece and her whole family were serfs. Given the count's general efforts to identify and claim his serfs, it was normal for him to inquire into the family's status once this allegation had been made, and when, writes Galbert, he "had learned from the judgement of the courts and the report of the elders of the realm that they—the Erembald clan—belonged to him beyond doubt, he set about trying to claim them as his serfs" ([7], 37/39; trans., 100).

Galbert goes on in chapters 7 through 13 to relate this family's efforts to resist their relegation to servile status and their growing desperation, culminating in their decision to kill the count. The whole first part of their story, as Galbert imagined it, is summarized in chapter 13:

> And so when he [Bertulf] became head of his family, he tried to advance beyond everyone in the fatherland his nephews who were well brought up and finally girded with the sword of knighthood. Trying to make their reputation

known everywhere, he armed his kinsmen for strife and discord; and he found enemies for them to fight in order to make it known to everyone that he and his nephews were so powerful and strong that no one in the realm could resist them or prevail against them. Finally, accused in the presence of the count of servile status, and affronted by the efforts of the count himself to prove that he and all his lineage were servile, he tried, as we have said, to resist servitude by every course and device and to preserve his usurped liberty with all his might. And when, steadfast in his determination, he could not succeed otherwise, he himself, with his kinsmen, carried through the treachery, which he had long refused to consider, with frightful consequences involving both his own kinsmen and the peers of the realm. ([13], 21/35; trans., 116)

According to Galbert, then, the investigation that "discovered" the Erembalds' servile origins and the count's subsequent efforts to reduce the family to its former status were not aimed exclusively or particularly at the Erembalds but were part of a more general effort to reestablish a hierarchy of authority in his realm, and it is perhaps significant that Galbert calls Charles "pious" in this context. The failing, in other words, was not in Charles but in the proud and twisted Erembalds:[48] Charles was murdered because he had, in the faithful prosecution of the office and duties, the ministerium, God had enjoined upon him, provoked the envy of the devil and the ire of the Erembalds.[49]

Galbert—and certain other contemporary sources[50]—thus portray Charles's murder as having been planned and carried out by the Erembalds, who were motivated by a fear that the count intended to return the family to its former, servile status. Other contemporary sources are less ready to hang the blame on them alone, however,[51] and there are indications, even in the *Passio,* of a more widespread conspiracy and dissatisfaction with Charles's rule. In the first chapter, for example, Galbert writes that after Charles had succeeded Baldwin VII in the countship, he "took such measures to strengthen the peace, to reaffirm the laws and rights of the realm, that little by little public order was restored in all parts, and by the fourth year of his reign, thanks to his efforts, everything was flourishing, everything was happy and joyful in the security of peace and justice" ([1], 11/15; trans., 83). In other words, and as we know from Walter's *Vita* ([7]–[9], 541–43), Charles's accession was contested by a coalition involving several important lords of Flanders and led by Baldwin's mother, Clémence of Burgundy, who wanted William of Ypres to succeed her son, and it took Charles four years to win the county by arms and restore peace.[52]

This "boon of peace" did not, however, make men better or produce universal approbation for Charles's reign, for although the inhabitants of Flanders subsequently "governed themselves in accordance with laws and justice, devising by skill and study every kind of argument for use in the courts," there were "many illiterate people [*multi illiterati*], endowed by nature herself with the gift of eloquence and rational methods of inference and argument, whom those who were trained and skilled in the rhetorical art were not able to resist or refute," who "through their tricks brought action in the courts against the faithful and the lambs of God, who were less wary" ([1], 22/33; trans., 84; trans. mod.). Seeing this, writes Galbert in chapter 2, God "deigned by the terror of omens to recall to penitence those whom He had foreseen as prone to evil [*pronos . . . ad malum*]. . . . But when men were not corrected in this way, neither lords nor serfs [*tam domini quam servi*], there came the hunger of sudden famine, and subsequently the scourges of death attacked them" ([2], 2/4, 14/16; trans. 84–85).

The evil men who provoked this divine wrath are not very clearly defined here-they were sly, rhetorically gifted illiterates, men "prone to evil," lords and serfs—but the passage suggests significant tensions within the county, and Galbert identifies these malevolent men as Charles's assassins at the beginning of chapter 3: "but the impious [*impii*] were not corrected in this way [by the scourges of famine and death], for it is said that at this very time they had plotted the death of the most pious [*piissimi*] count Charles" ([3], 1/2; trans., 87).

This group of conspirators immediately reappears in chapter 4 when the count confers "with the nobles and peers of his land" *(cum nobilibus et paribus terrae suae)* about whether he should accept the offer of the empire: "those evil traitors . . . who were threatening his life, advised him to assume the German kingship and its dignities, pointing out to him how much glory and fame would be his as king of the Romans. Those wretches were trying by this guile and trickery to get rid of him; later when they had been unable to remove him while he was alive, they betrayed him while he was contending with them on behalf of the law of God and men" ([4], 21/22, 26/32; trans., 91). Galbert alludes to them yet again in chapter 5 in connection with the offer of the kingdom of Jerusalem: "but he was unwilling . . . to desert the Fatherland of Flanders, which in his lifetime he was to govern well, and would have ruled even better if those evil traitors, full of the demon, had not slain their lord and father" ([5], 10/14; trans., 93). This group of sly, malevolent, illiterate conspirators, prone to evil, thus includes "both lords and serfs" and has representatives among the "nobles and peers of the land" whom Charles consults in connection with the offer of the empire.

Four other bits of evidence in the *Passio* support this impression of an important degree of discontent with Charles. First, the inquest ordered by William Clito in September 1127 ([87], 1/19; trans., 258–59) indicted more than one hundred and sixty people. Galbert does not tell us who they were, but a French translation of a more detailed record of this inquest or of a similar but earlier one is included in the so-called *Chronique de Baudouin d'Avesne* and confirms that a wide range of people were implicated in the murder or aided the assassins.[53] Galbert tells us, second, that "it was true that many, after the death of Count Charles, had gone over to him [William of Ypres], such as the chaplains and servants and mercenaries and serfs of the usual household of the count" ([79], 13/15; trans., 248); this suggests that the party that had wanted William of Ypres to succeed Baldwin was still alive and strong. Third, Galbert and Walter both include William of Wervik and Ingran of Esen among the core conspirators who swore and plotted to kill Charles, but neither of them, so far as we can tell, was related to the Erembalds.[54] This suggests that the assassination was motivated by more than the Erembalds' fear and frustration, that other men had reasons to want to get rid of the count, and that the conspiracy went beyond that family. This is also suggested, fourth, in the later parts of the *Passio* where Galbert, perhaps as a consequence of the inquest held on September 16, implicates Baldwin of Aalst, a peer of Flanders, and the knight Everard of Ghent in the conspiracy.[55]

If Charles was indeed trying to find out "who belonged to him, who were servile and who were free men in the realm," moreover, his efforts might well have been unpopular in the towns of Flanders which, Van Caenegem writes, "must have contained an important percentage of freemen of recent date—[this was] one of the reasons . . . the unfree Erembalds enjoyed a surprising measure of sympathy in Bruges, even after their treacherous deed: they were a symbol of what unfree people could achieve. . . . Liberty was a politically sensitive issue, and any move by a count-landlord to recover his serfs, whether they seemed emancipated and occupied high positions or had fled his manors, was bound to be watched closely and suspiciously by the freedom-loving townspeople."[56]

The Erembalds' servility was perhaps not as evident as Galbert and some other contemporary sources make it out to be, however. Galbert writes that Erembald was the "vassal and knight" *(homo et miles)* and closest confidant ([71], 4, 8/9; trans., 239) of the castellan of Bruges, but he nowhere calls him a "servus" (serf). As Sproemberg pointed out, moreover, "Erembald was appointed castellan of Bruges by Baldwin VI, served as castellan until his death, and was able to transform this office into a hereditary possession of his family,"[57] and Galbert himself tells us that "because the provost and his kin had not heretofore been molested or accused of servile status by the predecessors of the count, this would have been consigned to oblivion, having been laid to rest, as it were, and disregarded for so long, if it had not been brought to the attention of the courts by the challenge to combat" ([7], 39/41; trans., 100). Warlop and Declercq likewise note that the family could not have acquired and held the offices of castellan and provost without the support of the count.[58]

As Sproemberg suggests, then, the struggle between Charles and the Erembalds was probably not really a legal struggle over the family's status but a power struggle between the count and the most puissant family in the county, against a backdrop of more widespread discontent. The question of the family's status was simply something that Charles had dug up to use as one weapon in this struggle.[59]

The metaphysical explanation of the assassination purveyed by Galbert and other contemporary historians was thus an expedient, as well as a more gripping and narratively tractable, version in which the Erembalds were made to stand for all those who were unhappy with Charles's rule and who had conspired to at least some degree in the assassination. The attribution of Charles's assassination to the Erembalds, that is, was perhaps not unlike the attribution of certain twentieth-century assassinations to mad, lone gunmen. Galbert uses this same strategy, somewhat more transparently, in the account of the death of the young Count Arnold at the battle of Cassel in 1071, which he added during the summer or fall of 1127 to the long manuscript chapter consisting of modern chapters 66–72. The way Galbert tells this story, "the very servants [*servi*] who had armed him and knew in advance the markings on his arms unhorsed their young lord in the very tumult of battle and slew him with swords, as if they were strangers rather than servants" ([69], 59/62; trans., 236; trans. mod.), ignoring for the moment the fact that Arnold was fighting this battle against his uncle, Robert the Frisian, who had broken his oath not to harm his nephew, "had won over all the barons of the fatherland, and obtained their pledges of faith and loyalty" ([69], 46/47; trans., 235), and had invaded Flanders. One has to wonder, in fact, if the parallels between Arnold and Charles—murdered by servi but the objects of widespread dissatisfaction and a conspiracy involving at least some of the members of the nobility—were not part of the reason Galbert tells Arnold's story and associates his murder with that of Charles. Faced, not necessarily consciously, with a choice between a simpler, more comforting, more gripping story of the good prince and the wicked servi and a more complicated, more disturbing, more diffuse tale of wider dissatisfaction with Charles's reign and a wider conspiracy in his murder, Galbert and certain other historians understandably chose the former. It was the story that, given their narrative and political traditions and their desire to restore Charles's prestige and that of his office, they "naturally" saw in the events surrounding the assassination.

Even if the cause for Charles's murder lay in the devil's envy and the Erembalds' pride, however, it would have amounted to a triumph of evil over good unless Galbert could show that these evil designs had been taken up and woven into a greater providential one. Like Walter of Thérouanne, therefore, he immediately portrays the murder as a martyrdom—a divine reward for faithful service—in the long manuscript chapter (modern chapters 15–21) recounting the events of March 2,[60] and is careful to include in his record any subsequent events that confirm Charles's martyrdom and sanctity. He relates, for example, that the assassins, made uncomfortable by the corpse's incessant silent accusation, immediately invited the abbot of Saint Peter's abbey in Ghent to remove it to his abbey. The abbot arrived the next morning "after riding all night" ([22], 2; trans., 137), and his haste and repeated attempts to carry off the body[61] suggest that he thought it would have a more-than-dynastic appeal for future pilgrims. The citizens and clergy of Bruges seem to have thought so, too, and were ready to offer armed resistance to efforts to remove it.[62] Their attitude is expressed in two speeches addressed to Bertulf, one by the paupers who had gathered around the body in the hope of a distribution of alms, the other by one of the senior canons, both of which refer to the protection and divine favor the count's body would afford the church and town.[63] Galbert also notes that when these speeches were made "the sick and crippled were [already] lying under the bier" ([22], 56; trans., 139) in the hope, one presumes, of being healed.

This popular belief in Charles's sanctity is confirmed by two miracles. In the first case, as the citizens of Bruges were on the point of coming to blows with the Erembald party over the removal of the count's body, one of the sick and crippled lying under the bier, "a lame man, who was born with his foot attached to his buttocks, began to cry out and bless God, who, through the merits of the pious count, had restored his natural capacity to move, in the sight of all the bystanders" ([22], 57/60; trans., 139–40). Suitably chastised, the belligerents were calmed and blows avoided.

The second miracle occurred when Charles's body was exhumed and discovered to have suffered no corruption during its seven weeks of entombment.[64] Galbert is not quite so ebulient as Walter of Thérouanne, who writes that when the tomb was opened, "a great wave of a most sweet odor also poured forth divinely and filled the whole place and hardly anyone doubted that God wished to glorify his faithful man" ([47], 558, 36/38), but it is clear that he, too, sees this as a divine confirmation of the count's martyrdom and saintliness, and he concludes that as a result of Charles's "betrayal and martyrdom God . . . carried off to the place of the saints the one who had been killed in the cause of justice in the fatherland. . . . He immediately received among the blessed martyrs the one who died for the sake of justice" ([70], 8/10, 11/12; trans., 237).

Galbert also shows how the evil designs that brought about Charles's murder served good ends by chronicling minutely the inexorable punishment of the wicked servi, which he sums up nicely in an image of noose-tightening confinement in a passage that was probably added during the summer or fall of 1127 to the manuscript chapter devoted to April 19 (modern chapters 74 and 75):

For when they thought they had committed with impunity all they had treacherously done, and no man dared to inflict vengeance, vengeance was left to God alone who at once confined them and struck them with fear so that they did not dare to go out beyond the inhabited area of our place but decided instead to enclose the area and our town by palisade and ditch, as we have told above. On the eighth day after the count's death they were forthwith shut up in the castle by the siege; then when the castle was invaded by our men, they fled to the tower where they were more confined; finally thrown into prison, they were in such close quarters that they could not sit down at the same time unless at least three or four stood up. Darkness, heat, stench, and sweat undid them, and the horror of hopeless life and the shame of uncertain death to come. ([75], 7/19; trans. 243)

The corporate story of the wicked servi ends in chapter 81 with the precipitation from the tower of the count's house of the twenty-seven men who had been trapped in the tower and surrendered on April 19, but Galbert, like Walter, also tells the individual stories of the most important conspirators, Borsiard[65] and Isaac,[66] as well as those of lesser figures, like the mercenary Benkin or Borsiard's counselor, Lambert Archei,[67] who intrigued him for one reason or another. One of the more interesting is that of Robert the Young, whom Galbert is at great pains to exculpate insofar as possible, and to whom he attributes a maudlin, adolescent sentimentality.[68] The most important and most developed of these individual stories is that of Bertulf, whom Galbert portrays as the archtraitor, but for whom he nonetheless feels a certain admiration, respect, and pity.

The bulk of the additions that Galbert made to the end of the *Passio* at this time (chapters 86–91) relate the indictment and punishment of those conspirators who had escaped punishment in the immediate aftermath of the assassination.[69] They give Galbert the chance to demonstrate, and reassure his readers, that God does not hesitate to intervene directly to punish the wicked when human justice proves insufficient. "It was true," he writes, "that no one dared to raise a hand against Walter [of Vladslo] although he was accessory to the treachery, for he was a peer of the land, and next after the count. But God, to whom his punishment was left, removed him by a lingering death from the sight of the faithful" ([89], 27/31; trans., 263).[70] He also reports the bizarre "accidental" death of Baldwin of Aalst, "also a peer of the peers of Flanders, [and] branded with the stigma of the betrayal of his lord, Charles" ([91], 2/3; trans., 263–64), who had likewise escaped punishment because of his rank and power, and notes that he, too, was "slain by the sword of God" ([91], 11; trans., 264). The inhabitants of Flanders were struck by these events, he tells us, and "talked about the sudden death of those whom God alone had deprived of life after the death of lord Charles by such a swift sentence and had ordained that they should die from such trivial causes" ([91], 16/19; trans., 264).[71] Galbert added these accounts to the end of the *Passio,* not simply because these events had occurred, but because they provided information about the fate of men whom Galbert suspected of conspiring in the count's murder and confirmed his sense of a divine vengeance grinding increasingly small.

Galbert discovered yet another, complementary, way in which Charles's murder served providential ends at some point after he had begun his revision of his notes and added it in the margins, probably, of the manuscript chapter devoted to the events of April 17 (modern editorial chapters 66–72). When he began reworking his parchment notes, the entry for April 17 probably corresponded to: modern chapter 66, relating the report to the king in Bruges on that day of the new count's reception in Saint-Omer; modern chapter [67], 1/12,[72] recounting an attack on Aire; modern chapters [67], 12/16 and [72], 2/8,[73] recounting an attack on Oudenaarde; and modern chapter [72], 8/11,[74] relating an attempt to escape from the tower by one of the besieged.

The first addition Galbert made to this entry in the course of composing the *Passio* was probably modern chapters [68], 1/[69], 80,[75] which describe the dynastic history of Flanders from Baldwin V (1035–1067) onward. The addition of this historical parenthesis appears to have been motivated by the sentence of the original entry that immediately precedes it: "the Count of Mons [Baldwin IV of Hainaut] and his men had entered and fortified [the castle of Oudenaarde] for the purpose of invading the realm of Flanders, which by right of kinship more justly belonged to him" ([67], 13/16; trans., 231). Rereading his earlier work, Galbert evidently felt that he ought at this point to explain the basis of Baldwin's claim to the county of Flanders.

The highlight of this historical aside is the story, mentioned above, of Robert the Frisian's treacherous acquisition of the county through the murder of his nephew Arnold by his wicked servi. Perceiving, perhaps, a further parallel between Arnold's betrayal and that of Charles, Galbert went on to describe a subsequent falling out between Robert the Frisian and many of the barons who had helped him to overthrow Arnold, and the new count's punishment of his predecessor's betrayers and assassins (albeit they were also his former allies): "some were beheaded, some condemned to exile, and many proscribed" *(decollati sunt alii et alii exilio damnati, plures quippe proscripti)* ([70], 12/26),[76] a punishment recalling that of Charles's assassins and their accomplices who were likewise "proscribed, cast down, hanged, and beheaded" *(proscripti, praecipitati, suspensi et decollati)* ([80], 6; trans., 249–50).[77]

At some subsequent point, prodded perhaps by these parallels between Arnold's and Charles's betrayals, Galbert seems to have hit upon the biblical notion of old sins remembered and punished in subsequent generations and felt that he had been given a sudden insight into the divine economy of the events he had witnessed.[78] Flush with this insight, he added the following passage to the long manuscript entry, probably in the margin of the text:

And the prophecy concerning past treachery should be noted in connection with this deed [Robert's betrayal of Arnold] "since God is wont in the severity of his punishment to correct the iniquities of the fathers unto the third and fourth generation" [*Et notandum in hoc facto antiquae traditionis illud propheticum: "Quoniam Deus iniquitates patrum solet vindictae severitate corrigere in tertiam et quartam generationem"*].[79] And so that Robert who betrayed his nephew is numbered "the first," and his son Robert, who lies in Arras as "the second," in the succession and the countship. After him, his son Baldwin, who lies at Saint Omer, was the third. And after him, the best count of all the counts, the star and bright luminary of earthly splendor, was the fourth; in his betrayal and martyrdom God brought to an end the punishment of the old betrayal [*antiquae traditionis*], and carried off to the place of the saints the one who had been killed in the cause of justice in the fatherland, in the very place where formerly the oath had been sworn. And so God took care of two things in the second betrayal [*secunda traditione*]: He carried out vengeance for the old betrayal [*antiquae traditionis*], and He immediately received among the blessed martyrs the one who had died for the sake of justice. ([69], 80/[70], 12; trans., 237; trans. mod.)

Galbert seems to have realized at yet another moment that this same notion could explain the Erembalds' fate as well as Charles's, and he added another passage to this manuscript chapter—perhaps in the margin, perhaps on another piece of parchment—which was eventually inserted into the text just after the passage describing Robert's punishment of his rebellious former allies: "Finally," the passage begins, "(this is hardly worth hearing but should be recorded if only out of wonder), God subsequently avenged an old betrayal in the fourth or third generation of the family of the traitors with new dangers and a new kind of fall [*in quarta vel tertia generis linea Deus vindicavit consequenter in genere traditorum scilicet antiquam traditionem novis periculis, novo genere praecipitationis*].[80] Let me, therefore, trace the origins of the family of the provost and his nephews a bit further back" ([70], 27/[71], 2; trans., 238; trans. mod.). Galbert then goes on to recount how the knight Erembald, vassal and confidant of Boldran, the castellan of Bruges, entered into an adulterous liaison with Boldran's wife, Dedda, murdered Boldran by pushing him off a boat into a river while he was fully armed, married Dedda, became castellan himself, and fathered

> the provost, Bertulf, and Hacket, Wulfric Cnop, Lambert Nappin, the father of Borsiard, and also Robert, castellan after him in the second place. After Robert, his son Walter succeeded as heir to the office of castellan in the third place. After him, Hacket was castellan, in whose time Count Charles was betrayed. In this fourth degree, therefore, the old precipitation [*antiqua praecipitatio*] of Boldran was punished in the persons of Erembald's successors by this new precipitation [*nova ista praecipitatione*] which was accomplished from the battlements of the count's house in Bruges. And so, you might say, by the dispensation of God they were punished for the sins of their parents, as it is read in Exodus, where God speaks to Moses in the thirty-fourth chapter of the same Exodus where God gives out the laws for all, saying: "I, the lord your God, am a jealous God, visiting the iniquities of the fathers upon the sons, even unto the third and fourth generation of those who hate me [*Ego sum dominus Deus tuus fortis zelotes, visitans iniquitatem patrum in filiis, in tertiam et quartam generationem eorum, qui oderunt me*]." ([71], 23/36; trans., 239–40; trans. mod.)[81]

At this point the text returns to the original entry of the parchment notes: "now we should go back to the narration of the events at Oudenaarde . . ." ([72], 1/2; trans., 240).

Ultimately, then, Galbert suggests that God achieved five things through the murder: he rewarded Charles for his piety and service to the county and the Church with the gift of martyrdom; he gave this martyr to the church of Saint Donatian and the people of Bruges;[82] he punished—in the fourth generation—Robert the Frisian's usurpation of the county of Flanders and avenged the murder of the young Count Arnold; he also avenged—in the fourth generation—the murder of Boldran and punished the descendants of his assassin; and he purged the county of the wicked Erembalds and their accomplices.

The heart of the *Passio* is thus a fable of the good prince and the wicked servi whose simple moral Galbert announces toward the end of the Prologue: "if anyone reads this dry style and this little handful of a book, I ask and admonish that he not make fun of it or condemn it but wonder with fresh wonder at what is written down and what came to pass by the ordinance of God only in our time, and learn not to despise or kill earthly rulers [—Arnold, Boldran, Charles—] whom we are bound to believe were placed over us by the ordinance of God, as the apostle says: 'Let every soul be subject to every power, either to the king as supreme or to governors as sent by God'" ([Prol.], 35/43; trans., 80; trans. mod.).[83] This divinely sanctioned injunction to respect and obey authority is illustrated and reinforced through the *Passio*'s depiction of the good prince's heavenly reward, its exhaustive description of the divine punishment of his murderers, and its detailed images of the grief and desolation brought about by his death.[84] The true protagonist of the *Passio* is thus not Charles, Bertulf, Bruges, or Flanders, but a God whose infinite mind and omnipotence determine the course and character of history, endowing it with an absolute inevitability and an enigmatic but infinite meaningfulness.[85] And the *Passio* achieves its ideological work of moral reassurance by discovering and drawing attention to His structuring omnipresence in a series of events from which it might at first seem absent.

God's controlling presence in history was, to be sure, reiterated ad nauseam by twelfth-century historians, but few of them seem to have taken the idea as seriously as Galbert. "Only the most strenuously philosophic of minds," writes Partner,

> would attempt to work out the implications of their historical religion for their own, invariably disordered, time. European Christendom was old by the twelfth century [and] . . . the insistent and present sense of a large and inclu-

sive plan for mankind, the need for that sense, had subsided into a quiet acceptance of the *idea* of such a plan without the need for very specific understanding of its provisions. . . . Only a very few historians seem to have had the intellectual confidence or the interest to make systematically known their own understanding of any higher purpose informing recent history.[86]

Despite his determination "to connect his history with the true meaning immanent in, and higher than, human affairs," Ordericus Vitalis, for example, ". . . seems to have been sincerely content to record and wait for the figure in the carpet to appear, which it never did. . . . Orderic, and William of Newburgh, and other sincere Christian historians tended to wait for meaning to appear, reluctant to impose it or stage-manage it; hence, the shambling, slack quality of their writing which lacks the skeletal control of informing figures or the larger tropes of meaning."[87] Galbert, as Partner observes, was also exceptional in this regard.[88] He would not wait for the figure in the carpet to appear. He wanted to see it himself and help his audience to discover it as well.

The *Passio*'s work of moral reassurance naturally raises the question of the audience that it was intended to reassure. Galbert himself makes no clear statement on this point, describing his intended audience variously in the Prologue as the "the faithful" *(fideles)* ([Prol.], 17; trans., 80) "you[89] and all the faithful" *(vos et omnes fideles)* ([Prol.], 30/31; trans., 80), and "our posterity" *(posteros nostros)* ([Prol.], 34; trans., 80), where the "our" seems to refer to "all who suffered the same dangers with me" ([Prol.], 33/34; trans., 80). The intended audience thus seems to be, in the first instance, all the inhabitants of Bruges and, ultimately, all other Christians.

Ross did not think that Galbert had any precise public in mind when he began to write, but feels that the *Passio*'s "theme of martyrdom," "the strong religious tone and Biblical language of the parts added [during this second period of revision], and [Galbert's] interpretation of the tragedy as God's punishment of evil men, visiting the sins of the parents upon the children and manifesting the frightful consequences of disobedience to the powers that be" suggest that it was written for "the clergy of Saint Donatian," "a clerical audience," or "the clergy in general."[90] All historical writing of the time was necessarily "clerical," however, and the notions of divine retribution and divinely instituted political authority would have been reassuring to more than just the clergy. As Van Caenegem points out, moreover, the *Passio* was a formal oddity that did not fit easily into any "clerical" genre, such as hagiography, and Galbert criticizes and mocks certain of the clergy of Bruges.[91] This criticism and mockery is always aimed at individual clergy for specific misdeeds, however, and he respects and admires other clergy like Fromold Senior. He does not, that is, criticize the clergy as a whole, and one can imagine that some clergymen would welcome his exposure of specific clerical abuses. It is thus difficult to imagine that the *Passio* was intended exclusively for the clergy, but one should not therefore exclude all clergymen from its audience.

This is also true of the aristocracy, including the new count and the members of his court. As Van Caenegem points out, Galbert is likewise critical of many members of this group and does nothing to disguise their venality and self-interestedness.[92] He never condemns the aristocracy or the court as a group, however, and his portraits of William Clito and certain aristocrats, like Gervaise of Praet, are on the whole favorable in the *Passio.*

Sproemberg and Coué think Galbert wrote for the burghers of Bruges,[93] and Van Caenegem has suggested that his ideal audience was "the common folk, the general public, that long enjoyed the tales of Reinard the Fox and was embodied in Uilenspiegel," and who would have greatly appreciated his criticism of many members of the aristocracy and the clergy. The problem with this public, Van Caenegem observes, is that it was not Latinate, or even lettered.[94] As Galbert's record shows, however, the burghers were used to dealing with Latin documents in the course of their public affairs—and in what other language could he have written a historical account in 1127?

A bourgeois audience, and more specifically an audience consisting of the citizens of Bruges, is likewise suggested by Galbert's treatment of the Erembalds—the lords of Bruges—and especially by his treatment of Robert the Young. There is, for example, a note of admiration in his description of Borsiard's military ferocity, and his sympathy for Bertulf is real, even though it does not blind Galbert to his guilt. A comparison of Galbert's and Walter's treatment of Robert the Young is particularly revealing in this light. Walter, who has no attachments to Bruges, is categorical in his condemnation of Robert.[95] Galbert, on the other hand, goes to some pains to excuse him; indeed, Alan Murray suggests that the "main purpose" of Galbert's description of the conspiratorial dialogue in which Robert is tricked into assenting to the assassination without knowing it "seems to be to exonerate Robert from any part in the murder, and thus indirectly to excuse the public sympathy for him shown by the people of Bruges right up to his execution."[96] The representation of Robert the Young, in sum, suggests that the burghers of Bruges were a major part of the public Galbert had in mind when he wrote the *Passio.*

It thus seems likely that the burghers of Bruges figured most prominently in Galbert's mind while he was composing the *Passio,* but that his intended audience included all the inhabitants of Bruges, clergy and aristocrats as well, and even, albeit more vaguely, all the inhabitants of Flanders and any other of the faithful who might be interested in an account of Charles's death and the punishment of his murderers.[97] The public he anticipated at this point, that is, was a broad and general one, including everyone who could profit from the cautionary tale of the good prince and the wicked servi and a reminder of God's intimate presence in all their deeds and designs.

CHAPTER 4

The Art of History

Emulating a painter, he ought to sketch out the image first in ugly charcoal, so to speak, composing whatever he has undertaken to write purposefully and carefully in simple and uncultivated speech, and then apply a pleasing variety of colors to the sketched lines, dyeing each document. . . .

—Alberic of Monte Cassino, *De dictamine*[1]

The wise man's mind detects what is helpful or fitting in cases as they occur, nor does he shun fables, stories, or spectacles in general, providing that they possess the requirements of virtue and honorable utility.

—John of Salisbury, *Policraticus*[2]

For the benefit of those who will come after, I have also rescued from oblivion some of the remarkable events of our own times. This cannot be achieved without great labour, but I have enjoyed doing it. The research-work necessary if one is to find out just what really happened is not at all easy. Even when one has discovered the truth in all its detail, there still remains the task of ordering one's facts, and this is difficult, too. To maintain a correct balance from beginning to end, and, indeed, throughout the whole course of one's narrative, and to exclude all irrelevant material, is not easy.

—Gerald of Wales, *The Description of Wales*[3]

Galbert's efforts to assuage the troubling doubts that Charles's assassination raised about his abilities as a ruler, the providential nature of history, and the divine ordainment of political authority perhaps stand out somewhat from the similar efforts of other contemporary authors writing in response to similar crises by their rigor and intensity, but the ideological framework in which he casts his response to Charles's murder is essentially identical to that used by other authors—by, for example, Walter of Thérouanne in his *Vita Karoli.* Galbert's artistic achievement is more singular and greater—his chronicle is distinctly more original and more captivating than Walter's—but has been largely ignored because the *De multro* has been taken to be an unrevised diary and not a work of historical literature. In this and the next chapter, therefore, I will look closely at the literary qualities of the *Passio* in order to develop some idea of the degree and nature of Galbert's artistic achievement, which is largely responsible for the success of his chronicle with various audiences over the last five hundred years.

There is, I think, good reason to believe that Galbert revised his parchment notes extensively when he decided to transform them into a *Passio Karoli.* Some traces of this revision are obvious—the substantial additions he made to the beginning, middle, and end of his notes after May 22 (the Prologue and chapters 1–14, 68–71, 86–92), which have long been recognized as such;[4] a number of other additions that have gone largely unnoticed, or at least uncommented upon;[5] three cross-references;[6] several allusions to future events;[7] and the relative paucity of passages beginning with *et notandum* in the portions of the *Passio* corresponding to the primitive text[8]—but the surface of Galbert's text is generally so seamless, so well crafted, and so well rehearsed, that it is only by looking behind the scenes that one can glimpse the sophisticated machinery that makes it all work so smoothly.

If, for example, the *Passio* were a true journal, one would not expect to find in it any of the recurring motifs or themes that literary works use to make particular points or to guide their audiences' reception of the events they relate. Authorial preoccupations may well run through a journal and lead to a series of passages devoted to a single topic, and such preoccupations may indeed become themes as each new passage recalls and builds on the former ones, but the earlier passages cannot, in a true journal, anticipate later events or final conclusions. If they do, it suggests that one is not dealing with a true journal but with a literary work cast in journalistic form. One can, I think, identify at least three recurring motifs in the entries of the *Passio* corresponding to the primitive parchment notes, which thus suggest that these entries were revised after May 22.

Already in the last chapter we have seen that the theme of Charles's martyrdom, one of the most important aspects of the *Passio*'s ideological work, is developed principally in chapters corresponding to the primitive parchment notes.[9] It is of course possible, perhaps even likely, that Galbert immediately saw Charles as a martyr and that some elements of this theme were already in his parchment, or even his wax, notes; but the development of this motif in the *Passio,* especially in the long, and, as we will see below, obviously rewritten manuscript chapter recounting the events of March 2 (modern chapters 15–21), seems too careful, too literary, to be spontaneous, and suggests that Galbert reworked these passages in his primitive notes after he had decided to transform them into a *Passio Karoli.*

If it is possible that Galbert foresaw, at least to some degree, that martyrdom would be an important motif of his chronicle whatever its final form, and thus wove it into his notes even as he jotted them down, this is not the case with two other motifs woven through the *Passio*: the one focused on a silver cup and the other on the traitors' execution by precipitation.

The saga of the silver cup that Count Charles purchased at the fair in Ypres shortly before his murder is the vehicle for an exposé of clerical failings. Having recounted the count's assassination and the pursuit through and beyond Bruges of his friends and collaborators, Galbert describes the arrival of the news of his death that same day at the fair in Ypres where "merchants from all the kingdoms around Flanders had come together." To this fair had also come "merchants from the kingdom of the Lombards . . . from whom," he adds, rather inconsequentially given the circumstances, "the count had bought a silver cup [*argenteam kannam*] for twenty-one marks, which was marvelously made so that the liquid which it held disappeared as one looked at it." He then returns to the main topic, writing that "when the news reached all these people from various places who had come together at the fair, they packed up their goods and fled by day and by night" ([16], 53/62; trans., 123–24; trans. mod.). The cup obviously caught Galbert's eye, but it is difficult, at first, to understand why it was important enough to be mentioned here in his description of the immediate aftermath of the murder.

This cup reappears three times in the *Passio,* however, and these subsequent appearances motivate its introduction in chapter 16. It first reappears in chapter 61, dated to April 13, as a focus of ecclesiastical venality and priestly credulity:

It is true that the provost had received from his nephews as a kind of gift when the loot was divided, a golden goblet with its own lid, and a vessel, or rather a silver container for wine [*cannam scilicet argenteum vas vinarium*], and that he had presented these vessels to God for the service of the church in order to save his soul. Then when the siege was going on and the brothers were carrying the relics and shrines of the saints out of the castle, they had borne out those two vessels which had been secretly placed in a certain chest under the guise of relics along with the true relics of the saints. The dean [Helias] had entrusted that chest to the care of a certain simple priest, Eggard, in the church of the Holy Savior, indicating that it should be venerated as though it contained the most precious relics. How devoutly, in fact, that simple priest had received the chest and how, having placed it in the sanctuary, he poured forth prayers and begged for the salvation of his soul, was revealed by his fellow-priests in the same church; every night he placed before it tallow candles, wax candles, and lights and lighted lamps, believing he could not venerate those relics enough. (That priest had really done enough to deserve a drink or more of good wine from those vessels when they were handed over to the new count!). ([61], 19/38; trans., 219–20)

The vessel reappears as the devil's bait in chapter 83, dated to May 7, where it is again a source of clerical covetousness, corruption, and mendacity:

On May 7, Saturday, the dean, Helias, handed over to the new count the silver vessel [*kannam argenteam*] and the golden goblet, with the golden cover, belonging to Count Charles which the provost, Bertulf, had entrusted to the dean when he took flight. . . . Many people marveled at the artlessness of the dean Helias, however, how he had feigned the appearance of sanctity and simplicity, for although he had lived heretofore as if he were rigorous in sanctity, he had certainly strayed from the path in receiving this loot, since it is forbidden by the authority of God: "You shall not touch the unclean." For he gave that treasure up unwillingly to the count, showing in this way how much he had loved the loot. He also said that the provost Bertulf had given those vessels to Saint Donatian for the salvation of his soul, believing he could in this way plead his innocence. In this matter we all knew perfectly well that the provost had received the count's vessels for his own use in the division of the treasure, and when he was unable to carry them with him in flight, he left that wretched loot to his dean. ([83], 1/19; trans., 253–54)

In chapter 85, dated to May 21, finally, Galbert tells us that Helias's retention of the cup excited a general suspicion that the canons had received a substantial portion of the count's treasure: "it seemed likely to many, however—seeing that the dean, Helias, had already . . . handed over to the count the silver vessel [*cannam argenteam*] of the weight of twenty-one marks and the golden goblet with the golden cover of the weight of seven gold marks—that the dean as well as certain canons of his were still in possession of a lot of silver, as it later became clear" ([85], 13/19; trans., 257).[10]

This cup seems to have brought out the worst—covetousness, venality, mendacity, and credulity—in the provost and dean of Saint Donatian and a priest of the church of the Holy Savior, and thus serves as the focal point for an exposure and critique of ecclesiastical corruption, or at least ecclesiastical corruptibility. Since the cup was not handed over, and its story not known, until May 7, however, Galbert cannot have foreseen that it could serve as the vehicle for such an exposure and critique until then. He must, that is, have gone back and added the passages devoted to it to the primitive versions of chapters 16 and 61, recounting the events of March 2 and April 13, and mentioned it again in chapter 85, dated to May 21, so that this motif weaves through literally the whole of the *Passio* corresponding to his primitive parchment record, from its first entry, for March 2, to its last, for May 21.

Galbert's elaboration of a more complex and more important second motif focused on the traitors' execution by precipitation likewise attests to his revision of his primitive notes once he had decided to transform them into a passio. The assassins and conspirators who were still holed up in Saint Donatian were driven into the church tower on April 14 and surrendered on April 19. On May 5, the count and king ordered that they be thrown from the tower of the count's house in Bruges. Wulfric Knop, Bertulf's brother, was the first to be executed, and Galbert writes that the guards "hurled him down as he was gazing down at the steep descent that meant his death" *(mortis suae praecipitium deorsum prospicientem, . . . dejecerunt),* and that "he fell to earth broken and ruined in his whole body" *(decidit in terram toto corpore fractus et destructus)* ([81], 25/28; trans., 251).

This novel form of execution[11] made a strong impression on Galbert and, as two passages in the *Passio* attest, he eventually came to feel that its peculiar form had been inspired by God rather than occurring by accident. As we have seen in the preceding chapter, Galbert discovered the key to Charles's assassination sometime after May 22 in the biblical notion of old sins remembered and punished in subsequent generations. As he explains in the additions he made to the entry devoted to April 17, he thought he could discern the origin of the sad events of 1127 in the treacherous precipitation of two men over fifty years earlier. The first was Erembald's precipitation of Boldran from their ship into the Scheldt one night ("*domnum in profundum torrentis aquosi praecipitavit*"; [71], 17/18; trans., 239) some time around 1055, and the second was that of the young Count Arnold whose servants, suborned by Robert I, "threw down [*dejecerunt*] their young lord" from his horse before killing him at the battle of Cassel in 1071 ([69], 61; trans., 236). Charles's "betrayal" was punishment, in the fourth generation, for his ancestor Robert's "old betrayal [*antiquae traditionis*] [of Arnold] . . . in the very place [Saint Donatian] where formerly [Robert's] . . . oath [not to harm Arnold] had been sworn" ([70], 6/10; trans., 237; trans. mod.), while the "new precipitation [*nova ista praecipitatione*] [of the conspirators in Charles's murder] which was accomplished from the battlements of the count's house in Bruges" was likewise punishment in the fourth generation of Erembald's descendents for his "old precipitation [*antiqua praecipitatio*] of Boldran" ([71], 29/31; trans., 240; trans. mod.), as well as for the murder of Charles.

This discovery of the providential nature of the precise mode of the traitors' execution is also evident in Galbert's description of the death of Water of Vladslo in an undated chapter found between two chapters dated to September 17 and October 8. Walter, writes Galbert, was "hurled from his horse [*ab equo praecipitatus*] by its motion," and "altogether shattered [*totus confractus*] . . . and died a few days later" ([89], 3/4; trans., 262; trans. mod.). Galbert considered Walter an accessory to Charles's murder and, as the words he used to describe it show, he associated Walter's death with the execution of the captured traitors like Wulfric Knop, and felt that its mode confirmed Walter's complicity in the assassination. Able to escape human justice and the execution by precipitation that he ought to have shared with the other traitors, Walter was nonetheless precipitated from his horse by "the severe and horrible judgement of God . . . to whom his punishment was left" ([89], 1, 29/30; trans., 262, 263).

Since the mode of the traitors' execution was sufficiently novel that it could not have been foreseen much before May 5, and since Galbert's "discovery" that its peculiar mode signaled its participation in a vast providential scheme must have occurred at some point between May 5 and the death of Walter of Vladslo around the end of September, one would not expect to find any awareness of the mode of their execution or of this scheme in the entries devoted to events before May 5—if the *Passio* were a true journal.

In fact, however, the *Passio* contains a multistranded motif of providential economy focused on the traitors' execution by precipitation whose filaments are woven into entries written both before and after May 5. The "novelty" of the coming execution is hinted at in four different passages. In chapter 37, Galbert relates in indirect discourse the substance of a discussion between the "barons of the siege" and the "besieged," which he dates to March 17, 1127. In the course of this discussion, the barons set out the conditions under which the besieged who wished to come out of the castle and attempt to prove their innocence might do so, "but," the barons concluded, "no consideration of any kind would be granted to those guilty of committing such a great villany and a crime unheard-of before this [*ante hoc inauditum . . . crimen*]; on the contrary, they should suffer unheard-of destruction and a bitterness of dying unheard-of before this [*inaudito . . . exterminio et ante hoc inaudita moriendi acerbitate*]" ([37], 46/49; trans., 169; trans. mod.).

The notion of a "punishment unheard-of before this time" in retribution for an unheard-of crime recurs twice in chapter 52, dated to March 30, relating the return to Bruges of the barons of Flanders who had gone to Arras to consult with the French king over the election of a new count of Flanders. They brought with them a letter, a *mandatum,* from the king, which was read to the assembled citizens of Bruges and whose content was then expounded by none other than Walter of Vladslo. This passage begins with what Galbert seems to want us to believe is a verbatim transcription of the first part, at least, of the king's letter, in which, according to Galbert, the king writes: "'we have come to carry out vengeance with severity, rigor, and punishment unheard-of before this time [*inaudito ante hoc tempus supplicio*]'" ([52], 14/16; trans., 195; trans. mod.).[12] The chapter continues with Walter of Vladslo's paraphrase of the content of the rest of the letter, in which he at one point says that Charles's assassins "'can expect only the most terrible and heretofore unthought-of death [*gravissimam et inexcogitatam adhuc mortem*]'" ([52], 37/39; trans., 197; trans. mod.).

This same notion, and same language, reappear in chapter 6 (one of the introductory chapters added to the chronicle after May 22). There, in a passage praising Charles, Galbert writes: "Certainly there is no one so senseless, so stupid and obtuse, as not to sentence those traitors to the vilest and most unheard-of punishments [*penis infimis et inauditis*], . . . who by unheard-of treachery [*inaudita traditione*] did away with their lord" ([6], 19/22; trans., 95).

In each of these four cases, this recurrent phrase is applied to the punishment awaiting Charles's assassins and seems to refer to their indeed novel execution by precipitation.[13] In the first and last of these passages the notion of an "unheard-of punishment" can be attributed to Galbert (although he perhaps wanted us to attribute it to the barons in the first). The second and third are a bit problematic since Galbert seems to want us to attribute them to the king and (perhaps) Walter of Vladslo, but since the execution did not take place until over a month after the receipt of the king's letter, one must assume either that the king and Walter were prescient; or that, having declared more than a month earlier that the assassins' punishment would be unheard-of, they wracked their brains for a novel form of execution so they could live up to their word; or that Galbert attributed these words to the king and Walter in the course of a revision of chapter 52 sometime after May 5, 1127. The third explanation seems the most likely, especially given the irony of Walter of Vladslo's unconscious self-sentencing. Taken together, these passages create a certain expectation in the reader, which, when it is fulfilled, lends an air of inevitability to the traitors' death.

As we have seen, the inevitability and significance of the mode of the traitors' execution was revealed to Galbert, or at least confirmed for him, retrospectively by Walter of Valdslo's death from a fall toward the end of September. But its inevitability and significance are likewise *foreshadowed* in the *Passio* by the death of the knight Gilbert, who, when the castle was invaded on March 19, joined some of the besieged who tried to escape capture by slipping over the walls and "fell in sliding over and died" *(in labendo praecipitatus . . . expiravit)* ([41], 37/38; trans., 175). This death was perhaps noteworthy in and of itself and was perhaps already in Galbert's notes when he set out to revise them, but one has to wonder if the *praecipitatus,* at least, was not added in the course of revision. Had Gilbert been captured or shut up in the church and eventually the tower with the others who were besieged, he, too, would have been executed by precipitation on May 5. He fled, Galbert perhaps reminds us, but could no more escape God's wrath and his foreordained punishment than could Walter of Vladslo.

In yet another passage, dated to April 18, Galbert tells us that when the last conspirators had been shut up in the church tower, the king ordered it to be undermined, and within a day the work had advanced so far that he and his men

> were awaiting the fall and collapse of the tower [*casum et ruinam turris*] . . . and only a short time remained until after a little more cutting it would fall down in a tremendous collapse [*casum et ruinam gravissimam*]. . . . when they [the besieged] realized that the greater part of the tower had been demolished and the danger of collapse [*periculum ruinae*] was imminent—for at the summit of the tower they felt the reverberation and swaying at each blow of the hammers, and it seemed as if the tower were shaking and quaking—they were consumed with fear, and decided to surrender to the power of the king rather than to suffocate, buried by the collapse and fall of the tower [*oppressi in ruina et casu turris*]. ([73], 11, 20/[74], 7; trans., 241–42; trans. mod.)

They thus surrendered in order to avoid dying in the fall of the church tower only to die in a fall from the tower of the count's house a short time later.

A series of allusions to the traitors' (future) precipitation form another strand of this motif. The first is found in chapter 26, dated March 7, where Galbert writes: "for God had so blinded them [the traitors] that they no longer possessed any reason or prudence, but, cast down into every kind of evil [*praecipitati in omne malum*] and drunk with rage and wrath, they went astray in fear and dread, both those who had betrayed the count, and those who were lending them aid" ([26], 24/28; trans., 148). It is possible that Galbert's use of the word "cast down" *(praecipitati)* here is fortuitous, but it seems intended to suggest that the assassins and their allies had cast themselves down morally before they were cast down physically from the count's house, and that the fall from the count's house that killed their bodies was but the culmination and outward sign of a more important spiritual fall that had preceded it.

Galbert writes similarly in chapter 57, dated April 11, that "God, whom nothing can resist, . . . made clear to his faithful this inhuman turpitude and revealed the betrayers of such a great prince, and He damned and proscribed them and cast them down [*praecipitavit*]" ([57], 14/17; trans., 208–9). The use of "cast down" can hardly be fortuitous here and since this comment is made in the context of a discussion of William of Ypres's involvement in the conspiracy, and William was imprisoned but never executed, it, too, suggests that the physical precipitation of some of the conspirators was but a material sign of the spiritual precipitation of them all.

Another manifest allusion to the traitors' execution is found in chapter 80, which records events of May 1, but refers to the many who were "punished, proscribed, cast down [*praecipitati*], hanged, and beheaded!" ([80], 6; trans., 249–50) because of Borsiard.

The form of the traitors' execution was so clearly foreordained, Galbert felt, that he could perceive its shadow in the omens that foretold it. "When the bowmen among the besieged," he writes, "were aiming their arrows at the workmen from their position on the summit of the tower and the strings of the drawn bows were vibrating, a certain bow with its arrow in place fell [*decidit*] from the hands of a bowman just in the act of drawing. This was observed by the knights, who were standing by with their shields close to the work of the artisans to protect them as they skillfully operated the engines of war . . . and they prophesied a most unlucky consequence of the fall [*casu*] of the bow and arrow from the besieged" ([59], 5/14; trans., 214). Two of the three signs Bertulf received from God of his own death likewise involve falling objects. In the first instance, when Bertulf had once gone to visit the sick sacristan of Saint Donatian, "the beams broke [*confractae sunt*] which supported the roof right over his head, so that he thought he could barely escape from the room" ([84], 43/47; trans., 256; trans. mod.), while in the second, "the great beam in his house at Bruges fell down [*decidit*], not through the agency of man or wind, exactly on top of the chair and the seats next to it where the provost was accustomed to sit in his power and arrogance . . . and everything affected by the crash was smashed to bits [*confracta sunt omnia quaecumque in ipsa ruina comprehensa fuerant*]" ([84], 47/52; trans., 256).

Most distantly, finally, Galbert refers to the "ruin [*ruinam*] of the fatherland" that would have ensued if Charles had accepted one of the other crowns offered him ([4], 25; trans., 91) and to the "ruin" *(ruinam)*" ([52], 13; trans., 195) and "fall" *(casum)* ([64], 15; trans., 225) of Flanders that did in fact follow Charles's death, suggesting, perhaps, that it was right that those who had brought about the fall of Flanders should likewise die from a fall.

Galbert thus perceived a providential link between the deaths of the young Count Arnold, Boldran, the knight Gilbert, the traitors who were thrown from the count's house, and Walter of Vladslo, and he draws the reader's or listener's attention to this link by creating verbal parallels between these different events through his choice of words.[14] He uses the same technique to suggest a providential link between these deaths and other events—falling arrows and beams—or the moral events that caused or resulted from them—a fall into sin, the fall of the county—and thus weaves a multistranded motif throughout both the old and the new parts of the *Passio,* that is, throughout both the chapters corresponding to his primitive notes and the new passages he added after May 22. He could not have begun to do so, however, until after May 5, and it seems likely that he did not do so until substantially later, around the same time he "discovered" the biblical key to the events he had witnessed and the providential inevitability of the traitors' execution by precipitation, most probably in the early fall of 1127.

When we look behind the scenes of Galbert's descriptions—which stand out even in a century that was "pre-eminent for descriptive writing"[15] and are so brilliantly staged that they seem artless—we find further evidence that he made substantial revisions to his existing notes when he decided to transform them into a passio. His "technical" descriptions, like the following description of the construction of scaling ladders, are remarkable for their detail and clarity:

> Now the ladders were made in this way: at first a wider ladder with rungs was constructed according to the height of the castle walls; to the right and left, green branches, woven tightly together, formed a kind of "wall," and in front of the ladder a similar "wall" was woven. On this ladder another ladder, longer and narrower, and made in a similar way, was superimposed, lying on its side, so that after the erection of the bigger ladder, the smaller ladder could be slid over the wall of the castle and the woven "walls" to right and left and in front would protect the climbers on all sides. ([35], 46/54; trans., 164–65)

The description has a characteristically strong temporal and spatial order that permits us to reconstruct the image piece by piece in our mind. It is also characteristic of Galbert that when he mentions the "walls" protecting the ladders, he distinguishes and mentions separately the right wall, the left wall, and the wall in front, and that he refers to the walls of the smaller ladders in the same order as those of the larger ladders in the preceding sentences. He maintains the same spatial sequence in the description of the protective walls of the two ladders, that is, and does not refer to the right, left, front one time and the left, right, front (or front, right, left, or whatever) another. It is a small point, but it is a good example of the orderliness and precision of his descriptions. Other examples of this kind of technical description include passages devoted to the towers and roof of Saint Donatian ([37], 7/24; trans., 167–68), and the construction and use of a battering ram ([62], 1/38; trans., 220–22); indeed, these descriptions have been noted and praised by historians of material culture.[16]

According to Gransden, twelfth-century authors are noteworthy for their attention to urban and topographical features,[17] but here, too, Galbert excells. His descriptions of the topography of Bruges in the early twelfth century have been invaluable to urban historians and have in every instance proved to be exact.[18] His ability not only to visualize things in space but to communicate that vision in writing is likewise evident in the list he gives of the towns around Bruges: he starts to the northeast with Ijzendijke, and works his way counterclockwise to the southwest.[19] He is able, that is, to imagine the geography of the whole of northern Flanders and projects an itinerary through the countryside around Bruges like an AAA travel map or a Michelin guidebook.

Galbert's technical and topographical descriptions are thus characterized by a precision and orderliness that create a sense of "transparence" by enabling the reader to visualize clearly the things described. This same orderliness and sense of transparence are to be found in his descriptions of actions and events, like his well-known account of the ceremony of homage in chapter 56:

> On April 7, Thursday, homages [*hominia*] to the count were again performed; they were carried out in this order in expression of faith [*fidei*] and loyalty [*securitatis*]. First they did homage [*hominia fecerunt*] in this way. The count asked each one if he [*ille*] wished to become wholly his man, and the latter replied, "I so wish [*volo*]," and with his hands clasped and enclosed by those of the count, they were bound together by a kiss. Secondly, he who had done homage

pledged his faith [*fidem dedit*] to the count's spokesman [*prolocutori comitis*] in these words: "I promise on my faith that I will henceforth be faithful to Count William and that I will maintain my homage toward him completely against everyone, in good faith and without guile." And in the third place he swore an oath to this effect on the relics of the saints [*super reliquias sanctorum . . . juravit*]. Then the count, with a wand [*virgula*] which he held in his hand, gave investiture [*investituras donavit*] to all those who by this compact had promised loyalty and done homage and had taken an oath [*securitatem et hominium simulque juramentum fecerant*]. ([56], 1/12; trans., 206–7)

This seems, at first, a straightforward description of a textbook example of the ceremony of homage and investiture—perhaps in part because it has been *the* textbook example for some historians.[20] Closer examination, however, suggests that it is not an immediate, unreflective description of a ceremony Galbert witnessed, but a dramatization or reimagining, a representation, of one he had witnessed many times.

One should note, first, that the actor here is a generic *ille* (he) and that Galbert makes no claim to be describing a particular act that really took place. What he describes, in other words, is a generic act of homage that he has abstracted from the various individual acts of homage he has witnessed.

Second, the presence of the count's "spokesman/translator" *(prolocutor)* reminds us that the ceremony was not conducted in Latin and that Galbert is at least translating, and may be editing, what was said.[21]

Third, while the ceremony of homage may itself have been traditional and standardized, its description was not necessarily so. Each participant in, or spectator of, this ceremony undoubtedly had a mental model of how it should be conducted, but they had almost certainly constructed this model as much or more by observing it performed as by having it described to them. There was thus no reason for everyone's mental model to be the same, and no guarantee that they were so. It mattered little how each participant described the ceremony to himself or others, so long as he could perform the requisite acts in the requisite order. Each spectator or participant may well have described it differently if called upon to do so. The division of the ceremony into four moments—"first they did homage. . . . Secondly, he who had done homage pledged his faith. . . . And in the third place he swore an oath to this effect on the relics of the saints. Then the count, with a wand which he held in his hand, gave investiture to all those . . ."—is thus Galbert's analysis of what was essential to the ceremony: another observer might well have analysed the ceremony differently and have divided it into more or fewer parts.

Walter of Thérouanne, for example, mentions only one act of homage in his *Vita Karoli* and he does not analyze it at all, writing simply that William of Wervik "had secretly done homage" *(per subreptionem hominium fecerat)* to William of Ypres ([52], 560, 18). His description of this latter William's renunciation of the homage done to him by his vassal Alard of Warneton—"Then lord William . . . renounced the homage Alard had sworn to him [*hominium Alardi guerpivit*], defied him [*eo diffiduciato*], [and] repossessed his entire fief [*totum feodum eius saisivit*]" ([37], 554, 16/17)—suggests, however, that he would have divided the ceremony into three parts corresponding roughly to three of the four moments mentioned by Galbert: homage *(hominium),* faith *(fides),* and investiture *(investitura).*[22]

Galbert in fact himself provides two different analyses of the ceremony in the above-cited passage. In the first part of the passage, the order of the elements is: homage *(hominium),* faith *(fides),* oath *(jurare),* and investiture *(investitura).* In the last sentence of the passage, however, he writes: "then the count, with a wand which he held in his hand, gave investiture [*investituras donavit*] to all those who by this compact had promised loyalty and done homage and had taken an oath [*securitatem et hominium simulque juramentum fecerant*]." One of the first three elements is here called "loyalty" *(securitas)* rather than "faith" *(fides)* and their order is: loyalty *(securitas),* homage *(hominium),* and oath *(juramentum).*

Galbert's model of the ceremony of homage also underlies his description and analysis in the immediately preceding chapter of the agreement through which the king and the new count bought the support of the burghers of Bruges, and this description and analysis further demonstrate the model's flexibility, utility, and subjectivity. His account of this agreement runs as follows:

> There was also read the little charter of agreement [*chartula conventionis*] reached between the count and our citizens about the remission of the toll and the ground rent on their houses. As the price of their election and acceptance of the person of the new count, they were to receive from the count this liberty [*reciperent a comite libertatem*], that neither they nor their successors in our place

should pay toll or rent henceforth to the count or his successors. And having been granted [*donati*] this liberty in perpetuity, as it was written in the charter of agreement, they should receive confirmation of this same liberty by an oath [*juramentum*] which they demanded of both king and count, to the effect that neither king nor count, either in person or through their agents, would any longer disturb our citizens, or their successors in our place, about paying the toll and rent but would respect inviolably the privileges of the canons as well as the remission of tolls and rent, honestly and fairly, without reservation. Binding themselves to accept this condition, the king and count took an oath on the relics of the saints [*juraverunt . . . super sanctorum reliquias*] in the hearing of the clergy and the people. Subsequently the citizens swore fealty [*juraverunt fidelitatem*] to the count, according to custom, and did homage and promised loyalty [*hominia fecerunt . . . et securitates*] to him, as they had done formerly to his predecessors, the lawful princes and lords of the land. ([55], 27/46; trans., 203–4; trans. mod.)

One can distinguish five moments in the description of this event: first, the king and count "invested" the burghers with a liberty *(libertatem)* by means of a charter *(chartula;* which seems to stand, here, in the place of the wand [*virgula*] with which the vassals are enfeoffed in the next chapter);[23] second, they confirmed this liberty through an "oath" *(juraverunt);* third, the citizens "swore fealty" *(juraverunt fidelitatem);* fourth, they "did homage" *(hominia fecerunt)* to him; and, fifth, they "promised loyalty" *(fecerunt . . . securitates)* to him. Four of these five moments—the count's "investiture" of the citizens with a liberty, and the citizens' acts of "fealty" *(fidelitas),* "homage" *(hominium),* and "loyalty" *(securitas)*—seem to correspond to the four moments of ceremony of homage described in chapter 56: "homage" *(hominium),* "faith" *(fides),* "oath" *(jurare),* and "investiture" *(investitura).* The act of "faith" *(fides)* is again called "loyalty" *(securitas),* the "oath" *(jurare, juramentum)* is here called "swearing fealty" *(jurare fidelitatem),* the order of the elements is changed (perhaps the burghers realized the momentary strength of their position and insisted that the investiture precede the homage), and a new element—the count and king's "oath" *(jurare)* confirming the gift (perhaps also an addition that suggested itself to a merchant mentality)—is added,[24] but it is nonetheless clear that Galbert conceives of what passes between the king, the new count, and the burghers in terms of an act of homage and investiture and analyzes its elements in that way.[25]

One must wonder, however, if the king and count perceived this exchange in quite the same terms as did Galbert. Did they, too, think of what had passed between them and the burghers as an act of homage and investiture? How did the various witnesses to this exchange perceive it? If it was commonly perceived as an act of homage and investiture, then the elements of this ceremony as it was practiced in Flanders in 1127 were flexible. They had no fixed or necessary order and new elements could be added. If the exchange described by Galbert was not commonly perceived in terms of an act of homage and investiture, if, that is, Galbert is using his model of homage and investiture to describe what was perhaps an extraordinary agreement, it shows that the categories of his analysis and the moments of the ceremony were, in his mind at least, generative and could be used and recombined in new ways to fit new situations.

Heirbaut and Van Caenegem have pointed to another example of what one might term the metaphoric extension of the ceremony, or at least the concepts or vocabulary, of homage in the *Passio.* When William Clito first went to Saint-Omer, writes Galbert, he was met outside the town by a group of youths armed with bows and arrows who declared that they wanted the count to confirm their possession of "'a fief [*feodum*] that our boys had always held from your predecessors'" ([66], 11/12; trans., 228; trans. mod.). "The feodum they wanted to be renewed or confirmed," writes Van Caenegem, "was the right to hunt in the surrounding woods. It is clear that feodum does not stand here for a fief in the usual technical sense, as the youngsters of Saint-Omer were no comital vassals."[26] If Galbert is simply reporting the youths' speech, the "metaphoric" use of the term *feodum* would of course be theirs. It is more likely, however, that it is due to Galbert, who imagined the count's reception in Saint-Omer on the basis of reports he received. Walter of Thérouanne, who was based much closer to Saint-Omer than Galbert, says nothing of this request. Galbert likewise reports that immediately after Charles's murder William of Ypres seized the merchants who were in Ypres at that moment for the market—regardless of where they were from—and forced them to "swear faith and loyalty and do homage" *(fidem, securitatem et hominia facerent)* to him ([25], 15/18; trans., 144; cf. [20], 25/31; trans., 133), whereas Walter notes only that William made the citizens of the towns of which he took control "swear fealty" *(fidelitatem jurare/facere)* to him ([43], 557, 14/15; [48], 559, 11/12).[27] The concepts of homage were thus elastic and generative for Galbert, and he used its vocabulary metaphorically.[28] His descriptions of both noble and nonnoble homage are thus not the transparent, objective accounts of these social interactions that they have sometimes been taken to be, but instead carefully crafted analyses of them. These interactions, that is, have been understood, grasped, analyzed, and imagined by Galbert himself—and in terms that were not necessarily shared by his contemporaries.[29]

The "transparency" of Galbert's descriptions of these ceremonies, the impression they give the reader of "being there," are thus due to the penetration of his mind, which permitted him to seize and analyze the flow of life around him, and the literary work that synthesized and communicated this analysis in seemingly ingenuous descriptions. These same abilities are apparent throughout his descriptions of less structured actions as well, with the same result.[30] A concise and brilliant example of his abilities is to be found in two sentences at the end of chapter 63, which describes the invasion of Saint Donatian by the besiegers. When they finally manage to break through a wall with a ram, Galbert depicts the rush into the church in these terms:

> they hurled themselves through the middle of the opening in one rush, without order, without line of battle, without any thought for arms [*sine ordine, sine pugna, absque omni respectu armorum*], so that by rushing in all at once they could prevent the besieged from having any time or place in which to fight and kill anyone. For they kept rushing in without stopping until they had transformed themselves into a kind of bridge [*Non enim cessabant ruere donec sine interruptione quasi pontem se ipsos fecissent*], and, by the marvelous dispensation of God, they advanced without mortal danger to their lives, some dashing, some stumbling, some pushed in forcibly, some falling down and trying to get up again, some rushing in without order, as is usual in such a great tumult [*sine vitae suae periculo mortali ingressi sunt, alii ruendo, alii offendendo, alii intrusi violenter, alii surgere conantes a casu prosternentes, alii, sicut solet fieri in tanto tumultu, sine ordine irruentes*]. Not only the church but the whole castle and its vicinity was filled with the sound of their shouts and cries, with the noise of their passage, the crumbling of the wall and the clamor and crash of arms. Outside they were praising God and thanking him for this victory by which He honored [*honestavit*] the victors, exalted [*sublimavit*] the king and his men, glorified [*glorificavit*] his majestic name above all others, cleansed [*mundavit*]

the church in part from the defilers, and made it possible [*donavit*] at last for that glorious martyr, his count, to be mourned by the pious veneration of good men and to be sustained by the prayers of his faithful. ([63], 52/70; trans., 224; trans. mod.)

The last three of the four sentences of the English translation correspond to a single, remarkable Latin one in which the adrenalin-driven anarchy of the moment is depicted, indeed is made sensible, by the continuous action of the first verb ("for they kept rushing in without stopping until . . . [*non enim cessabant ruere donec sine interruptione . . .*]"); by the image of individual attackers melding themselves (in an animation-like blurring of individuals, distinct images, that, through the speed with which they pass, are perceived to form one continuous action) into the single mass of a human bridge; by the repetition of "without" *(sine),* beginning in the first sentence, emphasizing the attackers' feral energy; by the repetition of the indefinite plural "some" *(alii)* with a participle that distinguishes a series of different actions while maintaining a sense of their simultaneity and collective nature; by a similar repetition of verbs ending in *-avit* to suggest a varied but equally frenzied and continuous activity outside the church; and, finally, by the addition of a "sound track" describing the din inside the church ("not only the church but the whole castle and its vicinity was filled with the sound of their shouts and cries, with the noise of their passage, the crumbling of the wall and the clamor and crash of arms"), and its simultaneous echo outside ("outside they were praising God and thanking him"). This is a striking imposition of linguistic order on evenemential chaos in a way that renders it simultaneously sensible and comprehensible, and it is highly unlikely that it was achieved in a single pass.

Galbert's long description of the immediate aftermath of the count's murder likewise turns what must have been an even greater and more complex mass of action into a well-ordered set of events. In all the manuscripts, the murder and its immediate aftermath are described in a single long chapter covering all the events of March 2, 1127.[31] The first thirty lines (in my edition) of this original chapter (corresponding to the modern chapter 15) are devoted to the assassination of the count. The next six lines ([16], 1/6) are devoted to the murder of the castellan of Bourbourg who had (to his misfortune) accompanied the count to the church that morning. The castellan did not die immediately, however, but had time to confess and commune. The next three lines—"For immediately after killing the count, the swordsmen, leaving the corpse of the count and the castellan at the point of death in the gallery, went out to attack those of their enemies from the court of the count who happened to be present" ([16], 6/9; trans., 121)—back up one moment in time to the point after the castellan's wounding but before his confession and communion, explain why he had time to do so, and follow the assassins as they rush out of the church. Faced with a division of the action, that is, between the mortally wounded castellan who remains in the gallery of the church and the assassins who rush outside, Galbert follows one narrative thread, the story of the castellan, to its conclusion and then backs up to pick up the second thread, the subsequent actions of the assassins, at its beginning.

The assassins do not remain together as a single body, however, but divide up and pursue different people simultaneously. Galbert thus first relates to its conclusion the pursuit by some of the assassins of the knight Henry ([16], 10/16); then relates the simultaneous pursuit and murder by another group of assassins of the two sons of the castellan of Bourbourg ([16], 16/33), introducing this second narrative thread with the time expression "at the same moment" *(ipso momento);* and then goes on to describe, third, the unsuccessful simultaneous pursuit of Richard of Woumen ([16], 33/39). The narrative then follows the assassins back to the castle of Bruges: "the traitors, frustrated in their pursuit, returned to the castle" ([16], 39/40; trans., 122).

Galbert's description of this initial series of events may seem to be a simple reporting of the events as they happened, but this impression is a product of the narration and not of the events themselves. It is unlikely, for example, that these four men were the only ones pursued by the assassins bent on killing as many of their enemies as possible; indeed, Galbert, shortly afterward mentions an indefinite number of other friends of the count who were in hiding and names two others, Gervaise and John, who, like Richard, successfully escaped.[32] Galbert thus seems to have chosen these three pursuits as representative of a number of simultaneous ones, creating a symbolic order out of an evenemential heap.

Why did he choose these three? We can only speculate, of course, but the pursuit of Henry may have interested him because the knight is saved—ironically? poignantly?—by Haket, the castellan of Bruges, brother of the provost Bertulf and uncle of the assassin Borsiard. The pursuit and murder of the sons of the castellan of Bourbourg must have appealed to Galbert for their tragic overtones and for the pathos they lend a subsequent scene in which the dying castellan sends his last requests, through the abbess of Origny, to his wife and his sons who, although he does not know it, have already been murdered. I will suggest a bit later that one of the reasons the pursuit of Richard of Woumen interested Galbert was that it was unsuccessful, but it may also have interested him because Richard's family was allied by marriage with the family of Thancmar of Straeten, whose feud with Borsiard, of which Galbert here reminds us, was the immediate provocation for the assassination. Each of these pursuits, that is, has dramatic and thematic overtones that can perhaps explain why Galbert chose to relate it rather than others.

If these three pursuits occur more or less simultaneously, moreover, why did Galbert choose to relate them in the order he did? One reason probably has to do with spatial order. Henry is chased into the count's house where he throws himself at Haket's feet and begs for his protection. He never leaves the burg of Bruges. Galbert relates the pursuit of the sons of the castellan of Bourbourg next because they get further away before being caught: one makes it to the edge of the town before being pulled off his horse and killed; the other is murdered on the threshold of his own dwelling. The pursuit of Richard of Woumen comes last because he is chased "for a mile" ([16], 36; trans., 122) and is never caught. The three pursuits are arranged in a spatial progression from the burg of Bruges outward, from the closed space of a chapel in the gallery of the church where the count and castellan of Bourbourg are trapped and murdered outward to the freedom of the open Flemish plain.

Richard's pursuit is also placed last, I would suggest, because the failure to capture him and the assassins' frustration both allow the narrative focus to return to the burg with them and hint at their ultimate frustration and defeat in the coming days and weeks. This pursuit is placed third, that is, because of its narrative and thematic utility. The link between this pursuit and the beginning of the next section—"the traitors, frustrated in their pursuit, returned to the castle"—also provides us with another example of the way in which Galbert condensed his information for the sake of a coherent narrative by allowing one action to stand for many, for surely the various parties of assassins and their accomplices did not all return simultaneously from pursuing their various enemies.

The inner-to-outer, burg-to-countryside, wave that characterizes this first sequence of events continues in the next part of the long original chapter. Having brought his narrative focus back to the burg, Galbert mentions, first, the crowd of residents milling around the courtyard of the burg; second, the friends of the count who have gone into hiding (nearby it would seem); and third, Gervaise, a chamberlain, and John, the count's favorite servant, who have fled on horseback to the north and to Ypres, respectively ([16], 39/53). John brings news of the count's murder to Ypres, and Galbert goes on to describe the effect of this news on the merchants assembled there for a fair, who immediately pack up their goods and flee, carrying the news with them to the ends of the earth: "bearing with them word of the disgrace of our land and spreading it everywhere. And so every man of peace and honor who had heard of the fame of this count now mourned him" ([16], 62/[17], 2; trans., 124).

After this second wave of movement from the burg to beyond the borders of Flanders, Galbert returns once more to the burg—"but in our castle where our lord and most pious father was lying slain, no one dared openly to weep for his death" ([17], 2/4; trans., 124)—and picks up the narrative thread precisely where he had left it (note the use of "immediately" [*statim*] in the following passage), with the return of the frustrated assassins to the burg: "For when the nephews of the provost and that most criminal of men, Borsiard, with their accomplices, returned to the castle immediately after the flight of their enemies . . ." ([17], 8/11; trans., 125).

The series of events related in the next part of the original chapter all take place within the burg, but they, too, have a marked spatial rhythm. In this part of the chapter, Galbert relates three forays that groups of the assassins and their accomplices made into the church in search of their enemies. Having entered the church, first, to look for one of their principal antagonists, Walter of Loker, some of them come across the castellan of Bourbourg, "still breathing" ([17], 25; trans., 125), and drag him by the feet down the stairs and out into the courtyard, where they dismember him ([17], 24/31). The remaining searchers subsequently flush out Walter of Loker, who is likewise dragged outside and slain ([17], 31/54). A group of servants then enters the church a second time and discovers a number of people hiding in the sanctuary, most notably Fromold Junior ([18], 1/20). When they come back outside and report their discoveries, one of the leading assassins, Isaac, swears that he will kill Fromold Junior—his brother-in-law!—rushes into the church, seizes him, and drags him out to be killed. Fromold is spared, however, both because the assassins need his help to obtain the count's treasure and because, at the request of his uncle and the canons of Saint Donatian, the provost Bertulf intervenes on his behalf and takes him into his custody.

Were these the only forays into the church made by the assassins that day? It seems more likely that there was a constant coming and going within the church throughout the day, and there are several points in this passage suggesting that Galbert, as he did with the pursuit of the assassins' enemies, has deliberately reduced this confused activity to a relatively small and symbolically important series of discrete events.

Having related the extraction and death of the castellan of Bourbourg, for example, Galbert returns his narrative focus to the search for Walter of Loker with the sentence: "Meanwhile Walter of Loker was being hunted everywhere, inside and outside the church" ([17], 31/32; trans., 126), but Galbert says nothing more about any searching for anyone outside the church. One must assume, therefore, that he chose to concentrate on the search within Saint Donatian for the sake of narrative coherence.

After relating how Isaac dragged his brother-in-law Fromold Junior from the sanctuary and threatened to kill him, moreover, Galbert tells us that his life was momentarily spared while Isaac and Borsiard discussed how they might best extort "the whole treasure of the count from him and also from the chamberlain, Arnold, whom they had taken captive in the same place" ([18], 43/44; trans., 129). And shortly afterward, he writes that Bertulf "took all [*omnes*] those captured there [in the church] into his custody" ([19], 16; trans., 130; trans. mod.).

The "all" certainly suggests that there were more captives than just Fromold and Arnold—perhaps we are meant to understand that all the people discovered in the church during the second foray mentioned above were taken captive[33]—but Galbert says nothing about the capture of either Arnold or any of the others, choosing to relate exclusively the capture of Fromold Junior.

Galbert's desire to create a gripping and thematically unified historical narrative is also evident in the parallels he establishes between these three forays into the church. They are described in similarly energetic, and similar-sounding, terms—"now they rushed through the doors into the church" *(irruerunt igitur per januas intra templum)* ([17], 20/21; trans., 125), "running back into the sanctuary" *(iterum recurrentes in sanctuarium)* ([18], 1; trans., 127), and "then bursting through the doors Isaac rushed in at once" *(tunc discussis foribus, irruperat statim Isaac)* ([18], 29; trans., 129)—creating not only a parallel between the three actions, but a repeated impression of violent transgression. As a result of these incursions, three men, one after another, are dragged from the church. The first and second are killed in signally savage fashion—"They also killed the castellan of Bourbourg. First wounding him mortally, they afterward dragged him ignobly by his feet from the gallery . . . to the doors of the church and dismembered him outside with their swords" ([16], 1/4; trans., 120);[34] "And when they had led him [Walter of Loker] out into the court of the castle, pushing him from them, they threw him to their serfs to be killed. How quickly the serfs put him to death, beating him down with swords and sticks, clubs and stones" ([17], 51/54; trans., 127)—and the third, Fromold Junior, is threatened with a similar death ([18], 29/[19], 4; trans., 129–30). The dying castellan gives a ring to an abbess to pass on to his wife, and the seemingly doomed Fromold likewise gives a ring to a priest to pass on to his daughter ([17], 27/30; trans., 126; [18], 39/41; trans., 129). To Walter of Loker's pleas for pity, the assassins respond: "'We must repay you with the kind of pity you have deserved from us!'" *(talem tibi rependere debemus misericordiam, qualem erga nos promeruisti)* ([17], 50/51; trans., 127), and to Fromold Junior's pleas Isaac responds similarly: "'You are going to receive the mercy you have deserved for slandering us to the count!'" *(illam habiturus es veniam quam detrahendo apud comitem nobis promeruisti)* ([18], 35/36; trans., 129; trans. mod.). There is also a clerical presence in each case: the priests who hear the castellan's confession and give him the viaticum, as well as the abbess to whom he gives his ring ([16], 4/6, 16/17; [17], 27/30; trans., 120–21, 126);[35] the clergy who convince Borsiard not to kill Walter in the church itself ([17], 46/48; trans., 127); and the priest who hears Fromold's confession and to whom Fromold gives his ring ([18], 37/41; trans., 129).

These parallels were undoubtedly in the events themselves to some degree, but Galbert nonetheless had to grasp them, see them as parallels, and then relate them in such a way that his readers would sense them as well. And in the case of the direct speech he reports, he was at the least translating from Flemish into Latin and thus able to choose or change words to heighten the similarities between the assassins' two responses; perhaps he simply invented them.

Galbert's desire to make his narrative of this sequence of forays into the church gripping and thematically coherent is also evident in, and helps to explain, his decision to relate Fromold Junior's capture rather than that of Arnold or of any of the others hiding in the church. Fromold was a prominent person, one of the count's favorites. He may also have been someone whom Galbert knew particularly well or with whom he worked particularly closely if they both worked in the local fiscal administration of the castellany of Bruges. Fromold's capture was thus perhaps the most interesting one to Galbert because of his relation to Fromold and Fromold's relation to Charles. It was perhaps also interesting to Galbert for the above-mentioned parallels—which he grasped, or could at least forge—between it and the murders of the castellan and Walter of Loker, and for its pathos. For when Fromold first saw his brother-in-law Isaac coming toward him in the church, "he thought Isaac was going to save him from death, not take him captive, and he said: 'Isaac, my friend, I beg you, by the friendship which has so far existed between us, save my life, and take care of my sons, who are your nephews, by saving me, for if I am killed they will be without a protector'" ([18], 31/35; trans., 129), to which appeal Isaac responded by promising his death. Fromold's capture also provoked his uncle's plea to the provost to save his life, and permits Galbert to describe the behavior of the provost—who fascinated him—in a difficult moment ([19], 1/24; trans., 130–31). Fromold's capture may also have interested Galbert, finally, for its narrative utility and effect. Just as he had earlier narrated three pursuits, the last of which ended in the fugitive's escape, thus signaling the end of the pursuit of fugitives beyond the confines of the burg and leading the narrative back there, so here he narrates the extraction of three men from the church, of whom the first two are brutally murdered but the third survives thanks to the depth of the assassins' cupidity which makes them hesitate to kill him until they have extracted from him everything they can learn about the count's treasure. This hesitation saves his life and shows that the assassins' blood lust has been sated to a point where it is now no stronger than their greed. It thus has an important thematic function, marking the end of the violent simplification of social interaction inherent in the count's murder and the beginning of the reestablishment of a more normally complex social order.

The description of Fromold's capture also provides us with an example of Galbert's ability to present a series of simultaneous and therefore potentially confusing actions in an orderly sequence. While *(interim)* Fromold was being held captive by the assassins, Galbert tells us, a priest heard his confession and Fromold gave him a ring ([18], 37/41; trans., 129). While this was going on *(interim),* Isaac and Borsiard were discussing what should be done with Fromold ([18], 41/44; trans., 129). Meanwhile *(interea)* Fromold Junior's uncle and the canons of Saint Donatian were pleading with the provost to intervene with the assassins and save Fromold ([19], 1/18; trans., 130).

This relation of three simultaneous actions in two distinct locations also demonstrates both Galbert's analytic powers and his ability to combine material from various sources into a seamless whole. He might have been able simultaneously to *overhear* Isaac and Borsiard's conversation and to *watch* Fromold Junior confess and give his ring to a priest—assuming that both actions took place inside, or both outside, the church—but he cannot also have been present at the simultaneous pleadings of Fromold's uncle, which took place in the provost's house. Since Galbert does not place himself anywhere in the events of this day,[36] it is even possible that he did not himself witness any of these actions but learned of them later, perhaps from the priest who heard Fromold's confession, one of the canons who accompanied Fromold's uncle, and someone who overheard Borsiard and Isaac's conversation. He thus drew on at least one other source in his relation of these actions and yet manages to integrate this secondhand material into his account in such a way that we cannot distinguish what he himself witnessed from what he heard from others.

The long description of the forays into the church ends with another demonstration of Galbert's ability to narrate simultaneous action and combine seamlessly accounts from other sources with what he may himself have witnessed. Having imagined the thoughts and feelings of those who had been captured in the church and were now incarcerated in a room in the provost's house ([19], 30/44; trans., 131–32), he goes on to relate the simultaneous removal of the bodies of the castellan, his sons, and Walter, which "were carried out of the castle and immediately put on board ships . . . and they were conveyed to their respective houses and castles" ([20], 2/4; trans., 132), and efforts of the provost to disassociate himself from the murderers while walking around in his house with his canons ([20], 4/6; trans., 132). Following on the hesitation—due to a conflict between a lust for gold and a lust for vengeance—that saved Fromold's life and marks the end of the first wave of violence, this imprisonment of the captives, care for the bodies of the dead, and attempt at self-justification were also the beginnings of the negotiations necessary for the restoration of normal relationships, and thus have an important thematic function.

This long description ([17], 2–[20], 6) of the three forays into the church, the dismemberment of the castellan of Bourbourg, the murder of Walter of Loker, the capture of Fromold Junior, the imprisonment of Fromold and the others captured in the church, the removal of the bodies, and the provost's excuses provides us with evidence of Galbert's desire and efforts to give his narrative a symbolic order through the selection of representative actions and their arrangement in a rhythmic, dramatic, thematically coherent, rhetorically effective series. This series of events in the burg turns out, moreover, to be the first moment of yet a third wave of motion from the burg outward. After describing the provost's attempts to disinculpate himself, Galbert goes on to relate, first, an assault that the assassins and their accomplices made—"on the same day" ([20], 6; trans., 132)—against the stronghold of their enemy Thancmar at Straeten (now Sint Andries to the southwest of Bruges); second, the attacks made on merchants on the road to the fair at Ypres; and, finally, William of Ypres's efforts to make all the merchants who were already in Ypres pledge loyalty and fealty and do homage to him as a first step in his campaign to acquire the county ([20], 6/31; trans., 132–43). This movement outward is all the more striking when one realizes that Straeten lay on the road between Bruges and Ypres: the narrative thus follows the road from Bruges to Straeten and the assault on Thancmar's stronghold there, to the attacks made on merchants along it, and then ends in Ypres itself, providing further evidence of Galbert's ability to visualize space and communicate his vision.

Having described William's actions in Ypres, Galbert returns once more to Bruges, "late on the same day, toward evening" ([20], 31/32; trans., 134), to describe the assassins' acquisition of the count's treasure, the laying out of the count's body, and the assassins' plans for its removal from Bruges ([20], 32/38, [21], 1/20; trans., 134–35). "And so closed that day," he writes, "full of sorrow and misery" ([21], 20/21; trans., 135), before going on to describe the watch placed in and around the church during the night by the provost who fears lest the citizens invade the church ([21], 23/29; trans., 135).

This long chapter demonstrates Galbert's ability to combine information from various sources with what he himself had witnessed in such a way that we cannot distinguish the two, and of his ability to create a spatially, temporally, and thematically well-ordered narrative. For thematic or dramatic reasons, he has chosen a few actions to stand for the many that must have occurred that day and has arranged them in a coherent order: the attack on the count and castellan followed by a first pulse outward from the burg as the assassins pursue their enemies beyond the edges of the town, a movement that ends with the frustration of the third pursuit; a second outward pulse of news from the burg to Ypres, to the ends of the earth; a rhythmic, almost ritualistic, hunting down of trapped enemies that ends with the third victim when the spell is broken by the provost's intervention; a third pulse outward from the burg to Straeten to Ypres; then a final evening return to the burg, the disposition of the count's body, the fall of night, and the watch on the church. These passages are not the hastily scribbled notes of the small-minded, naive, neurotically anxious pen-pusher portrayed by Pirenne and Ross. They are the product of a rigorous mind that was able to forge from a chaotic flux of events a temporally and spatially coherent description so limpid that its careful structure is almost invisible.[37]

This description of the events of March 2 is not, moreover, unique. The *Passio* has many other equally vivid descriptions of crowd scenes and complex events like the discussion between the conspirators and their kinsman Robert the Young the night before the assassination ([11], 10/42; trans., 109–10), the invasion of the town by Gervaise's forces on March 9 ([28], 1/[29], 32; trans., 151–55), the storming of the castle ([40], 1/[41], 83; trans., 172–77), the execution of the provost Bertulf ([57], 1/93; trans., 208–12), the assault on the church ([62], 1/[64], 51; trans., 220–26),[38] and the battle of Ypres ([79], 1/12; trans., 248).[39]

What is even more extraordinary about many of these descriptions is that Galbert was almost certainly not a witness to the events he relates so vividly in them. As Alan Murray notes, for example, Galbert could not possibly have been present at the discussion he describes between the conspirators and Robert the Young: "given the alleged circumstances of this incident, the conspiratorial dialogue can only be a fabrication, or a construction deriving from a later account given by Robert himself."[40] Even if this dialogue—which represents the conspirators' unsuccessful efforts to include Robert in their plot to kill the count—is based ultimately on an account originating with Robert, it probably bears little relation to what was actually said. The only likely time for Robert to have given such an account was after he had surrendered with the other conspirators besieged in the church on April 19, 1127, and before he was removed from Bruges by the king of France on May 6 (and executed at Cassel shortly thereafter). At this point in time, Robert had every reason to concoct a version of the conspiracy that made him an unwitting and unwilling participant, and, as Murray observes, "the main purpose" of the dialogue recorded by Galbert "seems to be to exonerate Robert from any part in the murder," although he notes that it also serves "indirectly to excuse the public sympathy for him by the people of Bruges right up to his execution at Cassel on the orders of Louis VI."[41] Any account of this dialogue given by Robert may, moreover, have reached Galbert only second- or thirdhand, and Galbert probably did not write his version of the dialogue until after May 22. His account of it, that is, is the product of at least one revision—by Robert, more than six weeks after it took place, in desperate circumstances, and with a precise goal in mind—and may have been revised in one or more intermediate retellings and again by Galbert.

The scene, as Murray points out, has a distinctly literary quality to it, showing "Robert in a conflict of loyalties [torn between the loyalty he owes his kinsmen and that he owes the count] akin to those later beloved by writers of vernacular chivalric romance."[42] If Galbert himself imagined this scene, if, that is, he asked himself how people *should* behave and what they *should* say in such a dramatic situation, he could not help but find the answers in the models of speech and behavior that were circulated through both fictional and historical narratives. In fact, his account of this dramatic scene gains credibility by conforming to his contemporaries' shared expectations concerning dramatic behavior, expectations that were themselves created by shared narrative models of such behavior. It is even less surprising that such models should suggest themselves to Robert, if this account of the scene ultimately goes back to him, since his version of the story would have had the most fundamental of rhetorical goals: the evocation of sympathy.

The *Passio* contains other vivid and detailed descriptions of events that Galbert did not witness but imagined from other people's accounts of them, and in these, too, one often senses an underlying narrative model around which Galbert has built his account.[43] Chapters 57 and 58 provide two noteworthy examples of such descriptions, the first of Bertulf's execution in Ypres on April 11, 1127, and the second of the judicial duel between Guy of Steenvorde and Iron Herman that took place near Ypres on the same day. Galbert indicates the sources for these accounts in only the vaguest terms: "so they say" *(sic aiunt)* ([57], 20; trans., 209; trans. mod.), he writes at one point, and later adds: "So it was related by a squire who came to us and in the presence of the king told us of their fate; he had been present on that day and had seen the provost and Guy hanged at Ypres" ([58], 39/42; trans., 213). He probably composed his descriptions from several sources, although the squire may have been his principal informant, and he himself probably imagined much of their detail. It seems inevitable, that is, that, without suppressing or falsifying any of the information he was able to gather, Galbert imagined the events of the day on the basis of that information, creating what he deemed worthy and appropriate versions of the execution and duel. What we have is thus not Galbert's transcription of the testimonies he heard, but the visions of the events that he imagined on the basis of them, visions, moreover, that have been influenced by two ambient narrative models.

Since it is shorter and simpler, let me turn first to the second event Galbert relates, the judicial duel between Guy and Herman:

As soon as the provost was dead, everyone present went out to the manor where the combat between Herman the Iron and Guy had been called and where both sides fought bitterly. Guy had unhorsed his adversary and kept him down with his lance just as he liked whenever Herman tried to get up. Then his adversary, coming closer, disemboweled Guy's horse, running him through with his sword. Guy, having slipped from his horse, rushed at his adversary with his sword drawn. Now there was a continuous and bitter struggle, with alternating thrusts of swords, until both, exhausted by the weight and burden of arms, threw away their shields and hastened to gain victory in the fight by resorting to wrestling. Herman the Iron fell prostrate on the ground, and Guy was lying on top of him smashing the knight's face and eyes with his iron gauntlets. But Herman, prostrate, little by little regained his strength from the coolness of the earth, as we read of Antaeus, and by cleverly lying quiet made Guy believe he was certain of victory. Meanwhile, gently moving his hand down to the lower edge of the cuirass where Guy was not protected, Herman seized him by the testicles, and summoning all his strength for the brief space of one moment, he hurled Guy from him; by this tearing motion all the lower parts of the body were broken so that Guy, now prostrate, gave up, crying out that he was conquered and dying. ([58], 10/30; trans., 212–13)

The literary quality of Galbert's account is clear when one compares it, on the one hand, with Walter of Thérouanne's description of the same event and, on the other hand, with a description of a purely literary battle such as that between Arthur and Frollo in Geoffrey of Monmouth's *Historia regum Britanniae.* Walter describes the duel this way in his *Vita Karoli:*

After the provost had been killed, lord William left Ypres for the trial of Guy of Steenvorde who had recently been accused of the same crime, that he had, namely, agreed to, and conspired in, the count's death. When the judicial duel to determine the case between Guy and his accuser Herman, nicknamed the Iron, began, Guy had the better of the first and second exchanges of blows and fell on Herman and crushed him to the ground under the immense weight of his body and their arms (for Guy, like Herman, was armed with a heavy hauberk and a helmet). Then Herman, strengthened by God's virtue, got up as if he no longer felt anything weighing on him and, throwing down in turn him who, as was mentioned above, had previously had the upper hand, began to press him to confess the crime he had committed. What more can I say? He was ultimately vanquished by divine judgement and convicted of the crime of which he was accused and thus sentenced to die. ([39], 555, 1/12)

Walter's account is less detailed, less vivid, less dramatic. He seems less interested in the duel than Galbert and makes no effort to make the reader feel like he or she is there, in the presence of the combatants. His rhetorical "What more can I say?" in fact draws the audience's attention away from the scene and toward him, the narrator, whereas Galbert's description focuses the audience's attention steadily on the struggle.

Writing around 1135, Geoffrey of Monmouth described the battle of Arthur and Frollo, the Roman governor of Gaul, on an island in the Seine in these terms:

Arthur and Frollo were both fully armed and seated on horses which were wonderfully fleet of foot. It was not easy to foretell which would win. For a moment they stood facing each other with their lances held straight in the air: then they suddenly set spurs to their horses and struck each other two mighty blows. Arthur aimed his lance with more care and hit Frollo high up on his chest. He avoided Frollo's weapon, and hurled his enemy to the ground with all his might. Arthur then drew his sword from the scabbard and was just hurrying forward to strike Frollo when the latter leapt quickly to his feet, ran forward with his lance levelled and with a deadly thrust stabbed Arthur's horse in the chest, thus bringing down both horse and rider. . . . Arthur sprang quickly to his feet, covered himself with his shield, and rushed forward to meet Frollo. They stood up to each other hand to hand, giving blow for blow, and each doing his utmost to kill the other. In the end Frollo found an opening and struck Arthur on the forehead. It was only the fact that he blunted the edge of his swordblade at the point where it made contact with Arthur's metal helmet that prevented Frollo from dealing a mortal blow. When Arthur saw his leather cuirass and his round shield grow red, he was roused to even fiercer anger. He raised Caliburn in the air with all his strength and brought it down through Frollo's helmet and so on to his head, which he cut into two halves. At this blow Frollo fell to the ground, drummed the earth with his heels and breathed his soul into the winds.[44]

As this passage shows, the literary quality of Galbert's account of a duel is not limited to its vividness and detail, but includes his careful delimitation of the traditional moments of a literary duel—one or more initial passes on horseback with lances, followed by a long exchange of blows on foot with swords ending in a critical moment in which one of the combatants, often the one who appears to be losing, wins the contest by an extraordinary blow or effort—and his allusion to classical mythology (at the same point where Walter refers to divine virtue). There are, to be sure, certain elements of the fight—like resorting to fisticuffs, and the mighty testicle-tugging toss by which Herman vanquishes his enemy—that are out of harmony with the spirit of heroic literary duels and are unlikely to have been invented by Galbert, and the fight probably took place in much the way Galbert describes it. Guy probably did knock Herman off his horse and keep him down; Herman probably did then kill Guy's horse; they probably did fight with swords, then with fists; and so on. But here, as he did in his description of the ceremony in which the king and count "invest" the citizens of Bruges with a liberty and receive their "homage," Galbert has used an existing mental model—in this case, the narrative model of a duel—to grasp, analyze, and represent an event which, in this case, he has not witnessed and must imagine on the basis of other people's accounts. By inserting it in a narrative tradition, moreover, this model makes his description richer, more vivid, and more detailed than Walter's, and lends it a resonance and familiarity that Walter's lacks.

The account of Bertulf's execution in Ypres offers an even better example of Galbert's use of a literary model to grasp and represent an event he did not witness.[45] He describes the entry of the captive Bertulf into Ypres in this way:

> There was so much tumult and clamor and such a great concourse of people from Ypres and the whole vicinity around that one captive that there is nothing to which we can compare it. It is said that they went before and followed after the provost, leaping, dancing, applauding in various ways, and pulling him with long ropes from the left and right so that the line of pullers could move alternately forwards and sidewise; in this way that man, once so respected and powerful, could be insulted shamefully and ignominiously by everyone. He was pulled along nude except for breeches, the target of mud and stones. Except for the clergy and a few who had formerly known him as a religious man, no one took pity on him. . . . And so that man went along, once glorious but now ignominious, once respected and now disgraced, his face immobile and his eyes turned to Heaven, and, unless I am mistaken, he was invoking the aid of God; not with his voice but in the depths of his soul he

called upon him, the compassionate, with mercy towards that human condition which He had assumed when He reigned over men in the kingdom of the world. Then one of his persecutors, striking his head with a stick, said, "Oh, you proudest of men, why do you scorn to look at us and to speak to the barons and us who have the power of destroying you?" But he did not trouble to look at them, and he was hanged on a gallows in the middle of the market place at Ypres, like a thief or robber. . . . His arms were stretched out like a cross on the gibbet and his hands inserted, and his head thrust through the hole of the gibbet, so that the rest of his body, suspended by his own members, as if by a kind of noose, would expire by suffocation. ([57], 17/27, 55/64, 67/70; trans., 209, 210–11, 211)

The treatment the provost receives at the hands of the citizens of Ypres recalls the taunting and striking of Jesus;[46] his silence recalls Jesus' before Caiaphas, Pilate, and Herod;[47] Galbert's remark that he was put in a gallows "like a thief or robber" *(juxta supplicia furum et latronum)* recalls Jesus' remarks in Gethsemane to those who come to capture him[48] and the two thieves crucified with him; and the statement that Bertulf's arms were "stretched out like a cross" *(in crucem extensa)* on the gallows draws a parallel between the two instruments of execution. Bertulf's silent invocation of God (which necessarily springs from Galbert's imagination) is perhaps intended to echo Jesus' invocation of God while on the cross, and the provost's last words remind us that he, like Jesus, has been betrayed by one of his own men: "Now as he died the provost brought charges of treachery against Walter, a knight of Zarren and his vassal, who had betrayed him to the very death he was now suffering; he had deceived him when he should have lent him guidance" ([57], 87/90; trans., 211). There is also something vaguely reminiscent of Peter in William of Ypres's efforts to deny any complicity in the plot against the count and thus avoid the punishment of the conspirators. The—notably anonymous—figure who steps from the crowd to strike the provost on the head with a stick and ask: "'Oh, you proudest of men, why do you scorn to look at us and to speak to the barons and us who have the power of destroying you?'" is an intriguing bundle of allusions, most directly to one of Pilate's questions to Jesus,[49] but also to the Roman soldiers who strike Jesus on the head with a reed,[50] and his treatment before the High Council where he is struck and asked to tell who struck him.[51]

It is perhaps not surprising that an early twelfth-century Flemish cleric should imagine the public execution on a gallows of a major religious figure in terms of the Crucifixion, but it is also possible that Galbert was influenced here by Walter of Thérouanne's account of the same events, which runs as follows:

When the people of Ypres met him along the road and led him to Ypres, striking him pell-mell with their fists, sticks, stones, and the heads of sea fish—the ones they catch in that region are very big—and afflicting him with every kind of abuse, he bore all these things with unfailing patience, perhaps I should say with hardness, and in silence, and meditated continuously on the psalms almost until his death. Suspended by his neck and arms in a gibbet, slaughtered by the numerous blows of the enraged citizens, he was finally killed in this way. I do not think I should omit that while he prospered, he had a special horror of this kind of abuse and ridicule. For I learned truly from certain of those who were close to him that whenever the conversation among his household happened to turn to the redeeming passion of our Lord Jesus Christ and others praised His patience, he used to say: "I cannot understand why the Lord was willing to suffer such things. If that kind of rabble taunted me like that, believe you me, I'd pay them back quickly for their insults, especially if I were omnipotent, and at the very least I'd spit in the face of anyone who ridiculed me." See how for his greater misery he was forced to tolerate the very things he had judged altogether intolerable. ([38], 554, 35–49)[52]

A reading of the *Vita Karoli* may have suggested the comparison between Bertulf and Jesus to Galbert, but he both extended it—grasping or, more probably, creating more parallels between the two events than their protagonists' silence and patient long-suffering—and made it more subtle, eschewing explicit comparison in favor of a series of allusions.

A comparison of the two descriptions thus shows again the way in which Galbert used a narrative paradigm to understand, imagine, and represent an event he did not witness and how his use of that paradigm enabled him to write a more detailed, more vivid, more dramatic, and thematically richer description than Walter. The parallel Galbert establishes between Bertulf and Jesus is also more complex, and perhaps even more troubling, than Walter's, which seems intended not to create any affinity between Bertulf and Jesus or to inspire pity for Bertulf in the reader, but to emphasize just how spiritually humiliating and degrading Bertulf must have found his execution. Galbert, on the other hand, establishes a more intimate link between Bertulf and Jesus and does manage to inspire a pity for Bertulf and a horror at this execution that are not unakin to the pity and horror inspired by tragedy. Like Milton, Galbert makes us sympathize, in the end, with the great villain of his account.[53]

The vividness of his descriptions—of objects, places, and actions—is thus due to a profound narrative culture, the remarkable orderliness of his mind, and his equally remarkable talent for translating that mental order into Latin prose. He was able to grasp and analyze great masses of both first- and secondhand perceptual information and then to construct plausible, gripping narratives from them. The Flanders we imagine on the basis of his descriptions is not a first-draft world, not Flanders-as-it-was-in-itself, but Galbert's Flanders, Galbert's world. The subjective aspect of these descriptions, moreover, is not the simple and inevitable subjectivity that forms the ground of anyone's account of anything. It is a cultivated subjectivity, an artistic subjectivity, that embraces its world intensely and comprehensively and imagines and represents it according to its own capacities, structures, and interests. Galbert imagines his world so well and so thoroughly, in fact, that there are very few of the discordances that remind us of a writer's subjectivity, of the partiality of his or her vision, and Galbert himself does nothing to draw attention to them or to himself. The transparency of Galbert's accounts is thus not the product of his *not* having reshaped what he perceived, but of his having reshaped it so completely; it is the transparency *not* of immediate perception, but of an ordered mind to itself.

CHAPTER 5

God's Scribe

History itself is not to be numbered among human creations because things that have already occurred can not be undone but are held in the order of time [ordinem temporum], *whose founder and director is God.*
—Augustine, *De Doctrina Christiana*[1]

The themes Galbert weaves through his chronicle and the careful composition of its descriptions betray a desire to do more than merely expand and revise his notes when he set out to transform them into a *Passio Karoli.* They suggest that he wanted to compose a polished, sophisticated piece of historiographical art. This desire is also immediately evident in the fourteen-line-long first sentence of the Prologue he added at this time; in the rhythm of the beginning of its second sentence, which led J.-M. De Smet to suggest that Galbert had borrowed it from a poem on Charles's death;[2] in his rhetorical refusal to embellish his work with the ornaments of rhetoric ([Prol.], 14/16; trans., 80); in his deploration of his arid style ([Prol.], 16/17, 35/36; trans., 80); in his request for the reader's indulgence ([Prol.], 35/38; trans., 80); in his repeated assurances that he is telling the truth ([Prol.], 16, 33; trans., 80); and in his declaration that he has written his execrable little work only in order to pass on to the faithful and posterity a record of the extraordinary events he has witnessed (and thus not out of a desire for personal glory) ([Prol.], 17, 30/31, 34; trans., 80).[3] This desire to write highbrow historiography is likewise apparent in his allusions to, or citations of, or reminiscences of, biblical and classical texts: some of these are found in the passages corresponding to the primitive text—and thus may have been in Galbert's parchment notes[4]—but they are relatively more frequent in the long sections he added to his primitive text when he revised it,[5] suggesting that he consciously sought to introduce more of them into his chronicle at that time.

Another element of Latinate historiography that Galbert incorporated in the *Passio* was a series of discourses, which is one of its most striking and most accomplished features. Influenced by the *Passio*'s journalistic form and the variety and authentic tone of these discourses, scholars have often taken them to be more-or-less stenographic records of discourses that Galbert actually heard, or at least the product of his best efforts at reconstructing discourses he heard or that were reported to him. A careful study of these passages suggests, however, that they are not in fact stenographic or good-faith reproductions of "real" ones, but that Galbert, like almost every other medieval historian, invented or at least heavily rewrote the discourses he reports.[6] If the spoken discourses of the *Passio* differ from those found in the works of other historians and merit particular attention, it is thus not by virtue of their authenticity but, on the contrary, by virtue of their greater artifice. Galbert had a Shakespearean gift for composing such discourses, which he used both to lend his account an unusual liveliness and realism and to influence the reader's understanding of the events he relates, and his skill as a writer is nowhere clearer than in his use of them.

This aspect of the *De multro* has been studied recently by Alan Murray, who suggests three general functions for the forty passages of direct speech he identifies in the chronicle. First, Galbert's "use of direct speech is probably a genuine reflection of the public political processes described by Galbert, many of which, such as oaths, the settlement of disputes and acts of feudal defiance, revolved around the spoken, rather than the written, word."[7] As Murray shows, however, Galbert's use of direct discourse was not simply a reflection of these processes. He often chooses not to reproduce the direct speech involved in certain crucial events, even though it is clear that he could have done so.[8] It is likewise clear that Galbert must have invented, wholly or largely, some of the discourses he records.[9] Murray thus concludes that Galbert uses direct speech selectively and deliberately to heighten "the dramatic qualities of his narrative."[10] He also points to a third, thematic, function for direct discourse in the *De multro*. Charles the Good, remarkably, participates in none of the forty instances of direct discourse identified by Murray, whereas members of the Erembald clan participate in twelve of them. This is at first surprising, but, as Murray observes, the "speeches placed by Galbert into the mouths of the Erembalds give evidence of their overweening pride, their lack of compassion when asked for mercy, the implication of each other in their crimes, and admissions of guilt and remorse. Thus in most of these instances of direct speech the traitors are made to condemn themselves, or each other, out of their own mouths. These episodes serve to distance the people of Bruges from the Erembalds, on whom the blame for the murder is firmly fixed."[11] He suggests, in sum, that Galbert's use of direct speech is deliberately and consciously artistic, that it participates in the dramatic and thematic aspects of the *De multro* and contributes to the impression of "transparency" created by the account. By relaying the public political processes he describes in the medium in which they took place, Galbert simultaneously reinforces their credibility and creates the feeling that we are present at them.

Murray also suggests that, despite appearances, many of these instances of direct discourse are not verbatim records of what was said, but were constructed by Galbert. Given the speakers and their audiences, moreover, only one or two of the forty instances of direct speech noted by Murray could have been spoken in Latin. At the very least, then, Galbert must have translated almost all of these speeches from Flemish or French into Latin. "It is likely," writes Murray, "that Galbert was able to record key points and phrases spoken at public events on his tablets, and later built his speeches around these when he had the facilities to transcribe his notes. I would accept that in these cases Galbert was, like numerous medieval chroniclers, attempting to convey the general sense of what had been said rather than to reproduce exactly the *ipsissima verba* of the speaker or speakers concerned." He goes on to suggest, moreover, "that on occasion Galbert constructed ostensibly verbatim reports of other discourse which he could not possibly have heard."[12] Murray observes, for example, that

> in a passage explaining how in 1071 the county of Flanders was usurped from Arnulf III (son of Count Baldwin VI of Flanders and Richilda of Hainaut), by Baldwin VI's younger brother, Robert I "the Frisian[,]" Galbert relates how fearing such treachery, Baldwin VI had previously required Robert to swear fealty to Arnulf and his brother Baldwin (later count of Hainaut as Baldwin III). It is noteworthy that Galbert does not reproduce the actual words of the oath sworn by Robert, although presumably these would have been formulaic, and therefore memorable; only the preliminaries to the oath, spoken by Bald-

win VI, are represented as direct speech. Considering that these events occurred over fifty-five years before Galbert was writing, it is difficult to believe that this speech can be anything other than a construction on his part.[13]

Murray divides the passages of direct speech into four categories—oaths, readings ("the oral delivery of letters and messages"),[14] monologues, and dialogues—and writes that "the accuracy of the different categories of discourse probably varies considerably. Letters, as opposed to messages which were given and delivered orally, were presumably given a faithful rendition, in that Galbert, as a notary, had access to the comital archives. We should also expect a relatively accurate representation of oaths, in view of their formulaic and public character." It is in the monologues and dialogues, especially the longer ones, Murray suggests, and in a curious sort of corporate speech that "Galbert had greater opportunity, and[,] possibly, necessity for his own elaboration."[15] Let us turn first, then, to these less fixed forms of discourse in order to develop some idea of the degree to which Galbert reworked or constructed them.

A series of speeches attributed to corporate speakers like the paupers or the citizens of Bruges offer the most obvious examples of discourses that Galbert invented or revised.[16] When the paupers of Bruges learned that Bertulf was planning to have the count's body removed to Ghent, for example, Galbert writes that they "kept following the provost around wherever he went, crying out: 'Oh, lord, don't ever let it happen that the body of our father and of such a glorious martyr should be taken away from our place, because, if it does happen, the place and its buildings will be destroyed in the future without mercy. For the enemies and pursuers who come to this castle will have enough pity and mercy not to destroy completely the church in which the body of the blessed count has been reverently buried'" ([22], 14/21; trans., 138; trans. mod.). This humble appeal and plaintive evocation of the martyr's protective presence evokes a common image of the poor as helpless children. It is thus simultaneously plausible, since it comes from precisely those people most exposed to the vicissitudes of social upheaval, and agreeable to everyone in Galbert's potential audience who, unlike these poor, are likely to have had sufficient resources to have some control over their lives. It is comforting and conforms to a cultural stereotype of the poor. It is, however, unlikely that the paupers spoke in Latin, managed to make this appeal in unison, or could speak quite so eloquently of the pity and mercy inspired by the saints. They may well have appealed to the provost somewhat less articulately and more stridently in Flemish but, insofar as this speech is concerned, it seems likely that Galbert made himself their mouthpiece, interpreted their sentiments, and wrote the entire thing for them. The paupers, that is, may well have followed Bertulf around and spoken to him, but the words Galbert attributes to them are almost certainly his.[17]

Another interesting example of corporate speech occurs in the description of the murder of Walter of Loker. As he was being dragged from the church by some of the conspirators, Galbert writes, "captive and sure of death, [he] went along crying, 'Have pity on me, oh Lord!' They answered him, saying: 'We must repay you with the kind of pity you have deserved [*promeruisti*] from us!'" ([17], 48/51; trans., 127). This exchange poses the parties in the instantly recognizable postures of innocent victim and wicked persecutors common to both medieval moral tales and contemporary cinema and thus sounds, again, so authentic—what else would a medieval innocent have cried out as he was being dragged to his death by his enemies?—that one tends to overlook its artifice.[18] It is unlikely, however, that this same phrase occurred spontaneously to all the conspirators busy looting and flushing out their enemies, and that they all managed to say it with one voice. It is also remarkable that another conspirator, Isaac, says something very similar shortly thereafter to the notary Fromold Junior, likewise captured within the church, reinforcing the thematically rich parallels and differences between Walter's and Fromold's capture that were discussed in the last chapter.[19] Perhaps this was one of those moments where life imitates art and Galbert needed only to realize the dramatic qualities of the neatly configured scene fate had handed him and then record it, but it seems much more likely that he revised or even fabricated at least the conspirators' corporate response.

Discourses Galbert attributes to anonymous or otherwise unknown speakers form a second category of recorded speech, and here again it seems likely that Galbert has done more than translate them into Latin.[20] Chapter 22 relates how the efforts of the paupers of Bruges to prevent the removal of Charles's body were seconded by the canons of Saint Donatian. They confronted the provost, and one of the older ones spoke out in front of all the people: "Lord provost, if you had wished to act justly, you would not have given away without the consent and advice of the brothers such a precious martyr, such a great ruler, a great treasure of our church whom divine mercy and dispensation have granted to us as a martyr. There is no reason at all why he should be taken away from us, in whose midst he grew up and spent most of his life, and among whom, by God's ordinance, he was betrayed in the cause of justice; on the contrary, if he is taken away, we may well fear the destruction both of the place and of the church. For by means of his intervention God may spare us and have pity on our place, but if by chance he is taken from us, God may avenge without any mercy at all this treachery which has been committed among us." ([22], 32/43; trans., 138–39)

There were undoubtedly learned and eloquent men among the brothers of Saint Donatian who were capable of making such a speech, but why, one wonders, did Galbert not identify this senior canon? By the time Galbert stopped working on the *De multro,* there would certainly have been no shame, and there might well have been a fair amount of glory, in being recognized as the brother who had stood up to Bertulf on this matter. Perhaps Galbert had not been present when the confrontation had taken place. Perhaps no one could remember what exactly had been said. Perhaps several brothers had spoken and Galbert did not want to drag this scene out or was afraid of omitting someone. In any event, it seems likely that he has here constructed a discourse that he and others would have considered appropriate for the situation—the kind of discourse that *ought* to have been pronounced at this point by one of the senior brothers—and let it stand for the largely forgotten or more spontaneous but less appropriate words that were actually spoken. The speech also has obvious thematic and artistic functions—it emphasizes Bertulf's haughtiness and forms a nice pendant to the corporate discourse of the paupers, whose terms it echoes—and these, too, suggest that it is too good to be verbatim.[21]

Chapter 38 offers an example of an important discourse attributed to a nearly anonymous speaker. Galbert tells us that on March 17, 1127, in response to the castellan Haket's plea for mercy on behalf of the besieged, "a certain knight of the siege named Walter" stepped forward from the crowd of besiegers and asserted that all former bonds between the besiegers and the assassins had been broken "'because you betrayed the prince of this land, who died on behalf of the justice of God and men, in holy Lent, in a holy place, while he was prostrate in holy prayer to God [*in sacro quadragenario, in sacro loco, in sacris orationibus Deo prostratum*]'" ([38], 47/49; trans., 171). This is an important speech since it functions as a public indictment—a public judgment even—of the conspirators. It is thus surprising that an otherwise unknown knight was entrusted with the response to Haket's plea, and that he carried it off so well.

Walter's insistence on the triple sacrilege of the murder—committed in the holy time of Lent, in a holy place, and while the count was in holy prayer—echoes a passage from chapter 26, devoted to the events of March 7, 1127. There, Galbert describes Gervaise of Praet's first efforts to avenge the count in these terms: "And so gathering his wrath, with the whole strength of his following, he vented his rage against those criminals, those wretched serfs who had slain their lord, who had believed he would always be safe among them, the best of all princes, pious and just in the service of God, when he was humbly prostrate in veneration of Him and His saints, in the holy time of Lent, and in a holy place and in holy prayer [*ad venerationem sui et sanctorum suorum prostratum humiliter in sacro tempore quadragesimae, et in sacro loco, et in sacra oratione*]" ([26], 4/10; trans., 147–48; trans. mod.).

This theme is developed yet a third time in chapter 6, part of the fourteen-chapter introduction that Galbert probably composed in the fall of 1127. There he writes: "For in a holy place and in holy prayer, and in holy devoutness of heart, and in the holy time of Lent, and in the holy act of almsgiving, and before the sacred altar and the sacred relics of Saint Donatian, archbishop of Rheims, and Saint Basil the Great, and Saint Maximus [*in sacro loco, igitur, et in sacris orationibus, et in sacra cordis devotione, et in sacro quadragenarii tempore, et in sacra eleemosynarum largitione, et ante sacrum altare, et inter sacras reliquias sanctorum Donatiani archiepiscopi Remorum et beati Basilii magni et sancti Maximi*], the one who raised three dead, those foul dogs, full of the demon, those serfs, murdered their lord!" ([6], 13/19; trans., 94–95).

In two of these three instances, Galbert uses the rhetorical "in the holy . . . in the holy . . . in the holy" himself. In the third, he attributes it to the knight Walter in a passage of direct discourse. So who used it first, Galbert or Walter? The question is further complicated by the presence of a similar phrase in Walter of Thérouanne's *Vita Karoli.* In chapter 26 of that work, Walter adresses Charles's assassins and compares their crime to that of the Jews in crucifying Jesus. The assassins are more evil than the Jews, he writes, because the Jews had never acknowledged Jesus as their lord and had killed him more with their tongues than with their hands; "you, however, did not shy away from killing in a holy place, and a holy time [*in loco sancto et tempore sancto*], and with both your tongues and your hands him whom you had clearly recognized as your lord" ([26], 549, 33/35). It is impossible to know who first used this theme in connection with Charles's death—Galbert, Walter of Thérouanne, the knight Walter, or some unknown person from whom one or more of them borrowed it—and it is possible that it occurred spontaneously to all of them, but given its relative development in its three occurrences in the *Passio,* it seems more than likely that Galbert first inserted it in a revision of an original chapter 26, subsequently put it in the mouth of the knight Walter in a revision of chapter 38, and finally gave it its full development in chapter 6 when he wrote the introductory chapters during the fall of 1127. What is important here, in any case, is that the recurrence of the phrase suggests that Galbert has written, or at least rewritten, the knight Walter's speech for him. Indeed, this knight Walter, who cannot otherwise be identified, may simply have been invented by Galbert to serve as the voice of the besiegers—or one may wish to see in him a playful reference to Walter of Thérouanne from whom Galbert may have borrowed the phrase.[22]

Galbert also puts words in the mouths of prominent, identifiable people. In chapter 8, for example, the provost Bertulf expresses his rage and desperation in the face of the count's efforts to prove the servile origin of his family: "'That Charles of Denmark would never have succeeded to the countship if I had not been willing. But now, although he became count by my efforts, he does not remember how much I did for him but instead seeks to cast me and all my line back into serfdom, trying to find out from the elders whether we are his serfs. But let him try as much as he wants, we shall be free and we are free, and there is no man on earth who can make us into serfs!'" ([8], 7/13; trans., 101). This remarkable snippet of conversation gives the reader a clear sense of Bertulf's character and determination and sounds like a verbatim citation of a remark that made a strong impression on Galbert. Galbert does not, however, claim that Bertulf ever actually pronounced these words. He writes rather that Bertulf "often attacked the count in these terms" ([8], 7; trans., 101). This precise discourse, that is, was invented by Galbert to represent a number of similar tirades that he had perhaps himself heard. The speech is Galbert's, composed in Bertulf's style, in order to characterize the provost.

Alan Murray has suggested, reasonably, that the more formal, "fixed" discourses of the *De multro* like oaths or the reading of letters are more likely to be faithful renderings of the oral discourses they purport to record. The precise wording of these discourses was important since the oaths and, in many cases, the letters had legal effects, and they were likewise more easily verified by means of witnesses or the texts of the letters. As we have seen, however, some of these "fixed" discourses—like the knight Walter's response to Haket, discussed above, or the king's letter to the inhabitants of Flanders discussed in the preceding chapter—contain what one might term "wandering phrases": similar or identical expressions that show up in both a "fixed" discourse like a letter or an oath and in one or more other discourses attributed to different people. The recurrence of these phrases suggests that Galbert was perfectly ready to put words in the mouths of the barons of Flanders or the king of France, and to do so in passages that purport to be verbatim reports of public speeches and royal letters. In addition to constructing speeches for various corporate bodies and anonymous characters, Galbert evidently felt free to rewrite or reimagine to at least some degree any speech, oath, and letter he recorded and to put words not only in the corporate mouth of the anonymous paupers of Bruges, but in the mouths and letters of a whole series of identifiable figures, from the provost of Saint Donatian, to the barons of Flanders and the king of France.

In addition to developing its rhetorical armature and revising or introducing a series of discourses, Galbert increased the *Passio*'s sophistication by portraying the inner world of the human heart and mind as well as the outer world of events. He starts with himself, analyzing the process that led to his beginning work on the chronicle in the Prologue:

And, in fact, I did not have a favorable time or place when I turned my spirit to this work [*cum animum in hoc opere intenderem*], because our place at that time was so disturbed by fear and anxiety that the clergy and people without exception were threatened continually with loss of life and property. It was, therefore, in the midst of many calamaties and in the most constrained circumstances that I began to compose my mind [*mentem . . . compescere*], as unquiet [*fluctuantem*] as if it were tossed about in Euripus, and to subdue it to the discipline of writing. In this distress of spirit [*in qua animi mei exactione*], a little spark of love [*illa caritatis scintillula*], warmed and animated by its own fire, set aflame all the spiritual strength of my heart [*cordis*] and consequently endowed my bodily self, which had been seized by fear [*hominem meum, quem a foris timor possederat*], with the freedom to write. ([Prol.], 18/29; trans., 80, trans. mod.)

Initially, Galbert's *homo* (perhaps here intended to mean his whole self)[23] was possessed *a foris* (from the outside, via his senses) by fear. His *animus* (spirit)—which was, for him, the seat of the emotions and the will[24]—was in a state of *exactio* (distress), his *mens* (mind)—the seat of the intellect[25]—was *fluctuans* (unquiet). At this point a spark of *caritas* (divine love?) strengthened the forces of his *cor* (heart)—roughly synonymous with *animus*[26]—from the inside. This allowed him to control his *animus,* turning it to this work *(animum intendere),* and to compose his mind *(mentem compescere)* and subdue it to the discipline of writing. The human being is thus portrayed as a theater of conflict between external, material influences and internal, spiritual ones, and both the *animus/cor* and the *mens* must be calmed and focused on the intended work before it can begin.[27]

Galbert also imagines and analyzes other people's thoughts, feelings, and motives with a skill that, again, renders his work almost invisible. He describes in some detail, for example, the "languor of mind" *(mentis languore)* that possessed Fromold Junior and the other friends of the count captured in the church once they were imprisoned in the provost's house.[28] He made this up—the captives were alone in a locked room and could not, according to Galbert, express their emotions except in sighs and sobs—yet the passage sounds like speech, like Galbert had overheard and recorded some of the hyperbolic declamations to which sorrow had driven them.

Fromold Junior's affection for the count was apparently particularly strong and well known, and Galbert later devotes a long passage to a description of Fromold's sentiments when he is finally able to mourn at the tomb of his lord and friend.[29] Galbert seems to have known Fromold Junior well and may have observed this scene, or Fromold may even have subsequently described his feelings to Galbert. The passage is nonetheless remarkable for its rendition of them. J. M. De Smet has pointed out that the description of Fromold's longing to see his entombed lord has an Easter-like theme and tone,[30] and that the whole passage has a distinctly poetic quality. He has suggested that it may be based on a lost poem, perhaps one written by Fromold himself.[31] This is entirely possible, but in light of the literary talent that Galbert demonstrates elsewhere in the *Passio,* the poetic aspects of the passage, as well as its insight into the psychology of devotion, may well be due to Galbert himself.

Galbert probably felt some affinity with Fromold and the other friends of Charles captured in the church on March 2, all of whom worked in the count's administration in one way or another. His ability to interpret the feelings of members of this group is thus perhaps not so very remarkable since he himself belonged to it and probably shared them to some extent. Elsewhere in the *Passio,* however, he demonstrates similar insight into the motives and feelings of people with whom he was less identified. Noting at one point, for example, that "so many men with lances were standing in the market that the tops of the spears seemed like a very dense forest!," he explains that "it was not surprising, for everybody in the whole realm had poured into the town that day, some for loot, some for vengeance, some rather to steal the count's body, some out of sheer wonder at everything that was going on there [*tum pro praeda, tum pro vindicta, tum magis pro auferendo consulis funere, tum pro admiratione omnium quae ibidem fiebant*]" ([45], 30/33; trans., 183; trans. mod.).[32] In a series of parallel phrases creating an impression of complex simultaneity, Galbert here shows us his awareness of the range of human motivations and of how a variety of motives may contribute to what appears to be a single collective action.

His ability to empathize and his talent for mimicry are also apparent in what he writes about the conduct of the avenging barons during the siege:

> But the barons did not care what they promised to the besieged or how many oaths they swore but were concerned only with extorting from them the money and treasure of the good count. And they acted rightly in accepting from

the besieged the treasure of the count and also many gifts, since they were under no obligation to keep faith or to honor their oaths toward those serfs who had betrayed their lawful and natural lord. And yet those who had slain their lord, the father of the whole country, tried to get their enemies to respect to their advantage the faith and oaths which they in no way deserved! Certainly it was more just [*justius ergo*] for those who loved the count even in death, and who came to avenge him and there endured alarms and vigils, wounds, attacks, and all the hardships that must be suffered in a siege—more just for them, I say [*justius, inquam*]—to have obtained the castle and treasure and rights of the count after the death of their lord than those wretched traitors who destroyed both the place and its riches. In this vein the besiegers and the besieged often talked back and forth to each other [*hujusmodi ratione saepe colloquebantur sibi obsidentes et obsessi*]. ([29], 42/58; trans., 155–56)[33]

The last sentence makes clear that Galbert is not speaking in his own voice here and not expressing his own convictions, but is rather mimicking (perhaps parodying) the arguments with which the besiegers justified their greed. And yet once he takes on the role, he identifies with it to the degree that he starts to imagine himself one of them ("more just for them, I say"). This passage suggests that Galbert was a natural mime, a natural actor, who easily imagined other people's motives and feelings.[34]

Galbert thus offers us a rich and varied portrait not only of the events and actions that occurred in Flanders in 1127 and 1128, but of the feelings and motives of the actors and spectators as well. The complexity of Galbert's psychological self-representation has been noted,[35] but the well-developed psychological side of his whole work has not received much comment, perhaps because he moves so easily and seamlessly between the outer and the inner worlds, between physical events and states of mind and soul, and because his psychology is so plausible, so sound. Galbert was as gifted at describing the intricacies of the human soul as he was at describing intricate human actions, and, like his descriptions of events he could not have seen, his descriptions of the human soul were the products of his empathetic imagination.

Given Galbert's psychological insight and his powers of empathy and observation, it is not surprising that he excels in the creation of individual portraits. Some of these portraits, like those of the mercenaries Benkin and Weriot, are very brief, no more than a few lines. Others, like the portraits of Dedda and Erembald and the counts Arnold and

Robert, develop over a chapter or two. The portraits of the leading actors in the events of 1127–1128, the assassin Borsiard, the notary Fromold Junior, the castellan Gervaise, Robert the Young, or the provost Bertulf, are built up incrementally over several chapters in a series of well-chosen "close-ups" or vignettes.

What makes these portraits vivid and memorable is Galbert's selection of particular details or traits to characterize and distinguish each person. He notes, for example, Benkin's astonishing energy and the strength behind his arrows, and the fact that Weriot can throw stones to great effect using only his left hand ([36], 8/19; trans., 165–66). He emphasizes the lust, greed, and ambition that drove Dedda and Erembald to murder the castellan Boldran, her husband and his lord, by writing that they committed adultery "frequently" *(saepe),* that Boldran was "constantly" *(semper)* on the lookout for a chance to kill Boldran, by referring to them consistently as "the adulteress" *(illa adultera)* and "the adulterer" *(ille adulter),* and by the rhythm and rapidity of his summation of the consequences of the murder: "When Erembald returned, he married the adulteress, and bought the office of castellan with the plentiful resources of his lord. By this wife he begot the provost, Bertulf, Haket, Wulfric Cnop, Lambert Nappin, the father of Borsiard, and also Robert, castellan after him in the second place" ([71], 21/25; trans., 239; trans. mod.). Fromold Junior, as we have seen, is distinguished by his attachment to Count Charles. Borsiard is "furious" *(furibundus),* "filled with fury" *(furens),* "furious and ferocious in countenance" *(valde furibundus et ferocissimus vultus),* "huge and wrathful, ferocious and undaunted" *(immanis et iracundus, ferox et imperterritus).*[36] Robert the Young is an ingenu.[37]

The political skills of the new castellan, Gervaise, are demonstrated when the citizens of Bruges attack his house to rescue one of their number who had been arrested by one of his knights, and "cried out that they did not ever intend to suffer the lordship of anyone at all" *(conclamaverunt enim se nunquam velle pati dominium cujusquam)* ([59], 36/37; trans., 215).[38] Coming out into their midst, Gervaise pacified them with the following speech:

"You know, citizens and my friends, that in accordance with your request, the king and count recently installed me as viscount of your place, and it was according to the order of the king and barons that my knight just now seized the citizen, your neighbor, as a violator of the order; by this act you have personally shown contempt for my office, you have attacked the count's house and my household who are in it, and finally, without reason you have risen up in an armed band in the presence of the king. Therefore, if you wish, I will give up the viscountship, because of the injury done to me; I will dissolve the faith and loyalty affirmed between us, so that it may be clear to all of you that I do not seek to obtain lordship [*dominium*] over you. If it pleases you, let us put aside arms and come together in the king's presence so that he may judge between you and us." ([59], 40/51; trans., 216; trans. mod.)

The repetition of "lordship" *(dominium)*—a repetition which may of course be due to Galbert rather than Gervaise—is an effective rhetorical device and creates a strong impression of Gervaise's political gifts.[39]

The most striking of Galbert's portraits, however, is that of the provost Bertulf. He is first presented in chapters 7 through 13 as the head of his powerful family and the chief strategist in their efforts to disguise their servile origin and resist the count's attempt to reduce them again to servile status, and his rage, determination, and desperation are communicated vividly in the passage of direct discourse cited above ([8], 5/13; trans., 101). The rest of the portrait is scattered throughout the first fifty-eight chapters. Some of its elements are quite small, such as Galbert's observation that "it was his habit when someone whom he knew perfectly well came into his presence, to dissemble, in his pride, and to ask disdainfully of those sitting near him, who that could be, and then only, if it pleased him, would he greet the newcomer" ([13], 7/10; trans., 115; trans. mod.); the provost's remark to the captive Fromold Junior that "'You must know by now, Fromold, that you are not going to get possession of my provostship by next Easter, as you were hoping to do. I have not deserved your undermining me in this way'" ([19], 21/24; trans., 131);[40] or the glimpse Galbert gives us of Bertulf, late in the day of the murder, "walking up and down in his house with his canons, absolving himself as well as he could in words, on the grounds that he had known nothing about the treachery in advance" ([20], 4/6; trans., 132). Other elements are more considerable, such as Galbert's description of the aid Bertulf gave his nephew Borsiard when the latter attacked the stronghold of a family enemy ([9], 1/24; trans., 103–4), his description of the appeal to the provost to save the life of Fromold Junior and the provost's reaction to it ([19], 1/24;

trans., 130–31), of his efforts to have the count's body removed ([22], 1/73; trans., 137–40), and to secure allies and support for his family ([25], 1/71; trans., 143–47), of his escape from the castle and wanderings through Flanders ([46], 1/17; trans., 185–86), and of the omens he received of his death ([84] 42/57; trans., 256). The portrait culminates in the altogether remarkable account of the provost's execution in Ypres that was discussed in the preceding chapter, an account that demonstrates, and evokes, considerable sympathy for Bertulf without ever losing sight of his guilt or the justice of his punishment.[41]

Citing Beryl Smalley, who observes that "many [medieval historians] show an acute awareness of self-interest covered up by hypocrisy, which they revel in exposing,"[42] Nancy Partner notes that a skeptical sensitivity to motivation was characteristic of twelfth-century historians,[43] and here, too, Galbert is both typical and exemplary.[44] He was especially sensitive to the cupidity that he seems to have felt motivated most, if not all, of the people around him, and clearly believed, for example, that greed, rather than a desire for justice, motivated the barons and knights who gathered in Bruges to besiege the assassins. This is apparent in his record of the oaths they had to swear to the citizens of Bruges before they were permitted into the city,[45] in his account of their casuistical justifications for accepting money from the besieged, and in his accounts of the sacking of the castle and the church.[46]

Galbert also unmasks and mocks the pecuniary self-interest of the men who rush through the newly breached wall of Saint Donatian:

> But when the drivers of the ram, and other knights of the king, and the young men of our place, armed and avid for conflict, finally saw the besieged opposite them, they summoned all their courage, picturing in their mind's eye how noble it would be to die for father and fatherland [compare Horace, *C.* 3, 2], and how honorable a victory was set before the conquerors, and how infamous and criminal those traitors had been who had made a den for themselves out of the church of Christ, and, as seems more likely, how avidly and greedily they would rush against the besieged in order to seize the treasure and money of the lord count, and for this reason alone they were hastening forward [*quam egregie pro patre et patria moriendum foret et quam honesta victoria vincentibus praeposita esset, quamque scelesti et facinorosi fuissent traditores illi qui de templo Christi speluncam sibi fecissent, et, quod magis videbatur, quam avide et cupide propter thesauri et pecuniae domini consulis rapinam irruerent super obsessos ipsi et idcirco solummodo festinabant*]. ([63], 42/52; trans., 223–24; trans. mod.)[47]

Galbert in fact makes fun of the reader or listener here as well as of the besiegers who masked their greed with patriotism. There is nothing at the beginning of this passage to suggest that his description of their motives is ironic or facetious and, as the allusion to Horace emphasizes, this is the kind of discourse about heroic and patriotic motives that both literary and historical works have taught us to expect in the description of such actions. When Galbert suddenly shifts his tone ("and, as seems more likely . . ."), he exposes simultaneously a human tendency to disguise greed as something else, the discursive tradition that makes such disguises possible, and the reader's complicity in that tradition.[48]

Galbert's interest in the inner world of human beings also went hand in hand with a taste for the dramatic, even the melodramatic, that he shared with many contemporary historians.[49] He achieves his dramatic effects both structurally, through rhetorical means, and thematically, through the pathos of the events he relates.

A good example of the way Galbert produces a dramatic effect through the structure of the *De multro* is to be found at the end of the first fourteen introductory chapters. In the manuscripts, modern editorial chapter 1 through line 21 of chapter 12 form a single long chapter providing the background of the murder. It ends with the burning of Borsiard's house (chapter 10), the planning and swearing of the assassination (chapter 11), and a description of the movements of the assassins and the count in the early hours of March 2 ([12], 1/21) that culminates in an assassins'-eye view of the prostrate count praying in the gallery chapel. This description is remarkable for its dramatic qualities—the initial description of a dark, foggy morning, the two steps back in time (first to the count's rising and then to the night before and his evident foreboding), the description of the action (which Galbert could not have witnessed and must have invented, at least in part) mostly from the assassins' point of view, a strategy that, curiously, identifies the readers with the assassins and encourages them to share some of the assassins' feelings of tension and excitement[50]—but what comes next is an even more obviously deliberate effort to create a dramatic effect. For having brought the assassins, and his readers, to the upper chapel and the prostrate count, Galbert breaks off his narrative to relate, in another long manuscript chapter (modern chapters [12],

22–[14], 25; trans., 112–18), more about Charles's past and qualities, the speed with which the news of his death spread, and Bertulf's qualities and history. The next manuscript chapter (modern editorial chapters 15 through 21) starts up where chapter 12, line 21 left off: "In the year one thousand one hundred and twenty seven, on the sixth day before the Nones of March, on the second day, that is, after the beginning of the same month, when two days of the second week of Lent had elapsed, before daylight on Wednesday, on the fifth Concurrent, and the sixth Epact, about dawn, the count at Bruges was kneeling in prayer in order to hear the early Mass in the church of Saint Donatian, the former archbishop of Rheims. Following his pious custom, he was giving out alms to the poor, with his eyes fixed on reading the psalms, and his right hand outstretched to bestow alms" ([15], 1/10; trans., 118, trans. mod.). A suspension of the narrative at its moment of greatest tension, often just before a murder, is an obvious device still beloved of modern televison melodramas and advertisers. One may question Galbert's taste here, but it is clear that he had a sense of the dramatic and was seeking to manipulate his readers' emotions.

The shift in narrative focus between the end of chapter 62 and the beginning of chapter 63 offers another good example of a dramatic effect produced through structural means. Modern chapters 62 through 64 form a single chapter in the manuscripts. The first part of this chapter (modern chapter 62) describes the placement of a battering ram next to an upper wall of the church and the beginning of the work of breaching the wall. The point of view of the narration is that of the besiegers on the outside of the church. In the next part of the original chapter (the beginning of modern chapter 63: the transition is signaled by the word *interim* ["meanwhile"] and both Henschen and Van Papenbroeck and Köpke introduce chapter breaks at this point), the narrative point of view shifts to that of the besieged inside the church and relates their desperate attempts to disrupt the ramming. The point of view then shifts back to the besiegers ([63], 12; trans., 222, "but neither the number nor the size . . .") and continues to shift between various points inside and outside the church, pausing briefly for a close-up of Fromold Junior's mourning of his great friend, throughout the rest of the manuscript chapter. The drama of this chapter is thus created as much by this shifting narrative focus, which leaps like a cinematographer's camera from outside to inside, from besiegers to besieged, as it is inherent in the events themselves.

Galbert is also sensitive to the pathos of many of the events he describes, and able to communicate his sense of it to the reader. I have already mentioned one of the most dramatic passages in the *Passio*—the execution of Bertulf in Ypres—and a couple of distinctly pathetic ones—those relating the grief of Charles's friends and, especially, of Fromold Junior, and the castellan of Bourbourg's dying efforts to communicate his last wishes to his sons, unaware that they have already been killed. I wish to draw attention here to two further examples of Galbert's ability to grasp and render the pathos of the events he recounts: his description of the capture and murder of Walter of Loker and his exploitation of the potential for tragedy inherent in the Christian concept of history common at the time.

Walter of Loker's death evoked a sort of fascinated horror in Galbert, and he in turn makes us sense something of Walter's fear and misery through a careful selection of evocative details ([17], 20/54; trans., 125–27). He notes that Walter hid himself in an enclosed, presumably small space near the bodies of the dead count and the dying castellan (whose confession, last wishes, and groans he could perhaps hear) and that he remained in that space from dawn to noon. One can imagine his mental and emotional exhaustion after hours of listening intently to everything that was going on around him and trying to decide if it was safe to come out. Galbert also emphasizes the noise Borsiard and his men made in searching for Walter—the banging of their arms, their calling him by name and pushing around furniture—precisely because this was the aspect of their searching most perceptible to the hidden Walter. By describing the search in aural terms, Galbert solicits the reader's identification with Walter and sympathy for him.

Galbert's explanation of the assassins' hatred for Walter and his emphasis on their fury and savagery also help the reader imagine this scene from Walter's point of view. He knew the depth of their anger, knew that no negotiation was possible, knew that discovery meant death. When in his hiding place he thought of Borsiard, he undoubtedly imagined the furious, ravening, bloody-sworded figure portrayed by Galbert.

Walter's dramatic and ill-advised attempt to escape thus becomes comprehensible to us. Exhausted after hours spent listening acutely and fearfully to everything going on around him, and imagining the bodies of the count and castellan lying near him and Borsiard's implacable rage, he heard the searchers drawing nearer, calling him by name, coming upon the body of the castellan—only a few yards away—and dragging him outside to be dismembered. In this state of exhausted terror—what Galbert calls his "deathly distress" (my translation of *angustia mortis)*—all that was left to him was an appeal to supernatural forces: he thus made a desperate rush for the main altar while calling on God and the saints. The rest of the description—the brief chase, the berserk Borsiard, the momentary respite, the plea for help and mercy, the callous reply, the ignominous and painful death—are likewise well chosen to evoke horror and pity, to evoke in the readers an awareness of the reality of this event and the suffering it entailed.

It is once again worth citing Walter of Thérouanne's description of this murder in order to throw the qualities of Galbert's description into greater relief: "They were still unable to find Walter, however, despite much searching and were beginning to despair of ever finding him, when some boy is said to have betrayed him and shown the searchers the refuge that had been hiding him so opportunely in such great need. Sensing himself betrayed, he immediately fled with great speed and ran in fear to the altar of Saint Donatian and wrapped himself as best he could in the cloth that was spread out on the altar. The devil's minions pursued him there, seized him, and, having callously denied him his only request, that he be given the chance to confess, they dragged him from the church and killed him" *(Vita Karoli,* [28], 550, 38/44). Perhaps the greatest difference between the two descriptions, curiously, is Walter's diabolization of Borsiard and his men. Galbert's explanation of the reasons for their particular hatred for Walter of Loker, even if it does not excuse their actions, does provide some justification for them: What pity and understanding had Walter shown them when he had persuaded the count to reduce them to servile status? Galbert is more sensitive to the moral complexity of the situation, able to understand it from the point of view of the murderer as well as that of the victim—or, in the case of Bertulf's execution, from that of the justly condemned man as well as that of his judges and executioners—and to evoke in his readers a similarly complex and multifocused comprehension of the events he describes.

One of the basic tenets of the medieval Christian theology of history was that God is the sole author of history in all its complexity and multiplicity. He has planned everything, foreseen everything, arranged everything.[51] Everything he has recorded, Galbert writes in the Prologue, "came to pass by the ordinance of God" *(sunt . . . Dei ordinatione congesta)* ([Prol.], 38; trans., 80), and he reminds us of God's continuous and omnipresent control throughout the *Passio.*[52] Since human beings possess free will, however, all human actions are doubly motivated, willed simultaneously by God and by their actors. Galbert is explicit on this point in chapter 11 where he observes that the traitors acted "by the necessity of divine ordination, through free will" *(ex necessitate divinae ordinationis per liberam voluntatem)* ([11], 3/4; trans., 108).[53] Since God is the omnipotent and single author of history, however, humans must always *do* what he wills, regardless of their intentions. Or, perhaps better, the omniscient and omnipotent God has always already woven the designs and deeds of all his creatures, good and evil, into history in such a way that they contribute to the achievement of his ineluctable ends. One may *intend* to do evil, but can only *do* good, or, as Galbert puts it, citing a chestnut from Saint Paul: "All things work together for good" ([6], 12; trans., 94).[54]

This double motivation of human actions—willed by both God and their actors—endows them with a metaphorical and pathetic dimension. When an individual's intentions are congruous with the divine will, they may be said to stand in an "allegorical" relation to it and to be "comic." When Gervaise, for example, first took up arms against the Erembalds and attacked Raverschoot, it was not he who acted, but God through him: "On March 7, Monday, God unsheathed the swords of divine punishment against the enemies of His Church, and he moved the heart of a certain knight Gervaise to undertake vengeance" ([26], 1/3; trans., 147).[55] When the people of Bruges heard of this attack, they immediately attributed it, according to Galbert anyway, not to Gervaise, but to God: "hearing that God had begun the vengeance so quickly, [they] rejoiced [*gaudebant*]. . . . In their hearts they gave thanks to God who with merciful eyes had deigned to look again upon His faithful in this place of horror and confusion, and was hastening to exterminate the wicked murderers" ([27], 7/8, 11/13; trans., 150). They quickly sent messengers to Gervaise offering their help, and he and his men in turn "joyfully [*laetiore*] . . . received the words of the messengers, and rightly so, knowing that whatever they did in carrying out the vengeance had been ordained by God [*dispensatum a Deo fuisse quidquid in vindicando agerent*]" ([27], 22/23; trans., 150).

When an individual's intentions are discongruous with the divine will, however—when, that is, human beings delude themselves into thinking that they can realize their intentions independently of the will of God—they stand in an "ironical" relation to it and are thus "tragic."[56] Galbert offers a striking example of this kind of tragic irony in chapter 89. Here, he tells how Bertulf had married one of his grand-nieces to Walter of Vladslo's supposed son, "so that they [Bertulf and Walter] would stand together firmly under all circumstances by reason of that marriage, and would become bolder, stronger, and more powerful" ([89], 19/21; trans., 262). After Walter's death, however, his wife confessed that their true son had died at birth and the supposed son was actually the child of a cobbler and his wife, whom she had paid to exchange the dead infant for the living one.[57] "And so God's strategem [*arte Dei*]," concludes Galbert, "foiled the strategem of the provost [*ars praepositi*], who, when he wanted to exalt his family proudly and arrogantly by that marriage, joined it to the son of a cobbler, deceived by the strategem of God!" ([89], 25/27; 262–63).[58]

The outstanding example of this kind of irony, of course, is the Erembalds' decision to murder Charles in order to save themselves. The effect of their decision was exactly the opposite of what they intended and Galbert notes that through them, and despite their intentions, "the dispensation of God was accomplished" ([75], 5; trans., 243). In his omniscience and omnipotence, that is, God incorporated even their evil designs into his providential plan, and they were ultimately as much the agents of his will as Gervaise and Charles's other avengers. Caught between the millstones of an omnipotent dispensation, the Erembalds, as Dhondt observed, become tragic figures who cannot escape death despite frantic efforts[59]—and Galbert exploits the emotional potential of this structure.[60] As Alan Murray has pointed out, moreover, the "speeches placed by Galbert into the mouths of the Erembalds" enhance this tragic effect insofar as they "give evidence of their overweening pride, their lack of compassion when asked for mercy, the implication of each other in their crimes, and admissions of guilt and remorse. Thus in most of these instances of direct speech the traitors are made to condemn themselves, or each other, out of their own mouths."[61] The traitors' designs cannot inflect the divinely ordained course of history, and their very inefficacy makes them tragic, endowing their story with a pathos which, insofar as it evokes a degree of pity for the sinful traitors, actually works against the moral lesson it is ostensibly intended to teach.

Pizarro identified a medieval historiographical style going back to the sixth through the eighth centuries that was characterized by its "dramatic illusionism": by the visualization of scenes in concrete space and time, the systematic use of direct, seemingly spontaneous speech linked to "dramatic elements such as gesture . . . posture . . . [and] the presence of significant objects," and a "total absence of authorial moralizing," a "subordination of narrative to information and intelligibility" that leads to the effacement of the author and creates "the illusion that we are witnessing the events he describes."[62] Pizarro further suggests that because this style was "such a deep structure, it [was] not susceptible of pronounced evolution,"[63] and it is recognizably the same style—based on "an ethical commitment to mimetic accuracy . . . [and seeking] to convey . . . as direct and vivid an impression of the past and present reality as possible"—identified by Spiegel and attributed by her to "much medieval historical writing,"[64] and by Partner to Richard of Devizes, whose late twelfth-century history, she writes, "moves in dramatic scenes, with concrete but exaggerated detail, short bursts of pointed dialogue. . . . Speech is central to all events."[65] It is also Galbert's style, one that he manipulates with great mastery and that achieves some of its most accomplished expressions and fullest effects in the *Passio.*

Pizarro suggests that oral-traditional narrative may have been "the primary model of the new style," but that its fully developed form was the result of the "merging" of oral-traditional style with "classical models . . . in the hands of gifted writers."[66] This is particularly interesting insofar as Galbert's adult education, I have suggested, was probably primarily oral, as were his sources for what he did not himself witness. Galbert may have been educated, may have been literate, and may have written something almost every day of his adult life, but his culture was nonetheless fundamentally oral, and writing, for him, both in the course of his administrative work and in the composition of the

Passio, was probably only the ultimate precipitate of extended conversation. It is thus no wonder that he should feel so at home in a style based ultimately on oral-traditional narrative and should produce one of its chef-d'oeuvres. If readers of the *Passio* sometimes have the impression of being present at the events Galbert describes, of hearing words he heard spoken, of knowing the people he mentions, it is not because he was artless and candid, a sort of human recording device, but because he imagined everything he relates so clearly and so fully and communicated his imaginings so well in a historiographical tradition that encouraged "dramatic illusionism." He was a gifted author whose material accuracy, psychological insight, sense of the dramatic, and realization of the potential of a certain historiographical style make the *Passio* a conspicuous artistic achievement.

Everything we have seen in this and the two preceding chapters suggests that Galbert set out in the late summer or early fall of 1127 to write a sophisticated passio, whose purpose, although he would undoubtedly not have expressed it in this way, was to ground a set of earthshaking events in the very worldview they threatened to upset, to make what was strange familiar, to make what was threatening comforting. Like Walter of Thérouanne, he wanted to create "a sense that the political order was not in fact overturned by the death of the count and the resultant blow to the dignity of the comital office, but rather that it was momentarily assimilated with the Kingdom of God in a most rare and glorious manner."[67] Walter met this challenge by portraying Charles as a martyr and casting his account of the assassination in the generically reassuring form of a saint's life. Galbert likewise assimilated Charles to a martyr and demonstrated the reassuring providential economy of the events of spring 1127, but he did so within the generically bizarre form of journal, a form that would at first seem to work against both his desire to reassure his audience, to make the strange familiar, and his desire to write a sophisticated literary work.

This choice of form was not accidental or dictated by the circumstances in which the notes on which the work was based were taken. If, as I believe I have shown in the last chapters, he revised his parchment notes extensively during the summer and fall of 1127, he had the opportunity to rewrite them as a continuous, coherent narrative if he had wished to do so. He chose instead to retain their journalistic form and tells us as much in chapter 14, at the end of the introductory chapters he added in the course of this revision: "In this account of his passion, the reader will find the subject divided by days and the events of those days [*distinctiones dierum et gestorum quae in ipsis facta sunt diebus*], up to the vengeance, related at the end of this little work" ([14], 19/22; trans., 117). The degree to which Galbert carried out this intention to impose a journalistic order on his chronicle is evident in the surviving manuscripts, but has been obscured by the chapter divisions imposed on the text by its modern editors.[68] In the manuscripts, the brief prologue is followed by a single long chapter made up of the modern editorial chapters [1], 1/[12], 21. This is followed by a second introductory manuscript chapter consisting of modern chapters [12], 22/[14], 25, at the end of which Galbert announces the journalistic organization of the rest of the chronicle. The next manuscript chapter is the very long one (modern chapters 15–21) devoted to the events of March 2, 1127, and the remaining manuscript chapters, up to the end of the work, are—with rare exceptions[69]—devoted to a single day (modern chapter 22 to March 3; modern chapter 23 to March 4; modern chapter 24 to March 5; and so on). The journalistic organization of the *Passio* is thus due to a conscious decision on Galbert's part, one that he respected conscientiously throughout his work, and a substantial effort of organization and composition.

This was a highly original decision. Isidore of Seville, to be sure, mentions the actions of a single day *(unius diei gestio)* as one of the three categories under which events may be organized, thus suggesting the possibility of journalistic history, but this was a logical distinction that was not based on the historiographical practices of the time and seems to have had little influence on subsequent practice.[70] The only other journal known to have been written in the southern Low Countries before the end of the fourteenth century is the lost *journal intime* that Beatrice of Nazareth evidently kept between c. 1215 and 1236, but this was, according to the editor of her *Vita,* a record of her inner life, containing "little . . . about events in her community or in society."[71] The journalistic form of the *De multro* had no precedent in medieval Flemish historiography, and is indeed unique in Europe even in a century known for its historiographical experimentation.[72] How can we explain Galbert's decision?

One reason for maintaining the journalistic form of his notes when he rewrote them, of course, was that it was the easiest thing for him to do. Reconfiguring all the information he had gathered into a single narrative account would have been an immense undertaking.

He may also have been influenced by the Christian theology of history current at the time, which taught that, because God is indeed the sole author of history, events always already have an inherent *ordinem,* an inherent temporal structure. "History itself [*ipsa historia*]," writes Augustine,

> is not to be numbered among human creations because things that have already occurred can not be undone but are held in the order of time [*ordinem temporum*], whose founder and director is God. . . .
>
> The truth of logical rules was not, however, created by men—for it is inherent in the nature of things and was divinely created—but men have observed it and noted it down so that they might either learn it or teach it, just as someone who relates the order of time [*ordinem temporum*] does not himself compose it.[73]

Time, that is, is a structure and is significant in and of itself, qua time.[74] Galbert's accute sensitivity to the passage of time throughout his chronicle, his chronological awareness and precision, suggest that time was indeed significant in and of itself for him, too, that he thought an event's meaning and significance were based on its place in the structure of time, that this structure gave it a meaning it would not have in an unstructured flux, and that to ignore or overlook its place in time was to ignore or overlook its full significance.[75]

Within this concept of history, the human historiographer's role was first and foremost scribal: to create a faithful, accurate written representation of the temporally structured series of events, the order of time, ordained by God "so that," as John of Salisbury wrote, "the invisible things of God may be clearly seen by the things that are done [*ut per ea que facta sunt conspiciantur inuisibilia Dei*], and men may by examples of reward or punishment be made more zealous in the fear of God and pursuit of justice. . . . nothing, after knowledge of the grace and law of God, teaches the living more surely and soundly than knowledge of the deeds of the departed."[76] It is for this reason that "history," in Augustine's words, "relates past events faithfully [*fideliter*] and usefully," and, according to Hugh of Saint Victor, "follows the order of time [*ordinem temporis*]."[77] Indeed, the more narrative or thematic a chronicle becomes, the more it distorts and obscures the divinely instituted temporal *ordo* of history insofar as it seeks to encompass an ordo fashioned by an omniscent mind within a different ordo imagined by a limited human one. This is evident in the work of Ordericus Vitalis, whose method is characterized by a "departure from strict chronology to look backwards or forwards in time, grouping together a number of related episodes,"[78] and in Suger's *Deeds of Louis the Fat* whose "anagogic" or "architectural" structure precludes "a commitment to chronological progression through the reign" and produces a "confused chronology."[79] Having similarly chosen to follow an "artificial order" *(ordine artificiali)* rather than a "natural [that is, chronological] order" *(naturali . . . ordine)* in relating the events of Charles's life, Walter of Thérouanne is forced to "beg the reader not to displace any of [the events he relates] in any way, but, looking ahead some times and reviewing what has been said at others, to move an earlier one, when it is introduced subsequently in the artificial order of the narrative, forward in his mind to a suitable place, and to attach a later one, although it may come earlier in the narrative, where it belongs until reason will have finally determined the place of each event, and the time at which each thing occurred will appear clearly enough" ([Prol.], 538, 20/23). And he later observes that, because he has chosen a thematic rather than a strictly chronological order, "everything that occurred at one time could not be told at the same time" ([43], 556, 50/557, 1).[80] For a historian who believed profoundly in the providential structure of history, then, the journal would logically be the best form of historical record because it offers the most faithful representation of the temporal structure in which God has embedded events.

This belief in the providential structure of history also entails a belief in the divinely instituted interconnectedness of all events: they are all part of a single plot, a single story.[81] The journal would thus also be the best form of historical record insofar as it permits the historian to include in it everything that he witnesses or learns, even those events whose connections to other events are obscure to limited human minds.[82] This ability to encompass everything he had noted down undoubtedly made the journal form desirable to Galbert for other reasons as well. It enabled him to preserve everything he had written, a natural desire familiar to anyone who has eliminated cherished and belabored passages from a work-in-progress. It also corresponded to the fundamental factual conservatism that seems to have been shared by many medieval historians, and was born of a sense of the paucity of their knowledge, a deep-seated fear of forgetting, and a horror of empty time that led someone like Geoffrey of Monmouth to invent a past rather than have none.[83]

Galbert, as we have seen, also had a taste for the dramatic, even the melodramatic, that he shared with many contemporary historians.[84] He may thus also have decided to maintain the journal form of his parchment notes because he recognized its dramatic nature, the sense that it gives the reader, the sense it has given modern historians, of experiencing the events as they happened, of advancing into an unforeseen and unforeseeable future, of being there, in Bruges, in 1127.

Galbert's decision to maintain the journal form when he rewrote his notes was perhaps also motivated by other aesthetic propensities of his age. "In general," writes Karl Morrison, twelfth-century "texts have no unified narrative structure. . . . [W]orks were composed as anecdotes, short narratives, or clusters of narratives. There was a designed incompleteness in the structure of works as albums made of fascicles, or nuclei which enable viewers or readers to break components of a work apart and reassemble (or 'reconceptualize') them, perhaps with other materials, in a quite different order." These works "provided readers with an array of narrative options instead of . . . a single, clear narrative line moving toward closure. . . . The cognitive structure in our texts was never intended to take shape around a single thread of narrative, *narratio* being one of the briefest members of a discourse. Instead, the thread of narrative was considered to be woven into a basket, a web, or a garland, which contained historical materials contemplated, at option, from multiple points of view inside the structure."[85] The journal was the ideal genre for this sort of composition and we in fact have a brilliant example of the way in which components of the *Passio* were broken apart and reassembled by one of its late-medieval readers: in the late fifteenth century, Roland or Antoine de Baenst, members of a noble family prominent in both Bruges and Ghent, abstracted the bits and pieces of information on the Erembalds scattered throughout the *Passio* and reassembled them in a chronological résumé of the family's rise and fall which he copied into a family record book.[86]

One could indeed suggest that the *Passio*'s "central" narrative of the good prince and the wicked servi is really a bundle of three smaller narratives: a "comedy" of the good prince's life and martyrdom; a "romance" of Flanders (which itself incorporates the "romances" of Bruges, and even of Saint Donatian!)[87] which loses its good prince and, thus orphaned, falls on hard times, but ultimately, purged of its wicked parricides, experiences a resurrection of political order with the advent of his successor (or so it seemed in autumn 1127); and a "tragedy" of the Erembalds, a pathetic account of human beings seeking ignorantly and impotently to reweave the fabric of an enigmatic destiny.[88] The *Passio* is in fact as much a kaleidoscope of latent narratives of various dimensions and complexity[89] as it is a tumble of events and a work of moral reassurance, and its modern success is due more to its multifocal narrative richness, its provision of the materials for a remarkable number of narratives, than to the mere information it contains concerning the events of 1127—if it may be said to contain any *mere* information at all. The *Passio* achieves its ideological work of moral and political reassurance by providing a simple, latent "central" fable with an equally simple moral that condense and to some degree mask a more complicated and troubling reality, but it leaves this fable inchoate and embedded in a rich texture of events that contains other stories and morals as well.

The journal form thus respected the divinely ordained rythm and order of time—an entry per day, day after day—while simultaneously making allowances for the limits of human experience and understanding insofar as each entry could be expanded indefinitely. It thus opened up a potentially infinite space in which new information could be added as learned, in which new insights and connections could be recorded. The shallow human understanding of time—that comes slowly, at the price of much thought and many words spread thinly on the surface of the page, to a partial grasp of all that God has achieved from the depths of hell to the heights of heaven in an instant—finds in the journal its own axis, its own dimension, that can be expanded until some comprehension is attained without obscuring the true Axis and divine Dimension of time. The journal is, moreover, by nature a "scenic" form of composition, whose every scene has a natural beginning, middle, and end, and yet allows narrative threads to develop over time, weaving in and out of one another. It was in fact a form that corresponded to both the theology of history and the literary tastes, to both the ideas and the penchants, of the time.

Galbert's radical break with historiographical tradition is thus neither inexplicable nor, probably, the result of an act of creative genius. He probably did not, that is, set out from the very first to make historiographical history. The break was more probably the product of two different stages or moments. In the first, his situation, his habit of keeping fiscal journals, and a spur-of-the-moment and perhaps reflexive decision on the first or second day he took notes to head that day's entries with the date led to the creation of a substantial body of journalistically organized notes. When he set out to rewrite these notes, he probably maintained this organization out of a combination of sloth and intellectual and aesthetic considerations. Seen in this light, his decision to maintain the journalistic form of his parchment notes when he rewrote and expanded them appears reasonable and even likely, but it should not be taken for granted. Even if they had had the opportunity to write a journalistic history, there is no guarantee that other historians would have chosen to do so. At some level Galbert's decision must have been due both to a strong sense of the form's aesthetic and dramatic promise and to the ferocity of his belief in the divinely instituted ordo of history, coupled perhaps with a weak sense of the Latinate historiographical tradition.

Galbert thus produced a curious hybrid that does the ideological work of a vita or a passio and achieves a morally satisfying closure, and yet does not have a continuous narrative structure and includes a great deal of material extraneous to its "central" narrative. He managed to do this by providing and to some degree working up the materials one needs to construct a *Passio Karoli* while leaving them embedded among the materials for many other stories in the manifold temporal structure in which they occurred. His revisions, that is, manage to endow the journal with a latent "central" narrative that discovers and explains the troubling events it relates without obscuring the divinely ordained structure of time. The presence of this latent narrative gives the *Passio* a coherence, a continuity, and a revelatory and didactic dimension that a true journal or a simple *descriptio secundum rerum eventum* would have lacked, while the maintenance of a journalistic form permitted Galbert to continue to include in his chronicle other stories and other kinds of information that he would have had to exclude from a continuous narrative focused solely on a story of crime and punishment. The *Passio* is a cross between a journal and a narrative history and offers the reader both the eclectic information and the sense of immediacy of the one and the coherence and rhetorical dimension of the other.

Through its emphasis on a latent "central" narrative and its simple moral, embedded inchoately in the materials for less exalted narratives that rooted the whole in the rough texture of common experience, the *Passio,* albeit perhaps only vaguely or unconsciously, would have reassured and comforted its audience, in part through the very familiarity of its narrative models and political ideas, showing that all was still right with the world, that the events it relates fell within their received worldview. It reaffirms common ideas, renders the alien comfortable and familiar, and is, therefore, intellectually commonplace. Galbert was not writing a theoretical or learned treatise, not even popularizing learned ideas. He was repeating, asserting, confirming what everyone knew, and showing how it could be applied to the events of 1127. His ideas were perhaps borrowed as much from public discussion (in the curia, in the conventus, in the market) as from reading or from school, but the *Passio* does not offer us the narrative schemes or political saws through which this or that element of Bruges's population made sense of their experience. It offers us rather the narrative schemes and political saws by means of which a particular educated comital functionary addressing himself to a broad audience tried to articulate and reaffirm, in his terms, their shared ideas. The originality of Galbert's version of the events of 1127 thus lies not in its narrative schemes nor in its political ideas, but in the literary quality of its execution and in his ability to make these schemes and ideas sensibly present within the tumble of events he relates, to tell stories and communicate concepts within a journal form.[90] The *Passio* may be a hybrid and therefore somewhat confusing chronicle from a generic point of view, but it is neat, morally satisfying, and reassuring from a narrative and ideological one, and this is the key to its success.

CHAPTER 6

The Tyrant

Blessed be the name of God for ever and ever: for wisdom and might are his: And he changeth the time and the seasons: he removeth kings, and setteth up kings.

—Daniel 2.20–21

Therefore God, the author and giver of happiness, since He alone is truly God, gives earthly realms to both good and evil men, but, since He is God and not chance, He does not do so casually or haphazardly but according to the order of events and times, which is hidden from us, intimately familiar to him.

—Augustine, *The City of God*[1]

When kings are good, it is a gift of God; when they are evil, it is a result of the people's wickedness. For rulers' lives are in keeping with the merits of their people. . . . When God's wrath is aroused, the people receive the ruler their sins have deserved. And sometimes kings change because of the people's malice, so that those who were previously good do evil once they have become king.

—Isidore of Seville, *Sententiae*[2]

I have suggested that Galbert stopped work on the nearly finished *Passio* sometime around December 17, 1127, but that he probably intended to return to it in the spring when Zephyrus's sweet breath made it easier to work with quill and parchment. Galbert does seem to have gone back to work during the second week of March 1128, but when he did so it was not only to polish the *Passio* but to expand it. The first new entry he made, chapter 93, is dated, curiously, to "last August 13" *(idus Augusti retro)* ([93], 1; trans., 265; trans. mod.).[3] It describes how the citizens of Lille drove the new count from their town after he had tried to seize one of his serfs in the midst of the market (a violation of the special "peace" that enabled such markets to exist),[4] and how he returned, besieged the town, and forced the citizens to pay a large fine.

Ross explained this leap backward by suggesting that news of "revolts against the new count in Saint-Omer and Ghent in February, 1128, must have led [Galbert] to take up his pen [again], and he logically added [chapter 93] as a beginning" to his accounts of these revolts in chapters 94 and 95.[5] She thus suggested that Galbert conceived and wrote the first two new chapters and at least the first part of the third new one (93; 94; [95], 1/7) as a single unit at some point after the revolt in Ghent on February 16. Coué has likewise underscored the common conception and composition of these first new chapters, noting that they are linked by verbal echoes as well as by a common theme.[6] She thinks that Galbert conceived these chapters not in response to the revolts in Saint-Omer (February 8) and Ghent (February 16), but as a reaction to a letter (or message) proposing a sort of mutual defense treaty that Ivan of Aalst and Daniel of Dendermonde sent "to the towns of Flanders" ([95], 62/63; trans., 270) sometime between February 16 and March 8, and that he was inspired to do so precisely because it was a call to collective action, which she believes to be the essential theme of the *Passio.*[7] According to Galbert, the letter read (or message was): "'We will exchange hostages and guarantors with you, if you wish to live with honor in the land, so that if the count tries to attack you or us violently, we can come to each other's defense in any place whatsoever'" ([95], 63/66; trans., 270). It was probably a follow-up to Ivan's public indictment of William Clito in Ghent at some point between February 16 and March 8 in which, speaking "for the citizens" of Ghent ([95], 9; trans., 267), he declared the count an oath breaker and a criminal and summoned him to a hearing at which the barons and peers of Flanders along with representatives of the clergy and the people would decide if he should continue as count or not.[8] William, not surprisingly, reacted violently, and Ivan and Daniel probably felt that it would be wise to seek allies among the towns.

These first three new entries are also linked thematically and verbally to the first part of the existing chapter 88, dated to September 17, 1127. This chapter describes the count's demand that the burghers of Bruges pay the toll that he had remitted in April in order to gain their support, and, as Coué points out,[9] its final sentence[10] resembles, and perhaps served as the model for, the final sentences of chapters 93 and 94. Ivan of Aalst's references to the earlier incidents in Bruges (September 17), Lille (August 13), and Saint-Omer (February 8) in Galbert's rendition of his speech to the count, reported in chapter 95,[11] provide further evidence that Galbert wanted his audience to grasp these four chapters as a single unit in which, according to Coué, the beginning of chapter 88 (the count's demand for the toll in Bruges), chapter 93 (his attempt to seize a serf in Lille), chapter 94 (his imposition of an inimicable castellan on Saint-Omer), and the beginning of chapter 95 (his support of an unpopular castellan in Ghent) explain and justify Ivan's speech and his and Daniel's call to collective resistance in chapter 95: "Since the revolts, which are spread out from September [read: August], 1127, to February, 1128, are always summarized in the same words, one must conclude that the appeal for collective action against William of Normandy, and not the individual confrontations, was the source of Galbert's fresh start and that the confrontations with the towns were placed before the appeal for common action as if forming its foundations."[12]

Galbert thus began this second period of writing not with a single event or a single entry but with a series of events stretching over four towns and seven months related in a four-entry unit. He began to write, probably sometime after March 8, in response to a perception of a pattern of comital oppression and civil resistance stretching back to the previous August. The specific spark that ignited his perception of this pattern—in a moment of discovery like that in which the biblical passages concerning the punishment of sins in the third and fourth generation gave him a sudden insight into the reasons for Charles's murder—might have been struck by reports of the revolts in Saint-Omer and Ghent (on February 8 and 16), by a report of Ivan's speech in Ghent (which took place sometime between February 16 and March 8), by the letter Ivan and Daniel sent to the towns of Flanders (after Ivan's speech but before March 8), by the reappearance of William's earlier rivals for the countship ([96], March 11), or by the citizens of Bruges closing the town gates on William ([97], March 16) "for they no longer wished to consider him as count" ([97], 5/7; trans., 272). No one of these events, however, or even all of them combined, is sufficient to explain this perception of a pattern, this pulling together of a series of events stretching over four towns and seven months. The figure, that is, was not in the carpet itself, nor in the events themselves—they did not pull themselves together—but in Galbert's perception of them, and he perceived this figure because his work on the *Passio* during the preceding fall had predisposed him to do so.

Perhaps the principal lesson he had learned from working on the *Passio* was that history ultimately made sense and that he could discover, comprehend, and communicate at least part of that sense. Events were enigmas, puzzles for the historian to figure out, and since he had successfully explained the events of the preceding spring, he had probably found historical writing to be a pleasurable intellectual exercise. After his work on the *Passio,* that is, he expected history to make sense, would be unsatisfied when it did not, was confident of his ability to discover its sense, and was probably half on the lookout for another puzzle to solve.

His statement in chapter 14 that conspirators implicated in Charles's death were still being ferreted out and punished even as he finished writing in the fall of 1127, and his addition of accounts of the deaths of Walter of Vladslo, Baldwin of Aalst, and Isaac's brother Didier to the end of the *Passio* also suggest that he felt that the story was not yet over, that justice had not yet been done. And although the new pattern he perceived and that led to this new period of writing was not related to the punishment of any conspirators, this suspicion that there was more to come probably also made him alert to further events related to the ones he had recorded.

He had also learned that history was figural, that historical processes, which he viewed as expressions of the divine mind, may manifest themselves as patterns, through coincidence and recurrence. In the *Passio,* for example, he notes that Robert the Frisian's oath-breaking betrayal of Arnold was punished "in the very place where formerly the oath had been sworn."[13] He was also certain that the traitors' novel execution by precipitation had not been fortuitous. His work on the *Passio* had made him sensitive to patterns and coincidences in the events around him.

Galbert's belief in the significance of time in and of itself as a fundamental medium of divine creation had been confirmed and intensified by his work on the *Passio,* and, combined with a sense of the figural nature of history, this belief made him sensitive also to temporal cycles like anniversaries.[14] The anniversary of Charles's murder at the beginning of March was thus probably an important moment for him and made him hypersensitive to any hint of special significance in events at that time.

For these various reasons, then, Galbert must have scrutinized events in early March with intense interest and close attention, sifting them for any sign of a tell-tale pattern. The ill will created among his fellow citizens in Bruges by the count's demand for the toll the preceding September probably made him sensitive to reports of comital oppression in the news he received from elsewhere in the county, especially because such oppression violated the evidently widespread sentiment —which Galbert seems to have shared and which, as we have seen, forms the conceptual underpinnings of the *Passio*—that the count ought to respect the law, establish justice, serve the common utility, and rule by consensus.

I thus think it likely that Galbert decided to continue his chronicle not in order to record a specific, particularly striking event or even a series of striking events, but because his work on the *Passio* had predisposed him in a general way to look for patterns in the events going on around him, especially around the beginning of March, and had made him particularly sensitive to anything having to do with the count's conduct vis-à-vis his subjects. I suspect that something in the report he received of Ivan's speech in Ghent, combined perhaps with something in Ivan and Daniel's message and the closing of the gates of Bruges on the count, led him to perceive, suddenly, a pattern in the events in Lille, Bruges, Saint-Omer, and Ghent and made him feel that once again he was witnessing the hand of God at work in Flanders.

These first new chapters thus show us that the entries Galbert added to the *Passio* in spring 1128 (modern chapters 93–122) were more than a prolongation of his existing work. They were a development of it, written in dialogue with it. This influence of the *Passio* on the new entries is also evident in a small but important way in Galbert's use of echoes of it for rhetorical purposes in these later entries. The echoes of chapter 88 in chapters 93 and 94 have been discussed above. One finds two further rhetorically important echoes of the *Passio* in chapter 113. Galbert's statement there, first, that the people of

Bruges had suffered "so many evils, so much looting and burning of houses, and so many murders" *(tot mala, . . . tot praedas et domorum incendia, et . . . tot homicidia)* ([113], 36/37; trans., 295) during the preceding fifteen months echoes and recalls his descriptions in both the Prologue and chapter 35 of the circumstances in which he began work during the early part of the siege,[15] while his allusion there, second, to a "new and unheard-of kind of death" *(novo et inaudito mortis fine)* ([113], 43; trans., 296) to which the citizens of Bruges wanted to put Walter, the nephew of Thancmar, when he was captured by Gervaise, echoes and recalls the "unheard-of" punishment meeted out to Charles's assassins for their "unheard-of" crime.[16] These echoes remind the reader or listener of earlier passages in the *Passio,* just as the capture of Walter evokes memories of earlier events in the minds of the citizens of Bruges, and thus unite the reader with the citizens of Bruges through parallel acts of memory and association.

Yet another example of this echoing of the *Passio* for rhetorical purposes may be found in chapter 121 where Galbert's statement that "God righted such a great wrong [the election of William, rather than Thierry, to the countship in spring 1127], which no human power could or would correct, in accordance with the line of strict examination [*quia nulla potestas humana corrigere aut potuit aut voluit, secundam lineam districti examinis sui Deus correxit*]" ([121], 28/30; trans., 311) echoes and recalls passages in chapters 14 and 89 where Galbert also refers to God's direct intervention in human affairs to correct a wrong that could not be corrected by human efforts.[17] At this point in time, uncomfortable with the way the conflict between William and Thierry had resolved itself, Galbert probably found it reassuring to reassert the omnipresence of God's guiding hand in terms that would recall His earlier interventions and thus render William's death less exceptional and less thorny.

Falling is, as we have seen, an important theme in the *Passio,* and four thematically important instances of falling in the new entries provide another example of the existing chronicle's influence on Galbert's work in 1128. In chapter 102, Galbert describes how a gallery in which William and his barons were sitting in Ypres, "considering what they should do against the newly elected Thierry, count only of the people of Ghent and Bruges and their confederates, . . . fell to the ground [*decidit . . . in terram*] and also all those sitting in it, so that one of them almost died of suffocation in the crash [*casu*]" ([102], 33/37; trans., 280; trans. mod.). At this point in time, as we will see later, Galbert considered this a sign of the wrongness of William's cause and the rightness of Thierry's. In chapter 114, Galbert likewise refers to the "fall [*casum*] and misfortunes" ([114], 60; trans., 299; trans. mod.) that the people of Bruges had suffered through Thierry's defeat at the battle of Axpoel, a battle that Galbert seems to have perceived to be the equivalent of a judicial dual between the two pretenders and whose outcome was significant for his evaluation of their claims to the county. He refers again to the "the fall [*casu*] and misfortune and . . . flight" ([116], 44; trans., 303) suffered by the people of Bruges after he begins to distance himself from them and view Thierry and his supporters as being in the wrong. He likewise interprets the repeated fall of a large crucifix in the church of the Holy Virgin in Bruges on Sunday, June 24, as a sign of God's displeasure with the citizens of Bruges and their count Thierry.[18]

As I noted in an earlier chapter, some of the entries written in 1128 seem close to first parchment drafts, but even these often appear to be compound entries in which one or more later additions have been made to an initial entry.[19] I have already discussed the evolution of chapters 102 and 110, the first of which may have been composed in as many as five different moments and the second in as many as eight,[20] and Mohr has likewise drawn attention to the series of undated passages beginning with *notandum* ("it should be noted") or a similar expression that appear to have been added to the primitive entries of 1128 in order to explain how certain events can be brought into line with Galbert's fundamental concept of the providential nature of history.[21] Other entries written in 1128 contain passages that seem carefully crafted. These include a series of politically important speeches—Ivan's speech in Ghent ([95], 10/39; trans., 267–69), Gervaise's speeches to the citizens of Bruges and Thierry ([100], 7/17; trans., 276; [104], 5/21; trans., 281–82), and the "speech" of the citizens of Bruges in reply to the king's letter summoning them to send representatives to Arras ([106], 15/53; trans., 284–85)—and Galbert's descriptions of the battles of Axpoel ([114], 16/56; trans., 297–99)[22] and Oostkamp ([116], 1/31; trans., 301–2). These all seem to be set pieces that Galbert probably composed more or less at leisure on the basis of notes he had taken earlier and he seems to have aimed at a sophisticated historiographical style more quickly in spring 1128 than he had in spring 1127.

Some of the passages and entries added to the *De multro* in 1128 may thus be unrevised first transfers of wax notes to parchment, but other passages and chapters seem to have been added later, as Galbert received new information or reflected on the events he had witnessed, and yet others are as thoroughly revised as any part of the *Passio.* None of the entries of 1128 can be said to be naïve or immediate, however, precisely because they were written within the context, against the background, of the *Passio.* Some of these new entries may never have been revised, but they were all "prevised," so to speak: they were all written within the framework of an existing, nearly finished chronicle.

The most important lesson Galbert learned from writing the *Passio* was that events had meaning, told a story, taught a lesson, and the greatest influence of the *Passio* on the entries of 1128—and the greatest difference between them—is that the latter, unlike the former, began with a consciously grasped "central" narrative of comital oppression and civil resistance, a fable of the tyrant and the good citizens, which reaches its first climax in the speech Ivan of Aalst made to Count William Clito on behalf of the citizens of Ghent between February 16 and March 8, 1128.[23] On February 16, the burghers of Ghent "rose against their castellan because he continued to deal with them injuriously and wrongfully [*injuriose et perverse*]." The castellan fled to Count William, returned with him to Ghent, and William, "wishing to oppress [*oprimere*] the citizens and to impose the castellan on them violently [*violenter*], stayed there for several days." While he was there, the citizens, acting in league with two important nobles of the region, Daniel of Dendermonde and Ivan of Aalst, "called the count to a reckoning" *(posuerunt comitem ad rationem).* When "everyone in Ghent" *(universis in Gandavo)* had been called together, "Ivan was made spokesman for the citizens [*prolocutor civium*]" and addressed the count on their behalf.

According to Galbert, his speech began with an accusation:

"Lord count, if you had wished to deal justly with our citizens, your burghers, and with us their friends [*Domine comes, si cives nostros et vestros burgenses et nos amicos ipsorum jure volueratis tractasse*], you would not have imposed evil exactions upon us and acted with hostility toward us, but, on the contrary, you would have defended us from our enemies and treated us honorably. But now, contrary to law [*contra jus*], you have in your own person both broken the oaths [*sacramenta . . . fregistis*] that we swore in your name . . . and violated your faith [*fidem vestram . . . violastis*], and ours as well since we took the oath to this effect together with you. Everyone knows how many acts of violence and how much pillage [*violentiam et rapinam*] you have been responsible for in Lille, and how unjustly and wrongfully [*injuste et perverse*] you have persecuted the citizens of Saint-Omer. Now, if you can, you are going to maltreat the citizens of Ghent. But since you are our lord and that of the whole land of Flanders, you ought to deal reasonably [*rationabiliter*] with us, not violently, not wrongfully [*non violenter, non perverse*]."

And it concluded: "'Behold! you have dealt wrongfully [*perverse*], not only with us, . . . but also with the burghers of almost the whole of Flanders, contrary to the faith and oath [*contra fidem et jusjurandum*] sworn by the king and yourself, and subsequently by all of us, the barons of the land.'"[24]

Ivan also proposed a means for settling the question:

"Let your court, if you please, be summoned at Ypres, which is located in the middle of your land, and let the barons from both sides, and our peers and all the wiser men among the clergy and people, come together in peace and without arms, calmly and with due consideration, without guile or evil intent, and let them judge [*conveniant principes utrimque nostrique compares ac universi sapientiores in clero et populo in pace et sine armis, tranquillo animo et bene considerato, sine dolo et malo ingenio, et dijudicent*]. If [in the opinion of that court] you can in the future obtain the countship without violating the honor of the land, I want you to obtain it; if, however, you are in fact what I have said, that is, lawless, faithless, a deceiver, a perjurer, get out of the county, so that we can commend it to some suitable and lawful man [*sin vero tales estis, scilicet exlex, sine fide, dolosus, perjurus, discedite a comitatu et eum nobis relinquite idoneo et legitimo alicui viro commendandum*]."[25]

This striking and powerful speech—Van Caenegem has called it "one of the most important political speeches in the history of the Low Countries"[26]—is perhaps not so original as has sometimes been suggested but it is nonetheless a sophisticated piece of political oratory that makes a precise accusation. "Whoever fails to rule the republic by law [*non jure principatur*]," wrote Smaragdus of Saint Mihiel at the beginning of the ninth century, "is rightly called a tyrant,"[27] and although Ivan does not expressly call William a tyrant—as Galbert later does ([121], 37; trans., 312)—his allegations and choice of words make the nature of his accusation clear.

The problem facing Ivan and the citizens of Flanders—and Galbert—in 1128 was not deciding whether or not William was a tyrant—they were convinced that he was—but how they could justify a rebellion against him since the right to cast aside an unjust prince was not at all obvious at the time. As we have seen, the traditional, conservative, theocratic view held that because all power is granted or tolerated by God, tyrants are as much His ministers as good princes: "God," wrote Augustine, "the author and giver of happiness, since He alone is truly God, gives earthly realms to both good and evil men, but, since He is God and not chance, He does not do so casually or haphazardly but according to the order of events and times, which is hidden from us, intimately familiar to him."[28] And what reason can God have for setting up tyrannical rulers? "When kings are good," explained Isidore of Seville, "it is a gift of God; when they are evil, it is a result of the people's wickedness. For rulers' lives are in keeping with the merits of their people. . . . When God's wrath is aroused, the people receive the ruler their sins have deserved."[29] Rebellion was thus never justified: one had to submit to an obvious tyrant as readily as to a good prince insofar as both were divine ministers whose power came from God.

This view is wonderfully illustrated in John of Salisbury's anecdote about Attila:

All power is from the Lord God, and was always with him, and has been the foundation of all ordained power since before the beginning of time. Whatever the prince can do, therefore, is from God, so that power does not depart from God, but is wielded through an intermediary hand, teaching all men His justice or mercy. 'Whoever therefore resists power, resists what is ordained by God' [Rom. 13.2], who has the authority to confer power and, when he wishes, to remove or limit it. Indeed, a ruler does not have the power to be harsh to those whom he rules, when he wishes to do so, unless divine dispensation wills to punish or discipline his subjects. Whence Attila—when, during the Hunnish persecution, he was asked by the holy bishop of a certain city who he was—replied: "I am Attila, scourge of God." Venerating the divine majesty in him (it is written), the bishop said: "The minister of God is welcome"; and repeating "Blessed is he who comes in the name of God," he unbarred the gates of the church and admitted the persecutor through whom he also attained the palm of martyrdom. For he did not dare to keep out the scourge of God, knowing that His cherished son had been scourged and that there was no power to scourge him except from the Lord.[30]

This view was embraced, notably, by Henry IV and his supporters in the course of what Karl Leyser termed the German "crisis" of the 1070s:[31] the "three-cornered struggle," as I. S. Robinson puts it, between the Saxon nobles, the German king, and the pope,[32] whose essential point of contention was the nature of royal or, more generally, central authority.[33] In his *Leodicensium epistola adversus Paschalem papam* (1103), for example, the pro-Henry Sigebert of Gembloux wrote that "even if he [Henry] were what you [Paschal II] say he is [that is, "chief heretic, rebellious to God, an invader of the ecclesiastical kingdom, a worshipper of the simoniacal idol"], we should nonetheless suffer him to rule over us since we deserve this kind of ruler for our sins. But let us unwillingly concede that he is as you say. We should still not drive such a ruler out by taking up arms against him, but by pouring out prayers to God."[34] Citing Job ("He sets up a hypocrite as ruler on account of the peoples' sins" [Job 34.30, Vulgate]) and Gregory the Great's gloss on this passage (in which the pontiff explains that subjects get the rulers they deserve), he concluded: "We are not saying that our emperor is a hypocrite, but we are surprised that you, who do hold him to be a hypocrite, do not ask why He has set up a hypocrite as a ruler. Indeed, if the sin's cause came to an end, so would its punishment."[35] The force of this traditional view is illustrated by the reluctance the pro-Saxon Archbishop Werner of Magdeburg and Bishop Werner of Merseburg showed to leave Henry's entourage even after the Saxon rebels were released in the summer 1076 and they could have returned to their sees, "because they were afraid that by offending him [Henry], even though he was impious [that is, a tyrant], they would offend God, from whom all power comes."[36] The only legitimate way to resist a wicked ruler, from this point of view, is to correct one's ways, appease God, and pray, waiting for Him to remove him.

This was, however, high theory. No medieval prince was able to rule effectively or for long without the consent and active support of at least his most important subjects, and in reality, as King puts it, "[T]he great men of the kingdom [here the Visigothic kingdom] needed no elaborate doctrine of justified tyrannicide or deposition as an excuse to rise in arms. . . . The power and greed for further power of the *maiores* was the constant political reality with which, for all his theocratic status, the king had always to reckon and the rock on which policies based upon nothing more substantial than theoretical royal supremacy were bound sadly to founder."[37] The Saxons felt no compunction about besieging Henry in the Harzburg in 1073, a good portion of the Flemish abandoned William without any soul-searching in 1128, and English barons switched their loyalty from Stephen to Mathilda—and back again—without turning a hair after 1135.

A tendency to legitimate resistance to tyrants had thus always existed alongside the theocratic point of view,[38] and Ivan's speech—as Sproemberg noted,[39] but to an even greater degree than he suggested—seems particularly, if distantly, indebted to the justification for their rebellion that Saxon historians and polemicists built around the notion of a pact or contract between the king and his subjects during the reign of Henry IV.[40] While the papal party tended to justify their resistance to Henry on the basis of his disobedience and "inutility,"[41] the Saxon doctrine held that a king who becomes a tyrant, thus failing to fulfill his *ministerium,* simply ceases to be a king and thus himself absolves his subjects from loyalty and obedience to him.

Bruno of Magdeburg articulates this doctrine in his *Saxonicum bellum* (1081–1093) by means of the Isidorean derivation of the noun *rex* (king) from the verb *regere* ("to rule" in the sense "to set limits," "to keep in line") and from *recte facere* or *recte agere* ("to act rightly" or "to do right"). This etymology goes back to various Roman and patristic sources that were gathered and "popularized" by Isidore of Seville, who in one passage writes: "Kings [*reges*] get their name from ruling [*regendo*]. . . . He does not rule [*regit*], however, who does not correct [*corrigit*]. The name of king [*regis nomen*] is therefore acquired by doing right [*recte . . . faciendo*] and is lost by sinning [*peccando*]. Whence the ancient proverb: 'You will be a king, if you act rightly [*Rex eris, si recte facias*]; if you do not, you will not.'"[42]

This etymology is first alluded to in a speech that, according to Bruno, Otto of Nordheim made to the assembled Saxons at Hoetensleben in July 1073. "'Because you are Christians,'" said Otto,

"you are perhaps afraid to break the oaths you swore to the king. This is as it should be; but you swore your oaths to the king. While he was a king to me and acted as a king should [*dum michi rex erat et ea, quae sunt regis, faciebat*], I kept the faith I swore to him whole and unsullied. When he stopped being a king [*postquam vero rex esse desivit*], he was no longer the person with whom I was obliged to keep faith. I take up arms, therefore, and call upon you to take them up with me, . . . not against the king, but against the unjust thief of my liberty, not against the fatherland, but for the fatherland and my liberty."[43]

The following month, according to Bruno, Otto replied on behalf of the assembled Saxons to the king's emissaries at the Harzburg and declared that "they had not come together there in a hostile spirit or because they wanted to start a civil war; they would serve the king with complete fidelity—if only he would act like a king [*si rex esse vellet*]."[44]

Lampert of Hersfeld gives a more detailed account, in indirect speech, of the content of a Saxon embassy to the king at roughly the same time which he attributes corporately to a group of unnamed representatives. Having set forth various grievances, these men concluded that

they had sworn faith to him but only if he wished to be a king who would edify God's church rather than destroy it [*si ad aedificationem, non ad destructionem aecclesiae Dei rex esse vellet*];[45] only if he acted with justice [*juste*], lawfully [*legittime*], and according to ancestral custom; only if he maintained order for everyone, maintained his dignity, and maintained his laws safe and inviolate. If, however, he himself first infringed upon these laws, they would no longer consider themselves to be bound by their oath [*sin ista prior ipse temerasset se iam sacramenti huius religione non teneri*] but would immediately start a just war [*iustum . . . bellum*] against him as if he were a barbarous enemy or an oppressor of the Christian name and would fight for God's Church, the Christian faith, and their own liberty as long as a spark of life remained in them.[46]

This theoretical justification of rebellion against a tyrant achieved perhaps its fullest expression in Manegold of Lautenbach's *Ad Gebehardum Liber* (c. 1085). "When he who has been elected for the coercion of the wicked and the defense of the upright," wrote Manegold,

has begun to foster evil against them, to destroy the good, and himself to exercise most cruelly against his subjects the tyranny which he ought to repel, is it not clear that he deservedly falls from the dignity entrusted to him and that the people stand free of his lordship and subjection, when he has been evidently the first to break the compact for whose sake he was appointed? . . . [H]e who attempts not to rule men, but to drive them into confusion, [is] deprived of all the authority and dignity which he has received over men. . . . It is one thing to reign, another to exercise tyranny in the kingdom. For as faith and reverence ought to be given to emperors and kings for safeguarding the administration of a kingdom, so certainly, for good reason, if they break into the exercise of tyranny, without any breach of faith or loss of piety no fidelity or reverence ought to be paid them. . . . "King" is not the name of a nature, but of an office, like "bishop," "priest," or "deacon." And when any of these is deposed for good reasons from the office committed to him, he is no longer what he was, nor afterwards is the honor due to the office to be paid to him. . . . Since no one can make himself emperor or king, for this one thing the people raises someone above itself: that he govern and rule them according to just government, giving to each what he deserves, cherishing the pious, destroying the impious, weighing out justice for all. But if he ever breaks the pact under which he was elected, he will have brought about the disruption and confusion of the very things he was set up to control [*corrigere*], and by every just and reasonable consideration absolves the people from the duty of subjection, since it was he who first deserted his oath [*cum fidem prior ipse deseruerit*] by which they were bound by mutual fidelity. . . . If he persists, not in governing the kingdom, but under the appearance of governing, practises tyranny, destroys justice, upsets the peace, and deserts his faith, then the taker of the oath [of allegiance] is absolved from the binding force of his oath, and it is free for the people to depose him and to select another.[47]

There is some difference of opinion as to how widely these histories and the various polemical texts of the Investiture Contest were circulated,[48] but there were various other ways in which the ideas they express could have reached Flanders. The county was something of a frontline state during the Investiture Contest and the various popes and their supporters both addressed themselves directly to the counts —who, for their own reasons, were usually at least moderately supportive of the reform movement[49]—and disseminated their views through "Gregorian friendship circles," a network of men with whom the papal party was in regular touch, who acted as its eyes, ears, and voice throughout Europe, cells of which are known to have existed in Thérouanne, Saint-Omer, and Saint Hubert.[50]

The anti-imperial ideas of the Saxon aristocracy could likewise have reached Flanders through the manifold contacts between the Flemish and the German populations. The counts of Flanders nibbled continuously at the edges of the Holy Roman Empire throughout the eleventh and early twelfth centuries in a constant give-and-take with the German kings, who enfeoffed them, willingly or reluctantly, at various times with various bits and pieces of imperial lands. The counts' influence was preponderant in Zeeland throughout the eleventh century; the status of "imperial Flanders," that part of the country that lay to the east of the Scheldt, was regularized in 1056 (during the minority of Henry IV) when the count became the vassal of the king and henceforward held this territory in fief from him; and the counts were the effective and eventually recognized lords of the Cambrésis after c. 1071–1076.[51] The counts of Flanders were likewise bound to aristocratic German houses by family ties. Baldwin VI was educated at the German court and knighted by Henry IV's father, Henry III, then married Richilde, the widow of Count Herman of Hainaut, and thus became count of Hainaut (1051–1070) before succeeding his father as count of Flanders (1067–1070).[52] His descendants continued to rule over the Hainaut even after they had been dispossessed of Flanders by his brother, Robert I (1071–1093). Robert himself had married Gertrude, the widow of Count Floris I of Frisia and the daughter of Duke Bernhard II of Saxony in 1063,[53] and their eldest son, Robert II (1093–1111), married the daughter of the count of Burgundy, while their daughter Gertrude married, first, the count of Louvain and then the duke of Upper Lorraine. It thus becomes clearer why Charles, great-grandson of a duke of Saxony, nephew of a duke of Upper Lorraine, and imperial vassal, was at least considered as a candidate for emperor when Henry V died in 1125 and approached by some leading men of the Holy Roman Empire.[54] Trade between Flanders and Germany[55] and some emigration from the Low Countries to northern Germany beginning as early as the first decade of the twelfth century likewise assured contacts at a more modest level of the population.[56]

According to Robinson, moreover, the election of the German king in 1125, which set aside Henry V's nephew and heir, Frederick II of Staufen, in favor of Lothar of Supplinburg, duke of Saxony, may have been consciously modeled on the "free," "popular" election of the anti-king Rudolf of Rheinfelden in 1077,[57] and thus may have drawn new attention in the Empire and the surrounding territories to the Saxon ideas about the election of a ruler and the pact between him and his subjects. Galbert obviously took some interest in the election of 1125 since he reports that Charles was approached as a potential candidate, and, as we will see in the next chapter, he holds it up as one example of the right way to elect a count.

It is also possible that Flemish clerics gleaned political ideas from biblical commentaries on passages like Romans 13. Paul's epistles were among the biblical texts on which the greatest number of commentaries were written at the end of the eleventh and the beginning of the twelfth centuries,[58] and such commentaries, especially those on Romans 13, could well have served as a vehicle for the dissemination of political thought. Abelard's commentary on Romans 13, for example, although still fundamentally theocratic, seems to have been influenced by—and disseminated—anti-imperial justifications of rebellion against a tyrant. "It is one thing," he writes, "to resist the tyranny of an evil ruler, quite another to resist his just power [*iustae eius potestati*], which he receives from God. Indeed, when we resist him for doing by means of violence [*per uiolentiam*] something that does not pertain to his power and position [*potestatem et institutionem*], we oppose the tyrant rather than the power, the man rather than God, since he does not act in accordance with God's wishes, but out of his own presumption [*quia hoc ex se praesumit, non ex Deo agit*]. When, however, we resist him in the performance of those things for which he was legitimately established, then we contravene power."[59] It thus seems reasonable to think that the Saxon tsunami of the 1070s had had some effect on the rivers of thought in Flanders by 1128.[60]

These Saxon waters had also been fed by two other streams by the time they welled forth in Ghent in 1128. First, Ivan's contention that William deserved to be deposed because he had violated his faith, broken his oath, and attacked and robbed his subjects seems also to be rooted, in part at least, in an experience and understanding of "the feudal bond," which, in Van Caenegem's words, "was contractual, . . . implied duties and rights for both sides, and . . . explicitly granted those vassals who were treated unjustly by their lords the right to resist and released them from their duty of obedience. The main idea here was of a pact, a freely concluded contract that gave the subjects rights as well as duties and made them equals rather than inferiors."[61] Writing c.

1130, Paul of Bernried explicitly compared the feudal "pact" between a knight and his lord to the "pact" between the king (in this instance, Henry IV) and his subjects, and justified the subjects' rebellion against an unjust king by comparing it to a knight's breaking faith with an unjust lord: "What more can I say? Is not every knight who swears fealty to his lord subject to him according to the agreement [*eo pacto*] that the lord will not refuse him whatever a lord owes to a knight? If therefore the lord fails to give the knight what is due to him, can the knight not subsequently freely [*libere*] refuse to have him as lord? Most freely [*liberrime*], I say. Nor can anyone, I say, rightly accuse the knight of infidelity or perjury in this instance since he has done all that he promised, fighting for his lord as long as his lord treated him as a lord should a knight."[62]

Ivan's speech also seems to owe something to the communal movement that had been spreading throughout northern Europe in the preceding decades.[63] The influence of this movement, which was particularly strong in the archdiocese of Reims in general and in Flanders in particular,[64] is evident in the speech's origin in a sworn agreement between the burghers, Daniel and Ivan,[65] and the fact that it was pronounced, perhaps in the marketplace, on behalf of the burghers and in the presence of "everyone in Ghent." It is also apparent in a general way in the speech's identification of the burghers as the principal victims of William's tyranny and in its aversion to *violentia* and emphasis on *ratio* and peaceful deliberation,[66] but most precisely and tellingly in the specific accusation that gives it legal force: that William has violated his oath—and thus the oaths of his coswearers, including Daniel and Ivan's brother and predecessor, Baldwin—to respect the "laws and customs" recorded in the charters he granted to several Flemish towns. Ivan accuses him most specifically, that is, of having broken his oath to respect and uphold communal law—and thus of tyranny—and through Ivan the citizens were exercising "the right to resist [that] was a constant in the diocesan associations and the communes, both in order to force recalcitrants to swear to respect the established rules or peace law and in order to punish violators."[67] The new final clause that was added to the charter of Saint-Omer when the recently triumphant Count Thierry confirmed it in August 1128 spells out clearly the basis of Ivan's speech and the burghers' rebellion the preceding February:

"The aforementioned barons [including Ivan, Daniel, and the castellans of Saint-Omer, Bergues, Bourbourg, Ghent, and Bruges] further swear that if the count tries to dispossess the burghers of Saint-Omer of their customs and deal with them without the judgment of their aldermen, they [the barons] will abandon the count and ally themselves with them [the burghers] [*si comes burgenses Sancti Audomari extra consuetudines suas eicere et sine iudicio scabinorum tractare vellet, se a comite discessuros et cum eis remansuros*] until the count restores their customs in their entirety and permits them to be judged by the aldermen."[68]

A vassal's right to renounce his homage to an abusive lord—as Gervaise ([104], 1/21; trans., 281–82) and the men of Oostkerke ([101], 29/32; trans., 278) did theirs to William—and the communal habit of rising against one—as did the citizens of Lille the preceding August ([93], 1/11; trans., 265–66) and those of Saint-Omer on February 8 ([94], 1/14; trans., 266–67)—may thus have reinforced or smoothed the way for the thinking that inspired Ivan's speech and the rebellion it announced, but they cannot explain its "national" scope—Ivan is not speaking as a vassal of the count, or on behalf of only the burghers of Ghent, but for all the citizens of Flanders[69]—or its concept of princely authority. Protonationalism and protopopulism were perhaps simply in the water and the air to some degree in northwestern Europe during the late eleventh and early twelfth centuries[70]—and were thus immediately and independently available to both the Saxon rebels of the 1070s and the Flemish ones of the 1120s—but it is also likely that their expression in Ghent in 1128 was aided, however distantly, by rearticulations of the received "ministerial theocracy" in the context and aftermath of the German crisis of the 1070s that were disseminated in various ways and to varying degrees throughout western Europe in the subsequent decades.

Ivan and the citizens of Ghent could thus claim ample moral, theoretical, and legal justification for their rebellion and for William's deposition and replacement—if William was indeed the tyrant they claimed. The practical problem they faced was the absence of a mechanism or institution for proving his tyranny and deposing him. This was the essential problem of the medieval theory of the tyrant,[71] the same problem that had been faced by the Saxon and papal parties in the crisis of the 1070s, and here again their experience is informative.

Two mechanisms for the deposition of a tyrant had emerged from this crisis. Gregory VII, first of all, thought that the pope was competent to judge a king and, if warranted, to release his subjects from their allegiance to him, freeing them to elect another in his place.[72] The Saxon princes and bishops more or less endorsed and elaborated this model in the fall of 1076, when they swore that unless the ban of excommunication was lifted from Henry by the beginning of the following February, he could never again be king, and asked the pope to attend an assembly at Augsburg at the beginning of that month "so that," in Bruno's words, "once the case had been carefully examined before everyone, either he [Gregory] would release him [Henry] or, when he [Henry] had been bound yet more tightly, they would seek out another man, who knew how to reign, with his [Gregory's] accord [*cum ipsius consensu*]."[73] Lampert, who gives a slightly different version of this meeting and its deliberations, confirms that the Saxons declared that "although he [Henry] had never payed any attention to justice or laws in either war or peace, they nonetheless wished to deal with him according to the laws and, even if the crimes of which they accused him were well known to everyone, they would place the whole matter before the Roman pontiff. They would arrange for him to be at Augsburg on February 2 and there, at a thoroughly publicized assembly of the princes of the whole realm, once the allegations had been discussed by both parties, he [the pope] would condemn or absolve the accused by his judgement."[74] The Saxons thus proposed a sort of national assembly or court held before the pope where both the pro- and anti-imperial parties would present their cases and the pope would act as Henry's judge.

As Gregory was traveling to this meeting, he was intercepted in northern Italy by a penitent Henry IV and persuaded to lift the king's excommunication. The assembly never took place, and Gregory's unilateral action exposed the basic differences between him and the Saxons with respect to the king's deposition. The astonished Saxons objected that Gregory had no right to act without first consulting them ("*absque nostro consilio*"), especially since it was thanks to their efforts that Henry had been "compelled to worship your footsteps,"[75] and proceeded to elect Rudolf of Rheinfelden as anti-king at a meeting at Forchheim in March. Bruno notes the presence of a papal legate at this meeting (there in fact seem to have been two), but says that he was there only to "confirm with the authority of apostolic sublimity all those useful arrangements concerning the realm which our men made."[76] When the pope later decreed and ordered—"by the judgment of the Holy Spirit" *(Iudicio enim sancti Spiritus decrevimus et praecipimus)* no less!—that an assembly of bishops and laymen be called to discuss the respective claims of Henry and Rudolf in the presence of papal legates, the Saxons by-and-large ignored him,[77] as they did in their subsequent deliberations.[78]

Having attempted to realize the sophisticated two-step model of trying a king at a "national" court, perhaps presided over by the pope, before electing a new one in a "national" assembly, the disappointed Saxons reverted to the older, if messier, method for deposing a ruler: they simply abandoned the old one, freed themselves from their obedience to him, and chose a new one. This new election, as Kern pointed out, was the decisive and often the only formal legal step in this method of deposition—there was, in sum, no deposition—but the old ruler was rarely without support and this led to civil war which often—as in both this case and that of William and Thierry—could be decided only by the death of one of the parties.[79]

Ivan's proposition of a national court to try William was thus not altogether without precedent, and may owe something to the ghost of the proposed court of Augsburg or that of the assembly in the Kaufunger forest held some forty years earlier. Here, too, however, a reminiscence of past events was perhaps reinforced by current practices. Cases involving the count of Flanders were occasionally tried by his barons in his own court,[80] and it is noteworthy that the first members of the court proposed by Ivan, in the order in which they are enumerated in the speech, are "the barons . . . and . . . peers" of Flanders—the men who, from the feudal point of view, were most competent to judge another member of the high nobility.[81] The inclusion of "the wiser men among the . . . people" *(sapentiores in . . . populo)*[82] in the court that Ivan proposes to judge the count was perhaps influenced by the existence of aldermanic courts whose judgments, as we have seen, William had sworn to enforce against everyone, including himself, thus recognizing that, in some instances at least, representatives of the burghers could sit in judgment of him. The suggestion that "all the wiser men among *the clergy and people*" (my emphasis) should sit together with the barons and peers in judgment on William—the same people who ought, according to the Gregorian party, to elect freely a bishop—was perhaps also influenced by a tendency to model secular "offices" like that of the count on the office of a bishop,[83] and the subsequent conclusion that, since the "clergy and people" elected a count, they were his natural judges. Ivan's proposition was thus unusual but not unprecedented and was in the "logic" of other contemporary practices.[84] Like the court of Augsburg, however, this court never met and the usual civil war ensued.

It is almost certain that Galbert was not in Ghent to hear Ivan's speech,[85] but received accounts of it from travelers or messengers. As Sproemberg points out,[86] morever, Galbert is the only chronicler to mention the speech, suggesting that it was not "published," that is, an account of it was not circulated systematically throughout the county. The reports of it that reached Bruges may thus have been somewhat haphazard and informal and it is "difficult to believe," as Sproemberg puts it, that the speech's "wording was communicated to [Galbert], although it cannot be doubted, on the other hand, that he could quickly learn its contents."[87] It is unlikely, in sum, that the final wording of the speech in the *De multro* is a simple translation of the Flemish original. Its first clauses are strikingly similar to those of the speech, cited in an earlier chapter, made to Bertulf by an anonymous senior canon of Saint Donatian—"'Lord count, if you had wished to deal justly . . . , you would not have . . .'" *(Domine comes, si . . . jure volueratis tractasse, non . . .)*; "'Lord provost, if you had wished to act justly, you would not have . . .'" *(Domine praeposite, si juste volebatis egisse, non . . .)*—and the similarity suggests that Galbert composed at least the beginning of both. The speech's terms and form—the familiarity it evinces with political and juridical thought, its coherence, clarity, and vividness—seem learned, and it shows every sign of having been composed by someone who had spent a fair amount of time on a school bench, as Ivan presumably had not.[88]

Moreover, Galbert's contribution to the version of the speech recorded in the *De multro* may have gone beyond its diction and form. A peer of Flanders, Ivan presumably perceived his world in largely feudal terms and the influence of the conceptual world of vassalage on the speech recorded in the *De multro* can probably be attributed principally to him. It is also true that his base of power lay in imperial Flanders, the part of the county where the influence of the German crisis of the 1070s was likely to be the strongest, and he had perhaps been present when his brother and Daniel had cosworn to uphold the laws and the authority of various towns and was probably familiar in a general way with the contents of the charters granted to them. The speech's focus on the wrongs done to the burghers of Ghent, Lille, and Saint-Omer—its panbourgeois vision—is nonetheless surprising, even if Ivan was surrounded by the burghers of Ghent and speaking on their behalf, and suggests that parts of it may have been eroded and replaced with other sediments in bourgeois minds and mouths in the course of its transmission from Ghent to Bruges. The insistence on William's violation of law and the repetition of certain key terms also suggest a greater and more precise familiarity with learned tyrannology than Ivan is likely to have possessed,[89] while the proposition of a "supreme" national court to judge the count, especially one that included "all the wiser men among the clergy and people," seems less likely to have occurred spontaneously to Ivan than a feudal court made up of "the barons from both sides, and our peers."[90] It is thus possible that Ivan suggested only that a feudal court, made up of peers and barons, judge William, and that representatives of the people and clergy were added to it as an account of his speech roiled from the marketplace of Ghent to a parchment page in Bruges.

There is in sum no reason to doubt that Ivan of Aalst delivered a speech in the circumstances described by Galbert—it must have been heard by hundreds of witnesses, including the count of Flanders and some of the leading men of the county—and no reason to doubt that Ivan effectively suggested that Flanders would be better off with another count. Ivan thus probably meant what Galbert wrote—but he probably did not say what he meant in the words Galbert attributes to him. When Galbert heard a report, or perhaps several reports, of Ivan's speech, that is, he naturally assimilated its main points to his own ideas, influenced by his education and ideas and doctrines he had perhaps heard discussed rather than read, and had perhaps himself discussed, in both the burg and suburb of Bruges, and expressed them in the ringing terms and tones he thought they deserved. Given his situation and background, Galbert must have been relatively well bathed in the intellectual currents driven—principally by wagging tongues—across Flanders and must have had many ideas whose origins even he would have been hard put to discern. "Ivan's" speech is thus probably a composite one to which Ivan, the burghers of Ghent (and Bruges), and Galbert all contributed and which was influenced by feudal, clerical, and bourgeois traditions, attitudes, and concerns. Thanks to its occasion, setting, speaker, and means of transmission and preservation, in other words, the final version of the speech is probably broadly representative of the political ideas that were "in the water" in the urban centers of Flanders in 1128, but its striking capture and presentation of these fluid ideas is probably mostly Galbert's work.[91]

Given the consciously and strongly theocratic moral of the *Passio*'s fable of the good prince and the wicked *servi* and its "descending conception of law and government," to borrow Walter Ullmann's terms,[92] one may at first be surprised that Galbert gave the "populist" ideas of Ivan's speech and the "ascending conception of law and government" on which they are based such prominence and took such pains to articulate them so clearly and forcefully. At first, that is, he seems to have changed during the winter of 1127–1128 from a dyed-in-the-wool theocrat to a card-carrying populist.

This seeming contradiction or sudden shift can be explained in three ways. First, the fundamentally theocratic concept of government that underlies the *Passio* as a whole is considerably more nuanced and complicated than Galbert's rather bald declaration of theocratic principles at the end of the Prologue may suggest.[93] Galbert may have thought of himself as a confirmed theocrat, but the inhabitants of Flanders were not, and he probably shared many of their ideas and convictions, perhaps without ever realizing the ways in which they conditioned or even contradicted the theocratic moral of his political fable.

Indeed, two sentences after he makes this declaration, Galbert refers to Charles as "one in whom the residue of earthly authority [*terreni imperii reliqua potestas*] assumed the form of ruling well and the substance of serving God" ([Prol.], 49/51; trans., 81). It is not altogether clear what he means by "the residue of earthly authority" here. It may be a reminiscence of the beginning of the second book of the *Seven Books of History against the Pagans* in which Orosius distinguishes between "kingdoms" and the "remaining powers" *(reliquae potestates)* which proceed from them, and between "the power of the other kingdoms" *(reliquorum regnorum potestas)* and that of the series of "four chief kingdoms" *(regnum . . . maximum)* which, he suggests, have ruled the world one after another;[94] or, given the influence of the Investiture Contest on the political thought of the time, he may be contrasting Charles's limited power to "the fullness of power" *(plenitudo potestatis)* possessed by the pope.[95] In either case, the sentence suggests that the count's *potestas* is limited in some way by at least one other *potestas.*

The count's power is also limited by his obligation to carry out his divine ministerium. He must respect the law, establish justice, "provide," as Thierry of Alsace wrote, "for the common advantage and welfare," and defend his subjects, especially the Church and the poor, placing the county's welfare before his personal interests, even if it cost him his life.[96] He must, as David Van Meter has put it, combine in himself "the *figura* of the evangelical Christ . . . [and the] *figura* of the Lamb of the Apocalypse."[97]

The limitations to the count's power receive the most concrete possible demonstration in the concessions William Clito had to make in order to be elected. When they arrived in Bruges, Louis VI and William—who had already purchased his election in Arras by the barons of Flanders by conceding to them "the lands and estates of the traitors who, according to the judgement of all the barons, [had] been condemned by proscription and . . . irrevocably deprived of their goods" ([52], 36/39; trans., 197)—granted the citizens of Bruges a charter abolishing tolls and the ground rent on their houses "as the price [*pro pretio*] of their election and acceptance of the new count" ([55], 30/31; trans., 203), as Galbert unblushingly puts it.[98] He records that a similar charter was granted to the citizens of Aardenburg and we know that other charters were given to the citizens of Saint-Omer and, probably, Ghent.[99] The count and king evidently felt that the new count could not rule without the assent of the burghers as well as the assent of the magnates and were willing to make important material concessions in order to acquire it.[100]

This remission of the tolls for the citizens of Bruges was in fact one of the factors that led to William's downfall since the count's knights who had been enfeoffed with these tolls subsequently complained that he had no right to remit them without their consent. Under this pressure from his knights, the count "demanded the toll from our burghers" despite the charter ([88], 1/9; trans., 260), and thus began to lose their support. Far from being absolute, the new count's power, as this and subsequent events showed, resided in his ability to mediate between various social groups and their conflicting interests. The broadly consensual basis of the count's rule is also evident in Galbert's description of the mechanism of the inquest William ordered into Charles's murder: "the count ordered the best and most faithful men from among the citizens of Bruges and from all the vicinities around us and also the castellan, Gervaise, to swear that they would declare by true assertion, for the honor of the land, the names of those who had killed Count Charles. . . . Then after taking the oath they assembled [*post conjurationem consederunt simul*] in the count's house and they accused one hundred and twenty-five among us . . ." ([87], 2/5, 16/18; trans., 258–59).[101]

In the world of the *Passio,* then, the power of the count of Flanders is limited in a number of ways that qualify the starkly theocratic moral of the fable of the good prince and the wicked servi. The more comprehensive, but un- or semiconscious, political theory, if one may call it that, which underlies the whole *Passio* seems to be one of mutual obligation—is it too much to speak of a contract or a pact?—between the count and the inhabitants of the county. The inhabitants of Flanders owe their count absolute and unwavering loyalty and obedience, while he, entrusted with supreme public authority in the county, "should," as Hugh of Fleury wrote, "love . . . the people entrusted to him by God like himself," emptying himself of private desires and interests and pursuing his subjects' security and welfare, their common advantage, single-mindedly and wholeheartedly, even to the point of dying for them.[102]

Like his cocitizens, Galbert may have been half a populist already, without necessarily realizing it, and his shift toward populism in the spring of 1128 was perhaps not so abrupt or unprepared as it might at first seem. While it is true, moreover, that the theocratic concept of government looked askance at spontaneous human resistance to a tyrant—whose power, like that of the good prince, came from God and thus had to be suffered and obeyed—it did recognize that God Himself might limit or withdraw the power He had given a tyrant, once the tyrant had served His purposes, and ordain that the tyrant be deposed or killed, often through human agents.[103] The troublesome point, of course, was how to know if resistance to a tyrant was divinely ordained or a product of human pride. It was thus possible that the voice of Ivan, himself the voice of the burghers, was the voice of God—but it was also possible that it was the devil's.

The political moral of the *Passio* and the ideas advanced in Ivan's speech are contradictory or inconsistent, finally, only if one presumes that Galbert was using the *De multro* to advance a political theory or program. But this was not his purpose. He was a scribe: his primary goal was to note down as exactly as possible the events God had dictated and his secondary goal was to attempt to articulate the lessons He taught through them. Galbert was not trying, at least not consciously trying, to advance his own political vision but to understand God's as He revealed it in the events of 1127–1128. He thus recorded Ivan's speech and took great pains to articulate its contentions and suggestions as clearly as possible because Ivan was, perhaps, speaking with the voice of God. It was Galbert's passionate belief in the divine authorship of history—and not his own political penchants, political naiveté, or any scientific or personal disinterest—that led him to articulate this "popular" political thought so clearly at a time when, as a rule, "the [popular] groups or unions or sects has no spokesman capable of being a counterpart of the scholarly theocratic writer. Inarticulate the groups were indeed; largely unorganized; probably unaware of the issues they themselves raised; groping towards a goal rather than deliberately acting."[104] For at least a time at the beginning of 1128, Galbert was this popular spokesman, the popular counterpart of the educated theocratic writer (which he also was both earlier and later), not because he was himself a populist but because he thought, for a time, that God might be. It is in this sense and for this reason that Galbert was, as Sproemberg puts it, "the first democratic theorist of the medieval bourgeoisie,"[105] a theorist in something of the original meaning of the word. His task was to observe and interpret, to disclose what had been done and its significance.

William Clito did not think Ivan's voice was that of God, and he was ready to refer the matter immediately and directly to God for summary judgment. When Ivan had finished speaking, he "leapt forward and would have thrown back the *festuca* to Ivan, if he had dared to do so in the midst of the tumultuous crowd of citizens, and said: 'I wish, then, to make myself your equal by rejecting the homage you have done to me, and to challenge you without delay to combat, because as count I have thus far acted rightly and reasonably [*bene et rationabiliter*] in every way'" ([95], 39/43; trans., 269). Ivan refused the challenge, and, although some kind of gathering was fixed for Ypres on March 8, William had no intention of letting his subjects decide whether he should retain the county: "and so on the day set the count went to Ypres with an armed force, and filled it with knights and mercenaries, ready and girded for fighting" ([95], 50/52; trans., 270). Ivan's refusal of William's challenge, on the one hand, and William's refusal to permit the hearing proposed by Ivan, on the other, left the accusation of tyranny unadjudicated, and Galbert the theorist must have waited eagerly, stylus poised, to learn and record God's verdict.

To someone living in Bruges, He must have seemed to reveal His judgment and intentions fairly quickly. As we have seen, the citizens of Bruges closed the gates of the town on William on March 16. They did so again on March 24 ([98], 17/21; trans., 274) and two days later they received Thierry in the town "applauding his arrival" ([100], 23; trans. 276). On March 30, finally, "immediately after eating, the barons and the people came together [*tam principes quam populus convenerunt*] at the exit of the town, at the Sands, and there they all elected [*omnes ibique elegerunt*] Thierry of Alsace as count of all Flanders" ([102], 11/13; trans., 278).

Galbert obviously found it significant that "on the very same day, in the year before [*in anno praeterito, ista eadem feria*], the barons of the siege [*principes obsidionis*] had returned from Arras, the ones who had gone out from us to elect the count of the land according to the counsel and order of King Louis [*secundum regis Ludovici consilium ac praeceptum*]. . . . Coming back to us in happy spirits, they had announced to us that they, together with the king of France, had elected the young William of Normandy freely and lawfully [*denuntiaverunt nobis sese cum rege Franciae elegisse Willelmum puerum ex Nortmania libere et legitime*] as count and lord of our whole land" ([102], 23/31; trans., 279), and his description of the different parties involved in these two elections—

"the barons . . . according to the counsel and order of King Louis" in the election of 1127, "the barons and the people" in 1128—suggests that in Thierry's elevation to the countship he perceived a divine lesson concerning the right way to elect a count as well as a divinely ordained withdrawal of power from William. It was thus no accident that the second election took place in Bruges exactly one year after the result of the first was announced there—the coincidence is God's way of drawing attention to the differences between the two elections[106]—and Galbert reports the above-described collapse that same day of a gallery in which William and his barons were sitting in Ypres as if it were a divine confirmation of the new election, and new way of electing, in Bruges.

The installation of Thierry as count took place over the next two days and at this point the clergy, who are not mentioned in Galbert's description of his election, likewise became involved. On March 31, the newly elected count took an oath before the assembled "clergy and people" *(clerus et populus)* on the relics of Saint Donatian to "fulfill everything he had sworn and not consciously violate anything" ([103], 1/2, 5/6; trans., 280) and received the fealty of the citizens of Bruges and Ghent.[107] On April 1, finally, "Thierry was acknowledged as count, and he went in procession to the church of Saint Donatian in Bruges and entered in, according to the custom of the counts, his predecessors, and he dined in the hall and house of the counts" ([103], 10/13; trans., 280). Galbert finds further evidence of the favor with which God looked on the election of this new count in the fact that this ultimate recognition took place on "Sunday, *Laetare Hierusalem,* in the middle of Lent" ([103], 9/10; trans., 280) since it was a significant day in the ecclesiastical calendar and the text from which the celebration takes its name refers to a joyful Jerusalem, in direct contrast to the desolate Jerusalem, bereft of its ruler, which Galbert mentions at the beginning of chapter 5.[108]

This triumph of populism is neatly bracketed and illustrated by the castellan Gervaise's change of allegiance (and one may wonder if the bracketing was quite so neat in reality). On March 26, the day that Thierry first came to Bruges, Galbert tells us, "the castellan, Gervaise, decided he would stay no longer with our people in Bruges because they had forbidden the place and his castle to Count William, and had barred the gates against him, and, moreover, had put Thierry in his place as their count. Therefore Gervaise sent for the leading citizens and spoke to them as follows outside the castle at Bruges: 'Because I still keep faith with my only lord, Count William, from whom, according to secular law [*legem seculi*], I cannot be separated without loss of honor, I am no longer free to stay with you, who have shown such contempt for the count'" ([100], 1/10; trans., 275–76). At this point, that is, Gervaise felt that "secular law" required him to respect his oath to William and leave Bruges.

If he remained loyal to William and outside of Bruges, however, he risked losing his position as castellan once Thierry controled the city. As we have seen, the people of Bruges elected Thierry count on March 30, and Gervaise seems to have felt that this new election also released him, or allowed him to release himself honorably, from his oath to William.[109] On April 2, therefore,

> the castellan Gervaise came into the castle at Bruges to see count Thierry in the midst of his knights and of the burghers who had faithfully loved him, and standing before them all he said: "Lord Count Thierry! if God had granted us and the fatherland the favor of your presence right after the death of our lord and your cousin Charles, we would have acknowledged no one but you in the countship. Therefore I now give notice to all that I break completely with Count William, that I renounce the homage and faith and loyalty I have observed towards him up to now because the peers of the land and all the people have condemned that one who is still wandering about the land lawless, faithless, without regard for the justice of God or men, and they have acknowledged you with honor and love as the natural heir and rightful lord of the land [*eo quod pares terrae et omnis populus illum condemnaverit, sine lege, sine fide, sine justitia Dei et hominum adhuc in terra errantem, vosque heredem naturalem et dominum terrae justum cum honore et dilectione susceperint*]. I wish, therefore, to do homage and pledge my faith to you, as to the natural lord of the land and the one with whom we are in agreement; I wish to receive from you the office and fiefs that I formerly held from your predecessors." ([104], 3/18; trans., 281; trans. mod.)

The reference to a condemnation of William by the peers and all the people can be read as suggesting that some sort of hearing like that proposed by Ivan and planned for March 8 in Ypres may have taken place.[110] It is unlikely, however, that Galbert would have failed to mention such a gathering. It seems more likely that Gervaise conveniently interpreted the election of Thierry by Daniel, Ivan, and the people and clergy of Bruges and Ghent as a confirmation of the accusations leveled against William. It is clear, in any case, that he felt that this election freed him to break, the wording suggests that he even felt obliged to break, the ties binding him to William.[111] The judgment and will of the peers and people, his shift of allegiance suggests, is more authoritative than the "secular law" binding him to William.

The populist fable of the tyrant and the good citizens reaches its second and ultimate climax on April 10, 1128. On that day, the burghers of Bruges received their copy of a letter the king of France had sent to all the cities of Flanders inviting each of them to send eight representatives to Arras on Palm Sunday (April 15). "'In their presence and that of all my barons,'" the king wrote, "'I want to reconsider rationally the point at issue and the cause of the conflict between you and your count, William, and I shall try at once to bring about a peaceful settlement between you and him'" ([106], 9/12; trans., 283). "The citizens," writes Galbert, "at once began to argue and deliberate about sending a letter in reply, saying . . ." *(cives super remittendis litteris rationis et consilii studium inierunt, dicentes . . .)*, and he then records their response in thirty-nine lines of direct discourse.

The first part of this discourse ([106], 15/31; trans., 284, "'The king has perjured himself . . . from the land'") sets forth their complaints against Louis and William and ends with the declaration: "'For this reason we have just cause for expelling him from the land!'" ([106], 31; trans., 284). Having asserted their right to depose a tyrannical count who rules "'contrary to reason, contrary to the law of God and men'" *(sine ratione, sine lege Dei et hominum)* ([106], 27/28; trans., 284),[112] they go on in the second, brief, part of the discourse to assert their right to elect a new count: "'Now we have elected as our count a more rightful heir, the son of the sister of Count Charles's mother, a man faithful and wise; raised to power in accordance with the custom of the land, and strengthened by our faith and homage'" ([106], 31/35; trans., 284; trans. mod.). The third, and most remarkable, part of this discourse extracts an abstract principle from the events of 1127–1128, asserting the independence of Flanders and establishing a process for the election of a new count. At its heart is the declaration "that the king of France has nothing to do with electing or setting up a count of Flanders, whether the previous count has died with or without heirs. The peers of the land and the citizens have the power of electing the nearest of kin as heir to the count's authority, and they have the privilege of raising him to the countship [*terrae compares et cives proximum comitatus heredem eligendi habent potestatem et in ipso comitatu sublimandi possident libertatem*]'" ([106], 38/42; trans., 284–85; trans. mod.).[113]

This radical declaration, whose importance is perhaps best indicated by its inclusion as the very first entry in a seventeenth-century copy of a collection of "Treaties between France and Flanders,"[114] is, once again, probably due to Galbert's editorial work. As Murray has pointed out, the oral and corporate nature of the discourse suggest that it is a résumé of a debate, perhaps several debates, that took place among the citizens of Bruges.[115] The speech has, morever, a learned and literary quality, as if it had been carefully drafted by someone with a certain amount of education and political experience. Sproemberg calls it a "manifesto" whose third part is couched in "the solemn style of a charter and seeks to erect the following statements into a legal principle for all future times." "One immediately has the impression," he observes, "that one is dealing here with . . . the logical structure of a legal theory."[116] Given the discourse's learned, literary quality and the fact that Galbert situates it within the context of a discussion of a *written* reply to the king, it is possible that it is based on, and incorporates portions of, a written reponse from the citizens of Bruges to the king's letter.[117]

It is thus unlikely that this speech was ever pronounced. It is more likely a summary of one or more discussions among the citizens of Bruges and, perhaps, their written reply to the king. The "speech" is thus probably an artificial device Galbert used to represent and summarize this process of producing a corporate reply to the king's letter.[118] If this is the case, much of its precise articulation may be due to Galbert.[119] It is probably no more correct then to say that Galbert wrote this declaration than it is to say that Thomas Jefferson wrote the *Declaration of Independence.* Like Jefferson, Galbert was probably summarizing and giving form to a body of opinion expressed in debate and, perhaps, in writing, and he may have had some twelfth-century Benjamin Franklin looking over his shoulder. But it is nonetheless the form which these two writers gave to their respective summaries which make them such striking and memorable documents.

The clarity and forcefulness of the speech thus suggest that, when he wrote it, Galbert felt confident that he had indeed seen the hand of God at work again in Flanders and had been right in discerning in the events of August through March a divine withdrawal of power from a tyrant through the agency of a popular uprising and a divine conferral of power upon a new count through a free, popular election. The moral of this fable of the tyrant and the good citizens is thus that God works through popular consensus: it is through this consensus that princes are elected, tyrants deposed, and good princes sustained.[120] This model of government does not contradict the theocratic model of the *Passio* insofar as all power still resides with God, but it does delineate a sort of democratic theocracy in which God uses popular consensus as an instrument "to confer power and, when he wishes, to remove or limit it."[121]

The relatively long entry describing the receipt of the king's letter and the burghers' collective response is dated to April 10. The almost daily entries that Galbert had made since March 8 stop on April 11 with an entry recording two minor victories for the men of Bruges that seem to confirm that things were going in Thierry's favor ([107], 1/10; trans., 286). The next entry is dated April 23. This twelve-day interruption in his note taking suggests both that he wrote the final version of the burghers' reply to the king during this period and that he felt the pattern of political lessons he had discerned had culminated in this "spontaneous," "popular" articulation of the principles behind William's deposition and Thierry's election. In the middle of April, that is, Galbert probably felt that the events that had begun on March 2 the previous year—and the *Passio*—had finally come to their conclusion. Thierry did not yet control the whole county but his ultimate success, Galbert probably felt, was assured by the pattern of events he had discerned.

William was not, however, quite dead yet, nor had he been formally deposed; he still enjoyed substantial support in the county and had no intention of peacefully turning power over to Thierry and going quietly away. It is significant, in this light, that Galbert continues to call him count even after Thierry's election. I do not believe that he did so because his loyalties were divided—he is consistent, as we will see, in affirming that Thierry had the better claim to the county and was the better count—but because nothing had yet occurred that would allow him to affirm that William was no longer count. Both William and Thierry had been elected and recognized as count and, because neither had died or been formally deposed, both were count.[122]

There is nothing in Galbert's account of the burghers' reply to the king's letter to suggest that he had any doubts or reservations about its well-foundedness or the divine sanction of the popularism it promulgated, but both the *Passio*'s fable of the good prince and the wicked servi and the later entries of 1128 suggest that he was not personally inclined toward popularism. He had, as a conscientious scribe and theorist, carefully recorded and articulated the popularist lessons he perceived God to be teaching in the events of February, March, and early April 1128, but he was probably not altogether at ease with them, and the failure to depose William and his defiance of the will of the people—in fact the will of the burghers of Ghent and Bruges—probably nourished Galbert's doubts. He still found it a bit hard to believe that Ivan and the burghers of Bruges, whose discourses he so carefully relates, spoke with the voice of God.

His ambivalence is evident when he began taking notes again on April 23. He begins his entry for April 23 ([107], 11/28; trans., 286–87, "On April 23 . . . in the churches there") by recording that Thierry went to Lille that day and established control over the city and the region. He goes on to note, however, that Bruges was also attacked on that day and that Fromold Junior's house in Beernem was burned by Thancmar's nephews. The most upsetting news, though, was that William had consulted with the king and entered into an agreement with Bishop Simon of Noyon and Tournai whereby the latter would condemn "by the ban and word of excommunication . . . all citizens whatsoever of the land of Flanders who had received Thierry as count and elevated him to the power of the countship and had substituted him for count William violently and without judgement [*violenter et sine judicio*]" ([107], 23/26; trans., 287; trans. mod.), and that the bishop had in fact ordered the suspension of divine services in Ghent. This evidence of royal and episcopal support for William—and especially the accusation that Thierry had been substituted for William "violently and without judgement"—must have troubled Galbert and may be what led him to begin taking notes again.[123] He had begun to doubt his reading of the events of the previous months and suspected that God's lessons, and his task, were not yet over.

The next entry comes a week later on April 30 and records an event that seems to have been even more troubling for Galbert. On that day, Lambert of Aardenburg attacked Oostburg, where he and many of his men were killed. Galbert perceived their deaths to be a divine punishment, like that visited on Walter of Vladslo, Baldwin of Aalst, and Didier the preceding fall, and, initially, this confused him since Lambert had just acquitted himself of the charge of treason by the ordeal of hot iron before Thierry, and been reconciled to the new count, on April 6.[124] In a first reflective addendum to the original entry ([108], 28/48; trans., 288–89, "It should be noted . . . does not succumb"), Galbert explains the acquittal and subsequent death by arguing that Lambert had repented of his role in Charles's murder before the ordeal and thus been spared by "the mercy of God," but had subsequently failed to "carry out worthy acts of penitence, as he had promised God and the Church," had attacked an inferior force at Oostburg, and had refused mediation "without any regard for God or for the oath he had sworn to Count Thierry not to stir up any discord, either in his own person or through his men. And so he deserved to be killed . . . ," not for his role in the count's death, but because he had persisted in violence and broken faith with the count, the Church, and God.

Galbert suggests yet another reason for Lambert's death in what appears to be a second reflective addendum to the original entry ([108], 48/57; trans., 289, "It should be noted . . . his own land of Flanders"). Here, he writes that "those who were killed at Oostburg [Lambert and his men] had by their counsel and trickery [*consilio et dolis*] originally supported the cause of Count Thierry in Ghent and Bruges and put him in the place of Count William. And although Thierry is the natural heir to Flanders and a just and pious count, and William is, in fact, a dishonorable count of Flanders and an oppressor of the citizens of the land [*Theodericus heres sit naturalis Flandriae et justus comes et pius, Willelmus vero comes Flandriae sit inhonestus et civium terrae persecutor*], nevertheless, those who now miserably lie dead did not advise him rightly [*non juste consuluerunt*]; and they can not be called innocent of the betrayal of their lord [*traditione domini sui*] since Count William as a result of their counsel and cunning violence [*consilio et violentia doli*] is now a wanderer in his own land of Flanders" (trans. mod.). Lambert's death, that is, was a divine punishment not for his betrayal of Charles, but for his betrayal of William (as well as his violence and oath breaking).

The change in Galbert's attitude here is signal. First, he no longer attributes William's tyranny exclusively to William. It is due, rather, both to the count's unhappy inclinations and to a lapse on the part of those who ought to have counseled him "rightly" but failed to do so. If William had become a tyrant, Galbert now seems to think, it was because both he and his subjects had failed to live up to their obligations. Second, and more importantly, Galbert here characterizes Thierry's election as a "betrayal" of William accomplished by the "cunning violence" of some of his subjects, even though Thierry has the better claim to the county and is a better count. Galbert thus seems to have rejected—or, better, seems to have perceived God as rejecting—"Gervaise's" solution to the problem of the two counts, which viewed the simple election of Thierry as dissolving the bonds linking William and his subjects, without any formal process of deposition. He seems to have concluded, that is, that because God had not permitted William to die or be formally, legitimately deposed—because He had not withdrawn all power from William—the inhabitants of Flanders continued to owe him their allegiance and obedience, and that any effort to set Thierry up in his place before his death or formal deposition amounted to treason.[125]

Galbert returns to this new theme twice more in entries dated to May 5 and May 15. In the first entry, observing that May 5 was the anniversary of the execution of the conspirators in Charles's murder, he draws a direct parallel between them and the men who had been killed at Oostburg in punishment, he implies, for their betrayal of William: "On May 5, Saturday, after the revolution of a year, there came about the anniversary day of all those who had been hurled from the tower on account of the murder of Count Charles. And it should be noted that in the same week Lambert, the son of Ledewif,[126] was killed at Oostburg and with him more of those by whose counsel and treachery [*consilio et traditione*] Thierry of Flanders was violently [*violenter*] put in the place of William the Norman" ([110], 3/7; trans., 290; trans. mod.).

When William attacked Oostkamp on May 15, the burghers of Bruges marched out against him, but catching sight of his forces, Galbert writes, "our burghers fled, overcome by fear and alarm, and also because they knew in their hearts that they had unjustly expelled the same Count William and had betrayed him [*injuste expulerant et tradiderant*]" ([111], 15/17; trans., 293). The various skirmishes and raids that Galbert records between April 23 and May 15 were not militarily conclusive, although William might perhaps be said to have had slightly the better of the exchanges, but during this time Galbert came to the conclusion that the election of Thierry, even if he had the better claim and was the better count, had amounted to a violent betrayal of William, and that those who had participated in it were as much traitors as the conspirators in Charles's murder.

Galbert discovered celestial confirmation of this new idea in William's decisive victory at the battle of Axpoel on June 21 (related in chapter 114) and the strange incident of the falling cross (chapter 115), mentioned above, on June 24, and by the beginning of July he had become convinced that the divine lesson being taught in the events of August 1127 to June 1128 was in fact the same theocratic one that lay at the heart of the events of spring 1127. Returning in an addendum to the entry for July 9 to the passage from 1 Peter he had cited in the Prologue to the *Passio,* Galbert writes: "'Let every soul be subject to every power' says the apostle. Therefore, if in that place where the most wicked treacheries [*pessimae traditiones*] had come forth, there came to pass misfortunes, war, sedition, homicide, and the eternal disgrace of Flanders, did not that place rightfully deserve all those evils? And if the church of the brothers in Bruges suffered, was it not deservedly because the provost of that church bore responsibility for the evils? And . . . we heard and we knew for a fact that we had been deservedly placed under the ban and prohibition of divine services because we had substituted one count for another and had thus been responsible for an infinite number of deaths" ([116], 52/64; trans., 303–4). The logic of the passage is not straightforward, but Galbert's thinking here seems to be based on the theocratic concept that tyrants like William are as much the ministers of God as good princes like Charles and are visited upon wicked nations as a punishment for their sins. The fact that Bruges, having already been the site of Charles's betrayal and the nursery of his murderers, had now betrayed another count—rather than humbly accepting him as a deserved divine scourge—confirmed its wickedness, and had provoked a new, more painful punishment.[127]

Galbert's theocracy receives its ultimate expression in an anti-sacerdotal tirade and orgy of biblical citation in an entry composed between July 12 and 25. Bruges's tribulation, he writes, proved to be a good thing for those fawning priests [of Bruges] since, . . . bearing crosses and anathematizing Count William, they received their fee in candles and pennies and other offerings suitable only for bellies, and they acted as if they could bend God himself to injustice [*injustitiam*] by such fasting and offerings, even though the citizens were still persisting in their obstinacy by refusing absolutely to recognize their lord, and even though, as we have often said, "Every soul should be subject to every authority for the love of God." And the Lord himself answered Pilate (who was himself set over the Jews of Jerusalem by the Romans) at the very time of the Lord's Passion, "You would not have any power over me, if it had not been given to you from above by my Father"; and again, "Render unto God the things that are God's and unto Caesar the things that are Caesar's."[128] The citizens were, indeed, acting unjustly [*injuste*] in that while their lord was still alive they had put another lord in his place, and neither was the one justly cast down nor the other justly set up [*neutro quippe vel juste depulso vel suscepto*]. . . . How clear it became "that iniquity sprang forth from the elder judges who were supposed to rule over" the flock of the Lord![129] ([118], 18/42; trans., 305–6; trans. mod.)

And even after William's death, Galbert maintains that Thierry "had been put in his place unjustly and treacherously [*injuste et traditiose*]" ([120], 56/57; trans., 310).[130]

William was, in Galbert's opinion, a new Attila—a divine chastisement—who deserved to be deposed, but he could not be—at least not by the citizens of Flanders—because his power, like that of any other prince, good or bad, came from God, while Thierry was a good count with a better claim to the county whose election had been free, but he could not be legitimately enthroned until God permitted William to die. Only God could resolve this problem[131]—and he did so by ordaining the death of William from a wound he received while he and the duke of Louvain were besieging Thierry at Aalst on July 27 or 28, 1128.

William's death and Thierry's subsequent acquisition of the county led Galbert to a long reflection, added sometime after the events of July 27–29 and recorded in modern chapters [120], 15/[121], 43 (trans., 308–12, "And it should be noted . . . whenever they wished").[132] The order of this reflection is associational rather than logical, but it is organized around three main issues. Some people, it seems, had suggested that the burghers of Bruges and Thierry's other partisans were at least partially responsible for William's death insofar as they had rebelled against him and incited others to do so as well.[133] Galbert's first preoccupation was therefore to absolve the burghers of Bruges from all guilt in William's death, which he does by asserting that it was not only ordained by God, but was ordained by Him to occur in such a way that Thierry's supporters could not be blamed for it:

[God] slew Count William by the sword of His justice but in such a way that he died fighting not in his own cause but in that of another, that is, he was giving aid to that duke. Consequently we people of Bruges were considered guiltless of his death since in fact none of us had inflicted death on him. . . . For it was a marvelous dispensation of God which arranged for that prince to die in such a way that he went outside our county to aid the duke at the siege of Aalst. And although he was fighting on the side against our count and us, the responsibility for the siege and the conflict rested on the duke and no one else. And although Count William fought against us willingly on any occasion whatsoever, and for this very reason had gone to the aid of the duke, his fight and his death there, predetermined by God, cannot be attributed to anyone but the duke. For he was the duke's knight in this affair, and he died there fighting not for the countship itself but for the honor and safety of the duke, just like any mercenary. ([120], 18/41; trans., 308–9; trans. mod.)

Galbert's argument here is a bit complicated and depends on the fact that Aalst, where William and the duke of Louvain had besieged Thierry, was not located in "royal" Flanders, the original part of the county held in fief from the king of France, but in "imperial" Flanders, a later addition to the county held in fief from the emperor.[134] This allowed Galbert to argue that William had left Flanders to help the duke of Louvain besiege Thierry in Aalst and had died while serving a foreign prince in a foreign land. The citizens of Bruges and Thierry's other supporters were thus guiltless in William's death and simultaneously freed from their obedience to him. The explanation may seem specious and thoroughly self-interested to us, but I do not think Galbert advanced it in bad faith.[135]

This discussion of the responsibility for William's death at Aalst eventually focuses on the pretenders' reasons for being there, concluding with an acknowledgment that their motives were equally valid.[136] This leads Galbert, through something of an associational leap (from equally valid reasons for fighting at Aalst to equally valid claims to the county), to the second major issue of his postproelial reflection: "It may well be asked why, therefore, when God wished to restore the peace of the fatherland through the death of one of the two, He preferred that Count William should die, who had the more just claim [*justiorem causam*] to rule the land,[137] and why on the contrary Count Thierry did not die who seemed unjustly [*injuste*] put in his place; or by what justice [*qua justitia*] God granted the countship to the one who violently [*violenter*] seized the office. If, indeed, neither of them received the countship in the correct way [*bene*], by right [*jure*] both of them should have been removed" ([121], 1/7; trans., 310–11; trans. mod.).

Galbert's response to his own question was that the violent substitution of Thierry for William, while it might at first appear unjust, was in fact the just correction of William's unjust election as count, which had been flawed in two ways. First, the electors had not done their job. They had ignored the letters Thierry had sent to Flanders before William's election claiming the county for himself,[138] and they had chosen a candidate whose hereditary claim was weaker than Thierry's.[139] William's election was also flawed because the king of France had influenced the election unduly and "sold" the county, which William had "purchased" with a monetary relief.[140] Given Galbert's ideas about the "canonical" election of the count by the clergy and the people, this amounted, as Sproemberg points out, to a secular version of simony.[141] The election had not, therefore, been "free."

William's election had thus been "a great wrong" that God himself had "righted" since "no human power could or would" do so ([121], 28/29; trans., 311). "Therefore after so much controversy," Galbert concludes,

> we consider the more just cause [*justiorem causam*] to be that of Count Thierry who cannot justly [*juste*] be said to have been substituted for Count William; on the contrary, that dead count was most unjustly [*injustissime*] substituted for Thierry and, in return for a relief, forcibily made count through the king's power [*per coemptionem ex regis potestate potestative comes effectus*]. And so God rightfully [*jure*] preserved the life of Count Thierry in accordance with prior justice [*antiqua justitia*],[142] and restored him to his heritage, and removed the other one from the countship by death. ([121], 8/21; trans., 311; trans. mod.)[143]

The final problem with which Galbert wrestles in this penultimate chapter is alluded to in his report of Gervaise of Praet's speech to

Thierry on April 2. "Lord Count Thierry!" it begins, "if God had granted us and the fatherland the grace [*hanc gratiam*] of your presence right after the death of our lord and your cousin Charles, we would have acknowledged no one but you in the countship" ([104], 5/9; trans., 281; trans. mod.). If God intended, as was now evident, to grant the countship to Thierry eventually, why had He not done so immediately? What purpose had been served by William's sixteen-month reign?

In an addendum to the entry for July 9, as we have seen, Galbert seems to suggest that Bruges (at least) had had to suffer the afflictions of an evil ruler because it had been the site of Charles's betrayal and the cradle of his murderers, and had suffered particularly in the civil war between William and Thierry because, rather than humbly accepting the relatively mild scourge of a bad ruler, it had been one of the first and leading rebels against William.[144] In this penultimate entry, Galbert finds two other reasons for God's having sent a tyrant to reign over Bruges and Flanders:

> And therefore [God] turned his anger and the flails of his wrath against the men of Flanders, because earlier they had all had the opportunity to consider and foresee and discuss and seek out with all care the one whom they would set up as lord over themselves and the fatherland, and whom they would love and venerate once he was elected. And by contrition of heart and dedication of pious mind they could have pleased God in this matter. But because they failed to do so, they had to endure the tyrant and despoiler and evil exactor whom they had so rashly accepted as lord; and after his election and elevation to the countship, the barons and officials and counselors of the land did not guide him in the right path or teach him the honorable customs of the counts his predecessors, but instructed him in pillaging and in crafty and deceitful pretexts by means of which they could demand vast sums of money from the citizens and burghers of the land and extort it from them by violence whenever they wished. ([121], 30/43; trans., 311–12; trans. mod.)[145]

The Flemish failure to choose and advise a new count well was the source of all they had suffered in the past year.

And why had God finally seen fit to remove the tyrant and hand over the county to the rightful heir? Galbert suggests that He had been appeased by a change of heart on the part of the burghers of Bruges and thus removed the tyrant He had sent to punish them.[146] It is not clear what the burghers had repented of, or when or how they had done so,[147] however, and Galbert is perhaps only arguing backward here on the basis of the logic of tyrannology: since evil rulers were punishments God inflicted on wicked and unrepentant people, the removal of the tyrant was a sign that the people had repented.[148] When the people of Bruges repented, in sum, God removed the evil ruler He had set over them as a punishment and installed the rightful heir as count.

The flawed, indeed sinful election of William had displeased God and brought with it its own punishment—as well as a punishment for raising and abetting Charles's assassins—since through their error, the Flemish had elected a prototyrant, whom they had failed to correct by good counsel and had in fact made worse through bad, and then punished themselves further by plunging themselves into a civil war which they had to endure until they repented and God saw fit to remove the tyrant. In a sense, then, God had inflicted neither the tyrant nor the war on the Flemish; He had simply let them inflict them on themselves. A wicked nation had itself chosen wickedly the tyrant it deserved and thus imposed on itself the punishment it deserved for the wrong it had done Charles, Thierry, and itself. Thierry's challenge to William had been God's way of removing a tyrant and restoring justice after the people of Flanders, or at least of Bruges, had been punished, first, with a tyrant and then, when it rebelled, with a civil war, and had finally repented.

This long reflection thus answers the two essential questions posed by William's sudden death, a death that confirmed, at least for Galbert, that he had indeed been a tyrant. It explains what the people of Bruges and Flanders had done to deserve him—the sins for which he was their punishment—and why God had finally withdrawn power from him and allowed him to be killed. It also went one step further and argued that, this time at least, the inhabitants of Flanders could not be accused of complicity in the count's death and thus deserved no further Attilas. God could, therefore, finally permit Thierry, "the natural heir to Flanders and a just and pious count" *(heres . . . naturalis Flandriae et justus comes et pius)* ([108], 511/52; trans., 289), to rule.

The entries of spring 1128 thus complement the *Passio*'s theocratic fable of the good prince and the wicked servi. They begin with a fable of the tyrant and the good citizens whose apparently triumphant populism dissolves in the blood of four months of civil war and crystallizes, as the violence evaporates, in a fable of the tyrant and the wicked citizens-who-finally-come-to-their-senses-and-repent, and a new revelation of the theocratic basis of secular authority. The entries added in 1128 form a thematic and dramatic continuation of the *Passio* and the resulting work, the *De multro,* is a coherent chronicle that is also a sophisticated and extended attempt to understand contemporary events in terms of contemporary political thought. It is thus finished, at least as far as its general plan and argument are concerned: Bruges had been punished, the "mistake" of William's election had been corrected, the "natural," freely elected heir firmly installed as count, and the events' divine lessons elucidated. What Galbert did not do, as he had done the previous summer and fall, was go back and rewrite his work in order to create a more polished and rhetorically effective whole. The intellectual work was done; the rhetorical work was not, and Galbert never did it.

CHAPTER 7

"Sapiens"

And what he hath seen and heard, that he testifieth; and no man receiveth his testimony.

—John 3.32

The mind, enlightened by the guidance of reason, rises in the midst of virtues to which it is inclined by an innate predilection, however much it is abused by vices, and beholds the knowledge of God which towers like a citadel. . . . Because the judgements of God are inscrutable and we can neither know them all nor explain those we know, let me state that the rebuke of our Judge and God, in whatever form it may take, is justly undergone by those who know and likewise by those who know not.

—Orosius, *Seven Books of History against the Pagans*[1]

But we must write truthfully of the world as it is and of human affairs, and a chronicle must be composed in praise of the Creator and just Governor of all things. For the eternal Creator still works without ceasing and marvellously orders all things; and of his glorious acts let each one according to his ability and desire duly relate what is shown him from on high.

—Orderic Vitalis, *Ecclesiastical History*[2]

The rebellion against William and the ensuing civil war led Galbert to add a substantial series of new entries to his chronicle in 1128, but this addition of new entries did not preclude his going back to work on the existing *Passio,* as I have suggested he intended to do when he put down his pen in December 1127. The running entries for the roughly twenty-six weeks between February 3 and July 29, 1128 (chapters 94–[120], 14), take up only twenty-five pages of my edition (roughly one page per week), far less than the one hundred and two pages taken up by the entries for the roughly twelve weeks between March 2 and May 22, 1127 (chapters 15–85; roughly 8.5 pages per week). The entries for 1127 had probably been substantially expanded during summer and fall of that year, but it nonetheless seems likely that Galbert devoted much less time to drafting new entries in 1128 than he had in 1127 and thus had a fair amount of time that he could have devoted to continuing his revisions of the *Passio.*

I have listed in Appendix VI the passages that I believe Galbert added or substantially rewrote when he revised his basic notes after May 22, 1127 (there were probably many more that we cannot discern). It is almost impossible to date these passages with any precision—most of them were probably written during the summer and fall of 1127, although they could well have been added during the spring of 1128—but there are two series of passages that can with some probability be dated to spring 1128 and thus suggest that Galbert did indeed continue to work on the existing *Passio* at the same time he was drafting new entries concerning the events of that spring. There are, first, five passages in these chapters that begin with *"et notandum"* or a similar expression and may thus, like such passages in chapters 93–122, have been added in spring 1128.[3] These passages may, of course, be additions that he had jotted in the margins, between the lines, or on a piece of parchment late in 1127 and not yet had time to incorporate into the text when he stopped work. In most cases, it makes little difference whether they were added late in 1127 or in 1128, although it would be interesting to know when Galbert decided to "sign" his work by adding the passage in which he names himself to chapter 35, and it would likewise be interesting, and potentially significant for the history of the work's composition, to know when he added the long passage working out his sudden insight concerning the punishment of crimes in subsequent generations.

There are, second, two substantial sections of the *Passio,* both describing the election of rulers—the reports of the offers to Charles of the crowns of the Holy Roman Empire and the kingdom of Jerusalem (chapters 4 and 5) and the chapters describing William's election (47, 51–54)—that may have been reworked, or, in the case of chapters 4 and 5, added in 1128 in response to the events of that spring and would thus amount to a reinterpretation of earlier events in light of later ones.

As it is described in the *Passio,* William Clito's acquisition of the countship took place in several stages. The process was initiated by a letter from Louis VI that was received in Bruges on March 20. Writing from Arras, the king addressed his letter, according to Galbert, to "the princes and barons of the siege," and ordered them "'to come to my presence without delay and to elect by common agreement the kind of count who will be useful to you [*comitem utilem vobis*] and whom you will agree to let rule [*consenseritis praeesse*] over the land and its inhabitants'" ([47], 3, 19/21; trans., 186–87; trans. mod.). The letter thus suggests that the electors should be limited to the princes and barons, and that they should elect someone who will work for their advantage *(utilem vobis)* and further their group interests.[4] Elected by the magnates (only) and himself a noble (the same letter rejects William of Ypres as a candidate because he was born "of . . . an ignoble mother [*matre ignobili*] who continued to card wool as long as she lived"; [47], 18; trans., 187), the letter implies that the count should govern on behalf of, and for the benefit of, the nobility.

The barons left for Arras on March 21 and 22, and at the beginning of chapter 52 Galbert describes the return to Bruges on March 30 of the nobles "who had gone to the king to take counsel concerning the realm and to elect a count in accordance with the advice [*eligendo consule secundum consilium*] of King Louis, emperor of France, and the election of all his barons and those of our land, and after prudent consideration of what was likely to be of advantage to the fatherland [*omnium baronum ipsius et terrae nostrae electionem et juxta prudentem et patriae utilitati probabilem examinationem*]" ([52], 2/6; trans., 194–95; trans. mod.).[5] Later in the same chapter he has Walter of Vladslo (paraphrasing or translating a letter from the king) declare, more honestly, "the barons of France and the leading men of the land of Flanders, on the order and advice of the king, have elected as your count and the count of this land [*principes Franciae et primi terrae Flandriarum, jussu et consilio regio, elegerunt vobis et terrae*] the young William"; [52], 24/26; trans., 196). William was subsequently elected by the representatives of the citizens of Ghent (and by at least some of the representatives of the citizens of Bruges) on April 2, after having already been elected, probably, by the citizens of Lille and Arras (see [53], 11/14; trans., 199). He was acclaimed in Bruges on April 6 and in Saint-Omer around April 16.

William was thus first *designated* by the king of France, then *elected* by the barons of Flanders *and* France, and then, in a series of separate elections, *elected* yet again by the citizens of the towns of Flanders. There was not one election, but several; some were more important than others; and the whole process took place under the watchful eye of the king of France and his barons. The king "consulted" both the barons and the citizens and, as we have seen, made important material concessions to both in order to gain their support, but the process was, on the whole, a "descending" one in which Louis acted as a fedual overlord, enfiefing William with the county of Flanders.

A rather different process for electing a new count is outlined in a letter from Thierry of Alsace that was likewise received in Bruges on March 20, within minutes, astonishingly, of the king's letter.[6] This letter, or at least Galbert's version of it, contrasts with the king's in some precise and interesting points. It was addressed to "the barons of the siege and . . . all the inhabitants of the land [*omnes terrae inhabitatores*]," rather than to just "the princes and barons of the siege," and in it Thierry wrote: "'You all [*vobis omnibus*] know for a certainty that the realm of Flanders pertains to my lot and power by right of kinship after the death of my lord the count. Therefore I want you [*vos*] to take thought and proceed carefully concerning the election of my person. . . . If . . . you send back a favorable reply, I shall hasten to become your count, and I shall be just, peaceful, tractable, and a husbandman of the common utility and welfare [*utilitatis communis atque salutis provisor*]'" ([47], 25/34; trans., 188; trans. mod.). There is no mention of any designation by an overlord here—Thierry is designated by his genetic relation to the former count—and the "you all" seems to refer back to "all the inhabitants of the land" of the preceding sentence and to the "you" who will do the electing in the next one, suggesting that the count should be elected by *all* the inhabitants of the land in, it would seem, a single, simultaneous election. If he is elected, moreover, Thierry promises to attend not only to what is useful for the nobility but to provide for the *common* utility and welfare.[7]

The same model for the election of the count and the same concept of his duties reappear in Galbert's description of an oath that was sworn exactly one week later by the leading men of the region of Bruges, while the barons were still in Arras with the king:

On March 27, Palm Sunday, our burghers came together [*convenerunt burgenses nostri*] in the field that lies next to the town within the enclosure, after calling together the Flemings from the region all around us, and they swore together [*convocatis undecumque Flandrensibus circa nos, conjuraverunt simul*] on the relics of the saints as follows:

"I, Folpert, judge [*judex*], swear that I will elect as count of this land one who will rule the realm of his predecessors, the counts, usefully [*utiliter recturus regnum*], who will be able to maintain by force the rights of the fatherland against its enemies, who will prove himself to be kind and generous toward the poor and reverent before God, who will tread the narrow path of rectitude, and who will and can serve the common utility of the fatherland [*utilitati communiter patriae velit et possit prodesse*]."

Then following him all [*omnes*] the leading citizens swore. From Ijzendijke, Adalard, the *échevin,* with his following; from Oostburg, Haiolus with the leading men of that place; from Aardenburg, Hugo Berlensis and the strong men of that place; from Lapscheure, Oostkerke, Uitkerke, Lissewege, Slijpe, Gistel, Oudenburg, Lichtervelde, and Jabbeke, all the strong and influential men swore by a similar oath, and there was a great crowd of co-swearers to this effect [*omnes fortiores et meliores simili sacramento juraverunt. Eratque multitudo maxima conjurantium in idipsum*]. ([51], 1/16; trans., 193–94; trans. mod.)

One's first impression on reading this passage is that Galbert here provides us with a verbatim transcription of the oath sworn by these men that day, but the oath shows signs of having been composed by someone more learned than one would normally expect a citizen of Bruges, even a *judex,* to be.[8] The idea of the "common utility of the fatherland" *(utilitati communiter patriae)* as the end of government goes back, as we have seen, to Augustine and Cicero, while the desire to elect someone who "can" *(possit)* serve the common good, as well as being willing to do so, evokes the importance of the ruler's idoneity.[9] The oath's reference to a count "who will prove himself to be kind and generous toward the poor and reverent before God, who will tread the narrow path of rectitude" likewise recalls the traditional princely virtues mentioned in Hugh of Fleury's *Tractatus de regia potestate et sacerdotali dignitate.*[10] The idea that the ruler should "serve" *(prodesse)* his subjects, rather than "lord it over" *(praeesse)* them, goes back to Augustine, Saint Benedict, and Gregory the Great,[11] and the division of this couplet between the king's letter *(praeesse)* and Folpert's oath *(prodesse)* is a subtle but striking way of characterizing their different attitudes toward comital power.

Galbert's description of the circumstances in which this oath was taken also emphasizes the importance of collective consultation, agreement, and action, of, in a word, consensus (note especially the uses of *simul, omnes,* and of words beginning with the prefix *con-).*[12] This spirit of happy bourgeois solidarity continues in the next chapter, in which Galbert relates the return of the barons on March 30 and the public reading of the king's letter announcing William Clito's election as count, and ordering, asking, and advising the citizens to consent to it. When they had heard the letter, Galbert tells us, the citizens postponed making any response to it "until they could summon those Flemings with whom they had taken an oath concerning the election [*cum quibus eligendi sacramenta constituerant*] and could take joint action with them in approving or opposing the content of the royal message [*simul aut . . . facerent aut . . . refutarent*]" ([52], 49/52; trans., 197–98).

In chapter 53, he notes that the next day, March 31, "after the citizens had met with the other men of Flanders, they decided by common agreement" *(convenerant cives cum Flandrigenis, ex communi consilio consenserunt)* to send representatives to Raverschoot to meet with representatives of the king and of the burghers of Ghent on Saturday, April 2—"for the burghers of the cities and towns of Flanders were pledged to each other in loyalty and friendship so that they would neither accept nor reject anything in the matter of the election except in common [*nihil in electione nisi communiter consentirent aut contradicerent*]. In this matter our burghers would take no action without the counsel [*consilio*] of the men of Ghent who lived in their vicinity"—and that on that day "an agreement was reached between our men and the men of Ghent [*concorditer actum est inter nostros et Gendenses*] concerning the acceptance of the newly elected count to the effect that they would receive him as count and advocate of the whole land" ([53], 1/3, 6/10, 17/20; trans., 198–99).[13]

These same principles of decision by consensus, no designation of the ruler by a higher authority, a common election involving representatives of the entire population, and the prince's obligation to work for the advantage of everyone are also found in Galbert's descriptions of the "offers" of the crowns of the Holy Roman Empire and of the kingdom of Jerusalem to Charles in chapters 4 and 5, offers which, as Sproemberg and Alan Murray have shown, are in large part the product of his imagination.[14] In the first of these chapters, he writes that when Henry V died in 1125, "the wiser men among the clergy and the people [*sapientiores in clero et populo*] of the realm of the Romans and Germans . . . took counsel together [*inierunt consilium*]" and decided to offer the throne of the Empire to Charles "on behalf of the whole clergy and people [*ex parte totius cleri et ex parte totius populi*] of the kingdom and empire of the Germans. . . . For all the better men among both clergy and people [*omnes enim meliores tam in clero quam in populo*] were hoping, ardently and rightly, that he would be elected so that if, God willing, he deigned to come to them, they could elevate him unanimously [*unanimiter*] by the imperial coronation and establish him as king by the law of the preceding Catholic emperors" ([4], 4/20; trans., 90–91; trans. mod.).

In chapter 5, he tells us that when the king of Jerusalem was captured by Saracens in 1123, the Crusaders, who were none too fond of him, decided to replace him. They too, therefore, "took counsel together and by general consent [*inierunt ergo consilium et communi consensu*] sent a letter to Count Charles asking him to come to Jerusalem and receive the kingdom of Judaea, and in that place and in the holy city take possession of the crown of the Catholic realm and the royal dignity" ([5], 6/10; trans., 93; trans. mod.). And Galbert concludes chapter 5 by lamenting: "Alas, what sorrow, that they should rob the church of God of such a great man whom the church and the people of the Eastern Empire, and the holy city of Jerusalem and its Christian population [*ecclesiae et populus orientalis imperii et Hierosolimorum civitas sancta simul cum populo christianorum*], had preferred and chosen, and even demanded to have as king!" ([5], 14/18; trans., 93).

These various passages thus set forth two markedly different ideas about the election of the new count and the scope of his vocation. The king's letter suggests that the count should be elected by the magnates and serve their interests, while Thierry's letter, Folpert's oath, and the accounts of the two offers made to Charles suggest that he should be elected by all the inhabitants of Flanders (although neither the letter nor the oath have anything to say about the clergy) and should serve the common welfare. The splitting of the couplet *"praeesse"/"prodesse"* between the king's letter and Folpert's oath is an especially deft touch that simultaneously associates the two discourses in the (learned) reader's mind, locates them within the tradition of political thought, and underlines in a clear and memorable way the difference between a count chosen by the king and barons, who will "lord it over" the land and its inhabitants, and one elected freely and popularly who will "serve" the common utility.[15]

Over and beyond their differences with respect to the count's election and vocation, these discourses share a common set of political touchstones which they understand in different ways: the importance of consent and consensus; the prince's obligation, and the importance of his ability, to make himself useful; and the Augustinian distinction between serving and lording. These were all commonalities of learned political discourse in the twelfth century and, given that Louis VI's and Thierry's letters were drafted, presumably, by some cleric in their entourage, it is perhaps not surprising that they share common intellectual foundations. It is somewhat more surprising to discover that these learned commonalities had so permeated secular society that they also formed the basis of Folpert's thought, and the contrasts between the king's letter, on the one hand, and Thierry's letter and Folpert's oath, on the other, seem rather too pointed to be fortuitous. The common intellectual foundation of these passages might thus also, and perhaps more probably, be explained by their having been grasped together as part of an extended representation of the process of electing a count—of which they articulated the principles—and passed through the conceptual and linguistic sieve of a single mind. It seems likely, in sum, that Galbert is here assimilating a series of roughly similar ideas expressed by different people in different terms to his own, educated, ideas and terms, which he has placed in the letters, mouths, and minds of the king, the future count, and the burghers.[16]

As we saw in the preceding chapter, Thierry's letter plays a crucial role in Galbert's ultimate evaluation of the legitimacy of William's and Thierry's respective claims to the countship in the early summer of 1128,[17] and the electoral process described or proposed in it, in Folpert's oath, and in chapters 4 and 5—which, as I noted earlier, seem to be a later addition to the first version of the introduction, and may not have been added until 1128[18]—corresponds more or less to Galbert's description of the way in which Thierry was elected count that spring. It therefore seems possible that chapters 4–5, 47, and 51–54 were reworked in 1128 so that the existing chronicle would register Thierry's claim to the county at a legally important moment and announce and justify the method of his election in 1128.[19]

One may thus suspect that Galbert continued to revise the existing *Passio* in spring 1128—as he had probably planned to do—while simultaneously recording and writing up new events. If this was the case, if he continued to revise or add passages here or there throughout the whole chronicle even as he added more material to the end of it, one has to wonder why he never went back and rewrote the entire chronicle after Thierry had secured the county through William's death in July 1128. The complicated political fable had unraveled to its end, God's obscure judgment had been made clear, and Galbert had all the time in the world to polish the end of his chronicle as he had its beginning. Why didn't he do so?

Maybe he died, although, as we saw in chapter 1, his name perhaps appears in a charter dating to 1130. Maybe illness or old age sapped the energy he needed to finish his work. I think, however, that it is more likely that he did not do the rhetorical work he needed to do in order to present his history to the public because he no longer felt he had a public. The intellectual work he had done for himself, to satisfy his own curiosity and disclose the lessons of the events of 1128. The rhetorical work was useful only if he planned to publish his history, and he no longer planned to do so.

I have suggested that Galbert wrote the *Passio,* in the first instance, for the burghers of Bruges, and more generally, for all the inhabitants of Bruges, clergy and aristocrats as well, and ultimately, for all the inhabitants of Flanders and any other of the faithful who might be interested in an account of Charles's death and the punishment of his murderers. Galbert had, however, become thoroughly alienated from his fellow citizens during the spring and summer of 1128. His view on the necessity of formally deposing William and of remaining obedient to him until he died or was so deposed, first articulated in the entry dated to April 30, can hardly have been well received in Bruges, but the first signs of what must have been a growing impatience with the stubborn refusal of his fellow citizens to see the divine lessons in the events surrounding them do not appear until the entry dated to June 12, where he records their reaction to the capture of Walter, the nephew of Thancmar of Straeten:

The citizens of Bruges clapped their hands with joy, hardly able to express their high spirits over such a great success. For finally, after so many evils, so much looting and burning of houses, and so many murders which had been inflicted on us we had captured [*in nostros perpetrata, captus est . . . a nostris*] that Walter who was the source and beginning of all the misfortunes of our land [*terrae nostrae*], by whose cunning Count Charles had been betrayed; not that he himself had betrayed him but he had forced his enemies, Borsiard and his men, to the act of betrayal. I say this in accordance with the feeling of the people and with the rage of spirit of those [*secundum sensum vulgi et secundum furorem animi illorum*] who would have hanged that captive Walter without delay or destroyed him by some new and unheard-of kind of death, if the count had permitted it. ([113], 33/44; trans., 295–96)

In the first part of this passage, Galbert invites the listener or reader to sympathize with the citizens of Bruges in two ways. First, as I mentioned earlier,[20] he uses linguistic echoes to evoke his earlier descriptions of the circumstances in which he began work during the early part of the siege and of the "unheard-of" punishment meeted out to Charles's assassins, reminding the reader or listener of the events they describe just as the capture of Walter evoked memories of these events in the minds of the citizens of Bruges. He thus unites the listener or reader with the citizens of Bruges through parallel acts of memory. He also paraphrases the citizens' opinions (in what almost sounds like direct speech) and solicits the reader's acceptance of them by associating himself with the citizens ("on us . . . we had captured . . . our land"). At the end of the passage, however, he tells us that he is speaking not in his own voice, but "in accordance with the feeling of the people and with the rage of spirit of those who would have hanged that captive Walter without delay." He thus reveals the lynch-mob mentality of the "citizens of Bruges" in search of a scapegoat and the system of coercive emotional appeals dressed up as reason ("not that he himself had betrayed him but he had forced his enemies, Borsiard and his men, to the act of betrayal") with which that mentality seeks to justify and promulgate itself, and demonstrates how easy it was to share. The shift in his terms for the inhabitants of Bruges, from "citizens of Bruges" to "the crowd," his mention of their "rage of spirit" or "frenzy," and the implicit distinction between their "feeling" or "way of seeing things" *(sensum)* and his, all indicate, for the first time, a certain distance between Galbert and his fellow citizens and a critical attitude toward them.

We glimpse this same attitude again a few sentences later, where he records that when the "citizens of Bruges" got news that same day of the capture of a number of William's supporters in other engagements, they "attributed Thierry's successes and good fortune to a certain priest of his who by his anathema had excommunicated Count William and his partisans. But at Ypres," he notes, "a certain provost, Hildfred, was daily excommunicating all those who sided with or aided our Count Thierry. In this interchange," he adds ironically, "the anathema of our priest prevailed, and I do not think our priest intends to desist from the anathema until he has forced Count William with his supporters and his provost, Hildfred, into exile. And it is marvelous that a priest can cast a spell on God in such a way that, whether God wishes it or not, William may be thrown out of the countship [*et mirum est quod sacerdos ita Deum incantare possit ut, velit nolit Deus, Willelmus a comitatu ejiciatur*]!" ([113], 52/61; trans., 296).[21] Galbert here distances himself from the credulous crowd again, and this time his criticism extends to one of Thierry's priests who, in his opinion, had begun to act more like a sorcerer.

Galbert's impatience with the citizens and priests of Bruges reemerges in the next chapter, in an entry dating to June 22. Having suffered a decisive defeat at the battle of Axpoel and learning that "Count William, before going into battle, had dedicated himself humbly to God, and had received the sacrament of penance, and that he and all his men, after his misfortunes in war, had cut off their hair and cast off their superfluous garments, our citizens together with their Count Thierry *finally* [*tandem*] removed their hair and clothes, and those priests of ours also, following the example of the enemy, *finally* [*tandem*] preached penance" ([114], 68/74; trans., 299; trans. mod., my emphasis).

Galbert appears to have still had some hope at this point that his fellow inhabitants would come to their senses, but the following entry, dated to June 24, shows that it was quickly dashed. Having recounted the strange incident of the falling cross, he goes on to note that "our idiot priests [*nostri sacerdotes idiotae*] were again saying that the priest from Aartrijke and the priest from Knesselare and the cleric Odfrid had put Count Thierry and his men to flight in the battle by incantations [*per incantationes*], when in fact it is God who disposes and ordains all things!" ([115], 11/15; trans., 301; trans. mod.).

From this point on, Galbert's alienation from his fellow citizens deepens and becomes irremediable. In an addendum to the entry for July 9, after William's siege of Oostkamp and the withdrawal of many of the inhabitants of the region of Bruges into the relative security of the town, he writes:

> It should be noted, certainly, that no wise man [*nullus sapientium*] among us at Bruges dared to speak the truth [*vera profiteri*] about the calamity and misfortune and our flight. For if anyone uttered a word of the truth [*aliquid veritatis profitebatur*], they defamed him as a traitor to our place and a supporter of Count William and threatened him with sudden death. And it was no wonder, because God was hardening their hearts so that they did not want to hear the truth [*veritatem*] at all. By following the crosses and processions led by the clergy through the churches they actually provoked God to wrath rather than appeasing him, because they had risen up against the power set over them by God in their obstinacy of soul, evil doing, pride and strife. . . . Our priests and the clergy of our place had taken their stand in the fight with the people and the crowd [*cum populo et turba*], not remembering that they should stand like a wall for the house of Israel. ([116], 43/52, 64/66; trans., 303–4; trans. mod.)

This passage suggests that Galbert's impatience and irritation had grown to the point that he had finally said something to his fellow citizens. Perhaps he had explained that God was punishing them for their disobedience and their forcible substitution of Thierry for William, a lesson they were not likely to have received charitably.[22]

There are, significantly, only three entries for the eighteen days between this entry and the one for July 27, which begins with a passage that reads like a sigh of relief—"On July 27, the sixth day after the Transfiguration of the Lord on Mount Tabor, the Lord deigned to bring an end in a certain manner both to what he had foreseen and to what we had suffered in this strife" ([119], 1/4; trans., 307)—and goes on to relate the death of William Clito. Two of these entries are brief accounts of the handing over of hostages for the release of Thancmar's wounded nephew, Walter, on July 11, and of the healed Walter's return to captivity on July 25. The only substantial entry for this period of almost three weeks, dated to July 12, is given over almost entirely to an embittered criticism of the citizens and clergy of Bruges. The first, short sentence of this entry records the start of the siege of Aalst. Galbert then observes that "many lies were flying [*multa mendacia volitabant*] among the citizens of Bruges about the affair of the recent siege [the siege, probably, of Oostkamp]" ([118], 3/5; trans., 305; trans. mod.), and goes on to mention the collapse of a water-mill at Bruges that caused part of the moat around the castle to dry up. The citizens rushed to repair the damage, and "then they charged that the undermining of the mill had been done secretly by their enemies so that after the water flowed off . . . [,] the castle and their town would lie open to enemy attack. There were many soothsayers, both laymen and priests [*multi aderant divinatores et laici et sacerdotes*], who were flattering our citizens, foretelling whatever they knew the citizens wanted to hear. In fact, if anyone knowing the truth [*vero sapiens*] about the affair of the siege and the dangers threatening the place and the citizens spoke the truth [*verum profitebatur*], they brought base charges against him and he was silenced" ([118], 10/17; trans., 305). The entry ends with the passage, cited in the last chapter, that castigates the "fawning priests" of Bruges and asserts the essential importance of obedience to legitimate authority.[23]

Galbert's frustration and disgust with the citizens' unwillingness to hear "the truth"—the word occurs six times in the passages dated to July 9 and 12[24]—contrast strikingly with his attitude when he was working on the *Passio* the previous fall. In the Prologue, he stated his intention to relate "only the truth of things" *(rerum veritatem solummodo)* ([Prol.], 16; trans., 80), the "truth [*veritatem*] as it is known to all who suffered the same dangers with me, and I commit it to the memory of our posterity" ([Prol.], 33/35; trans., 80). In fall 1127, he had felt that he shared a common truth with his fellow citizens and had created a record of that common truth that could be passed down to their posterity as part of their common heritage. He had intended this record of commonly agreed-upon common experience to serve as a manifestation of, and perpetual catalyst for, the solidarity of the *Brugenses.* In fall 1127, a common truth had bound the community together, and him to the community. By the summer of 1128, however, he felt that the community was bound together by a common lie and, as a *sapiens* and speaker of truth, he felt himself to be excluded from it. He had become, as Jan Dhondt points out, an individual and isolated figure,[25] and the solitary, unpopular, truth-speaking *sapiens,* opposed to the "many soothsayers, both laymen and priests, who were flattering our citizens," is perhaps a self-portrait of the alienated Galbert, who seems here to be casting himself in the role of an Old Testament prophet preaching repentance to the wayward children of Israel.[26] With a "tyrant and despoiler and evil exactor" as its head; its "idiot," "fawning priests," who "received their fee in candles and pennies and other offerings suitable only for bellies, and . . . acted as if they could bend God himself to injustice"; its "barons and officials and counselors . . . [who] did not guide [the count] . . . in the right path or teach him the honorable customs of the counts his predecessors, but instructed him in pillaging and in crafty and deceitful pretexts by means of which they could demand vast sums of money from the citizens and burghers of the land and extort it from them by violence whenever they wished"; its countryside "so torn by dangers, by ravaging, arson, treachery, and deceit that no honest man could live in security" ([110], 15/16; trans., 291); and its citizens who "had risen up against the power set over them by God in their obstinacy of soul, evil doing, pride and strife," "even though . . . the Lord himself answered Pilate (who was himself set over the Jews of Jerusalem by the Romans) at the very time of the Lord's Passion, 'You would not have any power over me, if it had not been given to you from above by my Father'; and . . . were, indeed, acting unjustly in that while their lord was still alive they had put another lord in his place," Flanders, and above all Bruges, had become, in Galbert's eyes, what John of Salisbury soon thereafter called a "republic of the impious [*res publica impiorum*] . . . [whose] tyrannical head . . . is the image of the devil; its soul is formed of heretical, schismatic and sacrilegious priests . . . assailing the laws of the Lord; the heart of impious counsellors is like a senate of iniquity; its eyes, ears, tongue and unarmed hand are unjust officials, judges and laws; its armed hand is violent soldiers . . . ; its feet are those among the more humble occupations who oppose the precepts of the Lord and legitimate institutions."[27]

Galbert's near silence—except for this critical outburst aimed at the inhabitants of Bruges—for almost three weeks between July 9 and 27 can perhaps be explained in part by a shift in the conflict's principal theater of action to the southeast, but it nonetheless seems a heavy silence, a brooding silence, as if Galbert, disappointed and impatient with the fellow citizens for whom he had thought he was writing, rebuffed and even threatened by them, had decided that it was not worth continuing. William's death at Aalst, and the rapid and unlooked-for resolution to the conflict that it occasioned, did provoke Galbert into making four more manuscript entries,[28] but these entries, with the exception of the long reflection on God's dispensation, provide only the minimum possible conclusion to the work. One can perhaps sense some remnants of solidarity, or a forlorn effort to reestablish a solidarity, with the inhabitants of Bruges in the first part of the long reflection,[29] but it seems, on the whole, to be a private effort to understand God's plan. The *De multro* reads like a true journal at this point, and Galbert seems to be writing more for himself than for anyone else.

I would thus suggest that Galbert may have continued to tinker with the *Passio,* as well as to record new events, until as late as the second week of July 1128. After that point, he added five more entries—a very brief one noting Walter's return to captivity on July 25 ([118], 48/51); a substantial one relating William's death on July 27 ([119], 1/[120], 4); a brief one dated to July 29 relating Thierry's arrival in Ypres and the confusion of William's supporters in the area ([120], 5/14); the long, undated reflection explaining why God had slain William and given the county to Thierry ([120], 15/[121], 43); and a brief, undated final one recording Thierry's triumphal tour through Flanders and his performance of homage to the kings of France and England (122)—and then he quit. He did not revise the *De multro* and prepare it for publication because he no longer felt it had an audience. His work on this chronicle for the inhabitants of Bruges had made him a *sapiens,* had given him a quasi-prophetic insight into the ways of God and men, and had thus set him apart from the very fellow citizens for whom he had written it. In the end, he came to feel that his was a lonely voice crying in the urban wilderness of Bruges, and that, like all prophets, he was without honor—and thus without an audience—in his own country and in his own town.

A fairly good parchment copy of the *Passio* (Prologue-92) may have existed in December 1127, but the presence in this section of several passages beginning with *"notandum,"* the "tacked-on" feeling of chapters 86–91, and the addition of chapter 92 after the "end" of the text mentioned in the Prologue, suggest that this was still a working copy with a certain number of marginal or interlinear notes and perhaps one or more new leaves attached to its end. The obviously composite nature of many of the entries for 1128, and the relatively high number of passages beginning with *"notandum"* in this part of the *De multro,* suggest that the parchment record of these entries was in a more primitive state in July 1128, probably not so crowded and difficult to read as the first parchment record Galbert had faced in May 1127, but nonetheless full of notes and additions.

Henschen and Van Papenbroeck, who were the first to edit the complete text in 1668, wrote that their edition was based on a "most ancient manuscript from Galbert's time or not long afterward,"[30] and since the order of their text is the same as that in the surviving manuscript versions of it, a fair copy of the working, annotated parchment record Galbert left in 1128 must have been made relatively soon after he stopped work on it and was the ancestor of all the existing versions of the text. There is no reason to believe that Galbert himself made this fair copy, however, and the inconsequent situation of certain passages, especially some of those beginning with *"notandum,"* suggests that it was in fact made by someone else who inserted notes and additions where they appeared to belong without making a detailed study of the text.[31]

This fair copy of the *De multro* was a frozen, linear image of a living, incomplete, two-dimensional work-in-progress and imposed a premature and unnatural fixity and finality on it. One is tempted to compare this unfinished *De multro* to an insect trapped in amber or to the human body found in an Alpine glacier a few years ago: it is an incomplete life, pursuing eternally a set of unfulfilled and enigmatic intentions. The *De multro,* however, is not a single entity, not a single work, but a palimpsest on which three distinct works—the *descriptio,* the *Passio,* and the *De multro*—all of them unfinished, have been superimposed. Thanks precisely to its imperfection, this complex work thus tells one more tale in addition to all those enumerated in the preceding chapters. It is a historiographical bildungsroman, relating Galbert's efforts to grasp events in an intellectual construct that gave them meaning and order, the ways he sought to impose order on his account of those events and communicate their lessons to his fellow Flemings, and his growing sense of the nature and substance of history.

A marginal figure standing at the intersection of the clerical, secular, aristocratic, and popular worlds, Galbert extends the boundaries of twelfth-century historiography, taking certain of its tendencies and principles to an extreme. His dramatic, paratactic, speech- and scene-larded, self-effacing narratives, constructed around various ambient narrative models, are the happy fruits of the grafts historical writing had plucked from the storytelling that surrounded it. His unparalleled intellectual rigor, tenacity, and faith also led him, in an extreme application of the theology of history and authority that underlay all historical writing of the time, to crunch events like a philosophical dog, unwilling to let them go until he had found their providential marrow, and sucked from them their sapiential nourishment. But Galbert perhaps pushed the bounds of twelfth-century historiography back furthest simply by writing history, for his was a voice we would normally have never heard. He was not simple, naive, uneducated, or "a man of the people." He was, rather, educated, cultured, shrewd, a comital functionary who kept his ears and eyes open and had undoubtedly seen his share of human duplicity, cruelty—and kindness—and had thought more about them than many others. But like many other educated, well-informed, thoughtful people of his time—and ours—he had never been trained to write literature and had probably never had any serious thought or hope of doing so. The *De multro* thus stretches the boundary of twelfth-century historiography to include this one long reflection from a member of a group of people from whom we almost otherwise never hear, and demonstrates the richness of their lives and the sophistication of their minds. Galbert's efforts to understand an extended series of events in light of the theology of history and authority common in his day, and to apply that theology to the practice of historical writing, make the *De multro* one of the most "intellectual" and "experimental" histories of its time, while its style, form, and viewpoint make it one of the most "popular" ones: it is in its curious way one of the far outposts of early twelfth-century historical writing.

"Galbert insists," writes Nancy Partner, "at whatever cost of effort, that the surface reveal its inner meaning of right judgement and eternal truth. . . . he would not record the surface and leave the significance for a later generation." But she also writes in the same article that

> the only medieval "historian" to record both the literal and the allegorical levels of experience simultaneously and successfully was Dante, who freely created the literal reality of his story to correspond perfectly with what he knew to

be the eternal truth of the soul's pilgrimage to God. For historians of the intractable "given" of literal experience, the letter tended to remain very opaque and the spirit very elusive. When both levels of reality are fixed by the limits of experience and doctrine respectively, something (vitality, plausibility, coherence) will always be lost in the attempt to align them in relations necessary to *figura,* or allegory; the resources of classical rhetoric are not fully adequate (for writer or reader) to the task.[32]

We ought, I think, to add Galbert's name to this exclusive list of historians who were able to record simultaneously the dark empirical letter and the bright empyrean spirit of experience without sacrificing vitality, plausibility, or coherence, and he was able to do so, perhaps, precisely because he did not limit himself to the resources of classical rhetoric, but found new ones in his faith, the practices of the count's fiscal administration, and the tales and conversations, the raconteur culture, that had nourished his imagination. He thus succeeded astonishingly well in finding a form that would let him simultaneously record history and explain it, and one wishes his fellow citizens had been more willing to hear the truth. Their hostility put an end to Galbert's literary ambitions, and his poetic achievement is undoubtedly less than Dante's, but his intellectual achievement is greater insofar as he could not freely create the literal reality of his story to correspond perfectly with what he knew to be the eternal truths behind it, because he believed them both to have been dictated by a mumbling, infinitely subtle Author whose scribe he was, and whose knowledge he beheld like a towering citadel.

Appendices

APPENDIX I

Members of the "Conventus" of Saint Donatian and Clerics Active in the Count's Administration in Bruges (1089–1135)

Some of these identifications are tentative and should not be taken as established (I have not included evidence from suspect or forged charters). The identification of the members of the conventus of Saint Donatian, in particular, will need to be reviewed in light of Véronique Lambert's forthcoming edition of the charters of that church. I have not annotated this list or explained the various tentative identifications since it would take another book to do so adequately and a global impression of the overlap between the clerical members of the count's administration and the members of the conventus was sufficient for my purposes here. I have nonetheless decided to publish this list in the hope that it may be of some use to others who wish to undertake better and more detailed studies of these institutions.

ABBREVIATIONS

† member of conventus of Saint Donatian

£ active in count's administration in Bruges

DeH&V De Hemptinne, Thérèse, and Adriaan Verhulst. *De oorkonden der graven van Vlaanderen (Juli 1128–September 1191), II. Uitgave, v. 1: Regering van Diederik van de Elzas (Juli 1128–17 Januari 1168).* Académie Royale de Belgique, Commission royale d'histoire, Recueil des actes des princes belges/Koninklijke Academie van België, Koninklijke Commissie voor Geschiedenis, Verzameling van de Akten der Belgische Vorsten, 6. Brussels, 1988.

DeM De Marneffe, Edgar. *Cartulaire de l'Abbaye d'Afflighem et des monastères qui en dépendaient.* Analectes pour servir à l'histoire ecclésiastique de la Belgique, 2e section, Série des cartulaires et des documents étendues. Fasc. 1–5. Louvain, 1894–1901.

G&K Gysseling, M., and A. C. F. Koch. *Diplomata Belgica ante annum millesium centesium scripta.* Bouwstoffen en Studiën voor de Gescheidenis en de Lexicografie van het Nederlands, 1. 2 vols. Brussels, 1950.

L Lambert, Véronique. Forthcoming edition of the charters of Saint Donatian.

MB Muller, S., and A. C. Bouman. *Oorkondenboek van het Sticht Utrecht tot 1301.* Vol. 1. Utrecht, 1920.

MF Miraeus, Aubertus (= Aubert Le Mire). *Opera diplomatica et historica.* Vols. 1–2. 2nd ed. Jean François Foppens. Vols. 3–4. Jean François Foppens. *Diplomatum Belgicorum nova collectio, sive supplementum ad "Opera diplomatica" Auberti Miraei.* 4 vols. Louvain and Brussels, 1723–1748.

SOB, ms. 71 Stedelijke Openbare Bibliotheek, Bruges, manuscript 71. A tax list whose earliest entries perhaps date from c. 1127–1128 (and whose latest entries date from late in the century) is currently found on the endsheets of this manuscript. It is reproduced and discussed briefly by Strubbe, *Het Fragment,* 21–22, illustrations iv–v. See also Declercq, "Galbert van Brugge," 110–11.

T Tock, Benoît-Michel. Forthcoming edition of the charters of the bishops of Thérouanne.

V Vercauteren, Fernand. *Actes des comtes de Flandre, 1071–1128.* Brussels, 1938.

VdP&C Van de Putte, F., and Ch. Carton, eds. *Chronicon Vormeselense.* Recueil de chroniques, chartes et autres documents concernant l'histoire et les antiquités de la Flandre Occidentale publié par la Société d'Emulation de Bruges, 1ère série: Chroniques des monastères de Flandre. Bruges, 1847.

LIST OF MEMBERS

Albaldus (†) 1089, *canonicus* (V, 32); 1114, *Formoselensis prepositus* (V, 157–58).

Balduinus/1 (†) 1116, *{frater} Brugensis* (MB, 265); 1122 (?) (MB, 277); 1127, member of *conventus* of Saint Donatian (V, 302); 1129, member of *conventus* of Saint Donatian (VdP&C, 39).

Balduinus/2 (£) 1116, *capellanus curie* (V, 178); 1118–1119, *presbyter, capellanus* (V, 207); 1119, *capellanus* (T, 1119–22; ed. B. Guérard, *Cartulaire de l'abbaye de Saint-Bertin,* n° 28, 239–41); 1123, *capellanus* (V, 262); 1119–1127, *capellanus* (V, 285); 1127, *capellanus, sacerdos (De multro* [18], 4, 18; [23], 6); 1130, *capellanus* (DeH&V, 28); 1133, *notarius* (DeH&V, 47); 1133, *notarius* (DeH&V, 48); 1136, *cancellarius* (DeH&V, 60); 1136, *cancellarius* (DeH&V, 63).

Basilius (†£) 1127–1175, *notarius* (SOB, ms. 71); 1128, *notarius comitis (De multro,* [112], 16); 1129, member of *conventus* of Saint Donatian (VdP&C, 39); 1133, *clericus* (DeH&V, 45, 46); 1137, *cartator comitis* (DeH&V, 69); 1139–1147, *breviator comitis* (DeH&V, 167).

Bernardus (£) 1104, *capellanus* (V, 96); 1106, *capellanus* (V, 102); 1107, *capellanus* (V, 103); 1107, *capellanus* (V, 104); 1109, *capellanus* (V, 107); 1110, *capellanus* (V, 118); 1110, *capellanus* (V, 123); 1112, *capellanus* (V, 140); 1112, *capellanus comitis* (V, 145).

Bertinus (£) 1104, *capellanus* (V, 96); 1107, *capellanus* (V, 103); 1109, *capellanus* (V, 107); 1110, *capellanus comitis* (V, 109); 1115, *capellanus comitis* (V, 171).

Bertulfus/1 (†£) 1089, *canonicus* (V, 32); 1089, *capellanus* (V, 23); 1093, *prepositus Brugensis* (V, 41); . . . 1123, *prepositus Brugensis, archicapellanus* (V, 262) . . . 1127 *(De multro,* passim).

Bertulfus/2 (†) 1096 (G&K, 253); 1101, *diaconus* (V, 82).

Blitro (†) 1100, *canonicus* (L 13; MF, 3:313); 1100 (MF, 1:272–73; DeM, 19); 1116, *{frater} Brugensis* (MB, 265).

Blizonus (£) 1104–1106, *breviarius de Burgis* [*sic*] (V, xxxiv).

Cono (†£) 1093, *canonicus, capellanus* (V, 41); 1096, *capellanus* (V, 65); 1096, *clericus capellanus comitis* (V, 67).

Dodinus (†) 1089, *canonicus* (V, 32); 1096, *decanus* (G&K, 253); 1100, *decanus* (L 13; MF, 3:313); 1101, *decanus* (V, 82).

Ebrardus/Everardus (†£) 1127–1175 (?) (SOB, ms. 71); 1129, member of *conventus* of Saint Donatian, *magister* (VdP&C, 39); 1138/39 (?), *magister E. Casletensis* (DeH&V, 85); 1142/47 (?), *magister de Casleto* (DeH&V, 168); 1166/67 (?), *magister* (DeH&V, 437).

Erlaboldus (†) 1127, *canonicus* (V, 302); 1129, member of *conventus* of Saint Donatian, *presbyter* (VdP&C, 39).

Eustachius (£) 1127, *clericus (De multro,* [16], 15; [18], 16/17).

Everolfus (†) 1100, *canonicus* (L 13; MF, 3:313).

Fromoldus Senior/1 (†£) 1104, *inbreviator* (V, 96); 1107, *notarius* (V, 104); 1109, *canonicus* (V, 106); . . . 1111–1112, *prepositus Furnensis* (V, 136); . . . 1111–1115, *brivarius* (V, 175); . . . 1127, member of *conventus* of Saint Donatian (V, 302); . . . 1128, *presbyter (De multro,* [114], 79); 1129, member of *conventus* of Saint Donatian, *prepositus Furnensis* (VdP&C, 39).

Fromoldus Junior/2 (£) 1127, *notarius* (*De multro,* passim); 1127–1175, (SOB, ms. 71); 1128, *clericus* (DeH&V, 13); 1130, *breviator* (DeH&V, 31); 1129–1130, *notarius* (DeH&V, 37); 1132, *clericus* (DeH&V, 43); 1133, *clericus* (DeH&V, 45); 1132–1133, *notarius* (DeH&V, 49); 1137, *cartator comitis* (DeH&V, 69); 1139, *Brugensis* (DeH&V, 86); 1139, *notarius* (DeH&V, 89); 1141, *breviator* (DeH&V, 97).

Fulco/Folcardus (†£) 1127, *canonicus (De multro,* [46], 1/2); 1127–1175 (SOB, ms. 71); 1139, *cancellarius* (DeH&V, 86); 1144, *prepositus Ariensis* (DeH&V, 120).

Fulpertus/1 (†£) 1084, *clericus* (V, liii, n. 1); 1087, *capellanus* (V, 21); 1089, *canonicus* (V, 32); 1093, *canonicus, capellanus* (V, 41); 1096, *capellanus* (V, 65); 1100, *canonicus* (L 13; MF, 3:313); 1101, *presbyter* (V, 82).

Fulpertus/2 (†) 1113, *canonicus, diaconus* (V, 147); 1127–1175, *canonicus* (SOB, ms. 71).

Galbertus/1 (†) 1100, *canonicus* (L 13; MF, 3:313); 1100 (?), (MF, 1:272–73; DeM, 19); 1101, *diaconus* (V, 82); 1116 (?), *{frater} Brugensis* (MB, 265); 1127–1175 (?), *canonicus* (SOB, ms. 71); 1129 (?), member of *conventus* of Saint Donatian (VdP&C, 39).

Galbertus/2 (†) 1100, *canonicus* (L 13; MF, 3:313); 1100 (?), (MF, 1:272–73; DeM, 19); 1113, *clericus* (V, 147); 1116 (?), *{frater} Brugensis* (MB, 265); 1127–1175 (?), *canonicus* (SOB, ms. 71); 1129 (?), member of *conventus* of Saint Donatian (VdP&C, 39).

Galbertus/3 (£) 1130, *clericus* (DeH&V, 37).

Gerardus/1 (†£) 1123, *magister {Furnensis?}* (V, 262).

Gerardus/2 (†£) 1127–1175 (?), *presbyter* (SOB, ms. 71); 1130, *breviator* (DeH&V, 31); 1133, *clericus* (DeH&V, 45); 1141 (?), *canonicus* (DeH&V, 97).

Godbertus (£) 1124, *clericus* (V, 267); 1127, *clericus comitis (De multro,* [18], 5, 18; [23], 7); 1128, *clericus* (DeH&V, 13).

Gozelo (†) 1110, *canonicus* (V, 118); 1113, *clericus* (V, 147); 1116, *{frater} Brugensis* (MB, 265); 1122 (?) (MB, 277); 1127, member of *conventus* of Saint Donatian (V, 302); 1129, member of *conventus* of Saint Donatian (VdP&C, 39).

Gummarus (†£) 1093, *canonicus, capellanus* (V, 41); 1101, *subdiaconus* (V, 82; V. says that this is another Gummarus); 1105 (?), provost of Our Lady of Bruges (Derolez and Victor, *Corpus Catalogorum Belgii,* 1:29); 1110, *canonicus* (V, 118); 1113, *canonicus, prepositus* (of Our Lady of Bruges?) (V, 147); 1114, archdeacon of Tournai (see Pycke, *Le Chapitre cathédral Notre-Dame de Tournai,* 148–49, 329, 337); died in 1114 (?) (Derolez and Victor, *Corpus Catalogorum Belgii,* 1:29); 1122 (?), *filius Bertulfi,* former *clericus Brugensis* (MB, 276).

Helias (†) 1110, *decanus* (V, 118); 1113, *decanus* (V, 147); 1116, *decanus* (MB, 265); 1122, *decanus* (V, 246); 1127, *decanus* (*De multro,* passim); 1127, *decanus* (V, 302); 1129, *decanus* (VdP&C, 39).

Henricus (£) 1118, *cancellarius* (V, 194); 1122, *capellanus* (V, 250); 1139 (?), *notarius* (DeH&V, xliii, n. 97); 1140 (?), *breviator* (DeH&V, 96).

Hugo/1 (†) 1113, *canonicus, presbyter* (V, 147); 1127–1175 (?) (SOB, ms. 71).

Hugo/2 (£) 1127–1175 (?) (SOB, ms. 71); 1129, *clericus* (DeH&V, 25).

Huno (†) 1110, *presbyter* (V, 109).

Ingaricus/Iggricus (†£) 1085–1093, *clericus* (G&K, 301); 1089, *canonicus* (V, 32); 1105, *capellanus* (V, 97); 1111–1112, *notarius* (V, 136); 1115, *notarius* (V, 166).

Joseph (†) 1129, member of *conventus* of Saint Donatian (VdP&C, 39).

Lambertus (†) 1129, member of *conventus* of Saint Donatian, *presbyter* (VdP&C, 39).

Lambinus (£) 1129, *breviator {Furnensis?}* (DeH&V, 25).

Ledelinus (†£) 1087, *capellanus* (V, 21); 1089, *canonicus* (V, 32); 1093, *canonicus, capellanus* (V, 41); 1095–1096, *capellanus* (V, 70); 1096, *capellanus* (V, 65).

Letbertus/1 (†£) 1087, *capellanus* (V, 21); 1089, *prepositus Brugensis* (V, 23).

Letbertus/2 (†) 1089, *canonicus* (V, 32); 1101, *diaconus* (V, 82).

Letbertus/3 (†£) 1113, *clericus* (V, 147); 1127, member of *conventus* of Saint Donatian (V, 302); 1127–1175, *canonicus* (SOB, ms. 71); 1129, member of *conventus* of Saint Donatian (VdP&C, 39); 1136, *decanus, notarius* (DeH&V, 60); 1135–1145, *decanus* (see Declercq, "Dekens," 49–50).

Littera (†) 1113, *canonicus, prepositus* (V, 147); 1116, *{frater} Brugensis* (MB, 265); 1127, *canonicus (De multro,* [85], 8/9, 29).

Lugericus (£) 1093, *notarius* (V, 41).

Nicholas (†) 1129, member of *conventus* of Saint Donatian (VdP&C, 39).

Odgerus/1 (£) 1107, *notarius* (V, 103); 1111–1112, *notarius* (V, 136); 1112 (?) (V, 145); 1113, *cancellarius* (T 1113-1; MF, 4:192); 1113, *cancellarius* (V, 148); 1114, *notarius* (V, 150); 1114, *prepositus S. Audomari* (V, 158); 1115, *notarius* (V, 166); 1115, *cancellarius* (V, 174); 1116, *notarius* (V, 178); 1116, *cancellarius* (V, 184); 1117, *prepositus S. Audomari* (V, 188); . . . 1130, *gerulus sigilli* (DeH&V, 31); . . . 1137, [*gerulus sigilli*] (DeH&V, 72); . . . 1138, *prepositus S. Audomari* (DeH&V, 82); 1128–1142, *prepositus S. Audomari* (DeH&V, 101); 1134–1142, *prepositus S. Audomari* (DeH&V, 103).

Odgerus/2 (£) 1110, *capellanus* (V, 118); 1111–1115 (?), *clericus* (V, 172); 1112 (?) (V, 145); 1116, *capellanus curie* (V, 178); 1121, *prepositus Truncinensis* (V, 236); 1122, *prepositus Truncinensis* (V, 246); 1137, *prepositus Truncinensis* (DeH&V, 71); 1138, *prepositus Truncinensis* (DeH&V, 81).

Odgerus Junior/3 (£) 1127, *clericus* (*De multro,* [18], 7, 10, 16; [23], 6); 1128, *clericus* (DeH&V, 13); 1130, *notarius* (DeH&V, 28); 1139, *notarius* (DeH&V, 89); 1139, *notarius* (DeH&V, xliii, n. 97, xlv, n. 119); 1140, *breviator* (DeH&V, 95); 1140, *breviator* (DeH&V, 96); 1141, *cancellarius* (DeH&V, 100); 1128–1142, *cancellarius* (DeH&V, 101); 1142, *capellanus comitis* (DeH&V, 109); 1142, *notarius* (DeH&V, 113); . . . 1145, *scriba* (DeH&V, 147); . . . 1146, *notarius* (DeH&V, 152); 1147–1149, *notarius* (DeH&V, 184).

Radulfus/1 (†) 1089, *canonicus* (V, 32); 1110 (?), *canonicus* (V, 118).

Radulfus/2 (†£) 1110 (?), *canonicus* (V, 118); 1122 (?), *clericus* (V, 254); 1127, *magister (De multro,* [85], 10); 1129–1130, *canonicus, magister* (DeH&V, 37).

Radulfus/3 (†) 1127–1175, *presbyter* (SOB, ms. 71); 1129, member of *conventus* of Saint Donatian, *presbyter* (VdP&C, 39).

Radulphus Lupus (†) 1129, member of *conventus* of Saint Donatian (VdP&C, 39).

Rainlofus/1 (†) 1100, *canonicus* (L 13; MF, 3:313); 1101, *presbyter* (V, 82); 1114, *decanus Furnensis* (DeH&V, l, n. 167); 1123, *decanus Furnensis* (V, 262).

Rainlofus/2 (£) 1135, *notarius* (DeH&V, 56).

Reinarus/1 (†£) 1080, *vice cancellarius* (V, 16); 1089, *prepositus Brugensis* (V, 32).

Reinarus Parvus/2 (†£) 1089 (V, 23); 1089, *canonicus* (V, 32); 1093, *canonicus, capellanus* (V, 41); 1096 (?) (G&K, 253); 1096, *clericus capellanus comitis* (V, 67); 1100 (?), *canonicus* (L 13; MF, 3:313); 1100 (?), (MF, 1:272–73; DeM, 19); 1103, *capellanus comitis* (V, 89); 1105, *capellanus* (V, 97); 1110, *capellanus* (V, 118); 1116, *capellanus curie* (V, 178); 1119, *capellanus* (T, 1119-2; B. Guérard, *Cartulaire de l'abbaye de Saint-Bertin,* n° 28, p. 239–41).

Reinarus/3 (†£) 1096 (?) (G&K, 253); 1100 (?), *canonicus* (L 13; MF, 3:313); 1100 (?), (MF, 1:272–73; DeM, 19); 1101 (?), *subdiaconus* (V, 82); 1110, *notarius* (V, 119); 1112, *notarius* (V, 140); 1113 (?), *notarius* (Tock, 1113-3; Arch. dép. Pas-de-Calais, H Cercamp non coté, fol. 1–2).

Reinarus/4 (†£) 1096 (?) (G&K, 253); 1100 (?), *canonicus* (L 13; MF, 3:313); 1100 (?), (MF, 1:272–73; DeM, 19); 1101 (?), *subdiaconus* (V, 82); 1111–1112, *clericus* (V, 136); 1114, *clericus* (V, 150); 1115, *clericus* (V, 166); 1122, *clericus* (V, 254).

Rippertus (†) 1113, *canonicus, diaconus* (V, 147); 1116, *{frater} Brugensis* (MB, 265); 1122 (?) (MB, 277); 1127, member of *conventus* of Saint Donatian (V, 302); 1129, member of *conventus* of Saint Donatian, *presbyter* (VdP&C, 39).

Riquardus (†) 1113, *clericus* (V, 147); 1127–1175, (SOB, ms. 71).

Robertus/1 (†) 1127 (?), member of *conventus* of Saint Donatian (V, 302); 1127–1175, *canonicus* (SOB, ms. 71); 1129, member of *conventus* of Saint Donatian (VdP&C, 39).

Robertus/2 (†) 1127 (?), member of *conventus* of Saint Donatian (V, 302); 1129, member of *conventus* of Saint Donatian (VdP&C, 39).

Robertus/3 (†) 1119–1127, *feodum Roberti presbiteri* (V, 287); 1127, *custos, presbyter (De multro,* [85], 9, 19/20, 22, 24); 1127–1175, *presbyter, canonicus* (SOB, ms. 71).

Rodgerus (†£) 1127, *prepositus Brugensis (De multro,* [78], 16, 23); 1127, *prepositus Brugensis* (V, 302, pre), 1127–1175, *prepositus Brugensis* (SOB, ms. 71); 1128, *prepositus Brugensis* (DeH&V, 13); 1128, *prepositus Brugensis, cancellarius comitis* (DeH&V, 20); 1128, *prepositus Brugensis* (DeH&V, 23); 1129, *prepositus Brugensis* (VdP&C, 39); 1130, *prepositus Brugensis* (DeH&V, 31); . . . 1156, *prepositus Brugensis* (DeH&V, 251).

Salomon (£) 1123, *capellanus comitissae* (V, 262); 1124, *capellanus comitissae* (V, 267).

Siboldus (£) 1085–1093, *clericus* (G&K, 301); 1093, *notarius* (V, 41).

Simon (†) 1113, *clericus* (V, 147); 1116, *{frater} Brugensis* (MB, 265).

Tancradus (†) 1089, *canonicus* (V, 32); 1096 (G&K, 253); 1100, *canonicus* (L 13; MF, 3:313); 1100, (MF, 1:272–73; DeM, 19); 1101, *subdiaconus* (V, 82); 1110, *canonicus* (V, 118); 1111–1115, *canonicus* (V, 172).

Theodericus (£) 1106, *notarius* (V, 102); 1107, *notarius* (V, 103); 1107, *notarius* (V, 104); 1110, *notarius* (V, 123); 1116, *notarius* (V, 176).

Waldricus (£) 1124, *clericus* (V, 267).

Walterus/1 (†) 1113, *canonicus, presbyter* (V, 147); 1127 (?), member of *conventus* of Saint Donatian (V, 302).

Walterus/2 (†£) 1127 (?), member of *conventus* of Saint Donatian (V, 302); 1141, *clericus* (DeH&V, 97); 1142 (1150?), *capellanus* (DeH&V, 107); 1145, *canonicus* (DeH&V, 131); 1148, *clericus Rodgeri prepositi Brugensis* (DeH&V, 183); 1152, *capellanus, notarius* (DeH&V, 220); 1154, *prepositus Furnensis, capellanus* (DeH&V, 227); . . . 1166–1169, *prepositus Furnensis* (DeH&V, lvi).

APPENDIX II

Oral Sources

Chapter, ll. (Trans. p.)	Source Information reported
[3], 1/2 (87)	anonymous report ("it is said" [*aiunt*]) conspiracy against Charles
[12], 6/11 (111)	Charles's chaplains Charles's restlessness the night before his assassination
[12], 35/39 (113)	Charles what he learned while on Crusade
[12], 45/53 (114)	students from Bruges studying in Laon when word of Charles's death reached them
[12], 45/53 (114)	merchants from Bruges doing business in London when word of Charles's death reached them
[26], 38/40 (149)	escapees from the siege of Raverschoot the siege of the town by Gervaise
[39], 1/3 (171)	squires of the abbess of Origny Isaac's capture and execution in Thérouanne
[45], 1/2 (182)	anonymous report ("so they say" [*aiunt*]) the role of Thancmar's nephews in the count's death
[46], 6/11 (185)	anonymous report ("we have heard" [*audivimus*]) Bertulf's flight
[49], 1/4 (190)	Woltra Cruual false report of Henry I's support for William of Ypres
[57], 20/25 (209)	anonymous report ("it is said" [*aiunt*]) the captive Bertulf's reception in Ypres
[58], 39/42 (213)	a squire the deaths and hanging on a wheel of Bertulf and Guy of Steenvorde
[66], 1/36 (227)	anonymous report ("it was announced to the king" [*nunciatum est regi*]) Count William's reception in Saint-Omer

[71], 12/14 (239)	anonymous report ("it is said" [*aiunt*]) murderous agreement between Dedda and Erembald
[80], 1/4 (249)	anonymous report ("we heard" [*relatum est nobis*]) execution of Borsiard in Lille
[80], 15/17 (250)	anonymous report ("it is said" [*aiunt*]) the burning of a church in Oudenaarde in which many people had taken refuge
[84], 57/58 (256)	anonymous report ("we have heard" [*audivimus*]) Bertulf's execution in Ypres
[93], 1/11 (265)	implicit report events at the fair in Lille in August 1127
[94], 1/14 (266)	implicit report rebellion of Saint-Omer in February 1128
[95], 1/61 (267)	implicit report confrontation in Ghent and Ypres between Count William and Daniel and Ivan
[96], 1/5 (271)	anonymous report ("the news, which was true, reached us" [*fama vera nos percellebat*]) the reception of Thierry of Alsace in Ghent
[97], 16/19 (272)	Gervaise, castellan of Bruges Arnold, nephew of Charles, received as count for a second time by people of Saint-Omer
[98], 9/10 (273)	anonymous report ("the people of Bruges heard" [*audierant Brugenses*]) the count plans to come to Bruges from Aalter
[101], 10/13 (277)	anonymous report ("we heard" [*audivimus*]) released from prison in Lille, William of Ypres joins Count William's forces in Courtrai
[102], 9/11 (278)	anonymous report ("it was reported" [*relatum est*]) William of Ypres's release from prison
[110], 32/34 (291)	anonymous report ("they say" [*aiunt*]) Count Thierry's sickness after he has been sprinkled with water by a sorceress in Lille
[112], 1/3 (293)	anonymous report ("news reached us" [*fama retulit*]) word from Lens that Louis VI has withdrawn from the siege of Lille
[112], 3/5 (293)	implicit report a sorceress is eviscerated in Ghent

[112], 11/13 (293)	implicit report Count William raids Oostkamp
[113], 47/51 (296)	anonymous report ("on hearing all this news" [*auditis his omnibus*]) capture of Walter of Zomergem and his men at Aalter; success of Daniel and Ivan at Rupelmonde
[116], 59/64 (304)	anonymous report ("we heard" [*audivimus*]) Bruges laid under an ecclesiastical ban and anathema by archbishop of Reims and his suffragan bishops

APPENDIX III

Written Sources

Chapter, ll. (Trans. p.)	Source / Contents
[5], 6/10 (93)	letter *(litterae)* from Crusaders invitation to Charles to become king of Jerusalem
[21], 30/34 (135–36)	letter *(litterae)* from Bertulf to Simon, bishop of Noyon Bertulf sends greetings *(transmittit salutem)* to Simon and asks him to purify Saint Donatian
[25], 1/15 (144)	written message *(scriptus)* from William of Ypres to Bertulf and his party William sends greetings *(salutat)* to Bertulf and his party and offers them, in writing, aid and allegiance
[25], 38/43 (145)	letter *(litterae)* from Bertulf to Simon, bishop of Noyon (perhaps the same letter mentioned in [21], 30/34) Bertulf asserts his innocence with respect to the murder of Charles and asks the bishop to purify Saint Donatian
[25], 43/44 (145)	letter *(litterae)* from Bertulf to John, bishop of Thérouanne same as preceding letter
[45], 65/69 (185)	letters *(litterae)* from the barons of Flanders to those besieged in the tower of Saint Donatian, shot into the tower by arrow offers of friendship and aid
[47], 1/24 (187)	letter *(litterae)* from Louis VI in Arras to the princes and barons of the siege in Bruges the king sends greetings *(mandat salutem)* to the princes and barons and summons them to Arras in order to elect a new count
[47], 24/35 (188)	letter *(litterae)* from Thierry in Alsace to the princes of the siege and the inhabitants of Flanders Thierry sends greetings *(salutem)* to the barons of the siege and all the inhabitants of the land, and claims the countship

[49], 10/12 (191)	daily letters *(quotidianae litterae)* exchanged between William of Ypres and the Erembalds communications of their mutual desires and secret aims
[49], 23/25 (191)	a sealed letter *(litterae signatae)* from William of Ypres to Bertulf and his party (perhaps the same as [25], 1/15) William sends greetings *(mandat salutem)* to Bertulf and his party and offers them aid
[52], 7/52 (195)	a sealed letter or mandate *(litterae signatae, mandatum)* from Louis VI to the inhabitants of Flanders the king sends greetings and an assurance of fidelity *(salutem et fidem)* to the inhabitants of Flanders, describes the election of William Clito as count of Flanders, and solicits their consent to the election
[55], 10/27 (201–2)	charter *(charta)* of the liberty of the church and of the privileges of Saint Donatian no specific content mentioned other than the right to elect the provost
[55], 27/43 (203)	a charter *(chartula, charta)* of agreement between the count and the citizens of Bruges the count remits in perpetuity the toll and ground rent on houses in Bruges
[55], 49/82 (204–5)	a letter *(litterae)* from and charter *(charta)* drawn up by the leading men of Aardenburg the leading men of Aardenburg request a series of rights and privileges
[57], 6/9 (208)	mention of earlier letter *(mandat salutationem)* from William of Ypres to Bertulf and his party (see [25], 1/15)
[87], 1/19 (259)	inquest into the murder of Charles a list of the different charges to be considered by the jurors
[95], 62/66 (270)	letter (?) from Ivan and Daniel to the fortified towns of Flanders Iwan and Daniel send greetings *(transmittunt mandantes salutem)* to the towns of Flanders and propose a treaty of mutual defense against Count William
[98], 1/8 (273)	letter *(litterae)* from the men of Ghent, Ivan, and Daniel to the burghers of Bruges the authors ask the burghers of Bruges to choose definitively between William and Thierry within three days

[99], 3/12 (274)
letter (?) from Thierry of Alsace and his sister, the countess of Holland, to the clergy and people of Bruges
Thierry and his sister send greetings *(mandant salutem)* to the people of Bruges and solicit their support for his claim to the countship

[101], 29/32 (278)
letter (?) from knights of Oostkerke to Count William
the knights ("with their names inscribed on parchment" [*ex nomine inscriptos parchameno*]) renounce their faith and homage

[106], 5/13 (283)
letter *(litterae)* from Louis VI to the citizens of Bruges
the king asks that eight representatives be sent from Bruges (as from the other fortified towns of Flanders) to Arras on Palm Sunday to discuss the conflict between Count William and the towns

[107], 26/28 (287)
letter *(litterae)* from bishop Simon of Noyon to the people of Ghent
the bishop suspends divine services in the churches of Ghent

[113], 61/64 (296)
letter *(litterae)* from the citizens of Ypres to those of Bruges
the citizens of Ypres request a meeting to discuss measures they might take in common

[121], 9/14 (311)
mention of the letter *(litterae)* sent by Thierry of Alsace to the barons of Flanders (compare [47], 24/35)
Thierry claims countship

APPENDIX IV

Messages

Chapter, ll. (Trans., p.)	Source Contents
[4], 7/15 (90)	the wise and powerful men of the Holy Roman Empire send "suitable delegates" *(legatos idoneos)* to Charles they ask Charles to become emperor
[19], 7/10 (130)	Bertulf sends a messenger *(mittit nuntium)* from his residence to his nephews in Saint Donatian he forbids them to harm Fromold Junior
[21], 38/42 (136)	Bertulf sends a boy *(mandat per quemdam garcionem)* to Walter of Vladslo he sends Walter money and asks him to come to his aid
[22], 1/2 (137)	the Erembalds send a messenge *(transmittunt)* to the abbot of Saint Peter's Abbey in Ghent they ask him to come to carry off Charles's body
[22], 60/63 (140)	the Erembalds send a message *(mandant)* to the citizens of Bruges they will not try to remove Charles's body against the citizens' will
[25], 1/15 (143–44)	William of Ypres sends Godescalc Taihals as a messenger *(internuntius, nuntius)* to the Erembalds he greets the Erembalds publicly on William's behalf and brings a letter to them from William (see above in Appendix II)
[25], 33/35 (145)	Bertulf sends a message *(mandat)* to William of Ypres he promises the countship to William and encourages him to secure the homage of everyone he can
[25], 36/37 (145)	Bertulf sends a message *(transmandat)* to the men of Veurne he tells them to swear loyalty to William of Ypres
[25], 44/47 (145–46)	Bertulf sends a message *(mandat)* to Robert of Crecques he tells him to fortify his house

[25], 53/56 (146)	Bertulf sends a message *(mandat)* to the men of coastal Flanders around Veurne he asks them to come to his aid
[27], 15/26 (150)	a few leading men of Bruges send messengers *(summittunt internuntios)* to Gervaise they offer him their help and promise to open the gates of the city to him
[33], 6/10 (160)	the castellan of Ghent sends a message *(mandat)* from Bruges to the burghers of Ghent he asks them to assemble their forces and come to the siege
[47], 23/39 (188)	Thierry of Alsace sends a messenger *(nuntius)* to the barons of the siege in Bruges the messenger bears the letter in which Thierry claims the countship (see above in Appendix II)
[52], 18/52 (195)	Louis VI sends Walter of Vladso to the people of Bruges Walter bears the king's letter *(lator litterarum)* announcing the election of William Clito as count of Flanders
[52], 52/55 (198)	the citizens of Bruges send a message *(mandant)* to the people of Flanders they ask them to come to consider whether or not to approve the election of the new count
[53], 1/6 (198)	the king sends messengers *(nuntii)* to Raverschoot to meet with representatives from Bruges and Ghent negotiations concerning the election of William as count
[66], 8/10 (228)	Count William sends a messenger *(internuntius)* to the crowd of young men armed with bows who come toward him as he approaches Saint-Omer he asks them what they want with him
[69], 38/45 (235)	Robert the Frisian uses a cleric of his household as a courier *(internuntius)* to carry messages *(mandata deferre)* to the barons of Flanders communications concerning the plot to overthrow Robert's nephew Arnold
[95], 53/61 (270)	Ivan and Daniel send messengers *(praemittunt internuntios)* from Roeselare to Count William in Ypres they renounce their homage to him
[99], 16/17 (275)	the people of Bruges send a message *(transmittunt)* to Daniel they ask him to come to their aid

[100], 5/18 (101)	Gervaise sends a message *(mandat)* to the leading citizens of Bruges he asks them to meet with him outside the town walls
[108], 7/11 (288)	Count Thierry sends Gervaise as a messenger *(nuntius)* to Lambert of Aardenburg, and to the men of Oostburg and Aardenburg he wants them to refrain from battle and come to him to be reconciled
[120], 28/29 (309)	a messenger *(nuncius)* sent to Bruges (by Thierry of Alsace?) announces the death of William Clito

APPENDIX V

Parallel Passages from Walter of Thérouanne's "Vita Karoli" and Galbert of Bruges's "De multro"

I have listed the most obviously parallel passages in the two chronicles below. Many of these parallels are not especially telling in and of themselves. The first three, for example—an explanation of the chronicle's origin in a desire to record the acts of God for some "you" (John, bishop of Thérouanne, for Walter; an unknown person for Galbert) and posterity for whom the record will have a salutary moral effect, an apology for the aridity of one's style, and a renunciation of the colors of rhetoric—are prologic commonplaces; and yet the fact that all three are used by both authors and certain other verbal echoes make the prologues of the two works sound almost like a medieval call and response. This dialogic effect is further enhanced through common elements in Walter's and Galbert's descriptions of Charles's life and reign up to the moment of the assassination and in their common development of certain scenes and events, like the deaths of the castellan of Bourbourg, of his sons and Walter of Loker, the deaths of Bertulf and Guy of Steenvoorde, and so on.

The exact parallels between the two texts are never more than a few words or a phrase, but these tiny echoes can be striking. It is interesting, for example, that Walter uses the adjective *furibundus* (furious or raging) only once in the *Vita,* to describe Borsiard ([25], 549, 17), while Galbert uses it twice in the *De multro,* the first time to describe Borsiard ([12], 15; trans., 112), the second time to describe Borsiard and Isaac ([17], 42; trans., 126); that Walter writes that the mortally wounded castellan of Bourbourg was "still gasping his last breaths" *(palpitantem adhuc in extremis)* ([28], 550, 37) when he was dragged out of the church and killed, while Galbert writes that he was "still breathing" *(adhuc spirantem)* ([17], 25; trans., 125); that Walter writes that the plot to kill Charles was made "after the provost and his messengers had withdrawn [*corporaliter amoto*] so that he who did everything, would appear to do nothing [*qui totum faciebat, sic facere nichil videretur*]" ([23], 548, 20/21), while Galbert writes that "though the provost did not take part and acted as if he had done nothing [when Borsiard and his men raided Thancmar's stronghold], he actually did everything [*absens tamen et quasi nihil fecisset, . . . omnia fecit*] by direction and deception" ([9], 9/10; trans. 103); and that Walter refers to the provost as "the most splendid son of this subcelestial world and the wealthiest in all of this world's riches, and the most powerful of almost all this land, second only to the count" *(huius quidem seculi filium splendidissimum et omnibus mundi istius divitiis affluentissimum, et, post comitem solum, fere totius terre huius potentis-*

simum) ([39], 555, 22/26), while Galbert writes that "the provost . . . was more powerful than anyone in the realm except the count and more eminent in reputation and religion" *(post comitem in regno potentior et fama atque religione gloriosior)* ([8], 1/2; trans. 101).

In certain cases, Galbert's descriptions of scenes or events can be read as developing or illustrating or reworking Walter's descriptions of these same scenes and events. Walter, for example, twice notes that the "dark deeds" of the assassination were plotted at night,[1] whereas Galbert actually stages the scene at night.[2] Galbert's description of the hanging on a wheel of Bertulf's and Guy of Steenvorde's bodies[3] is likewise similar to Walter's,[4] and seems to betray simultaneously a desire to disguise that similarity[5] and to develop the idea of the traitors' embrace.

Galbert's account of Bertulf's execution also appears to develop two themes he found in Walter's text.[6] His description of the crowd's reception and treatment of Bertulf, first, seems inspired by Walter's, although Galbert is more graphic (except for the fish heads) and emphasizes both Bertulf's humiliation and the crowd's frenzy. He also emphasizes Bertulf's stoicism more (and, as we have seen, develops the comparison between Bertulf and Christ) by showing how it exasperated at least one member of the crowd. His description thus reads like an amplification of Walter's.

The *De multro* shares at least three important themes with the *Vita,* moreover. One of them, the sacrilegious character of the murder, which was committed in "a holy place and a holy time," is discussed in Chapter 5.[7] The second of these themes is a rhetorical question that Walter attributes to Borsiard. When the count returned to Ypres at the end of February, writes Walter, he was informed of the depredations perpetrated by the Erembalds (evidently) in the region of Bruges and, acting on the advice of his barons, he decided to go there and see the damage for himself "even though he was by no means unaware of their malicious machinations against him—especially because the aforesaid Burchard was accused of having already said some time before: 'If someone were to kill the count, who would avenge him?'" *(si quis comitem occideret, quis eum vindicaret?)* ([20], 547, 20/22). Galbert refers to this question, which he attributes to the Erembalds corporately, twice: in chapter 14 and in chapter 37.[8] The initial version of chapter 37 was written before the initial version of chapter 14 and it is possible that the assassins' "proverb" was first mentioned in the first version of chapter 37 and then mentioned again in chapter 14 in order to create a thematic link between the introduction and the body of the account. The passage in chapter 37—which says that the assassins "could remember" their proverb which had finally "achieved its just and full meaning"—seems to look back to the passage in chapter 14, however, suggesting that it was added to chapter 37, or at least that a first allusion to the proverb in chapter 37 was rewritten, after chapter 14 had been written. Here again, that is, Galbert may have been struck by a passage in the *Vita* which he developed in his own way in the *De multro.*

The third, and most important, theme that Galbert may have discovered in the *Vita* and developed in his own chronicle is that of God's punishing the sins of one generation in a subsequent one. Galbert develops this theme at two points in the passages (modern chapters 68–71) he intercalated toward the end of the primitive journal when he made his first set of additions to it. These passages relate how in Charles's death and the elimination of the Erembalds two ancient crimes were punished in the fourth generation of their perpetrators' descendants or successors.[9] This theme was obviously an important one for Galbert, and one can almost sense his excitement as he discovered its explanatory power. Since he introduced it in passages intercalated in the primitive journal during the first set of additions, however, he does not seem to have come across it until after May 1127. He could have discovered it in the first chapter of the *Vita* where Walter writes: "Indeed, on that day of that year the lives of many people were jeopardized through the life of one man and, according to God's just judgement, the deserved deaths of many men were engendered in a kind of horrible breeding [*terribili quadam generatione*] by the undeserved death of one man. For then, when the man upon whom, second only to God, the people's welfare had until then been founded was taken from them, the iniquity of our fathers was remembered in the sight of the Lord, as the prophet said, and our old sins were castigated with a new punishment [*tunc namque secundum prophetam in memoriam rediit iniquitas patrum nostrorum in conspectu Domini, et antiqua peccata nostra noua ceperunt ultione feriri*]" ([1], 539, 33/37). Walter's reference, it is true, is to Psalms 108.14 while Galbert's is to Exodus,[10] but we nonetheless find in Walter's text the key terms *(iniquitas patrum, antiqua peccata, noua ultio)*, and the essential idea (God punishes the crimes of one generation in subsequent generations) of Galbert's theme.[11]

Galbert never mentions Walter or the *Vita* and never cites the *Vita* verbatim. Thus it is impossible to prove that he had read Walter's chronicle before he finished his own. Each of the parallels found below, moreover, can probably be accounted for in other ways: common sources, a common reaction to a common event by men who were of relatively similar backgrounds and training, and so on. Taken together, however, the relatively large number of parallels and verbal echoes between the two texts nonetheless suggest, at least, a possible influence of the *Vita* on the *De multro.*

These parallels could also be explained, of course, by Walter's having read Galbert's text and been influenced by it before he completed the *Vita.* It seems more likely that Galbert was influenced by Walter, however, for four reasons. First, it is more likely that a clericus would be influenced by an archdeacon than an archdeacon by a clericus. Second, almost all the important information contained in the *Vita* is also found in Galbert's chronicle,[12] while the contrary is not true. Third, and most importantly, the parallel passages in the *De multro* are concentrated heavily in the chapters added to the primitive journal between May and December—and most probably between c. September 10 and c. December 17—1127 whereas the corresponding passages in the *Vita* are spread throughout the work. Fourth, the parallel themes or ideas are often more developed in the *De multro* than in the *Vita.*

Vita Karoli	*De multro*
Prologue, 537, 37/538, 4	Prologue, 29–43
Prologue, 538, 8/9	Prologue, 17, 35–36
Prologue, 538, 11/16	Prologue, 14/18
Prologue, 538, 20/23 (compare [43], 556, 49/557, 1)	[14], 19/25
[1], 539, 35/39 (see Chapter 3, pp. 71–72)	[69], 80/83, [71], 28/36
[2], 540, 14/19	[1], 3/6; [12], 29/41
[11], 544, 1/17	[2], 14/[3], 36
[12], 544, 33/37	[1], 20/22
[13], 545, 13/15	[6], 13/19
[19], 547, 3/7	[9], 30/32
[20], 547, 16/17	[10], 1/8
[20], 547, 20/23	[14], 5/11; [37], 28/33
[21], 547, 35/37 (compare [24], 548, 30)	[11], 43/54 (esp. 51)
[22], 547, 43/548, 9	[10], 28/47
[23], 548, 16/19	[11], 4/10
[23], 548, 19/22	[9], 9/10
[24], 548, 24/30 (compare [50], 559, 43/47)	[11], 1/43
[25], 549, 2/3	[15], 25/26
[25], 549, 17	[12], 15; [17], 42
[26], 549, 33/35 (see Chapter 5, pp. 117–19)	[6], 13/19; [26], 4/10; [38], 44/49
[27], 550, 18/20	[6], 7/10
[28], 550, 24/38	[16], 1/6, 16/33; [17], 24/31
[28], 550, 38/44 (see Chapter 5, pp. 129–30)	[17], 8/24, 31/54
[29], 551, 3/4	[21], 15/18
[29], 551, 6/13	[22], 7/21
[30], 551, 14/49	[22], 53/60
[38], 554, 21/49 (see Chapter 4, pp. 108–11)	[57], 1/93
[39], 555, 1/12 (see Chapter 4, pp. 106–8)	[58], 1/30
[39], 555, 18/21	[58], 30/39
[39], 555, 22/26	[8], 1/2
[43], 557, 1/5	[12], 43/55; [16], 49/[17], 2

[45], 558, 5/9
[46], 558, 13/21
[46], 558, 23/25
[46]/[47], 558, 24/40
[48]/[49], 559, 1/35
[50], 559, 37/42
[66], 1/38
[73], 13/17
[23], 20/22
[77], 1/23
[79], 1/12
[81], 3/52

APPENDIX VI

Passages in the "Passio Karoli" That May Have Been Revised or Added during the Transformation of the "Descriptio"

Chapter, ll. (Trans. p.)	Reason
[Prol.]/[14] (79–118)	provide background
[15] (118–19)	revised to emphasize Charles's "passion"?
[17], 12/14 (125)	refers to [7], 36/39; trans., 100
[17], 13/14 (125)	echoes [8], 10/13; trans., 101; [11], 27/28; trans., 109; [13], 28/30; trans., 116
[18], 28/29 (129)	refers to [7], 36/39; trans., 100
[22], 39 (139)	echoes [Prol.], 13; trans., 79; [38], 47; trans., 171; [68], 16; trans., 232; [70], 7/11; trans., 237
[25], 47/52 (146)	refers to [7], 22/35; trans., 99–100
[26], 6/10 (147–48)	echoes [6], 13/19; trans., 94; and [38], 48/49; trans., 171
[26], 9/10 (148)	echoes [Prol.], 13; trans., 79; [6], 22; trans., 95; [6], 35/36; trans., 96; [12], 22/23; trans., 112; [29], 47/48; trans., 156; [43], 36/38; trans., 180; [44], 5/6; trans., 181; [64], 16/17; trans., 225
[29], 47/48 (156)	echoes [Prol.], 13; trans., 79; [6], 22; trans., 95; [6], 35/36; trans., 96; [12], 22/23; trans., 112; [26], 9/10; trans., 148; [43], 36/38; trans., 180; [44], 5/6; trans., 181; [64], 16/17; trans., 225

[35], 14/19 (163)	added later? compare [37], 7/17; trans., 167
[35], 33/45 (164)	added later? begins with "and it should be known" *(et notandum)* and echoes [Prol.], 18/32
[35], 46/54 (164–65)	added later? unrelated to what comes before and after; set off in manuscripts from what comes before
[36], 1/19 (165)	added later? begins with "it should not be forgotten" *(hic non est praetereundum)*
[37], 7/17 (167)	added later? compare [35], 14/19; trans., 163
[37], 24/33 (168)	echoes [14], 5/11; trans., 117
[37], 33/[38], 56 (168–71)	added later? (1) begins with ("and it should be known" [*et sciendum*]); (2) contains elaborate speeches; (3) [37], 47/49; trans., 169, echoes [6], 21; trans., 95; [52], 15; trans., 195; and [52], 38/39; trans., 197; (4) [38], 47/48; trans., 171, echoes [Prol.], 13; trans., 79; [22], 39; trans., 139; [68], 16; trans., 232; [70], 7/11; trans., 237; and (5) [38], 48/49; trans. 171, echoes [6], 13/19; trans., 94; and [26], 6/10; trans., 148
[43], 36/38 (180)	echoes [Prol.], 13; trans., 79; [6], 22; trans., 95; [6], 35/36; trans., 96; [12], 22/23; trans., 112; [26], 9/10; trans., 148; [29], 47/48; trans., 156; [44], 5/6; trans., 181; [64], 16/17; trans., 225
[44], 5/6 (181)	echoes [Prol.], 13; trans., 79; [6], 22; trans., 95; [6], 35/36; trans., 96; [12], 22/23; trans., 112; [26], 9/10; trans., 148; [29], 47/48; trans., 156; [43], 36/38; trans., 180; [64], 16/17; trans., 225
[52], 15 (195)	echoes [6], 21; trans., 95; [37], 47/49; trans., 169; [52], 38/39; trans., 197
[52], 38/39 (197)	echoes [6], 21; trans., 95; [37], 47/49; trans., 169; [52], 15; trans., 195
[57], 15 (208)	biblical citation
[58], 23/24 (213)	allusion to classical mythology

[63], 46 (224)	reminiscence of Horace
[63], 48/49 (224)	biblical allusion
[64], 16/17 (225)	echoes [Prol.], 13; trans., 79; [6], 22; trans., 95; [6], 35/36; trans., 96; [12], 22/23; trans., 112; [26], 9/10; trans., 148; [29], 47/48; trans., 156; [43], 36/38; trans., 180; [44], 5/6; trans., 181
[68]/[72], 2 (231–40)	explain fate of Charles and Erembalds
[75], 1/31 (243–44)	added later? compare especially [75], 2/3 and [13], 2/5; trans., 114–15
[81], 50 (252)	allusion to Virgil
[83], 10/11 (254)	biblical citation
[84] (254–56)	added later? compare especially [84], 43/58; trans., 256, and [14], 1/2; trans., 117
[86]/[91] (258–64)	relate fate of previously unpunished traitors

APPENDIX VII

Allusions to Subsequent Events in Chapters 15–67, 72–85

Chapter, ll. (Trans. p.)	Date of Ms. Chapter	Reason
[16], 46/48 (122–23)	3/2	refers to Gervaise as an avenger and so could not have been written before 3/7–9 when Gervaise attacks Raverschoot and Bruges
[21], 20/23 (135)	3/2	refers to future troubles
[21], 30/38 (135–36)	3/2	deals with events of 3/6
[21], 42/43 (136)	3/2	written after Walter appears at the siege on 3/11
[25], 18/26 (144)	3/6	written after the choice of a new count (3/30) and after Charles has been avenged (5/5?)
[26], 24/28 (148)	3/7	the traitors are "precipitated" in moral turpitude; written after the execution of 5/5
[26], 46/50 (149)	3/7	written when it is clear that the traitors will be punished
[27], 3/4 (150)	3/8	Wulfric Knop is said to have sworn the death of the count, but this is first revealed by Isaac on 3/17
[27], 7/15 (150)	3/8	written when it is clear that the traitors will be punished, perhaps after 5/5

[29], 33/59 (155)	3/9	refers to the whole length of siege (ending 3/19 with the storming of the castle? or 4/14 with the invasion of the church gallery? or 4/19 with the surrender of the besieged?)
[35], 29/33 (164)	3/17	written after the storming of the church on 3/19
[42], 4/14 (177)	3/19	written later, after Bertulf's capture on 4/11?
[46], 1/17 (185–86)	3/19	added after Bertulf's capture on 4/11
[53], 10/20 (198–99)	3/31	written after meeting at Deinze on 4/2
[57], 12/17 (208–9)	4/11	written after 5/5 since it refers to the precipitation of the traitors
[61], 41/45 (220)	4/13	written after 5/7 since it alludes to the departure of the king on May 6 and the handing over of silver and golden vessels on May 7
[80], 4/6 (249–50)	5/1	written after 5/5 since it refers to the precipitation of the traitors

Notes

Bibliography

Index

Notes

NOTES TO INTRODUCTION

1. This résumé is found on folios 37r–37v of manuscript 442 of the Stedelijke Openbare Bibliotheek in Bruges. The manuscript is described by Pierre-Joseph Laude, in his *Catalogue méthodique, descriptif et analytique des manuscrits de la Bibliothèque publique de Bruges* (Bruges, 1859), 385–86, n° 442, and by Alphonse de Poorter, in his *Catalogue des manuscrits de la Bibliothèque publique de la ville de Bruges,* Catalogue général des manuscrits des bibliothèques de Belgique 2 (Gembloux, 1934), 500–501, n° 442. I have printed the résumé in its entirety in an appendix to my edition of the *De multro* (Galbert of Bruges [Galbertus Brugensis], *De multro, traditione, et occisione gloriosi Karoli comitis Flandriarum,* Corpus Christianorum, Continuatio medievalis 131, ed. Jeff Rider [Turnhout, 1994]), 173–75). On the fifteenth-century French translation, of which only the first third survives in a sixteenth-century manuscript, see my edition, xxxvi–vii, and Jeff Rider, "Galbert of Bruges' 'Journal': From Medieval Flop to Modern Bestseller," in L. Milis, V. Lambert, and A. Kelders, eds., *Verhalende Bronnen: Repertoriering, Editie en Commercialisiering,* Studia Historica Gandensia: Publicaties van de Opleiding Geschiedenis van de Universiteit Gent 283 (Ghent, 1996), 67–93.

2. Jacob de Meyer (Jacobus Meyerus), *Commentarii sive Annales rerum Flandricarum libri XVII* (Antwerp, 1561), 40r (all translations throughout the book are mine unless otherwise noted). This work was completed and published after de Meyer's death by his nephew Antoine de Meyer. It is interesting to note that Orderic Vitalis's *Ecclesiastical History* was likewise neglected "until he was rediscovered in the sixteenth century. . . . [I]t seems that Orderic's work was too varied, too individual, and at the same time too much of its own age, to arouse great interest outside the community for which it was written until the end of the middle ages" (Marjorie Chibnall, *The World of Orderic Vitalis* [Oxford, U.K., 1984], 216, 219; compare Orderic Vitalis, *The Ecclesiastical History of Orderic Vitalis,* 6 vols., ed. and trans. Marjorie Chibnall [London, 1969–1980], 1:113).

3. H. Jan Gooris, *Het Leven ende Martelie van den Heylighen Graef van Vlaenderen Carolus Bonus* (Bruges, 1629). For his sources, see vi; for a citation of Galbert, see 128.

4. André Duchesne, *Histoire généalogique des maisons de Guines, d'Ardres, de Gand et de Coucy* (Paris, 1631), 69–70, 196–97, 205–8, 234–35.

5. Godefroid Henschen and Daniel Van Papenbroeck, "De B. Carolo bono, comite Flandriae, martyre," *Acta Sanctorum,* March, 1 (Antwerp, 1668), 153.

6. Galbert of Bruges, "Historia vitae & passionis S. Caroli Com. Flandr. Auctore Galberto notario," ed. Jacob Langebek, *Scriptores rerum Danicorum medii aevi* 4 (1776; rpt. Nendeln, 1969), 110–11.

7. *Recueil des historiens des Gaules et de la France* 13 (1786; new ed., Paris, 1869), 347–92.

8. Galbert of Bruges, "Vie de Charles le Bon, Comte de Flandre," trans. François P. G. Guizot, in *Collection des mémoires relatifs à l'histoire de France depuis la fondation de la monarchie française jusqu'au XIIIe siècle* 8 (Paris, 1825), 237–433. An abridged version of this translation was published as Galbert of Bruges, *La Légende du bienheureux Charles le Bon, Comte de Flandre: Récit du XIIe siècle,* Bibliothèque des chemins de fer, 2 séries: Histoire et Voyages (Paris, 1853).

9. Galbert of Bruges, *Histoire du règne de Charles le Bon, précédée d'un résumé de l'histoire des Flandres,* trans. Joseph-Octave Delepierre and Jean Perneel (Brussels, 1830; rpt. 1831, 1844). On this translation, see Antoon Viaene, "Galbert van Brugge in eerste moderne vertaling: Een Vlaams initiatief van archivaris Delepierre," *Biekorf* 78 (1978): 193–99.

10. R. Köpke, "Vita Karoli comitis Flandriae," *Monumenta Germaniae Historica, Scriptores* 12 (Hannover, 1856), 533–34.

11. Alphonse Wauters, "Gualbert," *Biographie nationale* 8 (Brussels, 1884–1885), col. 393. Compare the remarks of Achille Luchaire, in *Louis VI le Gros, Annales de sa vie et de son règne (1081–1137)* (Paris, 1890), 314.

12. *Histoire du meurtre de Charles le Bon, comte de Flandre (1127–28),* ed. Henri Pirenne, Collection de textes pour servir à l'étude et l'enseignement de l'histoire 10 (Paris, 1891); *Patrologia latina* 166, 943–1046.

13. *The Murder of Charles the Good, Count of Flanders,* trans. James Bruce Ross, Records of Civilization, Sources and Studies 61 (1959; rev. ed., 1967; rpt. Medieval Academy Reprints for Teaching 12 [Toronto, 1982]). Since it was reprinted by the University of Toronto Press for the Medieval Academy Reprints for Teaching series, the translation has sold steadily at a rate of c. 900 copies a year. A fourth French translation of the chronicle and the first Dutch translation of it were published under the direction of Professor R. C. Van Caenegem in 1978 *(De Moord op Karel de Goede,* gen. ed. R. C. Van Caenegem, trans. Albert Demyttenaere [Antwerp, 1978]; *Le Meurtre de Charles le Bon,* gen. ed. R. C. Van Caenegem, trans. J. Gengoux [Antwerp, 1978]), and a new Dutch translation by Albert Demyttenaere has just appeared *(De Moord op Karel de Goede* [Leuven, 1999]).

14. Pirenne, ed., xii, xiii, xiv.

15. Pirenne, ed., xiv–xvii.

16. Pirenne, ed., vi–vii.

17. Pirenne, ed., viii, xvi–xvii, xiii.

18. Ross, trans., 64, 75.

19. "Of his qualities as a writer, the reader can best judge for himself. Evidence of training in the arts of grammar or rhetoric is slight: his sentence structure is clumsy, his locutions often obscure and incorrect, and his knowledge of the classics scanty. His conscious efforts at style in the parts added at leisure are lamentable. His real gift as a writer lies elsewhere and is largely unconscious: the power to tell a swift-moving story with precision and vitality, to describe a complex scene vividly, and to lay bare the motives of men through their actions" (Ross, trans., 74).

20. "Day by day he sets down a summary of events on wax tablets, and then as soon as possible he transcribes the information in more finished form. The immediacy of his recording is obvious not only from the internal evidence of the items themselves but from the tone of the narrative as a whole. In most cases only a few days seem to have elapsed between the events (and the original notations) and the entry as we now have it"; "it is clear that Galbert never went over his entries to eliminate repetitions and inconsistencies and to incorporate odds and ends of information that he had simply attached by *notandum*" (Ross, trans., 66–67, 70).

21. Ross, trans., 75.

22. Ross, trans., 66. Elsewhere, Ross observes that Galbert seems *"impelled"* to disclose his name "though *unwillingly,* by the very difficulties of his self-imposed task" (trans., 63–64); that "it seems to be the mention of his *precious* archives being removed from the castle, along with the relics of the saints, that *goads* Galbert into revealing himself and his new activity" (trans., 66); that Galbert's "notarial *impulse* to record, despite all obstacles, was

probably strengthened by Galbert's sense of the personal tragedy and drama enveloping the two figures who had *dominated* his life" (trans., 67); and that something "*impelled* him to resume his recording with the outbreak of the revolt against Count William in February, 1128" (trans., 70). My emphasis.

23. Beryl Smalley, *Historians in the Middle Ages* (London, 1974), 107–9. The influence of Pirenne's views on subsequent scholars can be seen neatly in a series of articles that François-Louis Ganshof wrote between 1924 and 1950: "Note sur les événements de 1127 en Flandre," *Handelingen van het Genootschap voor Geschiedenis Gesticht onder de Benaming "Société d'émulation" te Brugge* 67 (1924): 97–107; "Le Roi de France en Flandre en 1127 et 1128," *Revue Historique de Droit Français et Etranger*, 4th ser., 27 (1949): 204–28; "Trois Mandements perdus du roi de France, Louis VI, intéressant la Flandre," *Handelingen van het Genootschap voor Geschiedenis Gesticht onder de Benaming "Société d'émulation" te Brugge* 87 (1950): 117–33; and "Les Origines du concept de souveraineté nationale en Flandre," *Tijdschrift voor Rechtsgeschiedenis / Revue d'Histoire du Droit / The Legal History Review* 18 (1950): 135–58. In these articles, which are either about the *De multro* or rely heavily on it, Ganshof used and interpreted information provided by the chronicle as if it were an immediate, entirely objective, straightforward record, without any evident concern for Galbert's interests and ideas and the ways they may have shaped the collection and communication of that information.

24. Heinrich Sproemberg, "Das Erwachen des Staatsgefühls in den Niederlanden. Galbert von Brügge," in *L'Organisation corporative du Moyen Age à la fin de l'Ancien Régime*, Etudes présentées à la Commission Internationale pour l'histoire des assemblées d'états 3, Université de Louvain, Recueil de Travaux publiés par les Membres des Conférences d'Histoire et de Philologie, 2 série, 50 (Leuven, 1939), 31–89; Paul Bonenfant, "La Dépendance du Château d'Alost au XIIe siècle," in Robert Foncke et al., eds., *Album Dr Jan Lindemans* (Brussels, 1951), 169–73.

25. Jan Dhondt, "Une Mentalité du douzième siècle: Galbert de Bruges," *Revue du Nord* 39 (1957): 102, 104, 105, 107. In the second article, a discussion of medieval "solidarities" based on the *De multro*, Dhondt summarizes his thoughts on Galbert in this way: "Uncomplicated, intellectual by the standards of his time, tossed like so many others by the waves of events, he shows us (an exceptional sight for the period) a human being, a man who hesitates from day to day between an easy and total identification with his surroundings and a break with it, however sorrowful and dangerous that break might be. His environment is the crowd of Bruges. He is part of it; he shares its ideas. . . . Galbert has both a religious mind and a feeling for the concrete; he reasons and is thus constantly grappling with the serious problem of God's unfathomable Providence, a God who determines the actions of all men but not in the way Galbert thinks justice demands. From this comes his anxiety. . . . Identifying himself with his milieu, Galbert shares this crowd's 'political' conceptions, its now favorable, now unfavorable attitude toward the battling parties. . . . Despite everything, Galbert is an individualist to the extent—small, to be sure—that an average individual can free himself from his milieu. He has his personal ideas, his personal fears, if you prefer, which lead him one fine day when the fight seems uncertain to try to go it alone . . . [but] once the struggle in Flanders is over, he dives happily back into conformity" ("Les 'Solidarités' médiévales. Une société en transition: La Flandre en 1127–28," *Annales. Economies-Sociétés-Civilisations* 12 [1957]: 535–36; trans. F. L. Cheyette, in Cheyette, ed., *Lordship and Community in Medieval Europe* [New York, 1968], 272–73; translation modified [hereafter noted as "trans. mod."]).

26. Only one of these essays was published before his death ("Eine Rheinische Königskandidatur im Jahre 1125," in *Aus Geschichte und Landeskunde. Forschungen und*

Darstellungen, Franz Steinbach zum 65. Geburtstag gewidmet [Bonn, 1960], 50–70); the others were published posthumously in Heinrich Sproemberg, *Mittelalter und Demokratische Geschichtsschreibung. Ausgëwahlte Abhandlungen,* ed. Manfred Unger, Lily Sproemberg, and Wolfgang Eggert, Forschungen zur Mittelalterlichen Geschichte 18 (Berlin, 1971): "Galbert von Brügge—Stellung und Bedeutung" (1954), 278–372; "Die Bürger und der Staat in den Niederlanden zu Beginn des 12. Jahrhunderts" (1958), 223–38; and "Galbert von Brügge—Persönlichkeit und Werk" (1963–1964), 239–77.

27. "Pirenne has stated that Galbert evidently lacked the time and perhaps also the moral courage to revise and finish his work; it was not intended to be published in the form in which it has come down to us. . . . Pirenne also thinks the narrative is utterly artless, written in absolute good faith. The narrator speaks candidly; he never tries to recast the events, but reports them exactly as they were told to him. That means that Galbert simply 'received,' so to speak, what was reported; that he was not personally implicated in any way in the events and was altogether unbiased. I cannot agree with this interpretation. . . . Influenced in no small measure by Pirenne's interpretation, sketched out above, no one until now has made a serious effort to study our author's personality more closely, and this neglect has been of great consequence for the interpretation of the information he provides and, above all, of the statements in his work concerning constitutional law. It has also barely occurred to anyone to consider Galbert's role in the formulation or indeed the conception of these statements. This is all the more curious given, first, that one cannot deny its historical importance, and, second, as we have noted and as Pirenne too recognized, our author had a great deal of legal background and his narrative is remarkable for its unusual liveliness" (*Mittelalter,* 320–21; compare 261–63). Lorraine Elias has echoed Sproemberg recently, observing that "previous scholars have valued Galbert's book mainly for its content, paying little attention to the style of the text and the mind-set that conceived and controls its structure and development," and suggesting that Pirenne's and Ross's depictions of Galbert and the *De multro* may well "serve as a block to accepting the text as it is given by the author" ("Augustinian Elements in the Record of Galbert of Bruges," *Proceedings of the PMR [Patristic, Medieval and Renaissance] Conference* 18 [1993–1994], 35).

28. *Mittelalter,* 323; 328–31 (compare 233–34); 367–74 (compare 237–38); 374.

29. "Eine rheinische Königskandidatur," 62–63.

30. "Eine rheinische Königskandidatur," 65–66; compare *Mittelalter,* 78, 80, 367–74.

31. "We may indeed presume that Galbert reported the facts faithfully in his account and we can even verify this in some cases. The legal interpretation and formulation of his statements, however, are his own work; they go far beyond the ideas current at this time" (*Mittelalter,* 238).

32. *Mittelalter,* 324.

33. Nicolas Huyghebaert, "Galbert de Bruges," *Dictionnaire d'histoire et de géographie ecclésiastiques* 19 (Paris, 1981), 737–39; Walter Mohr, "Geschichtstheologische Aspekte im Werk Galberts von Brügge," in R. Lievens, E. Van Mingroot, and W. Verbeke, eds., *Pascua Mediaevalia: Studies voor Prof. Dr. Jozef-Maria De Smet,* Medievalia Lovaniensia 1.10 (Leuven, 1983), 246–62; Stephanie Coué, "Der Mord an Karl dem Guten (1127) und die Werke Galberts von Brügge und Walters von Thérouanne," in Hagen Keller, Klaus Grubmüller, and Nikolaus Staubach, eds., *Pragmatische Schriftlichkeit im Mittelalter: Erscheinungsformen und Entwickelungsstufen,* Münsterche Mittelalterschriften 65 (Munich, 1992), 108–29; Dirk Heirbaut, "Galbert van Brugge: Een Bron voor de Vlaamse Feodaliteit in de XIIde Eeuw," *Tijdschrift voor Rechtsgeschiedenis / Revue d'Histoire du Droit / The Legal History Review* 60 (1992): 49–62; Elias, "Augustinian Elements," 35–48; Alan V. Murray, "Voices of Flanders: Orality

and Constructed Orality in the Chronicle of Galbert of Bruges," *Handelingen van de Maatschappij voor Geschiedenis en Oudheidkunde te Gent,* n.s. 48 (1994): 103–19, and "The Divine and the Diabolic in Twelfth-Century Historiography: The Chronicle of Galbert of Bruges," paper read to the Research Association of the Center for Medieval Studies of the University of Leeds, July 1, 1997; Albert Demyttenaere, "Mentaliteit in de twaalfde eeuw en de benauwenis van Galbert van Brugge," in M. Mostert, R. E. Künzel, and A. Demyttenaere, eds., *Middeleeuwse cultuur: Verscheidenheid, spanning en verandering* (Hilversum, 1994), 77–129; Martina Häcker, "Mothers, Wives, and Witches: The Depiction of Women in Galbert of Bruges' Account of the Murder of Charles the Good," *Bulletin of International Medieval Research* 2–3 (1996–1997): 10–26; Laurence W. Marvin, "'Men Famous in Combat and Battle . . .': Common Soldiers and the Siege of Bruges, 1127," *Journal of Medieval History* 24 (1998): 243–58; Lisa H. Cooper, "Making Space for History: Galbert of Bruges and the Murder of Charles the Good," forthcoming in Laura L. Howes, ed., *Place, Space, and Landscape in Medieval Literature,* Tennessee Studies in Literature (I would like to thank Ms. Cooper for sending me a copy of her article prior to its publication).

34. *Galbert van Brugge en het recht,* Mededelingen van de Koninklijke Academie voor Wetenschappen, Letteren en Schone Kunsten van België, Klasse der Letteren 40.1 (Brussels, 1978); "The Ghent Revolt of February 1128," in Van Caenegem, *Law, History, the Low Countries and Europe,* ed. Ludo Milis et al. (London, 1994), 107–12 (first published as "De Gentse februari-opstand van het jaar 1128," *Spiegel Historiael: Maanblad voor Geschiedenis en Archeologie* 13 [1978]: 478–83); introduction to Galbert, *Le Meurtre* and *De Moord* (1978), revised in introduction to Galbert, *De Moord* (1999); "Galbert of Bruges on Serfdom, Prosecution of Crime, and Constitutionalism," in Bernard S. Bachrach and David Nicholas, eds., *Law, Custom, and the Social Fabric in Medieval Europe: Essays in Honor of Bryce Lyon* (Kalamazoo, Mich., 1990), 89–112; "Misdaad en Straf bij Galbert van Brugge," in *Liber Amicorum Jules D'Haenens* (Ghent, 1993), 321–31; "Law and Power in Twelfth-Century Flanders," in Thomas N. Bisson, ed., *Cultures of Power: Lordship, Status, and Process in Twelfth-Century Europe* (Philadelphia, 1995), 149–71; "Notes on Galbert of Bruges and His Translators," in Jean-Marie Duvosquel and Erik Thoen, eds., *Peasants and Townsmen in Medieval Europe: Studia in honorem Adriaan Verhulst* (Ghent, 1995), 619–29.

35. He observes that Galbert "was not a learned theologian, but had nonetheless received a good education in Latin literature and Holy Scripture—first in Bruges and afterwards in Laon?," and later notes "if . . . one is willing to apply the term 'jurist' to everyone who has to work with laws and courts in the daily practice of his profession, then one can indeed call Galbert a jurist" (*Galbert van Brugge,* 8, 12); elsewhere, he calls Galbert "cultured" and writes that "as a clerk, he had undoubtedly been educated in Latin, in a cathedral, abbey or chapter school, and had studied the Church Fathers, perhaps at the cathedral of Laon, where many young Flemings studied then" (Galbert, *Le Meurtre,* 65, 59).

36. "Galbert was able to evoke a mood in a few sentences" (Galbert, *Le Meurtre,* 63).

37. Galbert, *Le Meurtre,* 65; compare "Galbert of Bruges," 90: "[H]e was occasionally involved with legal matters and did not confine himself to reporting—with great accuracy—what happened, but also what, according to public opinion or his own judgement, should have happened and why." Van Caenegem also reminds us that "one should not forget, furthermore, that Galbert also has his own perception of legal problems and—what is especially fascinating—focuses on a single legal issue from very different points of view and thus fluctuates in a very obvious way according to the political situation" (*Galbert van Brugge,* 12).

38. In Galbert, *Le Meurtre,* 65–66; "Misdaad," 331, n. 31.

39. Dhondt, "Les 'Solidarités,'" 530; trans., 269.

40. Dhondt, "Une Mentalité," 102.

41. In Galbert, *Le Meurtre,* 59–60.

42. There is, of course, the previous question of how one recognizes an event as an event, or several events as forming a series. An author's preexisting narrative competence, his or her awareness of the narrative traditions of his or her culture, undoubtedly plays a productive role in this recognition of events and series of events. "Event," that is, is a narrative category rather than a material one, and every event, every collection of events, has a narrative potential.

43. There have been certain exceptions to this rule. In his review of Pirenne's edition, Charles de Smedt suggested that the first part of the text had been substantially revised (*Analecta Bollandiana* 11 [1892]: 194), and Father Huyghebaert likewise noted the "rather polished composition" of the Prologue and first twenty-three chapters of the *De multro* ("Galbert de Bruges," 738) but they did not go on (and given the format of their remarks—a review and a brief encyclopedia article—could not have been expected to do so) to study even this portion of the work for what it could tell us about Galbert's historiography. Sproemberg declared that the *De multro* was in fact finished as it stands (*Mittelalter,* 242–43, 321), but he, too, has nothing much to say about Galbert's historiography (unless it is that the purpose of historical writing is to provide political models). Only Murray has studied in any detail the ways in which Galbert uses literary and rhetorical devices to impose a particular form on the events he relates and to shape the readers' interpretation of them.

44. This book thus belongs to the no longer so *nouvelle vague* of what one might term the historiographical reaction to the "positivistic," "scientific," or "modern" approaches that dominated the study of medieval histories from c. 1870 to c. 1970. This is not the place to attempt a bibliography of the historiographical approach, but one might get a sense of it from the following sampling: Robert W. Hanning, *The Vision of History in Early Britain: From Gildas to Geoffrey of Monmouth* (New York, 1966); R. W. Southern, "Aspects of the European Tradition of Historical Writing," *Transactions of the Royal Historical Society,* 5th ser., 20 (1970): 173–96; 21 (1971): 159–79; 22 (1972): 159–80; 23 (1973): 243–63; Nancy Partner, *Serious Entertainments: The Writing of History in Twelfth-Century England* (Chicago, 1977); Bernard Guenée, *Histoire et culture historique dans l'Occident medieval* (Paris, 1980); R. H. C. Davis and J. M. Wallace-Hadrill, eds., *The Writing of History in the Middle Ages: Essays Presented to Richard William Southern* (Oxford, U.K., 1981); Chibnall, *The World of Orderic Vitalis;* Ernst Breisach, ed., *Classical Rhetoric and Medieval Historiography,* Studies in Medieval Culture 19 (Kalamazoo, Mich., 1985); Robert M. Stein, "Signs and Things: The *Vita Heinrici IV. Imperatoris* and the Crisis of Interpretation in Twelfth-Century History," *Traditio* 43 (1987): 105–19; P. W. Edbury, *William of Tyre, Historian of the Latin East* (Cambridge, U.K., 1988); Karl Frederick Morrison, *History as a Visual Art in the Twelfth-Century Renaissance* (Princeton, N.J., 1990); Antonia Gransden, *Legends, Traditions, and History in Medieval England* (London, 1992); Gabrielle Spiegel, *Romancing the Past: The Rise of Vernacular Prose Historiography in Thirteenth-Century France* (Berkeley, Calif., 1993); Richard Landes, *Relics, Apocalypse, and the Deceits of History: Ademar of Chabbanes, 989–1034* (Cambridge, Mass., 1995); Monika Otter, *Inventiones: Fiction and Referentiality in Twelfth-Century Historical Writing* (Chapel Hill, N.C., 1996); L. A. J. R. Houwen and A. A. MacDonald, eds., *Beda Venerabilis: Historian, Monk and Northumbrian* (Groningen, 1996); Leah Shopkow, *History and Community: Norman Historians in the Eleventh and Twelfth Centuries* (Washington, D.C., 1997); John O. Ward, "'Chronicle' and 'History': The Medieval Origins of Postmodern Historiographical Practice?" *Parergon* 14 (1997): 101–27.

45. Ward, "'Chronicle' and 'History,'" 122.

46. "We have simply lost contact, albeit willingly and rightly, with everything that could allow us to approach medieval histories naturally and directly. And yet those works have continued to be read by scholars variously puzzled, bored, critical, and intrigued, because they are the sources for information otherwise unavailable" (*Serious Entertainments*, 4).

NOTES TO CHAPTER I

1. *Historia Anglorum / The History of the English People*, ed. and trans. Diana Greenway, Oxford Medieval Texts (Oxford, U.K., 1996), 477.

2. Galbert, *De multro*, [12], 8/10; *The Murder*, 112. All references to the *De multro* will be to the chapter and line numbers of this edition and to the pages of this translation. The principal descriptions of Charles's final days, on which this introductory résumé is based, are Galbert's *De multro;* Walter of Thérouanne's "Vita Karoli comitis, auctore Waltero archidiacono Tervanensi," ed. R. Köpke, *Monumenta Germaniae Historica, Scriptores* 12 (Hannover, 1856), 537–61 (references will be to the chapter of the text and to the pages and lines of the edition); and Herman of Tournai's "Liber de restauratione monasterii Sancti Martini Tornacensis," ed. Georg Waitz, *Monumenta Germaniae Historica, Scriptores* 14 (Hannover, 1883), 274–317; Lynn H. Nelson, trans., *The Restoration of the Monastery of Saint Martin of Tournai*, Medieval Texts in Translation (Washington, D.C., 1996) (references to the chapter of the text, the pages and lines of the edition, and the pages of the trans.).

3. On the special importance and power of the castellan of Bruges, see W. Blommaert, *Les Châtelains de Flandre. Etude d'histoire constitutionelle* (Ghent, 1915), 10–38, esp. 33. Bertulf, writes Galbert, was "more powerful than anyone in the realm except the count and more eminent in reputation and in religion" ([8], 1/2; trans., 101), and the members of his family "were very powerful and noble men in the county" ([45], 39/40; trans., 184). Walter of Thérouanne calls Bertulf "the most splendid son of this subcelestial world and the wealthiest in all of this world's riches, and the most powerful of almost all this land, second only to the count" ([39], 555, 23/25). On Bertulf, see Georges Declercq, "Bertulf," *National Biografisch Woordenboek* (Brussels, 1990), 13:73–80; on the whole family, see James Bruce Ross, "Rise and Fall of a Twelfth- Century Clan: The Erembalds and the Murder of Count Charles of Flanders, 1127–28," *Speculum* 34 (1959): 367–90; and E. Warlop, *The Flemish Nobility before 1300*, 2 vols., 4 parts, trans. J. B. Ross and H. Vandermoere (Kortrijk, 1975–1976), 1:186–95.

4. Bertulf, at least, was afraid that Charles was planning to strip him of the provostship of Saint Donatian before Easter (April 3) (see *De multro*, [19], 19/24; trans., 130–31).

5. See Sandy Burton Hicks, "The Impact of William Clito upon the Continental Policies of Henry I of England," *Viator* 10 (1979): 1–21. The social and economic links between Flanders and England in the late eleventh and early twelfth centuries were extensive. On the Flemish settlement in England and, especially, Wales and the social and economic relations between the kingdom and the county, see Orderic Vitalis, *Ecclesiastical History* 13.17, 6:442; Giraldus Cambrensis (Gerald of Wales), *Itinerarium Cambriae* 2.11, ed. James F. Dimock, in *Opera* (London, 1868), 6:83; Lewis Thorpe, trans., *"The Journey through Wales" and "The Description of Wales"* (Harmondsworth, U.K., 1978), 141–42; John Edward Lloyd, *A History of Wales*, 2nd ed., 2 vols. (London, 1912), 2:424, 475; Hilary Jenkinson, "William Cade, a Financier of the Twelfth Century," *English Historical Review* 28 (1913): 209–27, 731–32; J. H. Round, "The Debtors of William Cade," *English Historical Review* 28 (1913): 522–27; Charles H. Haskins's comments, *English Historical Review* 28 (1913): 730–31; Gaston Dept, "Les Marchands flamands et le roi d'Angleterre (1154–1216)," *Revue du Nord* 12 (1926): 303–24; Robert H. George, "The Contribution of Flanders to the Conquest of England,

1065–86," *Revue Belge de Philologie et d'Histoire* 5 (1926): 81–97; Charles Verlinden, *Robert Ier le Frison, comte de Flandre. Etude d'histoire politique* (Antwerp, 1935), 107–12; L. Vercauteren–De Smet, "Etude sur les rapports politiques de l'Angleterre et de la Flandre sous le règne du comte Robert II (1093–1111)," in *Etudes d'histoire dédiées à la mémoire de Henri Pirenne par ses anciens élèves* (Brussels, 1937), 413–23; René Derolez, "British and English History in the *Liber Floridus,*" in Albert Derolez, ed., *Liber Floridus Colloquium* (Ghent, 1973), 64; Martin Brett, "John of Worcester and His Contemporaries," in Davis and Wallace-Hadrill, eds., *The Writing of History in the Middle Ages,* 101; Marjorie Chibnall, *Anglo-Norman England* (Oxford, U.K., 1986), 48; Lauran Toorians, "Wizo Flandrensis and the Flemish Settlement in Pembrokeshire," *Cambridge Medieval Celtic Studies* 20 (1990): 99–118; R. R. Davies, *The Age of Conquest: Wales 1063–1415* (Oxford, U.K., 1991), 98–99, 159–60; and David Nicholas, *Medieval Flanders* (London, 1992), 52–55, 107–8.

6. On Thierry, see Thérèse de Hemptinne and Michel Parisse, "Thierry d'Alsace, comte de Flandre: Biographie et actes," *Annales de l'Est* 43 (1991): 83–113.

7. See Jan Dhondt, "Développement urbain et initiative comtale en Flandre au XIe siècle," *Revue du Nord* 30 (1948): 133–56.

8. See Dhondt, "Développement urbain," 153–54, 156. Georges Declercq thinks that Dhondt's suggestion that counts founded chapters in these administrative centers in order to provide functionaries for their administration goes too far. He argues that the number of canons (c. 150) in comital chapters c. 1100 was far greater than was needed for the comital administration and suggests that other motives, including religious devotion, were involved in their foundation ("Sekuliere Kapittels in Vlaanderen," *De Leiegouw* 28 [1986]: 237–38). The fact that the number of canons attached to these chapters was greater than was needed for the comital administration does not, however, mean that none of them worked in it, nor does piety exclude practicality. As Declercq shows, most chapters founded by counts were in administrative centers and most administrative centers had a chapter founded by the counts, or at least, as in Ghent, a comital church (see Declercq's table on 241–42). The coincidence suggests some link between the count's administration and these clerical pools: there is no reason why the counts could not have appreciated both the brothers' prayers and their ability to write and keep accounts. It seems reasonable to think that the counts founded these chapter and churches in the administrative centers of the county both out of piety and in order to have at hand a pool of clerics to serve the needs of their administration.

9. The earliest evidence we have of the functioning of this administration comes from folios 147–53 of the autograph manuscript of Lambert of Saint-Omer's *Liber Floridus* (completed in 1120) that appear to have contained "old accounts of the counts of Flanders" before being erased and reused. A scrap of text—"Account of the revenues [*ratio*] from the count's manors [presumably in the castellany of Saint-Omer:] Chickens and Eggs"—and a few numbers survive in the fold of one of them (*Liber Floridus: Codex autographus bibliothecae universitatis Gandavensis,* ed. Albert Derolez, pref. Egied I. Strubbe and Albert Derolez [Ghent, 1968], ix, 298). The next piece of evidence we have is an account of the disbursements made between October 13, 1140, and January 24, 1141, by the comital functionary in charge of the "fodermolt" (a special "public" tax or revenue belonging to the count and going back perhaps to Carolingian times) in Bergues-Saint-Winnoc (see Egied Strubbe, *Het Fragment van een Grafeliijke Rekening van Vlaanderen uit 1140,* Mededelingen van de Koninklijke Vlaamse Academie voor Wetenschappen, Letteren en Schone Kunsten van België, Klasse der Letteren 12.9 [Brussel, 1950]). This record mentions that "after Epiphany" a messenger came to take "the pennies" to the chamberlain Arnold, who is already mentioned as Charles's chamberlain in 1127 (*De multro,* [18], 10/11, 16, 44; trans., 128–29) and appears

in this office as late as 1156–1166 in a charter of Thierry (Thérèse de Hemptinne and Adriaan Verhulst, eds., *De oorkonden der graven van Vlaanderen (Juli 1128–September 1191), II. Uitgave, v. 1: Regering van Diederik van de Elzas (Juli 1128–17 Januari 1168)*, Académie Royale de Belgique, Commission royale d'histoire, Recueil des actes des princes belges / Koninklijke Academie van België, Koninklijke Commissie voor Geschiedenis, Verzameling van de Akten der Belgische Vorsten 6 [Brussels, 1988], n° 262, p. 415). The *fodermolt* was a revenue in fodder, but the account records disbursements in both fodder and cash, so the pennies the functionary disbursed and the surplus ones the messenger had come to take away to Bruges presumably came from the sale of fodder that was not used or disbursed at Bergues-Saint-Winnoc (see Strubbe, *Het Fragment*, 15–16). For an overview of the administration of medieval Flanders, see Raymond Monier, *Les Institutions centrales du comté de Flandre de la fin du IXe siècle à 1384* (Paris, 1943), and *Les Institutions financières du comté de Flandre du IXe siècle à 1384* (Paris, 1948); F. L. Ganshof, "La Flandre," in Ferdinand Lot and Robert Fawtier, eds., *Histoire des institutions française au Moyen Age*, vol. 1: *Institutions seigneuriales* (Paris, 1957), 343–426; A. Verhulst and M. Gysseling, *Le Compte Général de 1187, connu sous le nom de "Gros Brief," et les institutions financières du comté de Flandre au XIIe siècle* (Brussels, 1962); and Bryce Lyon and A. E. Verhulst, *Medieval Finance: A Comparison of Financial Institutions in Northwestern Europe* (Providence, R.I., 1967), 12–40. See also L. Genicot, "Le premier siècle de la 'curia' de Hainaut (1060 env.–1195)," *Le Moyen Age* 53 (1947): 39–60.

10. On the evolution of the clerical side of the count's administration in late eleventh and early twelfth-century Flanders, see Henri Pirenne, "La Chancellerie et les notaires des comtes de Flandre avant le XIIIe siècle," in *Mélanges Julien Havet: Recueil de travaux d'érudition dédiés à la mémoire de Julien Havet* (Paris, 1895), 733–48; E. Reusens, "Les Chancelleries inférieures en Belgique depuis leur origine jusqu'au commencement du XIIIe siècle," *Analectes pour Servir à l'Histoire Ecclésiastique de la Belgique* 26 (1896): 57–133; Fernand Vercauteren, *Actes des comtes de Flandre, 1071–1128* (Brussels, 1938), xlix–lxvi; Egidius Strubbe, *Egidius van Breedene (11 . . –1270) Grafelijk Ambtenaar en Stichter van de Abdij Spermalie*, Rijksuniversiteit te Gent, Werken uitgeven door de Faculteit van de Wijsbegeerte en Letteren 94 (Bruges, 1942); Walter Prevenier, "La Chancellerie des comtes de Flandre dans le cadre européen à la fin du XIIe siècle," *Bibliothèque de l'Ecole des Chartes* 125 (1967): 34–93; Adriaan Verhulst and Thérèse De Hemptinne, "Le Chancelier de Flandre sous les comtes de la maison d'Alsace (1128–1191)," *Bulletin de la Commission royale d'histoire / Handelingen van de Koniklijke Commissie van Geschiedenis* 141 (1975): 267–311; Thérèse De Hemptinne and Maurice Vandermaesen, "De ambtenaren van de centrale administratie van het graafschap Vlaanderen van de 12e tot de 14e eeuw," *Tijdschrift voor Geschiedenis* 93 (1980): 177–209; Thérèse De Hemptinne, Walter Prevenier, and Maurice Vandermaesen, "La Chancellerie des comtes de Flandre (12e–14e siècle)," in Gabriel Silagi, ed., *Landesherrliche Kanzleien im Spätmittelalter: Referate zum VI. Internationalen Kongre für Diplomatik, München 1983*, Münchener Beiträge zur Mediävistik und Renaissance-Forschung 35, 2 vols. (Munich, 1984), 1:433–54; and De Hemptinne and Verhulst, *Oorkonden*, xxxv–lx. On the evolution of the count's administration in the thirteenth and fourteenth centuries, see Ellen E. Kittell, *From "Ad Hoc" to Routine: A Case Study in Medieval Bureaucracy* (Philadelphia, 1991).

11. Vercauteren, *Actes*, n° 9, p. 30. The charter is also printed by M. Gysseling and A. C. F. Koch, in their *Diplomata Belgica ante Annum Millesimum Centesimum Scripta*, Bouwstoffen en Studiën voor de Gescheidenis en de Lexicografie van het Nederlands 1, 2 vols. (Brussels, 1950), n°170, p. 295–98. On this charter, see Ganshof, "La Flandre," 381–82; Lyon and Verhulst, *Medieval Finance*, 12–13; and Verhulst and De Hemptinne, "Le Chancelier de Flandre," 272–73.

12. See Appendix I, and Verhulst and De Hemptinne, "Le Chancelier de Flandre," 272–80.

13. See Lyon and Verhulst, *Medieval Finance,* 16–17.

14. According to Lyon and Verhulst, "[T]he provost-chancellor was entrusted . . . with the keeping of the accounts of the fixed revenues of the count and with control over current expenditures of local rent-collecting centers. . . . [He] was simply an officer responsible for the collection and supervision of all the accounts of the local collectors, for which purpose he possessed some coercive jurisdiction" *(Medieval Finance,* 16, 17).

15. De Hemptinne and Verhulst, *Oorkonden,* n° 13, pp. 36–37.

16. A *preco* was a comital official, with judicial, police, and fiscal responsibilities in part of one of the *officia,* or administrative subdistricts, into which the castellanies were divided. See Ganshof, "La Flandre," 402; Verhulst and Gysseling, *Le Compte Général,* 103–6, 205; and Lyon and Verhulst, *Medieval Finance,* 24–25.

17. The ranks, described in the above-mentioned charter of 1089, were, from highest to lowest, notary, chapellan, and clericus. On these ranks and the career track through the curia, see Strubbe, *Egidius van Breedene,* 32–37; and De Hemptinne and Verhulst, *Oorkonden,* xxxv, xxxvii, xxxviii, xlviii–xlix, lvi. The ranks of the personnel of the episcopal chancellery of Arras in the twelfth century were, similarly, chapellan, master *(magister),* and clericus (sometimes qualified as clericus of the bishop's house or of the bishop's chapel [*clericus domus episcopi,* or *capelle episcopi*]) (Benoît-Michel Tock, *Une Chancellerie épiscopale au XIIe siècle: Le Cas d'Arras* [Louvain-la-Neuve, 1991], 191). In both cases, the clerici formed the lowest rank.

18. De Hemptinne and Verhulst suggest that, in the first half of the twelfth century, an educated member of the clergy of Saint Donatian like the schoolmaster (magister) must have played some role in the count's administration *(Oorkonden,* xxxvi, xlix). Tock shows that at least one magister, and probably others, worked in the episcopal chancery of Arras in the twelfth century (Tock, *Chancellerie épiscopale,* 189–91).

19. Georges Declercq reaches the same conclusions about this charter ("Galbert van Brugge en de Verraderlijke Moord op Karel de Goede," *Handelingen der Maatschappij voor Geschiedenis en Oudheidkunde te Gent,* n.s. 49 [1995]: 113–14).

20. The list of individually named aristocrats is too long to give here—Galbert names twenty-eight knights, for example—but they may be found in the index to my edition.

21. On Borsiard, see especially [17], 8/54; trans., 125–27; [41], 54/57; trans., 176; and [84], 1/9; trans., 254. On Gervaise, see especially [59], 14/53; trans., 214–16; [100], 1/18; trans., 275–76; and [104] 1/22; trans., 281–82.

22. On the court of the count of Flanders at this time, see Monier, *Institutions centrales,* 40–62; and Ganshof, "La Flandre," 379–84, 385–87.

23. In 1187, for example, six different kinds of revenues from the castellany of Bruges (and, for two of them, from an area slightly larger than the castellany) were received and accounted for in Bruges, making it the most important local center in the count's fiscal administration (see Verhulst and Gysseling, *Le Compte Général,* 90–100). For a description of the local fiscal administration of the castellany of Douai in the eleventh and twelfth centuries, see George Espinas, *Les Finances de la commune de Douai des origines au XVe siècle* (Paris, 1902), 5–30.

24. Sproemberg, *Mittelalter,* 338.

25. See Verhulst and Gysseling, *Le Compte Général,* 119–20; and Lyon and Verhulst, *Medieval Finance,* 28.

26. Verhulst and Gysseling, *Le Compte Général,* 41–47, 121; Lyon and Verhulst, *Medieval Finance,* 27–28.

27. Strubbe suggests the existence in the twelfth century of both what he calls "*officium*-notaries," "more-or-less independent" local functionaries each of whom oversaw one of the various fiscal divisions of the count's domain, and "court-notaries": "responsible for the smooth running of what then formed the central administration of the count's domain, they were really court functionaries, who did not enjoy much independence" *(Egidius van Breedene,* 38–39). It would be difficult, however, to maintain this distinction and identify any "court-notaries" devoted exclusively to the "national" administration of the domain in the first third of the twelfth century. At this time, at least, it seems more likely that "*officium*-notaries"—perhaps most often those based in Bruges—also served as "court-notaries" as the need arose: that the same people served both functions, although the two functions were in fact distinct.

28. For the evidence concerning these two men, see Appendix I, *s.v.* Basilius, Fromoldus Junior/2.

29. See Verhulst and Gysseling, *Le Compte Général,* 115, 149.

30. Lyon and Verhulst, *Medieval Finance,* 13–15. See *De multro* [18], 6/13, 41/44; trans., 128, 129.

31. See Verhulst and Gysseling, *Le Compte Général,* 110, 170.

32. He is called "Galbertus notarius Brudgensis" in the heading of manuscript *A* (and the two existing manuscripts copied from *A*). In my edition, I mistakenly stated that he was also called a notary in the heading of manuscript *B:* he is not.

33. "And it should be noted that in the midst of such a great tumult and the burning of so many houses—set on fire by lighted arrows shot onto the roofs of the town from within the castle, and also by brigands from the outside in the hope of looting—and in the midst of so much danger by night and conflict by day, even though I, Galbert, a notary [*ego Galbertus notarius*], had no suitable place for writing, I noted down on tablets a summary of events . . ." ([35], 33/38 [see variants]; trans., 164; trans. mod.). The other three early versions of the text—manuscript *B;* the seventeenth-century edition by Henschen and Van Papenbroeck ("Alia vita [B. Caroli boni comitis Flandriae], auctore Galberto notario," in *Acta Sanctorum,* March, 1 [Antwerp, 1668], 179–219); and the fifteenth-century French translation of the *De multro* (published facing the Latin text in my edition)—omit the word *notarius.*

34. At most four of the six receivers in Bruges in 1187 seem to have been notaries, and Verhulst and Gysseling have emphasized that while the count's receivers were often, they were not always, notaries (see *Le Compte Général,* 106–19, 149, 151, 170, 171, 175, 176; see also Lyon and Verhulst, *Medieval Finance,* 21–26; and Verhulst and De Hemptinne, "Le Chancelier de Flandre," 274).

35. "Galbert van Brugge," 107–8.

36. The title given to the work in the existing manuscripts is *De multro, traditione, et occisione gloriosi Karoli comitis Flandriarum (The Murder, Betrayal, and Assassination of the Glorious Charles, Count of the Flemish),* but as R. Köpke pointed out, Galbert probably intended to entitle his work, or at least one version of it, something like the *Passio Karoli comitis (The Passion of Count Charles),* the title Köpke gives his reprint of Henschen and Van Papenbroeck's edition, since in [14], 19 Galbert writes: "In this account of his [Charles's] passion . . ." [*in hac passionis subscriptione* . . .] (see Galbert, "Passio Karoli comitis, auctore Galberto," ed. R. Köpke, in *Monumenta Germaniae Historica, Scriptores* 12 [Hannover, 1856], 561, n. 88). Henschen and Van Papenbroeck—who edited the *De multro* in the second half of the seventeenth century and wrote that they had a manuscript, now lost, that dated "to Galbert's time or not long after"—called the work simply a *Vita [Karoli]* (Henschen and Van Papenbroeck, "De B. Carolo bono," 153; and Galbert, "Alia vita," 179). As we will see, someone other than

Galbert probably made the copy of his chronicle from which all later versions descend and this same person perhaps gave it the title it bears in the existing manuscripts.

37. See Declercq, "Galbert van Brugge," 107–8; Henschen and Van Papenbroeck, "De B. Carolo bono," 153; Galbert, "Alia vita," 179; and Rider in Galbert, *De multro,* xxix–xxxvi, xli–xliv.

38. See De Hemptinne and Verhulst, *Oorkonden,* lix–lx.

39. It is striking to find the name of "Lambertus notarius Brugensis" (Lambert, notary of Bruges), exactly the same title applied to Galbert in manuscript *A,* in a charter of Count Thierry dating to 1153–1157 (De Hemptinne and Verhulst, *Oorkonden,* n° 159, p. 257).

40. See Verhulst and Gysseling, *Le Compte Général,* 106–19; Lyon and Verhulst, *Medieval Finance,* 21–26; Verhulst and De Hemptinne, "Le Chancelier de Flandre," 274; and De Hemptinne and Vandermaesen, "De ambtenaren," 192–93.

41. [6], 10/11; trans., 94; Ov., *Met.* 3, 136/137.

42. [81], 50; trans., 252; Verg., *Aen.* 5, 709.

43. [63], 46; trans., 224; compare Hor., *C.* 3, 2.

44. [Prol.], 23/25; trans., 80; compare Mela, *De Chorographia* 2, 108; Sen., *Troad.* 838; [58], 22/24; trans., 213; compare Luc., *Bellum civile* 4, 594/660; [119], 27/28; trans., 308; compare Verg., *Aen* 7, 104; 9, 473/74; and Ov., *Fast.* 6, 527. Galbert's declaration that "Count William will confess, among the shades which he sent before him to the places of punishment [*inter umbras quas ad penalia loca praemisit*], that nothing remains to him of all he possessed in life except knightly fame" ([121], 25/27; trans., 311; trans. mod.) also has a classical ring to it.

45. "For 'as' is not used figuratively but demonstratively; it is used in Holy Writ for that which is true, for example, 'as or like a spouse' really means 'a spouse'" ([Prol.], 43/45; trans., 81); "They often asked themselves, if they killed the count, who would avenge him? But they did not know what they were saying, for 'who,' an infinite word, meant an infinite number of persons, who cannot be reckoned in a definite figure" ([14], 5/8; trans., 117); "Then finally they could remember their own saying, 'If we kill Charles, who will come to avenge him?' But, in fact, those coming to avenge him were infinite and the number of men was unknown, except to God; and therefore the word 'who,' interrogative and infinite in their saying, achieved its just and full meaning" ([37], 28/33; trans., 168).

46. "When I set out to describe the death of such a great prince [*tanti quidem principis mortem descripturus;* note the rhythm of this phrase], I did not seek to embellish it with eloquence [*eloquentiae ornatum*] or to display the modes of different styles [*diversorum colorum distinguere modos*] but I related only the truth of things, and even if my style is dry [*quamquam stilo arido*] I committed to writing for the memory of the faithful the strange outcome of his death" ([Prol.], 14/18; trans., 79–80); "Thanks to this boon of peace, men governed themselves in accordance with laws and justice, devising by skill and study every kind of argument for use in courts [*omnia ingeniorum et studiorum argumenta ad placita componentes*], so that when anyone was attacked he could defend himself by the strength and eloquence of rhetoric [*in virtute et eloquentia rhetoricae*], or when he was attacking, he might ensnare his enemy, who would be deceived by the wealth of his oratory [*colorum varietate oratorie*]. Rhetoric [*rhetorica*] was now used both by the educated and by those who were naturally talented, for there were many illiterate people, endowed by nature herself with the gift of eloquence [*eloquentiae modos*] and rational methods of inference and argument, whom those who were trained and skilled in the rhetorical art [*qui disciplinati erant et docti artem rhetoricam*] were not able to resist or refute" ([1], 22/31; trans., 84). As we will see in the following chapters, Galbert was, despite his protestations to the contrary, trained in rhetoric and used what he had learned in the composi-

tion of the *De multro.* Chapter 6, for example, a panegyric of Charles, begins with a traditional panegyrical topic—Curtius called it the "modesty" topic—in which the author states that he is not capable of praising his subject adequately (Ernst Robert Curtius, *European Literature and the Latin Middle Ages,* trans. Willard R. Trask [Princeton, N.J., 1953], 83–85).

47. His statement that, in Charles, "the residue of earthly authority assumed the form [*formam*] of ruling well and the substance [*materiam*] of serving God" ([Prol. 50/51; trans., 81) has a Scholastic ring to it, as do certain later passages: "It is a most grievous thing for a man to be in accord with his enemy, and against nature, for every creature flees what is inimical to itself, if it can" ([24], 17/19; trans., 143); "Finally our citizens questioned [*interrogabant*] Ivan and Daniel: 'Why, then [*Cur ergo*], did you bring Thierry around to us if all of us are not going to pledge faith and loyalty and do homage to him, you first and we second?' They replied: 'Because [*Responderunt: 'Quia*] when we came to Bruges . . ." ([101], 21/26; trans., 277); "It may well be asked why, therefore [*Queratur ergo . . . cur*], when God wished to restore the peace of the fatherland through the death of one of the two, He preferred that Count William should die, . . . and why [*et quare*] on the contrary Count Thierry did not die . . . ; or [*aut*] by what justice God granted the countship to the one . . ." ([121], 1/6; trans., 310). This is the vocabulary and technique of early Scholasticism and may be found, for example, in the *sententia* attributed to the late-eleventh and early twelfth-century "School of Laon" (see Martin Grabmann, *Die Geschichte der Scholastischen Methode,* 2 vols. [Berlin, 1957], 2:153–57; Wilfried Hartmann, "Manegold von Lautenbach und die Anfänge der Frühscholastik," *Deutsches Archiv für Erforschung des Mittelalters* 26 [1970]: 106–7; and Brian Lawn, *The Rise and Decline of the Scholastic "Quaestio disputata" with Special Emphasis on Its Use in the Teaching of Medicine and Science* [Leiden, 1993]). On Galbert's knowledge and use of dialectic, see also Sproemberg, *Mittelalter,* 323–24.

48. "In this distress of mind, a little spark of love, warmed and animated by its own fire, set aflame all the spiritual strength of my heart and consequently endowed my bodily self, which had been seized by fear, with the freedom to write" ([Prol.], 26/29; trans., 80); "Strength of mind and memory and even reason, the greater virtue of the mind, fail me . . ." ([6], 1/2; trans., 93). Compare Guibert of Nogent's analysis of Anselm of Bec's psychological teachings at the end of the eleventh century (*Autobiographie* [*De Vita sua, sive Monodiae*], 1.17, ed. and French trans. Edmond-René Labande, Classiques de l'histoire de France au Moyen Age 34 [Paris, 1981], 138–40; trans. John F. Benton, *Self and Society in Medieval France* [1970; rpt. Medieval Academy Reprints for Teaching 15 [Toronto, 1984], 89–90). Aelred of Rievaulx writes that the soul has three powers: "memory . . . , knowledge, love, or will" (*memoriam . . . , scientiam, amorem, sive voluntatem*) (*Speculum charitatis* 1.3, *Patrologia latina* 195, 507; compare abridged trans. Geoffrey Webb and Adrian Walker, *The Mirror of Charity* [London, 1962], 5).

49. A concentration on the trivium, and especially on grammar and rhetoric, was characteristic of the schools of northern Europe in the late eleventh and early twelfth centuries, where dialectic and the quadrivium were not much taught and "grammar was still . . . the art of speaking well and interpreting the poets and historians. *Lectio, narratio, declinatio* were still the basic techniques" (Pierre Riché, "Jean de Salisbury et le monde scolaire," in *Education et culture dans l'Occident médiéval,* 16 [Aldershot, 1993], 54). On the kind of education Galbert might have received c. 1100, see Philippe Delhaye, "L'Organisation scolaire au XIIe siècle," *Traditio* 5 (1947): 211–68; Luitpold Wallach, "Onulf of Speyer: A Humanist of the Eleventh Century," *Medievalia et Humanistica* 6 (1950): 35–56; Hartmann, "Manegold von Lautenbach"; Valerie Flint, "The 'School of Laon': A Reconsideration," *Recherches de Théologie Ancienne et Médiévale* 43 (1976): 97–100, 108; David L. Wagner, ed., *The Seven Liberal Arts in*

the Middle Ages (Bloomington, Ind., 1983); Julia Barrow, "Education and the Recruitment of Cathedral Canons in England and Germany, 1100–1225," *Viator* 20 (1989): 124–26; Pierre Riché, "L'Enseignement de Gerbert à Reims dans le contexte européen," in *Education et culture,* 6, and "Jean de Salisbury et le monde scolaire," 39–41, 54–55; Martin Irvine, *The Making of Textual Culture: 'Grammatica' and Literary Theory, 350–1100* (Cambridge, U.K., 1994); C. Stephen Jaeger, *The Envy of Angels: Cathedral Schools and Social Ideals in Medieval Europe: 950–1200* (Philadelphia, 1994), 128–64; and Suzanne Reynolds, *Medieval Reading: Grammar, Rhetoric and the Classical Text* (Cambridge, U.K., 1996).

50. By the end of the eleventh century, an education in the trivium was increasingly seen and used as preparation for an administrative or professional career: Paetow even speaks of a "'Business Course' at Medieval Universities" (Louis John Paetow, *The Arts Course at Medieval Universities with Special Reference to Grammar and Rhetoric* [Champaign, Ill., 1910], 67). On the role of the trivium in the growing clerical careerism of the time, see Delhaye, "L'Organisation scolaire," 213; Pierre Riché, *Les Ecoles et l'enseignement dans l'Occident chrétien de la fin du Ve siècle au milieu du XIe siècle* (Paris, 1979), 258–60, "La Vie scolaire et la pédagogie au Bec au temps de Lanfranc et de Saint Anselme," in *Education et culture,* 14, 214, and "Jean de Salisbury et le monde scolaire," 49–52; William D. Patt, "The Early 'Ars Dictaminis' as a Response to a Changing Society," *Viator* 9 (1978): 134, 146–47; R. W. Southern, "The Schools of Paris and the School of Chartres," in Robert L. Benson and Giles Constable, eds., *Renaissance and Renewal in the Twelfth Century* (Cambridge, Mass., 1982), 115–16; Karl Morrison, "Incentives for Studying the Liberal Arts," in Wagner, ed., *The Seven Liberal Arts,* 33; Barrow, "Education and the Recruitment of Cathedral Canons," 126; and Jaeger, *The Envy of Angels,* 36–75. The end of the eleventh century also saw the first concerted Scholastic development of the *ars dictaminis,* the ultimate administrative discipline, which was nonetheless "firmly rooted in the rhetorical tradition" (Patt, "The Early 'Ars Dictaminis,'" 152) and thus linked closely to the trivium (see James J. Murphy, *Rhetoric in the Middle Ages* [Berkeley, Calif., 1974], 194–268; Patt, "The Early 'Ars Dictaminis'"; Hans Szklenar, *Magister Nicolaus de Dybin. Vorstudien zu einer Edition seiner Schriften. Ein Beitrag zur Geschichte der literarischen Rhetorik im späteren Mittelalter* [Munich, 1981], 20–21; Janet Martin, "Classicism and Style in Latin Literature," in Benson and Constable, eds., *Renaissance and Renewal in the Twelfth Century,* 538–39; and Martin Camargo, "Rhetoric," in Wagner, ed., *The Seven Liberal Arts,* 107–10). Although the Scholarly elaboration of the *ars dictaminis* has traditionally been thought to have begun in Italy and not to have spread north until after Galbert's time, Patt has recently argued that it "was not a localized product which spread to the rest of Europe from individual centers which successively dominated the field, but rather a cultural development which occurred more or less simultaneously in Italy, France, Germany, and perhaps other parts of Europe as well" ("The Early 'Ars Dictaminis,'" 139).

51. "Marvelous to tell, although the count was killed in the castle of Bruges on the morning of one day, that is, the fourth day of the week, the news of this impious death . . . towards evening of the same second day . . . disturbed the people of Laon who live far away from us in France. We learned this through our students who at that time were studying in Laon" ([12], 45/51; trans., 113–14). Guibert of Nogent likewise mentions "two little boys [probably from Flanders] who could speak only the Germanic tongue" who were being taught French by a monk at the monastery of Barisis-aux-Bois near Laon c. 1109 *(Autobiographie* 3.5, ed., 300; trans., 159). Lyon and Verhulst have also noted that "the cathedral school of Laon, famous for the study of mathematics and the abacus" was a possible source of knowledge about the abacus and its usefulness in auditing accounts for both the clergy of Saint Donatian and the English exchequer *(Medieval Finance,* 39–40). On the schools of Laon

in the early twelfth century, see Emile Lesne, *Histoire de la propriété ecclésiastique en France,* vol. 5: *Les Ecoles de la fin du VIIIe siècle à la fin du XIIe* (Lille, 1940), 299–310; J. de Ghellinck, *Le Mouvement théologique du XIIe siècle,* 2nd ed. (Bruges, 1948), 133–48; Bernard Merlette, "Ecoles et bibliothèques, à Laon, du déclin de l'antiquité au développement de l'université," in *Enseignement et vie intellectuelle (IXe–XVIe siècle),* Actes du 95e Congrès national des sociétés savantes, Reims, 1970, Section de philologie et d'histoire jusqu'à 1610 (Paris, 1975), 1:21–53; Flint, "The 'School of Laon'"; Marcia Colish, "Another Look at the School of Laon," *Archives d'Histoire doctrinale et littéraires du Moyen Age* 61 (1986): 7–22; and Alain Saint-Denis, *Apogée d'une cité: Laon et le Laonnois aux XIIe et XIIIe siècles* (Nancy, 1994).

52. Albert Demyttenaere has taken this suggestion the furthest, discerning a potential influence of the teachings of the school of Laon in several passages in the *De multro* ("Mentaliteit in de twaalfde eeuw," 87, 108, 117–18).

53. Galbert refers twice to a building he calls the "school" *(scholae),* adjacent to the church of Saint Donatian ([17], 36/37; trans., 126; [42], 22/23; trans., 178; it should be noted that the first of these references is not altogether clear and there is a plausible variant reading of *scalarum* for *scholarum:* Walter of Loker, that is, may have jumped down from "the high vault [or arch] of the stairs" rather than from "the high alcove [or vault or arch] of the school" [trans., 126]). This school, Galbert tells us, was "adjacent to the church," near enough that the beseiged "hurled fire" onto its roof in an effort "to set fire to the provost's house which was next to it" ([42], 22/24; trans., 178). Since the dormitory was also next to the church and close enough to the western tower for the beseiged to throw millstones onto it from there (see [60], 4/5; trans., 217; [62], 3/5; trans., 220; [63], 3/12; trans., 222), the school seems to have been located next to the church between the dormitory (also adjacent to the church, to the east) and the provost's house (to the west), on at least the upper floor of a building in either the southwest corner of the cloister or immediately to the west of this corner. The schools of the cathedrals of Notre-Dame of Tournai and Saint-Etienne of Toulouse were similarly situated next to the church in the cloister. In Tournai, a stairway led from the northwestern corner of the nave down to the ground level of the cloister, ending immediately in front of the entry to the school which occupied the ground floor of the buildings on the western side of the cloister, whose upper floor was occupied by the refectory and kitchen (Jacques Pycke, *Le Chapitre cathédral Notre-Dame de Tournai de la fin du XIe à la fin du XIIIe siècle: Son organisation, sa vie, ses membres,* Université de Louvain: Recueil de travaux d'histoire et de philologie 6.30 [Louvain-la-Neuve, 1986], 38, 40). In Toulouse, the school was on the upper floor of a building that extended east from the northeastern corner of the cloister (the corner nearest the church) to the town wall: its ground level was occupied by the refectory (Yves Esquieu, "Les Batiments de la vie commune des chanoines," in Jean-Charles Picard, ed., *Les Chanoines dans la ville. Recherches sur la topographie des quartiers canoniaux en France* [Paris, 1994], 44; illustration in Quitterie Cazes, "Toulouse," in Picard, ed., *Les Chanoines dans la ville,* 346).

Two members of the *conventus* of Saint Donatian during the first half of the twelfth century—Radulfus (1110[?]–1129/30) and Ebrardus (1127/75[?]–1166/67[?])—are called *magister* (see Appendix I, *s.v.* Ebrardus/Everardus and Radulfus/2), and the fact that the one seems to succeed the other suggests that term refers here to the function of schoolmaster rather than to the possession of an academic degree. It is thus curious that the earliest catalogue of the chapter library of Saint Donatian (c. 1260–1270; ed. in Albert Derolez and Benjamin Victor, *Corpus Catalogorum Belgii: The Medieval Booklists of the Southern Low Countries,* vol. 1: *Province of West Flanders,* 2nd ed. [Brussels, 1991], 167–70) lists so few "textbooks" (no works of Donatus, Servius, Priscian, Cicero, Horace, Juvenal, Lucan, Ovid, Sallust, Statius, or Virgil; for a late-twelfth-century Parisian list of textbooks, see Charles Homer Haskins, "A List of Text-Books from the Close of the Twelfth Century," *Studies in the History of Mediaeval Science* [Cambridge, Mass., 1924], 356–76). Perhaps there was a school library distinct from the chapter library, as Barrow has suggested was normal in German cathedral schools of the twelfth century ("Education and the Recruitment of Cathedral Canons," 125).

54. For some idea of the classical works available for study in the dioceses of Arras, Noyon-Tournai, and Thérouanne at this time, see Birger Munk Olsen, *L'Etude des auteurs classiques latins aux XIe et XIIe siècles,* 4 vols. (Paris, 1982–89), 3.1: *s.v.* Arras (30–31), Bruges (58), Clairmarais (73–74), Cysoing (92–93), Dunes (94), Gand (116), St-Amand (216–20), St-Bertin (221–22), Tournai (255–57), and Watten (269). Collectively, these libraries contained various works of Apuleius, Cicero, Dares, Julius Frontinus, Homer, Horace, Hyginus, Juvenal, Lucan, Ovid, Persius, Pliny, Sallust, Seneca, Statius, Terence, and Virgil. For a broader picture of the works that might have been available to Galbert, one can turn to the surviving catalogues of twelfth-century libraries in the provinces of West Flanders, Liège, Luxemburg, and Namur: see Derolez and Victor, *Corpus Catalogorum Belgii,* 1:30–31 (Bruges, Our Lady); 1:156 (Bruges, Sint Andries, or Affligem); vol. 2, *Provinces of Liège, Luxemburg and Namur* (Brussels, 1994), 113–14 (Liège, Saint Laurence); 116–18 (unknown chapter or monastic library); 169–74 (Stavelot, Saint Remaculus); 218–19 (Brogne, Saint Gerard). For an overview of the clerical literary culture of Flanders from the tenth through the mid-fourteenth centuries, see E. de Moreau, "Kerk en geestelijk leven tot het Concordaat van Worms, 936–1122," *Algemene Geschiedenis der Nederlanden* 2 (Utrecht, 1950), 221–23; and Lieven van Acker, "De Latijnse literaire cultuur in Noorden en Zuiden van circa 1050 tot circa 1350," *Algemene Geschiedenis der Nederlanden* 3 (Haarlem, 1982), 328–42.

55. Notre-Dame of Tournai had a well-known schoolmaster, Odo of Orléans, from c. 1086–1092 (who left to found and serve as the first abbot of the abbey of Saint Martin of Tournai [1092–1105] and was eventually elected bishop of Cambrai [1105–1113]), and was generally happy in its choice of schoolmasters until 1136, although there was no "higher" school there (Pycke, *Le Chapitre cathédral Notre-Dame de Tournai,* 111–13, 270–74; compare Herman of Tournai, *Liber,* 1–4, ed. 274–77; trans., 13–19). Elias has speculated that Galbert was indeed taught by Odo or someone trained by him and discerns traces of his teaching in what she perceives to be Galbert's Augustinianism ("Augustinian Elements," 46–47, n. 13).

56. The list of his classical and patristic citations (ed., 192) is distinctly thin when compared to that of almost any other writer of the period (see, for example, the citations in Guibert of Nogent's *Autobiographie* [ed., 491] or those of the author of the *Vita Heinrici IV. imperatoris* [ed. W. Wattenbach and W. Eberhard, in Franz-Josef Schmale, gen. ed. and trans., *Quellen zur Geschichte Kaiser Heinrichs IV* (Darmstadt, 1974), 408–67, footnotes] or the *Gesta Stephani* [ed. and trans. K. R. Potter, Oxford Medieval Texts (Oxford, U.K., 1976), footnotes]).

57. He evidently cites the Bible from memory since he occasionally conflates or confuses passages (see [Prol.], 41/43; trans., 80; [2], 16/17; trans., 85; [6], 11/13; trans., 94; [6], 36/38; trans., 96; [12], 41/42; trans., 11; [57], 15; trans., 208; [63], 48/49; trans., 224; [69], 82/83; trans., 237; [71], 34/36; trans., 240; [83], 10/11; trans., 254; [116], 52/53; trans., 303; [118], 30/31; trans., 306; [118], 33/34; trans., 306; [118], 35; trans., 306), and the list of his biblical citations (ed., 191; to which should be added a citation of Dan. 13.5 in [118], 41/42, identified by Demyttenaere, *De Moord* [1999], 264, n. 238), which, as we will see, were mostly added in the process of rewriting his first draft and are concentrated in a few

chapters of the *De multro,* is risible when compared with that of a monastic historian like Guibert of Nogent *(Autobiographie,* ed., 489–91) or even that of the authors, probably secular clerics, of the *Vita Heinrici IV* (ed., footnotes) or the *Gesta Stephani* (ed., footnotes).

58. He sometimes notes dates, as do other historians of the period, by referring to the first words of the Introit of the Mass for that day (see *De multro,* [34], 2; trans., 161; [48], 2; trans., 189; [55], 1; trans., 201; [66], 1/2; trans., 227; [98], 9; trans., 273; [99], 2/3; trans., 274; [103], 9; trans., 280; and [110], 8; trans., 290), and he notes that the count was murdered after "the office of the first hour was completed and also the response of the third hour, when 'Our Father' is said" ([15], 12/14; trans., 119). Walter, archdeacon of the diocese of Thérouanne, however, is even more precise, noting that the count was killed while his chaplain "was singing the first and third hours of the day in ecclesiastical fashion and, having already said the Lord's prayer, recited to him the prayers of the third hour, and while he [the count] was reciting the fiftieth psalm, the fourth penitential one, having already said three of them" *(Vita Karoli,* [25], 549, 10/12).

59. B. Smalley, "Sallust in the Middle Ages," in R. R. Bolgar, ed., *Classical Influences on European Culture, A.D. 500–1500* (Cambridge, U.K., 1971), 172. Sallust's *Bellum Catilinae (The War with Catiline)* and *Bellum Iugurthinum (The War with Jugurtha)* were a regular part of the grammar curriculum at this time (see Smalley, "Sallust," 168; Riché, *Les Ecoles et l'enseignement,* 252; and Martin, "Classicism and Style," 549, who calls him "a school author"). Other classical historians were less taught, and their works were rarely found in chapter libraries (see Birger Munk Olsen, "La Diffusion et l'étude des historiens antiques au XIIe siècle," in Andries Welkenhuysen, Herman Braet, and Werner Verbeke, eds., *Mediaeval Antiquity,* Mediaevalia Lovaniensia 1.24 [Leuven, 1995], 33–34, 41). The works of Sallust are not, however, mentioned in the late-thirteenth-century catalogue of the chapter library of Saint Donatian, whose only historical works were *The City of God,* a copy of the "book of Paul Orosius" *(liber Pauli Orosii),* saints' lives, a "complete history of Alexander" *(historia plena de Alexandro),* and a "*coronica*" (Derolez and Victor, *Corpus Catalogorum Belgii,* 1:167–70).

60. Because he sought to restore confidence, in the wake of the fall of Rome, in the "idea of progress" commonly held in Christian circles—a belief that human life had become materially better since the advent of Christianity and that the end of history was the collective salvation, the collective perfection of humankind and its institutions—and in the even older and more widely held idea of "a commutative contract between God and man"—a belief that God rewards good deeds and punishes bad ones with relative alacrity in the here-and-now—Orosius had a greater influence on the writing of history in the Middle Ages than did Augustine, who rejected both ideas and suggested that the end of history was "the salvation of individual men, not of any collective groups or organizations" (Theodor E. Mommsen, "Saint Augustine and the Christian Idea of Progress: The Background of *The City of God,*" in his *Medieval and Renaissance Studies,* ed. Eugene F. Rice Jr. [Ithaca, N.Y., 1959], 277, 280, 293; see also his "Orosius and Augustine," in *Medieval and Renaissance Studies,* 325–48; Benoit Lacroix, *Orose et ses idées* [Montreal, 1965]; Karl Ferdinand Werner, "Gott, Herrscher und Historiograph. Der Geschichtsschreiber als Interpret des Wirkens Gottes in der Welt und Ratgeber der Könige [4. bis 12. Jahrhundert]," in Ernst-Dieter Hehl, Hubertus Seibert, and Franz Staab, eds., *Deus qui mutat tempora. Menschen und Institutionen im Wandel des Mittelalters. Feschrift für Alfons Becker zu seinem fünfundsechzigsten Geburtstag* [Sigmaringen, 1987], 1–31; and Orosius, *Histoires (Contre les Païens),* 3 vols., ed. and French trans. Marie-Pierre Arnaud-Lindet [Paris, 1990–1991], 1:xx–lxvi).

Galbert, like Augustine and Orosius, wrote in response to a historical crisis that challenged fundamental ideas about God's role in history. Elias has identified a number of ways in which he may have been influenced by the Augustinian concept of history ("Augustinian Elements," 35–48), but, overall, Galbert's interest in the collective fate of the inhabitants of Flanders, his efforts to restore confidence in the theology of history challenged by the crisis, his driving desire to "identify God's intentions in the earthly events he chooses to recount" (Lacroix, *Orose,* 205), to "prove beyond question that all these events were arranged according to the inscrutable, mysterious, and unfathomable judgements of God and that they were not brought to pass either by human agencies or by mere chance" (Orosius, *Histoires* 2.2.4, ed., 1:86; *Seven Books of History against the Pagans,* Records of Civilization, Sources and Studies 26, trans. Irving W. Raymond [New York, 1936], 73; compare trans. Mommsen, "Orosius and Augustine," 338; and *The Seven Books of History against the Pagans,* The Fathers of the Church, A New Translation 50, trans. Roy J. Deferrari [Washington, D.C., 1964], 45) and his sense that the events of 1127–1128 were a series of punishments and rewards for past deeds are more Orosian than Augustinian. As was mentioned above, the late-thirteenth-century catalogue of the chapter library of Saint Donatian lists both a copy of *The City of God* and a copy of the "book of Paul Orosius" *(liber Pauli Orosii),* but there is no evidence other than a couple of vague reminiscences that Galbert himself read the work of either author.

61. Chapters 68–71, which Galbert added to the *De multro* when he revised his first draft in the summer and fall of 1127, are the only ones that relate events that clearly occurred before his lifetime.

Chapters 68–70 provide a skeletal dynastic history of Flanders from c. 1051 (the marriage of the future Baldwin VI to Countess Richilde of Hainaut) to c. 1083 (an unsuccessful rebellion against Robert I), whose major focus is Robert I's treacherous acquisition of the county in 1071. Galbert's account of the unsuccessful rebellion of c. 1083 ([70], 12/26; trans., 237–38) echoes the account of the same rebellion in the *Life of Saint Arnulf (Vita Arnulfi episcopi Suessionensis auctore Hariulfo abbate Aldenburgensi,* ed. O. Holder-Egger, *Monumenta Germaniae Historica, Scriptores* 15, 2 [Hannover, 1888], 886–87), written in 1114 by Hariulf, abbot of Oudenburg (1105–1143)—who was known to Galbert at least by reputation, since he refers to him as "a devout and wise man" ([114], 18; trans., 297)—and it is possible that he was drawing on, or remembering, the *Vita* at this point, but overall the popular character of Galbert's account of Robert I's acquisition of the county—its sentimentality, Flandrocentrism (he never mentions King Philip of France, who played an important role in the conflict between Robert and his nephew, Arnold), colorful detail (Baldwin's speech to the assembled nobles, the story of the clerical messenger who feigns blindness, and the fact that Arnold was killed by the very servants who armed him)—becomes all the more evident when one compares it with Hermann of Tournai's later (1142), more succinct and matter-of-fact account *(Liber,* 12–13, ed., 279–80; trans., 27–28) of this same history. Gislebert of Mons's even later (1200–23/25) account likewise betrays a popular influence (in, for example, his characterisation of Robert the Frisian and the tale of the assassin Gerbodo's trip to Rome), although the popular memory of these events was rather different in the Hainaut than it was in Flanders *(Chronicon Hanoniense,* Scriptores rerum Germanicarum in usum scholarum, ed. Wilhelm Arndt [Hannover, 1869], 26–31).

Chapter 71 relates the rather ribald and otherwise unknown history of the origins of the Erembald family in its founder's adulterous relations with the wife of his lord and friend, Boldran, the castellan of Bruges. Since the suddenly omniscient Galbert tells us that "when the silence of the night had fallen, and the castellan had gone to the rim of the ship to urinate, Erembald, running up from behind, precipitated his lord into the depths of the rushing water, far from the ship . . . while the others were asleep . . . [so that] no one but the adulterer knew what had become of that castellan" ([71], 15/20; trans., 239), this part of the story, at least, was made up and seems to have been shaped at the rumor mill to titillate a popular palate.

62. See Appendix V.

63. See Declercq, "Gablert van Brugge," 112, n. 145. On the meaning of *conventus* in medieval Latin, see Pierre Michaud-Quantin, *Universitas: Expressions du mouvement communautaire dans le Moyen-Age latin,* L'Eglise et l'état au Moyen Age 13 (Paris, 1970), 107–9.

64. Baldwin (chaplain, notary, chancellor), Basil (clericus, notary), Bertulf (chaplain, provost), Fromold Sr. (notary), Ledbert (chaplain, former provost of Saint Donatian), Ralph (schoolmaster), and Roger (Bertulf's successor as provost of Saint Donatian). For the passages in which Galbert names these clerics, too numerous to cite here, see the indices to my edition and Ross's translation. For other evidence concerning these men and their role in the count's administration, see Appendix I, *s.v.* Balduinus/2, Basilius, Bertulfus/1, Fromoldus Senior/1, Letbertus/1, Radulfus/2, and Rodgerus.

65. Fulco (canon) is said to have had a brother who was a "crafty knight" *(militem subdolum)* and helped Bertulf escape ([46], 2; trans., 185), while Galbert reports that the remaining three, Helias (dean), Littera (canon), and Robert (priest and sacristan) all received money from the assassins (see [83], 1/19; trans., 253–54; [85], 8/30; trans.; 256–57). For other evidence concerning these men, see Appendix I, *s.v.* Fulco, Helias, Littera, and Robertus/3. The charter evidence indicates that Fulco may have served as a clericus and chancellor in the administration. It is thus perhaps significant that Galbert does not criticize him, only his brother, and does not identify him as a member of the administration.

66. Eustace (clericus; see [18], 17; trans., 128); Fromold Junior (clericus, notary; see [18], 30/35, 39/41; trans., 129, [19], 24/30; trans., 131; [24], 7/28; trans., 142–43; [25], 61/63; trans., 146–47; [107] 13/16; trans., 286); Godbert (the count's clericus; see [18], 5; trans., 128; [23], 7; trans., 141); Odger Junior (clericus, notary, chaplain, chancellor; see [18], 7; trans., 128; [23], 6/7; trans., 141). For other evidence concerning these men and their role in the count's administration, see Appendix I, *s.v.* Eustachius, Fromoldus Junior/2, Godbertus, and Odgerus Junior/3.

67. Eggard (priest of the church of the Holy Savior), Heribert (priest), Sigebod (priest, as we know from elsewhere, of the church of Saint Mary [see S. Muller and A. C. Bouman, eds., *Oorkondenboek van het Sticht Utrecht tot 1301,* vol. 1 (Utrecht, 1920), n° 286, 265]), Thancran (dean and priest [of the church of Saint Mary?]; see Muller and Bouman, *Oorkondenboek,* n° 301, 277)]), Thierry (priest). See [61], 15/38; trans., 219–20; [113], 51/61; trans., 296; [114], 74/95; trans., 299–301; [115], 11/15; trans., 301; [118], 17/27; trans., 305. Galbert also includes Fromold Senior, a member of both the conventus and the administration in the list of priests he castigates in chapter 114, but he identifies him there only as a priest and does not mention his connection with either of these institutions.

68. See Pirenne, ed., xiii. F. L. Ganshof wrote that "he belongs to the milieu of the burghers of Bruges and echoes their reactions" ("Les Origines du concept," 139; compare Ganshof's "Le Roi de France en Flandre," 207). Ross calls him "a true son of Bruges" (trans., 73–74), while Sproemberg suggests "that he came from a burgher family of the *suburbium* [the town surrounding the burg]," and notes his strong interest in the fate of merchants and many contacts with them *(Mittelalter,* 338–39; compare 229–30, 240, 356). Coué suggests that Galbert was more or less commissioned to write the *De multro* by the burghers of Bruges ("Der Mord," 123). Ross and Alan Murray both also note that Galbert shared the burghers' devotion to Robert the Young, a member of the Erembald clan (see trans., 109, n. 7, and 149, n. 7; A. Murray, "Voices of Flanders," 111–12).

69. Sproemberg suggests that Galbert's "description of the fighting in the burg makes it clear that he didn't live there; he probably owned a modest dwelling in the *suburbium*" *(Mittelalter,* 338). Fromold Junior, who is never named as a member of the conventus of Saint Donatian, had a family and children, a significant household (see *De multro,* [18], 30/35, 39/41; trans., 129, [24], 7/28; trans., 142–43; [25], 61/63; trans., 146–47), and as many as two houses, one of which was particularly magnificent *(De multro,* [19], 24/30; trans., 131, [107] 13/16; trans., 286). On Fromold Junior, see Reusens, "Les Chancelleries," 122, 124–25; Vercauteren, *Actes,* li and n. 3; Ross, trans., 130, n. 2; and De Hemptinne and Verhulst, *Oorkonden,* xli–xlii.

70. Folpert, a judge, ([51], 5; trans., 193), Gerbert ([48], 20/24; trans., 190), and Lambert Berakin ([16], 30/32; trans., 122).

71. The term comes from Dhondt's article, "Les 'Solidarités.'"

72. See Appendix I, *s.v.* Galbertus/1. The tax list of 1127/28–c. 1175 is a particularly interesting document which has been studied briefly by Strubbe *(Het Fragment,* 21–22) and Declercq ("Galbert van Brugge," 110–11).

73. At the beginning of chapter 19, for example, Galbert writes: "Meanwhile the canons of that place [*canonici loci illius*] ran to the uncle of Fromold Junior advising him to intercede with the provost for the life of his nephew whom they had seen placed in mortal danger, for Isaac had sworn his death. Then the older man, hastening to the provost, entered his house with the brothers of the church [*cum fratribus ecclesiae*], and kneeling at his feet, begged and beseeched him to protect the life of his nephew" ([19], 1/7; trans., 130). Galbert describes the canons of Saint Donatian here and elsewhere in the third person plural and there is no suggestion that I can sense that he belonged to this group. When he does use the first person plural, it is, as was mentioned above, to describe the inhabitants of Bruges. Compare his other references to the "brothers" or canons of Saint Donatian: [9], 16, 22; trans., 103, 104; [13], 12/21; trans., 115–16; [17], 22/23; trans., 125; [20], 4/5; trans., 132; [21], 5/11; trans., 134–35; [22], 27/53, 66/71; trans., 138–39, 140; [23], 1/11; trans., 141; [25], 38/43; trans., 145; [35], 1/13, 19/29; trans., 162–63, 16–64; [37], 6/7, 21/22; trans., 167, 168; [41], 67/68, 77/83; trans., 176, 176–77; [43], 49; trans., 180; [45], 58/60; trans., 184; [55], 1/6; 10/27, 39/40; trans., 201, 201–2, 203; [60], 1/7; trans., 216–17; [61], 23/30; trans., 219; [62], 1/10; trans., 220–21; [64], 36/43; trans., 226; [76], 7/11; trans., 245; [77], 1/15; trans., 245–46; [78], 7/16; trans., 247; [81], 4/5; trans., 250; [85], 1/30; trans., 256–57; [116], 57/58; trans., 303. James Murray has likewise suggested that Galbert's "ties with the church were not taut. He was a *notarius* and perhaps chapter scribe for St. Donatian's church, thus probably in minor orders and certainly not a canon or chaplain of the church. His concurrent work for the count may have required the bulk of his time, thus making him more a member of the comital household than church functionary" ("The Rites of Feudal Violence in Twelfth-Century Flanders," unpublished paper delivered at the 27th International Congress on Medieval Studies, Kalamazoo, Mich., May 1992.) I would like to thank Professor Murray for giving me a copy of this paper.

74. See De Hemptinne and Vandermaesen, "De ambtenaren," 201; Rider, ed., xiii–xv; and Appendix I, *s.v.* Balduinus, Bertulfus, Fromoldus, Fulpertus, Hugo, Letbertus, Odgerus, Radulfus, Rainlofus, Reinarus, and Walterus.

75. See Appendix I, *s.v.* Galbertus/2.

76. See Declercq, "Galbert van Brugge," 111–12.

77. As Declercq has done ("Galbert van Brugge," 115–16).

78. "In the house of the brothers in the church of Saint Donatian," he writes, "the canons had formerly been deeply religious men and perfectly educated, that is, at the begin-

ning of the provostship of this most arrogant prelate [c. 1091]. Restraining his pride, they had held him in check by advice and by Catholic doctrine so that he could not undertake anything unseemly in the church. But after they went to sleep in the Lord, the provost, left to himself, set in motion anything that pleased him and toward which the force of his pride impelled him" ([13], 14/21; trans., 115–16). In his description of Bertulf's capture and execution, Galbert likewise writes: "he could indeed have remembered, if he had wished, how after asserting himself forcibly and imposing himself unjustly while the provost Ledbert was still alive—an honorable man who endured everything for the sake of God—he had, contrary to God, usurped the prelacy in the Church of God" ([57], 32/35; trans., 209).

79. See his descriptions of the church at [35], 14/16; trans., 163; [37], 7/20; trans., 167–68; [78], 7/23; trans., 247–48.

80. See Appendix I, *s.v.* Basilius. De Hemptinne and Verhulst write that the notary Lambert, one of the six receivers of Bruges mentioned in the *Gros Brief* of 1187, was also a canon of Saint Donatian *(Oorkonden,* xlv), but in a recent e-mail message, Professor De Hemptinne has told me that there is in fact no concrete evidence that he was a canon of that church, although there was indeed a canon of that name at that time and the notary Lambert is always mentioned among the clergy—most often dignitaries and canons of Saint Donatian—in witness lists. She added, however, that another of the six receivers, William of Commines or Messines, is mentioned as a canon of Saint Donatian in a charter of Philippe of Alsace dating to 1176/77.

81. Thirty-one of the fifty-two members (60 percent) of the conventus whom I have been able to identify as being active between 1089 and 1135 seem never to have served in the administration, while twenty of the forty-one clerics (49 percent) whom I have been able to identify as being active in the count's administration in Bruges during this period have no apparent attachments to the conventus (see Appendix I).

The distinction between the two groups is underlined by the fact that only one of the eight men whom we can identify, from the *De multro,* as having accompanied the count to Saint Donatian on the morning of March 2—the priest and chaplain Baldwin (Balduinus/2)—may have been a member of the conventus ([16]–[18]; trans., 120–29). This Baldwin, moreover, hid (with the clerk Godbert) in obvious fear of his life that morning, whereas the priests and clergy of Saint Donatian seem to have moved about, and even to have stood up to Borsiard, with impunity ([16], 4/6; trans., 120–21; [17], 46/48; trans., 127; [18], 3/6, 37–41; trans., 127–28, 129): Baldwin's service to the count thus seems to have distinguished him from the regular priests of Saint Donatian.

De Hemptinne, Prevenier, and Vandermaesen note that even the personnel of the chancellery (which, as Strubbe emphasized, was not identical with the fiscal administration of the comital domain and was distinctly more clerical in nature [*Egidius van Breedene,* 38]) might be drawn from either "the prince's chapel . . . or . . . one of the numerous comital chapters created during the eleventh century" in connection with the division of Flanders into castellanies ("La Chancellerie," 443; see also De Hemptinne and Vandermaesen, "De ambtenaren," 192). It thus seems, and Strubbe likewise suggests, that some of the personnel of the count's administration entered that administration directly, while others were first, or were at least simultaneously, canons of this or that chapter. Strubbe further suggests that some of the clergymen who entered directly into the count's administration might later have been compensated with prebends in the conventus of Saint Donatian (see *Egidius van Breedene,* 29–30).

82. See under these names in Appendix I.

83. The members of this group are Basilius, Cono, Fulco, Ingaricus, Ledelinus,

Reinarus parvus/2, and Walter/2; Gerardus/2 and either Reinarus/3 or Reinarus/4 perhaps belong in this group as well. The distinction between ecclesiastical and administrative roles and ranks is likewise found in the episcopal chancellery of Arras in the twelfth century, whose clerici—the lowest adminstrative rank—included two priests, a deacon, a subdeacon, and an acolyte, as well as a number of men who are not given any ecclesiastical rank (Tock, *Chancellerie épiscopale,* 191–92).

84. A fairly large "lower" clerical pool of men at or below the rank of subdeacon may have been a common feature of Flemish chapters of the time. The chapter founded at Cassel by Robert the Frisian in 1085 included twenty "brothers" *(fratres)* of whom seven were to be priests and five deacons. Robert stipulated that "the eight remaining brothers will serve in the subdiaconate and other ranks, as the provost enjoins" *(in ordine subdiaconatus et caeterorum graduum, prout injunctum fuerit a praelato)* (Vercauteren, *Actes,* n° 6, p. 18). Pycke was unable to determine the ecclesiastical rank of 60 percent of the clergy of Notre-Dame of Tournai between 1100 and 1140 and suggests that "the large proportion of clerics whose rank is unknown between 1100 and 1140 might well indicate that a large number of canons had received only the tonsure and had no desire to accede to major orders" *(Le Chapitre cathédral Notre-Dame de Tournai,* 245; on the proportions of priests, deacons, subdeacons, and acolytes in collegial chapters in the eleventh and twelfth centuries, see also Georges Declercq, "Nieuwe Inzichten over de Oorsprong van het Sint-Veerlekapittel in Gent," *Handelingen der Maatschappij voor Geschiedenis en Ouheidkunde te Gent,* n.s. 43 [1989]: 61, n. 85, and 74, n. 155). It is possible that Saint Donatian had a similar lower clerical pool, some of whose members, as Strubbe suggested, were first and foremost comital functionairies for whom the count was able to secure a prebend or benefice in the conventus of Saint Donatian *(Egidius van Breedene,* 29–30).

It is interesting to note in this connection that the conventus of Veurne—the second largest local center of the count's fiscal administration—had eighteen canons in 1123, when Charles added a nineteenth (Vercauteren, *Actes,* n° 114, p. 261), providing for the new prebend with revenues from the comital domain. This suggests that the new canon may have been essentially a fiscal functionary, compensated from the count's revenues, whom he attached to the conventus because it was the center of the castellany's fiscal administration. It may thus have been the case that all (or at least most of) the members of this administration were attached to one or another conventus in some way, and the count's fiscal administration may have been a sort of parasite living within these various conventus, although the count saw to it that the resources of the conventus were sufficient to support both those members with liturgical duties and those with fiscal ones.

According to Dirk Heirbaut, "the household servants," "garrisons and court officials of the count [the secular wing of his administration] . . .were originally supported at their lord's court, where they received a prebend." By 1187 (perhaps even before 1089, Heirbaut suggests), this prebend had been transformed into a *feif-rent:* "a yearly income assigned on a source of revenue" that could, it seems, be an ecclesiastical prebend or property, but whose installments were paid by the comital treasury or one of the local receiverships of his domain ("The *Feif-Rente:* A New Evaluation, Based on Flemish Sources [1000–1305]," *Tijdschrift voor Rechtsgeschiedenis / Revue d'Histoire du Droit / The Legal History Review* 67 [1999]: 14, 17, 22). In the early twelfth century, in sum, the count's administration included both secular members, supported through the count's domanial revenues, and clerical members, some of whom were supported by the domanial revenues and some of whom were supported by ecclesiastical prebends. One's work, that is, did not clearly indicate how one was compensated, and the source of one's compensation did not clearly indicate what kind of work one did.

85. Galbert refers to the canons' "dormitory" *(dormitorium)* ([37], 21; trans., 168; [41],

67, 80; trans., 176, 177; [45], 60; trans., 184, [60], 1, 4; trans., 216–17, [62], 3, 7, 24; trans., [63], 4, 7/9, 14; trans., 222) and "refectory" *(refectorium)* ([9], 22; trans., 104, [37], 6; trans., 167, [45], 59; trans., 184)—the two buildings, as Esquieu points out, that are essential to a common life ("Batiments de la vie commune," 41)—so some of them, at least, seem to have lived a communal, if very comfortable, life (see Galbert's description of the contents of their cellar and the accouterments of the dormitory, [41], 76/83; trans., 176–77). In the charter of 1085, mentioned above, founding the chapter of Cassel, Robert the Frisian had decreed that "the same brothers will remain chaste, will eat together, sleep together, comport themselves religiously within the cloister, and carefully respect other observances pertaining to canons" *(eosdem fratres castitatem observare, simul commedere, simul jacere, cum habitu religionis infra claustrum incedere et caetera quae canonicorum sunt sollicite observare)* (Vercauteren, *Actes,* n° 6, p. 18–19), and, according to Pycke, a communal life was still probably observed, albeit with a growing laxness, in the region's collegial chapters in the 1120s, although it was gradually abandoned there over the course of the twelfth century. Galbert's frequent use of the term *frater* (instead of *canonicus)* to refer to the members of the conventus may also, according to Pycke, reflect the existence of a communal life, or at least the aspiration for such a life, within the conventus at this time *(Le Chapitre cathédral Notre-Dame de Tournai,* 107–8, 113–15).

Perhaps Galbert distinguished between the members of the conventus who were in major orders and those who were not, and referred only to the former as "canons" or "brothers." Declercq likewise seems to suggest that "canon" might be used in two senses in the charters of the time: in a restricted sense to refer only to senior members of the conventus and in a broader sense to refer to all its members ("Galbert van Brugge," 112–13).

86. The question as to whether or not the author Galbert was a canon is perhaps not so very significant insofar as the term "canon" had a variety of meanings in northwestern Europe at this time. "The technical vocabulary of medieval religious life," writes Giles Constable, "is complicated and elusive" and "one of the most confusing terms is 'canon' . . . . [I]n practice there were almost as many different types of canons, both regular and secular, as there were of monks, and each order and house had to some extent its own way of life." In some cases, secular and regular canons coexisted within a single community as they did at Saint Quiriace in Provins from c. 1140 to 1152 *(The Reformation of the Twelfth Century* [Cambridge, U.K., 1996], 9, 11, 55, 114–15). E. Lesne has observed that, on the one hand, "it does not seem that the payment of prebendal revenues was strictly subordinated to the fulfilment of [liturgical] functions," and, on the other, that various benefices could well be held from a chapter by men who were not canons ("Les Origines de la prébende," *Revue Historique de Droit Français et Etranger* 8 [1929]: 279–80, 285). In late-eleventh- and twelfth-century Flanders, according to Declercq, *canonicus* could even "be used to refer to a group of secular clergy who were attached to a non-collegial church" and *prebenda* could be used to refer to their benefices. The comital church of Sint-Veerle in the castle of Ghent, for example, was not a collegial church, but the clergy attached to it in the late eleventh and twelfth centuries—who seem to have been comital *capellani* and may have served as administrative functionaries as well as chapelains—were called *canonici* and their benefices *prebenda* ("Nieuwe Inzichten," 60–61; see 59–64, 69–70, 101). As Heirbaut has pointed out, even "the fief of the Saint-Omar castle guard was called: '*feodum et prebenda*'" in 1127 ("The *Fief-Rente,*" 22 n. 152). Identifying Galbert as a "canon" of Saint Donatian, in sum, tells us only that he was a cleric who was compensated from the resources of Saint Donatian; it does not tell us anything definite about his way of life or duties.

87. Ross likewise calls Galbert a "notary or fiscal functionary" ("Rise and Fall," 370).

88. Some of the count's charters were prepared by members of his administration, for

example, rather than their beneficiaries, and members of the fiscal administration might likewise have been called upon to be present at donations or other juridical acts in order to take notes that served as the basis for the subsequent composition of a charter or to help the count with his correspondance (see Tock, *Chancellerie épiscopale,* 86, 69–73; Strubbe, *Egidius van Breedene,* 38; De Hemptinne and Vandermaesen, "De ambtenaren," 188; and De Hemptinne, Prevenier, and Vandermaesen, "La Chancellerie," 441). Two of the three Odgers active in the count's administration between 1089 and 1135, for example, are termed both "notary," denoting a position in the fiscal administration, and "chancellor," keeper of the seal, or scribe, indicating some role in the elaboration of the count's charters or correspondance (see Appendix I, *s.v.* Odgerus/1, Odgerus Junior/3). Basilius and Fromold Junior are likewise called both notary and comital *cartator* (Appendix 1, *s.v.* Basilius, Fromoldus Junior/2). Verlinden also notes that when, in 1084, Robert I ordered the castellan of Bruges, Erembald of Veurne (Bertulf's father), and "the wise men" *(prudentes vires)* of the castellany to carry out an inquiry into murders that had been committed within the castellany and to report the results of the inquest in writing, they were probably aided by a clerical functionary, at least in the composition of their written report *(Robert Ier le Frison,* 35–36, 36 n. 1, 142; the charge is recorded in Hariulf, *Vita Arnulfi* 2.19, 890). The inquest carried out in September 1127 into Charles's murder likewise resulted in a written document, and the members of the fiscal administration may have helped in this kind of work as well (perhaps Galbert had a hand in writing up the results of this inquest). It seems reasonable to suppose, that is, that the comital administration in Bruges at this time employed a number of clerical workers whose principal, standing duties lay in the fiscal administration of the count's domain in the castellany of Bruges, but who were also called upon to carry out various other clerical duties when the need arose.

89. Galbert's distance from both the conventus and the curia, and his detached and slightly critical, almost reporter-like, attitude toward their members are neatly evident in his account of Charles's burial on March 4 ([23], 1/27; trans., 141–42).

90. Galbert's practical experience of comital government sets him apart from most other historians of the time. Writing about Orderic Vitalis, for example, Marjorie Chibnall notes that "abstract political thought . . . lay outside Orderic's intellectual experience. He had to feel his way towards abstract concepts by applying his knowledge of Scripture and the writings of the Fathers and earlier historians to his own experience of political reality and feudal and ecclesiastical custom" *(The World of Orderic Vitalis,* 191).

91. Smalley, *Historians in the Middle Ages,* 107. Bernard Guenée likewise characterizes Galbert as one of the first "bureaucratic" historians *(Histoire et culture historique,* 65–66).

92. *Galbert van Brugge,* 6; compare Galbert, *Le Meurtre,* 63.

NOTES TO CHAPTER 2

1. *Historia Pontificalis / Memoirs of the Papal Court,* Prologue, trans. Marjorie Chibnall (Edinburgh and London, 1956), 4.

2. *Didascalicon,* 6.2–3, ed. Charles Henry Buttimer (Washington, D.C., 1939), 113–14; *Didascalicon,* trans. Jerome Taylor (New York, 1961), 135–36.

3. "And, in fact, I did not have a favorable time or place when I turned my mind to this work, because our place at that time was so disturbed by fear and anxiety that the clergy and people without exception were threatened continually with loss of life and property. It was, therefore, in the midst of many calamities and in the most constrained circumstances that I began to compose my mind, as unquiet as if it were tossed about in Euripus, and to subdue it to the discipline of writing" ([Prol.], 18/26; trans., 80).

4. Pirenne, ed., viii.

5. Ross, trans., 66–67.

6. Van Caenegem proposes a similarly psychological explanation for Galbert's undertaking the *Descriptio*—"He simply started writing, obeying a simple need to put down in writing the interesting and dramatic events in which he found himself plunged"—adding more explicitly that by writing, Galbert "sought to understand what he had observed" (in Galbert, *Le Meurtre,* 63, 65).

7. This explanation is also advanced, in part, by Father Huyghebaert: "Galbert, who had lived many years in the prince's orbit and felt great admiration for him, seems to have decided to write the Life of a man whom he considered a martyr" ("Galbert de Bruges," 737).

8. "Der Mord," 114, 123–24, 117, 108–9, 117.

9. In a letter of October 5, 1997, in response to an earlier version of this discussion of Galbert's motives, Professor Van Caenegem wrote that "I myself started keeping a diary in the spring of 1944 when we felt that big events (D-day!) were on the way and I kept it till the liberation in September of that year, but I do not know why I did it. I had no particular model in mind, just the thought that these memorable events ought not to be lost forever." This impulse to record is undoubtedly widespread, but it is not always realized with equal assiduity and discipline.

10. Bede describes his method, which included an intermediate stage of circulating drafts of his work for comment by others, in the prologue to his *Vita Sancti Cuthberti:* "I have not presumed to write down anything concerning so great a man without the most rigorous investigation of the facts nor, at the end, to hand on what I had written to be copied for general use, without scrupulous examination of credible witnesses. Nay rather, it was only after first diligently investigating the beginning, the progress, and the end of his most glorious life and activity, with the help of those who knew him, that I began at last to set about making notes [*ad scedulas manum mittere*]. . . . Further, when my little work was arranged [*digesto*], though still kept in the form of notes [*sed adhuc in scedulis retento*], I often showed what I had written [to men who had known Cuthbert] . . . so that they might read and revise it at their leisure; and I diligently amended some things in accordance with their judgement. . . . And thus I made it my business to put down on parchment [*commendare menbranulis*] the results of my rigorous investigation of the truth . . ." (Bede, *Vita Sancti Cuthberti,* prologue, in Bertram Colgrave, ed. and trans., *Two "Lives" of Saint Cuthbert* [Cambridge, U.K., 1940], 142–45).

Citing Eadmer's comment that "when I had first taken the work [his biography of Saint Anselm] in hand, and had already transcribed onto parchment [*pergamenae . . . tradidissem*] a great part of what I had drafted in wax [*in cera dictaverim*], Father Anselm himself one day called me to him privately and asked what it was I was drafting and copying [*quid dictitarem, quid scriptitarem*]" *(The Life of Saint Anselm,* ed. and trans. R. W. Southern, corr. ed. [1962; Oxford, U.K., 1972], 149–50), M. T. Clanchy observes that "the process of composing on wax tablets is thus described in Latin by the word *dictitare* (literally, 'to dictate'), even though in Eadmer's case he was dictating to himself. The use of 'writing' *(scriptitare)* is confined to making the fair copy on parchment" *(From Memory to Written Record, England 1066–1307,* 2nd ed. [Oxford, U.K., 1993], 271).

The author of the *Vita Heinrici IV imperatoris,* written during the reign of Henry V (1106–1125), refers to the stylus with which he is writing (on, therefore, wax) and says, echoing Ovid, that as he begins his task, he "writes and rejects, notes and erases" *(Vita Heinrici IV imperatoris,* 1, ed., 414; *The Life of the Emperor Henry IV,* in Theodor E. Mommsen and Karl F. Morrison, trans., *Imperial Lives and Letters of the Eleventh Century* [New York, 1962], 105).

Orderic Vitalis relates that "Anthony, a monk of Winchester, recently passed this way with a copy [of a *Life* of Saint William], and showed it to our eager eyes. . . . But in truth, since the bearer was in haste to depart, and the winter cold prevented me from writing, I made a brief but accurate summary of it on tablets [*sinceram adbreuiationem sicut tabellis tradidi compendiose*], and now I will make an effort to commit it summarily to parchment [*membranae summatim commendare*]" (*Ecclesiastical History,* 6.3, 3:218; trans. mod.; on Orderic's note taking, see Chibnall in Orderic Vitalis, *Ecclesiastical History,* 1:99–100).

Gabrielle Spiegel observes that Suger had likewise "prepared notes for a Life of Louis VII" which death prevented him from completing (*The Chronicle Tradition of Saint-Denis: A Survey* [Brookline, Mass., 1978], 48).

Guibert of Nogent, on the other hand, tells us: "For the composition and writing [*dictando et scribendo*] of this [a commentary on Genesis] or my other works, I did not prepare a draft on wax tablets [*nullis impressa tabulis*], but committed them to the written page in their final form [*scribenda . . . immutabiliter paginis*] as I thought them out" (*Autobiographie,* 1.17, ed., 144; trans., 91): as Elisabeth Lalou has observed, the very fact that he deems this worthy of comment suggests that it was unusual ("Les Tablettes de cire médiévales," *Bibliothèque de l'Ecole des Chartes* 147 [1989]: 133–34).

On the stages of the composition of letters in the Middle Ages, see Peter the Venerable, *The Letters of Peter the Venerable,* 2 vols., ed. Giles Constable (Cambridge, Mass., 1967), 2:18–20; and Giles Constable, *Letters and Letter-Collections,* Typologie des sources du Moyen Age occidental 17 (Turnhout, 1976), 42–48; on those of the composition of charters, see Tock, *Chancellerie épiscopale,* 88–89; on the methods of composition in general, see Richard H. Rouse and Mary A. Rouse, "Wax Tablets," *Language and Communication* 9 (1989): 177–80; and Mary Carruthers, *The Book of Memory: A Study of Memory in Medieval Culture* (Cambridge, U.K., 1990), 194–212.

11. According to Constable, however, "the tablets themselves were occasionally sent as letters" and thus served as the final medium as well as the intermediary one (in Peter the Venerable, *Letters,* 45).

12. Clanchy, *From Memory to Written Record,* 118.

13. "Inventaire des tablettes médiévales et présentation générale," in Lalou, ed., *Les Tablettes à écrire de l'antiquité à l'époque moderne,* Bibliogia: Elementa ad librorum studia pertinentia (Turnhout, 1992), 234, 236. Concerning wax tablets, see also Lalou, "Les Tablettes de cire médiévales," 123–40; José Trenchs Odena and Maria José Carbonnel, "Tablettes de cire aragonaises (XIIe–XVe siècle)," *Bibliothèque de l'Ecole des Chartes* 151 (1993): 155–60; Constable, in Peter the Venerable, *Letters,* 44–45; and Bernhard Bischoff, *Latin Paleography, Antiquity and the Middle Ages,* trans. Dáibhí O Cróinín and David Ganz (Cambridge, U.K., 1990), 13–14, 18.

14. See Lalou, "Inventaire," 249. Another interesting example of this kind of codex is currently in Dublin. It dates from the 7th century, measures 75 mm by 210 mm, and contains six "leaves" on which are written Psalms 30–32 (see Lalou, "Inventaire," 256). In the early twelfth century, the French poet Baudry of Bourgueil composed a poem for his codex, which consisted of eight "leaves" (cited in Rouse and Rouse, "Wax Tablets," 187, and in their "The Vocabulary of Wax Tablets," *Harvard Library Bulletin,* n.s. 1.3 [Fall 1990]: 14). Lalou provides an inventory of all known surviving medieval tablets ("Inventaire," 248–78). For photos and illustrations of some tablets, see Lalou, "Inventaire," 281–85, and Sonia O'Connor and Dominic Tweddle, "A Set of Waxed Tablets from Swinegate, York," in Lalou, ed., *Les Tablettes à écrire,* 319–22.

15. Orderic tells us, for example, that Osbern, abbot of Saint Evroul "with his own hands . . . made the metal styles and wax-covered tablets [*scriptoria . . . tabulasque cera illitas*]

for the boys and beginners, and exacted the daily tasks from each individually" *(Ecclesiastical History,* 3, 2:106). See also Rouse and Rouse, "Wax Tablets," 175–77; and Lalou, "Les Tablettes de cire médiévales," 130–31.

16. Smaragdus of Saint-Mihiel (who lived in the ninth century) tells us that his students took lecture notes on wax tablets (Rouse and Rouse, "Wax Tablets," 183), while a student of Hugh of Saint Victor relates that he was commissioned by his fellow students to record Hugh's lectures on wax tablets and took his wax notes to Hugh once a week so that Hugh could correct and augment them (cited by Delhaye, in "L'Organisation scolaire," 245–46). Carruthers notes that writing on wax tablets was a common metaphor for memorizing and that writing on wax was used as an aide to memorization *(The Book of Memory,* 28, 74).

17. *From Memory to Written Record,* 118.

18. Walter Jarecki, ed., *Signa loquendi: Die cluniacensischen Signa-Listen eingeleitet und herausgegeben,* Saecula Spiritalia 4 (Baden-Baden, 1981), 131. I would like to thank Professor Ludo Milis of the University of Ghent for drawing my attention to this text and its significance.

19. Lalou, "Inventaire," 242.

20. Lalou, "Inventaire," 244. On the use of tablets in medieval accounting, see also Lalou, "Les Tablettes de cire médiévales," 131–33.

21. See Rouse and Rouse, "The Vocabulary of Wax Tablets," 17, and "Wax Tablets," 179. This association between wax tablets and what one might term the protochancelleries of the eleventh and early twelfth centuries is likewise suggested by the words with which Fulbert of Chartres (960–1028) conferred the charge of schoolmaster and chancellor at Chartres at the beginning of the eleventh century: "I give into your keeping the rod of the school and the chancellor's tablets [*cancelarii tabulas*]" (Delhaye, "L'Organisation scolaire," 247, n. 50). Galbert tells us that the canons of Saint Donatian bore "the accounts and records [*brevia et notationes*] of the revenues of the count" out of the castle on March 17 along with the relics of their church, but he does not tell us the support on which they were kept ([35], 9/10; trans., 163).

22. Cited by Rouse and Rouse, "Vocabulary of Wax Tablets," 17.

23. Ganshof in particular insisted on Galbert's status as an eyewitness. See Ganshof, "Note," 99; "*Coemptio gravissima mansionum* (Galbert de Bruges, c. 55)," *Bulletin Du Cange / Archivium Latinitatis Medii Aevi* 17 (1943 for 1942): 149; "Le Roi de France en Flandre," 207; "Trois Mandements," 118–19 and nn. 5–6; and "Les Origines du concept," 138–39. See also Ross, trans., 68. It is interesting that Galbert never places himself in the scenes he describes, although we seem to glimpse him listening in the crowd on certain occasions, or can at least imagine we do so. Reporting the executions of Bertulf and Guy of Steenvoorde, for example, he notes: "so it was related by a squire who came to us and in the presence of the king told us what had happened to them" ([58], 39/42; trans., 213; trans. mod.).

24. As we will see in Chapter 3, he describes events on the day of the assassination that occurred simultaneously in different parts of the town, and could not, therefore, have observed them all himself. Ross likewise observed that he included material he "heard . . . from [other] eyewitnesses in Bruges" (trans., 68).

25. On Galbert's sources, see also Pirenne, ed., xiii, and Ross, trans., 68.

26. An "implicit report" is, to be sure, a tenuous and elastic notion that could be stretched to include many kinds of information, and I ought perhaps to have excluded such reports from the list of oral sources. In the cases I have included, however, it seems clear to me that Galbert is recording something he has heard but has, for whatever reason, not pref-

aced with "they say" or "we have heard."

27. This supports Pirenne's suggestion that Galbert never left Bruges during 1127–1128 (ed., xiii). This list of oral sources should be considered alongside the instances of direct discourse in the *De multro* which A. Murray has listed in an appendix to his article on the "Voices of Flanders," 119. Galbert presumably heard many of these discourses, but he could not, as we will see, have heard all of them, and thus must in some cases have received an account of them from some unnamed source.

28. As Gabrielle Spiegel has pointed out, "[T]he chronicler would naturally . . . incorporate into his account whatever legends, miracles, or fictions circulated in the world he was attempting with mimetic fidelity to record. . . . [T]he 'untruths' of . . . contemporary observers easily entered the narrative without necessarily violating the chronicler's obedience to the first law of history—which was, of course, the pursuit of truth [*prima lex historiae veritas est*]. Indeed, to leave them out would have been neglectful of that obligation to truth. . . ." ("Genealogy: Form and Function in Medieval Historiography," in Spiegel, *The Past as Text: The Theory and Practice of Medieval Historiography* [Baltimore, 1997], 102).

29. On this document, see Van Caenegem, "Notes on Galbert of Bruges," 626.

30. On Galbert's written sources and his use of them, see Pirenne, ed., xiv; Ganshof, "Iets over Brugge gedurende de preconstitutionele periode van haar geschiedenis," *Nederlandsche Historiebladen* 1 (1938): 218–303, "*Coemptio gravissima mansionum,*" "Le Roi de France en Flandre," "Trois mandements," and "Le Droit urbain en Flandre au début de la première phase de son histoire (1127)," *Tijdschrift voor Rechtsgeschiedenis / Revue d'Histoire du Droit / The Legal History Review* 19 (1951): 387–416; Sproemberg, *Mittelalter,* 250–61; Ross, trans., 68–69; Coué, "Der Mord," 123–24; and A. Murray, "Voices of Flanders," 105.

31. If a document was in Latin, its public reading was accompanied, presumably, by its translation or summary for a non-Latinate audience. Perhaps only the translation or summary was given publicly (on the public reading of charters and their explanation in the vernacular, see Tock, *Chancellerie épiscopale,* 100–101). Given their senders and receivers, however, it is hard to believe that some of the written messages Galbert mentions were not written in Flemish. Were the "letters" *(litteras)* from the barons that were "shot into the tower [to the besieged] by arrows" ([46], 65/69; trans., 185), written in Latin? Were those from the citizens of Ghent and Ypres to the citizens of Bruges ([98], 1/8; trans., 273; [113], 61/64; trans., 296)?

32. He writes just after this that William's offer of aid was "in writing" *(scripto)* ([25], 14; trans., 144) and in a later allusion to what seems to be this message, he writes that "before the time of the siege he had clearly sent greetings and aid in a sealed letter [*litteris signatis*] to the provost and his kin" ([49], 24/25; trans., 191; trans. mod.). Galbert also refers, as we have seen above, to a series of letters exchanged between William and the Erembalds.

The written part of William's message may, however, have been limited to the passage cited by Galbert. As Constable has pointed out, letters sometimes served only to introduce a messenger, to whom a verbal message was entrusted (in Peter the Venerable, *Letters,* 2:25–28; Constable, *Letters,* 48; on the transportation and oral delivery of letters, see Constable, 52–55); at other times, the messenger carried both a written and a verbal message. In a letter sent to Rudolf of Rheinfelden in 1079, for example, Gregory VII wrote: "my legates [*legati*], if they make it safely to you thanks to a propitious God, will attest to and explain these and other things in person [*viva voce*] better than this letter" (cited by Bruno of Magdeburg, *Saxonicum bellum* 119, ed. Hans-Eberhard Lohman, in Schmale, *Quellen,* 384); and Henry IV wrote similarly to Paschal II in 1105: "Besides those things which have been written here, we have committed certain things to this, our most faithful envoy, to be said to you. You may believe them as truly as the things which have been written" *(Epistolae* 34 [1105], ed. Carl Erdman, in Schmale, *Quellen,* 110; *The Letters of Henry IV,* in Mommsen and Morrison, trans., *Imperial Lives,* 182).

33. Joaquín Martínez Pizarro suggests that this "use of envoys and ambassadors [in historical works] . . . to present the text of the messages they carry as if the sender were speaking directly" is "artificial" *(A Rhetoric of the Scene: Dramatic Narrative in the Early Middle Ages* [Toronto, 1989], 94), by which he seems to mean a literary convention not grounded in practice. The "performance" of messages by the messenger undoubtedly has a dramatic effect and certain of the public readings we find in histories may be literary inventions, but the literary convention of public readings, insofar as there was one, was probably elaborated from communicative practice.

34. For other examples of the public reading of written documents, see [47], 1/24, trans., 186–88; [52], 7/52, trans., 195–97; [55], 10/27, trans., 201–2; [55], 27/43, trans., 203–4; [55], 49/82, trans., 204–6.

35. Ganshof, "Trois Mandements," 117–33.

36. As medieval correspondents were well aware. "I am sorry," wrote Peter the Venerable (c. 1092–1156) to Bernard of Clairvaux, "that you have not yet given more certain signs [of your friendship] in the form of letters. I have said 'more certain' because a sheet is unable to change the words imprinted upon it, whereas a speaker's tongue often changes by adding and subtracting the truth that has been imposed upon it" *(Letters,* letter 65, 1:194–95; trans. Constable, 2:18).

37. The distinct, letterlike, status of the verbal messages carried by formal messengers is also suggested by the partly written, partly oral messages mentioned above, and by Bruno of Magedeburg's references to the "repeated embassies [*legationes*], now with letters, now without letters," that the Saxon princes sent to Henry IV *(Saxonicum bellum* 41, 246), and the "embassies with either letters or verbal messages [*vel litteris vel verbis*]" they sent to the king's supporters *(Saxonicum bellum,* 43, 250). On the use of messengers in general, see Constable in Peter the Venerable, *Letters,* 2:23–28; and Donald Queller, "Thirteenth-Century Diplomatic Envoys: Nuncii and Procuratores," *Speculum* 35 (1960): 196–213.

38. The evidence is limited and hard to evaluate. The small, six-leaved, 7th-century codex in Dublin, mentioned above in note 14, contains Psalms 30–32; Hadoard, ninth-century librarian of Corbie, collected texts on wax tablets for a florilegium he was composing, until the tablets "grew into the likeness of a book" *(Ut libri tandem redderet effigiem)*; Baudry of Bourgueil was able to record 112 verses on his eight-leaved codex in the early twelfth century; Anselm of Bec may have composed the entire *Proslogion* on wax tablets at roughly the same time (Rouse and Rouse, "Wax Tablets," 179, 187).

39. Coué's argument that he did not begin writing until March 17 is interesting in this context (although all the evidence she cites may also be explained by a subsequent revision of the first chapters after May 22), insofar as it suggests that he may have made his first transfer onto parchment at about this time ("Der Mord," 112–14).

40. Rouse and Rouse, "Wax Tablets," 179. The fourteenth-century Flemish author Jan van Ruusbroec was in the habit of noting down his thoughts on wax tablets while on walks but would sometimes not transpose them onto parchment for several weeks (Rouse and Rouse, "Wax Tablets," 180).

41. Lalou, "Inventaire," 244.

42. Lalou, "Inventaire," 256.

43. As we have seen, Orderic Vitalis likewise associates writing on wax with summarization, writing that "Anthony, a monk of Winchester, recently passed this way with a copy

[of the *Life of Saint William*], and showed it to our eager eyes. . . . But in truth, since the bearer was in haste to depart, and the winter cold prevented me from writing, I made a brief but accurate summary of it on tablets [*sinceram adbreuiationem sicut tabellis tradidi compendiose*]" (*Ecclesiastical History*, 6.3, 3:218; trans. mod.).

44. On abbreviations in medieval writing in general, see Bischoff, *Latin Paleography*, 80–82, 150–68. The letter of archbishop Renaud II of Reims to the abbey of Cysoing in 1129 is characteristic of letters of the time insofar as it "displays a clear concern for economy. The writing is tiny, with many abbreviations, reducing the names of people to their intials" (P. Demouÿ, *Actes des archevêques de Reims d'Arnou à Renaud II, 997–1139*, vol. 1: *Présentation* [Nancy, 1982], 151; cited in Tock, *Chancellerie épiscopale*, 69, n. 108).

The account of the expenditures of the *fodermolt* (see Chapter 1, note 9) of Bergues-Saint-Winnoc for 1140–1141 is highly abbreviated (*d.*, for example, stands for both *dies* and *denarius*) and must have been difficult to read even for a contemporary who was not familiar with its subject matter and system. "One has here," writes Strubbe, "a tradition of writing peculiar to a group of insiders: the writer is addressing himself to an experienced reader who already knows half of what is being reported to him" (*Het Fragment*, 7). This "insider" writing, or shorthand, was probably common throughout the count's fiscal administration and suggests something about the degree of abbreviation Galbert may have used in his wax notes.

45. Compare Van Caenegem, *Galbert van Brugge*, 5; and Sproemberg, *Mittelalter*, 249–50. The account of the expenditures of the *fodermolt* of Bergues-Saint-Winnoc of 1140–1141 is in journal form—each day's expenditures are dated and listed separately with a brief description—and its method of dating its entries recalls that used by Galbert to date his (see Strubbe, *Het Fragment*, 7, 18, 25–26). The earliest surviving annual account of the count's revenues and expenses, the *Gros Brief* of 1187, was drawn up in Ypres over the course of at least nine days (June 1–9). It is organized both according to fiscal circumscriptions (the account for Bergues, then that for Diksmuide, for Ghent, and so on) and journalistically. The accounts for Bergues, Diksmuide, and Ghent, for example, were drawn up on Monday, June 1; those for Aalter and Rupelmonde on Tuesday, June 2; and so on, and each account begins with a notation of the date on which and the place where it was drawn up: "1187. The account of Richard [for Bergues], in the count's house in Ypres, the Monday before the feast of Saints Marcellinus and Peter [June 1]"; "1187. The account of Weitin [for the cereal revenues of Bruges], in the count's house in Ypres, the Wednesday after the feast of Saints Marcellinus and Peter [June 3]"; and so on. See Verhulst and Gysseling, *Le Compte Général*, 141–93.

46. [35], 33; [36], 1; [42], 4; [75], 1; [78], 19/20; [102], 23; [102], 31; [108], 28; [108], 48; [110], 3; [110], 20; [110], 29; [114], 84; [116], 43; [120], 15; trans., 164, 165, 177, 243, 247, 279, 288, 289, 290, 291, 300, 303, 308.

47. "On March 30 . . . those who had sworn with them" (trans., 278).

48. "Now this day was Friday . . . in the previous year" (trans., 278).

49. "On the same day . . . and the honor of the land" (trans., 278–79).

50. Many of the passages beginning with "eodem die" or a similar expression may be later additions to earlier entries. See [12], 49; [12], 52; [20], 6; [28], 6; [39], 1; [54], 10; [54], 27; [56], 13; [56], 16; [58], 40; [59], 1; [59], 14; [61], 44; [72], 8; [77], 24; [78], 17; [78], 19; [85], 29; [97], 4; [97], 23; [97], 26; [98], 17; [98], 21; [100], 18; [100], 21; [101], 10; [102], 8; [103], 7; [106], 5; [109], 7; [113], 19; [113], 47; [113], 49; [113], 61; [116], 40; [120], 26; trans., 114, 132, 171, 200, 207, 213, 214, 220, 240, 246, 247, 257, 272, 273, 274, 276, 277, 278, 280, 283, 290, 295, 296, 303, 309.

51. "And it should be noted . . . and lord of our whole land" (trans., 279).

52. "And it should be noted . . . in the crash" (trans., 279–80).

53. "On May 5 . . . the murder of Count Charles" (trans., 290).

54. "And it should be noted . . . in the place of William the Norman" (trans., 290).

55. See Mohr, "Geschichtstheologische Aspekte," 259. He suggests that these first two passages were written in the opposite order: the mention of the anniversary of the execution being written after, and inspired by, the mention of the death of those who had betrayed William, but the *et notandum* with which the passage begins and the fact that the battle had already been discussed at length in chapter 108 suggest the opposite order.

56. "In this same week . . . and which he should establish" (trans., 290–91).

57. "At this time . . . to descend on them" (trans., 291).

58. "And it should be noted . . . or has responded" (trans., 291).

59. Ross, trans., 291, n. 4.

60. "And it is worth remembering . . . burnt her up" (trans., 291–92).

61. "From that time . . . and those of their knights" (trans., 292).

62. Bernard Guenée cites examples of historians who took notes on single leaves and small pieces of parchment, whose information was not, in at least one case, always recopied in the right order *(Histoire et culture historique,* 112–13). See also Spiegel, *The Chronicle Tradition,* 41.

63. Brett notes that the "chief feature [of the second stage of John of Worcester's revision of his chronicle] was an intensive use of Malmesbury's *Deeds of the Bishops* in marginal notes, corrections and interlineations. Some of these insertions are not skillfully managed. . . ." ("John of Worcester," 105).

64. Constable observes that, in the case of letter collections, "it is not certain . . . whether they [the copies of letters] were kept in bound volumes, on quires of parchment for later binding, or on separate leaves. . . . John of Salisbury . . . seems to have kept his drafts or copies on separate sheets, from which his collection was later compiled" (in Peter the Venerable, *Letters,* 2:8–9).

65. John T. Appleby in Richard of Devizes, *Cronicon Richardi Divisensis de tempore Regis Richardi Primi,* ed. John T. Appleby (London, 1963), xix–xxi; see also Partner, *Serious Entertainments,* 208–10. The surviving autograph manuscripts of other historians have a similar appearance. The autograph of John of Worcester's early twelfth-century chronicle "is a working text, in which innumerable changes and additions have been made to the original narrative. It reveals a steady accretion of new material, and in its pages we can watch the compiler at work with most unusual clarity" (Brett, "John of Worcester," 122; see also Antonia Gransden, *Historical Writing in England c. 550 to c. 1307* [Ithaca, N.Y., 1974], 146–47). The autograph of William of Malmesbury's *Gesta Pontificum* (1125) "is pocket-size, suitable for . . . journeys. It was obviously written piecemeal (this is shown by the many changes in the shade of ink) and William's alterations can be seen in the text itself, and additions are crowded in the margins" (Gransden, *Historical Writing,* 175; see also her "Prologues in the Historiography of Twelfth-Century England," in her *Legends, Traditions, and History,* 141). Spiegel describes another historiographical manuscript (BN Lat. 12,710) as "a collection of *cahiers* containing a series of notes written in different hands of the late twelfth century. The writing is cramped and abounds with abbreviations, and often fragments of parchment are used in an obvious attempt at economy"; it appears to have been compiled for the sake of writing a chronicle known as the *Nova Gesta Francorum (The Chronicle Tradition;* 41–42).

66. It is possible, as I noted above, that Galbert was able to record quite a bit of information on his tablets before transferring it to parchment; it is even conceivable that he was able to record all the information pertaining to the events of March 2 to May 22 on wax be-

fore transferring it to parchment. The final parchment document, however, would have looked much the same regardless of whether this transfer took place in one, ten, or twenty moments: Galbert would have had to move serially through his wax notes and add to existing parchment entries information pertaining to those days that he had learned after that day.

NOTES TO CHAPTER 3

1. *Vita Heinrici IV,* 5, 426; *The Life of the Emperor Henry IV,* 113.

2. Gerald of Wales, *Itinerarium Cambriae,* 2.2, 111; *"The Journey through Wales" and "The Description of Wales,"* 170.

3. Based on this passage, Köpke entitled the work the *Passio Karoli comitis* (Galbert, "Passio," 561, n. 88). This title is ill-suited both for the first version of the chronicle and for its final state, but it does apply well to this second version and was perhaps the title Galbert intended for it.

4. "And therefore after these two barons of the land [*principes terrae*] had died, not far apart in time or space, they were remembered and discussed by the inhabitants of the land; they talked about the sudden death [*subita morte*] of those whom God had deprived of life after the death of lord Charles by such a swift sentence [*Deus tam veloci sententia a vita privaverat*]" ([91], 14/18; trans., 264).

5. Clanchy, *From Memory to Written Record,* 119; Orderic Vitalis, *Ecclesiastical History,* 6.3, 3:218 (trans. mod.). Orderic likewise writes, at the end of the fourth book of the *Ecclesiastical History* that "[m]ortal men are oppressed by many misfortunes, which would fill great volumes if the whole tale of them were written down. But now, numbed by the winter cold, I turn to other pursuits; and, weary with toil, resolve to end my present book here. When the warmth of sweet spring returns I will relate in the following books everything that I have only briefly touched upon, or omitted altogether" (4, 2:360).

6. Demyttenaere also thinks that Galbert had not yet finished reworking the text of 1127 when he started taking new notes in 1128 ("Mentaliteit in de twaalfde eeuw," 80).

7. See Verhulst and Gysseling, *Le Compte Général,* 141–93.

8. Strubbe, *Het Fragment,* 18; compare Verhulst and Gysseling, *Le Compte Général,* 119–20; Lyon and Verhulst, *Medieval Finance,* 28.

9. As was mentioned above, chapter 86, the first new entry after May 22, is dated to September 10. The reference to the "the suspect and the guilty and those who have fled in all directions and gone into exile" in [14], 13/14 (trans., 117) suggests that this passage was written in the aftermath of the final stage of the inquest on September 17–18 (see chapters 87–88), while the probable allusion at the end of that same chapter ([14], 21/25; trans., 117–18) to the death of Baldwin of Aalst on October 24, 1127, suggests that it was written or revised after that date.

10. Compare Huyghebaert, "Galbert of Bruges," 738; Mohr, "Geschichtstheologische Aspekte," 246; and J. Marotta, "Teaching Medieval Narrative," in H. Chickering, ed., *1983 NEH Institute Resource Book for the Teaching of Medieval Civilization* (Amherst, Mass., 1984), 23.

11. *Contra Faustum,* 22.75, ed. J. Zycha, in *Corpus scriptorum ecclesiasticorum latinorum* 25 (Vienna, 1891), 673; compare *Reply to Faustus the Manichaean,* trans. Richard Stothert, in *A Select Library of Nicene and Post-Nicene Fathers of the Christian Church,* ed. Philip Schaff, vol. 4: *St. Augustin: The Writings against the Manichaeans and against the Donatists* (1887; rpt. Grand Rapids, Mich., 1956), 301.

12. *De civitate Dei* 5.11, Corpus Christianorum, series latina 47–48, 2 vols., ed. B.

Dombart and A. Kalb (Turnhout, 1955), 1:142; *Concerning the City of God against the Pagans,* trans. Henry Bettenson (Harmondsworth, U.K., 1972), 196. On the theocratic concept of the origin of power, see R. W. Carlyle and A. J. Carlyle, *A History of Medieval Political Theory in the West,* 6 vols. (Edinburgh, 1903–1936), 1:89–98 and 147–60, 2:146–48, and 3:92–105; Wilfrid Parsons, "The Medieval Theory of the Tyrant," *Review of Politics* 4 (1942): 130–34; Fritz Kern, *Gottesgnadentum und Widerstandsrecht im Früheren Mittelalter: Zur Entwicklungsgeschichte der Monarchie,* 2nd ed., ed. Rudolf Buchner (Darmstadt, 1954), 6–10, 176, 359–62; Ewart Lewis, *Medieval Political Ideas,* 2 vols. (New York, 1954), 1:142–43; H.-X. Arquillière, *L'Augustinisme politique: Essais sur la formation des théories politiques du Moyen-Age,* 2nd ed. (Paris, 1955), 67–71, 89–94; Walter Ullmann, *Principles of Government and Politics in the Middle Ages* (London, 1961), 117–37, *The Growth of Papal Government in the Middle Ages,* 2nd ed. (London, 1962), 344–58, 382–412, and *The Individual and Society in the Middle Ages* (Baltimore, 1966), 3–50; Karl Morrison in Mommsen and Morrison, trans., *Imperial Lives,* 5–34; Hans Hubert Anton, *Fürstenspiegel und Herrscherethos in der Karolingerzeit,* Bonner Historische Forschungen 32 (Bonn, 1968), 357–83, 388–90; Werner Affeldt, *Die weltliche Gewalt in der Paulus-Exegese: Röm. 13, 1–7 in den Römerbriefkommentaren der lateinischen Kirche bis zum Ende des 13. Jahrhunderts* (Göttingen, 1969); P. D. King, *Law and Society in the Visigothic Kingdom,* Cambridge Studies in Medieval Life and Thought 3.5 (Cambridge, U.K., 1972), 23–36; and Marcel Pacaut, *La Théocracie. L'Eglise et le pouvoir au Moyen Age* (Paris, 1989).

13. MGH. Concil. ii. 2, 651–2, cited and translated by Ullman, in *The Growth of Papal Government,* 130; trans. mod. On the elaboration of the concept of the king's *ministerium,* see Lewis, *Medieval Political Ideas,* 1:145–47; Ullmann, *The Growth of Papal Government,* 119–42; E. Buschmann, "Ministerium Dei—Idoneitas," *Historisches Jahrbuch* 82 (1963): 70–102; Anton, *Fürstenspiegel,* 369–77, 404–19; Jürgen Hannig, *Consensus fidelium: Frühfeudale Interpretationen des Verhältnisses von Königtum und Adel am Beispiel des Frankreiches* (Stuttgart, 1982), 258–75; P. D. King, "The Barbarian Kingdoms," in J. H. Burns, ed., *The Cambridge History of Medieval Political Thought c. 350–c. 1450* (Cambridge, U.K., 1988), 137, 143–44; and Joseph Canning, *A History of Medieval Political Thought, 300–1450* (London, 1996), 18–22, 47–59.

14. *Tractatus de regia potestate et sacerdotali dignitate* 1.4, ed. E. Sackur, *Monumenta Germaniae Historica, Libelli de lite imperatorum et pontificum,* 3 vols. (Hannover, 1881–1897), 2:468–69. Two centuries later still (c. 1275–1283), Raymond Lulle observed similarly that "a prince is a man raised by election to lordship over other men in order to keep peace among them through fear of justice" *(Doctrine d'enfant* 80, ed. Armand Llinarès [Paris, 1969], 173).

15. *Tractatus de regia potestate* 1.6, 2:473.

16. Wippo, chaplain to the emperor Conrad II, crystallized this principle in three verses written c. 1028: "It befits the king to know the law. / Let the king hear what the law teaches. / To reign is to serve the law" *(Decet regem discere legem. / Audiat rex, quod praecepit lex. / Legem servare est regnare) (Proverbia,* 1–3, in *Die Werke Wipos,* 3rd ed., ed. Harry Bresslau [Hannover, 1915], 66), while in the following century, John of Salisbury wrote that "he who receives power from God serves the laws and is the slave of justice and right" *(legibus seruit et iustitiae et iuris famulus est) (Policraticus I–IV,* 3.15, Corpus Christianorum, continuatio medievalis 118, ed. K. S. B. Keats-Rohan [Turnhout, 1993], 230; *Policraticus,* trans. Cary J. Nederman [Cambridge, 1990], 25; compare *Policraticus,* 2 vols., ed. Clemens C. I. Webb [1909; rpt. Frankfurt, 1965], 1:232; *Frivolities of Courtiers and Footprints of Philosophers: Being a Translation of the First, Second, and Third Books and Selections from the Seventh and Eighth Books of the "Policraticus" of John of Salisbury,* trans. Joseph B. Pike [1938; rpt. New York, 1972],

211). On the ruler's obligation to respect and uphold the law, see Carlyle and Carlyle, *History,* 1:162–64, 2:150–51, 3:30–40, 125–46, 181–85; Parsons, "The Medieval Theory," 137–38; Kern, *Gottesgnadentum,* 3–11, 121–37, 152–53; Anton, *Fürstenspiegel,* 404–19; King, *Law and Society,* 26–44; D. E. Luscombe, "Introduction: The Formation of Political Thought in the West [c. 750–c. 1150]," in Burns, ed., *Medieval Political Thought,* 163–65; and Janet Nelson, "Kingship and Empire," in Burns, ed., *Medieval Political Thought,* 213–29.

We find striking evidence of the practical application of this concept in early twelfth-century Flanders in William Clito's promise, recorded in the first article of the charter he granted to the citizens of Saint-Omer in 1127 in exchange for their support, to enforce the sentences of their aldermen against anyone—including himself ("*erga me ipsum*") (Georges Espinas, "Le Privilège de Saint-Omer de 1127," *Revue du Nord* 29 [1947]: 45; compare Van Caenegem, "Law and Power," 156).

17. Summarizing a passage from Cicero's *Republic* (1.25.39, ed. and French trans. Esther Bréguet, *La République,* 2 vols. [Paris, 1980], 1:222), Augustine writes: "Scipio . . . defines 'the community' [*populum*] as meaning not any and every association of the population, but 'an association united by a common sense of right and a community of interest' [*coetum iuris consensu et utilitatis communione sociatum*]" (*De civitate Dei,* 2.21, ed., 1:53; trans., 73; compare 19.21, ed. 2:687–88; trans., 881). Clinton Walker Keyes translates *coetum . . . utilitatis communione sociatum* as "a partnership for the common good" (Cicero, *De re publica / De legibus,* Loeb Classical Library, ed. and trans. Clinton Walker Keyes [Cambridge, Mass., 1970], 65; on this passage in Cicero, see Karl Büchner, *M. Tullius Cicero, De re publica, Kommentar* [Heidelberg, 1984], 123–24). On the concept of public or common utility in tenth- and eleventh-century imperial episcopal circles, see Jaeger, *The Envy of Angels,* 37–39. In his *Theologia Christiana,* Galbert's contemporary Abelard writes that the state "whose administration strives for the common utility [*ad communem geritur utilitatem*] truly deserves the name 'republic'" (*Theologia Christiana* 2.49, in *Opera Theologica,* Corpus Christianorum, continuatio medievalis 11–13, 3 vols., ed. E. M. Buytaert and C. J. Mews [Turnhout, 1969–87], 2:151), while in his commentary on Paul's Epistle to the Romans, he declares that one should obey rulers "on account of the manifest utility [*pro manifesta utilitate*] that you reap from the ministry of princes [*ministerium principum*]" (*Commentaria in Epistolam Pauli ad Romanos* 4 [XIII, u. 5], in *Opera Theologica,* 1:287). The somewhat younger John of Salisbury echoes the idea that "the prince is the minister of the public utility [*publicae . . . utilitatis minister*] and the servant of equity," and he later observes that knights and laborers are likewise obliged to work for the "public utility" (*publica utilitas*) (*Policraticus,* 4.2, 6.8, 6.20, ed. Webb, 1:238, 2:23, 2:59; trans. Nederman, 31, 116, 126; compare ed. Keats-Rohan, 235; *The Statesman's Book of John of Salisbury: Being the Fourth, Fifth, and Sixth Books, and Selections from the Seventh and Eighth Books, of the "Policraticus,"* trans. John Dickinson [1927; rpt. New York, 1963], 7, 199–200, 243). According to the author of the *Gesta Stephani,* the citizens of London who elected Stephen were preoccupied with choosing someone who would work "for the common utility" (*communis utilitatis*) (*Gesta Stephani* 2, 6–7). See also Ullmann, *The Growth of Papal Government,* 425; and Peter Hibst, *Utilitas Publica—Gemeiner Nutz—Gemeinwohl: Untersuchungen zur Idee eines politischen Leitbegriffes von der Antike bis zum späten Mittelalter* (Frankfurt, 1991).

18. On the concept and importance of the ruler's idoneity, see Kern, *Gottesgnadentum,* 48–50, 59–60; Ullmann, *Principles of Government and Politics,* 68–69; Buschmann, "Ministerium Dei—Idoneitas"; Anton, *Fürstenspiegel,* 411; Edward Peters, *The Shadow King: "Rex Inutilis" in Medieval Law and Literature, 751–1327* (New Haven, Conn., 1970), 42, 61,

65–67, 70; and Hannig, *Consensus fidelium,* 202, 300.

19. See Peters, *The Shadow King;* and Cary J. Nederman, "The Changing Face of Tyranny: The Reign of King Stephen in John of Salisbury's Political Thought," *Nottingham Medieval Studies* 33 (1989): 13, 15.

20. *Tractatus de regia potestate* 1.4, 2:469.

21. *Tractatus de regia potestate* 1.4, 2:470.

22. *Tractatus de regia potestate* 1.4, 2:469, 470.

23. *Tractatus de regia potestate* 1.9, 2:476–77.

24. "Le Meurtre du seigneur dans la société féodale. La mémoire, le rite, la fonction," *Annales. Economies. Sociétés. Civilisations* 45 (1990): 253, 250, 256–58.

25. This was the "crucial ideological work," as David Van Meter has put it with respect to Walter's *Vita Karoli,* that both Galbert and Walter set out to do ("Eschatology and the Sanctification of the Prince in Twelfth-Century Flanders: The Case of Walter of Thérouanne's *Vita Karoli comitis Flandriae,*" *Sacris Erudiri* 35 [1995]: 131).

26. He tells us that Charles was "renowned for . . . his royal blood" ([Prol.], 9; trans., 79). He returns to this topic two other times in the introduction, reminding us that Charles was the "son of Canute, king of Denmark, and born of a mother who was descended from the blood of the counts of the land of Flanders" ([1], 1/3; trans., 81), and noting finally that "his ancestors were among the best and most powerful rulers who from the beginning of the Holy Church had flourished in France, or Flanders, or Denmark, or under the Roman Empire," and that "he never departed from the noble habits of his royal ancestors" ([12], 23/26, 28; trans., 112).

27. [1], 11; trans., 82; [4], 12; trans., 90; [6], 27; trans., 95; [7], 6; trans., 96; [12], 27; trans., 112; [12], 36; trans., 113; [14], 10/11; trans., 117; [15], 5, 7; trans. 118 (the first occurrence of the word is not translated); [16], 56; trans., 123; [17], 3; trans., 124; [19], 32; trans., 131.

28. [Prol.], 48; trans., 81; [4], 35; trans. 91; [6], 6; trans., 94.

29. [Prol.], 48; trans., 81; [4], 35; trans., 91.

30. When Charles "saw that such a great boon of peace made everyone happy," Galbert writes, "he gave orders that throughout the limits of the realm all who frequented markets or dwelt in towns should live together in quiet and security without resort to arms; otherwise they would be punished by the very arms they bore. To enforce this, bows and arrows and subsequently all arms were laid aside not only in those places already protected by the count's peace but in other places as well. Thanks to this boon of peace, men governed themselves in accordance with laws and justice, devising by skill and study every kind of argument for use in the courts, so that when anyone was attacked he could defend himself [*se defensaret cum impetitus fuisset*] by the strength and eloquence of rhetoric, or when he was attacking [*impeteret*], he might ensnare his enemy, who would be deceived by the wealth of his oratory" ([1], 16/26; trans., 83–84). The rule of law did not make men better—it did not stop them from attacking one another in the courts—but the substitution of rhetoric for arms, emphasized by the terms Galbert uses to describe legal conflicts (*se defensare,* "to defend oneself," *impetere,* "to attack"), is exact (Coué likewise draws attention to this passage as an expression of the burghers' desire to be ruled by law rather than by violence ["Der Mord," 118–19]).

31. [Prol.], 10; trans., 79; [Prol.], 49; trans., 81; [6], 26; trans., 95.

32. He notes that "the count tried in every way possible to take care of the poor, distributing alms in the towns and throughout his domain, both in person and by his officials. At the same time he was feeding one hundred paupers in Bruges every day; and he gave a

sizable loaf of bread to each of them from before Lent until the new harvests of the same year. And likewise in his other towns he had made the same provisions" ([3], 3/9; trans., 87). He then goes on to describe the count's order that peas and beans be sown in place of bread grains, his prohibition of brewing to save grain, and his fixing of prices.

33. [Prol.], 10; trans., 79; [4], 23/24; trans., 91; [5], 13; trans., 93; [6], 25/27; trans., 95; [10], 3; trans., 105; [17], 3/6; trans., 124; [19], 32, 37; trans., 131.

34. Perhaps to attend Louis VI's Christmas court or the marriage of William Clito to Queen Adela's half-sister in January. It is also possible that Charles accompanied William when he went to Gisors in late January or early February to lay claim to Normandy (see Orderic Vitalis, *Ecclesiastical History,* 12.45, 6:368–70).

35. Compare [9], 26/32; trans., 104.

36. See [27], 23/26; trans., 150, "And Gervaise and his men . . . of our land"; [31], 7/18; trans., 158–59, "Now after meeting with our citizens . . . taking part in the siege"; and [33], 17/26; trans., 161, "When they had reached the gates . . . and send the others away."

37. The influence and importance of physical presence on the acquisition, distribution, and application of power are also apparent in William of Ypres's and Thierry of Alsace's failure to secure the countship in 1127 because, according to Galbert, they did not come to Bruges (the center of Galbert's Flanders). Galbert is explicit about this in the case of William, writing that "certainly William would have been raised to the countship at this time if he had gone at once to Bruges to avenge his lord and cousin, the betrayed count" ([25], 20/23; trans., 144). The importance of distance is also implicit in the barons' reasons for disregarding Thierry's initial claim, by letter, to the county—"but the barons . . . , asserting that it [the letter] was not genuine, did not take the trouble to reply because the common welfare was in danger, and the king was making haste to call an assembly nearby [*e vicino*], and they did not see how they could manage to elect that kinsman without a great deal of effort [*longa opera*]" ([47], 34/39; trans., 188)—and Galbert reports that Gervaise of Praet later said to Thierry that "'if God had granted us and the fatherland the favor of your presence [*vos . . . praesentem*] right after the death of our lord and your cousin Charles, we would have acknowledged no one but you in the countship'" ([104], 6/9; trans., 281). Stephen of Blois, on the other hand, rushed to London when he heard of Henry I's death and was elected, in part, according to the author of the *Gesta Stephani,* because the citizens "had no one at hand [*in manu*] who could take the king's place and put an end to the great dangers threatening the kingdom except Stephen, who, they thought, had been brought among them by Providence" *(Gesta Stephani* 2, 6–7). Thierry learned his lesson the first time around and, in 1128, was in Ghent less than three weeks after the February 16 uprising there.

Written at roughly the same time (c. 1130–1133), Orderic's description of the aftermath of William the Conqueror's death *(Ecclesiastical History* 7.16, 4:102) is more succinct than Galbert's of that of Charles's death, but reminiscent of it.

38. Flanders is called a "fatherland" *(patria)* or Charles its "father" *(pater)* in the introduction in [Prol.], 10; trans., 79; [1], 3; trans., 81; [4], 23/24, 25, 34; trans., 91; [5], 11, 13; trans., 93; [11], 32; trans., 110; [13], 4; trans., 115; [13], 23; trans., 116. Galbert calls Flanders a "land" *(terra)* in [Prol.], 47; trans., 81; [1], 2; trans., 81; [2], 28, 35; trans., 86; [3], 20; trans., 88 (trans. as "townspeople and countrypeople"); [4], 22, 37; trans., 91; [4], 41; trans., 92. He calls it a "realm" or "kingdom" *(regnum)* in [1], 10; trans., 82; [1], 12, 17; trans., 83; [2], 2; trans., 84; [7], 7, 8; trans., 96; [7], 37; trans., 100; [8], 2; trans., 101; [9], 30, 31; trans., 104; [13], 27, 34; trans., 116. On this theme, see Monier, *Institutions centrales,* 13–23; Van Caenegem, *Galbert van Brugge,* 18–22, "Galbert of Bruges," 103–4, "Govern-

ment, Law and Society," in Burns, ed., *Medieval Political Thought*, 185–88, and "Law and Power," 162–63; Jean Dunbabin, *France in the Making, 843–1180* (Oxford, U.K., 1985), 318–19; Demyttenaere, "Mentaliteit in de twaalfde eeuw," 89–94; and Geoffrey Koziol, *Begging Pardon and Favor: Ritual and Political Order in Early Medieval France* (Ithaca, N.Y., 1992), 142–43, 171–72, 241–47, 250–51, 267. Koziol points out that Flanders was already described as a *monarchia* in the reigns of Baldwin IV and V (988–1067) and that the sacralization of the count's authority seems to have been uniquely intense and concerted in Flanders and to have lasted longer there than elsewhere in France. This perhaps in part explains—and is in part explained by—the fact that, as Van Caenegem observes, Flanders never underwent the disintegration that other territorial principalities did in the 11th century ("Government, Law and Society," 176–77, 185). The theme was, in any case, well established by the time Galbert was writing.

39. [19], 31/41; trans., 131.

40. [64], 1/18; trans., 224–25. See also Galbert's descriptions of Fromold Senior's grief ([23], 7/13; trans., 141), and that of Gervaise ([54], 14/19; trans., 200).

41. One can perhaps add to these examples Galbert's account of the reaction when Charles is offered the crown of the Holy Roman Empire: "those who had rightly cherished and loved him, and who venerated him as a father, began to grieve and to lament his departure, predicting that it would prove the ruin of the fatherland if he should desert it," and the count eventually decided to remain in Flanders "because of the insistence of those who loved him, seeking and establishing for all, so far as possible, the peace and well-being of the fatherland" ([4], 24/25, 33/35; trans., 91).

42. Compare, for example, Hugh of Fleury's abstract portrait of the ideal prince *(Tractatus de regia potestate* 1.3–4, 6–7, 2:468–72, 473–75); the portraits of Henry IV in the *Carmen de bello Saxonico* 1.11–24 (ed. O. Holder-Egger, in Schmale, *Quellen*, 144) and the *Vita Heinrici IV* 1 (ed. 408–14; *The Life of the Emperor Henry IV*, 101–5); and his anti-portrait, or portrait as a bad king, in Lampert of Hersfeld's *Annales* 1076 *(Lamperti monachi Hersfeldensis opera*, ed. Oswald Holder-Egger, Scriptores rerum Germanicarum in usum scholarum [Hannover and Leipzig, 1894], 277–78). According to Ian Stuart Robinson, this ideal portrait goes back to the ninth chapter of the pseudo-Cyprianic *De duodecim abusivis saeculi*, a treatise that "had had considerable influence on Carolingian political thought . . . [and whose] account of the duties of the king . . . seems to have been common to the political thinking of both the supporters and the opponents of Henry IV" *(Authority and Resistance in the Investiture Contest: The Polemical Literature of the Late Eleventh Century* [Manchester, U.K., 1978], 115–16; also see 114–24). See also Arquillière, *L'Augustinisme politique*, 146–53; and Riché, *Les Ecoles et l'enseignement*, 288–92.

43. Galbert here evokes what Van Meter has termed a well-developed medieval "religio-political ideology" that portrayed the divinely ordained ruler as "the barrier to the advent of the Antichrist that St. Paul speaks of in his second epistle to the Thessalonians. By the early twelfth century," he writes, ". . . this exegesis of 2 Thessalonians 2, 1–8 was well on its way to becoming something of a common-place of political theology. . . . To follow the logic of a contemporary political treatise by the Norman Anonymous, the dignity and continuity of the Roman Empire are symbolically vested in all legitimate secular rulers, and the figure of the Antichrist may be discerned in those who would seek to usurp their authority" ("Eschatology," 115–16). This ideology also shaped the reactions to Charles's murder of Walter of Thérouanne (see *Vita Karoli*, 24, 548, 24/25), Anselm of Gembloux, and Herman of Tournai *(Liber* [30], 286, 15/17; trans., 45) (see Van Meter, "Eschatology," 116–18, 121–24). For the influence of this same ideology on the *Vita Heinrici IV*, see Stein, "Signs and Things,"

116–17. As Piet Leupen points out, the equation of a Christian sociopolitical entity, here the county of Flanders, with the Church of God is a Carolingian idea ("La 'Sainte Eglise de Dieu' [du VIIIe au XIe siècle]," in Ludo Milis, ed., *La Chrétienté des origines à la fin du Moyen Age* [Paris, 1998], 71–72).

44. Just as Gervaise and his men subsequently act as God's agent in avenging the murder (see Chapter 5, pp. 131–32). Ross observes that "*Superbia* is the keynote of his [Bertulf's] career" ("Rise and Fall," 383; see 383–84), and Alan Murray develops this line of thought in his paper on "The Divine and the Diabolic in Twelfth-Century Historiography: The Chronicle of Galbert of Bruges" (I would like to thank Dr. Murray for giving me a copy of this paper), noting that Bertulf's "defining characteristics" in the *De multro* "are pride and arrogance, and these characteristics lead him to challenge and betray his master, and in doing so, he does the work of the devil in attempting to subvert the order of Flanders and destroy God's church. However, what is striking is that Bertulf is not only shown as a tool of the devil in the perennial struggle between good and evil, but in his characterisation as full of *superbia* [pride] is portrayed as a kind of surrogate Satan himself." Just as the prince is God's "image" *(imago)* on earth, as John of Salisbury put it *(Policraticus* 4.1; ed. Keats-Rohan, 232; trans. Nederman, 28; compare ed. Webb, 1:236; trans. Dickinson, 4), so does the provost become Satan's. Galbert thus represents the struggle between the count and provost as an allegorical manifestation of that between God and the devil. Elias suggests that, influenced by Augustine's concept of the two cities, Galbert perceived the struggle between Charles and the Erembalds as one between "members of the *civitas Dei* and the *civitas terrena*" ("Augustinian Elements," 37).

45. [5], 13; trans., 93; [6], 18; trans., 95.

46. [26], 3; trans., 147; [26], 16; trans., 148; [27], 13/15; trans., 150; [64], 44; trans., 226.

47. Chibnall observes similarly that "as Orderic saw the world, all human acts had significance in the perpetual battle of demons for the souls of men. But they also had their place in the visible changes of everyday life. . . . So rebellion might be the result of sin; but it was also the work of the disinherited or overambitious" *(The World of Ordericus Vitalis,* 181–82; compare Guenée, *Histoire et culture historique,* 209–10).

48. Walter calls them "twisted men" *(pravi homines)* who were so "badly tormented within . . . by envy, [that] they complained that whatever [the count] tried to do for the common good was in fact done to oppress them" *(Vita Karoli,* [21], 547, 34; [17], 546, 19/21).

49. Initially, at least, the structure of the *Passio* is thus fundamentally the same as that of Suger's *Life of Louis VI,* "in which," writes Spiegel, "historical action is inaugurated by a disturbance to an existing situation, followed by the king's attempt to deal with the consequences of that disturbance, and concludes with the restoration of 'correct' order, viewed either as a return to the previously existing situation or as the institution of a new and ethically more just arrangement. . . . The offense to royal majesty represents a deformation of hierarchical order and unleashes Louis's vengeance against the pillaging, despoiling, overweening, ravening disturbers of the peace of the kingdom so familiar to all readers of the *Vita Ludovici*" ("History as Enlightenment: Suger and the *Mos Anagogicus,*" in *The Past as Text,* 166, 169). But whereas Louis goes on from triumph to triumph, Charles is murdered in the process of restoring order and the story changes to one of vengeance and punishment, in which God replaces his murdered minister and restores order Himself.

50. See Warlop, *The Flemish Nobility,* 1:196, to which one might add Suger, *Vie de Louis VI le Gros,* 30, ed. and French trans. Henri Waquet, Les Classiques de l'Histoire de France

au Moyen Age 11 (Paris, 1929), 242; *The Deeds of Louis the Fat,* trans. Richard Cusimano and John Moorhead (Washington, D.C., 1992), 138–39.

51. See Warlop, *The Flemish Nobility,* 1:196, to which one might add Ordericus Vitalis, *Ecclesiastical History* 12.45, 6:370, and Henry of Huntingdon, *Historia Anglorum* 7.37, 476.

52. On Clémence of Burgundy and this episode, see Jan Dhondt, "Vlaanderen van Arnulf de Grote tot Willem Clito, 918–1128," *Algemene Geschiedenis der Nederlanden* 2 (Utrecht, 1950): 90–91; Heinrich Sproemberg, "Clementia, Gräfin von Flandern," *Revue belge de philologie et d'histoire* 42 (1964): 1203–41; Huyghebaert, "Les Femmes laïques dans la vie religieuse des XIe et XIIe siècles dans la province ecclésiastique de Reims," in *I Laici nella "Societas christiana" dei secoli XI e XII. Atti della terza Settimana internazionale di studio, Mendola 21–27 agosto 1965,* Miscellanea del Centro di Studi Medioevali 5 (Milan, 1968), 378–79; Thérèse de Hemptinne, "Clementia van Bourgondië, gravin van Vlaanderen," *Nationaal Biografisch Woordenboek* (Brussels, 1981), 9:148–50, and "Les Epouses des croisés et pèlerins flamands aux XIe et XIIe siècles: L'Exemple des comtesses de Flandre Clémence et Sibylle," in *Autour de la première croisade. Actes du Colloque de la Society for the Study of the Crusades and the Latin East (Clermont-Ferrand, 22–25 juin 1995),* ed. Michel Balard (Paris, 1996), 89–92.

53. *Chronicon Hanoniense quod dicitur Balduini Avennensis,* ed. J. Heller, *Monumenta Germaniae Historica, Scriptores* 25 (Hannover, 1880), 441–43. On this chronicle, see most recently Godfried Croenen, "Princely and Noble Genealogies, Twelfth to Fourteenth Century: Form and Function," in Erik Kooper, ed., *The Medieval Chronicle: Proceedings of the First International Conference on the Medieval Chronicle. Driebergen/Utrecht 13–16 July 1996* (Amsterdam, 1999), 84–95. I have prepared a new edition of this record of the inquest in connection with my forthcoming edition of Walter of Thérouanne's *Vita Karoli* and *Vita b. Ioannis episcopis Morinensis* for the Corpus Christianorum series.

Alan Murray has argued that the inquest into Charles's murder was "a fairly complex and long-drawn out process" consisting of "two distinct parts." The first was "the process of gathering evidence to determine which individuals should be charged." It was "carried out under the authority of the king and count," and thus took place between the king's arrival at Arras in late March and his departure from Bruges on May 6. The second part of the inquest, "the process of answering charges and sentencing[,] was carried out by William Clito at Ypres," probably on Saturday and Sunday, September 17–18. What Galbert records in chapter 87 (September 16), Murray argues, are "new statements of accusation" ordered by the count, "a public re- affirmation of charges originally made April/May, probably as a formal preliminary to the meeting of the court at Ypres which was due to start the next day" ("The Judicial Inquest into the Death of Count Charles the Good of Flanders [1127]: Location and Chronology," *Tijdschrift voor Rechtsgeschiedenis / Revue d'Histoire du Droit / The Legal History Review* 60 (2000): 56–57. I would like to thank Dr. Murray for sending me a copy of his article prior to its publication).

54. Galbert, [11], 1/2; trans., 108; Walter, [24], 548, 27. On these two men, see Warlop, *The Flemish Nobility,* 1:129–32, 199, 202, 205–6.

55. See [88], 31/34; trans., 261; [91], 2/3; trans., 263–64. In his study of the descriptions of seven contemporary assassinations in northeastern France, Jacob observes that, regardless of how the authors of these descriptions eventually explained the murder, "the [true] motive for the crime, as the sources tell us expressly or as is unequivocally clear from the context, was indeed a reaction against the victim's abuse of power," and he characterizes Charles's assassination as "a revolt of nobles." Elsewhere he remarks that "the murder of a lord is a formal gesture. It does not belong to those that are left to chance; the action is, in

general, collective and premeditated" ("Le Meurtre du seigneur," 249, 253; compare 258). Jacob's study suggests that the news of Charles's assassination would have been greeted, at least outside Flanders, with the presumption that Charles had been murdered as a result of a relatively widespread reaction to an abuse of power: according to Henry of Huntingdon, for example, Henry I of England was told that Charles had been "murdered by his nobles in the church at Bruges" *(Historia Anglorum* 7.37, 477). The energy and intellectual resources with which Galbert and Walter sought to defeat this presumption suggest that it perhaps contained a grain of truth.

56. "Law and Power," 167–68.

57. *Mittelalter,* 334–35.

58. Warlop, *The Flemish Nobility,* 192–95; Declercq, "Bertulf," 74. Ross is also doubtful about the Erembalds' servility ("Rise and Fall," 378–79). Warlop notes that Erembald appears "in the company of and perhaps as the presiding officer of the aldermen of the castellany of Veurne" in a charter of c. 1085–1093 and suggests that he may have been simultaneously castellan of Veurne and Bruges *(The Flemish Nobility,* 114, 116, 122). Since, as Pycke shows, the town and aldermancy of Tournai were dominated before the mid-twelfth century by four prominent families, each of whom "ran" (and took their name from) a part of the town, and whose members were "for the most part . . . knights" *(Le Chapitre cathédral Notre-Dame de Tournai,* 43–44), it does not seem unreasonable to suggest that Erembald's family may have held a similar position in Veurne before he seized the opportunity to implant the family in the richer and more powerful town of Bruges. Veurne remained the "hometown" of the Erembalds, however: Bertulf's wife, to whom he fled when he escaped from Bruges, lived there ([46], 5/6; trans., 185); and his first appeal for aid in the wake of the assassination is to "the men of Veurne, who were allied to him in friendship" ([25], 6/37; trans., 145). Veurne was also the second largest local center of the count's fiscal administration and its *conventus* was overseen from c. 1111 to c. 1129 by the provost Fromold Senior who was bound to the Erembalds by both professional and family ties: he himself remained a canon of Saint Donatian and a notary even after he became provost of Veurne—he was the canon who saw to it that "the accounts and records of the revenues of the count" *(De multro,* [35], 9/10; trans., 163) were carried out of the church on March 17—while his nephew, Fromold Junior, had married one of Bertulf's nieces and was evidently seen as a possible successor to the provost. The Erembalds thus maintained strong connections with Veurne and substantial influence over its comital institutions even after they were implanted in Bruges.

59. *Mittelalter,* 337; Van Caenegem is of the same opinion ("Galbert of Bruges," 97–99; "Law and Power," 169). On the insecurity of Charles's position, see also Dhondt, "Vlaanderen," 91–92; and Ross, "Rise and Fall," 389–90.

60. "And so God gave the palm of martyrs to the count, washed clean in the rivulets of his blood and the course of his life brought to an end in good works. In the final moment of his life and at the onset of death, he had most nobly lifted his countenance and his royal hands to heaven, as well as he could among so many blows and thrusts of the swordsmen; and so he surrendered his spirit to the Lord of all and offered himself as a morning sacrifice to God. . . . Whosoever has heard the circumstances of his death has mourned in tears his pitiable death and has commended to God such a great and lamented prince, brought to an end by the fate of the martyrs" ([15], 20/30; trans., 119; trans. mod.). Compare [Prol.] 13/14; trans., 79; [22], 39; trans., 139; [23], 23/27; trans., 142; [38], 47/48; trans., 171; and [70], 6/12; trans., 237.

61. Frustrated by the clergy and people of Bruges in his first attempt on March 3, he, or at least the citizens of Ghent and his monks, made two more attempts to steal the body

([43], 1/33, [50], 1/21; trans., 178–79, 192–93).

62. See [22], 21/53; trans., 138–39; [43], 16/28; trans., 179; and [50], 10/21; trans., 192–93.

63. Both speeches are cited below, Chapter 5, pp. 115–17. On the importance and theft of relics during the period 800–1100, see Patrick Geary, *Furta Sacra: Thefts of Relics in the Central Middle Ages,* 2nd ed. (Princeton, N.J., 1990). Jennifer Welsh has discussed in detail the struggle over the count's body and the popular perception of his sanctity in a paper entitled "The Count's One Body: Struggles for and around the Corpse of Charles the Good of Flanders," which she read at last year's (2000) International Medieval Congress at Leeds. I would like to thank Ms. Welsh for sending me a copy of her paper.

64. "When seven weeks since his first burial had passed, the tomb of the count in the gallery was broken open, and his body was reverently removed, with thyme and frankincense and unguents. For the brothers of the church believed that the body was already rotting and that no one could stand the mortal stench, because it had already been committed to the tomb from the day of burial in the gallery, on the first Friday, up to the Friday which came afterwards on April 22. Therefore they had arranged in advance that during the removal of the body from the tomb they would burn thyme and frankincense in a fire lighted close by the place where the body lay, so that if any stench arose from the tomb, it would be overcome by the strength of the salubrious odors. But when they removed the stone and smelt nothing bad, they placed the body wrapped in the deerskin on a bier in the middle of the choir" ([77], 1/15; trans., 245–46).

65. Borsiard's participation in the murder is recounted mainly in chapters 10, 11, 12, 17, and 18; his fate after the siege has begun is detailed in chapters 28, 41, 48, 61, 80, 84, and 90.

66. Isaac's complicity in the crime is told in chapters 11, 17, and 18; his flight, capture, and execution in chapters 28, 29, 30, 39, 48, and 84.

67. For Benkin, see chapters 36, 75, 77; for Lambert Archei, chapter 48.

68. For the story of Robert the Young, see chapters 11, 26, 28, 41, 44, 45, 60, 61, 65, 73, 74, 82, 83, and 84.

69. These seven entries, added to the end of the chronicle between c. September 10 and c. December 17, relate the transfer of the captive William of Ypres from Ypres to Bruges ([86], shortly after September 10); the count's attempt to exact the toll, which he had remitted in order to gain their favor, from the burghers of Bruges; the second part of the inquest into the assassination and the attempt to enforce its results ([87]–[88], September 16–17); the death of Walter of Vladslo ([89], no precise date); the transfer of William of Ypres to Lille ([90], October 8); the death of Baldwin of Aalst ([91], October 24); and the death of Didier, the brother of Isaac ([92], December 17).

70. Compare [89], 1/4; trans., 262, "it came about by the severe and horrible judgement of God . . . in a shattered condition."

71. Compare [14], 21/23; trans., 117–18, "up to the vengeance . . . the punishment of death."

72. "Also at this time . . . and gained five horses" (trans., 230–31).

73. "At the same time . . . belonged to him" (trans., 231); "Because the count of Mons . . . ardent supporters of his" (trans., 240).

74. "On the same day at Bruges . . . the day of his destruction" (trans., 240–41).

75. "Now in order to tell . . . does not seem effective" (trans., 231–37).

76. "But after that Robert . . . and many proscribed" (trans., 237–38).

77. This parallel between the punishment of those who had plotted Arnold's and

Charles's murders did not exist at all before the executions of May 5, of course, but it was more precise after the inquest held on September 16, which suggests that this passage may have been added after that date. The falling out Galbert mentions between Robert the Frisian and the barons who had helped him overthrow Arnold probably refers to a rebellion that Robert I put down c. 1083, twelve years after he had seized power (see Hariulf, *Vita Arnulfi* 2.13, 886–87; Verlinden, *Robert Ier le Frison,* 148–49; and Nicholas, *Medieval Flanders,* 56). Some of the barons who helped Robert in 1071 may well have risen against him in 1083, but the two events were probably not as closely connected as Galbert portrays them: his interpretation of these events seems to have been influenced here by his desire to find in them parallels to the present, and he enhances and draws attention to these parallels by linguistic means.

78. It is possible that Galbert's memory was also prodded by a reading of the first chapter of Walter of Thérouanne's *Vita Karoli.* The number of commonalities between the *Passio* and the *Vita Karoli* is striking, running from the events and scenes they choose to record to certain small verbal echoes, and suggests that Galbert may have read a version of the *Vita* before he completed the *Passio* (see the summary and discussion in Appendix V). In the form we have it, however, the *Vita* could not have been completed before the late summer of 1127, since Walter mentions that Pope Honorius told him of the donation Charles's half-brother William, duke of Apulia, made to the Holy See on his deathbed, and William died on July 26, 1127 *(Vita Karoli,* [2], 540, 8/14), but it was certainly finished before the death of John of Warneton, the bishop of Thérouanne at whose request Walter wrote the *Vita,* in January 1130, and probably completed before the struggle between William Clito and Thierry of Alsace in the spring of 1128, since Walter never mentions Thierry or any of the troubles of that spring. It is thus possible that Galbert saw a copy of the *Vita* as early as September 1127, at a time when he had perhaps already begun to revise his notes but had probably not finished doing so.

79. Köpke, followed by Pirenne, began a new chapter (70) at this point, and I reproduced this chapter division in my edition so that readers seeking passages referred to in these earlier editions could find them more easily. The manuscripts, however, do not have a break at this point and I do not believe Galbert intended to have one here.

80. Köpke, followed by Pirenne, introduced another chapter division (71) here, which has thoroughly obscured the structure and meaning of this passage. There is no division in the manuscripts at this point and when one reads the passage with an eye uninfluenced by the modern division, it is clear, I think, that this sentence ("Finally . . .") does not refer backward to the Flemish traitors who helped Robert seize the county—as the modern chapter division suggests and as Pirenne (ed., 115, n. 1), Ross (trans., 238, n. 10), and I (ed., xxiv–xxv), influenced by it, mistakenly believed—but forward to the following passage in which Galbert discusses Erembald's murder of Boldran.

81. On Erembald's murder of Boldran, see G. Blancquaert, "L'Expédition flamande contre Anvers en 1055 et les premiers châtelains de Bruges," *Annales de la Société royale d'archéologie de Bruxelles* 46 (1942–1943): 167–71. Galbert's account of the provost's family history is vaguely reminiscent of Ordericus Vitalis's account of that of the sycophantic Ranulf Flambard, who rose "from low origins" to be bishop of Durham, "chief manager of the king's [William Rufus'] wealth and justice," and immensely wealthy. Bertulf's mother, the adulteress Dedda, is matched by Ranulf's, who was, according to Ordericus, "a sorceress and had often conversed with the devil" *(Ecclesiastical History* 10.19, 5:313). Bertulf's father, Erembald, seems to be a moral ancestor of Robert Fitz Hildebrand, "a man of low birth indeed but also of tried military qualities," who, according to the author of the *Gesta Stephani,* was sent by Matilda to help William de Pont de l'Arche in his struggle with the bishop of

Winchester, became William's confidant, seduced his wife, and eventually imprisoned him in the dungeon, "enjoying his castle, wealth, and wife." Robert was, of course, punished by God through a lingering and painful illness and death *(Gesta Stephani* 77, 150–52). These vague similarities suggest that Galbert's account of the Erembalds has been influenced by an ambient narrative model linking inferior social status, strong sexual and acquisitive appetites, deceit and treachery.

Galbert's account of the Erembalds' family romance in order to explain how their punishment is related to the sins of their ancestors is all the more striking because he declares expressly that he is not going to relate this information in the course of describing Bertulf's execution in chapter 57: "And although I may seem to have a convenient place here to recount his genealogy, nevertheless, it seems to me I should let the work I have undertaken suffice and omit such an account, for I have set out to relate the outcome of the siege and not the adulterous origin of the family of the provost and his kin" ([57], 50/55; trans., 210). This latter passage probably belongs to the first parchment record and the contradiction between the two passages shows the difference between Galbert's earlier intentions when he first transferred his notes to parchment and his later ones when he set to work on the *Passio.* The planned *Descriptio* was concerned with a description of events in the present, while the *Passio* was intended to provide the background and an explanation of those events. The subsistence of the two contradictory passages in the existing *De multro* is also evidence that Galbert never finished the *Passio.*

82. Upbraiding Bertulf for his efforts to have Charles's body removed to Ghent, one of the senior canons of the church declares it "a great treasure of our church whom divine mercy and dispensation have granted to us as a martyr" ([22], 35/37; trans., 138). The value of the martyr's presence is also apparent in the readiness of the people of Bruges to resort to arms to keep it in their town.

83. As was mentioned at the beginning of this chapter, 1 Peter 2.13–14, which Galbert cites here, was one of the biblical cornerstones of the theocratic concept of princely authority (see Carlyle and Carlyle, *History,* 1:91; Kern, *Gottesgnadentum,* 176; and Anton, *Fürstenspiegel,* 359).

84. The theme of the "princeless land" is evoked at the very outset of the *Passio,* in Galbert's reference in the Prologue to the death without heirs of both Charles and the Emperor Henry V and the ruling Henry I of England's lack of a (male) heir ([Prol.], 1/7, 12; trans., 79). It appears again at the beginning of Galbert's accounts of the offers made to Charles of the Holy Roman Empire and the kingdom of Jerusalem in chapters 4 and 5. The two chapters begin in similar ways—"while the marquis Charles was reigning in his county of Flanders in the splendor of peace and fame, Henry, the Roman emperor, died, and the realm of that empire was made desolate and left without a heir to the throne" *(et desolatum est regnum imperii illius et sine herede exheredatum)* ([4], 1/4; trans., 90); "during his lifetime it happened that the king of Jerusalem was taken captive by the Saracens, and the city of Jerusalem sat desolate without her king" *(et desolata sedebat civitas Hierusalem absque rege suo)* ([5], 1/3; trans., 92)—and while the contrast between the desolate empire and kingdom and the peaceful and glorious county of Flanders is obviously intended as a testimonial to Charles's abilities as a ruler, it also evokes the dangers a realm faces when it lacks a prince.

85. Jacob notes that regardless of whether the murder of a lord was portrayed as a martyrdom or a punishment, its "overarching significance is always the same: the fertile presence of the divine will in the working out of human destinies" ("Le Meurtre du seigneur," 250).

86. *Serious Entertainments,* 221.

87. "The New Cornificius: Medieval History and the Artifice of Words," in Breisach, ed., *Classical Rhetoric,* 49, 50.

88. "Most observers would surely not have been moved to attempt [to explain Lambert of Aardenburg's death in battle after he had cleared himself by ordeal of a charge of treason (see Chapter 6, p. 175), but Galbert] . . . will not allow signs to lie, because their meaning has to depend on a God who is just, reasonable, and consistent. Galbert will not accept a dramatic reality tolerated by a God of rhetorical gestures; . . . Galbert insists, at whatever cost of effort, that the surface reveal its inner meaning of right judgement and eternal truth. . . . he would not record the surface and leave the significance for a later generation. His voice throughout reminds us of an intelligible higher order, known to every Christian and not invented by him. His is the authentic voice of serious realism in medieval terms" ("The New Cornificius," 50, 52).

89. This "you" is perplexing. The most obvious reference is the "the clergy and people" ([Prol.], 22; trans., 80) of Bruges to whom Galbert refers shortly before and to whom he clearly refers in the expressions "our place" *(noster locus)* ([Prol.], 20; trans., 80) and "our posterity" *(posteris nostris)* ([Prol.], 34; trans., 80) shortly before and after this line.

90. Ross, trans., 69–70.

91. See "Galbert of Bruges," 92; *Galbert van Brugge,* 6; and in Galbert, *Le Meurtre,* 61–62.

92. "Galbert of Bruges," 92; *Galbert van Brugge,* 6; and in Galbert, *Le Meurtre,* 61.

93. Sproemberg writes: "one must bear in mind above all that Galbert is writing in Bruges and for the burghers of Bruges" ("Erwachen des Staatsgefühls," 51; compare his *Mittelalter,* 352–57). For Coué, see Chapter 2, pp. 30–31.

94. *Galbert van Brugge,* 6–7; compare in Galbert, *Le Meurtre,* 61–62; "Galbert of Bruges," 92.

95. Walter includes him among the core conspirators who swear to murder Charles ([24], 548, 25/28) and reaffirms his guilt when he describes his execution ([50], 559, 43). It is particularly interesting to compare the passages describing the swearing of the conspiracy in the two works: *Vita Karoli,* [24], 548, 24/30; *De multro,* [11], 1/43; trans., 108–10.

96. "Voices of Flanders," 112.

97. Smalley concludes similarly that "Galbert addressed himself to the men of Bruges and to 'all the faithful'. He had a sense of solidarity with his fellow townsmen, in spite of their misbehaviour, which he was the first to recognize. . . ." *(Historians in the Middle Ages,* 108).

NOTES TO CHAPTER 4

1. Alberic of Monte Cassino, *De dictamine,* 2, in Ludwig Rockinger, ed., *Briefsteller und Formelbücher des elften bis vierzehnten Jahrhunderts,* Quellen und Erörterungen zur bayerischen und deutschen Geschichte 9, 2 vols. (1863–1864; rpt. New York, 1961), 1:30.

2. *Policraticus* 1.8, ed. Keats-Rohan, 55; trans. Pike, 38–39; compare ed. Webb, 1:48.

3. *Descriptio Kambriae, Praefatio secunda,* ed. James F. Dimock, in *Opera,* ed. J. S. Brewer et al. (London, 1868), 6:163; *"The Journey through Wales" and "The Description of Wales,"* 216.

4. See Pirenne (ed., viii–ix), followed by Ross (trans., 64–65, 69) and all later scholars (for example, Van Caenegem, *Galbert van Brugge,* 4).

5. See Appendix VI. Some of these additions echo or refer to passages in the introductory material that was added at this time and seem intended to link the old and the new material and increase the coherence of the different parts of the *Passio* ([17], 12/14; trans., 125; [17], 13/14; trans., 125; [18], 28/29; trans., 129; [22], 39; trans., 139; [25], 47/52; trans.,

146; [26], 6/10; trans. 147–48; [26], 9/10; trans., 148; [29], 47/48; trans., 156; [37], 24/33; trans., 168; [37], 33/[38], 56; trans., 168–71; [43], 36/38; trans., 180; [44], 5/6; trans., 181; [52], 15; trans., 195; [52], 38/39; trans., 197; [64], 16/17; trans., 225.). In some of these cases it is possible that the newly added introductory material echoes the existing passages, but it generally seems to be the other way around: Galbert appears to have rewritten the earlier passages in order to link them to the new introduction. The other additions are of various kinds and varying importance. None of them are of a journalistic nature, or at least of a purely journalistic nature.

The additions (chapters 68–71) Galbert made to the long manuscript entry for April 17 (chapters 66–72) have been discussed in the preceding chapter. The long manuscript entry devoted to the events of March 17 (modern editorial chapters 35–39) offers another excellent example of the way Galbert expanded an existing entry. The first version of this chapter probably consisted of [35], 1/14 (trans., 162–63, "On March 17 . . . to be taken out"); [35], 19/33 (trans., 163–64, "Then after everything . . . the invasion of the church"); [36], 20/[37], 7 (trans., 166–67, "There was indeed . . . into the church"); [37], 17/24 (trans., 168, "In the western part . . . for fighting outside"); and [39], 1/23 (trans., 171–72, "On the same day . . . the very bowels of the earth"). The remaining passages (see Appendix VI) may have been added in as many as seven different moments.

Ross notes (trans., 96, n. 1) that the first sentence of chapter 7—"now after the clemency of God had withdrawn the scourges [*flagella*] and completely removed the troubles of the time . . ." ([7], 1/2; trans., 96)—refers back to the "scourges *(flagella)* of famine and . . . death" ([2], 1; trans., 84; trans. mod.) mentioned and described in chapters 2–3, suggesting that chapters 4–6, consisting of accounts of the offers of the Holy Roman Empire and the kingdom of Jerusalem to Charles, and a eulogy of the murdered prince, are later additions to the long introductory manuscript chapter represented by modern chapters [1]/[12], 21. Thierry of Alsace was installed as count the following year on "Sunday, *Laetare Hierusalem,* in the middle of Lent" ([103], 9/10; trans., 280) and the text from which the celebration takes its name refers to a joyful Jerusalem, in direct contrast to the image of a desolate Jerusalem, bereft of her king ("*et desolata sedebat civitas Hierusalem absque rege suo,*" [5], 2–3; trans., 92) with which chapter 5 begins. It is thus possible that chapters 4 and 5, at least, were not added until spring 1128 (see Chapter 7, below).

The evolution of this introductory material is probably still more complicated, however. In the manuscripts, it is divided into three chapters corresponding to the Prologue, modern chapters [1]/[12], 21 (trans., 81–112, "Charles, son of Canute . . . pennies to the poor"), and modern chapters [12], 22/[14] (trans., 112–18, "Now it should be known . . . through to the end"). Chapters 1–6 are devoted to Charles. Chapters [7]/[12], 21 are devoted to the history of Charles's struggle with the Erembalds and end with a vision of Borsiard and his accomplices in the upper gallery of the church, ready to kill the count. Chapter [12], 22/55 adds new information about Charles's past and the consequences of his death, chapter 13 adds new information about Bertulf's past and his struggle with Charles, while chapter 14 returns to some prologue-like reflections on the hardheartedness of the assassins, God's role in history, and the organization of the chronicle. This third manuscript chapter is thus something of a grabbag which, although it serves a dramatic function (discussed in the next chapter), may well be a later addition to the first version of the introduction. One might thus suggest that a first version of the introduction consisted of the Prologue and chapters 1–3 and [7]/[12], 21, to which chapters 4–6 and [12], 22/[14] were added in two or more subsequent moments.

6. In chapter 61, dated to April 13, Galbert mentions that Helias surrendered the gold

and silver vessels to the count "as we are about to tell" ([61], 45; trans., 220), but the story is not related until chapter 83, dated to May 7. The other two cross-references are to information that Galbert has provided earlier and thus do not provide any chronological evidence of rewriting. In chapter 57, dated to April 11, Galbert notes that William of Ypres had sent a messenger to the provost after the murder, "as we have noted above" ([57], 6; trans., 208). The reference is to chapter 25, dated to March 6. In chapter 75, dated to April 19, he mentions the construction of a palisade and ditch around Bruges, "as we have told above" ([75], 12; trans., 243). The reference is again to chapter 25.

7. I have attached a list of all these allusions in Appendix VII (many of them are also discussed by Coué, "Der Mord," 112–14. See also Pirenne, ed., vii; Ross, trans., 155, nn. 5 and 6; 164, n. 7; 186, n. 5; 220, nn. 7 and 8.). Some of them—[16], 46/48; trans., 122–23 ("Gervaise . . . his kinsmen"); [21], 30/38; trans., 135–36 ("On Sunday . . . very much for himself"); [21], 42/43; trans., 136 ("But Walter . . . and his nephews"); [27], 3/4; trans., 150 ("a brother of the provost, who had sworn the death of the count"); [35], 29/33; trans., 164 ("Then all good men . . . invasion of the church"); and [53], 10/20; trans., 198–99 ("And so they went . . . advocate of the whole land")—allude to events that lie only a few days in the future and thus show only that they were written or rewritten at least a few days after the events they relate. Two passages—[21], 20/23; trans., 135 ("And so closed that day . . . in the future"); [85], 13/19; trans., 257 ("It seemed likely . . . as it later became clear")—allude vaguely to future troubles and future revelations, while a third—[29], 33/59; trans., 155–56 ("In the same way . . . excuses for their treachery")—is dated to March 9, but refers to the whole length of the siege (ending 3/19 with the storming of the castle? or 4/14 with the invasion of the church gallery? or 4/19 with the surrender of the besieged?) and may thus have been written or rewritten as few as ten days after the events it relates or as many as six weeks later. A series of passages—[25], 18/26; trans., 144 ("Now this was done . . . the most pious count"); [26], 46/50; trans., 149 ("It would take too long . . . his vengeance impartially"); [27], 7/15; trans., 150 ("Our burghers . . . and every kind of disorder")—alludes to the future punishment of Charles's assassins, but cannot clearly be shown to have been written or rewritten after their execution. A long manuscript chapter (modern chapters 41–46), dated March 19, contains two passages concerning Bertulf's escape from the siege—[42], 4/14; trans., 177 ("The names of those . . . where he should flee or to whom"); [46], 1/17; trans., 185–86 ("Now on Thursday night . . . within his own boundaries")—that include details that could only have been known after his capture on April 11, showing that this chapter must have been written or rewritten at least three weeks after the bulk of the events it relates. Chapter 61, dated to April 13, contains an allusion to events that occurred on May 6 and 7—[61], 41/45; trans., 220 ("That is why the king . . . about to tell")—and thus must have been written or rewritten after the latter date.

Three final allusions to future events ([26], 24/28; trans., 148; [57], 14/17; trans., 208–9; [80], 6; trans., 249–50) are particularly interesting insofar as they are linked to the theme of falling. They are discussed below.

8. The sixty-seven modern chapters that represent the first version of the *Passio* (15–67, 72–85) make up roughly 57 percent of the text but contain only three passages introduced by the phrases *et notandum* or *notandum* (in chapters 35, 75, and 78; these three passages may, moreover, be later additions made during the late fall of 1127 or 1128; see Chapter 7). The thirty modern chapters written during the spring of 1128 (93–122), in contrast, make up only about 20 percent of the text but contain nine passages introduced by this phrase (chapters 102 [twice], 108 [twice], 110 [twice], 114, 116, and 120). This phrase is more likely to be found in an earlier stage of composition than in a later one, and its relative paucity in

these first chapters (it does not appear at all in the first twenty chapters [15–34] and appears only once in the first fifty-six [15–67, 72–74]), compared to its relatively frequency in the final chapters, suggests that the initial parchment record of chapters 15–67 and 72–85 was indeed rewritten.

9. The theme is developed in the Prologue and chapters 15, 22, 23, 38, 43, 50, 70, and 77. See Chapter 3, pp. 67–68.

10. Helias went on to become a bishop in Denmark. See Michael H. Gelting, "Un Prélat flamand au Danemark au XIIe siècle: Hélie, évêque de Ribe (1142–1162)," *Handelingen van het Genootschap voor Geschiedenis Gesticht onder de Benaming "Société d'émulation" te Brugge* 122 (1985): 159–79. Galbert's use of the silver cup as the focus of a moral tale recalls Guibert of Nogent's similar use of similar vessels in his autobiography *(Autobiographie* 1.11, ed. 64–70; trans. 60–61).

11. Novel, at least, in Flanders. In 1090, Henry I, William Clito's uncle, had defenestrated the rebel burgher Conan from a window of the tower of the castle of Rouen. Van Caenegem has suggested that this may have been a regular form of execution among the Normans (see Orderic Vitalis, *Ecclesiastical History* 8.15, 4:224–27; and Van Caenegem, "Misdaad," 324).

12. In an article devoted to a study of this *mandatum* and two others that appear in the *De multro,* Ganshof argued that this "transcription," while based on a true *mandatum,* preserves only certain phrases of the original letter and that much of it is due to Galbert ("Trois Mandements," 132; compare 120).

13. For a discussion of this notion of "punishment unheard-of before this time" from a legal point of view, see Van Caenegem, "Misdaad," 324–26.

14. Galbert never cites Proverbs 16.18—"Pride goes before destruction, and a haughty spirit before a fall" *(contritionem praecedit superbia: et ante ruinam exaltatur spiritus)*—but one can't help but wonder if it didn't play some role in shaping his perception of this theme in the events he describes. Elias ("Augustinian Elements," 39–40) suggests that his perception of this theme may also have been influenced by Augustine's description of the precipitation of the angels of darkness in *De civitate Dei* 9.33 (ed. 2:352–54; trans., 468–69).

15. Antonia Gransden, "Realistic Observation in Twelfth-Century England," in her *Legends, Traditions, and History,* 176. Gabrielle Spiegel has suggested that the emphasis on accurate and detailed description in much medieval historical writing resulted from a concept of history and historiography that led to "an ethical commitment to mimetic accuracy . . . the historian in the Middle Ages viewed his text as a transparency through which he sought to convey to his prospective audience of readers or auditors as direct and vivid an impression of the past and present reality as possible" ("Genealogy: Form and Function in Medieval Historiography," in *The Past as Text,* 101). "The point" of medieval history, writes Partner, "was to get close enough to see for yourself or, more commonly, to give that impression" ("The New Cornificius," 12).

16. On the scholarly use of Galbert's descriptions of Saint Donatian, for example, see H. Mansion, "A propos de l'ancienne église Saint-Donatien à Bruges," *Revue Belge d'Archéologie et d'Histoire de l'Art* 8 (1938): 99–112; Jacques Vincent, "Au sujet de la tour et du 'solarium' de l'ancienne église Saint-Donatien à Bruges," *Revue belge d'archéologie et d'histoire de l'art* 14 (1944): 47–55; Jean De Sturler, "Note sur l'emploi de poteries creuses dans les édifices du moyen âge. A propos de la première église de Saint-Donatien à Bruges," *Le Moyen Age* 63 (1957): 241–65; Paul Rolland, "La Première Église de Saint-Donatien à Bruges (quelques remarques)," *Revue belge d'archéologie et d'histoire de l'art* 14 (1944): 101–11; J. Mertens, "Quelques édifices religieux à plan central découverts récemment en Belgique," *Genava,* n.s.

11 (1963): 141–61; and Luc Devliegher, "De voorromaanse, romaanse en gotische Sint-Donaaskerk: Evolutie en invloeden," in Hubert De Witte, ed., *De Brugse Burg* (Bruges, 1991), 118–36, and "De voorromaanse Sint-Donaaskerk en de romaanse westelijke kloostervleugel (onderzoek 1955 en later)," in De Witte, ed., *De Brugse Burg*, 46–92.

17. See Gransden, "Realistic Observation," 188–91.

18. For historians' use of topographical information provided by Galbert, see Guy de Poerck, "Trois Points litigieux dans la topographie de Bruges d'après Galbert," *Annales de la Fédération Archéologique et Historique de Belgique* 28, Congrès d'Anvers (1930), fasc. 1, 73–75; J. De Smet, "De oude hydrografie van de stad Brugge," *Handelingen van het Genootschap voor Geschiedenis Gesticht onder de Benaming "Société d'émulation" te Brugge* 86 (1949): 5–22; Jan Dhondt, "De vroege topografie van Brugge," *Handelingen der Maatschappij voor Geschiedenis en Oudheidkunde te Gent* n.s. 11 (1957): 3–30; A. C. F. Koch, "Brugge's topografische ontwikkeling tot in de 12e eeuw," *Handelingen van het Genootschap voor Geschiedenis Gesticht onder de Benaming "Société d'émulation" te Brugge* 99 (1962): 5–67; Egidius Strubbe, "Van de eerste naar de tweede omwalling van Brugge," *Handelingen van het Genootschap voor Geschiedenis Gesticht onder de Benaming "Société d'émulation" te Brugge* 100 (1963): 271–300; M. Coornaert, "Over de hydrografie van Brugge," in *Album Albert Schouteet* (Bruges, 1973), 23–25; Marc Ryckaert, "De Oudeburg te Brugge," in *Album Albert Schouteet*, 155–68, "Die Topographie der flandrischen Hafenstädte bis 1300: Das Beispiel von Brügge," *Lübecker Schriften zur Archäologie und Kulturgeschichte* 7 (1983): 47–55, and *Brugge*, Historische Stedenatlas van België (Brussels, 1991); Luc Devliegher, "Galbert et la topographie de Bruges," in Galbert, *Le Meurtre*, 254–64 (revised version, "Brugge in het dagboek van Galbert," in Galbert, *De Moord* [1999], 91–106); and Luc Goeminne, "Het verhaal van Galbertus over de moord op Karel de Goede en de grafelijke watergraanmolen te Brugge in 1127," *Molenecho's* 10.3 (1982): 96–97.

19. [51], 11/14; trans., 193–94. The order of the towns is: Ijzendijke, Oostburg, Aardenburg, Lapscheure, Oostkerke, Uitkerke, Lissewege, Slijpe, Gistel, Oudenburg, Lichtervelde, and Jabbeke.

20. See, for example, F. L. Ganshof, *Feudalism*, trans. Philip Grierson (London, 1952), 65–71, 110–11; Joseph Strayer, *Feudalism* (Princeton, N.J., 1965), 122; David Herlihy, *The History of Feudalism* (New York, 1970), 98; and Jacques Le Goff, "The Symbolic Ritual of Vassalage," in *Time, Work and Culture in the Middle Ages*, trans. Arthur Goldhammer (Chicago, 1980), 239–63. Galbert's description of this ceremony has been analyzed from the point of view of legal history by Heirbaut, in "Galbert van Brugge," 54–56; elsewhere, Heirbaut has observed that "nearly every general work on European feudalism seems to use well-known texts from Galbert of Bruges as sources describing some abstract European feudalism, while neglecting the specifically Flemish [and, one might add, specifically Galbertian] elements in these texts" ("The *Fief-Rente*," 8 n. 52).

21. Demyttenaere suggests that this prolocutor "is an experienced jurist who knows what words and gestures are important here for the legality of the agreement. He appears as a sort of master of ceremonies and not as an interpreter (William knew Dutch: he was brought up at the court of the then Dutch-speaking Flemish counts)" (in Galbert, *De Moord* [1999], 190, n. 127).

22. Gervaise of Praet likewise divides the ceremony into these three parts—homage *(hominium)*, faith *(fides)* and investiture—in Galbert's version of his speech to Thierry of Alsace when he returns to Bruges and becomes the new count's vassal: "'I wish . . . to do homage and pledge my faith to you [*volo . . . hominium et fidem vobis facere*], as to the natural lord of the land and the one with whom we are in agreement; I wish to receive from you the

office and fiefs [*officium et feoda . . . a vobis recipere volo*] that I formerly held from your predecessors'" ([104], 15/18; trans., 281).

The author of the *Gesta Stephani* mentions homage *(hominium)* three times, referring to gifts and lands in return for homage and an oath *(iusiurandum)* *(Gesta Stephani* 5, 12); an oath *(iuramentum)* and homage (41, 90); and faith *(fides)*, oath *(iuramentum)*, and homage (55, 112).

Orderic Vitalis mentions homage *(hominium/homagium)* in twenty-two passages. In ten of these, he mentions homage only *(Ecclesiastical History* 4, 2:310; 7.15, 4:88; 7.15, 4:92; 10.19, 5:318; 10.19, 5:314; 11.10, 6:58; 12.26, 6:302; 12.39, 6:352; 12.43, 6:364; 12.44, 6:366); in six others, he mentions only homage and fealty *(fidelitas)* (4, 2:304; 4, 2:356; 5.19, 3:184; 6.10, 3:306; 7.15, 4:84; 10.15, 5:290). In the remaining passages, he mentions homage and military service *(militare)* (9.17, 5:186); homage, faith *(fides)*, and fealty *(fidelitas)* (12.39, 6:352); homage in return for estates, dignities, and gifts (10.16, 5:298); homage and fealty *(fidelitas)* in return for provisions, escort, and support (9.6, 5:48); homage *(hominium)*, fidelity *(fidelis)*, and military service *(militare seruitium)* in return for gifts (7.15, 4:88); and an oath *(iurare)* without homage (9.6, 5:50).

Heirbaut's discussion of Galbert's description of this ceremony also shows how it can be analysed differently by other medieval authors and by modern scholars ("Galbert van Brugge," 54–56). I would like to thank Professor Fred Cheyette of Amherst College for initially drawing my attention to the subjective element in Galbert's description of these acts.

23. The tolls and rents remitted through this agreement had constituted the fiefs of some of the count's knights: the count, as these knights later objected, had transferred their fiefs to the burghers without their consent (see [88], 1/11; trans., 260). By remitting the tolls and rents, the count effectively enfeoffed the burghers with what had previously been knightly fiefs.

24. The citizens of London and Stephen likewise agreed to a "pact" *(pactione)* confirmed by an "oath taken on both sides" *(mutuo iuramento)* *before* they elected him king *(Gesta Stephani* 2, 6–7).

25. When Galbert reports the analogous reception and election of Thierry of Alsace by the people of Bruges the following year (March 30 to April 2, 1128), he breaks it into four somewhat different moments or stages: first, "the count took an oath" *(juravit)*, then Ivan of Aalst and Daniel of Dendermonde "were named as pledges between the count and the clergy and people" *(dati sunt inter consulem et clerum et populum obsides)*, then the citizens "swore fealty to the count" *(fidelitatem jurabant)*, and, finally, they "performed homages" *(hominia fecerunt)* ([103], 1/7; trans., 280).

26. "Notes on Galbert of Bruges," 625; compare Heirbaut, "Galbert van Brugge," 58–59.

27. Galbert in fact mentions more instances of nonnoble homage than he does instances of noble homage (for descriptions of nonnoble homage, see [20], 25/31; trans., 133; [25], 15/18; trans., 144; [54], 6/10; trans. 199–200; [66], 36/38; trans., 230; [94], 6/8; trans., 266–67; [103], 6/7; trans., 280; [106], 31/36; trans., 284; [107], 6/10; trans., 286; and [122], 1/5; trans., 312; for descriptions of noble homage, see [52], 33/35; trans., 197; [55], 82/85; trans., 206; [69], 3/6; trans., 233; [104], 15/24; trans., 281; for descriptions of mixed or indeterminate homage, see [25], 33/37; trans., 145; [53], 11/14; trans., 199; [88], 37/38; trans., 261; [99], 21/22; trans., 275; [101], 4/7, 22/25; trans., 276–77; [102], 3/6, 11/15; trans., 278–79). The number of separate moments or acts he mentions in connection with these ceremonies varies from one to five, and their names are not constant.

28. "Conventional conceptions of homage and fealty dissolve," wrote Ross in 1959,

"when confronted by Galbert's evidence of the varied use of pledges" ("Rise and Fall," 388, n. 163) and Susan Reynolds cites Galbert as a witness to "creative" uses of the ceremony of homage in the twelfth century (my point here is that the creativity may be as much Galbert's as that of the people involved in the ceremony), noting that "throughout the century the significance of oaths and ceremonies seems to have depended on circumstances and the status of the parties, and so did the meaning of words like *homagium, hominium, dominus ligius* or *homo ligius,* and *commendare*" (*Fiefs and Vassals* [Oxford, U.K., 1994], 268–69). On the metaphoric extension of the concepts or vocabulary of homage in the *De multro,* see also Heirbaut, "Galbert van Brugge," 59–62. On the flexibility, adaptability, and polysemy of such ceremonies, see Koziol, *Begging Pardon and Favor,* 8, 14, 296, 303–8, who has emphasized that "the history of ritual is . . . the history of perceptions, not, as is usually thought, because rituals provide a window onto the perceptions of participants, but because their perceptions determine the meaningfulness of their rituals" (107).

29. For other examples of Galbert's analyses of fixed, formal actions, see his descriptions of: the renunciation of homage and disinvestiture ([38], 37/54; trans., 170–71; [95], 39/43, 53/61; trans., 269, 270; [101], 29/32; trans., 278; and [104], 9/11; trans., 281; for a discussion of Galbert's description of this ceremony, see Marc Bloch, "Les Formes de la rupture de l'hommage dans l'ancien droit féodal," *Nouvelle Revue Historique du Droit Français et Etranger* 36 [1912]: 141–77; and Heirbaut, "Galbert van Brugge," 56–58); the new count and king's "joyous entries" into Saint-Omer and into Bruges ([66], 1/37; trans., 227–30 and [55], 1/51; trans., 201–4; on this "joyous entry," see James M. Murray, "The Liturgy of the Count's Advent in Bruges, from Galbert to Van Eyck," in Barbara A. Hanawalt and Kathryn Reyerson, eds., *City and Spectacle in Medieval Europe,* Medieval Cultures 6 [Minneapolis, 1994], 137–52; on this ceremony in general, see Wilfried Dotzauer, "Die Ankunft des Herrschers. Der fürstliche 'Einzug' in die Stadt [bis zum Ende des Alten Reichs]," *Archiv für Kulturgeschichte* 55 [1973]: 245–88; and Koziol, *Begging Pardon and Favor,* 133–34); and the charge to the jury responsible for conducting the inquest into Charles's murder ([87], 2/19; trans., 258–59).

30. Van Caenegem writes that Galbert's descriptions of the punishments meted out to various malefactors are so numerous and so "graphic . . . that we seem to have entered a 'chamber of horrors' when we read his journal" ("Misdaad," 323).

31. Köpke, followed by Pirenne, divided this manuscript chapter into seven chapters numbered 15 to 21.

32. Walter of Thérouanne writes that after Borsiard and his men had mortally wounded the castellan of Bourbourg, "each of the conspirators immediately appeared with his men and, scouring the whole town, which was as crowded and large as a city, and meeting no resistance, they hunted around for the others whom they had already marked for death" ([28], 550, 26/29). Suger declares that the assassins "slaughtered every member of the garrison [*quoscumque castellanos,* which might also be translated as 'every castellan'] and everyone of the count's noble barons whom they could find in the church or outside of the castle" (*Vie de Louis VI le Gros* 30, ed., 244; trans., 139).

33. Galbert names six men: Baldwin (chaplain and priest), Godebert (clerk of the count), Odger (clerk), Fromold Junior (notary and courtier), Arnold (chamberlain), and Eustace (clerk) ([18], 4/17; trans., 128).

34. Compare [17], 24/26; trans., 125–26, where the castellan's extraction and murder are again described.

35. Walter of Thérouanne also describes the castellan's death but he makes no mention of the castellan's giving his ring to the abbess of Origny and his effort to communicate his last wishes to his family through her (*Vita Karoli,* [28], 550, 24/38).

36. Sproemberg suggests that Galbert may not have been present at the assassination (*Mittelalter,* 338).

37. Sproemberg calls this description of the assassination a "work of art" (*Mittelalter,* 338).

38. This description forms a single long chapter in the manuscripts.

39. It is interesting to compare Galbert's descriptions of the battles of Ypres ([79], I/12; trans., 248), Axpoel ([114], I/68; trans., 297–99), and Oostkamp ([116], I/40; trans., 301–3) at which he was not present, with Suger's description of the siege of Le Puiset (*Vie de Louis le Gros* 19, ed., 136–40; trans., 87–89), at which Suger was, and with the descriptions of the sieges of Lincoln and Winchester in the *Gesta Stephani* (55, 63–68, pp. 113, 126–36). Galbert has recently been used as a source for the history of warfare by C. Gaier, "When the Crossbow Was a Novelty: Reflections on Its Role as a Military Weapon from the 10th Century to the 13th Century," *Le Moyen Age* 99 (1993): 224–25, n. 40; W. T. S. Tarver, "The Traction Trebuchet: A Reconstruction of an Early-Medieval Siege Engine," *Technology and Culture* 36 (1995): 146, n. 46; and Laurence W. Marvin, "'Men Famous in Combat and Battle . . . ,'" 243–58. I would like to thank Professor Marvin for sending me a copy of his article prior to its publication.

40. Murray, "Voices of Flanders," 112.

41. Murray, "Voices of Flanders," 112.

42. Murray, "Voices of Flanders," 112.

43. In addition to the ones discussed below, one finds examples of such descriptions in Galbert's account of the reception of William Clito in Saint-Omer ([66], I/38; trans., 227–30; Pirenne suggests that this account is highly inaccurate and refers to its "poetic trappings"; ed., 107–8, n. 2]; Ross likewise calls it a "poetic account" [trans., 229, n. 5]) and of the battle of Ypres ([79], I/12; trans., 248). Examples may likewise be found in the accounts Galbert added in spring 1128 of Ivan's speech to William Clito in Ghent and the events surrounding it ([95], I/45; trans., 267–69); of the battle of Axpoel ([114], I/68; trans., 297–99; the literary quality of this account is especially striking: compare it, for example, with Geoffrey of Monmouth's account of the battle between Arthur and Lucius Hiberius in the *Historia regum Britanniae* X.vi–xii, ed. Acton Griscom [London, 1929], 481–95; *The History of the Kings of Britain,* trans. Lewis Thorpe [Harmondsworth, U.K., 1966], 246–57); and of the battle of Oostkamp ([116], I/40; trans., 301–3).

44. *Historia regum Britanniae* IX.xi, ed., 449–50; trans., 224–25.

45. For a discussion of the popular traditions that are evident in Galbert's description of Bertulf's execution, see Van Caenegem, "Misdaad," 327.

46. Mt. 26.67–68, 27.28–31; Mk. 14.65, 15.19; Lk. 22.63–65, 23.11; Jn. 18.22, 19.1–3.

47. Mt. 26.63, Mk. 14.61; Mt. 27.14, Mk. 15.5; Lk. 23.9.

48. Mt. 26.55; Mk. 14.48, Lk. 22.52.

49. Jn. 19.9–11.

50. Mt. 27.30, Mk. 15.19.

51. Mt. 26.67–68, Lk. 22.63–64.

52. Notice again how Walter consistently draws attention to himself and his work—"perhaps I should say . . . ," "I do not think I should omit . . . ," "For I learned truly . . ."—whereas Galbert almost never does so.

53. Other scholars have likewise noted the presence of various narrative paradigms behind Galbert's descriptions of people and events. Martina Häcker has shown that his representation of the few women who appear in the *De multro* has been heavily influenced by "mysogynous didactic litterature, to which in his time ecclesiastics especially were exposed

in the course of their education," above all in "his reports of events not witnessed by himself" ("Mothers, Wives, and Witches," 25–26).

In his paper on "The Divine and the Diabolic in Twelfth-Century Historiography: The Chronicle of Galbert of Bruges," Alan Murray concludes that "in the depiction of his antihero Bertulf [as "a kind of surrogate Satan"], [Galbert] weaves into the story a quite subtle narrative strand which, for those who had ears to hear, would give a clue to his contemporaries as to the interpretation of this figure." Galbert's implicit comparison of Bertulf and Jesus and the sympathy he evokes for the provost in this description of his death are thus even more shocking in light of this earlier diabolization. Galbert's portrait of Bertulf is reminiscent in many ways of Guibert of Nogent's earlier one of Bishop Gaudry of Laon (*Autobiographie* 3.1–10; ed., 268–360; trans., 145–84) and of the later one of Bishop Roger of Salisbury drawn by the author of the *Gesta Stephani* (34–36, pp. 73–81), suggesting that all three portraits were built up from a common model of a "proud and worldly prelate."

In an article they are preparing for publication and have tentatively entitled "Dead Dogs and Punished Provosts: History in the Fabliau 'Du Provost à l'Aumuche' and Fabliau History in 'The Murder of Charles the Good,'" Lisa H. Cooper and Mary Agnes Edsall will suggest that the *De multro* shows signs of having been influenced by popular narrative traditions like one finds embodied in the fabliaux, and that Galbert's work may in turn have influenced these traditions. Ms. Cooper and Professor Edsall will deliver a preliminary version of this article at the International Medieval Congress in Leeds this coming summer (2001). I want to thank them for discussing with me the ideas for their article in advance of its appearance.

Galbert was clearly not unique in his use of existing narrative paradigms to understand, imagine, and represent the events he relates. Gabrielle Spiegel's description of the structure of the chapters of Suger's *Life of Louis the Fat*—"each chapter contains the narration of a single 'event-unit.' . . . Study of these narrative units . . . discloses a virtually identical internal structure in which historical action is inaugurated by a disturbance to an existing situation, followed by the king's attempt to deal with the consequences of that disturbance, and concludes with the restoration of 'correct' order, viewed either as a return to the previously existing situation or as the institution of a new and ethically more just arrangement" ("History as Enlightenment," 166)—would apply equally well to the structure of almost any contemporary romance. For discussions of other examples, see Partner, *Serious Entertainments,* 195–96; R. H. C. Davis, "William of Poitiers and His History of William the Conqueror," in Davis and Wallace-Hadrill, eds., *The Writing of History in the Middle Ages,* 83–84; Chibnall, in Orderic Vitalis, *Ecclesiastical History,* 1:38, and in *The World of Orderic Vitalis,* 204–8; and Spiegel, "Genealogy," 103, and "Political Utility in Medieval Historiography: A Sketch," in *The Past as Text,* 89–90, 98.

NOTES TO CHAPTER 5

1. *De Doctrina Christiana* 2.28.44, ed. and trans. R. P. H. Green (Oxford, U.K., 1995), 106–7; trans. mod.

2. "Bij de latijnsche gedichten over den moord op den Glz. Karel den Goede Graaf van Vlaanderen," in *Miscellanea historica in honorem Alberti de Meyer,* Université de Louvain, Recueil de Travaux d'histoire et de philologie 3.22, 2 vols. (Leuven, 1946), 1:440.

3. On these prologic commonplaces and historiographical prologues in general, see Gransden, "Prologues"; Guenée, *Histoire et culture historique,* 18–19, 27–29, 215; Milada Buda, *Medieval History and Discourse: Toward a Topography of Textuality* (New York, 1990), 31–32; and Spiegel, "Political Utility," 87–89.

Galbert also uses the motif "and so closed that day" four times in the chapters corresponding to the primitive parchment record: "And so that day closed" *(et sic clausus est ille dies)* ([21], 20/23; trans., 135; trans. mod.); "that day, too, closed" *(clausus est quoque ille dies)* ([22], 71/72; trans., 140; trans. mod.); "And finally that day closed" *(et tandem clausus est ille dies)* ([45], 56/57; trans., 184; trans. mod.); "then God brought that day to its conclusion" *(conclusit ergo Deus diem illum)* ([64], 43; trans., 226). The primary function of this motif seems to be emotive, that is to say, rhetorical, but its repetition also emphasizes the temporal and narrative unity of a day (which has a beginning, a middle, and an end) and it seems to emanate from the same conception of time and history, discussed below, that led Galbert to give his chronicle a journalistic organization.

For other examples of rhetorical devices, see [6], 1/3 (trans., 93: Galbert declares that he is inadequate to the task); [7], 33/35 (trans., 100: repetition of "indoluit" [mourned]); [14], 16/17 (trans., 117: truth claim); [60], 19/20 (trans., 217: "inordinabiliter . . . ordinatis" [order . . . disorderly]); and [63], 52/70 (trans., 224: the length and structure of sentence; see above, Chapter 4, pp. 93–94). The examples could be multiplied ad infinitum et nauseam.

4. [57], 15; trans., 208; [58], 23/24; trans., 213; [63], 46; trans., 224; [63], 48/49; trans., 224; [81], 50; trans., 252; [83], 10/11; trans., 254.

5. [Prol.], 25; trans., 80; [Prol.], 41/43; trans., 80; [2], 16/17; trans., 85; [5], 2/3; trans., 92; [6], 10/11; trans., 94; [6], 11/13; trans., 94; [6], 36/38; trans., 96; [12], 41/42; trans., 113; [69], 82/83; trans., 237; and [71], 34/36; trans., 240.

6. "The use of imagined speeches" in medieval histories, Marjorie Chibnall writes, "was a popular device; in such speeches a historian was allowed to invent as an orator would invent, and his readers were assumed to be sufficiently sophisticated to know what he was doing" *(The World of Orderic Vitalis,* 197); see also Chibnall in Orderic Vitalis, *Ecclesiastical History,* 1:78–84; and Partner, *Serious Entertainments,* 207. According to Pizarro, the use of direct speech was characteristic of the new style of historical writing introduced in the early Middle Ages *(A Rhetoric of the Scene,* 55, 69–105).

7. Murray, "Voices of Flanders," 105; compare 114–17.

8. Murray, "Voices of Flanders," 105–6.

9. Murray, "Voices of Flanders," 106–7, 111–12.

10. Murray, "Voices of Flanders," 105.

11. Murray, "Voices of Flanders," 111.

12. Murray, "Voices of Flanders," 106.

13. Murray, "Voices of Flanders," 107; see *De multro,* [69], 1/24; trans., 233–34.

14. Murray, "Voices of Flanders," 107.

15. Murray, "Voices of Flanders," 109.

16. Such corporate discourses were, according to Pizarro, part and parcel of the "new," "scenic" style of historical writing elaborated in the sixth through the eighth centuries. "The dramatic illusionism that underlies the conception and design of many scenes in these historical narratives," he writes, "is supported by a number of practical conventions. Groups of people, sometimes large crowds, are made to speak with a single voice. . . . a mob [may act] . . . as one man" *(A Rhetoric of the Scene,* 92–93).

The *Annales* of the Saxon historian Lampert of Hersfeld (c. 1077–1079) offer a good example of the use of this device. Surrounded by disgruntled Saxons at Goslar in August 1073, Henry IV sent a messenger to them offering to meet with them and address their grievances at a later time if they would put down their arms and go peacefully away. Lampert relates the messenger's speech in indirect discourse, but gives the reply in a longish passage of corporate direct discourse ("To these propositions, they replied: 'The causes inciting us to rebellion,' they said, 'are not the same for us as they are for other princes of the realm. . . .'" [*Annales* 1073, 154–55]).

Another Saxon historian, Bruno of Magdeburg, relates a similar, perhaps the same, response to royal messengers in indirect discourse in his *Saxonicum bellum* (1081–1093), attributing it to the Saxon leader Otto of Nordheim ("Duke Otto responded to them on behalf of all the Saxons, saying that they had not come together there in a hostile spirit or because they wanted to start a civil war. . . ." [*Saxonicum Bellum* 27, 228]). The choice of direct or indirect discourse, of a single or a corporate speaker, was thus a matter of style, of the effect the author wished to produce at that point in his narrative.

On Galbert's corporate discourses, see Murray, "Voices of Flanders," 115–17, 119. Examples of these discourses are found in [11], 27/30 and 36/41; trans., 109, 110 (the conspirators); [17], 50/51; trans., 127 (the conspirators); [22], 15/21; trans., 138 (the paupers of Bruges); [43], 28/32; trans., 179 (the "sensible men" at the siege); [55], 53/78; trans., 204–6 (the citizens of Aardenburg); [66], 10/17; trans., 228 (the "boys" of Saint-Omer); [95], 69/77; trans., 270–71 (the citizens of Flanders); [101], 22/25; trans., 277 (the citizens of Bruges); [106], 15/53; trans., 284–85 (the citizens of Bruges).

17. Walter of Thérouanne attributes a similar corporate speech to "the clergy and lay people" of Bruges at a similar point in his *Vita Karoli:* "'If you took our lord away from us so that he would not live,' they said, 'why should you snatch him away now that he is dead? Since you made sure we would not have him alive, let us at least have him now that his life is over. Since he was our defender and protector while he was alive, we are certain that he will be a much more faithful intercessor for us with God now that he is dead and a martyr'" ([29], 551, 9/13).

18. Galbert's descriptions of the murders of Charles and Walter recall Guibert of Nogent's description of the murder of Gérard of Quierzy in the cathedral of Notre Dame in Laon in 1110 at several points (*Autobiographie* 3.5, ed., 296–304; trans., 157–60). Although Gérard, for example, initially resisted being cast in the role of victim, telling the first man to seize him to "'Get out of here you dirty lecher!'" (thereby confirming Guibert's observation that he had a "lively . . . mind and tongue" and was given to "biting jests in filthy language against those about him"), he finally accepted it once he knew "he was done for" and "in desperation he cried out with all his strength, 'Holy Mary, aid me!'"

These similarities can be found in accounts of other medieval assassinations (see, for example, Gregory of Tours's description of the murder of Bishop Praetextatus of Rouen at a morning mass [*Libri historiarum x,* 8.31, ed. alteram Bruno Krusch and Wilhelm Levison, *Monumenta Germaniae historica, Scriptores rerum Merovingicarum,* 1.1 (Hannover, 1951), 397–98; *The History of the Franks,* trans. Lewis Thorpe (Harmondsworth, U.K., 1974), 463]; and Jacob's "Le Meurtre du seigneur," which includes discussions of Galbert's account of Charles's assassination and Guibert's of the assassination of Gérard of Quierzy) and they undoubtedly owe something to the practical considerations of assassination at the time. They also suggest that a mental model of "an assassination in a church," based both on these practical considerations and other, propagandistic and symbolic, ones—and comparable to the modern mental model of "an assassination at a political rally"—may have been common throughout northwestern Europe during this period (compare Jacob, "Le Meurtre du seigneur," 253–58). Such a model—Jacob calls it a "liturgy"—would have been the common reference for the assassins (it gave them a model for carrying out an assassination), the victims (it taught them what victims should do), and the members of the murder's "audience." It thus also, as Jacob observes, "prepared [the deed] symbolically for entry into the [collective] memory, or, better, the two [collective] memories, the providential system of the clerks and the imagination of the people" ("Le Meurtre du seigneur," 253). Authors of accounts of murders thus made their descriptions more credible and moving to their audiences by leaving out elements of the deed that did not correspond to the model and adding to their descriptions elements of it that the actors, in the heat of improvisation, had omitted.

19. Isaac says: "'You are going to receive the mercy you have deserved [*promeruisti*] for slandering us to the count!'" ([18], 35/36; trans., 129; trans. mod.). For further discussion of these events, see Chapter 4, pp. 97–100.

20. These discourses are found in [22], 33/43; trans., 138–39 (a canon of Saint Donatian); [25], 3/5; trans., 143 (Godescalc Taihals); [38], 37/51; trans., 170–71 (a knight Walter); [57], 61/62; trans., 210 (a citizen of Ypres).

21. This speech also resembles the one in Walter's *Vita,* cited above in n. 17, and may likewise have been inspired by it. Galbert, that is, may have taken the speech by the "clergy and lay people" he found in the *Vita* and transformed it into two similar speeches in his own work, one by the paupers and the other by the senior canon. It is also possible that Walter, or his source, conflated the two speeches. In either case, the more concrete visualization and melodrama of Galbert's account demonstrate his theatrical bent.

22. Sproemberg suggests that *both* the castellan Haket's plea for mercy on behalf of the beseiged and the knight Walter's reply were drafted by Galbert: "given its legal elegance, the formulation of this answer [that is, Walter's answer], like that of the castellan's speech, should be attributed to Galbert. I have no doubt that Bertulf's brother asked pardon for him and his men and that the besiegers did not grant it. But I find it very hard to believe that either speech had such a polished legal form. One recognizes here the hand of a learned legal scholar—and this is important for the appreciation of other speeches found in Galbert's work" *(Mittelalter,* 345).

23. Aelred of Rievaulx distinguishes between the "inner" and "outer man" *(interiorem hominem, exteriorem hominem)* in his *Vie de recluse* (1 and 33; *La Vie de recluse. La Prière pastorale,* ed. and French trans. Charles Dumont, Sources chrétiennes 76 [Paris, 1961], 42, 168). Compare Romans 7.22 and Ephesians 3.16.

24. Galbert uses *animus* generally to refer to a person's mood or feelings about someone or something (when Thierry of Alsace first came to Bruges, it was to discover "in what mood [*quo animo*] the people of Bruges would receive him"; [101], 27; trans., 278), or to a disposition toward certain kinds of action (the traitor Isaac, trapped in a monastery and about to be captured, said to the abbot, "'My lord, if my mind were set on fighting [*si animus mihi esset pugnandi*], I would not allow myself to be taken without killing a lot of people'"; [84], 18/19; trans., 255). In a more restricted sense, it means courage or determination (describing the fighting that took place in the passageway between the count's house and the church of Saint Donatian, Galbert writes that both sides were "putting their strength and courage [*animos*] to the test"; [41], 51/52; trans., 175–76).

25. This intellect also has moods—Galbert refers to a "state of mind" *(statum mentis)* ([26], 41; my translation, compare trans., 149) that may "*mutare*" (change), to a "sadness of mind" *(tristitia mentis)* ([19], 36; my translation, compare trans., 131), to a "languor of mind" *(mentis languore)* ([19], 42; my translation, compare trans., 131), and to a "great anguish and confusion of spirit" *(acriori mentis angustiati confusione)* ([119], 13/14; trans., 307)—and may be "unquiet" *(fluctuantem)* ([Prol.], 24; trans., 80), "perplexed and disturbed" *(confusa et turbata)* ([12], 9; trans., 111), or "attentive" *(intenta)* ([35], 43; my translation, compare trans., 164). The *mens* also has a spiritual side open to divine manipulation: Galbert mentions the "penitence of a pious mind" *(piae mentis sacrificio)* ([121], 33/34; my

translation, compare trans., 312) and writes that "God smites the minds [*mentes*] of the evil" ([79], 19; trans., 249).

Galbert refers to the *Passio* itself, interestingly, as a *mentis studio* (study, discipline, or application of the mind; [Prol.], 30; my translation, compare trans., 80). According to Ward, John of Salisbury refers similarly to "the activity of being a historian . . . simply as 'studium'" in his *Historia pontificalis* (John O. Ward, "Some Principles of Rhetorical Historiography in the Twelfth Century," in Breisach, ed., *Classical Rhetoric,* 107).

26. *Cor* likewise refers to the seat of the emotions and will (before they killed him, Charles's assassins were "already murderers at heart" *(in corde)*; [15], 16/17; trans., 119), although it also has more specific associations. It is the site of what one might term spiritual virtues—Galbert refers to the "spiritual strength of the heart" *(virtutes spirituales cordis)* ([Prol.], 27; trans., 80; trans. mod.), to a "holy devoutness of [the] heart" *(sacra cordis devotione)* ([6], 14; trans., 94), to a "contrition of [the] heart" *(cordis contritione)* ([64], 3; trans., 225), to a "contrite heart" *(contrito corde)* ([121], 33; my translation, compare trans., 312), to a "penitence of [the] heart" *(cordis sacrificio)* ([120], 17; trans., 308), and to a "prayer of . . . [the] heart" *(cordis oratione)* ([64], 9; trans., 225)—and is an organ through which God manipulates human behavior (God, for example, "moved the heart [*commovit cor*] of a certain knight Gervaise to undertake vengeance"; [26], 2/3; trans., 147).

27. Galbert conceived of the psychological world as a sort of inner person, complete with voice, face, and eyes, in an enclosed space in which representation takes place: almost like a spectator in a theater. He writes that the besiegers held an image "before the eyes of the heart" *(prae oculis cordis)* ([63], 45; my translation, compare trans., 224), and that as Bertulf was being dragged to the gallows, he "could with justice have called up before his mind's face [*mentis faciem*] everything he had done" ([57], 29/30; trans., 209; trans. mod.), "could indeed have pictured with his mind's eye [*mentis . . . oculus*]" all the favors God had bestowed upon him ([57], 41; trans., 210; trans. mod.), and "called upon [God] in the secret place of his mind [*in secreto mentis . . . invocaverat*]" ([57], 59; trans., 210; trans. mod.).

28. "Now when they were held in captivity, shut up and locked in, at any rate they had time and place to mourn the pious count, who in his intimacy with them had been like an equal, a father rather than a lord, and toward the rich and poor of the realm had been merciful, humble, gentle, and benevolent. In their sorrow the captives could not speak to each other except with sighs and sobs, which came from the profound sadness of their hearts. What a deplorable crime, when servants cannot die with their lord and father, but must live on in greater misery after him! They might have done better to pass from the world with him in a death which was noble and honorable toward God and men rather than live on with the sorrow of their lord's death and, God forbid!, to see the traitors flourish under the rule of another count" ([19], 30/41; trans., 131).

29. "Now at last Fromold Junior was able to do what had not been possible before and what he had long and ardently desired, to offer prayers to God for the salvation of his lord, the count, to make a sacrifice in tears and contrition of heart, and to rejoice greatly in the sight of the place where his lord, buried, was resting in peace; and so for the first time he was preparing funeral rites for his lord whom he had not been able to see since he was buried, that is for forty-four days. Since he could not see his body but only the outside of the tomb, he wished and implored with the prayer of both lips and heart that God on the day of common resurrection would permit him finally to see his lord and prince, Charles, raised to double glory among the faithful rulers and highest princes of his present Church, and to stay with him and be blessed with him eternally in the glory of the contemplation of the Holy Trinity. Therefore he considered it a great boon to be able to mourn the death of his

lord at his tomb, to lament the ruin of the fatherland, and to perform with the greatest love the last rites for one whom he had cherished in life, now betrayed by his serfs. He did so, indeed, not without tears" ([64], 1/18; trans., 224–25).

30. Charles was killed on March 2, 1127; Easter fell on April 3; and Fromold Junior was finally able to view the tomb on April 14.

31. "Bij de latijnsche gedichten," 1:440–43.

32. Compare this insight into the range of human motives with Galbert's reference to the gawkers who came to watch the assault on the castle ([40], 4/5; trans., 173).

33. Compare this passage to Galbert's analysis of the motives of the besiegers who rushed through the breached wall of the church ([63], 45/52; trans., 224; see below, pp. 126–27) where he likewise sees the self-interest hidden behind seemingly nobler sentiments.

34. Nancy Partner oberves that Richard of Devizes (1189–92) likewise "shifts, chameleon-like, from one persona to the next" in his chronicle ("The New Cornificius," 47).

35. See Dhondt, "Une Mentalité," 101–9; Van Caenegem in Galbert, *Le Meurtre,* 59–67, and *Galbert van Brugge,* 3–9; Huyghebaert, "Galbert de Bruges," 737–39; and Murray, "Voices of Flanders," 117–18.

36. [12], 15; [17], 41, 42; [41], 55; trans., 112, 126, 176; trans. mod. On Borsiard, see also Ross, "Rise and Fall," 373–74.

37. See [11], 13/42; [41] 57/64; [60], 28/40; [82], 1/11; [84], 58/61; trans., 109–10, 176, 218, 253, 256. On Robert the Young, see also Ross, "Rise and Fall," 376–77.

38. The citizens of Bruges here echo the Norman peasants who rose up against their lords during the reign of Richard II, c. 1000, swearing "that they did not ever intend to have a lord or advocate" *(que ja mais par lur volunté / n'avrunt seinur ne avoé).* Richard, less politically sensitive or gifted than Gervaise, solved the problem by capturing the leaders, pulling the teeth of some, gouging out the eyes of others, cutting off the hands of yet others, roasting some alive, and boiling others in lead (Wace, *Le Roman de Rou* 815–958, 3 vols., ed. A. J. Holden [Paris, 1970], 1.191–96).

39. See also his speech to the citizens of Bruges when he leaves them to join William Clito ([100], 1/18; trans., 275–76), and his speech when he returns and switches to Thierry's side ([104], 1/22; trans., 281–82). Gervaise seems to have been less effective when it came to his own family: on his daughter's vagaries, see Huyghebaert, "Les Femmes laïques," 370–71.

40. Note the expression "*my* provostship" (praepositurum *meam*): Bertulf had probably been provost of Saint Donation for about thirty-six years at that point and the provostship must indeed have seemed like *his* to him.

41. Galbert portrays Bertulf as a rather solitary figure, who is nonetheless deeply committed to the interests of his extended family. Yet Bertulf seems to have had a wife who was still alive and residing in Veurne in 1127 (see [46], 5/6; trans., 185) and the Gummar who first appears in 1093 as a canon of Saint Donatian and a comital chapelain, and went on to become provost of Our Lady of Bruges c. 1105 and archdeacon of the see of Tournai in 1114 can perhaps be identified with the Gummar who is referred to in a charter of 1122 as a former clericus of Bruges and "Bertulf's son" (see Appendix I, *s.v.* Gummar).

42. "Sallust," 172.

43. *Serious Entertainments,* 191–92.

44. Galbert's irony and humor have been noted by other scholars. Dhondt attributes to him "an almost Voltairian way of looking at things" ("Une Mentalité," 105), while Van Caenegem observes that "Galbert's tone is sometimes mischievous and sarcastic" (in Galbert, *Le Meurtre,* 65) and points out several examples of his irony and raillery.

45. They must promise "to respect as inviolate the area and property of the town" and to carry on the siege "without violating the property of the citizens" ([31], 10/11, 17; trans., 158, 159).

46. See [41], 64/83; trans., 176–77; [43], 1/7; trans., 178; [45], 7/16; trans., 182–83; [75], 31/47; trans., 244–45.

47. See also his account of the king's and new count's efforts to secure as much of Charles's treasure as possible ([61], 15/45; trans., 219–20; [83], 1/7; trans., 253; [85], 1/30; trans., 256–57) and of the knights' reaction to the report that the assassin Isaac had buried "money in a deep hole at the roots of an oak tree in the orchard adjoining his house" ([39], 19/23; trans., 172; trans. mod.).

48. Galbert uses this same sort of ironic manoeuvre in [113], 33/44; trans., 295–96, written in spring 1128.

49. The theatricality of the *De multro* has been detailed and discussed in Cooper's forthcoming article, "Making Space for History."

50. "When he [Charles] had set out on his way toward the church of Saint Donatian, the serfs who had been watching for his exit ran back and told the traitors that the count had gone up into the gallery of the church with a few companions. Then that raging Borsiard and his knights and servants, all with drawn swords beneath their cloaks, followed the count into the same gallery, dividing into two groups so that not one of those whom they wished to kill could escape from the gallery by either way, and behold [*et ecce*]! they saw the count prostrate before the altar, on a low stool, where he was chanting psalms to God and at the same time devoutly offering prayers and giving out pennies to the poor" ([12], 11/21; trans., 112). The *et ecce!* in particular encourages readers to visualize themselves as present in the chapel, thus decreasing their objectivity and distance from the scene.

51. There is, writes Augustine, an "order of events in history, . . . completely hidden from us, but perfectly known to God himself. Yet God is not bound in subjection to this order of events; he is himself in control, as the master of events, and arranges the order of things as a governor" *(De civitate Dei* 4.33, ed., 1:126; trans., 176). "In the Middle Ages," Bernard Guenée observes, "everyone knew that what came to pass came to pass through the will of God" *(Histoire et culture historique,* 29).

52. See, for example, [Prol.], 40/41; "earthly rulers . . . ordinance of God," trans., 80; [13], 1/5; "it was ordained by God . . . and of great wealth," trans., 114–15; [22], 36–39; "'whom divine mercy . . . in the cause of justice,'" trans., 138–39; [24], 19/24; "and so when he had eaten . . . the most pious count," trans., 143; [25], 23/26; "but because it was not so disposed by God . . . the most pious count," trans., 144; [57], 41/45; "he could indeed have pictured . . . his by right," trans., 210; [63], 56/59; "for they did not cease . . . to their lives," trans., 224; [73], 13/17; "by the marvelous dispensation of God . . . and foul odor," trans., 241; [80], 8/11; "and it was a happy dispensation . . . taken captive," trans., 250.

53. Elias ("Augustinian Elements," 36) points out that Galbert's concept of the coexistence of the "necessity of divine ordination" and "free will" is influenced, although perhaps only indirectly, by *De civitate Dei* 5.9–10 (ed., 1:136–41; trans., 190–95).

54. "In his [God's] will rests the supreme power," wrote Augustine, "which assists the good wills of created spirits, sits in judgement on the evil wills, orders all wills, granting the power of achievement to some and denying it to others. Just as he is the creator of all natures, so he is the giver of all power of achievement, but not of all acts of will. Evil wills do not proceed from him because they are contrary to the nature which proceeds from him. . . . all bodies are subject above all to the will of God, and to him all wills are also subject, be-

cause the only power they have is the power that God allows them" *(De civitate Dei* 5.9, ed., 1:139; trans., 193; compare 5.10, ed., 1:141; trans., 195). "Using men's spirits [*animis*] according to their intentions [*voluntatibus*] and merits," explained Sigebert of Gembloux, "God assigns appropriate tasks to the appropriate men so that the appropriate men may reap the appropriate awards: good men receive good ones for good works, evil men evil ones for evil works" *(Leodicensium epistola adversus Paschalem papam* 3, ed. E. Sackur, in *Monumenta Germaniae Historica, Libelli de lite,* 2:453). According to Hugh of Fleury, "The omnipotent God and Lord of all creation so ordered his creation that he uses both good and evil creatures well. God, I say, who does and disposes all things justly, uses good and evil creatures well. And he arranges things in such a way that even the evil angel and the evil man fight in the service of divine providence even though they may not know what good the divine providence or will achieves through them" *(Tractatus de regia potestate et sacerdotali dignitate* 1.4, 2:469). Abelard likewise distinguished between what could be and was done by evil men and their intentions: "'There is no authority [*potestas*],' whether it seem good or evil, 'except from God,' that is, established by his dispensation. . . . Whence even the power [*potestas*] of the devil or of any impious man may be said to be good, however evil their intention or perverse their deed. For their power comes from God, their evil intention from themselves" *(Commentaria* 4 [XIII, u. 1], 1:285–86). Aelred of Rievaulx, finally, writes that "God is not the creator or instigator of evil, but He is its most prudent governor. Why should my most gentle and most omnipotent God not allow evil to exist, since it cannot in any way infirm His eternal design? Indeed, His omnipotence appears all the more manifest, his wisdom more marvelous, his mercy more sweet when He omnipotently turns evil things to good ends, wisely governing the ungoverned, mercifully granting happiness to the wretched" *(Speculum charitatis* 1.2, 507; compare abridged trans., 4).

55. Compare [16], 47/48; trans., 122–23, "Gervaise . . . the death of his lord"; [26], 46/50; trans., 149, "it would take too long . . . vengeance impartially"; [54], 19/21; trans., 200, "and in that place Gervaise . . . to a happy conclusion."

56. "Men are often misled and mislead others," Orderic Vitalis writes, "when the Lord of Hosts disposes otherwise, for the thoughts of men, clouded with the darkness of ignorance, are without effect"; and elsewhere "but indeed sinners in their guilty blindness cannot see or understand the things which the heavenly king rightly ordains for his creation, until sinful man is captured like a fish on a hook or a bird in a net and entangled in sufferings beyond hope of escape. Indeed when he hopes for long life, happiness, and honour, he suddenly experiences death, wretchedness, and ruin. . . ." *(Ecclesiastical History* 10.14, 5:283; 12.26, 6:303). The author of the *Gesta Stephani* likewise observes that "every man is blind and altogether ignorant with regard to God's providence and his judgements" *(Gesta Stephani* 72, 142; compare 56, 114). On the metaphorical nature of human actions within this theology of history and its potential for comic and ironic effects, see also M. D. Chenu, "Theology and the New Awareness of History," in *Nature, Man, and Society in the Twelfth Century: Essays on New Theological Perspectives in the Latin West,* ed. and trans. Jerome Taylor and Lester K. Little (Chicago, 1968), 171; Partner, *Serious Entertainments,* 188; Stein, "Signs and Things," 105–7; and Buda, *Medieval History and Discourse,* 6.

57. For other examples, from the end of the eleventh and end of the twelfth centuries, of the purchase (or rental) of an infant to replace a dead one for reasons of inheritance, see P. Le Cacheux, "Une Charte de Jumièges concernant l'épreuve par le fer chaud (fin du XIe siècle)," *Mélanges (Société de l'Histoire de Normandie)* (1927): 206, 213; and Adam of Eynsham, *The Life of St Hugh of Lincoln / Magna Vita Sancti Hugonis* 4.5, 2 vols., ed. Decima L. Douie and Hugh Farmer (London, 1961–1962), 2:20–27.

58. The deaths of the knight Gilbert, the traitors who were thrown from the count's house, and Walter of Vladslo, discussed in the preceding chapter, are other instances of this kind of tragic irony.

59. "Les 'Solidarités,'" 534; trans., 272. Galbert compares God more or less explicitly to the Fates when he writes that some of the men who were executed were not guilty of the count's murder (although they were guilty of helping the murderers after the deed): "but because fate had caught them [*fata eos trahebant*], or rather because Divine vengeance coerced them [*divina ultio coegit*], they were cast down along with those who were guilty of the treachery" ([80], 50/52; trans., 252). The notion that "fate" is another name for God's will may owe something to Augustine's discussion of the two in *De civitate Dei* 5.8: "What they mean by 'destiny' [*fatum*] is principally the will of the supreme God" (ed., 1.135–36; trans., 188–89).

60. As does Walter of Thérouanne. "The broader theme of [the second half of the *Vita Karoli*]," writes Van Meter, ". . . is the loosing of God's swift and terrible justice upon the generation that had threatened the peace of Flanders and the safety of the Church. . . . [B]y focusing on the attempts of three leading conspirators to flee, and on their subsequent apprehension and execution, he emotively illustrates the puny nature of even great and powerful men when they futilely try to squirm away from the intent of divine will. The effect of these three vignettes is to create a dramatic tension: despite the incontrovertible guilt of the fugitives, Walter skillfully—and with remarkable sensitivity and pathos—relates their plight and ineluctable deaths in such a manner as to elicit a profound feeling of pity" ("Eschatology," 129).

61. Murray, "Voices of Flanders," 111.

62. Pizarro, *A Rhetoric of the Scene,* 92, 14, 34, 213, 13.

63. Pizarro, *A Rhetoric of the Scene,* 14.

64. "Genealogy," 101.

65. "The New Cornificius," 47.

66. Pizarro, *A Rhetoric of the Scene,* 61, 57.

67. Van Meter, "Eschatology," 131. "Royal history as written at Saint-Denis," had a similar ideological function according to Spiegel: it "furnished an interpretive strategy for understanding the basic character and dynamic of French kingship, and it treated royal action as part of an eternal pattern of behavior which was rooted in the spiritual nature of political society as established by God. The chronicler's task was to delineate that pattern in such a way that made its underlying character apparent and thereby bespoke its inherent legitimacy" *(The Chronicle Tradition,* 45; compare "History as Enlightenment," 174–75).

68. I have indicated the manuscript divisions, as well as the chapter breaks, introduced by Köpke and reproduced by Pirenne, in my edition of the *De multro.*

69. The exceptions fall into three categories.

First, there are six manuscript divisions that do not correspond to new days ([35], 45; [84], 1; [108], 28; [116], 43; [120], 15; [122], 1). These are probably due to later additions to the first version of the text, or to the insertion of marginal entries when the text was recopied.

Second, when there is a short entry for one or two days, it may be combined in a single manuscript chapter with information about a preceding day or a following day ([47], 49/52; [50], 1/2; [110], 1/44; [114], 1/15). Never are more than three days grouped together, and they are kept in chronological order. Since Galbert does respect the daily divisions at a number of other points even when it leads to very short manuscript chapters ([33], 1/2; [56], 20/21; [56], 30/33; [76], 12/14; [78], 1/3; [78], 4/6; [81], 1/2; [85], 31/34; [105], 1/4;

[111], 1/4; [112], 1/5; [112], 11/13; [113], 1/4; [118], 48/51), some of these multiple-day manuscript chapters may have been created through the omission of the original divisions when the text was recopied.

Third, some manuscript chapters contain information pertaining to a later date ([21], 30/48; [42], 7/14; [53], 10/20; [61], 41/45; [93], 1/11). These passages provide complementary information concerning events mentioned in the chapter and appear to be due to a second organizational principle, that of narrative completeness, overriding the chronological one. These all are, necessarily, later interpolations.

Three chapters ([95], 43/79, [113], 17/18; [114], 62/95) fall into both categories two and three insofar as they include information pertaining to more than one day, but the days are kept in order and the information concerning the later day completes information given concerning the earlier day.

There nonetheless remain two violations of the principle of chronological order ([46], 1/17; [48], 3/24) that have no obvious explanation.

70. *Etymologiarum sive originum libri xx,* 2 vols., ed. W. M. Lindsay (Oxford, U.K., 1911), 1.44.1.

71. *The Life of Beatrice of Nazareth, 1200–1268,* ed. Leonce Reypens, trans. Roger De Ganck (Kalamazoo, Mich., 1991), xxiv, xxvi, xxxi, 4.34, 274.19, 276.39.

72. See Van Caenegem, *Galbert van Brugge,* 3–5, and in Galbert, *Le Meurtre,* 59, 62; and Gransden, "Prologues," 146. For surveys of the Flemish historical writing of the time, see L. Genicot and P. Tombeur, gen. eds., *Index Scriptorum Operumque Latino-Belgicorum Medii Aevi: Nouveau répertoire des oeuvres médiolatines belges,* 4 vols. (Brussels, 1973–1979), and the on-line bibliography of *The Narrative Sources from the Southern Low Countries, 600–1500* at the University of Ghent <http://www.lib.rug.ac.be/n-exec.html>; click first on "Secundaire Bronnen / Secondary Sources" and then on "Narrative Sources").

73. *De Doctrina Christiana* 2.28.44, 2.32.50, ed. and trans., 106–7, 112–13; trans. mod.

74. "For Augustine," writes Jan Davidse, "everything is focused on the order of time, and this is what prevents events from dropping out of sight and becoming incomprehensible to us. The order of time is God's work, and that is why *historia* is not a human institution, even though it concerns matters human. Because history as such *(historia ipsa)* transcends man's domain, it is more than a narrative formulation of the past, and more than a subjective idea which consciousness imposes upon meaningless events; on the contrary, history precedes all human interpretation. For Augustine, interpretation can be nothing other than the indication of the relation of the *facta* to the order of time, created and controlled by God, and which contains their 'meaning.' . . . For Augustine it is not a question of whether events have meaning, but rather to what extent they illustrate the dynamics of the *historia ipsa.* . . . That a *historia* is in process is evident from the fact that the course of time . . . is bound to an order. . . . Events are related to this order through their temporality" ("On Bede as Christian Historian," in Houwen and MacDonald, eds., *Beda Venerabilis,* 9–11). Compare Theodor E. Mommsen: "From Augustine's conception of the course of history it follows that every particular event that takes place in time, every human life and human action, is a unique phenomenon which happens under the auspices of Divine Providence and must therefore have a definite meaning. . . . To [Augustine] . . . history was the *operatio Dei* in time" ("Saint Augustine," 276).

75. M. D. Chenu finds evidence of this belief in the work of Hugh of Saint Victor as well, for whom history "was a *series,* a sequence, and an organized sequence, an articulated continuity, whose themes made sense, which was exactly the object of the intelligibleness of

history—not Platonic ideas, but the initiatives of God within the time of mankind, the events of salvation. Henceforth, time and place became part of history, in events and in the understanding of their significance. . . . In its profound—and put simply, mysterious—reality, this *series* resulted from a whole plan, a conscious disposition with a preconceived goal to be realized in the course of time, a plan for which time, as opposed to eternal ideas, was an essential condition" ("Theology," 168–69).

Galbert's chronologically sensitivity is all the more remarkable because "a dearth of dates is typical of Latin rhetorical historiography from antiquity onward" (Roger Ray, "Rhetorical Scepticism and Verisimilar Narrative in John of Salisbury's *Historia Pontificalis,*" in Breisach, ed., *Classical Rhetoric,* 91): as Spiegel observes, for example, Suger eschews dates altogether in his *Life of Louis the Fat* ("History as Enlightenment," 170). Ross, too, notes that Galbert's "chronological precision is unusual for the age, even in documents, and displays an almost unparalleled 'taste for exactitude.'" "He is," she writes, "highly conscious of 'the revolution of the year,' the anomalies of Leap Year, and the occurrence of anniversaries" (trans., 67–68). On March 23, for example, he notes that Issac was captured and hung "three weeks after the slaying of the count" ([48], 2/3; trans., 189). On April 14, he observes that the count had been entombed for forty-four days ([64], 7; trans., 225). When the count's body is exhumed on April 22, he writes that "seven weeks since his first burial had passed," and that the body "had been committed to the tomb for seven weeks, from the first Friday, the day of its burial in the gallery, up to the Friday which came afterwards on April 22" ([77], 1/2, 6/9; trans., 245, 246). On Friday, March 30, 1128, he remarks that, because 1128 was a leap year, March 30 had fallen on a Wednesday in the preceding year ([102], 6/7; trans., 278) and that exactly one year before this day, on which the people of Bruges elected Thierry as count, the Flemish barons had returned from Arras to announce the election of William Clito ([102], 23/28; trans., 279). On April 2, 1128, he again remarks on the difference in the calendar between 1127 and 1128 ([104], 1/2; trans., 281), and on May 5, 1128, he notes the anniversary of the precipitation of the traitors ([110], 1/3; trans., 290).

76. John of Salisbury, *Historia Pontificalis* Prologue, 3. Compare Gransden, "Prologues," 134–35; and Partner, *Serious Entertainments,* 188. "For the medieval chronicler," writes Spiegel, "the events he recorded were also the structure of his history, determining a priori the shape of his narrative. . . . The medieval chronicler thus began with a belief in the mimetic identity of his narrative to the events it recounted, with a belief, in other words, in the metaphoric validity of his text. From this flowed a concern with establishing correct order, not conjecture about causes or conceptual interpretation, as the chief task of the historian, and he was construed to be most faithful to that task when displaying, in their proper places, the plethoric variety and variability of human occurrences. That such a view of the historian's task tended to result in what appears, at least to us, to be an unfortunate narrative clutter was an unavoidable concomitant of an ethical commitment to mimetic accuracy" ("Genealogy," 100–101).

77. *De Doctrina Christiana* 2.28.44, ed. and trans., 106–7; trans. mod.; *Didascalicon* 6.6, ed., 123; trans., 145.

78. Chibnall in Orderic Vitalis, *Ecclesiastical History,* 1:52.

79. Spiegel, "History as Enlightenment," 165–66. She later adds that, to sustain his theme of the royal restoration of order, Suger "willfully violates chronological order, conflating events or deferring the conclusion of a chapter until he can properly narrate the resolution of the disturbance and the restoration of order, always carefully marked by the repetition of lexical formulae of 'recovery,' 'return,' 'restoration,' and the like. The chronological looseness of the *Vita Ludovici,* therefore, is the result not of confusion but of narrative inten-

tion—for the sake of which, it might be added, Suger avoids mentioning any dates at all" ("History as Enlightenment," 169–70). See also Cusimano and Moorhead in Suger, *The Deeds of Louis the Fat,* 7–8.

80. On the *ordo artificialis* and the *ordo naturalis,* see Tony Hunt, "Tradition and Originality in the Prologues of Chrestien de Troyes," *Forum for Modern Language Studies* 8 (1972): 332–34; and James A. Schultz, "Classical Rhetoric, Medieval Poetics, and the Medieval Vernacular Prologue," *Speculum* 59 (1984): 8. When Galbert and Walter wrote, according to Hunt, the *ordo artificialis* "was regarded as superior to the *ordo naturalis* and less common" (334): the Latinate rhetorical models of the day were not especially friendly to historiography.

81. History is in this way like Scripture, another of God's "books." To the student tempted to object: "'I find many things in the histories [principally the historical books of the Bible] which seem to be of no utility: why should I be kept busy with this sort of thing?'" Hugh of Saint Victor responded: "Well said. There are indeed many things in the Scriptures which, considered in themselves, seem to have nothing worth looking for, but if you look at them in the light of the other things to which they are joined, and if you begin to weigh them in their whole context, you will see that they are as necessary as they are fitting. Some things are to be known for their own sakes, but others, although for their own sakes do not seem to be worthy of our labor, nevertheless, because without them the former class of things cannot be known with complete clarity, must by no means be carelessly skipped. Learn everything; you will see afterwards that nothing is superfluous" *(Didascalicon* 6.3, ed., 115; trans., 137).

82. Elias observes astutely that the *De multro* can be divided into, on the one hand, what she terms "secular sections" where Galbert "chronicles and analyzes events . . . from a purely secular perspective . . . [and, on the other hand,] passages where Galbert presents facts under the aegis of God's ordination," and she associates these two different historical paradigms with, respectively, "the new secularism [of, for example, Berengar of Tours and Peter Abelard]" and "the older Augustinianism . . . the two movements operating in Galbert's own world." Although "the overall mode and controlling motive of his text still remains more Augustinian than secular," she suggests that the new paradigm influenced his thinking and the organization of his chronicle just as it had influenced social and historical thought generally ("Augustinian Elements," 38, 41). Galbert clearly thought he had discovered the overriding providential structure that explained the principle events of 1127, but it is likewise true that he records many events that he is unable to situate within that structure. A great Order thus shines through some passages while it is, in others, still wrapped in the veil of random event. I do not think, however, that Galbert believed that any event was "secular" and lay outside the providential structure of time. He demonstrated as much of that structure as he could discover, but he recorded everything because he believed that everything had its place in that structure, even those events whose place was not yet apparent.

Even Augustine remarked, with respect to the "historical" events of the Old Testament, "these hidden meanings of inspired Scripture we track down as best we can, with varying degrees of success; and yet we all hold confidently to the firm belief that these historical events and the narrative of them have always some foreshadowing of things to come, and are always to be interpreted with reference to Christ and his Church, which is the City of God. . . . To be sure, we must not suppose that all the events in the narrative are symbolical; but those which have no symbolism are interwoven in the story for the sake of those which have this further significance. For it is only the share of the plough that cuts through the earth; but the other parts of the plough are essential to make this operation possible. . . . Similarly, in the prophetic history some things are recorded which have no prophetic significance in themselves; but they are there for the significant events to be attached to them, moored to them, as we might say" *(De civitate Dei* 16.2, ed. 2:500–1; trans., 652–53).

83. Galbert's inclusion of everything he had noted down also contributes to the reader's impression of the opacity and objectivity of his chronicle since the inclusion of seemingly unnecessary or insignificant events and details makes "us feel that we are witnessing an unedited slice of life . . . introduce[s] a fake imbalance in the composition of the scene. The narrator uses this apparent lack of critical control to efface the traces of his own activity: the facts are speaking to us 'by themselves'" (Pizarro, *A Rhetoric of the Scene,* 63).

84. Morrison notes that "over and over, [twelfth-century historiographers] . . . drew analogies between history and theater" *(History as a Visual Art,* xv). The third book of Guibert of Nogent's autobiography begins, for example, with a reference to his earlier promise "to tell the story of the people of Laon, or rather to present their tragedy on the stage [*tragoedias acturi*]" *(Autobiographie* 3.1, ed., 268; trans., 145), while Orderic distinguishes his work from both tragedy and comedy, writing: "I neither compose a fictitious tragedy [*fictilem tragediam*] for the sake of gain, nor entertain cackling parasites with a wordy comedy [*loquaci comedia*], but truly record events of different kinds for studious readers" *(Ecclesiastical History* 7.16, 4:106). The dramatic propensities of medieval histories have also been noted by Partner, who characterizes Richard of Devizes as a "promptor, actor, and director of a theatrical world of gesture" ("The New Cornificius," 47); by Spiegel, who writes that the medieval historian viewed "his text as a transparency through which he sought to convey to his prospective audience of readers or auditors as direct and vivid as impression of the past and present reality as possible" ("Genealogy," 101); and by Pizarro, whose whole book is an investigation of these propensities in early medieval historical writing.

85. Morrison, *History as a Visual Art,* 25, 103–4, 246, 249. Partner writes similarly that "*parataxis*[,] . . . the juxtaposition of essentially equal elements without causal or temporal connectives and without the subordination of one element or another[,] . . . is the single characteristic that most strikingly distinguishes medieval from classical or modern narrative; encountered in historical narrative, it is profoundly disturbing, both aesthetically and intellectually. . . . It was clearly the preferred form for narrative of all kinds, the form readers and auditors expected and enjoyed" *(Serious Entertainments,* 197, 202; see also "The New Cornificius," 15–21). She also suggests that one of the "web of factors" that combined to encourage this style of composition was "the tendency to search for meaning above or after, rather than in, events," a tendency that Galbert carried to an extreme ("The New Cornificius," 42).

Spiegel notes that "the mimetic goals of the medieval chronicler," goals that, again, Galbert carried to an extreme, "affected the nature of his method as well as the style of his narration. I would like to suggest that the historian in the Middle Ages viewed his text as a transparency through which he sought to convey to his prospective audience of readers or auditors as direct and vivid as impression of the past and present reality as possible. In considering his text as transparent, a lucid medium of transmission, the chronicler apprehended history itself as a perceptual field, to be seen and represented instead of constructed and analyzed, an object more of perception than of cognition. . . . considering medieval historiography in this way . . . helps to explain, for example, the privileged status of eyewitness testimony as evidence; the virtual absence of epistemological concerns (*what* is seen and known being more important than *how*); the seemingly dispersed, paratactic construction of the narrative, as the chronicler shifts his gaze over the historical landscape; and the lack of explicit causal analysis, as modes of representation take precedence over modes of explanation" ("Genealogy," 101).

Pizarro identifies this fascicular, cluster, or paratactic style of composition—which he terms "scenic" composition—as one of the elements of the new style of historical writing developed in the sixth to eighth centuries. He defines "a scene in narrative" as "the representation of a transaction between particular characters in their own words and actions, without the mediation of authorial commentary," and observes that "the far greater frequency of scenes in early medieval narrative . . . eliminates the sense of a continuous chronological sequence created by the classical narrator's summaries." It creates instead a sense of narrative "homogeneity" and allows the author "to display little control of the form of the story, [and] contributes to the self-effacing quality of the narrator's voice in the new style: the sense of choice, of strategy . . . is absent here. . . . The lack of any indication of what the narrator considers the central moment (since every moment is a scene here) makes for an opacity of representation that . . . is kept up in the detail of the story" *(A Rhetoric of the Scene,* 19, 63, 32–33).

86. The text of the résumé is printed in my edition of the *De multro,* 173–75. See also Rider, "Galbert of Bruges' 'Journal,'" 79–81.

87. Saint Donatian's story begins with its desecration by the murder (chapters 15 and 21), continues with its occupation by the murderers (chapters 35, 37, 43, 64), and ends with its cleansing and reconciliation (chapters 76 and 78).

88. As was just mentioned, the tragedy of the Erembalds was perceived as a separate story by a member of the De Baenst family at the end of the fifteenth century. Ross likewise felt that this tragedy formed the core of the *Passio:* "Galbert's intense concern with the history and fate of the Erembalds, especially his master, Bertulf, gives his record a unifying theme, not lacking in epic character, which serves to bind together the daily jottings of his journal" ("Rise and Fall," 371).

These three tales are essentially the same ones Walter of Thérouanne tells in his *Vita Karoli.* Relating that Charles could not be persuaded that his life was in danger and thus took no special precautions on the morning of the attack, Walter adds: "I easily and truly believe that he was prevented from taking these rumors seriously by the just and hidden judgement of God insofar as, in keeping with his merits, our sins, and their abominable crimes, to him the palm of martyrdom, to us sadness, and to those traitors just vengeance was quickly granted. It was right, and ought to be piously believed, that he was thus given the longed-for rest, and we, who were unworthy of him, were deprived of a defender and protector, and those scoundrels were punished with fitting hardships. O how wonderful is the dispensation of omnipotent God in all things!" ([24], 548, 35/40). These three tales, that is, are that of the good prince, the bereft nation, and the wicked servi. These stories are also set forth, in a less succinct form than in the *Vita,* in a passage from the end of the introduction to the *De multro,* most of which I cited at the begining of chapter 3 ([14], 11/19; trans., 117, "Not even yet . . . with the saints" [see above, p. 51]). Here we find, first, an allusion to the punishment of the murderers ([14], 11/14; "Not even yet . . . and gone into exile"), then an allusion to the loss of the nation of Flanders ([14], 14/15; "and so we, the inhabitants of the land of Flanders, who mourn the death of such a great count and prince"), and finally an allusion to the count's martyrdom and sanctity ([14], 18/19; "pray earnestly for the eternal glory of the life of his soul and his everlasting blessedness with the saints"). The tripartite structure of this fable recalls that of a theatrical performance (the protagonistic Charles, the antagonistic Erembalds, and the chorus formed by the citizens of Bruges or Flanders) and suggests again that Galbert's historical vision had a fundamentally theatrical bias.

89. Jan Dhondt provided a remarkable résumé of many of the stories told by the *De multro:* "Galbert's narrative is not the mere tale of a murder, a siege, the punishment of the murderers, and, in the end, a war between pretenders to the throne. Nor is it simply the story of the attempt by the King of France to extend his power over this great fief, or the illumination of one episode among many in the fight between France and England (for the King of England continuously intervened to oppose the aims of Louis VI). Nor is it primarily the story of the different neighboring princes who, of course, rushed in for the spoils. It is the story of a race for a throne (not limited to the two pretenders already named), a headlong race for treasure (the enormous treasury of the Flemish counts); for relics (the body of the assassinated Count, who is considered a martyr); and for the murderers' vast wealth, coveted by the barons of the kingdom. On a different level it is, in addition, the story of a private war (between the assassins, the Erembalds, and their neighbors, the lords of Straten), of a fight between clans at the count's court—the Erembalds on one side and various newcomers on the other—for the count's favor and high offices. It is also a full-fledged tragedy, the story of a family of servile origin (the Erembalds) who have found their way to the top ranks of the county and are threatened with being plunged back into servitude. To all this Galbert's psychology adds yet more: the working out of a plan of divine vengeance against a dynasty that won the Flemish throne by perjury and treason (the accession of Robert the Frisian) and against a family (again the Erembalds) who won their way by adultery and murder and were likewise soaked in the 'treason' of Robert the Frisian. There is a final aspect of capital importance: it is the first time the cities claim to play a predominant role in the conduct of the county" ("Les 'Solidarités,'" 533–35; trans. 271–72; trans. mod.).

Ross likewise observes that Galbert traces "day by day the many intertwining threads of this tightly woven story: the narrowing stages of the siege, culminating in the precipitation from a tall tower of the surviving traitors, about thirty in number; the frenzied but futile hunt for the count's vast treasure of gold and silver; the progressive self-assertion of barons and burghers; the confused struggle for the countship; the waxing and waning of the king's influence in Flemish affairs; the civil war and social demoralization" ("Rise and Fall," 369).

90. What the Carlyles said about Cicero—that he "is a political writer of great interest, not because he possesses any great originality of mind, or any great power of political analysis, but rather because, in the eclectic fashion of an amateur philosopher, he sums up the commonplaces of the political theory of his time. . . . [W]hen we read him . . . we learn how the honourable and right-minded and reasonably intelligent politician of his time tended to think, what were the conceptions which the public of that time would have applauded as being just and edifying with regard to the nature of society and the principles underlying social relations" *(History,* 1:3–4)—could also be said, mutatis mutandis, about Galbert. The principle difference is that the *De multro* is not a theoretical treatise but a description of a social and political crisis, and Galbert is not, in Demyttenaere's words, "a thinker who set forth a grand speculative system, but a man who stubbornly held fast to a series of postulates and tried with their help to discover a meaningful and coherent pattern in concrete historical events" ("Mentaliteit in de twaalfde eeuw," 129). This means, on the one hand, that the political ideas upon which his analysis of the crisis is founded are not presented in a systematic way, and, on the other, that these descriptions necessarily combine the political ideas that motivated the actors of the events they describe with Galbert's own ideas: what we have, in sum, is his interpretation of their ideas—many of which, presumably, he shared, although he perhaps articulated them differently.

NOTES TO CHAPTER 6

1. *De civitate Dei* 4.33, ed., 1:126; trans., 176; trans. mod.

2. *Sententiarum libri tres* 3.48.11, *Patrologia latina* 83, 720.

3. All the early versions of the text read "idus Augusti" (the ides of August, or August 13) here, which Köpke, followed by Pirenne, corrected to "kal. Augusti" (the kalends of August, or August 1) because the text continues "and so on the feast of Saint Peter in August, at the time of the fair in Lille" ([93], 1/2; trans., 265), and the feast of Saint Peter's Chains falls on August 1. A cycle of five major fairs—at Ypres, Bruges, Thourout, Lille, and Messines—was established in Flanders by 1200 and, at that time at least, the fair at Lille ran from August 15 to September 14 (see Simone Poignant, *La Foire de Lille,* Bibliothèque de la Société d'Histoire du droit des pays flamands, picards et wallons 6 [Lille, 1932], 35–36, 53, 87, 101, 106; Jan A. Van Houtte, "Les Foires dans la Belgique ancienne," *Essays on Medieval and Early Modern Economy and Society* [Leuven, 1977], 88; and Masahiko Yamada, "Le Mouvement des foires en Flandre avant 1200," in Jean-Marie Duvosquel and Alain Dierkens, eds., *Villes et campagnes au Moyen Age: Mélanges Georges Despy* [Liège, 1991], 773–89). The text is, therefore, contradictory, but two of the three indications of the date (the ides of August, at the time of the faire in Lille) suggest that the confrontation took place around August 13–15.

4. This attempt to capture a serf perhaps also violated a typical communal principle that no one except the town authorities could seize someone within the town (see Albert Vermeesch, *Essai sur les origines et la signification de la commune dans le nord de la France (XIe et XIIe siècles),* Etudes présentées à la Commission Internationale pour l'Histoire des Assemblées d'Etats 30 [Heule, 1966], 142–45; and the reaction of the citizens of Bruges when one of their number is arrested by one of the castellan's knights, [59], 14/53; trans., 214–16), or the rule that "town air makes a man free," that is, that a serf became a freeman if he lived in a town for a year and a day—if this rule was known in Lille at this time, and if this serf had lived in the town for more than a year (see Van Caenegem, "Galbert of Bruges," 96).

5. Ross, trans., 265, n. 1.

6. Coué, "Der Mord," 115–16. Chapters 93 and 94 end with similar sentences—"This was the source of great ill will between those citizens and the count so that henceforth both sides regarded each other with suspicion" *(unde concitata est maxima invidia inter cives illos et comitem ita ut deinceps sibi suspecti utrimque starent)* ([93], 9/11; trans., 266; trans. mod.); "this was the source of great ill will between those citizens and the count, and henceforth they regarded each other with suspicion" *(unde maxima invidia excitata est inter civos illos et comitem et deinceps facti sunt sibi suspecti)* ([94], 13/14; trans., 267; trans. mod.)—while chapters 94 and 95 begin similarly—"The burghers of Saint Omer rose in rebellion against the count because the count unjustly wished to set over them as castellan of that place one who had seized the goods and substance of those citizens by force and was still trying to despoil them" *(insurrexerunt burgenses in Sancto Audomaro contra comitem eo quod injuste volebat comes praeferre illis castellanum loci illius qui violenter res et substantiam civium illorum dirripuerat et adhuc rapere satagebat)* ([94], 2/5; trans., 266; trans. mod.); "the men of Ghent rose in rebellion against their castellan because he continued to deal with them wrongly and perversely" *(insurrexerunt Gendenses contra castellanum suum eo quod injuriose et perverse semper egisset contra ipsos)* ([95], 2/3; trans., 267; trans. mod.).

7. "Der Mord," 115–17.

8. [95], 10/39; trans. 267–69, "'Lord count . . . the barons of the land." The speech is discussed below.

9. "Der Mord," 115.

10. "This was the source of ill will between the citizens [and the count] and between the count and his knights" *(unde invidia concitata est inter cives {et comitem} et inter comitem militesque suos)* ([88], 9/11; trans., 260; trans. mod.; the text probably needs the emendation Ross introduced into her translation here).

11. "But now you have acted contrary to law and in your own person you have broken the oaths that we swore in your name concerning the remission of the toll, the maintenance of peace and the other rights which the men of this land obtained from the counts of the land, your good predecessors—especially in the time of Lord Charles—and from yourself; you have violated your faith and done injury to ours since we took the oath to this effect together with you. Everyone knows how many acts of violence and how much pillage you have been responsible for in Lille, and how unjustly and wrongfully you have persecuted the citizens of Saint Omer. Now, if you can, you are going to maltreat the citizens of Ghent" ([95], 14/23; trans., 268). The reference to the remission of tolls seems intended to evoke the incident in Bruges on September 17, since tolls are not mentioned in the other incidents.

12. "Der Mord," 116.

13. That is, in Saint Donatian. See [69], 6/24; trans., 233–34; [70], 9/10; trans., 237.

14. See above, Chapter 5, n. 75.

15. "It was there, in the midst of many calamaties and the most constrained circumstances" *(ibi inter tot adversa et angustissimos locorum fines)* ([Prol.], 23/24; trans., 80; trans. mod.); "in the midst of such a great tumult and the burning of so many houses . . . and in the midst of so much danger by night and conflict by day" *(in tanto tumultu rerum et tot domorum incendiis . . . et inter tot noctium pericula et tot dierum certamina)* ([35], 34/37; trans., 164).

16. Mentioned in [6], 21; trans., 95; [37], 47/49; trans., 169; [52], 15; trans., 195; and [52], 38/39; trans., 197. See Chapter 4, pp. 83–84.

17. At the end of chapter 14, he refers to the "the vengeance, related at the end of this little work, which God alone wrought against those barons of the land whom He has exterminated from this world by the punishment of death [*quam solus Deus exercuit in principes terrae quos ab hoc seculo mortis districtione exterminavit*], those by whose aid and counsel the treachery was begun and carried through to the end" ([14], 21/25; trans., 117–18). In chapter 89, he records that "it came about by the severe and horrible judgement of God that Walter of Vladslo . . . hurled from his horse by its motion . . . died after a few days. . . . It was true that no one dared to raise a hand against Walter although he was accessory to the treachery. . . . But God, to whom his punishment was left, removed him by a lingering death from the sight of the faithful [*factum est igitur Dei districto et horribili examine quod Walterus ex Florerdeslo . . . ex proprio cursu suo ab equo praecipitatus . . . in paucis diem obierit. . . . Nemo vero ausus fuit manum mittere contra Walterum quamvis traditionis conscius fuisse. . . . At Deus, cui vindicta relinquebatur, morte languida a fidelium aspectu exterminavit illum*]" ([89], 1/4, 27/31; trans., 262, 263).

18. "On June 24, Sunday, on the feast of Saint John the Baptist, in the church of the Holy Virgin, a crucifix which was standing on the floor to be adored by the faithful rose from the place where it had been firmly fixed, by itself and through the power of God; and it would have fallen [*decidisset*] to the pavement if one of the sacristans of the church had not caught it in his hands as it fell. This sacristan placed the crucifix again in its usual place, but when he had left, again, just as before, it rose up from its stand and began to fall [*ruere ceperat*]. Then all who were standing around in worship ran up and set it in its place again, thinking that the fall [*casum*] had come about from the carelessness of the one who had placed it. But on looking around they were satisfied that no lack of care could account for this" ([115], 1/11; trans., 301). Guibert of Nogent likewise relates the inexplicable fall of a gilded eagle "standing above the chest which contains the reliquaries of the saints" in the

cathedral of Laon, which he interprets (retrospectively) as a sign that the bishop would soon die and that Laon would "fall" *(ruisse) (Autobiographie* 3.13, ed., 392–94; trans., 197).

19. I am speaking here of manuscript entries or chapters. Most of the modern editorial chapters 93–122 are made up of more than one manuscript entry or chapter.

20. See Chapter 2, pp. 43–48.

21. "Viewed as a whole," he writes, "the second part of Galbert's work [chapters 93–121] is full of conflicting opinions, sometimes set in direct juxtaposition. Immediate impressions are here mixed with later reflections. It is thus extremely difficult for us to establish the chronological development of Galbert's narrative. Clues to a solution are provided by the fact that some chapters contain particular additions that begin with '*Et notandum*' ['and it should be noted'], '*Hic notandum*' ['here it should be noted'] and the like. Such additions sometimes contradict what has come just before, and one may suppose that Galbert intended to revise these chapters in order to bring what is reported there into conformity with his view of God's plan, as it appeared to him once it had been fully accomplished, and as he understood it to give meaning to what had happened when he looked back over events in the next to the last chapter [chapter 121]" ("Geschichtstheologische Aspekte," 252). The passages beginning with *et notandum* and the like are to be found in chapters [102], 23; trans., 279; [102], 31; trans., 279; [108], 28; trans., 288; [108], 48; trans., 289; [110], 3; trans., 290; [110], 20; trans., 291; [114], 84; trans., 300; [116], 43; trans., 303; [120], 15; trans., 308.

22. Galbert's description of this battle served as the basis for an article on medieval warfare by J. F. Verbruggen, "La Tactique militaire des armées de chevaliers," *Revue du Nord* 29 (1947): 161–80.

23. [95], 10/39; trans., 267–69. I have modified the translation at several points in the following citations. On this speech, see Sproemberg, "Erwachen des Staatsgefühls," 62–70, and *Mittelalter,* 232–33, 262; Ganshof, "Les Origines du concept," 144–49; Kern, *Gottesgnadentum,* 364–66; Van Caenegem, "Galbert of Bruges," 104–7, "The Ghent Revolt," 107–12, and "Law and Power," 155–56; and Murray, "Voices of Flanders," 103–19. Bert Demyttenaere has discussed this speech most interestingly in the more general context of Galbert's ideas about "meeting culture" in a paper entitled "Meeting Culture and Some Aborted Assemblies in Twelth-Century Flanders," which he delivered at last year's (2000) International Medieval Congress at Leeds. I would like to thank Professor Demyttenaere for sending me a copy of his paper.

24. The charter William granted to the citizens of Saint-Omer in 1127 begins with the declaration: "I, William, by the grace of God count of the Flemish . . . grant them [the burghers of Saint-Omer] the following laws or customs [*lagas seu consuetudines*] by perpetual right, and order that they remain in force." There then follows a list of twenty-one articles, and the charter concludes: "[the following] promised faithfully and confirmed by oath" *(fide promiserunt et sacramento confirmaverunt)* that they would enforce the charter's articles. This is followed by a list of co-swearers that includes King Louis VI of France, William, and a series of Flemish barons, among them Daniel of Dendermonde and Baldwin of Aalst, the brother of Ivan (Espinas, "Le Privilège de Saint-Omer," 45, 48). These are the faith and oath, pledged and sworn in connection with this and similar charters, and binding William to respect a set of written laws, that Ivan accused William of violating.

25. The translation of this passage is taken in part from Van Caenegem, "Law and Power," 163. Ivan's speech, writes Van Caenegem, presents "in a nutshell, the twelfth-century formula of the *Rechtsstaat:* all classes under the law, as enforced by the prince, and the prince himself bound by the law, as enforced by a supreme court" ("Law and Power," 163).

26. "Galbert of Bruges," 105.

27. *Commentaria in regulam Sancti Benedicti* 27, *Patrologia latina* 102, 853. In the elaborate, albeit inchoate, tyrannology of John of Salisbury, writes Cary Nederman, "tyranny is the peculiar vice of those who use to excess any power with which they are endowed, and who thus further their own interests at the expense of the liberty of others . . . tyrants exist in all facets of human life, since tyranny is simply the conjunction of license and power" ("The Changing Face," 9, 15). On the medieval theory of the tyrant, see Carlyle and Carlyle, *History,* 1:172–73, 221–22, 229–34, 250–52, 3:38, 52–73, 112–46, 166; Parsons, "The Medieval Theory," 129–43; Kern, *Gottesgnadentum,* 334–38, 356–57; Richard H. Rouse and Mary A. Rouse, "John of Salisbury and the Doctrine of Tyrannicide," *Speculum* 42 (1967): 693–709; Jan Van Laarhoven, "Thou Shalt *Not* Slay a Tyrant! The So-Called Theory of John of Salisbury," in Michael Wilks, ed., *The World of John of Salisbury* (Oxford, 1984), 319–41; Cary Nederman, "A Duty to Kill: John of Salisbury's Theory of Tyrannicide," *Review of Politics* 50 (1988): 365–89, and "The Changing Face"; Cary Nederman and Catherine Campbell, "Priests, Kings, and Tyrants: Spiritual and Temporal Power in John of Salisbury's *Policraticus,*" *Speculum* 66 (1991): 572–90; and Kate Langdon Forhan, "Salisburian Stakes: The Uses of 'Tyranny' in John of Salisbury's *Policraticus,*" *History of Political Thought* 11 (1990): 397–407.

28. *De civitate Dei* 4.33, ed., 126; trans., 176; trans. mod. See Arquillière, *L'Augustinisme politique,* 69, 121–41.

29. *Sententiae* 3.48.11, *Patrologia latina* 83, 720. Commenting on Rom. 13.1, Abelard elaborated: "'There is no authority [*potestas*],' whether it seem good or evil, 'except from God,' that is, established by His dispensation. When princes are good, it is a divine gift. When, however, they are evil, they are instituted by God—who makes good use of even the greatest impiety [Isidore of Seville refers to tyrants as "impious" *(Etymologiae* 2.29.7)]—either for the punishment of perverse men or for the purification or testing of good ones. Whence even the power [*potestas*] of the devil or of any impious man may be said to be good, however evil his intention or perverse his deed. For his power comes from God, his evil intention from himself" *(Commentaria* 4 [XIII, u. 1], 1:285–86). Compare John of Salisbury, *Policraticus* 8.20 (ed. Webb, 2:374; trans. Nederman, 207; trans. Dickinson, 368); Kern, *Gottesgnadentum,* 186–88; Arquillière, *L'Augustinisme politique,* 123–24; Rouse and Rouse, "John of Salisbury," 698; Horst Fuhrmann, "'Volkssouveränität' und 'Herrschaftsvertrag' bei Manegold von Lautenbach," in Sten Gagnér, Hans Schlosser, and Wolfgang Wiegand, eds., *Festschrift für Hermann Krause* (Cologne, 1975), 38; Robinson, *Authority and Resistance,* 121–22, 135–39; and Nederman, "A Duty to Kill," 377–78.

Augustine answered the question of why God set up tyrannical rulers in a different fashion—"The Reason why God gives worldly dominions both to the good and the evil is this: to prevent any of his worshippers who are still infants in respect of moral progress from yearning for such gifts from him as if they were of any importance" *(De civitate Dei* 4.33, ed., 1:126; trans., 177)—but this answer seems to have fallen on ears deafened by the well-established concept of "a commutative contract between God and man" (Mommsen, "Saint Augustine," 280) vehiculated, notably, by Orosius (see Chapter 1, p. 23, n. 60).

30. *Policraticus* 4.1, ed. Keats-Rohan, 232–33; trans. Nederman, 28–29; trans. mod.; compare ed. Webb, 1:236; trans. Dickinson, 4.

31. See Karl Leyser, "The Crisis of Medieval Germany," *Proceedings of the British Academy* 69 (1983): 409–43.

32. I. S. Robinson, "Pope Gregory VII, the Princes and the *Pactum,* 1088–80," *English Historical Review* 94 (1979): 756. His suggestion of a three-cornered, as opposed to two-sided, conflict was taken up by Leyser, who writes that while "the Ottonian ideas of king-

ship were negated by the Reformed Papacy, its practice was destroyed by the East Saxon nobles' rebellion" ("The Crisis," 442–43). It would perhaps be even better to think of this crisis as a four-cornered struggle between the king, the pope, the Saxon nobles, and the imperial bishops, who had their own interests and sought to maintain their independence from Rome by playing the king off against the pope (see Walter Ullmann, *The Growth of Papal Government,* 349–52; Robinson, "'Periculosus homo': Pope Gregory VII and Episcopal Authority," *Viator* 9 [1978]: 103–31; and Uta-Renate Blumenthal, *The Investiture Controversy: Church and Monarchy from the Ninth to the Twelfth Century* [Philadelphia, 1988], 118–19).

33. "The crux of the debate about the *regnum* in the polemic literature of the Investiture Contest . . . ," writes Robinson, was "whether rebellion against the *regnum* was ever justified" (Robinson, *Authority and Resistance,* 121). The Saxon complaint, that Henry was infringing on their traditional liberties, was in fact akin to the German bishops' complaint that Gregory was infringing on theirs: the core of the conflict in both instances was represented as a contest between traditional, local authority and new, centralizing authority. Ideologically, Henry and Gregory had much in common and were divided principally by their differing views as to who occupied the pinnacle of power, while the Saxons and the German bishops were likewise united in their opposition to what they perceived as a central authority's unprecedented effort to micromanage their affairs. The Saxons, however, viewed Henry as the authoritarian innovator, and thus saw in Gregory an ally whose power they could use to weaken Henry's, while the German clergy who were in favor of the traditional Catholic hierarchy saw Henry as a "local" ally in their struggle against a centralizing papacy (see Robinson, "'Periculosus homo,'" 131). For a summary of the struggle in Germany 1077–1122, see Ian Stuart Robinson, *The Papacy 1073–1198. Continuity and Innovation* (Cambridge, U.K., 1990), 398–441.

34. Hugh of Fleury wrote similarly that "evil kings are rather to be resisted with spiritual prayers than with carnal weapons" *(Tractatus de regia potestate* 1.4, 2:471), as did John of Salisbury: "tyrants are ministers of God . . . even the tyrants of the gentiles" and "the most useful and the safest" way of removing them is to "humbly resort to the protection of God's clemency and . . . [raise] up pure hands to the Lord in devoted prayer" *(Policraticus* 8.20, ed. Webb, 2:378; trans. Nederman, 209; compare trans. Dickinson, 373). See Rouse and Rouse, "John of Salisbury," 699; and Van Laarhoven, "Thou Shalt *Not,*" 326.

35. *Leodicensium epistola* 9–10, 2:461–62. About sixty years later, John of Salisbury observed that "tyrants are demanded, introduced, and raised to power by sin, and are excluded, blotted out, and destroyed by repentance" *(Policraticus* 8.20; ed. Webb, 2:374; trans. Dickinson, 368; compare trans. Nederman, 207). See Kern, *Gottesgnadentum,* 186–88; Arquillière, *L'Augustinisme politique,* 123–24; Rouse and Rouse, "John of Salisbury," 698; Fuhrmann, "'Volkssouveränität,'" 38; Robinson, *Authority and Resistance,* 121–22, 135–39; and Nederman, "A Duty to Kill," 377–78.

36. Bruno of Magdeburg, *Saxonicum bellum* 86, 324–26.

37. *Law and Society,* 50–51. On the Merovingian and Carolingian nobility's ability to resist the king, see Hannig, *Consensus fidelium.* Karl Morrison contrasts "the theoretical king" of the polemical literature surrounding the Investiture Contest with the real king "who found it necessary to bow to the commands of the princes, the king who begged and bribed to gain support, the king who was more subject to his subjects than they to him" (Morrison, in Mommsen and Morrison, trans., *Imperial Lives,* 5–6). The real position of Henry IV comes to the fore, for example, in a letter of 1076 pleading for the support of the German bishops *(Epistolae* 13, 68; trans. Mommsen and Morrison, *Imperial Lives,* 151–52). For examples of clerical resistance to ecclesiastical superiors, see Alfred Cauchie, *La Querelle des Investitures*

dans les diocèses de Liège et de Cambrai, 2 vols. (Leuven, 1890–1891), 1:9–12; Otto Gerhard Oexle, "Conjuratio und Gilde im frühen Mittelalter. Ein Beitrag zum Problem der sozial geschichtlichen Kontinuität zwischen Antike und Mittelalter," in Berent Schwineköper, ed., *Gilden und Zünfte. Kaufmännische und gewerbliche Genossenschaften im frühen und hohen Mittelalter* (Sigmaringen, 1985), 165–88; and Jaeger, *The Envy of Angels,* 202–10.

38. Even in the "mid-ninth century," writes Janet Nelson, "literate men . . . striving to articulate the relationship between the king and his constituency . . . [came] close to contract theory and a right of resistance" ("Kingship and Empire," 229). "Of kings, Pope Nicholas I [858–867] wrote to Aventius, bishop of Metz, 'See whether they govern according to right; if they do otherwise, they are to be considered tyrants, rather than to be regarded as kings. We are bound to resist these men, and to rise up against them, rather than to be subject to them'" (MGH Epp. Kar. Aev., IV, 299, no. 31, cited by Morrison in Mommsen and Morrison, trans., *Imperial Lives,* 35).

39. Sproemberg, *Mittelalter,* 233–38, 367–68; "Erwachen des Staatsgefühls," 77–83; "Eine rheinische Königskandidatur," 64–66. See also Van Caenegem, "Galbert of Bruges," 105.

40. See Robinson, *Authority and Resistance,* 128–35.

41. See Peters, *The Shadow King,* 30–80; and Robinson, *Authority and Resistance,* 131–35, and *Papacy,* 312–17. According to Gregory VII, "a Christian kingdom must be ruled by 'a suitable king for the honour of holy Church . . . [one, that is, who] is obedient, humbly devoted and useful to holy Church.' . . . the first duty of a king, as of a bishop, was *oboedientia.* . . . A king must be 'useful' *(utilis)* as well as obedient, the pope being the judge of his usefulness. . . . [In] the final version of Gregory's political thought . . . [t]he king must be 'suitable' *(idoneus)* for the duties prescribed by the church; he must be 'obedient, humbly devoted and useful to holy Church'; he must serve the pope as his feudal lord" (Robinson, *Papacy,* 312, 410, 411).

42. See Isidore, *Etymologiae* 9.3.4; see also 1.29.3; 7.12.17; 9.3.1, 6; Anton, *Fürstenspiegel,* 384–404.

43. Bruno of Magdeburg, *Saxonicum bellum* 25, 224.

44. Bruno of Magdeburg, *Saxonicum bellum* 27, 228. Robinson *(Authority and Resistance,* 132) seems to suggest that this articulation of the Saxon justification of their rebellion on the basis of the Isidorean etymology was perhaps due, in the first instance, to Archbishop Werner of Magdeburg, who sent a letter to various pro-Henry clergy in the wake of the Saxon defeat in June 1075 and asked them to "discuss these matters [the burning of churches and other depredations practiced by Henry's forces during their subsequent invasion of Saxony] calmly with our lord, and persuade him to think of himself as a king, and teach him why he is called a king *(ut se regem esse cogitet, suadete et, unde rex sit appellatus, edocete)*" (Bruno, *Saxonicum bellum* 49, 260). It is true that this letter, although it was written two years after Otto's speeches, antedates Bruno's *account* of those speeches by at least six years, and it is also true that Otto's speeches, only the first of which is given in direct discourse, are perhaps due more to Bruno than to Otto since his account of them was written at least eight years after they were made and the first one, in direct discourse, contains citations from Sallust. It is plausible, that is, to think that the "Isidorean" justification of the rebellion was first articulated in the archbishop's letter and that Bruno, a member of the archbishop's inner circle, was influenced by the letter (and by discussions in the archbishop's entourage) and added the allusions to the etymology to his account of Otto's speech when he wrote it up a number of years later (although, as we will see below, Lampert, writing 1077–1079, attributes a similar notion to a Saxon embassy of July/August 1073). Bruno may himself have played a

role in drafting the letters of the archbishop (or rewritten them somewhat when he inserted them there: see Schmale, ed., *Quellen,* 30–31, and Leyser, "The Crisis," 425). Bruno, that is, may well have participated in the collective elaboration of the "Isidorean" justification of the rebellion in the *familia* of Archbishop Werner.

Devoted to contemporary events, many of which its author had himself witnessed, punctuated by speeches in direct discourse and the texts of various letters, Bruno's chronicle resembles the *De multro* in a number of ways. There does not seem to be any possibility of direct influence since the *Saxonicum bellum* seems to have circulated only slightly more than the *De multro,* but Bruno's chronicle offers an interesting point of contrast for Galbert's: it is the kind of chronicle Galbert might have written had he decided to abandon a journalistic format.

45. This phrase, *si . . . rex esse vellet,* is perhaps yet another allusion to the above-mentioned Isidorean etymology of the word *rex.* If so, it suggests that the "Isidorean" justification of the rebellion was known to Lampert when he composed his annals in 1077–1079, and was thus perhaps a common doctrine among at least the learned supporters of the Saxon party. There is another Isidorean allusion (to the difference between a king and a tyrant; see *Etymologiae* 1.31; 2.29.7), and language that echoes that of this passage, in the content of another, later embassy to the king which Lampert attributes to Otto *(Annales* 1076, 270, lines 20–23).

46. Lampert, *Annales* 1073, 152.

47. *Ad Gebehardum Liber,* 30, 43, 47, 48, ed. Kuno Francke, in *Monumenta Germaniae Historica, Libelli de lite,* 1:365, 385, 391–92; trans. Lewis, *Medieval Political Ideas,* 1:165, and Parsons, "The Medieval Theory," 136; trans. mod. "Manegold's '*pactum* theory,'" writes Robinson, "cannot be traced in earlier reforming literature"; its "inspiration . . . is rather to be sought in the anti-Henrician propaganda justifying the conduct of the Saxon nobility who rebelled against their king in 1073. . . . Manegold's 'contractual argument' was, therefore, not an original idea but rather the clearest extant expression of the solution which had been canvassed among the aristocracy for at least a decade to the problem of a king who did not respect the rights of the *populus:* that is, of his most powerful subjects" *(Authority and Resistance,* 128–31). See also Fuhrmann, "'Volkssouveränität,'" 40, 42.

Echoing both Manegold and Isidore, Paul of Bernried offers a capsule version of this Saxon justification in his *Vita Gregorii VII* of c. 1130: "Free men [*liberi homines*], moreover, made Henry their king with the understanding [*pacto*] that he would try to judge his electors justly and be governed by royal providence. But afterwards, he consistently disregarded this understanding [*pacto*] and violated its spirit, oppressing all sorts of innocent people with tyrannical cruelty [*tyrannica crudelitate*]. . . . The princes, therefore, might have reasonably deposed him, even without the judgement of the Holy See, since he failed to fulfill the pact to which he had agreed in exchange for their electing him: since he had not fulfilled it, he could not be king [*nec rex esse poterat*]. For he can in no way be king, who does not rule his subjects but seeks to lead them into error [*rex nullatenus esse poterit, qui subditos suos non regere, sed in errorem mittere studuerit*]" ("Gregorii P. P. VII vita" 97, ed. Johann Matthias Watterich, *Pontificum Romanorum qui fuerunt inde abe exeunte saeculo IX usque ad finem saeculi XII vitae,* 2 vols. [Leipzig, 1862], 1:531–32).

It is striking that the same ideas were preached in almost the same terms in another revolutionary setting almost seven hundred years later. Speaking from his Boston pulpit on January 30, 1750, Dr. Jonathan Mayhew, taking Rom. 13 as his text, told his congregation: "if we attend to the nature of the argument with which the apostle here inforces the duty of submission to *the higher powers,* we shall find it to be such an one as concludes not in favor of submission to all who bear the *title* of rulers, in common; but only, to those who *actually* perform the duty of rulers, by exercising a reasonable and just authority, for the good of human society. . . . If those who bear the title of civil rulers, do not perform the duty of civil rulers, but act directly counter to the sole end and design of their office; if they injure and oppress their subjects, instead of defending their rights and doing them good; they have not the least pretence to be honored, obeyed and rewarded. . . . If it be our duty, for example, to obey our king, merely for this reason, that he rules for the public welfare, . . . it follows, by a parity of reason, that when he turns tyrant, and makes his subjects his prey to devour and to destroy, instead of his charge to defend and cherish, we are bound to throw off our allegiance to him, and to resist. . . . as soon as the prince sets himself up above the law, he loses the king in the tyrant: he does to all intents and purposes, unking himself, by acting out of, and beyond, that sphere which the constitution allows him to move in. And in such cases, he has no more right to be obeyed, than any inferior officer who acts beyond his commission. The subjects' obligation to allegiance then ceases of course: and to resist him is no more *rebellion,* than to resist any foreign invader" *(A Discourse Concerning Unlimited Submission and Non-Resistance to the Higher Powers* [Boston, 1750], 20, 22–23, 29–30, 45–46; *Early American Imprints,* 1st ser. [New York, 1985], Evans n° 6549).

48. Initially, according to Robinson, the "polemics were addressed to a very small audience within the ruling caste: to bishops and princes whose obedience was considered vital to the survival of either the papal or the imperial party. . . . The survival of certain *Libelli de lite* in more than one manuscript can usually be attributed not to wide circulation during the Investiture Contest, but rather to incorporation in a twelfth-century schoolbook; for the *Libelli* were used in the teaching of grammar and rhetoric in twelfth-century German cathedral schools" *(Authority and Resistance,* 8–9; see also Robinson, "The 'Colores Rhetorici' in the Investiture Contest," *Traditio* 32 [1976]: 209–38, and "The Dissemination of the Letters of Pope Gregory VII during the Investiture Contest," *Journal of Ecclesiastical History* 34 [1983]: 175–93). For the opposite point of view, that is, that the *libelli* were widely known, see Fuhrmann, "'Volkssouveränität,'" 27. In a first article originally published in 1965, Karl Leyser suggested that the *libelli* were widely circulated ("The Polemics of the Papal Revolution," in Leyser, *Medieval Germany and Its Neighbors, 900–1250* [London, 1982], 138–41), but he seems to have revised his views and wrote in a subsequent one that "most of the tracts in the *Reich* were written by bishops, well-schooled clerks, regular canons, or monks and addressed to their like" ("The Crisis," 418). This polemical literature, writes Canning, was "the first such publicistic exchange in the Middle Ages, with protracted discussion leading to a sharpening of political and ecclesiological ideas. The impact of individual tracts varied widely and their oral audience is unknowable; but the overall effect was that the issues involved in the dispute were exhaustively dissected in political and ecclesiastical circles for half a century" *(History,* 97). See also Luscombe, "Introduction," 171; and Pacaut, *La Théocracie,* 82–90.

49. Robert I, for example, was instrumental in the division of the see of Cambrai and Arras into two separate sees in 1092–1094, while his son, Robert II, invaded the region of Cambrai in 1102 at the request of Archbishop Manasses II and Paschal II—who in 1103 urged him to attack Liège as well, provoking Sigebert of Gembloux's *Leodicensium epistola adversus Paschalem papam* (see A. Giry, "Grégoire VII et les évêques de Térouane," *Revue Historique* 1 [1876]: 387–409; Cauchie, *La Querelle des Investitures,* 2:156–63, 178–80; P. Allossery, "Intervention flamande, à Cambrai, dans la querelle des investitures," *Annales de de la Fédération Archéologique et Historique de Belgique* 16 [1903]: 380–94; Verlinden, *Robert Ier le Frison,* 113–29; Nicolas Huyghebaert, "Un Légat de Grégoire VII en France: Warmond de

Vienne," *Revue d'Histoire Ecclésiastique* 40 [1944–1945]: 187–200; and Irven M. Resnick, "Odo of Cambrai and the Investiture Crisis in the Early Twelfth Century," *Viator* 28 [1997]: 83–98).

50. See I. S. Robinson, "The Friendship Network of Gregory VII," *History* 63 (1978): 18–19, and "Dissemination," 192–93; and Giry, "Grégoire VII," 392–99.

51. See Allossery, "Intervention flamande, à Cambrai"; Henri Pirenne, *Histoire de Belgique,* vol. 1: *Des origines au commencement du XIVe siècle,* 5th ed. (Brussels, 1929), 85, 103–18; Verlinden, *Robert Ier le Frison;* François-Louis Ganshof, "Les Origines de la Flandre Impériale. Contribution à l'histoire de l'ancien Brabant," *Annales de la Société Royale d'Archéologie de Bruxelles* 46 (1942–1943): 99–137, *La Flandre sous les premiers comtes,* 3rd ed. (Brussels, 1949), 33–52, and "La Flandre," 349–52; Jan Dhondt, "Vlaanderen," 79–80, 85–86; Marinette Bruwier, "Le Hainaut, le Cambrésis et l'Empire au XIIe siècle," *Annales de la Fédération Archéologique et Historique de Belgique* 36 (1955–1956): 207–26; Thérèse de Hemptinne, "Vlaanderen en Henegouwen onder de erfgenamen van de Boudewijns 1070–1244," *Algemene Geschiedenis der Nederlanden* 2 (Haarlem, 1982), 372–98; and Nicholas, *Medieval Flanders,* 45–61.

52. Nicholas, *Medieval Flanders,* 49–50.

53. See Nicholas Huyghebaert, "Gertrude de Saxe, comtesse de Flandre (ca. 1033–1113)," *Biographie nationale de Belgique* (Brussels, 1976), 39:429–32.

54. See *De multro,* [4], 1/36; trans., 90–91; and Sproemberg, "Eine rheinische Königskandidatur."

55. See Pirenne, *Histoire de Belgique,* 1:182, 186–87; Ganshof, *La Flandre sous les premiers comtes,* 72–74; H. van Werveke, "De opbloei van handel en nijverheid," *Algemene Geschiedenis der Nederlanden* 2 (Utrecht, 1950), 417–24; Ross, trans., 114, n. 13; and Nicholas, *Medieval Flanders,* 112–15.

56. See Emile de Borchgrave, *Histoire des colonies belges qui s'établirent en Allemagne pendant le douzième et le treizième siècle* (Brussels, 1865), 53–158; Pirenne, *Histoire de Belgique,* 1:156–57; J. F. Niermeyer, "Emigratie," in L. Voet, "Het platteland, maatschappelijk en economisch," *Algemene Geschiedenis der Nederlanden* 2 (Utrecht, 1950), 469; and Nicholas, *Medieval Flanders,* 108–9.

57. *Papacy,* 441–42.

58. See Riché, "La Vie scolaire," 217; and Flint, "The 'School of Laon,'" 91–94; ninety-two of the one hundred and twenty-eight *sententiae* that can be attributed to Anselm of Laon are on the epistles of Paul, and one commentary on the epistles is attributed to a Manegold that may be Manegold of Lautenbach (Flint, "The 'School of Laon,'" 94, 93).

59. Abelard, *Commentaria* 4 [XIII, u. 2], 1:286. The late-thirteenth-century catalogue of the chapter library of Saint Donatian mentions three copies of Paul's epistles, at least one of them "glosate" (Derolez and Victor, *Corpus Catalogorum Belgii,* 1:167). See also Affeldt, *Die weltliche Gewalt in der Paulus-Exegese,* and D. E. Luscombe and G. R. Evans, "The Twelfth-Century Renaissance," in Burns, ed., *Medieval Political Thought,* 317 (on Robert of Melun's *Quaestiones de epistolis Pauli* [c. 1145–1155]).

60. Like Belgium today, medieval Flanders was something of an intellectual crossroads—"during the 12th and 13th centuries," wrote Pirenne, "even more than during the 11th, Belgium was the broker, so to speak, in the intellectual commerce between the two great States [France and Germany] whose border passed through its territory" *(Histoire de Belgique,* 1:176)—and it lay at the heart of the region of Europe that could, according to John Ward, "lay strongest claim during the middle ages to a special place in the transmission of the duties of the Christian monarch and of the idea of imperial succession that made

up the essence of civilization as it was understood at that time" (Ward, "'Chronicle' and 'History,'" 117).

61. Van Caenegem, "Galbert of Bruges," 103. See also Van Caenegem, "Misdaad," 323; and Heinrich Mitteis, *Lehnrecht und Staatsgewalt: Untersuchungen zur mittelalterlichen Verfassungsgeschichte* (Cologne, 1974), 534–46.

62. "Gregorii P. P. VII vita" 97, 531–32. On the influence of vassalage on the concept of the relation between the prince and his subjects, see Carlyle and Carlyle, *History,* 3:75–86; Kern, *Gottesgnadentum,* 219–25, 362–64; Ullmann, *Principles of Government and Politics,* 150–92, and *The Individual and Society,* 63–98; and Dunbabin, *France,* 232–37, 358–65. "The road leading from the feudal *point d'appui* to constitutionalism [of which Ivan's speech may be considered a precocious example]," remarks Ullmann, "is marked by steady evolution" *(Principles of Government and Politics,* 24). For an analysis of the influence of the model of vassalage on the conflict between William and his subjects in particular, see Heirbaut, "Galbert van Brugge," 60–62.

63. On the development of the communal movement, see Cauchie, *La Querelle des Investitures,* 1:14–16; 2:158–63, 193–205; Vermeesch, *Essai;* André Chédeville, "De la cité à la ville," in Georges Duby, ed., *Histoire de la France urbaine,* vol. 2, ed. Jacques Le Goff, *La Ville médiévale des Carolingiens à la Renaissance* (Paris, 1980), 164–76; Société Académique de Saint-Quentin, *Les Chartes et le mouvement communal. Colloque régional (octobre 1980)* (Saint-Quentin, 1982); Oexle, "Conjuratio," 151–214, and "Die Kultur der Rebellion. Schwureinung und Verschwörung im früh- und hochmittelalterlichen Okzident," in Marie Theres Fögen, ed., *Ordnung und Aufruhr im Mittelalter. Historische und juristische Studien zur Rebellion* (Frankfurt, 1995), 119–37; and Alain Saint-Denis, "L'Apparition d'une identité urbaine dans les villes de commune de France du Nord aux XIIe et XIIIe siècles," forthcoming in Marc Boone and Peter Stabel, eds., *Shaping Urban Identity in Late Medieval Europe: The Use of Space and Images. Papers Presented at the Fourth International Conference of Urban History (Venice, September 1998).*

64. See Chédeville, "De la cité à la ville," 171; Carolus-Barré, "Origine et sens du mot 'commune,'" in Société Académique de Saint-Quentin, *Les Chartes,* 99; and P. Desportes, "Le Mouvement communal dans la Province de Reims," in Société Académique de Saint-Quentin, *Les Chartes,* 105. Pirenne and Oexle cite a capitulary of Louis the Pious from 821 that mentions the existence even then of "sworn alliances of serfs [*conjuration(es) servorum*] which are formed in Flanders and Mempiscus and other maritime territories"; Pirenne suggests that these societies were formed to resist the serfs' lords or the comital administration; Oexle suggests that they were self-defense societies, formed perhaps in reaction to Viking invasions (Capitula missorum c. 7, MGH Capitularia regum Francorum 1, p. 301; cited by Pirenne, *Histoire de Belgique,* 1:36, 154; Oexle, "Conjuratio," 152, n. 13).

65. "Then the citizens, as they had pledged to do [*pepigerant*] with the prince Daniel and Ivan, the brother of Baldwin, called the count to a reckoning" ([95], 7/8; trans., 267; trans. mod.). On the importance of the oath in collective actions and law, see Michaud-Quantin, *Universitas,* 233–45; and Yvonne Bongert, *Recherches sur les cours laïques du Xe au XIIIe siècle* (Paris, 1949), 205–10.

66. On the ways in which bourgeois practices and interests served to limit the ruler's power, see Ganshof, "Les Origines du concept," 155–57; Ullmann, *Principles of Government and Politics,* 215–30; and Coué, "Der Mord," 120–21.

67. Vermeesch, *Essai,* 112.

68. De Hemptinne and Verhulst, *Oorkonden,* n° 2, p. 17.

69. By the end of his speech, at least: the beginning of the speech, up to the point

where he evokes the count's abuses in Lille and Saint-Omer, could be understood to pertain only to the situation in Ghent.

70. The years 1100–1500, writes R. I. Moore, were an "inordinately active period" of "community formation" of all sorts, "perhaps the only time in European history we are dealing with a world which constructed far more of itself than it inherited" ("Heresy, Repression, and Social Change in the Age of Gregorian Reform," in Scott L. Waugh and Peter D. Diehl, eds., *Christendom and Its Discontents. Exclusion, Persecution, and Rebellion, 1000–1500* [Cambridge, 1996], 37). The pan-bourgeois uprising against William in 1128, which also involved the elements of the aristocracy whose interests were most closely tied up with those of the town-dwellers, can perhaps be seen as an example of the creation of what Moore has termed a "middle" community between the "little" "producing communities, relatively undifferentiated in their internal structure and generally communicating with one another only at the level of local exchange" and the "great" community of pan-European aristocracy represented by king and bishop ("Literacy and the Making of Heresy, c. 1000–c. 1150," in Peter Biller and Anne Hudson, eds., *Heresy and Literacy, 1000–1530* [Cambridge, U.K., 1994], 26). "The origin of this kind of 'rebellion,'" writes Oexle, "is the desire to restore order to a society ['société d'ordres'] that has fallen into a state of social disorder and whose order can no longer be restored in another way in the opinion of the 'conspirators.' . . . It is thus a matter of a conflict between two cultures . . . not between order and rebellion but between two 'orders,'" between a local order and a universal order represented "by the king or the Church" ("Kultur," 131–33).

71. See Kern, *Gottesgnadentum,* 146–50; compare 138, 145–50, 195, 243; Rouse and Rouse, "John of Salisbury," 702–4; Nelson, "Kingship and Empire," 246–47; Nederman, "A Duty to Kill," 368–69, 378.

72. See Robinson, *Papacy,* 405–10. Stephen of Blois in fact sought confirmation of his coronation as king of England from the pope in 1136, and the dispute between him and Matilda was evidently brought before Pope Innocent II at the Second Lateran Council of 1139, although, as Morey and Brooke point out (112, n. 2), political considerations forced the pope to end the hearing without a decision, tacitly approving the status quo (see Gilbert Foliot, *The Letters and Charters of Gilbert Foliot,* letter 26, ed. Z. N. Brooke, Adrian Morey, and C. N. L. Brooke [Cambridge, U.K., 1967], 60–66; John of Salisbury, *Historia pontificalis* 42, ed. and trans., 83–85; Adrian Morey and C. N. L. Brooke, *Gilbert Foliot and His Letters* [Cambridge, U.K., 1965], 105–23; Constable in Peter the Venerable, *Letters,* 2:252–56).

73. Bruno of Magdeburg, *Saxonicum bellum* 88, 330. It is important to distinguish the judgment of the sitting ruler—which, according to Gregory and, for the moment, the Saxons, fell within the pope's competence—from the election of the new ruler, which was the right of his subjects (although they hoped, of course, that the pope would endorse their choice).

74. *Annales* 1076, 281.

75. Bruno of Magdeburg, *Saxonicum bellum* 108, 356.

76. *Saxonicum bellum* 91, 332. Paul of Bernried, writing some fifty years later, says that through his legates the pope asked the Saxon princes to put off electing anyone until he could be present "if they thought this could be done without danger." The Saxons replied that "there would be a most dangerous and irrevocable schism throughout the realm, unless they hastened to forestall it, united in raising up a new leader at that assembly, as they had agreed." The legates answered that, if the election could in fact not be delayed, the future of the realm "lay less in their counsel than in the judgement of the princes . . . who held the republic in their hands and could best foresee what would ruin or profit the realm. . . . Con-

vinced that they were not required by the pope to wait, but that this matter had been left to their judgement" and that the pope had absolved them from their oaths to Henry, the princes proceeded to elect Rudolf king ("Gregorii P. P. VII vita" 94–95, 529–30). A bit later, Paul writes that "the princes . . . might have reasonably deposed him, even without the judgement of the Holy See, since he failed to fulfill the pact to which he had agreed in exchange for their electing him" ("Gregorii P. P. VII vita" 97, 532), suggesting that it was in their power to judge and to depose the king as well as to elect him.

77. Bruno, *Saxonicum bellum* 113–15, 370–78. See Robinson, "Pope Gregory VII," 746–47.

78. After Rudolf's death in October 1080, Henry made plans for a military excursion to Rome in order to have himself crowned emperor and Wibert consecrated as pope. For obvious reasons, he wanted to leave Germany in as peaceful a state as possible and invited Saxon representatives to a meeting "at which princes elected from both parties would discuss the common welfare [*de communi bono*]" (Bruno of Magdeburg, *Saxonicum bellum* 126, 396). This national meeting in the Kaufunger Forest in February 1081 brought together both "great and small" *(magnis et parvis),* bishops, "'most noble princes and most strong knights'" *(nobilissimi principes et fortissimi milites),* and even "common knights" *(milites . . . plebei)* (Bruno of Magdeburg, *Saxonicum bellum* 126, 396; 127, 398; 128, 402), who obviously felt themselves competent, even in the absence of any papal representatives, to judge Henry since Archbishop Gebhard of Salzburg, speaking for the Saxons, ended his speech to Henry's representatives by declaring: "'This is the essence of our request: that either you show us convincingly [*probabiliter ostendatis*] that Lord Henry can rightly rule [*iure posse regnare*] or you allow us to show you truly [*veraciter ostendere*] that he cannot do so; and that when either one or the other will have been demonstrated, you will stop persecuting us with fire and sword'" (Bruno of Magdeburg, *Saxonicum bellum* 127, 400). Neither side was able to convince the other, and when the Saxon princes and their army met the Swabians at Ochsenfurt in August 1081, "they took counsel together concerning their common business of electing a king and, after much discussion they all agreed unanimously that they should elect Herman king" *(de communi negotio regis constituendi communi consilio tractaverunt et post multo tractatus, ut Herimannum regem eligerent, unanimiter omnes consenserunt)* (Bruno of Magdeburg, *Saxonicum bellum* 130, 402)—in the absence, again, of any papal representative and without, evidently, any thought for Gregory's opinion. See Fuhrmann, "'Volkssouveränität,'" 39, n. 41; and Paul of Bernried, "Gregorii P. P. VII vita" 93–97, 529–32.

79. See Kern, *Gottesgnadentum,* 146–50. Galbert's description of the "offer" of the kingdom of Jerusalem to Charles also provides an example of this method of deposing a tyrant: the offer was made to Charles not only because the ruling king had been captured by Saracens, but because his subjects hated him "because he was grasping and penurious, and had not governed the people of God well" *(eo quod tenax et parcus fuisset . . . nec bene rexisset populum Dei).* They therefore met and decided to offer the throne to Charles "by general consent" *(communi consensu)* without bothering to formally depose the captured king in any way ([5], 5–7; trans., 93).

80. Two such cases are mentioned in the comital charters from the period 1071–1128. In 1096, a canon representing the chapter of Saint Martin of Tours accused Robert II of having kept for himself a land rent belonging to the chapter. The count said he had no knowledge of the matter, but the canon was obstinate and, evidently, annoying, so the count convened "bishops, abbots, our nobles, and everbody else whom we had heard knew anything about the matter" and was "convinced by their counsel and judgement" *(eorum consilio et judicio recognovi)* that the canon was right. The witnesses to the charter include the bishops of Thérouanne and Arras; their archdeacons; the abbots of Saint Vaast of Arras, Saint Sauveur

of Ham, Mont-Saint-Eloi, and Saint Denis of Reims; and Walter, "formerly castellan of Douai, but now a cleric," as well as the countess, the castellan of Lille, the count's steward, and other laymen (Vercauteren, *Actes,* n° 19, p. 60–62).

In 1117, the abbot of Saint Amand appeared before Baldwin VII to accuse his father, the now-deceased Robert II, "of blessed memory," of having appropriated for his own use, "on the advice of depraved men," a forest belonging to the abbey which happened to be contiguous with one of the count's forests. Baldwin referred the matter to the judgement of his "barons" (who are named in the charter and include the potential pretenders Charles and William of Ypres) and on their "advice" a group of men was chosen who, on a given day, walked the boundary between the two forests, followed by the count, who was carrying the saint's relics (Vercauteren, *Actes,* n° 85, p. 190–92; on the judicial function of the count's court, see Monier, *Institutions centrales,* 53–62; Ganshof, *La Flandre sous les premiers comtes,* 103–4, and "La Flandre," 410–11).

Ivan and the burghers might also, of course, have brought a complaint against William in the court of his lord, the king of France. When Baldwin VII refused to confirm the gifts of land his father, Robert II, had made to his mother, Clémence, for example, she demanded that "you [Baldwin] fix a day to hear her complaint and that, having called together the barons [*comites*] of your land and the castellans whom she wishes to be present at this hearing, the case be decided to her satisfaction by their judgement in your court, or, [if you do not do so] she is ready to pursue the matter in the court of the king of the French" (Bishop Lambert of Arras to Baldwin VII [1113], *Epistolae Lamberti episcopi Atrebatensis et aliorum ad ipsum* 126, *Patrologia latina* 162, 693; see Sproemberg, "Clementia," 1221, n. 1; it is possible that *comites* refers to the counts of Saint-Pol, Hesdin, Boulogne, and Guines). Louis VI in fact first tried to resolve the conflict between William and the burghers by convening an assembly of representatives from the towns of Flanders on April 15, 1128 ([106], 5/13; trans., 283), and eventually summoned "archbishops, bishops, and all synodal persons among the clergy, and abbots, and the most responsible persons from both the clergy and people, counts and barons and other leading men" to convene at Arras on May 6, 1128, "to hold a council concerning those two counts and decide which of them he should drive out by his royal authority and which he should establish" ([110], 7/13; trans., 290–91).

81. See Carlyle and Carlyle, *History,* 3: 52–74; and Bongert, *Recherches,* 62–71. When the counts of Flanders refer to the judgement of their court in legal matters in the comital charters of 1071–1128, they usually refer to "the counsel" *(consilio)* or "the judgement" *(judicio)* "of my barons" *(baronum meorum),* "of the princes of my land" *(principum terre mee),* "the more prudent men of the fatherland" *(prudentioribus patrie),* or "the leading men of our court" *(primoribus curie nostre)* (Vercauteren, *Actes,* n° 50, p. 128; n° 52, p. 131, 132; n° 82, p. 186; n° 95, p. 214; n° 106, p. 242; n° 108, pp. 249–50).

82. "The wiser men among the . . . people" is of course an elastic term that might in some circumstances mean only members of the upper nobility. Since Ivan has just mentioned "the barons . . . and . . . peers" of Flanders, however, "the wiser men among the . . . people" seems to refer here to representatives of at least the lesser aristocracy and probably, since Ivan was surrounded by the people of Ghent as he spoke, to representatives of the burghers as well.

83. As becomes clear from Robinson's discussion of Gregory VII's struggles with independently minded, or, in Gregory's terms, disobedient bishops whose clergy and people he regularly absolved "from their duty of obedience" to them ("'Periculosus homo,'" 104–25), Gregory applied an episcopal model to the office of the emperor and was in fact dealing with Henry IV in the same way he had already dealt with several disobedient bishops when he deposed him in 1076. According to Robinson, the famous twenty-seventh *sententia* of the

Dictatus papae of March 1075—which declares that the pope "'can absolve subjects from fealty to wicked men' . . .[—]may well refer to the subjects of bishops as much as to the subjects of kings. This *sententia* is more probably a reflection of the case of Bishop Otto of Constance—to whose subjects the pope wrote, 'For so long as he is a rebel against Almighty God and the apostolic see, you are bound to pay him no fealty'—than a prognostication of the case of King Henry IV in 1076" ("'Periculosus homo,'" 116). When faced with disobedient bishops or priests, Gregory's normal tactic was to absolve their subjects from their oaths of fealty and encourage them to rebel. In January 1075, for example, he wrote to Rudolf of Rheinfelden and other German princes commanding them "'in no way [to] recognize as priests those whom you know either to have been promoted and ordained simoniacally or to be accused of fornication. . . . and, to the utmost of your power, you are to prevent such men from administering the sacred mysteries—even, if necessary, by violence.'" He also wrote along these lines to Robert I of Flanders, and the Lenten synod of 1075 decreed that "'those who are not corrected through the love of God and the dignity of their office may be brought to their senses through the shame of the world and the rebuke of the people'" ("'Periculosus homo,'" 115). Although Gregory's ultimate goal was to establish a great chain of obedience stretching from the people through the princes, clergy, emperor, and bishops to the pope, his practice of setting subjects against disobedient bishops (and emperors) in order to attain these ends seems also to have encouraged protopopulism in both politics and the church.

Manegold of Lautenbach likewise suggests an analogy between secular and ecclesiastical offices when he writes that "'king' is not the name of a nature, but of an office, like 'bishop,' 'priest,' or 'deacon'" *(Ad Gebehardum liber* 43, 385), and Paul of Bernried makes the comparison explicit, declaring that "once the pope had absolved all Christians from that oath [their oath of fealty to Henry IV], it imposed no more subjection to him who had been deposed and excommunicated than is owed to a bishop, likewise excommunicated, after he is deposed" ("Gregorii P. P. VII vita" 97, 531). On the equation of a ruler with a bishop, and of the deposition of a tyrant with that of a bishop, see also Peters, *The Shadow King,* 126; and Robinson, *Authority and Resistance,* 103–9.

84. According to Oexle, sworn alliances like that formed between "the burghers of the cities and towns of Flanders" with respect to the election of the count in 1127 ([53], 6/9; trans., 198) or the mutual defense pact between the "towns of Flanders" proposed by Ivan and Daniel in 1128 ([95], 62/69; trans., 270) normally "produce . . . specific institutions, involving representation and delegation and institutionalised forms of behavior, in which public opinion can be formed, conflicts settled, and consensus forged like the so-called 'Parlement' in the case of the Norman commune [of c. 1000]" ("Kultur," 131)—or like the court proposed by Ivan.

85. He does not assign any precise date to the speech, and, given his habitual chronological precision, this omission alone makes it almost certain that he did not hear it. Sproemberg also concludes that "there is no evidence that Galbert heard it" in Ghent *(Mittelalter,* 262). In fact, as Pirenne notes, there is no indication anywhere in the *De multro* that he ever left Bruges during the period covered by his chronicle (ed., xiii).

86. *Mittelalter,* 232.

87. *Mittelalter,* 262.

88. Sproemberg remarks that "the first impression one has in reading Ivan's speech is that it is not in any way a passionate phillipic but is rather a formally concise, logically consistent legal plea" ("Erwachen des Staatsgefühls," 64); "one recognizes the hand of a learned jurist so clearly in the dialectical form of this accusation," he writes in a later article, "that

one naturally wonders who formulated it," and noting that Galbert, as a comital functionary, "had an abundance of legal and political knowledge and experience at his disposal," he concludes that ". . . the legal significance and formulation of these declarations [this one and that of the citizens of Bruges discussed below] are his own work" *(Mittelalter,* 233, 262, 238). Van Caenegem likewise observes that the speech "deserves a special place beside the celebrated political and military addresses in Livy's Roman history" ("The Ghent Revolt," 109), while Ganshof remarks that "through Galbert we know, if not the words, at least the gist of the speech that Ivan of Aalst, as spokesman, made to the count," suggesting that he, too, thought that the *words* attributed to Ivan are in fact Galbert's ("Les Origines du concept," 145).

89. Noting that Thierry, like Manegold of Lautenbach, came from Alsace, however, Van Caenegem has suggested that Manegold's ideas may have been brought to Flanders by Thierry and his counsellors and thus influenced Ivan more-or-less directly ("Galbert of Bruges," 105–7).

90. The charters for 1071–1128 suggest that the judicial functions of the count's court were usually carried out by its most prominent secular members, although the count might then ask that members of the clergy "add excommunication" *(excommunicationem adhibeant)* to his seal in order to ratify and enforce their judgement (Vercauteren, *Actes,* n° 108, p. 250; compare n° 85, p. 191). As we have seen, clergymen do seem to have participated in the court's judicial deliberations when the canon of Saint Martin of Tours brought a case against Robert II in 1096. In this instance, the count convened "bishops, abbots, our nobles, and everbody else whom we had heard knew anything about the matter" and was "convinced by their counsel and judgement" *(eorum consilio et judicio recognovi)* that the canon was right (Vercauteren, *Actes,* n° 19, pp. 60–62).

Another charter, however, relates a similar case from 1116 in which the abbot and monks of Saint Amand complained to Baldwin VII that Walter, the castellan of Tournai, had broken an agreement made between them in the days of Baldwin's father, Robert II. Baldwin convened "my men who, at the command of my father, had been present at this agreement, and Walter's men along with the men of Saint Amand" in order to determine what the terms of the agreement had actually been. Walter, however, refused to accept their rendition of the agreement until "he was compelled to give up by the judgement of my barons" *(judicio baronum meorum compulsus est abnuere)* (Vercauteren, *Actes,* n° 82, pp. 185–86). This latter case suggests that the clergymen mentioned in the charter of 1096 may have been convened by Robert II primarily as informants, and that the actual judgment in the case was his. The charter recording the resolution of the case brought against the deceased Robert II in the court of Baldwin VII in 1117 (see above, n. 80) includes a list of the "barons" who acted as judges, all of whom are secular nobles (Vercauteren, *Actes,* n° 85, pp. 190–92).

On the makeup of the court of Hainaut at this time, see Genicot, who notes that clerical attendance at that court was relatively rare before c. 1150 ("Le Premier Siècle," 48–54).

91. The literary quality of Galbert's description of Ivan's chastisement of Count William before, and on behalf of, the assembled burghers of Ghent becomes more evident when one compares it with the description of Turnus's chastisement of King Latinus before, and on behalf of, the assembled burghers of Laurente in the *Roman d'Enéas,* the medieval French adaptation of the *Aeneid,* which was written about thirty years later than the events Galbert describes *(Le Roman d'Enéas,* ed. Aimé Petit [Paris, 1997], 3868–967; compare *Eneas. Roman du XIIe siècle,* 2 vols., ed. J.-J. Salverda de Grave [Paris, 1925, 1931], 1:3785–880). A comparison of the two passages also demonstrates, of course, the historical

quality of the passage from the *Enéas,* and the two together suggest the existence in the twelfth century of an ambient narrative model of "a public chastisement of a lord by one of his barons acting as spokesman for his people."

92. See, for example, *Principles of Government and Politics,* 20–21: "There is the ascending conception of government and law according to which . . . power is concentrated in the people itself, so that one can speak of law and governmental power as rising or ascending. . . . Opposed to this ascending conception is the descending conception of government and law. Accordingly, governmental authority and law-creating competency descend from one supreme organ: power is distributed 'downwards.' . . . This one supreme organ, in whom all power is located and who hands it 'downwards', is God Himself. . . ."

93. "I ask and admonish [the reader to] . . . wonder with fresh wonder at what is written down and what came to pass by the ordinance of God only in our time, and learn not to despise or kill earthly rulers whom we are bound to believe were placed over us by the ordinance of God, as the apostle says: 'Let every soul be subject to every power, either to the king as supreme or to governors as sent by God'" ([Prol.], 35/43; trans., 80; trans. mod.)

94. Orosius, *Histoires* 2.1.3–4, ed. 1:84; trans. Deferrari, 44; compare trans. Raymond, 72 (Orosius likewise alludes to Rom. 13.1 [or 1 Peter 2.13] in this passage). Galbert has just asserted, however, that the emperor Henry V and King Henry I of England were less powerful and less famous *(minoris potentiae et famae; minoris quoque famae ac virium)* than Charles ([Prol.], 4/5; trans., 79).

95. See Robert L. Benson, "Plenitudo potestatis: Evolution of a Formula from Gregory IV to Gratian," *Studia Gratiana* 14 (1967): 195–217; I. S. Robinson, "Church and Papacy," in Burns, ed., *Medieval Political Thought,* 269–70, 282–88; Luscombe, "Introduction," 172; Canning, *History,* 32, 108–9, 118–19. Manegold of Lautenbach distinguishes "apostolic power" *(apostolica potestas)* from "the earthly imperium" *(terreno imperio)* and declares the former superior to the latter *(Ad Gebehardum liber* 44, 1:386), which suggests that Galbert, too, is here distinguishing the pope's fullness of power from the count's limited power.

96. At the end of the thirteenth century, Raymond Lulle wrote: "you should know, my son, that no man is so obligated to his office as is a prince, for I and you and the lesser people are obligated to only one man—to our king or prince or count or some other earthly lord—but the king is obligated to me and to you and to everyone else in his realm" *(Doctrine d'enfant* 80, 173).

97. "Eschatology," 126–27. At the end of chapter 6, Galbert writes that Charles "died like a Christian ruler, seeking the justice of God and the welfare of those over whom he ruled. But the men whom he trusted tripped him up and betrayed him, as it is said in the Psalm: 'Even my bosom friend in whom I trusted, who ate of my bread, has lifted his heal against me'" ([6], 33/38). Noting that Jesus cites this same Psalm (41.9) in reference to Judas during the Last Supper (Jn. 13.18) and that Galbert shows the count distributing wine to those present in his house on the last evening of his life ([10], 41/47), Demyttenaere suggests that Galbert may have been thinking of the Last Supper, and thus more or less consciously comparing Charles's betrayal and sacrifice to Jesus', when he wrote these chapters (in *De Moord* [1999], 120, n. 29, and 125, n. 37).

98. The charter William granted to Saint-Omer begins with only slightly more veiled frankness: "I, William, count of Flanders by the grace of God, not wishing to oppose the request [*petitioni*] of the burghers of Saint-Omer—especially because they readily [*libenti animo*] accepted my claim [*meam . . . petitionem*] to the countship of Flanders, and because they have always conducted themselves more honestly and faithfully towards me than other inhabitants of Flanders—concede to them by perpetual right [*perpetuo . . . jure*] the following

laws or customs [*lagas seu consuetudines*] and order that they remain in force" (Espinas, "Le Privilège de Saint-Omer," 45).

The Flemish burghers' consent to William's election in return for charters granting them the right to form what effectively amounts to a commune (and is explicitly so-called in the charter of Saint-Omer) is thus the equivalent of the money the citizens of Laon, Amiens, and, perhaps, Valenciennes, paid to this same king (and, in the case of Laon, to the bishop) in return for similar charters (see Guibert of Nogent, *Autobiographie* 3.7, 14; ed., 322, 400; trans., 168, 200; Vermeesch, *Essai*, 117–18; and Carolus-Barré, "Origine," 101).

The charter which the king and new count granted to the citizens of Bruges was read publicly on Wednesday, April 6, and must, therefore, have been drafted and copied before then. It seems likely that the concessions it spells out—"the price" of the citizens' "election and acceptance of the new count"—had been negotiated and agreed upon at the meeting between representatives of the king, count, and men of Bruges and Ghent at Raverschoot on Saturday, April 2, and that the charter had been prepared on April 3–5 (on the advance preparation of various kinds of "spontaneous" public ceremonies at the time, see Gerd Althoff, "*Colloqium familiare—Colloquium secretum—Colloquium publicum:* Beraten im politischen Leben des früheren Mittelalters," *Frühmitteralterliche Studien* 24 [1990]: 145–67, and "Demonstration und Inszenierung. Spielregeln der Kommunikation in mittelalterlicher Öffentlichhkeit," *Frühmittelalterliche Studien* 27 [1993]: 27–50). It also seems likely that a ceremony like that which took place in Bruges on April 6, when the king and count ratified the charters of both Saint Donatian and Bruges, and the citizens, in return, did homage to the new count and pledged him their faith and loyalty, had already taken place in Ghent on April 3 or 4. It seems likely, in sum, that Galbert learned the terms of the agreement between the king, the count, and the burghers on April 2 or 3 (when the representatives of Bruges returned from Raverschoot and began to prepare the charter to be presented to the king and count on April 6), and that he also learned of the public reception and election of the new count in Ghent no later than the evening of April 5, when the royal party arrived in Bruges. He makes no mention whatsoever of the king and count's reception and sojourn in Ghent, however—although he does describe his subsequent reception in Saint-Omer (before April 17)—and does not disclose any of the terms of the agreement between the king, the count, and the burghers until he describes the public reading of the charter on April 6. It thus seems likely that he suppressed this information in order to increase the drama of his description of the public ceremony in Bruges on April 6 (and perhaps, too, out of a sense of civic pride and rivalry). It is fairly clear, that is, that he has deliberately suppressed the "staging" and "rehearsal" of this ceremony in order to make his account of it more dramatic and illustrative of an ideal of political harmony—which the ceremony, too, was intended to manifest to those in attendance. It thus seems that we have here another case where, as Alan Murray has put it, Galbert's account is an imitation, a literary representation, a rhetorical reenactment of "the public political processes" it describes ("Voices of Flanders," 105).

99. See Ganshof, "Le Droit urbain"; Van Caenegem, *Coutumes et législation en Flandre au XIe et XIIe siècles* (Brussels, 1968), 245–79, and "De Keure van Sint-Omaars van 1127," *Tijdschrift voor Rechtsgeschiedenis / Revue d'Histoire du Droit / The Legal History Review* 50 (1982): 253–62; and Alain Derville, "Les Institutions communales de Saint-Omer," in Société Académique de Saint-Quentin, *Les Chartes,* 149–59.

100. On the new count and king's purchase of noble support, see Ross, "Rise and Fall," 380.

101. The importance of ruling by consent is also illustrated by Galbert's affirmation that Baldwin VI, when he was worried about how he might control his problematic brother,

Robert the Frisian, took "counsel [*consilio*] with the barons, knowing that it would be advantageous [*utile*] both to the fatherland and himself" ([69], 6/7; trans., 233).

102. This implicit theory is not unlike that articulated some thirty years later by John of Salisbury. On the one hand, John wrote, "the prince is the public power and a certain image on earth of the divine majesty. . . . For all power is from the Lord God, and is with him always, and is his forever. Whatever the prince can do, therefore, is from God, so that power does not depart from God, but it is used as a substitute for His hand, making all things learn His justice and mercy. 'Whoever therefore resists power, resists what is ordained by God' [Romans 13.2]." On the other hand, the prince "believes himself to be the minister of the people he rules by his judgement . . . [and is] concerned with the burdens of the entire community. . . . [He] loves justice, cherishes equity, procures the utility of the republic, and in all matters prefers the advantage of others to his private will. But who in public affairs may even speak of the will of the prince, since in such matters he is not permitted his own will unless it is prompted by law or equity, or brings about judgements for the common utility? . . . The prince is therefore the minister of the public utility and the servant of equity. . . ." (*Policraticus* 4.1–2, ed. Webb, 1:235–38; trans. Nederman, 28–31; compare trans. Dickinson, 4–7).

103. John of Salisbury, for example, thought that "the most useful and the safest" way of removing tyrants was to "humbly resort to the protection of God's clemency and . . . [raise] up pure hands to the Lord in devoted prayer," but he was nonetheless certain that God always punishes tyrants and brings them "to a bad end," sometimes miraculously "with His own lance," other times mundanely "with what seems to be a human lance" *(quasi hominis telo) (Policraticus* 8.18, 8.20, 8.21; ed. Webb, 2:358–60, 378, 379; trans. Nederman, 201–2, 209, 210; trans. Dickinson, 350–51, 373, 375; trans. mod.). Humans ought not, that is, take it upon themselves to rid themselves of a divinely ordained tyrant, but God sometimes acted through them to do so. Compare the remarks of Hugh of Fleury, cited above (Chapter 3, pp. 55–56), and Rouse and Rouse, "John of Salisbury," 702–4, 709; Van Laarhoven, "Thou Shalt *Not,*" 324–26; Nederman, "A Duty to Kill," 375; Forhan, "Salisburian Stakes," 405–6; and Nederman and Campbell, "Priests, Kings, and Tyrants," 583.

104. Ullmann, *Principles of Government and Politics,* 227–28.

105. *Mittelalter,* 374.

106. Guibert of Nogent likewise believed that God used anniversaries to signal connections between two events, noting that Bishop Gaudry conspired to overthrow the commune of Laon—and thus brought about his own destruction and, in and through it, the punishment of the misdeeds of his predecessors back to Adalberon—on Maundy Thursday, the same day Adalberon had betrayed Charles of Lorraine *(Autobiographie* 3.1; ed., 268, 330; trans., 146, 171). Benton notes (trans., 146, n. 3) that Guibert's date for Adalberon's treachery is different from that of other historians and suggests that "he may have changed the record here" in order to create this parallel.

107. The ceremony on March 31 was probably similar to that which had taken place on April 6 in the preceding year. See [55], 7/85; trans., 201–6.

108. As we will see in the next chapter, it is possible that chapter 5 was added to the *Passio* at roughly this time and the contrast between the two Jerusalems may have been deliberate. Rudolf of Rheinfelden was likewise consecrated on *Laetare* Sunday and Bruno of Magdeburg remarks the coincidence, writing that all the faithful were invited to be joyous *(Saxonicum bellum* 92, 334).

109. "The formula of fidelity (or the feudal oath) [*formam fidelitatis*]," writes John of Salisbury, "should be observed above all else" *(Policraticus* 6.25, ed. Webb, 2:75; trans. Nederman, 138; trans., Dickinson, 261; see Nederman, "A Duty to Kill," 381), and breaking the

oath one had sworn to the old ruler seems to have been the most difficult and delicate part of shifting allegiance to a new one. Otto of Nordheim, as we have seen, addressed this point directly in his attempt to convince the Saxons assembled at Hoetensleben in July 1073 to rise against Henry IV, noting that "'because you are Christians, you are perhaps afraid to break the oaths you swore to the king'" (Bruno of Magdeburg, *Saxonicum bellum* 25, 224), and providing them with an "honorable" excuse for doing so by arguing that they had sworn fealty to an office rather than to a man and thus owed no fealty to the man once he had ceased to fulfill his office.

Manegold of Lautenbach (*Ad Gebehardum liber* 47–49, 391–99) and Paul of Bernried ("Gregorii P. P. VII vita" 97, 531–32) likewise discuss this problem at some length and conclude, similarly, that one must indeed respect one's oath—but only so long as the ruler is, as Manegold puts it, "a devoted and present companion and helper, keeping the realm on course, preserving justice, establishing peace" (*Ad Gebehardum liber* 48, 392), although they both suggest that the pope is best suited to judge when the ruler has ceased to be a ruler. "No one," Paul writes, "can rightly accuse King Rudolf and his princes of perjury, even though they had long ago sworn fealty to the deposed king. For that oath was binding only so long as he ruled the realm. Once the pope had absolved all Christians from that oath, it imposed no more subjection to him who had been deposed and excommunicated than is owed to a bishop, likewise excommunicated, after he is deposed" ("Gregorii P. P. VII vita" 97, 531).

110. See Van Caenegem "Law and Power," 152; and Heirbaut "Galbert van Brugge," 61, n. 109.

111. It is impossible, of course, to say exactly what part of these speeches is due to Gervaise and what part to Galbert. Gervaise undoubtedly left Bruges on March 26 (perhaps both out of a sense of duty and because, at that point, he thought that William was ultimately likely to maintain his control over Bruges); he undoubtedly returned on April 2, after Thierry's election, and became the new count's vassal (both out of a sense of solidarity with the citizens of Bruges and in order to preserve his office and interests there); and Galbert consistently portrays him as a gifted politician and orator and speeches like the one he made in front of Thierry were in fact carefully prepared ahead of time (see Althoff, "*Colloqium familiare,*" and "Demonstration und Inszenierung"). It seems likely, however, that the precise words Galbert attributes to him in chapters 100 and 104 are due in some part to Galbert, and that Gervaise's intuitive and self-interested resolution of this conflict was transformed, in Galbert's hands, into an informed, articulate, and principled one.

112. Compare this to Gervaise's statement that William is "'lawless, faithless, without regard for the justice of God or men'" (*sine lege, sine fide, sine justitia Dei et hominum*) ([104], 12/13; trans., 281), and to Ivan's that he is "'lawless, faithless, a deceiver, a perjurer'" (*exlex, sine fide, dolosus, perjurus*) ([95], 31; trans., 268).

113. The citizens of London likewise claimed a special right to elect the new king in 1135: "Moreover, they said, it was their own right and peculiar privilege that if their king died from any cause a successor should immediately be appointed by their own choice" (*Gesta Stephani* 2, 6–7).

114. Paris, *Bibliothèque Nationale,* Français 17,849 (= St-Germain Harlay 205^{6}), f. 1r°–1v°. On this manuscript, see Rider, ed., xxxi; Pirenne, ed., 153, n. 1 (Pirenne mistakenly lists the manuscript as Français 17,489). Since the texts contained in this collection stop in 1326, it is possible that it was put together as early as the fourteenth century. "One is faced here," writes Ganshof, "with what is certainly one of the oldest texts where the concept of a contract between a ruler and his subjects is invoked in a conflict over the exercise of his powers" ("Les Origines du concept," 155), and Coué has termed this declaration the cul-

mination of the self-consciousness and confidence of the citizens of Bruges ("Der Mord," 122).

115. Murray, "Voices of Flanders," 114–15. Chibnall notes that in Orderic Vitalis's *Ecclesiastical History,* similarly, "direct speech, whether in the form of a dialogue or a single harangue, is [often] a statement of a widely held point of view: the quintessence of a debate, or of many much less articulate discussions" (in *Ecclesiastical History,* 1:83).

116. Sproemberg, "Erwachen des Staatsgefühls," 71, 72, 73. He also notes that "the significance of these legal principles is founded above all on the fact that, on the one hand, they draw the ultimate consequences from a concrete situation and, on the other, they contain an ambitious program for the future" ("Erwachen des Staatsgefühls," 82). Elsewhere, he writes that "this is an exceptionally well composed piece of writing that shows the hand of a learned jurist" *(Mittelalter,* 234).

117. Pirenne thought that "it is unlikely that the inhabitants of Bruges sent the manifesto recorded by Galbert to Louis VI. The tone is too aggressive and the style too distant from the ordinary style of charters" (Pirenne, ed., 153, n. 1), but as Sproemberg observes, "from the effect on the king, one can conclude that the manifesto was sent to him in an extremely blunt form, for in Arras he had the archbishop of Reims and his suffragan bishops suspend all divine services in the territory under Count Thierry's control" ("Erwachen des Staatsgefühls," 81). The résumé Galbert records may not have been sent to the king, but something like it may well have been.

118. The *ars dictaminis,* which was introduced throughout northern Europe in the twelfth century, was, writes Patt, "firmly rooted in the rhetorical tradition. Although the similarity between an oration and a letter may not be immediately obvious, it becomes clear if one remembers that medieval letters were intended to be read aloud, often to an audience" (Patt, "The Early 'Ars Dictaminis,'" 152). Constable likewise observes, that "the art of public speaking and the art of writing letters were therefore closely related and merged in what later came to be called diplomacy" *(Letters,* 54). The task of writing this speech, that is, would have been more or less the same as that of composing a letter to be read aloud to the king.

119. According to Sproemberg, "the legal significance and the formulation of these statements [this one and the one attributed to Ivan of Aalst, discussed above] are [Galbert's] own work; they go far beyond the ideas current at this time" *(Mittelalter,* 238). Pirenne and Ganshof likewise acknowledge that the *form* of the discourse as it is recorded in the *De multro* is probably due to Galbert. Pirenne suggested that he "probably reproduces in his own way the contents of the answer that was sent to the king" (Pirenne, ed., 153, n. 1), and Ganshof wrote that "through Galbert, we know the gist and perhaps to a certain degree the form of their answer" ("Les Origines du concept," 153–54), suggesting that the form is also due, in some measure, to Galbert.

120. As we have seen, the burghers declare that Thierry is "strengthened by our faith and homage." Before Stephen is elected king, according to the author of the *Gesta Stephani,* he and the citizens swear a "pact" *(pactione)* whereby "as long as he lived the citizens would aid him with their resources and protect him with their power, while he would gird himself with all his might to pacify the kingdom for the benefit of them all" *(Gesta Stephani* 2, 6–7).

121. John of Salisbury, *Policraticus* 4.1, ed. Webb, 1:236; trans. 29; trans. mod.; compare trans. Dickinson, 4.

122. After Rudolf of Rheinfelden's election by the Saxons and Swabians in 1077, Gregory VII similarly referred to both Rudolf and Henry IV as king in his letters until he finally deposed the latter for good in 1080. See, for example, the letter of May 31, 1077, where

he refers to "both kings, namely Henry and Rudolf," and the Saxons' 1077/78 letter to the pope, where they write that "when, as a result of the election of a king—and not of kings—great hope had sprung up among us for the revival of the Empire, behold! your letters arrived unexpectedly, announced that the kingdom had two kings and sent an embassy to both of them" (both cited by Bruno of Magdeburg, *Saxonicum bellum* 105, 108, 348–50, 356). See also Robinson, "Pope Gregory VII," 755–56, and *Papacy*, 405–10.

123. It is perhaps significant that in the Concordat of Worms (1122), Pope Calixtus II (the brother of Countess Clémence of Flanders) affirms that episcopal elections should take place in the presence of the emperor, but must proceed "without simony and without any violence" *(absque simonia et aliqua violentia) (Monumenta Germaniae Historica, Constitutiones et acta publica imperatorum et regum* 1, ed. L. Weiland [Hannover, 1893], 161). Perhaps Galbert, who, as we have seen, seems to share the tendency to model the count's office on that of a bishop, had the principles of the Concordat in mind here.

124. On this ordeal, see Van Caenegem, "Law and Power," 160.

125. Ordericus Vitalis seems to have shared Galbert's sentiment that "once a prince, always a prince," regardless of one's actions and irrespective of the value of other pretenders' claims. "Coronation mattered," writes Chibnall, "and to Orderic it was of supreme importance. He was indeed extremely reluctant to approve any arguments for deposing an anointed king. Harold's death in battle was represented as God's judgement on his perjury; in any case, it was not a deposition. William's victory was shown as a sign of God's will; he remained morally subject to God's judgement on the last day for the acts of his government, but once crowned he was king until he died. . . . [F]rom the moment that Stephen was crowned at Winchester, Orderic referred to him as king; the very last mention of him in the epilogue, when he was still imprisoned in fetters, called him king of England. . . . For many years after the victory at Tinchebray in 1106 Henry I ruled Normandy without using the ducal title in his charters; and though he had begun to do so by 1120 Orderic never gave it to him until Robert Curthose was dead" *(The World of Ordericus Vitalis,* 188–89). The author of the *Gesta Stephani* likewise "considered Stephen the legitimate king because he had been chosen by the magnates, and they had done homage to him" (Gransden, *Historical Writing,* 191; see the description of Stephen's election [*Gesta Stephani* 2, 4–7] and, for example, 41, 90–91).

126. It seems clear that this Lambert, the son of Ledewif, who was killed at Oostburg "that same week" (that is, the week of April 29 to May 5) is the same as the Lambert of Aardenburg mentioned in chapter 108 who was killed while attacking Oostburg on April 30. This supports Penelope Adair's conclusion that Lambert Nappin (a son of Erembald and Dedda, and the father of Borsiard) and Lambert of Aardenburg, son of Ledewif, were two different men ("Lambert Nappin and Lambert of Aardenburg: One Fleming or Two?," *Medieval Prosopography* 11.1 [1990]: 17–34).

127. This theme of double treachery is also found in the *Vita Karoli* where Walter observes that William of Ypres was defeated and captured by the king and William Clito only because "some of the burghers, who had sworn oaths of loyalty to him not once but many times, had plotted with some other of his men to betray him, had sent messengers to the king, and had pledged that they would open the gates to him and betray William. O what an affliction such offenses are to the world! or rather what an affliction traitors are to Flanders! It is wondrous and no less pitiful that the unhappy land that had lost its lord to treachery could not obtain another except through treachery" ([48], 559, 11/6).

128. These three biblical passages, Rom. 13.1 (or 1 Pet. 2.13), Jn. 19.11, and Mt. 22.21 (or Mk. 12.17 or Lk. 20.25) were among the scriptural foundations of the theocratic

concept of government (see Carlyle and Carlyle, *History,* 1:89–98, and Anton, *Fürstenspiegel,* 357–62) and Galbert's citation of all three in a single entry is something of a theocratic broadside.

It is interesting to compare this—unspoken—sermon with that preached in Laon by Archbishop Raoul of Reims in the wake of the uprising and the murder of Bishop Gaudry there in 1112: "During mass he preached a sermon about these accursed communes in which, contrary to right and justice, serfs withdraw from the rule of their lords. '"Serfs," said the Apostle, "be subject to your masters with all fear." And lest serfs plead as an excuse that their masters are hard and greedy, they should hear how it continues, "and not only to the good and gentle, but also to the froward" [1 Pet. 2.18]. In the authoritative canons, those people are damned with anathema who teach serfs to disobey their masters for the sake of entering religion, or to fly anywhere, much less to resist'" (Guibert of Nogent *Autobiographie* 3.10, ed., 360; trans., 183–84).

129. Galbert's citation of the apocryphal Daniel 13.5 here is thought-provoking. This book of Daniel recounts the story of Susanna, the virtuous wife of Joachim, who is accused of adultery by two senior judges, also referred to as "priests" *(presbyteri)* (verses 28, 34, 36, and so on), when she refuses to sleep with them. Galbert thus alludes to a biblical example of priests who, motivated by concupiscence, make a false accusation and bear false witness precisely here where he accuses the priests of Bruges of pandering to the citizens by anathematizing William in order to satisfy their bellies.

130. Compare [120], 60/61; trans., 310, where Galbert writes that the county had been "handed over to him [Thierry] but not in a proper way [*oblique tradito*]."

131. Galbert is explicit about this in the penultimate manuscript chapter (modern chapters [120], 15–[121] 43; trans., 308–12, "And it should be noted . . . whenever they wished") where he writes that "the town of Bruges stood in such great peril that the citizens believed there was no remedy possible except through God" *(ut cives nullo consilio sibi posse, nisi a solo Deo, mederi credidissent)* ([120], 15/17; trans., 308), and "therefore God righted such a great wrong, which no human power could or would correct [*nulla potestas humana corrigere aut potuit aut voluit*], in accordance with the line of strict examination" ([121], 28/30; trans., 311).

132. The modern chapter divisions at the end of the work make it difficult to perceive the flow of Galbert's thought at this point.

133. "Some argue that our people, after expelling Count William, substituted Count Thierry for him and that, after establishing the latter by means of silver and persuasion and in every possible way by use of influence and money everywhere in towns and all places in which they could find supporters, they set him to resisting William. For this reason, according to this argument, they can not be proved innocent of his death" ([120], 42/48; trans., 309–10; trans. mod.).

134. On this distinction, see Bonenfant, "La Dépendance du Château d'Alost."

135. The fact that William was a tyrant also excused to some degree those who compassed his death: no "blame," writes John of Salisbury a few decades later, is "attached to any of those by whose valor [in killing a tyrant] a penitent and humbled people was thus set free" *(Policraticus* 8.20; ed. Webb, 2:374; trans. Dickinson, 369; compare trans. Nederman, 207).

136. I think that Ross's translation misrepresents Galbert's thought in an important way in relation to this point. Discussing the motives of the combattants at Aalst, he writes: "Et ideo utrimque poterant rationabiliter et comes Willelmus pro causa ducis et pro propria injuria ibidem recte occubuisse, et comes Theodericus pro dote a duce expostulata juste et

pro comitatu oblique tradito ibidem restitisse et duci et Willelmo comiti" ([120], 57/61). Ross translates this: "And therefore on both sides they could argue rationally, on the one hand that Count William rightly succumbed there both in support of the duke and as a result of his own injurious acts, and on the other that Count Thierry fought there against the duke and the Count William for the sake of the dowry which was justly demanded from the duke, and for the sake of the countship which had been handed over to him but not in a proper way" (trans., 310). The translation suggests that Galbert has here decided that William is in the wrong (he "rightly succumbed there . . . as a result of his own injurious acts") and Thierry in the right, but Galbert is, I think, trying rather to show that they each had a weaker and a stronger reason to be fighting there.

William's weaker reason for being there was to support the duke; his stronger reason was to defend his countship. I would translate "propria injuria," that is, not as "his own injurious acts" but "his own injuries," the injuries done to him by Thierry in attempting to seize the countship, to which Galbert refers in the preceding sentence. These two reasons are implicitly contrasted by the chiasmatic structure of the two prepositional phrases beginning with "pro" which sets "ducis" ("the duke's") in opposition to "propria" ("his own").

Thierry's stronger reason is his attempt to reclaim the substantial part of Flanders which had formed the dowry of the Countess Clemence, widow of Count Robert II, when she married the duke of Louvain after her son's death in 1119; his weaker reason is his attempt to claim the countship which has been handed over to him; and again these two reasons are implicitly contrasted in the structure of the two prepositional phrases beginning with "pro" which sets "juste" ("justly") in opposition to "oblique" ("indirectly" or "improperly").

The balance between the two pretenders' motives is stressed and demonstrated by the four prepositional phrases beginning with "pro" and the chiasmatic structure of the whole sentence: William's weaker reason, followed by his stronger reason; Thierry's stronger reason, then his weaker one. The "recte" ("rightly") of the first clause is somewhat problematic, but I would suggest that it stands in counterpoint to the "juste" ("justly") of the second clause and that the two together are intended to communicate that both pretenders could be viewed as being in the right. One might thus translate "comes Willelmus pro causa ducis et pro propria injuria ibidem recte occubuisse" as "Count William succumbed there [while fighting] for the duke's cause and, rightly, in defense of his own interests." The sentence is carefully structured and aims precisely at demonstrating the equal justice of the pretenders' motives.

137. William's claim was "more just" not for any essential or hereditary reason but because he had been elected first and the inhabitants of Flanders had sworn oaths of loyalty to him.

138. "Before the election of that William, who is now dead, he had claimed that it [the county] belonged to him [Thierry] by letters sent to the barons of Flanders—although at that time they did not listen to him" ([121], 10/12; trans., 311). Galbert describes the receipt of one such letter from Thierry in Bruges, its contents, and the barons' decision to ignore it in [47], 23/29; trans., 187–88).

139. In the letter from Thierry which, according to Galbert, was received in Bruges on March 20, 1127, Thierry claimed that "the realm of Flanders pertains to my lot and power by right of kinship [*jure cognationis*]" ([47], 27/29; trans., 188; as we will see in the next chapter, Galbert may have added the passage describing the receipt of this letter in spring 1128); in his version of Gervaise's speech to Thierry on April 2, 1128, Galbert has the castellan declare that Thierry is "'the natural heir and rightful lord of the land'" *(heredem*

naturalem et dominum terrae justum) ([104], 14; trans., 281; trans. mod.); in their response to the king of France on April 10, Galbert has the citizens of Bruges state that Thierry is the "more rightful heir" *(justiorem . . . heredem)* ([106], 32); and he himself writes in this penultimate chapter that "the countship pertained by hereditary right [*jure hereditario*] to Count Thierry" ([121], 8; trans., 311). Thierry's claim was in fact slightly better since his grandfather, Robert I, had been count of Flanders whereas William had to go back to his and Thierry's great-grandfather, Baldwin VI, before he could number a count of Flanders among his ancestors. Count Baldwin IV of Hainault probably had a better claim than either of them, however, since he descended in a direct male line from Baldwin VI and they did not. In chapter 67, Galbert recognizes that "by right of kinship [*jure cognationis*] the realm of Flanders . . . more justly [*justius*] belonged to him [Baldwin IV of Hainault]" than it did to William, at least ([67], 15/16; trans., 231; trans. mod.).

140. In his version of their reply to Louis VI on April 10, Galbert has the citizens of Bruges say that King Louis VI "has perjured himself because he swore before the recognition of Count William that he neither wished to receive nor was entitled to receive any relief or payment [*nullam coemptionem vel pretium*] for the election of that count, but afterwards he openly received one thousand marks as payment and relief [*pro pretio et coemptione*]." They then go on to declare, in Galbert's rendition of their deliberations, that "when a count dies his successor shall give to the king, for the right to those lands which the former held in fief from the king, only a relief of arms [*armaturam*] for that same fief. The count of the land of Flanders owes nothing beyond this to the king of France, nor does the king have any right forcibly to impose a count on us for a relief or for a payment, or to prefer one candidate to another [*neque rex habet rationem aliquam ut potestative seu per coemptionem seu per pretium nobis superponat consulem, aut aliquem praeferat*]" ([106], 15/19, 42/47; trans., 284, 285; trans. mod.). Galbert echoes this declaration in the penultimate chapter where he writes that the county was "unjustly sold by the king of France" *(injuste a rege Franciae vendita)* and William, "in return for a relief, forcibily made count through the king's power" *(per coemptionem ex regis potestate potestative comes effectus)* ([120], 14, 18; trans., 311; trans. mod.).

141. "Erwachen des Staatsgefühls," 78. It is possible that Galbert's evaluation of the justice of the two pretenders' claims to the county is here again influenced by the terms of the Concordat of Worms. If the election of Thierry and the effort to impose him as count had been marred by "violence"—one of the two conditions that, according to the Concordat, invalidated an episcopal election—William's election had been marred by the other one, "simony" (see above, nn. 83 and 123). At first, then, as Galbert writes, it appears that since "neither of them received the countship in the correct way [*bene*], by right [*jure*] both of them should have been removed."

When various Saxon princes tried to barter their support for the election of Rudolf of Rheinfelden in return for promises of specific favors in 1077, one of the papal legates declared that the imposition of specific conditions in exchange for their support was tantamount to simony: "He said that if they continued along that road and he was elected by means of individual promises, that election would not appear valid [*sincera*] but polluted with the poison of the simoniacal heresy" (Bruno of Magdeburg, *Saxonicum bellum* 91, 332–34). Elected as bishop of Laon in 1106 "in a vain hope of profit," according to Guibert of Nogent, Gaudry's flawed election, like William's, worked "to the ruin of the city and the detriment of the whole province" *(Autobiographie* 3.4; ed., 280–84; trans., 151–53).

142. The injustice done to Thierry, when his claim to the county was ignored, preceded, was older, than the injustice done to William, when Thierry was set up in his place by some of the citizens of Flanders. When God removed William and elevated Thierry to the

countship, therefore, he was correcting the older of the two injustices, was restoring the older justice that had been the first one to be upset. Both this passage and the one cited above, in which Galbert writes that William's right to rule was "more just" because he had been elected before Thierry, demonstrate, once again, the importance of time for Galbert.

143. "To the contemporary mind," writes Van Caenegem, ". . . [William's] fate amounted to some sort of an ordeal, a judgement of God, as battles were often interpreted as being won or lost *justo judicio Dei*" ("Law and Power," 156).

144. See above, p. 177, and [116], 52/64; trans., 303–4.

145. Galbert had already noted the Flemish failure to provide William with good counsel and advice in an addendum to the entry for April 30 (see above, p. 175, and [108], 48/57; trans., 289). Galbert's notion that "the barons and officials and counselors of the land" are supposed to "guide [the count] . . . in the right path . . . [and] teach him the honorable customs of the counts his predecessors" anticipates John of Salisbury's concept of the senate, which forms the "heart" of the body politic and "from which proceeds the beginning of good and bad works" *(Policraticus* 5.2, ed. Webb, 1:283; trans. Nederman, 67; compare trans. Dickinson, 65; compare *Policraticus* 5.9, ed. Webb, 1:318–22; trans. Nederman, 81–85; trans. Dickinson, 108–13; and Nederman, "A Duty to Kill," 370–75). In the last quarter of the thirteenth century, Raymond Lulle wrote similarly that "just as bad members make a body sick, so do bad counselors make a prince bad and worse. And just as bad subjects create a bad lord, so do good subjects create a good one" *(Doctrine d'enfant,* 174).

146. "And it should be noted that when the town of Bruges stood in such great peril that the citizens believed there was no remedy possible except through God's aid and therefore appeased God by penitence of heart, He came to their rescue with his customary dispensation. For He slew Count William by the sword of his justice . . ." ([120], 15/19; trans., 308–9). This, too, is in keeping with the theocratic tyrannology of the time, "for penitence," wrote John of Salisbury, "annihilates, drives out and kills those tyrants whom sins obtain, introduce and encourage" *(Policraticus* 8.20; ed. Webb, 2:374; trans. Nederman, 207; compare trans. Dickinson, 368).

147. Perhaps on June 22, when, after the defeat at Axpoel, the citizens of Bruges "cut off their hair and cast off their superfluous garments" and their priests "preached penance, and . . . called for a universal fast" ([114], 68/75; trans., 299).

148. Galbert's account of the tribulations of the burghers of Bruges seems influenced by the biblical portrayal of those of "the children of Israel," who, writes John of Salisbury, "were time without number in bondage to tyrants. . . . And when the allotted time of their punishment was fulfilled, they were allowed to cast off the yoke from their necks by the slaughter of their tyrants" *(Policraticus* 8.20; ed. Webb, 2:374; trans. Dickinson, 368–69; compare trans. Nederman, 207; compare Rouse and Rouse "John of Salisbury," 698, and Nederman, "A Duty to Kill," 378; on the use of the Israelites as a model for the Carolingians, see Riché, "Les Clercs carolingiens au service du pouvoir," in *Education et culture,* V, 14).

This analogy between the inhabitants of a city and the wayward Israelites is also invoked by Sigebert of Gembloux in connection with Robert II's projected attack on Liège—Sigebert notes that "whenever the sons of Israel [compared here, evidently, to the Liégois] sinned, God stirred up enemies who wore the sinners down" *(Leodicensium epistola* 3, 2:453)—and seems likewise to have influenced Guibert of Nogent's representation of the people of Laon, whose troubles, he writes, go back to "the errors of the bishops of Laon. . . . Nevertheless, in spite of . . . [these errors], worldly prosperity attended the city and the city's bishop, God putting off the day of punishment," until the advent of Bishop Gaudry when "seeing that masters and subjects were by act and will partners in wickedness, God could no longer restrain his judgement and at last permitted the malice that had been conceived to break out into open rage" *(Autobiographie* 3.1, 7; ed., 268–70, 328; trans., 145, 146, 171).

Galbert's Brugocentrism comes to the fore in these final entries where he tends to confound Bruges with Flanders and to view events affecting the entire county as responses to the actions and attitudes of the burghers of Bruges.

NOTES TO CHAPTER 7

1. Orosius, *Histoires* 6.1.1, 7.41.10, ed., 2:162, 3:123; trans Raymond, 262, 393; compare trans. Deferrari, 228, 359.

2. *Ecclesiastical History* 6.1, 3:215.

3. These passages are [35], 33/45; trans., 164, "And it should be known . . . to commit to writing" (on this passage, see also above, pp. 20–21, 29–30, 30–31); [69], 80/[72], 1; trans., 237–40, "In connection with this deed . . . at Oudenaarde because" (on this passage, see above, pp. 71–72); [75], 1/31; trans., 243–44, "It should be noted here . . . distorted by hunger"; [78], 19/23; trans., 247–48, "And it should be recorded . . . in the same church"; [90], 5/11; trans., 263, "It should be noted . . . in any way avenge him."

4. The use of *utilem vobis* (useful to you) here in place of the more common and expected *utilem communi* (useful to everyone) or *utilem patriae* (useful to the fatherland) seems intended to suggest a distinctly aristocratic vision of the count's role and the constituents to whom he is accountable.

5. The statement that "the advantage of the fatherland"—rather than that of just the barons—was considered in the election of the new count suggests a more expansive, more democratic political vision, but it is not clear to whom it should be attributed. This passage seems to be in Galbert's voice, but it may incorporate terms from the royal letter communicating the results of the election in Arras or from Walter the Butler's prologue to its reading or to his summarization of it. It is also possible that the sentence is ironic, or cynical, contrasting the king's solicitation of the barons' consent (Come to me and we will choose someone who will look to your advantage) with the king's or the barons' solicitation of the citizens' consent (We have chosen someone who will look to the entire country's advantage).

6. Galbert's description of the dramatic arrival of the second letter on the heels of the first—"and when [the king's] letter had been read in the presence of all, behold! [*ecce!*], before they had replied to it saying whether they were coming or not, another messenger arrived suddenly from a kinsman of Count Charles . . ." ([47], 23/25; trans., 187–88; trans. mod.)—which suggests that he, too, finds the coincidence astonishing, can also be read as an attempt to render a fabrication, or at least an elaboration of the truth, credible.

7. As we have seen (Chapter 3, p. 58), Galbert likewise describes Charles as having been "useful for [both] the rich and poor of the realm" *(divitibus et pauperibus in regno utilem)* ([19], 33/34; trans., 131; trans. mod.).

8. Kern suggested that Folpert's oath repeats almost exactly the terms of the oath sworn by the counts of Flanders upon their accession to the countship (their *Regierungsgelübde) (Gottesgnadentum,* 308). This seems improbable—why would Galbert relate the count's oath indirectly through Folpert's rather than directly in his accounts of the recognition of William and Thierry in Bruges and their confirmation of the citizens' privileges? (see chapters 55 and 99–103)—but it does show that Kern, too, sensed that the oath's terms were unlikely to have occurred spontaneously to Folpert.

9. See Chapter 3, pp. 54–55.

10. See Chapter 3, p. 54.

11. Explaining the etymology of the word *bishop,* Augustine concludes: "Hence a 'bishop' who has set his heart on a position of eminence rather than an opportunity for service [*qui praeesse dilexerit, non prodesse*] should realize that he is no bishop" *(De civitate Dei* 19.19, ed., 2:687; trans., 880; compare *Contra Faustum* 22.56, 652; trans., 294). Compare Saint Benedict: "Once he has been constituted, let the Abbot . . . know that his duty is rather to profit his brethren than to preside over them [*sibi oportere prodesse magis quam praeesse*]" *(Regula monachorum* 64.8, ed. Jean Neufville, French trans. Adalbert de Vogüé, *La Règle de Saint Benoît,* 7 vols. [Paris, 1971–1977], 2:650; trans. Leonard Doyle, *St. Benedict's Rule for Monasteries* [Collegeville, Minn., 1948], 90); Gregory I: "all who are superiors . . . should find their joy not in ruling over men, but in helping them [*nec praeesse se hominibus gaudeant, sed prodesse*]" *(Regula pastoralis* 2.6, intro. Bruno Judic, ed. Floribert Rommel, French trans. Charles Morel, *Règle Pastorale,* 2 vols. [Paris, 1992], 1:204; trans. Henry Davis, *Pastoral Care* [Westminster, Md., 1950], 60); and R. A. Markus, "The Latin Fathers," in Burns, ed., *Medieval Political Thought,* 120. All three, it is worth noting, are speaking of ecclesiastical "rulers"—Augustine and Gregory of a bishop, Benedict of an abbot. The application of these terms here to secular rulers is another example of—Galbert's?—tendency to think of secular offices in terms of religious ones. On the role of this distinction between *praeesse* and *prodesse* in tenth- and eleventh-century notions of episcopal (and, more generally, adminstrative) functions in the Empire, see Jaeger, *The Envy of Angels,* 37–39, 133–34, 205–11.

12. Ganshof ("Les Origines du concept," 140–44) and Coué ("Der Mord," 116–17) have drawn particular attention to the importance of this theme in these chapters. On the theme in general, which was particularly dear to Carolingian authors, see Carlyle and Carlyle, *History,* 3:148–50, 153–60; Kern, *Gottesgnadentum,* 129–31, 269–76; Ullmann, *Principles of Government and Politics,* 215; Michaud-Quantin, *Universitas,* 135–41, 147–66, 269–76; Hannig, *Consensus fidelium;* Luscombe, "Introduction," 162–64; Nelson, "Kingship and Empire," 226–29, 242, 249; and Canning, *History,* 59–64.

13. The theme of consensus is not limited to expressions of bourgeois solidarity. One also finds examples of it in the oath sworn by the barons in connection with the siege ([31], 7/18; trans., 158–59), in their oath not to accept William of Ypres as count ([34], 18/20; trans., 162), in their common election of William Clito ([47], 19/21, [52], 24/35; trans., 187, 196–97), and in the oath sworn on May 22 by the count, Gervaise, Walter of Vladslo, and the knights of Flanders to maintain peace in Flanders ([85], 31/34; trans., 258).

Galbert's account of the events of Saturday, April 2, is divided between two chapters ([53], 10/20; [54], 6/21; trans., 198–99, 199–200) and, uncharacteristically, somewhat hard to follow, perhaps because these events occurred outside of Bruges and he had to depend on various reports of what had gone on. Between Wednesday, March 30, and Saturday, April 2, the king and the new count traveled from Arras to Lille, where "homages were done to the count," and then on "to the village of Deinze on the road [they were] . . . to take to Ghent." When they reached Deinze (on Friday, April 1, or Saturday, April 2?), they "waited [there] for the men of Ghent who were to accept the new count according to his [the king's] order and the election of the barons of the land." On Saturday, April 2, while the king and count were, evidently, waiting at Deinze (where, on that day, they installed Gervaise as castellan of Bruges), their representatives met with those of the men of the castellanies of Bruges and Ghent at Raverschoot and reached "an agreement . . . concerning the acceptance of the newly elected count." That same day, the representatives of Ghent "who had returned [to Ghent] from the conference elected William as their count and count of the fatherland, doing homage and pledging faith and loyalty to the count," as did certain of the representatives of Bruges, who, after the conference was over, had perhaps returned to Bruges, or had perhaps accompanied the representatives of Ghent when they returned to that city in order to stand shoulder to shoulder with them when they welcomed the king and the new count. Once the agreement had been reached and the new count had been elected by the representatives of Ghent (and at least some of those of Bruges), Louis and William proceeded to Ghent (arriving late on Saturday, April 2, or on Easter Sunday, April 3). The king and new count then went on to Bruges on Tuesday, April 5, arriving "at twilight."

14. Sproemberg, "Eine rheinische Königskandidatur," 62–63; A. Murray, "Baldwin II and His Nobles: Baronial Factionalism and Dissent in the Kingdom of Jerusalem, 1118–1134," *Nottingham Medieval Studies* 38 (1994): 71, 72–73.

15. Galbert's description of the arrival of Gertrude, widowed countess of Holland and half-sister of Thierry of Alsace, and her young son, Thierry IV of Holland, at the siege of the castle of Bruges on March 16, 1127—two weeks before Louis's and Thierry's letters arrived—also merits attention in this context, especially since Ross's translation has, I think, obscured its significance somewhat.

According to Galbert, the countess "sperabat enim omnes obsidionis principes electuros filium ejus in comitem eo quod illud ei cives nostri et plures principium suggessissent. Habebat quippe magnas gratias eis comitissa et laborabat omnium procerum animos convertere in amicitiam sui dando et promittendo multa" ([34], 4/8]). Ross translates this passage: "Now she was hoping that all the barons of the siege would elect her son as count, because our citizens and many of the barons had suggested it to him. The countess expressed her thanks for this, and she tried hard to secure the friendship of all the barons, bestowing many gifts and making many promises" (161–62). The "ei" to whom the citizens of Bruges and certain of the magnates had suggested this manoeuvre ought perhaps to be translated "to her," that is, to the countess, rather than "to him," that is, to her son, while the objects of the countess' gratitude ("eis"), who are not mentioned in the translation, seem to include both the citizens and the magnates who suggested she come to Bruges. The "omnes proceres" whose support she tried to secure might likewise be understood to include the leading citizens as well as the magnates. The fifteenth- century French translation captures these nuances better: the countess arrived "esperants que les princes alors presents ou siege esliroient son filz en la contee, comme plusieurs bourgois et princes luy avoient conseillié; et veritablement trouvoit grandes graces vers eulx et labourait par dons et promesses d'acquerre leur benevolence et bon vouloir" (Rider, ed., [34], p. 78). One might thus suggest that the English translation should read: "Now she was hoping that all the barons of the siege would elect her son as count, because our citizens and many of the barons had suggested it to her. The countess was very grateful to them for this, and she tried hard to secure the friendship of all the important men, bestowing many gifts and making many promises."

The prime mover behind this effort to elect Thierry of Holland thus seems to have been a coalition of the citizens of Bruges and some of the nobles of Flanders, just as the coalition of the citizens of Ghent, Ivan of Aalst, and Daniel of Dendermonde was the principal promoter of Thierry of Alsace's candidacy the following spring. Galbert does seem to suggest that her efforts to secure support for her son were directed mainly at the princes of the siege who were not already converted to his cause, but this could be either because she already knew she could count on the burghers' support or because she believed that the as yet unconverted nobles would play the decisive role in the election. It is clear, in any case, that the citizens of Bruges played an important role in the effort to have Thierry of Holland elected as count, and Galbert's description of their participation in this initiative further emphasizes the extremism of the king's notion that a new count should be elected by an exclusively noble body assembled under his watchful eye.

16. It is also possible, of course, that Galbert—or even Folpert—had the king's and Thierry's letters in mind when the oath was sworn or written down and borrowed their terms. But the antithetic relation between the king's letter and the other two discourses and the way in which together they foreshadow the ultimate failure of the king's choice for count, William, and the ultimate success of the burgher's choice, Thierry, seem too good to be true—unless of course they are manifestations of God's omnipotent prescience.

17. See [121], 9/14; trans., 311, "and if he seems to have seized it . . . by the king of France."

18. See Chapter 3, n. 84, and Chapter 4, n. 5.

19. A model for the election of a prince similar to that found in chapters 4–5, Thierry's letter, and Folpert's oath is likewise to be found in the *Gesta Stephani*'s description, written c. 1148, of the election of Stephen by the citizens of London in 1135. In this case, "the elders and those most shrewd in counsel summoned an assembly, and taking prudent forethought together for the utility of the state of the kingdom [*deque regni statu . . . utilia in commune prouidentes* (compare Thierry's promise to be *utilitatis communis . . . provisor)*], . . . they agreed unanimously [*unanimiter*] to choose a king. . . . So, when these arguments [in Stephen's favor] had been heard and favourably received by all without any open objection, they made a common [*in commune*] decree admitting him to the sovereignty and appointed him king with universal approval" *(Gesta Stephani* 2, 6–7; trans. mod.). A bit later, the author of the *Gesta* reports a speech by William, archbishop of Canterbury, in which he declares: "'just as a king is chosen to rule all, and, once chosen, to lay the commands of his sovereign power on all, assuredly in like manner it is fitting that all should meet together [*omnes pariter conuolent*] to ratify his accession and all should consider in agreement what is to be enacted and what rejected'" *(Gesta Stephani* 4, 10–11).

20. Chapter 6, pp. 146–47.

21. Van Caenegem likewises senses Galbert's irony in this passage ("Misdaad," 331, n. 31).

22. Dhondt likewise suggests that "one fine day . . . [Galbert tried] to go it alone. Too bad for his fellow burghers! These men do not tolerate such betrayal, of course, and our Galbert must have passed a few bad days" ("Les 'Solidarités,'" 536; trans., 273).

23. [118], 17/38; trans., 305–6, "But it proved to be a good thing . . . nor the other justly set up." See above, pp. 177–78. The solidarity between the citizens of Bruges and their priests, who "had taken their stand in the fight with the people and the crowd," is a reminder and an illustration of the close identification between a community and its parishes especially "during the exuberant decades on either side of 1100" (Moore, "Heresy," 38), as well as of the important ecclesiastical role and presence in the formation of urban communes in northern France and the southern Low Countries (see Vermeesch, *Essai,* 25–77, 176). Galbert's harsh words about these "fawning priests" who profited from popular superstition and the burghers' need for scapegoats is echoed by William of Newburgh who recorded the case of a "Christian looter of Jewish houses (at Stanford in 1190), who was killed in a squabble over the plunder and then revered as a local saint. . . . the cult began with the dreams of some poor, old person (not the sort of witness William trusts) and the 'illusory appearance of false signs'; he uses the word *praestigiis,* which suggests tricks as well as illusions. But if the cult arose through suggestible ignorance, it was nurtured by venal fraud: 'It was welcomed by certain clerks who saw that there was money to be gotten out of the superstition'" (Partner, *Serious Entertainments,* 192–93).

24. [116], 44, 45, 48, 61; trans., 303–4; [118], 15/17; trans., 305.

25. Dhondt finds the last short passage cited above ([118], 13/17; trans., 305) "profoundly revealing of Galbert's own agitation, torn between his most profound convictions

and driven by his individualism from the human community in which he was deeply rooted but whose political loyalties he no longer shares and whose belief in the possiblity of assuring victory through supernatural means he cannot accept" ("Une Mentalité," 107).

26. As we have seen (Chapter 6, n. 148), Galbert's description of the trials of the burghers of Bruges in the late spring and summer of 1128 seems influenced by the biblical portrayal of those of the recalcitrant "children of Israel," and his reference to the story of Susanna and the elders, in which the prophet Daniel exposes the false accusation and testimony of the "senior judges" or "priests" of Babylon, in chapter [118], 41/42 (trans., 306) likewise suggests that he may be thinking of himself as a prophet faced with a wayward people and their corrupt priests.

27. *Policraticus* 8.17, ed. Webb, 2:348–49; trans. Nederman, 193–94; compare trans. Dickinson, 339. Demyttenaere suggests that since the passage from Daniel 13.5 that Galbert cites in chapter [118], 41/42 (trans., 306) contains a reference to the iniquity of Babylon (although Galbert omits the reference to Babylon in his citation), he may be thinking of Bruges as a "new Babylon" at this point (in Galbert, *De moord* [1999], 264, n. 238).

28. An account of William's death ([119], 1/[120], 4; trans., 307–8, "On July 27 . . . or some other means beforehand"), a report of Thierry's capture of Ypres and the defensive preparations of William's supporters in the region of Bruges ([120], 5/14; trans., 308, "Therefore Count Thierry . . . were made ready"), the long reflection on the divine intentions behind William's death ([120], 15/[121], 43; trans., 308–12, "And it should be noted . . . whenever they wished"), and a brief conclusion relating Thierry's taking control of the county and his recognition by the kings of France and England ([122]; trans. 312).

29. Where Galbert recounts their repentance and absolves them from any responsibility for William's death (see [120], 15/48; trans., 308–10, "And it should be noted . . . be proved innocent of his death").

30. Henschen and Van Papenbroeck, "De B. Carolo bono," 153.

31. Richard of Devizes's *Cronicon* survives in two manuscript copies, the "author's draft" (probably) and a roughly contemporary "fair copy" of this draft made "when Richard himself was not present to be consulted, either because the copy was made at a different place . . . or because it was made . . . after Richard's death." The scribe of this copy reproduced the marginalia of Richard's draft as marginalia (see the discussion by Appleby in Richard of Devizes, *Cronicon,* xxi–xxiii).

Although the De Baenst register testifies to the existence of the *De multro* at the end of the fifteenth century, the incomplete sixteenth-century manuscript of the French translation and the mutilated late-sixteenth or early seventeenth-century Arras manuscript of the Latin text are the earliest surviving witnesses that give us more than a few passages from the text and allow us to form some idea of its structure. Were it not for Henschen and Van Papenbroeck's statement that they consulted a manuscript "from Galbert's time or not long afterwards," therefore, one might be tempted to suggest that the fair copy of Galbert's text that is at the origin of all subsequent versions may not have been made until the sixteenth century, perhaps by Jacob de Meyer. Since I have indulged this first fancy, and know that others have shared my suspicions, I will likewise confess here that I have, in the occasional dark hour, wondered if the *De multro* might not in fact be a sixteenth-century hoax. I do not, ultimately, think it is—and will look very silly indeed if it is one day proved to be one—but the fact that I, and others who know the text at least as well as I, have had these fleeting doubts says something about its originality and literary qualities. It is so surprising and so well done that one has to wonder at one time or another if it is not too good to be true.

32. "The New Cornificius," 50, 52, 21.

NOTES TO APPENDIX 5

1. "The sun . . . abandoned those parts of the world which it had been illuminating with its rays, . . . and gave the sons of darkness [*filiis tenebrarum*] the opportunity for which they longed to carry out dark deeds [*opera tenebrarum*]. He who does evil indeed hates the light" ([21], 547, 33/37); "And these things were decided at night as befitting deeds not of light but of darkness [*non lucis sed tenebrarum opera*]" ([24], 548, 30).

2. "As soon as they had entered, they put out the fire that was burning in the house so that those who had been awakened in the house should not find out from the light of the fire who they were and what sort of business they were carrying on at that time of night, contrary to custom. Then, safe in darkness [*securi igitur in tenebris*], they took counsel about the act of treason to be done as soon as dawn came . . ." ([11], 43/54; trans., 110–11).

3. "After this they placed the bodies of both men on the wheel of a cart, fastened to a high tree [*rotae plaustri superposita in malo altissimo fixae*], and exposed them to the gaze of all the passers-by; bending their arms around each other's necks as if in a mutual embrace [*brachiaque mutuis quasi amplexibus ad colla flectentes*], they made those dead men look as if they were plotting and conspiring for the death of their lord, the most glorious and pious count Charles, even after they had been dead for three days" ([58], 34/39; trans., 213).

4. "So they set up a tall pole and fixed a cartwheel to it [*arborem excelsam erexerunt et rota plaustri desuper imposita*] and set the two of them on it, sewed up in cowhides so that they would last longer, and joined together as if united in a mutual embrace [*eos invicem coniunctos, et quasi mutuo complexu colligatos*]" ([39], 555, 18/21).

5. *Malo altissimo* instead of *arborem excelsam*; *superposita* instead of *desuper imposita*; *brachiaque mutuis quasi amplexibus ad colla flectentes* instead of *eos invicem coniunctos, et quasi mutuo complexu colligatos.*

6. See *De multro* [57], 17/70; trans., 209–11; *Vita Karoli,* [38], 554, 35–49. The two passages are discussed in Chapter 4, pp. 108–11.

7. See above, pp. 117–19. The theme is found in [26], 549, 33/35 in the *Vita* and in [6], 13/19; trans., 94; [26], 4/10; trans., 148; and [38], 44/49; trans., 171 in the *De multro.*

8. In chapter 14, describing the conspiracy and the hard-heartedness of the conspirators, he writes: "they often asked themselves, if they killed the count, who would avenge him [*si comitem interficerent, quis eum vindicaret*]? But they did not know what they were saying, for 'who,' an infinite word, meant an infinite number of persons, who cannot be reckoned in a definite figure; the fact is that the king of France with a numerous army and also the barons of our land with an infinite multitude came to avenge the death of the most pious count!" ([14], 5/11; trans., 117). He returns to this theme in chapter 37 when he describes the conspirators' efforts to fortify the burg: "they labored day and night to make themselves safer inside because they had now learned that they would have to fight against the whole world. Then finally they could remember their own saying, 'If we kill Charles, who will come to avenge him [*si interfecerimus Karolum, quis vindicaturus veniet illum*]?' But, in fact, those coming to avenge him were infinite and the number of men was unknown, except to God; and therefore the word 'who,' interrogative and infinite in their saying, achieved its just and full meaning" ([37], 26/33; trans., 168).

9. *De multro,* [69], 80/[70], 12; trans., 237; [70], 27/30; trans., 238. These passages are discussed in Chapter 3, pp. 71–72.

10. Galbert appears in fact to have conflated several passages: Ex. 20.5 and 34.7, Num. 14.18, and Deut. 5.9.

11. This was not, of course, an uncommon theme. Guibert of Nogent explains Bishop Gaudry's murder as a consequence of his and his predecessors' cumulative "errors" (see *Auto-*

biographie 3.1, 7; ed., 268–70, 328; trans., 145–46, 171), and the author of the *Gesta Stephani* suggests that God punished Earl Robert of Gloucester's sins in his son (*Gesta Stephani* 74, 148).

12. The only major points completely omitted by Galbert are the fates of Ingran of Esen and William of Wervik, which Walter relates in the last two chapters of the *Vita Karoli* (51 and 52). His exposition of Borsiard's death ([80], 1/4; trans., 249) is also significantly shorter and less developed than Walter's ([40]/[42], 555, 31/556, 47). It is possible that Galbert read an earlier version of the *Vita* than the one we now possess and that these chapters were added to this earlier version.

Bibliography

PRIMARY SOURCES

Abelard, Peter. *Commentaria in Epistolam Pauli ad Romanos.* In Abelard, *Opera theologica,* 1:41–340.

———. *Opera theologica.* Edited by E. M. Buytaert and C. J. Mews. 3 vols. Corpus Christianorum, Continuatio medievalis 11–13. Turnhout, 1969–1987.

———. *Theologia Christiana.* In Abelard, *Opera theologica,* 2:71–372.

Adam of Eynsham. *The Life of St Hugh of Lincoln / Magna Vita Sancti Hugonis.* Edited by Decima L. Douie and Hugh Farmer. 2 vols. London, 1961–1962.

Aelred of Rievaulx. *La vie de recluse. La prière pastorale.* Edited and French translation by Charles Dumont. Sources chrétiennes 76. Paris, 1961.

———. *The Mirror of Charity* (abridged translation of *Speculum charitatis*). Translated by Geoffrey Webb and Adrian Walker. London, 1962.

———. *Speculum charitatis. Patrologia latina* 195, 501–620.

Alberic of Monte Cassino. *De dictamine.* In *Briefsteller und Formelbücher des elften bis vierzehnten Jahrhunderts,* ed. Ludwig Rockinger, 2 vols., Quellen und Erörterungen zur bayerischen und deutschen Geschichte 9, 1–2 (1863–1864; reprint, New York, 1961), 1:29–46.

Augustine of Hippo (Saint). *Concerning the City of God against the Pagans.* Translated by Henry Bettenson. Harmondsworth, U.K., 1972.

———. *Contra Faustum.* Edited by J. Zycha. In *Corpus scriptorum ecclesiasticorum latinorum* 25 (Vienna, 1891), 251–797.

———. *De civitate Dei.* Edited by B. Dombart and A. Kalb. 2 vols. Corpus Christianorum, Series latina 47–48. Turnhout, 1955.

———. *De Doctrina Christiana.* Edited and translated by R. P. H. Green. Oxford, U.K., 1995.

———. *Reply to Faustus the Manichaean.* Translated by Richard Stothert. In *A Select Library of Nicene and Poet-Nicene Fathers of the Christian Church,* ed. Philip Schaff, vol. 4: *St. Augustin: The Writings against the Manichaeans and against the Donatists* (1887; reprint, Grand Rapids, Mich., 1956), 151–345.

Bede the Venerable (Saint). *Vita Sancti Cuthberti.* In *Two "Lives" of Saint Cuthbert,* ed. and trans. Bertram Colgrave (Cambridge, U.K.,1940), 142–307.

Benedict of Nursia (Saint). *Regula monachorum / La règle de Saint Benoît.* Edited by Jean Neufville. French translation by Adalbert de Vogüé. 7 vols. Paris, 1971–1977.

———. *St. Benedict's Rule for Monasteries.* Translated by Leonard Doyle. Collegeville, Minn., 1948.

Bruno of Magdeburg. *Saxonicum bellum.* Edited by Hans-Eberhard Lohman. In Schmale, ed., *Quellen,* 192–405.

Carmen de bello Saxonico. Edited by O. Holder-Egger. In Schmale, ed., *Quellen,* 144–89.

Chronicon Hanoniense quod dicitur Balduini Avennensis. Edited by J. Heller. *Monumenta Germaniae Historica, Scriptores* 25 (Hannover, 1880), 419–67.

Chronicon Vormeselense. Edited by F. Van de Putte and Ch. Carton. Recueil de chroniques, chartes et autres documents concernant l'histoire et les antiquités de la Flandre Occidentale publié par la Société d'Emulation de Bruges, 1ère série: Chroniques des monastères de Flandre. Bruges, 1847.

Cicero. *De re publica / De legibus.* Edited and translated by Clinton Walker Keyes. Loeb Classical Library. Cambridge, Mass., 1970.

———. *La république.* Edited and French translation by Esther Bréguet. 2 vols. Paris, 1980.

Concordat of Worms. In *Monumenta Germaniae Historica, Constitutiones et acta publica imperatorum et regum* 1, ed. L. Weiland (Hannover, 1893), 159–61.

De Baenst, Roland or Antoine. Résumé of portions of the *De multro,* Ms. 442, 37r–37v. Stedelijke Openbare Bibliotheek, Bruges. Edited by Jeff Rider. In Galbert of Bruges, *De multro,* 173–175.

De Hemptinne, Thérèse, and Adriaan Verhulst. *De oorkonden der graven van Vlaanderen (Juli 1128–September 1191), II. Uitgave, v. 1: Regering van Diederik van de Elzas (Juli 1128–17 Januari 1168).* Académie Royale de Belgique, Commission royale d'histoire, Recueil des actes des princes belges / Koninklijke Academie van België, Koninklijke Commissie voor Geschiedenis, Verzameling van de Akten der Belgische Vorsten 6. Brussels, 1988.

De Marneffe, Edgar. *Cartulaire de l'Abbaye d'Afflighem et des monastères qui en dépendaient.* Analectes pour servir à l'histoire ecclésiastique de la Belgique, 2e section, Série des cartulaires et des documents étendues. Fasc. 1–5. Leuven, 1894–1901.

Eadmer. *The Life of Saint Anselm.* Edited and translated by R. W. Southern. Corrected edition. Oxford, U.K., 1972.

Eneas. Roman du XIIe siècle. Edited by J.-J. Salverda de Grave. 2 vols. Paris, 1925, 1931.

Espinas, Georges. "Le privilège de Saint-Omer de 1127." *Revue du Nord* (1947): 43–48.

Galbert of Bruges. "Alia vita [B. Caroli boni comitis Flandriae], auctore Galberto notario." Edited by Godefroid Henschen and Daniel Van Papenbroeck. In *Acta Sanctorum,* March, 1 (Antwerp, 1668), 179–219.

———. *De Moord op Karel de Goede.* Introduction by general editor R. C. Van Caenegem. Translated into Dutch by Albert Demyttenaere. Antwerp, 1978.

———. *De Moord op Karel de Goede.* Translated into Dutch by Albert Demyttenaere. Leuven, 1999.

———. *De multro, traditione, et occisione gloriosi Karoli comitis Flandriarum.* Edited by Jeff Rider. Corpus Christianorum, Continuatio medievalis 131. Turnhout, 1994.

———. "Ex alia ejusdem B. Caroli Vita auctore Galberto Brugensi notario coaevo." *Recueil des historiens des Gaules et de la France* 13. 1786; new ed., Paris, 1869. 347–92.

———. *Histoire du meurtre de Charles le Bon, comte de Flandre (1127–28).* Edited by Henri Pirenne. Collection de textes pour servir à l'étude et l'enseignement de l'histoire 10. Paris, 1891.

———. *Histoire du règne de Charles le Bon, précédée d'un résumé de l'histoire des Flandres.* Translated by Joseph-Octave Delepierre and Jean Perneel. Brussels, 1830.

———. "Historia vitae & passionis S. Caroli Com. Flandr. Auctore Galberto notario." Edited by Jacob Langebek. *Scriptores rerum Danicorum medii aevi* 4. 1776; reprint, Nendeln, 1969. 110–92.

———. *La légende du bienheureux Charles le Bon, comte de Flandre: Récit du XIIe siècle.* Bibliothèque des chemins de fer, 2 sér.: Histoire et Voyages. Paris, 1853.

———. *Le meurtre de Charles le Bon.* Introduction by general editor R. C. Van Caenegem. French translation by J. Gengoux. Antwerp, 1978.

———. *The Murder of Charles the Good, Count of Flanders.* Translated by James Bruce Ross. Records of Civilization, Sources and Studies 61. 1959; rev. ed., 1967; reprint, Medieval Academy Reprints for Teaching 12, Toronto, 1982.

———. "Passio Karoli comitis, auctore Galberto." Edited by R. Köpke. In *Monumenta Germaniae Historica, Scriptores* 12 (Hannover, 1856), 561–619.

———. "Vie de Charles le Bon, comte de Flandre." French translation by François P. G.

Guizot. In *Collection des mémoires relatifs à l'histoire de France depuis la fondation de la monarchie française jusqu'au XIIIe siècle* 8 (Paris, 1825), 237–433.

———. "Vita altera [B. Caroli boni comitis Flandriae], auctore Galberto notario." *Patrologia latina* 166, 943–1046.

Geoffrey of Monmouth. *Historia regum Britanniae.* Edited by Acton Griscom. London, 1929.

———. *The History of the Kings of Britain.* Translated by Lewis Thorpe. Harmondsworth, U.K., 1966.

Gerald of Wales (Giraldus Cambrensis). *Descriptio Kambriae.* Edited by James F. Dimock. In Gerald of Wales, *Opera,* ed. J. S. Brewer et al., vol. 6 (London, 1868), 155–227.

———. *Itinerarium Cambriae.* Edited by James F. Dimock. In Gerald of Wales, *Opera,* ed. J. S. Brewer et al., vol. 6 (London, 1868), 3–152.

———. *"The Journey through Wales" and "The Description of Wales."* Translated by Lewis Thorpe. Harmondsworth, U.K., 1978.

Gesta Stephani. Edited and translated by K. R. Potter. Oxford Medieval Texts. Oxford, U.K., 1976.

Gilbert Foliot. *The Letters and Charters of Gilbert Foliot.* Edited by Z. N. Brooke, Adrian Morey, and C. N. L. Brooke. Cambridge, U.K., 1967.

Gislebert of Mons. *Chronicon Hanoniense.* Edited by Wilhelm Arndt. Scriptores rerum Germanicarum in usum scholarum. Hannover, 1869.

Gregory I (Pope). *Pastoral Care.* Translated by Henry Davis. Westminster, Md., 1950.

———. *Regula pastoralis / Règle pastorale.* Introduction by Bruno Judic. Edited by Floribert Rommel. French translation by Charles Morel. 2 vols. Paris, 1992.

Gregory of Tours. *The History of the Franks.* Translated by Lewis Thorpe. Harmondsworth, U.K., 1974.

———. *Libri historiarum x.* Editionem alteram by Bruno Krusch and Wilhelm Levison. *Monumenta Germaniae Historica, Scriptores rerum Merovingicarum* 1.1 (Hannover, 1951).

Guibert of Nogent. *Autobiographie (De vita sua, sive Monodiae).* Edited with French translation by Edmond-René Labande. Classiques de l'histoire de France au Moyen Age 34. Paris, 1981.

———. *Self and Society in Medieval France.* Translated by John F. Benton. 1970; reprint, Medieval Academy Reprints for Teaching 15, Toronto, 1984.

Gysseling, M., and A. C. F. Koch. *Diplomata Belgica ante annum millesium centesium scripta.* Bouwstoffen en Studiën voor de Gescheidenis en de Lexicografie van het Nederlands 1. 2 vols. Brussels, 1950.

Hariulf. *Vita Arnulfi episcopi Suessionensis auctore Hariulfo abbate Aldenburgensi.* Edited by O. Holder-Egger. *Monumenta Germaniae Historica, Scriptores* 15, 2 (Hannover, 1888), 872–904.

Henry IV (Emperor). *Epistolae.* Edited by Carl Erdman. In Schmale, ed., *Quellen,* 52–141.

———. *The Letters of Henry IV.* In Mommsen and Morrison, trans., *Imperial Lives,* 138–200.

Henry of Huntingdon. *Historia Anglorum / The History of the English People.* Edited and translated by Diana Greenway. Oxford Medieval Texts. Oxford, U.K., 1996.

Herman of Tournai. "Liber de restauratione monasterii Sancti Martini Tornacensis." Edited by Georg Waitz. *Monumenta Germaniae Historica, Scriptores* 14 (Hannover, 1883), 274–317.

———. *The Restoration of the Monastery of Saint Martin of Tournai.* Translated by Lynn H. Nelson. Medieval Texts in Translation. Washington, D.C., 1996.

Hugh of Fleury. *Tractatus de regia potestate et sacerdotali dignitate.* Edited by E. Sackur. In *Monumenta Germaniae Historica, Libelli de lite,* 2:465–94.

Hugh of St. Victor. *Didascalicon.* Edited by Charles Henry Buttimer. Washington, D.C., 1939.

———. *Didascalicon.* Translated by Jerome Taylor. New York, 1961.

Isidore of Seville. *Etymologiarum sive originum libri xx.* Edited by W. M. Lindsay. 2 vols. Oxford, U.K., 1911.

———. *Sententiarum libri tres. Patrologia latina* 83, 538–738.

Jarecki, Walter, ed. *Signa loquendi: Die cluniacensischen Signa-Listen eingeleitet und herausgegeben.* Saecula Spiritalia 4. Baden-Baden, 1981.

John of Salisbury. *Frivolities of Courtiers and Footprints of Philosophers: Being a Translation of the First, Second, and Third Books and Selections from the Seventh and Eighth Books of the "Policraticus" of John of Salisbury.* Translated by Joseph B. Pike. 1938; reprint, New York, 1972.

———. *Historia Pontificalis / Memoirs of the Papal Court.* Translated by Marjorie Chibnall. Edinburgh and London, 1956.

———. *Policraticus.* Edited by Clemens C. I. Webb. 2 vols. 1909; reprint, Frankfurt, 1965.

———. *Policraticus I–IV.* Edited by K. S. B. Keats-Rohan. Corpus Christianorum, Continuatio medievalis 118. Turnhout, 1993.

———. *Policraticus.* Translated by Cary J. Nederman. Cambridge, U.K., 1990.

———. *The Statesman's Book of John of Salisbury: Being the Fourth, Fifth, and Sixth Books, and Selections from the Seventh and Eighth Books, of the "Policraticus."* Translated by John Dickinson. 1927; reprint, New York, 1963.

Lambert of Arras (Bishop). *Epistolae Lamberti episcopi Atrebatensis et aliorum ad ipsum. Patrologia latina* 162, 647–702.

Lambert of Saint-Omer. *Liber Floridus: Codex autographus bibliothecae universitatis Gandavensis.* Edited by Albert Derolez. Preface by Egied I. Strubbe and Albert Derolez. Ghent, 1968.

Lampert of Hersfeld. *Annales.* In *Lamperti monachi Hersfeldensis opera,* ed. Oswald Holder-Egger, Scriptores rerum Germanicarum in usum scholarum (Hannover and Leipzig, 1894), 58–304.

Le roman d'Enéas. Edited by Aimé Petit. Paris, 1997.

The Life of Beatrice of Nazareth, 1200–1268. Edited by Leonce Reypens. Translated by Roger De Ganck. Cistercian Fathers Series 50. Kalamazoo, Mich., 1991.

The Life of the Emperor Henry IV. In Mommsen and Morrison, trans., *Imperial Lives,* 101–37.

Manegold of Lautenbach. *Ad Gebehardum liber.* Edited by Kuno Francke. In *Monumenta Germaniae Historica, Libelli de lite,* 1:300–430.

Mayhew, Jonathan. *A Discourse Concerning Unlimited Submission and Non-Resistance to the Higher Powers.* Boston, 1750. *Early American Imprints,* 1st ser. New York, 1985. Evans n° 6549.

Miraeus, Aubertus (Aubert Le Mire). *Opera diplomatica et historica.* Vols. 1 and 2. 2nd ed. Jean François Foppens. Vols. 3 and 4. Jean François Foppens. *Diplomatum Belgicorum nova collectio, sive supplementum ad "Opera diplomatica" Auberti Miraei.* 4 vols. Leuven and Brussels, 1723–1748.

Mommsen, Theodor E., and Karl F. Morrison, trans. *Imperial Lives and Letters of the Eleventh Century.* New York, 1962.

Monumenta Germaniae Historica, Libelli de lite imperatorum et pontificum. 3 vols. Hannover, 1881–1897.

Muller, S., and A. C. Bouman. *Oorkondenboek van het Sticht Utrecht tot 1301.* Vol. 1. Utrecht, 1920.

Orderic Vitalis. *The Ecclesiastical History of Orderic Vitalis.* Edited and translated by Marjorie Chibnall. 6 vols. Oxford, U.K., 1969–1980.

Orosius. *Histoires (Contre les Païens).* Edited with French translation by Marie-Pierre Arnaud-Lindet. 3 vols. Paris, 1990–1991.

———. *Seven Books of History against the Pagans.* Translated by Irving W. Raymond. Records of Civilization, Sources and Studies 26. New York, 1936.

———. *The Seven Books of History against the Pagans.* Translated by Roy J. Deferrari. The Fathers of the Church, A New Translation 50. Washington, D.C., 1964.

Paul of Bernried. "Gregorii P. P. VII vita." In *Pontificum Romanorum qui fuerunt inde abe exeunte saeculo IX usque ad finem saeculi XII vitae,* ed. Johann Matthias Watterich, 2 vols. (Leipzig, 1862), 1:474–546.

Peter the Venerable. *The Letters of Peter the Venerable.* Edited by Giles Constable. 2 vols. Cambridge, Mass., 1967.

Raymond Lulle. *Doctrine d'enfant.* Edited by Armand Llinarès. Paris, 1969.

Richard of Devizes. *Cronicon Richardi Divisensis de tempore Regis Richardi Primi.* Edited by John T. Appleby. London, 1963.

Schmale, Franz-Josef, gen. ed. and trans. *Quellen zur Geschichte Kaiser Heinrichs IV.* Darmstadt, 1974.

Sigebert of Gembloux. *Leodicensium epistola adversus Paschalem papam.* Edited by E. Sackur. In *Monumenta Germaniae Historica, Libelli de lite,* 2:449–64.

Smaragdus of Saint Mihiel. *Commentaria in regulam Sancti Benedicti. Patrologia latina* 102, 689–932.

Suger. *The Deeds of Louis the Fat.* Translated by Richard Cusimano and John Moorhead. Washington, D.C., 1992.

———. *Vie de Louis VI le Gros.* Edited with French translation by Henri Waquet. Les Classiques de l'Histoire de France au Moyen Age 11. Paris, 1929.

Vercauteren, Fernand. *Actes des comtes de Flandre, 1071–1128.* Brussels, 1938.

Vita Heinrici IV. imperatoris. Edited by W. Wattenbach and W. Eberhard. In Schmale, ed., *Quellen,* 408–67.

Wace. *Le roman de Rou.* Edited by A. J. Holden. 3 vols. Paris, 1970–1973.

Walter of Thérouanne. "Vita Karoli comitis, auctore Waltero archidiacono Tervanensi." Edited by R. Köpke. *Monumenta Germaniae Historica, Scriptores* 12 (Hannover, 1856), 537–61.

Wippo. *Die Werke Wipos.* Edited by Harry Bresslau. 3rd ed. Hannover, 1915.

SECONDARY SOURCES

Adair, Penelope. "Lambert Nappin and Lambert of Aardenburg: One Fleming or Two?" *Medieval Prosopography* 11, no.1 (1990): 17–34.

Affeldt, Werner. *Die weltliche Gewalt in der Paulus-Exegese: Röm. 13, 1–7 in den Römerbriefkommentaren der lateinischen Kirche bis zum Ende des 13. Jahrhunderts.* Göttingen, 1969.

Album Albert Schouteet. Bruges, 1973.

Allossery, P. "Intervention flamande, à Cambrai, dans la querelle des investitures." *Annales de de la Fédération Archéologique et Historique de Belgique* 16 (1903): 380–94.

Althoff, Gerd. *"Colloqium familiare—Colloquium secretum—Colloquium publicumx:* Beraten im politischen Leben des früheren Mittelalters." *Frühmitteralterliche Studien* 24 (1990): 145–67.

———. "Demonstration und Inszenierung. Spielregeln der Kommunikation in mittelalterlicher Öffentlichhkeit." *Frühmittelalterliche Studien* 27 (1993): 27–50.

Anton, Hans Hubert. *Fürstenspiegel und Herrscherethos in der Karolingerzeit.* Bonner Historische Forschungen 32. Bonn, 1968.

Arquillière, H.-X. *L'Augustinisme politique: Essais sur la formation des théories politiques du Moyen-Age.* 2nd ed. Paris, 1955.

Barrow, Julia. "Education and the Recruitment of Cathedral Canons in England and Germany, 1100–1225." *Viator* 20 (1989): 117–38.

Benson, Robert L. "*Plenitudo potestatis:* Evolution of a Formula from Gregory IV to Gratian." *Studia Gratiana* 14 (1967): 195–217.

Benson, Robert L., and Giles Constable, eds. *Renaissance and Renewal in the Twelfth Century.* Cambridge, Mass., 1982.

Bischoff, Bernhard. *Latin Paleography, Antiquity, and the Middle Ages.* Translated by Dáibhí O Cróinín and David Ganz. Cambridge, U.K., 1990.

Blancquaert, G. "L'expédition flamande contre Anvers en 1055 et les premiers châtelains de Bruges." *Annales de la Société royale d'archéologie de Bruxelles* 46 (1942–1943): 167–71.

Bloch, Marc. "Les formes de la rupture de l'hommage dans l'ancien droit féodal." *Nouvelle Revue Historique du Droit Français et Etranger* 36 (1912): 141–77. Reprinted in Marc Bloch, *Mélanges Historiques,* 2 vols. (Paris, 1963), 2:189–209.

Blommaert, W. *Les châtelains de Flandre. Etude d'histoire constitutionelle.* Ghent, 1915.

Blumenthal, Uta-Renate. *The Investiture Controversy: Church and Monarchy from the Ninth to the Twelfth Century.* Philadelphia, 1988.

Bonenfant, Paul. "La dépendance du Château d'Alost au XIIe siècle." In Robert Foncke et al., eds., *Album Dr Jan Lindemans* (Brussels, 1951), 169–73.

Bongert, Yvonne. *Recherches sur les cours laïques du Xe au XIIIe siècle.* Paris, 1949.

Breisach, Ernst, ed. *Classical Rhetoric and Medieval Historiography.* Studies in Medieval Culture 19. Kalamazoo, Mich., 1985.

Brett, Martin. "John of Worcester and His Contemporaries." In Davis and Wallace-Hadrill, eds., *The Writing of History in the Middle Ages,* 101–26.

Bruwier, Marinette. "Le Hainaut, le Cambrésis et l'Empire au XIIe siècle." *Annales de la Fédération Archéologique et Historique de Belgique* 36 (1955–1956): 207–26.

Büchner, Karl. *M. Tullius Cicero, "De re publica," Kommentar.* Heidelberg, 1984.

Buda, Milada. *Medieval History and Discourse: Toward a Topography of Textuality.* New York, 1990.

Burns, J. H., ed. *The Cambridge History of Medieval Political Thought c. 350–c. 1450.* Cambridge, U.K., 1988.

Buschmann, E. "Ministerium Dei—Idoneitas." *Historisches Jahrbuch* 82 (1963): 70–102.

Camargo, Martin. "Rhetoric." In Wagner, ed., *The Seven Liberal Arts,* 96–124.

Canning, Joseph. *A History of Medieval Political Thought, 300–1450.* London, 1996.

Carlyle, R. W., and A. J. Carlyle. *A History of Medieval Political Theory in the West.* 6 vols. Edinburgh, 1903–1936.

Carolus-Barré, Louis. "Origine et sens du mot 'commune.'" In Société Académique de Saint-Quentin, ed., *Les chartes,* 83–104.

Carruthers, Mary. *The Book of Memory: A Study of Memory in Medieval Culture.* Cambridge, U.K., 1990.

Cauchie, Alfred. *La Querelle des Investitures dans les diocèses de Liège et de Cambrai.* 2 vols. Leuven, 1890–1891.

Cazes, Quitterie. "Toulouse." In Picard, ed., *Les chanoines dans la ville,* 345–55.

Chédeville, André. "De la cité à la ville." In Georges Duby, gen. ed., *Histoire de la France urbaine,* vol. 2: *La ville médiévale des Carolingiens à la Renaissance,* ed. Jacques Le Goff (Paris, 1980), 29–181.

Chenu, M. D. "Theology and the New Awareness of History." In M. D. Chenu, *Nature, Man, and Society in the Twelfth Century: Essays on New Theological Perspectives in the Latin West,* ed. and trans. Jerome Taylor and Lester K. Little (Chicago, 1968), 162–201.

Chibnall, Marjorie. *Anglo-Norman England.* Oxford, U.K., 1986.

———. *The World of Orderic Vitalis.* Oxford, U.K., 1984.

Clanchy, M. T. *From Memory to Written Record, England 1066–1307.* 2nd ed. Oxford, U.K., 1993.

Colish, Marcia. "Another Look at the School of Laon." *Archives d'Histoire doctrinale et littéraire du Moyen Age* 61 (1986): 7–22.

Constable, Giles. *Letters and Letter-Collections.* Typologie des sources du Moyen Age occidental 17. Turnhout, 1976.

———. *The Reformation of the Twelfth Century.* Cambridge, U.K., 1996.

Cooper, Lisa H. "Making Space for History: Galbert of Bruges and the Murder of Charles the Good." In Laura L. Howes, ed., *Place, Space, and Landscape in Medieval Literature,* Tennessee Studies in Literature, forthcoming.

Coornaert, M. "Over de hydrografie van Brugge." In *Album Albert Schouteet,* 23–25.

Coué, Stephanie. "Der Mord an Karl dem Guten (1127) und die Werke Galberts von Brügge und Walters von Thérouanne." In Hagen Keller, Klaus Grubmüller, and Nikolaus Staubach, eds., *Pragmatische Schriftlichkeit im Mittelalter: Erscheinungsformen und Entwickelungsstufen,* Münsterche Mittelalterschriften 65 (Munich, 1992), 108–29.

Croenen, Godfried. "Princely and Noble Genealogies, Twelfth to Fourteenth Century: Form and Function." In Erik Kooper, ed., *The Medieval Chronicle. Proceedings of the First International Conference on the Medieval Chronicle. Driebergen/Utrecht 13–16 July 1996* (Amsterdam, 1999), 84–95.

Curtius, Ernst Robert. *European Literature and the Latin Middle Ages.* Translated by Willard R. Trask. Princeton, N.J., 1953.

Davidse, Jan. "On Bede as Christian Historian." In Houwen and MacDonald, eds., *Beda Venerabilis,* 1–15.

Davies, R. R. *The Age of Conquest: Wales, 1063–1415.* Oxford, U.K., 1991.

Davis, R. H. C. "William of Poitiers and His History of William the Conqueror." In Davis and Wallace-Hadrill, eds., *The Writing of History in the Middle Ages,* 71–100.

Davis, R. H. C., and J. M. Wallace-Hadrill, eds. *The Writing of History in the Middle Ages: Essays Presented to Richard William Southern.* Oxford, U.K., 1981.

De Borchgrave, Emile. *Histoire des colonies belges qui s'établirent en Allemagne pendant le douzième et le treizième siècle.* Brussels, 1865.

Declercq, Georges. "Bertulf." *National Biografisch Woordenboek* 13 (Brussels, 1990), 73–80.

———. "Galbert van Brugge en de Verraderlijke Moord op Karel de Goede." *Handelingen der Maatschappij voor Geschiedenis en Oudheidkunde te Gent,* n.s. 49 (1995): 71–117.

———. "Nieuwe Inzichten over de Oorsprong van het Sint-Veerlekapittel in Gent." *Handelingen der Maatschappij voor Geschiedenis en Ouheidkunde te Gent,* n.s. 43 (1989): 49–102.

———. "Sekuliere Kapittels in Vlaanderen." *De Leiegouw* 28 (1986): 235–42.

De Ghellinck, J. *Le mouvement théologique du XIIe siècle.* 2nd ed. Bruges, 1948.

De Hemptinne, Thérèse. "Clementia van Bourgondië, gravin van Vlaanderen." *Nationaal Biografisch Woordenboek* 9 (Brussels, 1981), 148–50.

———. "Les epouses des croisés et pèlerins flamands aux XIe et XIIe siècles: L'exemple des comtesses de Flandre Clémence et Sibylle." In Michel Balard, ed., *Autour de la première croisade. Actes du Colloque de la Society for the Study of the Crusades and the Latin East (Clermont-Ferrand, 22–25 juin 1995)* (Paris, 1996), 83–95.

———. "Vlaanderen en Henegouwen onder de erfgenamen van de Boudewijns 1070–1244." *Algemene Geschiedenis der Nederlanden* 2 (Haarlem, 1982), 372–98.

De Hemptinne, Thérèse, and Michel Parisse. "Thierry d'Alsace, comte de Flandre: Biographie et actes." *Annales de l'Est* 43 (1991): 83–113.

De Hemptinne, Thérèse, Walter Prevenier, and Maurice Vandermaesen. "La chancellerie des comtes de Flandre (12e–14e siècle)." In Gabriel Silagi, ed., *Landesherrliche Kanzleien im Spätmittelalter: Referate zum VI. Internationalen Kongreß für Diplomatik, München 1983,* Münchener Beiträge zur Mediävistik und Renaissance-Forschung 35, 2 vols. (Munich, 1984), 1:433–54.

De Hemptinne, Thérèse, and Maurice Vandermaesen. "De ambtenaren van de centrale administratie van het graafschap Vlaanderen van de 12e tot de 14e eeuw,." *Tijdschrift voor Geschiedenis* 93 (1980): 177–209.

Delhaye, Philippe. "L'organisation scolaire au XIIe siècle." *Traditio* 5 (1947): 211–68.

De Meyer, Jacob (Jacobus Meyerus). *Commentarii sive Annales rerum Flandricarum libri XVII.* Antwerp, 1561.

De Moreau, E. "Kerk en geestelijk leven tot het Concordaat van Worms, 936–1122." *Algemene Geschiedenis der Nederlanden* 2 (Utrecht, 1950), 203–30.

Demyttenaere, Albert. "Mentaliteit in de twaalfde eeuw en de benauwenis van Galbert van Brugge." In M. Mostert, R. E. Künzel, and Albert Demyttenaere, eds., *Middeleeuwse cultuur: Verscheidenheid, spanning en verandering* (Hilversum, 1994), 77–129.

De Poerck, Guy. "Trois points litigieux dans la topographie de Bruges d'après Galbert." *Annales de la Fédération Archéologique et Historique de Belgique* 28, Congrès d'Anvers (1930): fasc. 1, 73–75.

De Poorter, Alphonse. *Catalogue des manuscrits de la Bibliothèque publique de la ville de Bruges.* Catalogue général des manuscrits des bibliothèques de Belgique 2. Gembloux, 1934.

Dept, Gaston. "Les marchands flamands et le roi d'Angleterre (1154–1216)." *Revue du Nord* 12 (1926): 303–24.

Derolez, Albert, and Benjamin Victor. *Corpus Catalogorum Belgii: The Medieval Booklists of the Southern Low Countries.* Vol. 1: *Province of West Flanders.* 2nd ed. Brussels, 1991. Vol. 2: *Provinces of Liège, Luxemburg and Namur.* Brussels, 1994.

Derolez, René. "British and English History in the *Liber Floridus.*" In Albert Derolez, ed., *Liber Floridus Colloquium* (Ghent, 1973), 59–70.

Derville, Alain. "Les institutions communales de Saint-Omer." In Société Académique de Saint-Quentin, ed., *Les chartes,* 149–59.

De Smedt, Charles. Review of Pirenne, *Histoire du meurtre de Charles le Bon. Analecta Bollandiana* 11 (1892): 188–97.

De Smet, J. "De oude hydrografie van de stad Brugge." *Handelingen van het Genootschap voor Geschiedenis Gesticht onder de Benaming "Société d'émulation" te Brugge* 86 (1949): 5–22.

De Smet, J. M. "Bij de latijnsche gedichten over den moord op den Glz. Karel den Goede Graaf van Vlaanderen." In *Miscellanea historica in honorem Alberti de Meyer,* 2 vols., Université de Louvain, Recueil de travaux d'histoire et de philologie 3.22 (Leuven, 1946), 1:418–43.

Desportes, P. "Le mouvement communal dans la Province de Reims." In Société Académique de Saint-Quentin, ed., *Les chartes,* 105–112.

De Sturler, Jean. "Note sur l'emploi de poteries creuses dans les édifices du Moyen Age. A propos de la première église de Saint-Donatien à Bruges." *Le Moyen Age* 63 (1957): 241–65.

Devliegher, Luc. "De voorromaanse, romaanse en gotische Sint-Donaaskerk: Evolutie en invloeden." In De Witte, ed., *De Brugse Burg,* 118–36.

———. "De voorromaanse Sint-Donaaskerk en de romaanse westelijke kloostervleugel (onderzoek 1955 en later)." In De Witte, ed., *De Brugse Burg,* 46–92.

———. "Galbert et la topographie de Bruges." In Galbert, *Le meurtre,* 254–64.

De Witte, Hubert, ed. *De Brugse Burg.* Bruges, 1991.

Dhondt, Jan. "Développement urbain et initiative comtale en Flandre au XIe siècle." *Revue du Nord* 30 (1948): 133–56.

———. "De vroege topografie van Brugge." *Handelingen der Maatschappij voor Geschiedenis en Oudheidkunde te Gent,* n.s. 11 (1957): 3–30.

———. "Les 'solidarités' médiévales. Une société en transition: la Flandre en 1127–28."

Annales. Economies-Sociétés-Civilisations 12 (1957): 529-60. Translated by F. L. Cheyette as "Medieval 'Solidarities': Flemish Society in Transition, 1127–28," in F. L. Cheyette, ed., *Lordship and Community in Medieval Europe* (New York, 1968), 268–90.

———. "Une mentalité du douzième siècle: Galbert de Bruges." *Revue du Nord* 39 (1957): 101–9.

———. "Vlaanderen van Arnulf de Grote tot Willem Clito, 918-1128." *Algemene Geschiedenis der Nederlanden* 2 (Utrecht, 1950), 66–93.

Dotzauer, Wilfried. "Die Ankunft des Herrschers. Der fürstliche 'Einzug' in die Stadt (bis zum Ende des Alten Reichs)." *Archiv für Kulturgeschichte* 55 (1973): 245–88.

Duchesne, André. *Histoire généalogique des maisons de Guines, d'Ardres, de Gand et de Coucy.* Paris, 1631.

Dunbabin, Jean. *France in the Making, 843–1180.* Oxford, U.K., 1985.

Edbury, P. W. *William of Tyre, Historian of the Latin East.* Cambridge, U.K., 1988.

Elias, Lorraine. "Augustinian Elements in the Record of Galbert of Bruges." *Proceedings of the PMR {Patristic, Medieval and Renaissance} Conference* 18 (1993–1994): 35–48.

Espinas, George. *Les finances de la commune de Douai des origines au XVe siècle.* Paris, 1902.

Esquieu, Yves. "Les batiments de la vie commune des chanoines." In Picard, ed., *Les chanoines dans la ville,* 41–46.

Flint, Valerie. "The 'School of Laon': A Reconsideration." *Recherches de Théologie Ancienne et Médiévale* 43 (1976): 89–110.

Forhan, Kate Langdon. "Salisburian Stakes: The Uses of 'Tyranny' in John of Salisbury's *Policraticus.*" *History of Political Thought* 11 (1990): 397–407.

Fuhrmann, Horst. "'Volkssouveränität' und 'Herrschaftsvertrag' bei Manegold von Lautenbach." In Sten Gagnér, Hans Schlosser and Wolfgang Wiegand, eds., *Festschrift für Hermann Krause* (Cologne, 1975), 21–42.

Gaier, C. "When the Crossbow Was a Novelty: Reflections on Its Role as a Military Weapon from the 10th Century to the 13th Century." *Le Moyen Age* 99 (1993): 201–29.

Ganshof, François-Louis. "*Coemptio gravissima mansionum* (Galbert de Bruges, c. 55)." *Bulletin Du Cange / Archivium Latinitatis Medii Aevi* 17 (1943 for 1942): 149–61.

———. *Feudalism.* Translated by Philip Grierson. London, 1952.

———. "Iets over Brugge gedurende de preconstitutionele periode van haar geschiedenis." *Nederlandsche Historiebladen* 1 (1938): 218–303.

———. "La Flandre." In Ferdinand Lot and Robert Fawtier, eds., *Histoire des institutions française au Moyen Age,* vol. 1: *Institutions seigneuriales* (Paris, 1957), 343–426.

———. *La Flandre sous les premiers comtes.* 3rd ed. Brussels, 1949.

———. "Le droit urbain en Flandre au début de la première phase de son histoire (1127)." *Tijdschrift voor Rechtsgeschiedenis / Revue d'Histoire du Droit / The Legal History Review* 19 (1951): 387–416.

———. "Le roi de France en Flandre en 1127 et 1128." *Revue Historique de Droit Français et Etranger,* 4 ser., 27 (1949): 204–28.

———. "Les origines de la Flandre impériale. Contribution à l'histoire de l'ancien Brabant." *Annales de la Société Royale d'Archéologie de Bruxelles* 46 (1942-1943): 99–137.

———. "Les origines du concept de souveraineté nationale en Flandre," *Tijdschrift voor Rechtsgeschiedenis / Revue d'Histoire du Droit / The Legal History Review* 18 (1950): 135–58.

———. "Note sur les événements de 1127 en Flandre." *Handelingen van het Genootschap voor Geschiedenis Gesticht onder de Benaming "Société d'émulation" te Brugge* 67 (1924): 97–107.

———. "Trois mandements perdus du roi de France, Louis VI, intéressant la Flandre." *Handelingen van het Genootschap voor Geschiedenis Gesticht onder de Benaming "Société d'émulation" te Brugge* 87 (1950): 117–33.

Geary, Patrick. *Furta Sacra: Thefts of Relics in the Central Middle Ages.* 2nd ed. Princeton, N.J., 1990.

Gelting, Michael H. "Un prélat flamand au Danemark au XIIe siècle: Hélie, évêque de Ribe (1142–1162)." *Handelingen van het Genootschap voor Geschiedenis Gesticht onder de Benaming "Société d'émulation" te Brugge* 122 (1985): 159–79.

Genicot, L. "Le premier siècle de la 'curia' de Hainaut (1060 env.–1195)." *Le Moyen Age* 53 (1947): 39–60.

Genicot, L., and P. Tombeur, gen. eds. *Index Scriptorum Operumque Latino-Belgicorum Medii Aevi: Nouveau répertoire des oeuvres médiolatines belges.* 4 vols. Brussels, 1973–1979.

George, Robert H. "The Contribution of Flanders to the Conquest of England, 1065–86." *Revue Belge de Philologie et d'histoire* 5 (1926): 81–97.

Giry, A. "Grégoire VII et les évêques de Térouane." *Revue Historique* 1 (1876): 387–409.

Goeminne, Luc. "Het verhaal van Galbertus over de moord op Karel de Goede en de grafelijke watergraanmolen te Brugge in 1127." *Molenecho's* 10, no. 3 (1982): 96–97.

Gooris, H. Jan. *Het Leven ende Martelie van den Heylighen Graef van Vlaenderen Carolus Bonus.* Bruges, 1629.

Grabmann, Martin. *Die Geschichte der Scholastischen Methode.* 2 vols. Berlin, 1957.

Gransden, Antonia. *Historical Writing in England c. 550 to c. 1307.* Ithaca, N.Y., 1974.

———. *Legends, Traditions, and History in Medieval England.* London, 1992.

———. "Prologues in the Historiography of Twelfth-Century England." In Gransden, *Legends, Traditions, and History,* 125–51. Originally published in Daniel Williams, ed., *England in the Twelfth-Century: Proceedings of the 1988 Harlaxton Symposium* (Woodbridge, 1990), 55–81.

———. "Realistic Observation in Twelfth-Century England." In Gransden, *Legends, Traditions, and History,* 175–97. Originally published in *Speculum* 47 (1972): 29–51.

Guenée, Bernard. *Histoire et culture historique dans l'Occident medieval.* Paris, 1980.

Häcker, Martina. "Mothers, Wives, and Witches: The Depiction of Women in Galbert of Bruges' Account of the Murder of Charles the Good." *Bulletin of International Medieval Research* 2–3 (1996–1997): 10–26.

Hannig, Jürgen. *Consensus fidelium: Frühfeudale Interpretationen des Verhältnisses von Königtum und Adel am Beispiel des Frankreiches.* Stuttgart, 1982.

Hanning, Robert W. *The Vision of History in Early Britain: From Gildas to Geoffrey of Monmouth.* New York, 1966.

Hartmann, Wilfried. "Manegold von Lautenbach und die Anfänge der Frühscholastik." *Deutsches Archiv für Erforschung des Mittelalters* 26 (1970): 47–149.

Haskins, Charles H. "Comments on Jenkinson, 'William Cade, a Financier of the Twelfth Century.'" *English Historical Review* 28 (1913): 730–31.

———. "A List of Text-Books from the Close of the Twelfth Century." In Charles H. Haskins, *Studies in the History of Mediaeval Science* (Cambridge, Mass., 1924), 356–76.

Heirbaut, Dirk. "The *Fief-Rente:* A New Evaluation, Based on Flemish Sources (1000–1305)." *Tijdschrift voor Rechtsgeschiedenis / Revue d'Histoire du Droit / The Legal History Review* 67 (1999): 1–37.

———. "Galbert van Brugge: Een Bron voor de Vlaamse Feodaliteit in de XIIde Eeuw." *Tijdschrift voor Rechtsgeschiedenis / Revue d'Histoire du Droit / The Legal History Review* 60 (1992): 49–62.

Henschen, Godefroid, and Daniel Van Papenbroeck. "De B. Carolo bono, comite Flandriae, martyre." In *Acta Sanctorum,* March, 1 (Antwerp, 1668), 152–62.

Herlihy, David. *The History of Feudalism.* New York, 1970.

Hibst, Peter. *Utilitas Publica—Gemeiner Nutz—Gemeinwohl: Untersuchungen zur Idee eines politischen Leitbegriffes von der Antike bis zum späten Mittelalter.* Frankfurt, 1991.

Hicks, Sandy Burton. "The Impact of William Clito upon the Continental Policies of Henry I of England." *Viator* 10 (1979): 1–21.

Houwen, L. A. J. R., and A. A. MacDonald, eds. *Beda Venerabilis: Historian, Monk, and Northumbrian.* Groningen, 1996.

Hunt, Tony. "Tradition and Originality in the Prologues of Chrestien de Troyes." *Forum for Modern Language Studies* 8 (1972): 320–44.

Huyghebaert, Nicolas. "Galbert de Bruges." *Dictionnaire d'Histoire et de Géographie Ecclésiastiques* 19 (Paris, 1981), 737–39.

———. "Gertrude de Saxe, comtesse de Flandre (ca. 1033–1113)." *Biographie nationale de Belgique* 39 (Brussels, 1976), 429–32.

———. "Les femmes laïques dans la vie religieuse des XIe et XIIe siècles dans la province ecclésiastique de Reims." In *I Laici nella "Societas christiana" dei secoli XI e XII. Atti della terza Settimana internazionale di studio, Mendola 21–27 agosto 1965,* Miscellanea del Centro di Studi Medioevali 5 (Milan, 1968), 346–89.

———. "Un légat de Grégoire VII en France: Warmond de Vienne." *Revue d'Histoire Ecclésiastique* 40 (1944–1945): 187–200.

Irvine, Martin. *The Making of Textual Culture: "Grammatica" and Literary Theory, 350–1100.* Cambridge, U.K., 1994.

Jacob, Robert. "Le meurtre du seigneur dans la société féodale. La mémoire, le rite, la fonction." *Annales. Economies-Sociétés-Civilisations.* 45 (1990): 247–63.

Jaeger, C. Stephen. *The Envy of Angels: Cathedral Schools and Social Ideals in Medieval Europe: 950–1200.* Philadelphia, 1994.

Jenkinson, Hilary. "William Cade, a Financier of the Twelfth Century." *English Historical Review* 28 (1913): 209–27, 731–32.

Kern, Fritz. *Gottesgnadentum und Widerstandsrecht im Früheren Mittelalter: Zur Entwicklungsgeschichte der Monarchie.* 2nd ed. Edited by Rudolf Buchner. Darmstadt, 1954.

King, P. D. "The Barbarian Kingdoms." In Burns, ed., *Medieval Political Thought,* 123–53.

———. *Law and Society in the Visigothic Kingdom.* Cambridge Studies in Medieval Life and Thought 3.5. Cambridge, U.K., 1972.

Kittell, Ellen E. *From "Ad Hoc" to Routine: A Case Study in Medieval Bureaucracy.* Philadelphia, 1991.

Koch, A. C. F. "Brugge's topografische ontwikkeling tot in de 12e eeuw." *Handelingen van het Genootschap voor Geschiedenis Gesticht onder de Benaming "Société d'émulation" te Brugge* 99 (1962): 5–67.

Köpke, R. "Vita Karoli comitis Flandriae." *Monumenta Germaniae Historica, Scriptores* 12 (Hannover, 1856), 531–37.

Koziol, Geoffrey. *Begging Pardon and Favor: Ritual and Political Order in Early Medieval France.* Ithaca, N.Y., 1992.

Lacroix, Benoit. *Orose et ses idées.* Montreal, 1965.

Lalou, Elisabeth. "Inventaire des tablettes médiévales et présentation générale." In Lalou, ed., *Les tablettes à écrire,* 233–85.

———, ed. *Les tablettes à écrire de l'antiquité à l'époque moderne.* Bibliogia: Elementa ad librorum studia pertinentia. Turnhout, 1992.

———. "Les tablettes de cire médiévales." *Bibliothèque de l'Ecole des Chartes* 147 (1989): 123–40.

Landes, Richard. *Relics, Apocalypse, and the Deceits of History: Ademar of Chabbanes, 989–1034.* Cambridge, Mass., 1995.

Laude, Pierre-Joseph. *Catalogue méthodique, descriptif et analytique des manuscrits de la Bibliothèque publique de Bruges.* Bruges, 1859.

Lawn, Brian. *The Rise and Decline of the Scholastic "Quaestio disputata" with Special Emphasis on*

Its Use in the Teaching of Medicine and Science. Leiden, 1993.

Le Cacheux, Paul. "Une charte de Jumièges concernant l'épreuve par le fer chaud (fin du XIe siècle)." *Mélanges (Société de l'Histoire de Normandie)* (1927): 205–16.

Le Goff, Jacques. "The Symbolic Ritual of Vassalage." In Jacques Le Goff, *Time, Work, and Culture in the Middle Ages,* trans. Arthur Goldhammer (Chicago, 1980), 237–87.

Lesne, Emile. *Histoire de la propriété ecclésiastique en France,* vol. 5: *Les ecoles de la fin du VIIIe siècle à la fin du XIIe.* Lille, 1940.

———. "Les origines de la prébende." *Revue Historique de Droit Français et Etranger* 8 (1929): 242–90.

Leupen, Piet. "La 'Sainte Eglise de Dieu' (du VIIIe au XIe siècle)." In Ludo Milis, ed., *La Chrétienté des origines à la fin du Moyen Age* (Paris, 1998), 70–91.

Lewis, Ewart. *Medieval Political Ideas.* 2 vols. New York, 1954.

Leyser, Karl. "The Crisis of Medieval Germany." *Proceedings of the British Academy* 69 (1983): 409–43.

———. "The Polemics of the Papal Revolution." In Karl Leyser, *Medieval Germany and Its Neighbors, 900–1250* (London, 1982), 138–160. Originally published in Beryl Smalley, ed., *Trends in Medieval Political Thought* (Oxford, U.K., 1965), 42–64.

Lloyd, John Edward. *A History of Wales.* 2nd ed. 2 vols. London, 1912.

Luchaire, Achille. *Louis VI le Gros, Annales de sa vie et de son règne (1081–1137).* Paris, 1890.

Luscombe, D. E. "Introduction: The Formation of Political Thought in the West [c. 750–c. 1150]." In Burns, ed., *Medieval Political Thought,* 157–73.

Luscombe, D. E., and G. R. Evans. "The Twelfth-Century Renaissance." In Burns, ed., *Medieval Political Thought,* 306–38.

Lyon, Bryce, and A. E. Verhulst. *Medieval Finance: A Comparison of Financial Institutions in Northwestern Europe.* Providence, R.I., 1967.

Mansion, H. "A propos de l'ancienne église Saint-Donatien à Bruges." *Revue Belge d'Archéologie et d'Histoire de l'Art* 8 (1938): 99–112.

Markus, R. A. "The Latin Fathers." In Burns, ed., *Medieval Political Thought,* 92–122.

Marotta, J. "Teaching Medieval Narrative." In H. Chickering, ed., *1983 NEH Institute Resource Book for the Teaching of Medieval Civilization* (Amherst, Mass., 1984), 13–35.

Martin, Janet. "Classicism and Style in Latin Literature." In Benson and Constable, eds., *Renaissance and Renewal in the Twelfth Century,* 537–68.

Marvin, Laurence W. "'Men Famous in Combat and Battle . . .': Common Soldiers and the Siege of Bruges, 1127." *Journal of Medieval History* 24 (1998): 243–58.

Merlette, Bernard. "Ecoles et bibliothèques, à Laon, du déclin de l'antiquité au développement de l'université." In *Enseignement et vie intellectuelle (IXe–XVIe siècle),* Actes du 95e Congrès national des sociétés savantes, Reims, 1970, Section de philologie et d'histoire jusqu'à 1610, vol. 1 (Paris, 1975), 21–53.

Mertens, J. "Quelques édifices religieux à plan central découverts récemment en Belgique." *Genava,* n.s. 11 (1963): 141–61.

Michaud-Quantin, Pierre. *Universitas: Expressions du mouvement communautaire dans le Moyen-Age latin.* L'Eglise et l'état au Moyen Age 13. Paris, 1970.

Mitteis, Heinrich. *Lehnrecht und Staatsgewalt: Untersuchungen zur Mittelalterlichen Verfassungsgeschichte.* Cologne, 1974.

Mohr, Walter. "Geschichtstheologische Aspekte im Werk Galberts von Brügge." In R. Lievens, E. Van Mingroot, and W. Verbeke, eds., *Pascua Mediaevalia: Studies voor Prof. Dr. Jozef-Maria De Smet,* Medievalia Lovaniensia 1.10 (Leuven, 1983), 246–62.

Mommsen, Theodor E. *Medieval and Renaissance Studies.* Edited by Eugene F. Rice Jr. Ithaca, N.Y., 1959.

———. "Orosius and Augustine." In Mommsen, *Medieval and Renaissance Studies*, 325–48.

———. "Saint Augustine and the Christian Idea of Progress: The Background of *The City of God*." In Mommsen, *Medieval and Renaissance Studies*, 265–98. Originally published in *Journal of the History of Ideas* 12 (1951): 346–74.

Monier, Raymond. *Les institutions centrales du Comté de Flandre de la fin du IXe siècle à 1384*. Paris, 1943.

———. *Les institutions financières du comté de Flandre du IXe siècle à 1384*. Paris, 1948.

Moore, R. I. "Heresy, Repression, and Social Change in the Age of Gregorian Reform." In Scott L. Waugh and Peter D. Diehl, eds., *Christendom and Its Discontents. Exclusion, Persecution, and Rebellion, 1000–1500* (Cambridge, U.K., 1996), 19–46.

———. "Literacy and the Making of Heresy, c. 1000–c. 1150." In Peter Biller and Anne Hudson, eds., *Heresy and Literacy, 1000–1530* (Cambridge, U.K., 1994), 19–37.

Morey, Adrian, and C. N. L. Brooke. *Gilbert Foliot and His Letters*. Cambridge, U.K., 1965.

Morrison, Karl Frederick. *History as a Visual Art in the Twelfth-Century Renaissance*. Princeton, N.J., 1990.

———. "Incentives for Studying the Liberal Arts." In Wagner, ed., *The Seven Liberal Arts*, 32–57.

Munk Olsen, Birger. "La diffusion et l'étude des historiens antiques au XIIe siècle." In Andries Welkenhuysen, Herman Braet, and Werner Verbeke, eds., *Mediaeval Antiquity*, Mediaevalia Lovaniensia 1.24 (Leuven, 1995), 21–43.

———. *L'etude des auteurs classiques latins aux XIe et XIIe siècles*. 4 vols. Paris, 1982–1989.

Murphy, James J. *Rhetoric in the Middle Ages*. Berkeley, Calif., 1974.

Murray, Alan V. "Baldwin II and His Nobles: Baronial Factionalism and Dissent in the Kingdom of Jerusalem, 1118–1134." *Nottingham Medieval Studies* 38 (1994): 60–85.

———. "The Judicial Inquest into the Death of Count Charles the Good of Flanders (1127): Location and Chronology." *Tijdschrift voor Rechtsgeschiedenis / Revue d'Histoire du Droit / The Legal History Review* 68 (2000): 47–61.

———. "Voices of Flanders: Orality and Constructed Orality in the Chronicle of Galbert of Bruges." *Handelingen van de Maatschappij voor Geschiedenis en Oudheidkunde te Gent*, n.s. 48 (1994): 103–119.

Murray, James M. "The Liturgy of the Count's Advent in Bruges, from Galbert to Van Eyck." In Barbara A. Hanawalt and Kathryn Reyerson, eds., *City and Spectacle in Medieval Europe*, Medieval Cultures 6 (Minneapolis, 1994), 137–52.

The Narrative Sources from the Southern Low Countries, 600–1500. University of Ghent. <http://www.lib.rug.ac.be/n-exec.html>.

Nederman, Cary J. "The Changing Face of Tyranny: The Reign of King Stephen in John of Salisbury's Political Thought." *Nottingham Medieval Studies* 33 (1989): 1–20.

———. "A Duty to Kill: John of Salisbury's Theory of Tyrannicide." *Review of Politics* 50 (1988): 365–89.

Nederman, Cary J., and Catherine Campbell. "Priests, Kings, and Tyrants: Spiritual and Temporal Power in John of Salisbury's *Policraticus*." *Speculum* 66 (1991): 572–90.

Nelson, Janet. "Kingship and Empire." In Burns, ed., *Medieval Political Thought*, 211–51.

Nicholas, David. *Medieval Flanders*. London, 1992.

Niermeyer, J. F. "Emigratie." 469–72. In L. Voet, "Het platteland, maatschappelijk en economisch,"*Algemene Geschiedenis der Nederlanden* 2 (Utrecht, 1950), 450–86.

O'Connor, Sonia, and Dominic Tweddle. "A Set of Waxed Tablets from Swinegate, York." In Lalou, ed., *Les tablettes à écrire*, 307–22.

Odena, José Trenchs, and Maria José Carbonnel. "Tablettes de cire aragonaises (XIIe–XVe siècle)." *Bibliothèque de l'Ecole des Chartes* 151 (1993): 155–60.

Oexle, Otto Gerhard. "Conjuratio und Gilde im frühen Mittelalter. Ein Beitrag zum Problem der sozial geschichtlichen Kontinuität zwischen Antike und Mittelalter." In Berent Schwineköper, ed., *Gilden und Zünfte. Kaufmännische und gewerbliche Genossenschaften im frühen und hohen Mittelalter* (Sigmaringen, 1985), 151–214.

———. "Die Kultur der Rebellion. Schwureinung und Verschwörung im früh- und hochmittelalterlichen Okzident." In Marie Theres Fögen, ed., *Ordnung und Aufruhr im Mittelalter. Historische und juristische Studien zur Rebellion* (Frankfurt, 1995), 119–37.

Otter, Monika. *Inventiones: Fiction and Referentiality in Twelfth-Century English Historical Writing.* Chapel Hill, N.C., 1996.

Pacaut, Marcel. *La théocracie. L'eglise et le pouvoir au Moyen Age.* Paris, 1989.

Paetow, Louis John. *The Arts Course at Medieval Universities with Special Reference to Grammar and Rhetoric.* Champaign, Ill., 1910.

Parsons, Wilfrid. "The Medieval Theory of the Tyrant." *Review of Politics* 4 (1942): 129–43.

Partner, Nancy. "The New Cornificius: Medieval History and the Artifice of Words." In Breisach, ed., *Classical Rhetoric,* 5–59.

———. *Serious Entertainments: The Writing of History in Twelfth-Century England.* Chicago, 1977.

Patt, William D. "The Early 'Ars Dictaminis' as a Response to a Changing Society." *Viator* 9 (1978): 133–55.

Peters, Edward. *The Shadow King: "Rex Inutilis" in Medieval Law and Literature, 751–1327.* New Haven, Conn., 1970.

Picard, Jean-Charles, ed. *Les chanoines dans la ville. Recherches sur la topographie des quartiers canoniaux en France.* Paris, 1994.

Pirenne, Henri. *Histoire de Belgique,* vol. 1: *Des origines au commencement du XIVe siècle.* 5th ed. Brussels, 1929.

———. "La chancellerie et les notaires des comtes de Flandre avant le XIIIe siècle." In *Mélanges Julien Havet: Recueil de travaux d'érudition dédiés à la mémoire de Julien Havet* (Paris, 1895), 733–48.

Pizarro, Joaquín Martínez. *A Rhetoric of the Scene: Dramatic Narrative in the Early Middle Ages.* Toronto, 1989.

Poignant, Simone. *La foire de Lille: Contribution à l'étude des foires flamandes au Moyen-Age.* Bibliothèque de la Société d'histoire du droit des pays flamands, picards et wallons 6. Lille, 1932.

Prevenier, Walter. "La chancellerie des comtes de Flandre dans le cadre européen à la fin du XIIe siècle." *Bibliothèque de l'Ecole des Chartes* 125 (1967): 34–93.

Pycke, Jacques. *Le chapitre cathédral Notre-Dame de Tournai de la fin du XIe à la fin du XIIIe siècle: Son organisation, sa vie, ses membres.* Université de Louvain: Recueil de travaux d'histoire et de philologie 6.30. Louvain-la-Neuve, 1986.

Queller, Donald. "Thirteenth-Century Diplomatic Envoys: Nuncii and Procuratores." *Speculum* 35 (1960): 196–213.

Ray, Roger. "Rhetorical Scepticism and Verisimilar Narrative in John of Salisbury's *Historia Pontificalis.*" In Breisach, ed., *Classical Rhetoric,* 61–102.

Resnick, Irven M. "Odo of Cambrai and the Investiture Crisis in the Early Twelfth Century." *Viator* 28 (1997): 83–98.

Reusens, E. "Les chancelleries inférieures en Belgique depuis leur origine jusqu'au commencement du XIIIe siècle." *Analectes pour Servir à l'Histoire Ecclésiastique de la Belgique* 26 (1896): 57–133.

Reynolds, Susan. *Fiefs and Vassals.* Oxford, U.K., 1994.

Reynolds, Suzanne. *Medieval Reading: Grammar, Rhetoric, and the Classical Text.* Cambridge, U.K., 1996.

Riché, Pierre. *Education et culture dans l'Occident médiéval.* Aldershot, U.K., 1993.

———. "Jean de Salisbury et le monde scolaire du XIIe siècle." In Riché, *Education et culture,* XVI.

———. "La vie scolaire et la pédagogie au Bec au temps de Lanfranc et de Saint Anselme." In Riché, *Education et culture,* XIV.

———. "L'enseignement de Gerbert à Reims dans le contexte européen." In Riché, *Education et culture,* VI.

———. "Les clercs carolingiens au service du pouvoir." In Riché, *Education et culture,* V.

———. *Les ecoles et l'enseignement dans l'Occident chrétien de la fin du Ve siècle au milieu du XIe siècle.* Paris, 1979.

Rider, Jeff. "Galbert of Bruges' 'Journal': From Medieval Flop to Modern Bestseller." In L. Milis, V. Lambert, and A. Kelders, eds., *Verhalende Bronnen: Repertoriering, Editie en Commercialisiering,* Studia Historica Gandensia: Publicaties van de Opleiding Geschiedenis van de Universiteit Gent 283 (Ghent, 1996), 67–93.

Robinson, Ian Stuart. *Authority and Resistance in the Investiture Contest: The Polemical Literature of the Late Eleventh Century.* Manchester, U.K., 1978.

———. "Church and Papacy." In Burns, ed., *Medieval Political Thought,* 252–305.

———. "The 'Colores Rhetorici' in the Investiture Contest." *Traditio* 32 (1976): 209–38.

———. "The Dissemination of the Letters of Pope Gregory VII during the Investiture Contest." *Journal of Ecclesiastical History* 34 (1983): 175–93.

———. "The Friendship Network of Gregory VII." *History* 63 (1978): 1–22.

———. *The Papacy, 1073–1198. Continuity and Innovation.* Cambridge, U.K., 1990.

———. "'Periculosus homo': Pope Gregory VII and Episcopal Authority." *Viator* 9 (1978): 103–31.

———. "Pope Gregory VII, the Princes, and the *Pactum,* 1088–80." *English Historical Review* 94 (1979): 721–56.

Rolland, Paul. "La première église de Saint-Donatien à Bruges (quelques remarques)." *Revue belge d'archéologie et d'histoire de l'art* 14 (1944): 101–11.

Ross, James Bruce. "Rise and Fall of a Twelfth-Century Clan: The Erembalds and the Murder of Count Charles of Flanders, 1127–28." *Speculum* 34 (1959): 367–90.

Round, J. H. "The Debtors of William Cade." *English Historical Review* 28 (1913): 522–27.

Rouse, Richard H., and Mary A. Rouse. "John of Salisbury and the Doctrine of Tyrannicide." *Speculum* 42 (1967): 693–709.

———. "The Vocabulary of Wax Tablets." *Harvard Library Bulletin,* n.s. 1, no. 3 (1990): 12–19.

———. "Wax Tablets." *Language and Communication* 9 (1989): 175–91.

Ryckaert, Marc. *Brugge.* Historische Stedenatlas van België. Brussels, 1991.

———. "De Oudeburg te Brugge." In *Album Albert Schouteet,* 155–68.

———. "Die Topographie der flandrischen Hafenstädte bis 1300: Das Beispiel von Brügge." *Lübecker Schriften zur Archäologie und Kulturgeschichte* 7 (1983): 47–55.

Saint-Denis, Alain. *Apogée d'une cité: Laon et le Laonnois aux XIIe et XIIIe siècles.* Nancy, 1994.

———. "L'apparition d'une identité urbaine dans les villes de commune de France du Nord aus XIIe et XIIIe siècles." In Marc Boone and Peter Stabel, eds., *Shaping Urban Identity in Late Medieval Europe: The Use of Space and Images. Papers Presented at the Fourth International Conference of Urban History (Venice, September 1998),* forthcoming.

Schultz, James A. "Classical Rhetoric, Medieval Poetics, and the Medieval Vernacular Prologue." *Speculum* 59 (1984): 1–15.

Shopkow, Leah. *History and Community: Norman Historians in the Eleventh and Twelfth Centuries.* Washington, D.C., 1997.

Smalley, Beryl. *Historians in the Middle Ages.* London, 1974.

———. "Sallust in the Middle Ages." In R. R. Bolgar, ed., *Classical Influences on European Culture, A. D. 500–1500* (Cambridge, U.K., 1971), 165–75.

Société Académique de Saint-Quentin, ed. *Les chartes et le mouvement communal. Colloque régional (octobre 1980).* Saint-Quentin, 1982.

Southern, R. W. "Aspects of the European Tradition of Historical Writing." *Transactions of the Royal Historical Society,* 5th ser., 20 (1970): 173–96; 21 (1971): 159–79; 22 (1972): 159–80; 23 (1973): 243–63.

———. "The Schools of Paris and the School of Chartres." In Benson and Constable, eds., *Renaissance and Renewal in the Twelfth Century,* 113–37.

Spiegel, Gabrielle M. *The Chronicle Tradition of Saint-Denis: A Survey.* Brookline, Mass., 1978.

———. "Genealogy: Form and Function in Medieval Historiography." In Spiegel, *The Past as Text,* 99–110. First published in *History and Theory* 22 (1983): 43–53.

———. "History as Enlightenment: Suger and the *Mos Anagogicus.*" In Spiegel, *The Past as Text,* 163–77. First published in Paula Gerson, ed., *Abbot Suger and Saint-Denis: A Symposium* (New York, 1986), 151–58.

———. *The Past as Text: The Theory and Practice of Medieval Historiography.* Baltimore, 1997.

———. "Political Utility in Medieval Historiography: A Sketch." In Spiegel, *The Past as Text,* 83–98. First published in *History and Theory* 14 (1975): 314–25.

———. *Romancing the Past: The Rise of Vernacular Prose Historiography in Thirteenth-Century France.* Berkeley, Calif., 1993.

Sproemberg, Heinrich. "Clementia, Gräfin von Flandern." *Revue belge de philologie et d'histoire* 42 (1964): 1203–41. Reprinted in Sproemberg, *Mittelalter,* 192–220.

———. "Das Erwachen des Staatsgefühls in den Niederlanden. Galbert von Brügge." In *L'organisation corporative du Moyen Age à la fin de l'Ancien Régime, Etudes présentées à la Commission Internationale pour l'histoire des assemblées d'états* 3, Université de Louvain, Recueil de Travaux publiés par les Membres des Conférences d'Histoire et de Philologie, 2 série, 50 (Leuven, 1939), 31–89.

———. "Eine Rheinische Königskandidatur im Jahre 1125." In *Aus Geschichte und Landeskunde. Forschungen und Darstellungen, Franz Steinbach zum 65. Geburtstag gewidmet* (Bonn, 1960), 50–70.

———. *Mittelalter und Demokratische Geschichtsschreibung. Ausgëwahlte Abhandlungen.* Edited by Manfred Unger, Lily Sproemberg and Wolfgang Eggert. Forschungen zur Mittelalterlichen Geschichte 18. Berlin, 1971.

Stein, Robert M. "Signs and Things: The *Vita Heinrici IV. Imperatoris* and the Crisis of Interpretation in Twelfth-Century History." *Traditio* 43 (1987): 105–19.

Strayer, Joseph. *Feudalism.* Princeton, N.J., 1965.

Strubbe, Egied I. *Egidius van Breedene (11. .–1270) grafelijk ambtenaar en stichter van de abdij Spermalie; bijdrage tot de geschiedenis van het grafelikje bestuur en van de cistercienser orde in het dertiendeeuwsche Vlaanderen.* Rijksuniversiteit te Gent. Werken uitgegeved door de Faculteit van de Wijsbegeerte en Letteren 94. Bruges, 1942.

———. *Het Fragment van een Grafeliijke Rekening van Vlaanderen uit 1140.* Mededelingen van de Koninklijke Vlaamse Academie voor Wetenschappen, Letteren en Schone Kunsten van België, Klasse der Letteren 12.9. Brussel, 1950.

———. "Van de eerste naar de tweede omwalling van Brugge." *Handelingen van het Genootschap voor Geschiedenis Gesticht onder de Benaming "Société d'émulation" te Brugge* 100 (1963): 271–300.

Szklenar, Hans. *Magister Nicolaus de Dybin. Vorstudien zu einer Edition seiner Schriften. Ein Beitrag zur Geschichte der literarischen Rhetorik im späteren Mittelalter.* Munich, 1981.

Tarver, W. T. S. "The Traction Trebuchet: A Reconstruction of an Early-Medieval Siege Engine." *Technology and Culture* 36 (1995): 136–67.

Tock, Benoît-Michel. *Une chancellerie épiscopale au XIIe siècle: Le Cas d'Arras.* Louvain-la-Neuve, 1991.

Toorians, Lauran. "Wizo Flandrensis and the Flemish Settlement in Pembrokeshire." *Cambridge Medieval Celtic Studies* 20 (1990): 99–118.

Ullmann, Walter. *The Growth of Papal Government in the Middle Ages.* 2nd ed. London, 1962.

———. *The Individual and Society in the Middle Ages.* Baltimore, 1966.

———. *Principles of Government and Politics in the Middle Ages.* London, 1961.

Van Acker, Liever. "De Latijnse literaire cultuur in Noorden en Zuiden van circa 1050 tot circa 1350." *Algemene Geschiedenis der Nederlanden* 3 (Haarlem, 1982), 328–42.

Van Caenegem, R. C. *Coutumes et législation en Flandre au XIe et XIIe siècles.* Brussels, 1968.

———. "De Keure van Sint-Omaars van 1127." *Tijdschrift voor Rechtsgeschiedenis / Revue d'Histoire du Droit / The Legal History Review* 50 (1982): 253–62.

———. "Galbert of Bruges on Serfdom, Prosecution of Crime, and Constitutionalism." In Bernard S. Bachrach and David Nicholas, eds., *Law, Custom, and the Social Fabric in Medieval Europe: Essays in Honor of Bryce Lyon* (Kalamazoo, Mich., 1990), 89–112.

———. *Galbert van Brugge en het recht.* Mededelingen van de Koninklijke Academie voor Wetenschappen, Letteren en Schone Kunsten van België, Klasse der Letteren 40.1. Brussels, 1978.

———. "The Ghent Revolt of February 1128." In Van Caenegem, *Law, History, the Low Countries and Europe,* ed. Ludo Milis et al. (London, 1994), 107–12. First published as "De Gentse februari-opstand van het jaar 1128," *Spiegel Historiael: Maanblad voor Geschiedenis en Archeologie* 13 (1978): 478–83.

———. "Government, Law and Society." In Burns, ed., *Medieval Political Thought,* 174–210.

———. "Law and Power in Twelfth-Century Flanders." In Thomas N. Bisson, ed., *Cultures of Power: Lordship, Status, and Process in Twelfth-Century Europe* (Philadelphia, 1995), 149–71.

———. "Misdaad en Straf bij Galbert van Brugge." In *Liber Amicorum Jules D'Haenens* (Ghent, 1993), 321–31.

———. "Notes on Galbert of Bruges and His Translators." In Jean-Marie Duvosquel and Erik Thoen, eds., *Peasants and Townsmen in Medieval Europe: Studia in honorem Adriaan Verhulst* (Ghent, 1995), 619–29.

Van Houtte, Jan A. "Les foires dans la Belgique ancienne." In Jan A. Van Houtte, *Essays on Medieval and Early Modern Economy and Society* (Leuven, 1977), 81–108. First published in *La Foire, Recueils de la Société Jean Bodin* 5 (1953): 175–207.

Van Laarhoven, Jan. "Thou shalt *not* slay a tyrant! The So-Called Theory of John of Salisbury." In Michael Wilks, ed., *The World of John of Salisbury* (Oxford, U.K., 1984), 319–41.

Van Meter, David. "Eschatology and the Sanctification of the Prince in Twelfth-Century Flanders: The Case of Walter of Thérouanne's *Vita Karoli comitis Flandriae.*" *Sacris Erudiri* 35 (1995): 115–31.

Van Werveke, H. "De opbloei van handel en nijverheid." *Algemene Geschiedenis der Nederlanden* 2 (Utrecht, 1950), 417–49.

Verbruggen, J. F. "La tactique militaire des armées de chevaliers." *Revue du Nord* 29 (1947): 161–80.

Vercauteren-De Smet, L. "Etude sur les rapports politiques de l'Angleterre et de la Flandre sous le règne du comte Robert II." In *Etudes d'histoire dédiées à la mémoire de Henri Pirenne* (Brussels, 1937), 413–23.

Verhulst, Adriaan E., and Thérèse De Hemptinne. "Le chancelier de Flandre sous les comtes de la maison d'Alsace (1128–1191)." *Bulletin de la Commission royale d'histoire / Handelingen van de Koniklijke Commissie van Geschiedenis* 141 (1975): 267–311.

Verhulst, Adriaan E., and M. Gysseling. *Le Compte Général de 1187, connu sous le nom de "Gros brief," et les institutions financières du comté de Flandre au XIIe siècle.* Brussels, 1962.

Verlinden, Charles. *Robert Ier le Frison, comte de Flandre. Etude d'histoire politique.* Antwerp, 1935.

Vermeesch, Albert. *Essai sur les origines et la signification de la commune dans le nord de la France (XIe et XIIe siècles).* Etudes présentées à la Commission Internationale pour l'Histoire des Assemblées d'Etats 30. Heule, 1966.

Viaene, Antoon. "Galbert van Brugge in eerste moderne vertaling: Een Vlaams initiatief van archivaris Delepierre." *Biekorf* 78 (1978): 193–99.

Vincent, Jacques. "Au sujet de la tour et du 'solarium' de l'ancienne église Saint-Donatien à Bruges." *Revue belge d'archéologie et d'histoire de l'art* 14 (1944): 47–55.

Wagner, David L., ed.. *The Seven Liberal Arts in the Middle Ages.* Bloomington, Ill., 1983.

Wallach, Luitpold. "Onulf of Speyer: A Humanist of the Eleventh Century." *Medievalia et Humanistica* 6 (1950): 35–56.

Ward, John O. "'Chronicle' and 'History': The Medieval Origins of Postmodern Historiographical Practice?" *Parergon* 14 (1997): 101–27.

———. "Some Principles of Rhetorical Historiography in the Twelfth Century." In Breisach, ed., *Classical Rhetoric,* 103–65.

Warlop, E. *The Flemish Nobility before 1300.* Translated by J. B. Ross and H. Vandermoere. 2 vols., 4 parts. Kortrijk, 1975–1976.

Wauters, Alphonse. "Gualbert." *Biographie nationale* 8 (Brussels, 1884–1885), 392–94.

Werner, Karl Ferdinand. "Gott, Herrscher und Historiograph. Der Geschichtsschreiber als Interpret des Wirkens Gottes in der Welt und Ratgeber der Könige (4. bis 12. Jahrhundert)." In Ernst-Dieter Hehl, Hubertus Seibert and Franz Staab, eds., *Deus qui mutat tempora. Menschen und Institutionen im Wandel des Mittelalters. Feschrift für Alfons Becker zu seinem fünfundsechzigsten Geburtstag* (Sigmaringen, 1987), 1–31.

Yamada, Masahiko. "Le mouvement des foires en Flandre avant 1200." In Jean-Marie Duvosquel and Alain Dierkens, eds., *Villes et campagnes au Moyen Age: Mélanges Georges Despy* (Liège, 1991), 773–89.

Index

www.ingramcontent.com/pod-product-compliance
Lightning Source LLC
LaVergne TN
LVHW090148080826
844660LV00013B/714/J